Fundamentals
of
Philosophy

A Study of Classical Texts

Fundamentals
of
Philosophy

A Study of Classical Texts

ERROL E. HARRIS
Northwestern University

HOLT, RINEHART AND WINSTON, INC.
New York   Chicago   San Francisco   Atlanta
Dallas   Montreal   Toronto

Copyright Acknowledgments

The author is grateful for permission to use the copyrighted material below.

Selection from John Watson's translation of *The Philosophy of Kant* reprinted by permission of Jackson Son & Co. (Booksellers) Ltd., Glasgow.

"Logical Atomism" reprinted from *Logic and Knowledge* by Bertrand Russell. By permission of George Allen & Unwin, Ltd.

Selections from Berkeley's Dialogues between *Hylas and Pilonous* and selections from Hume's *Treatise of Human Nature* reprinted by permission of the Clarendon Press, Oxford.

Preface

The student of philosophy has five things to learn: first and foremost to philosophize; secondly, to recognize and appreciate the main questions and topics with which the subject has traditionally been concerned; thirdly, to understand the sort of answers, with their supporting arguments, which have been given to the problems in the past; fourthly, to acquire a perspective of the historical development of philosophical theory; and fifthly, to read intelligently, to analyze and to assess critically philosophical texts. That he will learn all this sufficiently and satisfactorily from the perusal of this book is hardly to be expected, but I hope it may serve to introduce him to all five of these necessary facets of philosophical knowledge.

The first requisite, which is indispensable, cannot strictly be taught. Philosophizing is a skill not to be imparted by precept or instruction but to be acquired only by serving an apprenticeship in company with the great masters. In part it is an intellectual gift, in part it may be acquired by practice; but it will not be acquired without a genuine interest in the issue, and without hard and sincere thinking. Given these prerequisites, the best form of apprenticeship is a study of the works of the great philosophers of the past. In the course of this study the student must try to grasp the problems and think himself into and through the arguments. He must observe how the work of each philosopher advances upon that of his predecessors. He must criticize them and notice their shortcomings, and then try to form his own view of the problems discussed.

Accordingly, the study of suitably selected texts is the best method of achieving our five objectives. That is the method to be followed in this book, and the texts I have selected represent some of the most significant in western philosophical thought, both ancient and modern. In discussing them I shall not enter deeply into the history of philosophy but I shall try to put them in their historical context by suitable allusions, comments, and explanations, while concentrating primarily on the problems they raise and attempt to solve. The successive discussions will provide material for the construction in outline of a comprehensive theory in the light of more recent thinking and discovery.

This last, however, can properly be reached only by reviewing the present state of scientific and philosophical knowledge, as well as the aims and objectives of art and religion, and then by reflecting upon their mutual influences and compatibilities and the demands for coherence and consistency. Obviously this is the work of a lifetime, to which philosophers *pur sang* devote themselves. I hope that this book may help some students with philosophical inclinations to make a beginning, and others, who will not devote their whole lives to this task, to understand its interest, its fascination, and its importance even for those who are not professionally involved.

Indeed, philosophy has some appeal to everybody. However remote some of the more technical questions may seem from the affairs of our daily lives, there is a connection between them and other philosophical issues which have direct practical implications. Every philosophy is ultimately a way of life (whatever its proponents may say of it) and every way of life implies some philosophy, for after all, philosophy is nothing more nor less, in the last resort, than the effort to think as clearly, as rigorously, as coherently, and as effectively as we can about the matters most important to us. When we fail to do this we fail as philosophers.

The beginner in philosophy is apt to be bewildered by the criticism of successive theories, many of them at first appealing and attractive, which are nevertheless shown to lead to no firm ground. The critique appears to leave nothing standing. Disappointment that final answers are not forthcoming at the start and that no progress appears to be made, should not be allowed to degenerate into impatience with the method and despair of good results. With each rejected theory something is gained, not only the negative advantage of knowing what mistakes to avoid, but also positive advance pointing towards the next step to take — if it be no more than to explore some opposite alternative that may also have a contribution to make.

The initial discouragement will be less persistent if the student is himself genuinely seeking answers to the questions raised, so that he asks not only in what respects each author's theory fails to satisfy, but, how the theories may help toward the solution of his own problems. If, in this spirit, he approaches the texts selected for examination, he may hope to gain some profit from this introduction, which, if it succeeds, should whet his appetite for more detailed and more extensive study.

E. E. H.

Evanston, Illinois
December 1968

Contents

Fundamentals
of
Philosophy

A Study of Classical Texts

CHAPTER 1

Introduction

1. LEARNING BY DOING

Philosophy is a word much used and little understood — a fact which is perhaps not very surprising, because philosophers themselves disagree about its precise meaning, as they do about much else. This uncertainty of meaning and disagreement among the experts is not the only characteristic bewildering to the beginner; there is also a technicality and obscurity in the subject matter and its treatment which is apt to repel. Yet, if the right sort of approach is made, there should be no cause for discouragement on account of these seemingly forbidding aspects of the subject; for the study is really about the most familiar matters, and what is difficult and unfamiliar is only the exacting analysis of well-known conceptions which the method demands.

To attempt at the outset to define philosophy would be useless because any satisfactory definition would be intelligible only to the advanced student; nothing that a beginner could easily comprehend

1

would be adequate or correct. The only way to discover what philosophy is, is to do it—just as doing is the only way of learning to swim —and so to construct a definition as we proceed. We may begin with something naïve and provisional and then qualify and modify our definition as we become better acquainted with the discipline. This is the traditional and correct method of philosophizing: a continual debate, or running self-criticism, in which insights are acquired and evolved by continuous discussion. This is why philosophers always appear to disagree, because they are pursuing this method of developing a theory by progressive criticism, and their disagreement accordingly is not a sign of stupidity, ignorance, or ineptitude, but rather of progress and vitality in the pursuit of the proper method of acquiring knowledge and wisdom.

Though not always clearly apparent, the same is true of every intellectual discipline. All knowledge advances by discussion, even in the sciences. What is agreed upon and accepted is what is no longer of vital interest. The growing point of every branch of knowledge is a region of perpetual debate. It is more obviously the case in philosophy, because that is the intellectual discipline *par excellence* — what Hegel called "the thinking study of things" — and, in some sense, the growing point of all knowledge. Accordingly every science at its furthermost point of advance in the interpretation of its factual discoveries becomes philosophical.

We must not, therefore, be dismayed at the disagreement of philosophers, even about the character and object of their own study, for this is precisely the method of advance in the subject: a method which seeks to define some concept provisionally, as it appears to common sense, then to examine the definition, develop its implications to discover whether they are self-consistent, and correct it wherever it is found wanting. So we arrive at a rival definition—and a new theory of the conception defined—and proceed with a new critique, creating an appearance of disagreement by our natural process of advance. We shall find this form of discussion in the course of every good philosophical treatise—it is what Plato called "the dialogue in the soul." Even the individual philosopher, if he is worthy of his calling, argues with himself, and also criticizes the work of his predecessors and his colleagues, seeking not just to refute them but to discover what is reasonable, coherent, and true. Thus the history of philosophy also becomes a dialogue and a discussion, one which is never stale or dead because the issues are always current and, in some way, directly or indirectly, the concern of every thinking person.

2. THE BRANCHES OF PHILOSOPHY

This is most obvious in moral philosophy because morality is something none of us can escape. What we ought to do and how we ought to live are questions with which we are perennially confronted, whether or not we are habitually aware of them. As soon as we try to answer them, — and, by implication we answer them one way or another every time we act deliberately — we raise philosophical questions; for example we raise the question: By what criterion do we prefer one course of action to its alternatives? Or, when we express a preference, we raise the question: If we say A is better than B, what is our standard of evaluation? Such questions at once lead us further into philosophy. What are the principles of value? What is the source of moral obligation to act one way rather than another?

Questions like these are implicit in any and every practical decision we make. They are essentially philosophical questions, and thus philosophy, so far as it deals with value and with morals, deals with the most familiar matters. Value theory, moreover, is a large and important branch of philosophy; some thinkers have held it to comprise the whole subject. We shall see presently, however, that the branches of philosophy are not really separable — even though we can and must distinguish between them — so that the enthusiast for any one branch is apt to claim (not without justification) that the whole subject falls within it. Some have said that all philosophy is moral philosophy, and others that it is all logic, and yet others that it is all metaphysics. The truth is that these disciplines overlap. None can do without the rest and each is indispensable to all.

This is easy to illustrate without going very deeply into the subject matter of any branch of philosophy. Moral questions, we have seen, lead swiftly and directly to questions of moral philosophy and value theory, but they do not stop there. If I am concerned about what I ought to do, I at once become involved in the question of the criterion by which I judge. If I can discover a criterion of moral value, I do so by evaluating evidence and argument and by reasoning about these. But then I must be concerned to reason correctly and to argue soundly and I must know what evidence is to count. By what principles is some reasoning sound and valid and other reasoning sophistical and fallacious? By what principles do I decide that some evidence is relevant and that other evidence is beside the point? These are questions of logic, but ethics cannot do much without at least assuming that answers to them can be given.

Again my practical decisions are never made in a vacuum. I act in a definite situation, some features of which I must know about in order to act intelligently and deliberately. How do I acquire knowledge of the facts and how far is my knowledge reliable? As soon as I raise this question, I implicitly demand a theory of knowledge and I am embarked upon the study of epistemology, a distinct branch of philosophy, yet one on which all others are intimately dependent because they all seek to know and thus all assume that an answer to the question, "What is knowledge?" is at least possible.

In two ways at least any theory of knowledge involves yet another branch of philosophy: metaphysics. Sometimes this has been thought the most fundamental of all the sciences, and at other times it has been scoffed at as utterly meaningless and mystifying. In either case it is equally unavoidable. First, knowledge is commonly held to be our grasp of actuality and of what the world and things in it really are. If so we must be able to distinguish what they really are from what they only appear to be. This implies that we have a criterion of reality. What is it? The answer to this question (*whatever* it is) implies a metaphysical theory—a theory about the nature of reality. Secondly, a theory of knowledge is a theory of the relation between our minds and the world at large, so it involves a theory of mind as well as one of the world. Both such theories belong to metaphysics—the first, the theory of the mind, because it tells us what sort of entity can know, what it is to be capable of awareness, judgment, and knowledge. This is not just a psychological theory because psychology is a natural (or empirical) science, a branch of knowledge of the same kind and order as chemistry, physics, or biology. All such sciences assume before they begin that the answers to philosophical questions, such as those of which we have given examples, have already been given, or, if not, that some answer could be given. For if this were not the case, these sciences would be impossible. If there were no criterion of truth, of knowledge, or of reality; if it were in principle impossible to say what sort of entity could have knowledge or what relation between a mind and the world constitutes knowledge, then no claim to knowledge of any kind could ever be made. It is because there are sciences, and because we do claim to know some things and to be able to distinguish the true from the false, that we raise philosophical questions and search for answers which must in principle be possible.

If on the one hand we admit metaphysics to be the fundamental science, clearly we shall not try to avoid it but shall confess it to be required by every other discipline, because the ultimate questions about the nature of things are metaphysical questions. If, on the other hand, we renounce metaphysics and allege that it is worthless and devoid of meaning (as Hume and the Positivists did), we must do so on the ground of some conception or other of the general nature of things, of ourselves, and of knowledge – but that too will be or will imply a metaphysical theory.

Whatever metaphysical position we adopt is bound to have implications for epistemology and ethics and even (though attempts have been made to deny this) for logic. What the world and the mind are will determine what knowledge is. They will also determine what human action is and how it can be good or bad, right or wrong. If we say that metaphysics is nonsense, we imply a theory of knowledge and a criterion by which to decide what has sense. This again will have ethical repercussions. Once again, we find, every kind of philosophical thinking involves and requires every other. The subject is really one and indivisible, although it has distinct aspects and phases of which some appeal more strongly to some philosophers while others are more interesting to others.

3. PHILOSOPHICAL METHOD

The methods characteristic of all branches of philosophy have certain common features. There is much debate at the present time, and there has been also in the past, about whether philosophy can be "scientific" in its methods. It is not necessary to enter into this controversy here, for it will be sufficient to state at the outset those points on which there is agreement. Philosophy is like science in so far as it is essentially rationalistic, in the sense that it takes nothing merely on authority without investigation and criticism. No philosophical theory is accepted as merely intuitively compelling without any rational grounds, even if these be no more than that every possible means of investigation fails to reveal such grounds, so that the proposition in question must be accepted as primary. Secondly, the philosopher reaches his conclusions (when he does so legitimately) only by rigorous argument and valid reasoning. So far as he fails to demonstrate them he can offer them only as problematical. In short, philosophical theorizing is systematic thinking, as is all scientific theorizing. Nothing is scientific which is not systematic. What precisely is meant by systematic thinking and what sort of systematic thinking is peculiar to empirical science as distinct from philosophy are themselves philosophical questions that fall within the provinces of logic and epistemology.

R. G. Collingwood identified the relation between science and philosophy as one of degree of reflectiveness. The empirical scientist, he said, investigates – thinks about – an object directly. The philosopher investigates the scientist's thinking about that object; he thinks about the object in relation to the scientist's thinking. The astronomer, for instance, measures the distance of the earth from the moon. The philosopher of science asks what precisely a scientist is doing when he measures. "What is measurement?" So the philosopher's thinking is of the "second degree." Second degree thinking has first degree thinking as its object, and so it is reflective thinking.

It is to be noticed that when in everyday activities we measure something, or when as astronomers we compute the distance of a heavenly body, we assume that the answer to the qustion, "What is measurement?" is already known, and we proceed with the measurement as if we were clearly aware of what we were about. When we arrive at our result we say we *know* what it is, and we know it because we have measured. Unless we made these assumptions we could not begin to investigate things scientifically. When the philosopher raises the second degree questions, "What is measurement?" "How does it enable us to know?" he is attempting to bring these tacit assumptions to light, to face them, and to test their validity. He is not content simply to detect presuppositions; he considers how far they are mutually consistent, and if he finds that they are not he strives to criticize and correct them. Philosophy, thus, is the investigation of the presuppositions of common thinking and action and of scientific thinking. Not only science but every field of human activity involves presuppositions, and the various branches of philosophy relate to different fields of human thought and action.

For example, the simple act of coming to class is based on a number of unstated presuppositions. Anybody who performs this act presupposes that others will also do it. Since there must be at least a teacher and a student to make a class, the presupposition of the action is that at least one other person will come. It is presupposed also that some system of education is being implemented which requires the class to be held at a certain time and place. These presuppositions answer questions which the person acting has not (necessarily) raised; he has (as a rule) tacitly assumed the answers. Another presupposition, if the agent has come deliberately, is that he has some reason for doing so and therefore that he does so in preference to alternatives. That again presupposes that there is some standard or criterion of preferability and that he knows what it is.

Most people in such a simple case, if they were asked by what criterion they judged one action preferable to others, would cite some purpose which it served and which they wanted to realize; but if pressed for the reasons why they adopted this purpose, they would probably be at a loss for an answer. The investigation of these more fundamental presuppositions of deliberate action is at least part of ethics. Investigation of the presuppositions of aesthetic preferences would lead us to aesthetics. Similarly, investigation of the presuppositions of scientific method leads to epistemology and logic, and of the deliverances of scientific theory to metaphysics.

In all these cases we come in the last resort to the investigation of criteria of judgment. In ethics we become concerned with the criteria of rightness and goodness of action, in aesthetics with the criteria of beauty, in epistemology with the criteria of sound knowledge, in logic with those of validity, and in metaphysics with the criteria of reality (as contrasted with mere appearance). Philosophy has accordingly been called the body of criteriological sciences, and to the extent that it is, it always in some sense deals with values. Being a critical investigation of presupposed criteria, it is never purely descriptive, but always in a significant degree normative or prescriptive. To reveal what criteria are presupposed is not by itself sufficient. It is further necessary to find out whether they are mutually consistent and, if not, how they require modification. When this is determined we say not only what is presupposed in fact but what ought to be presupposed to make our thought and action consistent.

An example of this is Aristotle's investigation in the first book of the *Politics* of the institution of slavery among his Greek contemporaries. What, asks Aristotle in effect, would justify the use of a man as a slave? What is presupposed by such enslavement of another human being? His answer is that to use a man as a slave is to use him as a mere instrument, and that one would be justified in doing that only if the man were not capable of directing his own activities. A man who is so incapable, Aristotle maintains, is a slave by nature, and to enslave such a man would be justifiable. Aristotle leaves the matter so and assumes without further question that there are such people and that they may rightly be used as "living instruments." It did not occur to him that, according to his own theory of human nature and ethics, such a man would not be a responsible agent and would be incapable of virtue. In short, he would not be a man, properly speaking. So incapable an individual, even if there were such, would be useless as a slave. The presuppositions of slavery thus prove to be incoherent, and the injunction that no man ought be enslaved is shown to have good grounds.

When Kant spoke of philosophy as "critical" he was referring primarily to critical analysis of presupposed criteria. For him presuppositions were *a priori*, indicating that they were logically prior to the knowledge, action, or judgment under consideration. Nothing, he declared, not even religion, was so sacrosanct as to be immune to philosophical criticism. In other words, the value, validity, or authenticity of anything can be established only by critical analysis, and anything that claims exemption or withdraws at once becomes suspect, for if it cannot survive criticism, its claim to authenticity is hollow. Criticism is the fire in which its validity is proved.

4. PHILOSOPHY AND THE HISTORY OF PHILOSOPHY

Like every other civilized pursuit philosophy is rooted in history and can be properly understood only in the light of its past. We cannot fully understand contemporary philosophy or what modern philosophers are doing apart from their historical background, because what they write is the product in large measure of their reflection upon the work of their predecessors. This is also true to a greater extent than is usually realized of the work of scientists, but in the case of philosophy it is marked and inescapable. Nobody can develop an adequate philosophy for himself in complete ignorance of the philosophy of the past. If he could it would probably be something similar to the ideas produced by the Greeks in the sixth century B.C. Even this, however, is quite impossible, because philosophy begins from our ordinary everyday ideas and experience, which are already the products of a civilized way of living that has developed through past centuries and is saturated with concepts that past thinkers, scientists, and philosophers have contributed throughout its history. These we have incorporated "unconsciously," without clear awareness of their origins, into ways of thinking and acting which we take to be "natural" to us. For instance, we take it for granted today that no theory about what happens in the world around us is of much value unless it is based upon, and can be tested by, observation and experiment; but before the seventeenth century this would not normally have occurred even to highly intelligent people, who would have been prone to discount personal observations in the face of statements backed by high authority. Our modern attitude has been assimilated from our predecessors of the Renaissance, even though we are not necessarily aware of the fact, but take it as the natural attitude of all intelligent persons.

It is such ideas that we are called upon to examine in philosophy, and we cannot do so effectively if we take them in confused popular forms and in ignorance of their historical origin and development. They are, for the most part, philosophical theories which, in the course of time, have become accepted commonplaces. To understand them we must know their origins in, and as, past theories. But to understand their history we must not only recount past theories but must rethink them, redevelop them in our own thought, and by doing so enable ourselves to formulate new ideas that go beyond those of our predecessors.

The best introduction to philosophy is, therefore, to study the works of the great philosophers of the past. One defect of much contemporary philosophy is that it has developed from the work of certain brilliant mathematicians who had little interest in, and (in some cases) little knowledge of, the history of philosophy. So they and their followers have made mistakes, which had been made and corrected before, and of which they ought to have been forewarned had they paid more attention to earlier philosophy. Be that as it may, our plan in this book is to examine some of the works of past philosophers. We shall begin with Plato.

The way in which we shall proceed is to read the text of the *Phaedo*, and after each section of the argument we shall examine the essential issues in a brief commentary. When we have dealt with Plato we shall turn to modern philosophers and deal in the same way with the texts of Descartes's *Meditations,* some chapters of Locke's *Essay Concerning Human Understanding*, Berkeley's *Three Dialogues between Hylas and Philonous*, and extracts from Hume's *Treatise of Human Nature.* Then we shall look at some selections from Kant's *Critique of Pure Reason,* and finally at Bertrand Russell's essay on *Logical Atomism.*

"Why," you may ask, "should we go so far back in history as Plato?" Surely, our own age is so different from that of the Greeks and our knowledge so far in advance of theirs, that there is little or nothing we can learn from them — apart from the historical information we can gain about them. Is not Greek philosophy simply obsolete?

These objections rest on a misapprehension not only of the nature of philosophical thinking but also of the value of historical knowledge. History is not simply of antiquarian interest. We study it because in doing so we study the process by which our own age has come into being, and this is a process in which the earlier phases are taken up and preserved in the later. By studying past history we are learning at the same time about certain elements still present and at work in our own culture. Three main roots of modern Western culture are Greek thought, Hebraic religion, and Roman law. To study the first is far from being a waste of time, if we want to understand ourselves and the culture to which we belong and in which we have been nurtured. Many of the scientific, as well as the moral and political, ideas that influence us today — to mention only these — originated among the ancient

Greeks, and their philosophy is by no means irrelevant to our situation, nor are the answers they gave to fundamental questions obsolete or inapplicable to modern predicaments. Whether or not they are, or to what extent, can in any case be decided only by examining them, and whatever the outcome, that enterprise can hardly be unfruitful.

But to turn to the philosophical reasons for reading Plato, we may legitimately say that even if Plato's philosophy were "obsolete" (whatever that word is intended to mean in this context) that would be no reason for neglecting to study it. Philosophy is an activity, not just a theory. It is the activity of philosophizing; and to do it well requires practice. One way of practicing is to apprentice oneself to a master of the art, to watch him at work, and to imitate his technique. In reading Plato we come simultaneously into contact with two of the greatest masters of philosophical method, Socrates, who is dramatically presented in the dialogues, practicing the method that he made famous and which goes by his name, and Plato himself, who is at once a consummate dramatic and literary artist and an unrivaled philosopher.

Moreover, the problems we find being discussed by Socrates and his friends in Plato's dialogues are still being discussed by philosophers, although the intervening contributions of 2000 years have modified them and our contemporary approach to them. If we are to understand clearly what they are and how they arise, we shall find Plato as good a guide as any and better than most.

SUGGESTIONS FOR FURTHER READING

A. Sinclair, *Introduction to Philosophy*. New York: Oxford University Press, 1944.

C. J. J. Webb, *The History of Philosophy*. Oxford: Home University Library, 1947.

C. H. Perelman, *An Historical Introduction to Philosophical Thinking*. New York: Random House, 1965.

A. C. Ewing, *The Fundamental Questions of Philosophy*, Chapter I. New York: Macmillan, 1958.

PART I

Plato

CHAPTER 2

The Greek Background

We cannot simply begin with Plato, for just as our study of the Greeks helps us to understand the moderns, so to understand Plato we must seek the earlier origins of his thought. To understand Plato's writings we must approach them in the same historical spirit we have hitherto advocated, for Plato's philosophy is the product of reflection upon the thought of the two preceding centuries—one of the most intellectually productive periods in the world's history. There are four main influences of which we must take special note: (a) early Ionian "physical" philosophy, (b) the Pythagorean development of the Ionian philosophy, (c) the philosophy of Heraclitus, and (d) the Eleatic philosophy, founded by Parmenides along with the method of argument developed by his follower Zeno in its defense.

At the end of the sixth century B.C. a group of thinkers at Miletos in Ionia initiated the true beginning of scientific investigation. Prior to them, men had been content to tell stories to explain the world and the natural phenomena they experienced. Thus arose the wealth of mythology that has come down to us from every center of human culture. The Greeks seem to have been the first to ask for, and to be satisfied only with, rational explanations of experienced facts.

13

To understand a fact rationally is to see it as the consequence of a general principle in a system such that all explanation ultimately stems from a single universal principle. This has been the ideal of science from its beginnings and it still is. For example, the contemporary physicist Werner Heisenberg says: "The physicists today try to find a fundamental law of motion for matter from which all elementary particles and their properties can be derived mathematically."[1]

1. THE IONIANS

The first man to try to discover a single principle which would explain all terrestrial phenomena was Thales. He asked himself what the ultimate substance of all things might be, and decided that it must be water. The precise reasons that brought him to this conclusion we do not know (though there is some evidence supporting various reconstructions and surmises that were made by later historians), nor need they concern us here. The significance of Thales' pioneering thought is that it was the first with any scientific flavor. His immediate followers, about whom we know more, made this scientific endeavor plainly apparent.

Anaximander developed an elaborate and plausible cosmological theory derived from a small number of first principles, from which he rationally deduced explanations of astronomical phenomena. He postulated as the origin of all things an indeterminate "Boundless," which he thought of in a vague way as a sort of amalgam of all special and determinate material qualities. This Boundless was in constant vibratory motion, as a result of which opposite qualities separated out. They were the hot, the cold, the dry, and the moist. In combination these opposites give fire (hot and dry), air (hot and moist), water (cold and moist) and earth (cold and dry).[2] Further separation produced concentric layers of these substances with earth at the center, water next above earth, air above water, and fire in the outermost layer. But the heat of the fire was thought to expand the air and to cause a pressure which burst the outermost shell, so that the fiery exterior of the world was broken up into rings, each surrounded by a tube of cloud (moist or steamy air), through the apertures of which it shone as stars and other heavenly bodies.

---

[1]*Physics and Philosophy* (New York, Harper & Row, 1958; London, Unwin, 1959), p. 60.
[2]Earth, air, fire and water later came to be called "elements."

Anaximander was a more advanced and subtle thinker than his immediate successor and pupil Anaximenes, who adopted a simpler hypothesis more akin to Thales', but he changed the original principle from water to air. He seems, however, to have faced a further question that arises out of the one that Thales originally raised. If one asks what it is from which all things derive and finds what seems to be a satisfactory answer in a single substance, whether it be water or air (or, as Heraclitus later proposed, fire), the question naturally arises: If all things are basically made of the same stuff, why are they so different from one another? What is the explanation of the variety in the world? How does the one basic substance come to take so many divergent forms?

Anaximenes answered this question by saying that the differences were due to condensation and rarefaction of air, fire being more rarefied, water and earth more condensed. The differences between things thus depended upon the quantity of the original stuff contained in a given volume of space. Anaximenes' hypothesis thus turned the attention of thinkers toward the notions of quantity and number.

2. THE PYTHAGOREANS

A younger contemporary of Anaximenes, who spent his early life in the island of Samos, developed the Ionian ideas in a new and most far-reaching way. Pythagoras, experimenting with musical tones, discovered that the notes and harmonies of the scale depended upon the numerical proportions borne to one another by the lengths of the string of the monochord. This seems to have impressed upon Pythagoras the importance of the numerical aspect of things, as opposed to what things were made of. Consequently, he became the founder of theoretical mathematics, thus advancing beyond the empirical discoveries of certain numerical relationships already made by the Egyptians and Chaldeans.

We know very little about Pythagoras himself, but we do know that he was the head of a great scientific and philosophical movement which spread all over Greece and became a sort of religious sect, with "lodges" and schools in many places. We need not go into the precise details of the various doctrines that the school developed. It will be sufficient to list the more important ideas that emerged.

Pythagoras is credited with the dictum that "all things are numbers" and, as has been said, the numerical aspect of things was the main interest of the school. But at that early date there was no systematic numerical notation and numbers were represented by dots or pebbles

in the sand. The Pythagoreans became interested in the spatial arrangement of these dots and classified the numbers in accordance with
them. Thus the odd numbers were

square:

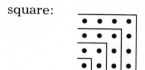

the even, oblong:

Triangular numbers

had special properties, giving a sort of visual formula for obtaining the
sum of consecutive integers. Consequently, the numbers were called
"schemata" (figures) or "$\epsilon'\iota\delta\eta$" (forms). What is chiefly noticeable
about these forms are the differences in qualitative character that go
along with the quantitative differences (squareness, triangularity, and
the like); Pythagoras had found a concomitance between the qualitative differences of sound and the quantitative differences of the sound-
ing objects. Next, the geometrical shapes were seen to possess special
geometrical properties (for example, the special relations between the
sides of a right angled triangle). Thus a solution of the problem set by
the Ionians was suggested: What accounts for the qualitative differences of things? Not their matter (what they are made of), but the
number or form that makes them specifically what they are.

Another important point to notice is that the mathematical concepts
represented by the forms are unchanging and eternal. Squareness
does not change into circularity or circularity into triangularity, although material things may be changed from one of these forms to
another by modification of the quantities of their constituents. The
square is an eternal idea and so is the circle. Numbers also are eternal,
each being peculiarly and unchangeably itself, with its own special
numerical properties. Likewise qualitative forms are insusceptible of
change: Middle C, redness, and the like. The material things assume or
display these qualities which are the same wherever they are met, and

the things change merely by changing from one to another in consequence of alterations in the quantity (and *ipso facto* in the arrangement) of their matter.

With this theory of numbers the Pythagoreans combined various doctrines which they had inherited from the Ionians. They made great play with the notion of opposites derived from Anaximander, extending the number much beyond four to constitute a list of ten pairs of categories ranged under one main opposition — that between the Unlimited (or indefinite) and the Limit. Here, too, we see the influence of Anaximander's theory of the Boundless, which was indefinite as to quality. For the Pythagoreans, definitive qualities within the Unlimited were produced by the imposition upon it of number or form, or precise limitiation. In this list of opposites, the third opposition was that of Many and One aligned under Unlimited and Limit. Thus the antitheses of matter and form became associated with that between the Unlimited and the Limit as well as with the Many and the One, where the unlimited was thought of as indefinite and unintelligible and the limit as that principle (or *logos*) that made things intelligible by delimitation. The intelligible principle was the one, and the unintelligible, the unordered manifold. These ideas were to bear fruit in later philosophy, especially in the work of Plato and Aristotle.

Pythagoreanism was not only a scientific school but also a religious sect, its religious beliefs having much in common with the Orphic religion of Greece. The main religious tenet was belief in the divinity of the human soul. The Pythagoreans believed that the soul was a divine and immortal being, imprisoned in the material body by which it was polluted and from which it must be freed by purification. Purification depended largely upon the individual's conduct and especially upon his observing a code of prescribed rules. If the soul was not purified, it passed, on the death of the body, into another body, possibly of some other species of animal, but if purification could be achieved, the soul was released altogether from its connection with the body and returned to the abode of the gods.

The Orphic version of this cult included elaborate purification rites involving the use of music to induce an emotional state of ecstasy through which purification was thought to be attained. The Pythagoreans seem to have refined the earlier practices. Possibly they considered the music the most important factor and its mathematical aspect as having magical properties. Eventually they came to think of the study of the mathematical aspect as affording the proper process of purification. For it seemed to the Pythagoreans that such intellectual activity was the truest and purest activity of the soul, so that devotion to it would release and withdraw the soul from the body altogether and thus enable it to attain its true immortality. Mathematics for the Greeks was synonymous with learning and the Pythagoreans included in it all knowledge and wisdom. Thus the love of wisdom (*philosophia*) and the way of philosophy came to be regarded as the true means of attaining purification of the soul and immortality.

3. HERACLITUS

A contemporary of Pythagoras, whose philosophy (so far as it has come down to us) is of enormous interest and which deserves far more attention than can be given to it here, is Heraclitus. He took the primary substance of things to be fire and identified fire with the soul. The universe, he believed, was a perpetual cyclic flux, nothing remaining the same for any length of time, but everything being in a state of constant change. The universe was a perpetual conflagration in which solid earth melted to water and evaporated into air, which sublimated into flame, and then as smoke and ash was precipitated again to earth to be rekindled into fire. "This world," he wrote, ". . . is an ever-living fire, with measures of it kindling, and measures going out."

For our purpose, the importance of the Heraclitean doctrine lies in the corollaries drawn from it by one of Heraclitus' later followers, Cratylus. If all things are in flux, what precisely are they? Any description that can be given by way of identifying any particular object becomes false as soon as it is enunciated, for the thing has then changed and the description is no longer applicable. At best we may make vague approximations, but any attempt at exactitude or precision will be defeated by the flux of the object of our reference. If this is so, exact science becomes impossible. We can have no precise knowledge about anything, no statement will ever be completely true, and the degree of its error can never be precisely determined. Cratylus, therefore, is said to have refused to make statements at all; in answer to questions he would merely wag (or, perhaps, point) his finger.

Here it is clear that certain presuppositions (which we commonly make) about knowledge are operative. It is assumed that only what is true can rank as knowledge and that truth is absolute — either all or nothing; what is not quite true is strictly not true at all, and therefore not knowledge. Again, what is true is true always, so that the object of knowledge must be eternal and unchanging. What constantly changes, therefore, cannot be an object for knowledge.

We may recall that for the Pythagoreans the intelligible objects were numbers—eternal, unchanging forms or ideas—and the unlimited, the many, and the indefinite were the unintelligible elements of things. The Heracliteans confirm this, for change is a manifold; but they refuse to admit the existence of anything else and assert that everything is always in flux. What changes never remains (and so never properly *is*) what at any moment it is said to be. It is constantly becoming something else—what it is not. It neither is, nor is not, precisely anything, and yet it is both something and something else—a very confusing state of affairs which does not lend itself to precise description or exact knowledge. It is hardly surprising that the next great thinker went to the opposite extreme and denied the possibility of change altogether—with at least as devastating an effect as the denial of permanence.

4. PARMENIDES

The philosopher who denied the existence of change was Parmenides of Elea (the founder of the Eleatic school of philosophy). He seems to have made a careful study of the work of the Pythagoreans and to have been much impressed by the power of deductive reasoning, perhaps because of their mathematical proofs. But for this very reason he believed that the Pythagoreans (and other philosophers) had allowed themselves to be led too far astray by appearances. Purely deductive reasoning seems to give us reliable—in fact indubitable—knowledge, without any appeal to the senses or to empirical confirmation. Once one has proved the theorem that the square on the diagonal of a right-angled triangle is equal to the sum of the squares on the other two sides, there is no need to measure; and if one did measure and found a discrepancy, it is the measurement one would suspect and not the proof. Whether or not this was in Parmenides' mind, he stated unequivocally that "it is the same thing that can be thought and that can be." In effect, he held that what is conceivable is real and true (in the strict sense of conceivable—not just what is imaginable, but what is conceivable logically and without contradiction). And what is not thinkable cannot be.

Now not-being (in Parmenides' language, "that which is not") cannot strictly be conceived, for whatever we conceive, we conceive as something, as some sort of object. To think of nothing is strictly not to think. So Parmenides concludes that there is no such thing as not-being—"That which is not, is not"—and that all previous philosophers who have treated nonbeing as an alternative reality to "that which is" have been mistaken and in consequence have fallen victim to illusion.

Such a conclusion, moreover, includes ordinary common sense as well, so that virtually all our common experience turns out to be illusory. Before we see that this follows, however, more explanation is needed.

The Pythagoreans treated the Unlimited, the opposite of the Limit, as unintelligible, and so associated it with darkness, fog, and mist. In Ionian thought the Unlimited again was associated with air. In the thought of the earlier philosophers there was considerable confusion between mist, darkness, and void or nothingness, for obviously what is dark does not appear to the senses, nor does the void, nor does air (and we may remember the parallel between the Boundless of Anaximander and the air of Anaximenes). All, therefore, gave some place in their systems to the void, or its equivalent; in short, to that which is not.

Now comes Parmenides, who declares that there is no void. He thought in strictly material terms. All that exists is "what is," and the universe therefore is a plenum, for "what is not" cannot be thought.

The corollaries of this dictum are completely revolutionary. I shall summarize the sort of argument that follows from it in my own way without attempting to reproduce exactly what is known of Parmenides' writings. What is could never have come into being, because that would imply a time when it was not—when nothing was—which is impossible. It could not come into being from what is other than being, because there is nothing other than being. For the same reason "what is" cannot cease to be, for then it would pass into what is not being, and that is impossible also. It follows further that there can be no change, because whatever is is, and to become something other would be to become something other than what is, that is to say, what is not.

Again if "what is not, is not," then the plenum of what is (of being) cannot be divided, because what could divide any one portion of it from any other could only be "what is not." If it were anything else it would be identical with being and there would be no division. It follows that no part of being can be other than, or different from, any other part of being, because what is other would be other than being—not-being—and there is no not-being; so no other.

We conclude, thus, that being is one, uncreated, and indestructible. There is no "other" and so there cannot be "a many" or more than one. Likewise there cannot be change or difference within the one. So there can be no movement, for movement is a form of change. There is no void in which to move, and it is impossible for anything to go from where it is to where it is not because "where it is not" has no meaning. There is no place where "what is" is not and so "what is" cannot move to any such place.

Consequently all variety, movement, change, multiplicity, difference, and divisibility is illusory and mere appearance. The theories describing the world in these terms are what Parmenides called "The Way of Belief," as opposed to "The Way of Truth," according to which the real is one, spherical, undifferentiated whole. (The allegation that it is spherical is strictly an inconsistency which was corrected by Melissus, one of Parmenides' disciples.)

Heraclitus declared that all was motion and change, which led Cratylus to the conclusion that nothing was knowable and no true statement could be made. Parmenides argues that only that is true which can be thought (or known), therefore there is no change or movement, and that only the eternal, uncreated, indestructible, unchanging One is real.

Why then do we experience change, variety, and movement? To this question Parmenides offers no answer. It is, he says, mere appearance and illusion, but what the source of the illusion could be his theory gives no clue. If all is one and unchanging, how can it appear to be many and variable? If the appearance occurs it must somehow be explicable and the explanation must be rooted in the real. The real must be such as to make the appearance possible. According to Parmenides' theory, no such appearance could occur, and our experience is therefore left unexplained by it. The best that Parmenides' followers could do to meet this objection (or its equivalent) was to show that no other theory could do any better. None could give any coherent account of multiplicity, movement, or change. The paradoxes of Parmenides' pupil, Zeno, were designed to demonstrate this.

5. ZENO

Although we remember Zeno chiefly for his paradoxes, he was better known among his contemporaries as the author of a special method of argument called dialectic. This was the method of exploring the logical consequences of a thesis or statement to show that it led equally to two inconsistent conclusions, then examining the opposite thesis in the same way to discover whether it would yield any better result.

The critics of Parmenides asserted that his thesis, that the real is one, led to absurdity and paradox; Zeno set out to show that the contrary position was even more absurd and analyzed the thesis "that there is a Many" to demonstrate that it too leads to contradictions.[3]

---

[3]Cf. Plato, *Parmenides*, 128c.

Now the philosophers who maintained that there is a Many were almost certainly the Pythagoreans. They were probably the original butt of Parmenides' criticism and very likely the people who objected that his thesis led to absurdities. They maintained that all things are numbers, but it is not easy to see what such a statement could mean if it did not at least imply that all things had distinct and numerable parts; and if their essential nature depended on their number, that must be something definite and precise, so that each thing must have certain ultimate parts or units of construction, on the number of which its essential nature would depend. The difficulty then arises of determining what constitutes a unit.

Zeno argued that if things are a Many, and that means a number of units, it would be impossible to say what things are unless we knew what a unit is. But every attempt to say what a unit is breaks down. The unit cannot be divisible because, if it were, it would be two or more and not one (or a unit). But if it is indivisible then there can never be a finite number of units in any material thing, because of any quantity one can always take half, and likewise of any portion of it, however small. So whatever number of units you may assign to things will be insufficient. Consequently, one has to say that if units are indivisible they must be infinite in number. But if infinite they can have no magnitude (for if they have they will be divisible), and if they have no magnitude, nothing which has magnitude can be composed of them (any number of zeros amount to no more than zero). If you deny that they have no magnitude, you have to say that things are infinite in size, because there must be an infinity of indivisible units. On the other hand, if you deny that units are infinite in number, you must assert that they are divisible in quantity.

Thus, if things are a Many, they can be neither finite in number nor infinite in number — or alternatively you will have to assert both with equal cogency.

Similarly motion, which Parmenides denied, cannot be made intelligible. To show this Zeno introduced his famous paradoxes. A moving body (for example, an arrow) must at each instant coincide with the space it occupies (that is, the points that make up its length); therefore at each instant it must be stationary, as is the space it occupies. But points and instants are indivisible, so between one set of points and the next, nothing intervenes; and between one instant and the next, there is no time in which the arrow can change its position. Therefore it cannot change its position or move at all.

Again, a body cannot traverse a given space (or length) unless it first traverses half of the space; but it cannot traverse half unless it first traverses half of that, and so on *ad infinitum*. Therefore a body cannot begin to move.

Likewise Achilles trying to overtake the tortoise can never do so, for when he reaches the point at which the tortoise started, it will have moved some distance forward to a new point ahead; and when Achilles gets to that point it will have moved forward again. However small the interval, it must take some time to cover, and however short the time, the tortoise will have moved some distance forward. So Achilles can never catch up.

In each case we are faced with the necessity of traversing seriatim an infinite number of parts (or units) in a finite time, which is an impossibility. If we attempt to avoid the difficulty by saying that the units have no magnitude, then the space to be traversed becomes nothing and cannot be traversed. No movement is possible in no space. Yet if we admit that the units have size, then the space becomes infinite and can never be traversed.

Alternatively, if we try to maintain that the units are finite in number and have a definite magnitude, then they must be divisible, or continuous motion is impossible, for before it can move from one unit of space to the next, a body must pass over half (or some portion) of the succeeding unit. For continuous motion the units of time must be similarly divisible, but as we saw, divisible quantities are not units: each would have to be a many. Let us try, then, to say that motion is discontinuous —but then how can it be motion? For at every instant the allegedly moving body must be stationary, in the place where it is, and between places and instants (the indivisible parts of space and time) there is no interval to traverse and no time in which to move.

Zeno concludes accordingly that even less sense can be made out of the thesis that things are a many than can be made out of the thesis that all being is one. Little wonder then that a new set of thinkers arose who maintained that no theory was any better than any other. Before we take notice of Zeno's successors, however, let us review the development of Greek thought to this point, in order to list the more important influences exerted upon Plato. The account given thus far has omitted many important thinkers and theories, for our purpose is not to give an exhaustive history of early Greek philosophy, but only to trace the origins of the most important of Plato's ideas. We have altogether omitted the Pluralists, Empedocles, and Anaxagoras; nor have we mentioned the Atomists, Leucippus, and Democritus. The latter thinkers hardly influenced Plato at all, but we shall have occasion to refer to Anaxagoras later.

6. SUMMARY

We may now list the ideas which have been developed thus far as follows:

(a)   the idea of some kind of primary matter, suggested by the Ionians: a unitary substratum underlying all the differences and variety of things.

(b)   the Pythagorean idea of numbers as schemata or forms determining the qualitative differences and intelligible characters of things, by the imposition of definite limits or proportions upon the indefinite material substratum.

(c)   the Heraclitean notion of perpetual flux leading to the conclusion that nothing material is precisely knowable.

(d)   the Parmenidean conception of a transcendent One which alone is knowable and thinkable, as opposed to the many and changeable, which are merely apparent and illusory.

(e)   the Pythagorean belief in an immortal soul imprisoned in a material body, condemned to flit from one body to another until by purification it can escape to some form of Elysium.

(f)   the Pythagorean theory of purification as the study of mathematics, the purest form of activity of the soul.

(g)   finally, the dialectical method of Zeno of developing the logical consequences of contrary theses to see whether or not they are self-consistent.

We shall find all of these ideas developed in an interesting and significant way in the work of Plato.

7. THE SOPHISTS

So many conflicting views had by now been put forward by the Greek philosophers that a number of teachers appeared who argued that no opinion was any better than any other. Not only were there conflicting philosophical theories, all seeming to lead to paradox, but also a number of competing religions, while it was obvious to all intelligent people that the old traditional stories about the gods were hopelessly inconsistent. The upshot was scepticism both as to the possibility of knowledge and with respect to morals. The idea became current that all one needed to do to succeed in life was to make one's case appear the better one whenever a dispute arose — the question of actual truth did not, and could not, arise.

So the new body of teachers, called Sophists, who toured from city to city, teaching for fees, claimed to be able to train young men in "virtue," by which was meant that skill in public speaking which would enable one to make a good case on whichever side of the debate one might be.

The Sophists asserted the relativism of truth and moral goodness, and were for the most part sceptical in their views. The two greatest and most famous of the Sophists, Protagoras and Gorgias, each left writings, brief fragments of which have come down to us. Though they seem to have maintained opposite theses, the fragments that have been preserved give the impression that their conclusions were equally sceptical.

Protagoras is quoted as writing: "Man is the measure of all things; of those that are, that they are; of those that are not, that they are not," which is as much as to say that, as things seem to man, so they are, and every opinion is as true as every other. The difference between appearance and reality is here denied. If all opinions are equally true, even when they contradict one another, then all truth is at an end and it is all one whether we say that all or none are true.

Gorgias' pronouncements were: "Nothing exists. If anything does exist, it cannot be known. If anything were knowable, it could not be communicated." The grounds for these statements are not elaborated. Possibly Gorgias concluded that the arguments of Parmenides showed the impossibility of knowing anything about the real. What we do seem to know is utterly different from what the Eleatics claimed to be intelligible. It answered more precisely to the Heraclitean description of flux, which was now seen to be unknowable. Cratylus was also considered by some to be a Sophist. So we cannot know if anything exists or communicate what we do experience.

It seems to follow from this that there can be no objective standards of judgment. Right and wrong are what men make them out to be. As the opinion of each is true for him, so each goes out for his own enjoyment and satisfaction and the strongest gets his own way, compelling the weaker to do his will and imposing rules upon him that he must perforce obey. These rules are called moral rules and to comply with them is called justice, but they are no more than the stronger imposes in his own interest, and in the last resort might is right; or rather, the question of right simply does not arise.

In many ways the age of the Sophists is not unlike our own. Relativism was the fashionable doctrine, traditional religion and morality were discredited by the rising generation, and the metaphysical type of philosophy was despised. As today mathematics and the natural sciences are respected for their precise methods, so in those days mathematics was considered the ideal form of knowledge; the sciences of nature, having not yet developed, were still metaphysical. The Sophists, like many contemporary philosophers, though in not quite the same way, devoted much of their attention to language, its forms and usages, and logic-chopping was much practiced, almost as a fashionable pastime.

8. SOCRATES

In the midst of this situation there arose a critic of the times, of the Sophists, and of current morals and politics, whose influence marked a revolution in philosophy. He was Socrates, who believed it to be his divine mission in life to combat the process of degeneration both in morals and in knowledge, which, he held, were inseparable or even identical. This he did in personal conversation, by a process of question and answer, a method which owed something to Zeno. He demanded precise definitions and then analyzed them logically to see whether they were self-consistent.

As the Sophists claimed to teach "virtue," it was for the definition of moral terms that Socrates constantly asked. But he was concerned not only with the Sophists, but primarily with the conduct of the citizens and politicians of Athens. He questioned all and sundry, frequently asking those who posed as experts in any field to define the subject of their expertise. He would then press further questions, forcing his companions to qualify their definitions until they proved untenable. At that point a new and better definition was sought which would avoid the defects of the first, and so on, resulting usually in the failure of the company to produce any satisfactory account of the matter under examination. Socrates claimed that to have arrived at this point was a gain, for to recognize one's own ignorance is much better than to believe one knows what one does not, and such recognition is the soundest starting point for learning and wisdom. It was, in fact, all the wisdom Socrates himself ever claimed. He never wrote anything and never made long speeches or gave lectures, and he objected when others did so; because, he pretended, he had a poor memory and needed to examine one point at a time to see where that led, before considering another.

It is to be noticed, however, that there are several very positive presuppositions in this Socratic method of procedure. It is assumed that properly to know something you must be able to define it clearly, precisely, and consistently; if you can, the definition will state just what is clearly intelligible in the subject. To establish such definitions (in morals and other fields) would then give us firm standards and criteria on which to found our knowledge. In geometry we do this. We define our terms in a precise and self-evident way and then proceed by strict deduction to reliable conclusions. But the definition gives us only the concept or "form" of the definiendum and none of the examples we can produce exactly fits it. They are all in some degree only approximations. Moreoever, they are changeable and imprecise and to that extent unintelligible. Whereas the definition is one and unchanging, the examples that fall under it are many and various. There is thus a sharp distinction between the intelligible concept and the sensible objects to which it applies. The latter are not intelligible in the same way as the concept and are intelligible only so far as they emobody the idea. Here the idea or form (what is stated in the definition) corresponds to the intelligible One of Parmenides and the sensible many to the Heraclitean flux.

At least, this seems to have been the way in which Socrates' pupil Plato saw the implications of his method of questioning, and we may best examine it as he presents it to us in the dialogues which represent Socrates in conversation with his fellow Greeks.

SUGGESTIONS FOR FURTHER READING

John Burnet, *Greek Philosophy from Thales to Plato*. New York: Macmillan, 1960.

A. E. Taylor, *Socrates*. New York: Anchor Books, 1960.

A. H. Armstrong, *Introduction to Ancient Philosophy*. London: Methuen, 1957.

R. G. Collingwood, *The Idea of Nature* (Part I). New York: Galaxy Books, Oxford University Press, 1965.

E. E. Harris, *Nature, Mind and Modern Science* (Part I). London: Allen and Unwin, 1954; New York: Humanities Press, 1954.

Werner Jaeger, *Theology of the Early Greek Philosophers*. New York: Oxford University Press, 1960.

CHAPTER 3

Virtue and Knowledge

Phaedo[1]

Persons of the Dialogue

PHAEDO, *who is the narrator*   APOLLODORUS
of the Dialogue to   SIMMIAS
Echecrates of Phlius   CEBES
SOCRATES   CRITO
ATTENDANT OF THE PRISON

SCENE: The Prison of Socrates

PLACE OF THE NARRATION: Phlius

57   ECHECRATES. Were you yourself, Phaedo, in the prison with Socrates on the day when he drank the poison?

PHAEDO. Yes, Echecrates, I was.

ECH. I should so like to know what he said during his last hours, and the

---

[1]The translation is by Benjamin Jowett. The numbers in the margin are the page numbers of the Stephanus edition of Plato's works.

28

manner of his death. No Phliasian goes much to Athens now, and it is a long time since any stranger has come from there who could give us a trustworthy account. We heard that he died by taking poison: but that was all.

58   PHAED. Did you not hear of the proceedings at the trial?

ECH. Yes; someone told us about the trial, and we could not understand why, having been condemned, he should have been put to death, not at the time, but long afterwards. What was the reason of this?

PHAED. An accident, Echecrates: the stern of the ship which the Athenians send to Delos happened to have been crowned on the day before he was tried.

ECH. What is this ship?

PHAED. It is the ship in which, according to Athenian tradition, Theseus went to Crete when he took with him "the fourteen," and was the saviour of them

b   and of himself. And they are said to have vowed to Apollo at the time, that if they were saved they would send a yearly mission to Delos. Well, the custom has continued without a break to this day, and the whole period of the voyage to and from Delos, beginning when the priest of Apollo crowns the stern of the ship, is a holy season, during which it is strictly forbidden to pollute the city by

c   executions; and when the vessel is detained by contrary winds, the time spent in going and returning is very considerable. As I was saying, the ship was crowned on the day before the trial, and this was the reason why Socrates lay in prison and was not put to death until long after he was condemned.

ECH. What was the manner of his death, Phaedo? What was said or done? And which of his friends were with him? Or would the authorities forbid them to be present—so that he had no friends near him when he died?

d   PHAED. No; there were some with him, in fact a good many.

ECH. If you have nothing else to do, I wish that you would tell me what passed, as exactly as you can.

PHAED. I have nothing at all to do, and will try to give you the facts. To be reminded of Socrates is always the greatest delight to me, whether I speak myself or hear another speak of him.

ECH. You will have listeners who are of the same mind with you; just try to relate everything as precisely as possible.

e   PHAED. I had a singular feeling at being in his company. For I could hardly believe that I was present at the death of a friend, and therefore I did not pity him, Echecrates; he died so fearlessly, and his words and bearing were so noble and gracious, that to me he appeared blessed. I thought that even in going to the other world he could not be without a divine call, and that he would be happy, if any man ever was, when he arrived there; and therefore no feeling of

59   pity for him entered my mind, as might have seemed natural at such an hour. Nor on the other hand did I feel pleasure that we were occupied as usual with philosophy (that was the theme of our conversation). My state of mind was curious, a strange compound of pleasure and pain, as I reflected that he was soon to die; and this double feeling was shared by us all; we were laughing and

b   weeping by turns, especially the excitable Apollodorus—you know what kind of man he is?

ECH. Yes.

PHAED. He was quite beside himself; and I and all of us were greatly moved.

ECH. Who were present?

PHAED. Of native Athenians there were, besides Apollodorus, Critobulus and his father, Hermogenes, Epigenes, Aeschines, Antisthenes; likewise Ctesippus

of the deme of Paeania, Menexenus, and some others; Plato, if I am not mistaken, was ill.

ECH. Were there any strangers?

c   PHAED. Yes, there were; Simmias the Theban, and Cebes, and Phaedondes;
Euclides and Terpsion, who came from Megara.

ECH. And was Aristippus there, and Cleombrotus?

PHAED. No, they were said to be in Aegina.

ECH. Anyone else?

PHAED. I feel fairly sure that these were all.

ECH. Well, and what did you talk about?

PHAED. I will begin at the beginning, and endeavour to repeat the entire con-
d   versation. During the whole time we had all been used to visit Socrates daily,
assembling early in the morning at the court in which the trial took place as it
was not far from the prison. There we would wait talking with one another until
the opening of the doors (for they were not opened very early); then we went in
and generally passed the day with Socrates. On the last morning we assembled
e   sooner than usual, having heard on the day before when we quitted the prison
in the evening that the sacred ship had come from Delos; and so we arranged to
meet very early at the accustomed place. On our arrival the jailer who answered
the door, instead of admitting us, came out and told us to wait until he called us.
"For the Eleven," he said, "are now with Socrates; they are taking off his chains,
and giving orders that he is to die today." He soon returned and said that we
60   might come in. On entering we found Socrates just released from chains, and
Xanthippe, whom you know, sitting by him, and holding his child in her arms.
When she saw us she uttered a cry and burst out in true feminine fashion:
"O Socrates, this is the last time that you will converse with your friends, and
they with you." Socrates turned to Crito and said: "Crito, let someone take her
home." Some of Crito's people accordingly led her away, crying out and beating
her breast. When she was gone, Socrates, sitting up on the couch, bent and
b   rubbed his leg, saying, as he was rubbing: How singular is the thing mankind
call pleasure, and how curiously related to pain, which might be thought to be
the opposite of it; for they are never present to a man at the same instant, and
yet he who pursues and gets either is generally compelled to get the other; their
bodies are two, but they are joined by a single head. And I cannot help thinking
c   that if Aesop had remembered them, he would have made a fable about God
trying to reconcile their strife, and how, when he could not, he fastened their
heads together; and this is the reason why when one comes the other follows:
as I know by my own experience now, when after the pain in my leg which was
caused by the chain pleasure, it seems, has succeeded.

Upon this Cebes said: I am glad, Socrates, that you have mentioned the name
d   of Aesop. For it reminds me of a question which has been asked by many,
and was asked of me only the day before yesterday by Evenus—he will be sure
to ask it again, and therefore if you would like me to have an answer ready for
him, you may as well tell me what I should say to him: he wanted to know for
what conceivable reason you, who never before wrote a line of poetry, now that
you are in prison are turning Aesop's fables into verse, and also composing that
hymn in honour of Apollo.

Tell him, Cebes, he replied, what is the truth—that I had no idea of rivalling
e   him or his poems; to do so, as I knew, would be no easy task. But I wanted to
see whether I could satisfy my conscience on a scruple which I felt about the

meaning of certain dreams. In the course of my life I have often had intimations
in dreams "that I should make music." The same dream came to me sometimes
in one form, and sometimes in another, but always saying the same or nearly
the same words: "Set to work and make music," said the dream. And hitherto
I had imagined that this was only intended to exhort and encourage me in the
61 study of philosophy, which has been the pursuit of my life, and is the noblest and
best of music. The dream was bidding me do what I was already doing, in the
same way that the competitor in a race is bidden by the spectators to run when
he is already running. But I was not certain of this; for the dream might have
meant music in the popular sense of the word, and being under sentence of
death, and the festival giving me a respite, I thought that it would be safer for
me to satisfy the scruple, and, in obedience to the dream, to compose a few
b verses before I departed. And first I made a hymn in honour of the god of the
festival, and then considering that a poet, if he is really to be a poet, should not
only put together words, but should invent stories, and that I have no invention,
I took some fables of Aesop, which I had ready at hand and knew by heart—the
first that occurred to me—and turned them into verse. Tell this to Evenus,
Cebes, and bid him farewell from me; say that I would have him come after me
if he be a wise man, and not tarry; and that today I am likely to be going, for the
c Athenians say that I must.
    Simmias said: What a message for such a man! Having been a frequent com-
panion of his I should say that, as far as I know him, he will never take your
advice unless he is obliged.
    Why, said Socrates, is not Evenus a philosopher?
    I think that he is, said Simmias.
    Then he, or any man who has the spirit of philosophy, will be willing to die;
but he will not take his own life, I conceive, for that is held to be unlawful.
    Here he changed his position, and put his legs off the couch on to the ground,
d and during the rest of the conversation he remained sitting.
    Why do you say, inquired Cebes, that a man ought not to take his own life,
but that the philosopher will be ready to follow one who is dying?
    Socrates replied: And have you, Cebes and Simmias, who are the disciples of
Philolaus, never heard him speak of this?
    Yes, but his language was indefinite, Socrates.
    My words, too, are only an echo; but there is no reason why I should hesitate
e to repeat what I have heard: and indeed, when a man is going to the other world,
it seems highly proper for him to reason and speculate about the nature of our
sojourn there. What could one do better in the interval between this and the
setting of the sun?
    Then tell me, Socrates, why is suicide held to be unlawful? as I have certainly
heard Philolaus, about whom you were just now asking, affirm when he was
staying with us at Thebes; and there are others who say the same, although I
have never heard anybody give a definite reason.
62 Do not lose heart, replied Socrates, and the day may come when you will hear
one. I suppose that you wonder why, when other things which are evil may be
good at certain times and to certain persons, death is to be the only exception,
and why, when a man is better dead, he is not permitted to be his own bene-
factor, but must wait for the kindness of another.
    Very true, said Cebes, laughing gently and speaking in his native Boeotian.
b I admit the appearance of inconsistency in what I am saying; but there may

not be any real inconsistency after all. There is a doctrine whispered in secret that man is a prisoner who has no right to open the door and run away; this is a great mystery, not to be easily apprehended. Yet I too believe that the gods are our guardians, and that we men are a chattel of theirs. Do you not agree?

Yes, I quite agree, said Cebes.

c   And if one of your own chattels, an ox or an ass, for example, took the liberty of putting itself out of the way when you had given no intimation of your wish that it should die, would you not be angry with it, and would you not punish it if you could?

Certainly, replied Cebes.

Then, if we look at the matter thus, there may be reason in saying that a man should wait, and not take his own life unless God sends some constraint such as that which has now come upon me.

Yes, Socrates, said Cebes, there seems to be truth in what you say. And yet
d how can you reconcile this seemingly true belief that God is our guardian and we his chattels, with the uncomplaining willingness to die which you were just now attributing to the philosopher? That the wisest of men should leave without reluctance a service in which they are ruled by the gods, who are the best of rulers, is not reasonable; for surely no wise man thinks that when set at liberty he will be able to take better care of himself. A fool may perhaps think so—he
e may argue that he had better run away from his master, not considering that he ought not to run away from the good but to cling to it, and that there would therefore be no sense in his running away. The wise man will want to be ever with him who is better than himself. Now this, Socrates, looks like the reverse of what was just now said; upon this view the wise man should sorrow and the fool rejoice at passing out of life.

63   The earnestness of Cebes seemed to please Socrates. Here, said he, turning to us, is a man who is always inquiring, and is not so easily convinced by the first thing which he hears.

And to me too, added Simmias, the objection which he is now making does appear to have some force. For what can be the meaning of a truly wise man wanting to fly away and lightly leave a master who is better than himself? And I rather imagine that Cebes is referring to you; he thinks that you are too ready to leave us, and too ready to leave the gods whom you acknowledge to be our good masters.

Yes, replied Socrates; there is justice in what you say. And so you think that
b I ought to answer your indictment as if I were in a court?

We should like you to do so, said Simmias.

Then I must try to make a more successful defence before you than I did before the judges. For I am quite ready to admit, Simmias and Cebes, that in meeting death without resentment I should be doing wrong, if I were not persuaded in the first place that I am going to other gods who are wise and good (of which
c I am as certain as I can be of any such matters), and secondly (though I am not so sure of this last) to men departed, better than those whom I leave behind; and therefore I do not resent it as I might have done, for I have good hope that there is yet something remaining for the dead, and as has been said of old, some far better thing for the good than for the evil.

But do you mean to take away your thoughts with you, Socrates? said Simd mias. Will you not impart them to us?—for they are a benefit in which we too are entitled to share. Moreover, if you succeed in convincing us, that will be the answer to the charge against yourself.

I will do my best, replied Socrates. But you must first let me hear what Crito wants; he has long been wishing to say something to me.

Only this, Socrates, replied Crito: the attendant who is to give you the poison has been telling me, and he wants me to tell you, that you are not to talk much; talking, he says, increases heat, and this is apt to interfere with the action of the
e poison; persons who excite themselves are sometimes obliged to take a second or even a third dose.

Never mind him, said Socrates, let him be prepared to give the poison twice or even thrice if necessary; that is all.

I knew quite well what you would say, replied Crito; but he has been worrying me about it for some time.

Never mind him, he repeated; and went on. Now, O my judges, I desire to prove to you that the real philosopher has reason to be of good cheer when he
64 is about to die, and that after death he may hope to obtain the greatest good in the other world. And how this may be, Simmias and Cebes, I will endeavour to explain. For I deem that the true votary of philosophy is likely to be misunderstood by other men; they do not perceive that of his own accord he is always engaged in the pursuit of dying and death; and if this be so, and he has had the desire of death all his life long, why when his time comes should he repine at that which he has been always pursuing and desiring?

Simmias said laughingly: Though I am not altogether in a laughing humour,
b you have made me laugh, Socrates; for I cannot help thinking that the many when they hear your words will say how truly you have described philosophers, and our people at home will likewise say that philosophers are in reality moribund, and that they have found them out to be deserving of the death which they desire.

And they are right, Simmias, in thinking so, with the exception of the words "they have found them out"; for they have not found out either in what sense the true philosopher is moribund and deserves death, or what manner of death
c he deserves. But enough of them: let us discuss the matter among ourselves. Do we attach a definite meaning to the word "death"?

To be sure, replied Simmias.

Is it not just the separation of soul and body? And to be dead is the completion of this; when the soul exists by herself and is released from the body, and the body is released from the soul. This, I presume, is what is meant by death?

Just so, he replied.

There is another question, which will probably throw light on our present
d inquiry if you and I can agree about it: Ought the philosopher to care about such pleasures – if they are to be called pleasures – as those of eating and drinking?

Certainly not, answered Simmias.

And what about the pleasures of love – should he care for them?

By no means.

And will he think much of the other ways of indulging the body, for example, the acquisition of costly raiment or sandals, or other adornments of the body? Instead of caring about them, does he not rather despise anything more than
e nature needs? What do you say?

I should say that the true philosopher would despise them.

Would you not say that he is entirely concerned with the soul and not with the body? He would like, as far as he can, to get away from the body and to turn to the soul.

Quite true.

First, therefore, in matters of this sort philosophers, above all other men, may
65 be observed in every sort of way to dissever the soul from the communion of
the body.

Very true.

Whereas, Simmias, the rest of the world are of opinion that to him who has
no taste for bodily pleasures and no part in them, life is not worth having; and
that he who is indifferent about them is as good as dead.

Perfectly true.

What again shall we say of the actual acquirement of knowledge? Is the
body, if invited to share in the inquiry, a hindrance or a help? I mean to say,
b have sight and hearing, as found in man, any truth in them? Are they not, as
the poets are always repeating, inaccurate witnesses? and yet, if even they are
inaccurate and indistinct, what is to be said of the other senses? — for you will
allow that they are the best of them?

Certainly, he replied.

Then when does the soul attain truth? — for in attempting to consider anything in company with the body she is obviously deceived by it.
c   True.

Then must not true reality be revealed to her in thought, if at all?

Yes.

And thought is best when the mind is gathered into herself and none of these
things trouble her — neither sounds nor sights nor pain, nor again any pleasure,
— when she takes leave of the body, and has as little as possible to do with it,
when she has no bodily sense or desire, but is aspiring after true being?

Certainly.

And here again it is characteristic of the philosopher to despise the body; his
d soul runs away from his body and desires to be alone and by herself?
That is true.

Well, but there is another thing, Simmias: Is there or is there not an absolute
justice?

Assuredly there is.

And an absolute beauty and absolute good?

Of course.

But did you ever behold any of them with your eyes?

Certainly not.

Or did you ever reach them with any other bodily sense? — and I speak not of
these alone, but of absolute greatness, and health, and strength, and, in short,
of the reality or true nature of everything. Is the truth of them ever perceived
e through the bodily organs? or rather, is not the nearest approach to the
knowledge of their several natures made by him who so orders his intellectual
vision as to have the most exact conception of the essence of each thing which
he considers?

Certainly.

And he attains to the purest knowledge of them who goes to each with the
intellect alone, not introducing or intruding in the act of thought sight or any
66 other sense together with reason, but with the intellect in its own purity
searches into the truth of each thing in its purity; he who has got rid, as far as
he can, of eyes and ears and, so to speak, of the whole body, these being in his
opinion distracting elements which when they associate with the soul hinder

her from acquiring truth and knowledge — who, if not he, is likely to attain to the knowledge of true being?

What you say has a wonderful truth in it, Socrates, replied Simmias.

And when real philosophers consider all these things, will they not be led to
b make a reflection which they will express in words something like the following? "Have we not found," they will say, "a path of thought which seems to bring us and our argument to the conclusion, that while we are in the body, and while the soul is mixed with the evils of the body, our desire will not be satisfied? and our desire is of the truth. For the body is a source of countless distractions by reason of the mere requirement of food, and is liable also to diseases
c which overtake and impede us in the pursuit of truth: it fills us full of loves, and lusts, and fears, and fancies of all kinds, and endless foolery, and in very truth, as men say, takes away from us the power of thinking at all. Whence come wars, and fightings, and factions? whence but from the body and the lusts of the body? All wars are occasioned by the love of money, and money has to be acquired for
d the sake of the body and in slavish ministration to it; and by reason of all these impediments we have no time to give to philosophy; and, last and worst of all, even if the body allows us leisure and we betake ourselves to some speculation, it is always breaking in upon us, causing turmoil and confusion in our inquiries, and so amazing us that we are prevented from seeing the truth. It has been proved to us by experience that if we would have pure knowledge of anything
e we must be quit of the body — the soul by herself must behold things by themselves: and then we shall attain that which we desire, and of which we say that we are lovers — wisdom; not while we live, but, as the argument shows, only after death, for if while in company with the body the soul cannot have pure knowledge, one of two things follows — either knowledge is not to be attained at all,
67 or, if at all, after death. For then, and not till then, the soul will be parted from the body and exist by herself alone. In this present life, we think that we make the nearest approach to knowledge when we have the least possible intercourse or communion with the body, and do not suffer the contagion of the bodily nature, but keep ourselves pure until the hour when God himself is pleased to release us. And thus getting rid of the foolishness of the body we may expect to be pure and hold converse with the pure, and to know of our-
b selves all that exists in perfection unalloyed, which, I take it, is no other than the truth. For the impure are not permitted to lay hold of the pure." These are the sort of words, Simmias, which the true lovers of knowledge cannot help saying to one another, and thinking. You would agree; would you not?

Undoubtedly, Socrates.

But, O my friend, if this be true, there is great reason to hope that, going whither I go, when I have come to the end of my journey I shall fully attain that which has been the pursuit of our lives. And therefore I accept with good hope
c this change of abode which is now enjoined upon me, and not I only, but every other man who believes that his mind has been made ready and that he is in a manner purified.

Certainly, replied Simmias.

And does it not follow that purification is nothing but that separation of the soul from the body, which has for some time been the subject of our argument; the habit of the soul gathering and collecting herself into herself from all sides out of the body; the dwelling in her own place alone, as in another life, so also
d in this, as far as she can; the release of the soul from the chains of the body?

Very true, he said.

And this separation and release of the soul from the body is termed death?
To be sure, he said.

And the true philosophers, and they only, are ever seeking to release the soul.
Is not the separation and release of the soul from the body their especial study?
That is true.

e And, as I was saying at first, there would be a ridiculous contradiction in men
studying to live as nearly as they can in a state like that of death, and yet repining
when death comes upon them.

Clearly.

In fact, the true philosophers, Simmias, are always occupied in the practice of
dying, wherefore also to them least of all men is death terrible. Look at the matter thus: if they have been in every way estranged from the body, and are wanting to be alone with the soul, when this desire of theirs is being granted, how
inconsistent would they be if they trembled and repined, instead of rejoicing at
their departure to that place where, when they arrive, they hope to gain that
68 which in life they desired—and their desire was for wisdom—and at the same
time to be rid of the company of their enemy. Many a man who has lost by death
an earthly love, or wife, or son, has been willing to go in quest of them to the
world below, animated by the hope of seeing them there and of being with those
for whom he yearned. And will he who is a true lover of wisdom, and is strongly
persuaded in like manner that only in the world below he can worthily enjoy
b her, still repine at death? Will he not depart with joy? Surely he will, O my
friend, if he be a true philosopher. For he will have a firm conviction that there,
and there only, he can find wisdom in her purity. And if this be true, he would
be very absurd, as I was saying, if he were afraid of death.

He would indeed, replied Simmias.

And when you see a man who is repining at the approach of death, is not his
c reluctance a sufficient proof that after all he is not a lover of wisdom, but a lover
of the body, and probably at the same time a lover of either money or power,
or both?

Quite so, he replied.

And then, Simmias, is not the quality we term courage most characteristic of
the philosopher?

Certainly.

There is temperance again—I mean the quality which the vulgar also call by
that name, the calm disdain and control of the passions—is not temperance a
virtue belonging to those only who disdain the body, and who pass their lives in
philosophy?

d   Most assuredly.

For the courage and temperance of other men, if you care to consider them,
are really a paradox.

How so?

Well, he said, you are aware that death is regarded by men in general as a
great evil.

Very true, he said.

And do not courageous men face death because they are afraid of yet greater
evils?

That is quite true.

Then all but the philosophers are courageous only from fear, and because they are afraid; and yet that a man should be courageous from fear, and because he is a coward, is surely a strange thing.

e   Very true.

And are not the self-restrained exactly in the same case? They are temperate because in a sense they are intemperate — which might seem to be impossible, but is nevertheless the sort of thing which happens with this fatuous temperance. For there are pleasures which they are afraid of losing; and in their desire to keep them, they abstain from some pleasures because they are overcome by others; and although to be conquered by pleasure is called by men intemper-
69 ance, to them the conquest of pleasure consists in being conquered by pleasure. And that is what I mean by saying that, in a sense, they are made temperate through intemperance.

Such appears to be the case.

Yet perhaps the exchange of one fear or pleasure or pain for another fear or pleasure or pain, of the greater for the less as if they were coins, is not the right exchange by the standard of virtue. O my dear Simmias, is there not one true coin for which all these ought to be exchanged? — and that is wisdom; and only
b   in company with this do we attain real courage or temperance or justice. In a word, is not all true virtue the companion of wisdom, no matter what fears or pleasures or other similar goods or evils may or may not attend her? But the virtue which is made up of these goods, when they are severed from wisdom and exchanged with one another, is perhaps a mere facade of virtue, a slavish quality, wholly false and unsound; the truth is far different — temperance and
c   justice and courage are in reality a purging away of all these things, and wisdom herself may be a kind of baptism into that purity. The founders of the mysteries would appear to have had a real meaning, and were not devoid of sense when they intimated in a figure long ago that he who passes unsanctified and uninitiated into the world below will lie in a slough, but that he who arrives there after initiation and purification will dwell with the gods. For "many," as
d   they say in the mysteries, "are the thyrsus-bearers, but few are the mystics." — meaning, as I interpret the words, "the true philosophers." In the number of whom, during my whole life, I have been seeking, according to my ability, to find a place; whether I have sought in a right way or not, and whether we have succeeded, we shall know for certain in a little while, if God will, when we arrive in the other world — such is my belief. And therefore I answer that I am right, Simmias and Cebes, in not grieving or repining at
e   parting from you and my masters in this world, for I believe that I shall equally find good masters and friends in another world. If now I succeed in convincing you by my defence better than I did the Athenian judges, it will be well.

1. GOODNESS AND VOLUNTARY ACTION

Plato's primary purpose in the *Phaedo* is to discuss the question of the immortality of the human soul, but the doctrines and arguments introduced to prove that the soul is immortal are interesting and important in their own right, quite apart from any merits or defects of the various proofs of immortality which he offers.

The dialogue is a dramatic presentation of Socrates' last day on earth, spent in philosophical discussion with his closest friends, and in it, restatements are given of some familiar Socratic teachings and reference is made to some theories which most commentators today attribute to Plato rather than to Socrates, even though these too are presented here as commonplace among Socrates' intimate circle. First, there is the doctrine that virtue is knowledge, which is restated at the beginning of the dialogue in a new and more radical form. This is a typically Socratic doctrine, but in some more naïve interpretations it is very unsatisfactory.

There is a popular and somewhat trivial version of the doctrine that virtue is knowledge which is almost certainly false. It is the contention that if a man knows what is good he cannot willingly choose to do anything else, so that vice is always and only ignorance — not knowing any better — and nobody is ever voluntarily vicious. The argument by which it is supported is somewhat as follows. Whatever anybody does knowingly and voluntarily he does because he wants to do it in preference to the possible alternatives. That means that he thinks it better than any of the possible alternatives. Whatever, therefore, he considers best among the courses of action open to him (that he can carry out), that is what he will do — unless he is forced to do otherwise against his will or acts without knowledge or inadvertently. Thus, the agent always does what he thinks or knows to be good and never does what he knows to be evil. If he ever acts badly it is through ignorance.

Most of us believe that it is possible, and is often the case, that we know what is good, but fail to do it, and what is bad, but do it nevertheless. And we usually think that although we may always choose what we prefer, we often prefer what we know to be morally wrong because it is more congenial, or easier to do, or safer, or for some similar reason. The doctrine as stated above, that virtue is knowledge, seems to rest on a confusion concerning the meaning of "good."

2. THE RIGHT AND THE EXPEDIENT

We sometimes use this term "good" in a strictly moral sense to mean "what is virtuous (or morally right)," and we sometimes use it to mean "what is good for the agent," in the sense of being to his advantage. The Greeks did not always distinguish these two senses clearly, at times simply due to confusion, but at times because they actually believed them to coincide. In the *Gorgias* Plato represents Polus, and in the first book of the *Republic*, Thrasymachus, as holding that to do whatever one wants, whatever one sees to be advantageous (and has the power to do), is to do good (or is "justice," or doing right). Socrates, on the other hand, is also represented as holding that what is good for one is morally good or right, but in the sense that nothing is good for one (or advantageous) except what is morally right.

In contrast to this, we usually distinguish what is right from what is expedient, though we admit that they sometimes coincide, and we should think it obviously untrue either that people always do what they think to be morally right (otherwise there would be no vice), or that they always do what they believe to be expedient (otherwise there would be no virtue). For we usually think that doing right involves resisting the temptation to do what is expedient, unless it happens to coincide with what is morally good—that is, that moral rightness and expediency are distinguished by different criteria.

Sometimes, however, popular moralists teach that "honesty is the best policy" and that "crime does not pay," implying that in the long run virtue and expediency do coincide. But these catchwords can also be given a questionable sense (as Plato shows in the second book of the *Republic*) to the effect that the only good reason for acting virtuously would be for the sake of consequences which were pleasant and beneficial in the long run. This, again, is a position that many of us would want to deny, although it is typical of a large body of ethical theory.

Some moral philosophers (of whom Socrates is one) do claim to prove that moral goodness and expediency in the last analysis are the same thing. But in doing so they modify the common usage of these terms and reinterpret them in rather special ways. To do this is perfectly legitimate if it happens in the course of demonstrating that the presuppositions of our common usages are mutually inconsistent and can be made compatible only by the proposed modifications.

But let us return to the theory that virtue is knowledge. We have shown thus far that the naïve interpretation begs questions arising out of the meaning of "being good" and "being good for." It further leaves obscure what it is to know what is good (or best). Most people would agree that it is possible to choose what you think is best and to be mistaken. Yet most of us, likewise, would not call such mistaken judgment vice. If the mistake were made in good faith, we should count it as an excuse exonerating the agent from blame. Real vice, we consider, is doing something wrong although we know it to be wrong. Socrates was inclined to argue that in such cases the agent does not *really* know the act to be bad. He thinks it is to his advantage, or he would not do it, and his real mistake is in not knowing that being morally wrong, it cannot really be to his advantage.

In either case, however, knowing what is right or what is advantageous is seldom complete knowledge. We know these things, if at all, only in degree, and most of our choices are between alternatives neither of which is good in either sense without qualification. In deciding which is better, we choose according to our lights, but in varying degrees are apt to go wrong. To say simply that we always choose to do what we think is, on the whole, the best alternative, and that this is doing good or acting virtuously, is to make the choice between moral good and evil impossible, for the good would then be simply whatever one chooses to do and the evil whatever one chooses to forego. This is certainly not what Socrates or Plato meant by the doctrine.

The main question that has so far been neglected is what criterion we are using to decide what is good morally or otherwise. This is the question to which Socrates and Plato are really addressing themselves. The treatment of the problem in the *Phaedo* makes this clear and should be compared with the teaching of the fourth book of the *Republic* where the question "What is Justice?" (or right action) is being answered.

3. KNOWLEDGE AND GOODNESS

In the opening passages of the *Phaedo* Socrates stresses the fact that the pursuit of knowledge requires discipline and the control of bodily desires and passions. The body interferes with this pursuit, first, because it distracts the mind from the endeavor by the insistence of its appetites, which are not only constantly importunate but also, when felt intensely, confusing and bewildering to the intellect. Our feelings and desires distort our powers of judgment and infect them with prejudice, and the pursuit of physical pleasures distracts us from serious study. Secondly, our senses, which are dependent upon bodily sense organs, constantly mislead us and subject us to illusion. If we are to know — to discover the truth about things — we can do so only by seeking to grasp the essential ideas or forms of them, which are not sensible but only intelligible. Therefore the soul must withdraw itself from the body, must concentrate itself in intellectual activity, disregard and suppress the passions, appetites, and desires to which the body gives rise, and exert itself in the purest form of its peculiar activity — thinking.

This is the gist of the argument in the *Phaedo*, the details of which we

shall presently examine more closely. It provides a basis for an entirely
new version of the doctrine that virtue is knowledge.

What the philosopher seeks, so it is maintained, is wisdom and
truth, and to this end he must keep his soul pure of bodily contamination, from passion and desire, and free himself from sensuous
illusion—separate soul from body. He can never hope to do this completely until he dies, for death *is* the separation of soul from body.
Consequently, he will welcome, and will never fear, death.

True courage is this fearlessness of death because it is known to be a
benefit and not an evil, although it is beneficial only to the philosopher
who has always sought purity of soul and who realizes that the ultimate
good is knowledge. The sort of courage which faces one evil because it
fears another greater evil is not true courage at all but a sort of cow-
ardice. The true virtue of courage, therefore, springs from the pursuit
of knowledge and from the possession of the knowledge that death is
something not to be feared but to be sought.

This teaching must be taken along with the correlative doctrine that
what is good for a man is what perfects his soul and not what titillates
his bodily appetites. Socrates is made to proclaim this view in several of
the dialogues—in the *Apology* and the *Gorgias,* especially—so that
harm can come to one only through what corrupts the soul, not through
what injures the body. Accordingly, bodily injury is not to be feared
because it does not harm the soul, whereas to behave wrongly morally
does corrupt the soul, and what is really to be feared is vice. To suffer
injustice does one no harm, but to commit it is truly harmful.

In *Republic* IV Socrates defines courage as the right opinion about
what ought to be feared; here we are being told what that opinion
should be and are given the grounds for holding it.

A similar account can be given of temperance, which for the Greeks
meant as much what we should call self-control as moderation in
indulging the appetites. Moderate indulgence is justified on the ground
that, at least in this life, we cannot do without the body. But only such
indulgence as is necessary to life and health is approved. The motive
for seeking more than that would be pleasure, which, as we have seen,
is a great distraction from the pursuit of the one end that is taken to be
good for man—wisdom. True temperance, therefore, is moderation and
self-restraint, not for the sake of the unpleasant physical consequences
of self-indulgence (like the after-effects of drunkenness, or the ill-
effects on digestion and health of gluttony), but for the love of wisdom
and its pursuit. Fear of the physical consequences would itself be a
kind of intemperence, but restraint for the sake of knowledge and
wisdom would be true temperance.

This account of temperance carries to a natural conclusion what Plato hints at, or expounds less radically, in other dialogues (such as *Charmides* and *Republic* IV). In the *Republic* temperance is the subjection of the lowest part of the soul to the dictates of wisdom through the exercise of the spirited element, and the restriction of that lowest part of the soul to its proper function of maintaining bodily health and physical well-being. But the reason given in the *Republic* is that the intellect is the part best fitted to rule, as it is the faculty of self-direction. In the *Phaedo* a more fundamental reason is offered in the ultimate value of wisdom for its own sake.

Yet the reason why wisdom is rated as the ultimate good is again prefigured in the first book of the *Republic* toward the end of the argument with Thrasymachus, though in that context justice takes the place given to wisdom in the *Phaedo*. As we see in the fourth book of the *Republic* and in the present discussion, the substitution of justice for wisdom makes no great difference, for justice in the end turns out to be the subordination of all other human capacities to the direction of the intellect and the pursuit of wisdom. Wisdom is taken to be the ultimate good because thinking and knowing are alleged to be the pure activity of the soul, of doing what it can do best and what it can do better than any other agent. Thus, wisdom is the peculiar virtue of man and the realization of one's peculiar virtue is what constitutes one's peculiar good.[3].

To conclude, then, we may say that virtue is knowledge because knowledge is the purification of the soul which we seek for its own intrinsic value and for the sake of which we value all virtues. Moreover, knowledge is the enlightenment that enables us to understand its own value and the way in which the other virtues are valuable as contributory to it.

4. CRITICISM

The moral philosopher, however, will ask why we should take knowledge or wisdom to be the ultimate good, as that which gives value to all ends. Why should we pursue knowledge rather than, say, pleasure? It may (or may not) be the case that this pursuit involves a withdrawal of the soul from the body, but that does not necessarily make it a good. If, with Plato, we believe that the soul is immortal and

---

[3] Cf. *Republic* I, 352e *ad fin.*

divine and is prevented by association with the body from returning to the home of the gods and attaining blessedness, then it will follow that what purifies and releases it will be good; and if the pursuit of knowledge does this, the argument is vindicated, but what proof is there that any such doctrine is true? The remainder of the dialogue is largely devoted to demonstrating that it is.

Nevertheless, is there not a circular argument in what has been thus far maintained? If knowledge purifies the soul, it is not good for its own sake but for the sake of immortality and the "blessedness" to which it is the means. But we are also told that immortality is desirable because it is only in purified and etherealized form that the soul can know the truth without distortion. The philosopher seeks wisdom and is hindered from attaining it by his bodily needs and passions; for this reason he welcomes death as a means of escape from corporeal bondage and as the gateway to immortality and the attainment of truth. Yet if his search for wisdom is for the sake of immortality and immortality is sought for the sake of knowledge, we have argued in a circle.

In *Republic* II, 363b, Adeimantus argues that the young are taught to be virtuous because virtue is rewarded in Heaven and the next life is depicted as an eternal debauch. Virtue is thus represented as a means to an end which in this life is said to be vicious. Pleasure could more securely be sought in this life. If it is held out as a reward for virtue later, why is it to be regarded as vicious now? Why not have the reward at once and neglect the alleged virtue altogether? Socrates is made to reject this notion by arguing that the next life (and the life of the gods) cannot be evil and that virtue (or justice) is good for its own sake. But from the outset he has asserted that it is also good for the sake of its consequences, and he then proceeds to demonstrate this in Book X (608d–614b) by explaining that virtue is the health of the soul and fits it for a better life after death, whereas vice mutilates it and condemns it to repeat its earthly life in probably some more debased animal form.

Our questions, then, must be (1) is wisdom good for its own sake or for the sake of immortality? — in which case we will have to show why immortality is good — or (2) is immortality desirable for the sake of the knowledge obtainable only after death? — in which case we need some assurance that the soul is immortal and that knowledge is an intrinsic good.

In the *Phaedo* (70) Cebes takes up this last point. Before we turn to it, however, let us consider a little more closely certain features of Socrates' argument in the earlier portion of the dialogue.

5. IDEAS AND THE KNOWLEDGE OF REALITY

In the course of the argument we are reminded of the unreliability of sense perception as a means of reaching the truth. "Is there any certainty," asks Socrates, "in human sight and hearing?" (65b) Sensory illusion is familiar enough, though it is not just illusion as an exceptional experience to which Plato is alluding here. The reference to illusion is nevertheless very relevant because it raises the question of how we distinguish between the illusory and the veridical. This is the central question of epistemology and it challenges us immediately when we attempt to form a theory of sense perception. If asked how we determine what is actual—what is really the case—we are apt to answer, in the last resort by observation, by seeing, hearing, and feeling. But then we are met by the occurrence of sensory illusion and we must find another criterion and cannot simply refer the questioner to sense perception.

What, we may ask, do we actually see, hear, and feel: material things or only colors and shapes, sounds, and tactual sense qualities? Many modern philosophers draw attention to the ambiguity of our use of perceptual verbs. We commonly talk of seeing material objects and would deny that we could "see" an object if it were not there to be seen. But there are numbers of occasions when we "see" objects that are not "there," as when we imagine that we see them, or suffer from illusions or dreams. If our common usage is loose, we then try to make it more precise either by saying that, in such cases, we only think we see the objects and do not really see them; or we say that we do see the colors and shapes but that they are centrally stimulated or wrongly interpreted. This leads to our alleging that we never really "see" any material objects strictly speaking, but only sense data which we take to belong to real things. If this is so, then Plato is right in saying that the senses mislead us, for they give us only untrustworthy sense data and the relation of these to real things is at best questionable and must be discovered by some other means than sense.

Some philosophers, however, reject this suggestion as ridiculous and as a violation of the rules of common usage, and persist in asserting that what we properly mean by "seeing x" is that x is a present, material, visually perceptible thing. But if this is so, other difficulties arise. If x is a real material thing it must have a back (which we do not see from the front elevation), an inside (which may be altogether inaccessible to sight), and a past history (which is not an object of visual perception at all); yet all of these are included in the material thing, which we claim to perceive. The use of our other senses may help us to become simultaneously aware of some of these other attributes of the material thing, which we cannot see at one and the same time, but they can never all be presented to us at once. How, then, do we know that they all belong together? How do we know the way in which they are actually related in one and the same material thing? Sense perception can never give us the answers to these questions immediately and without the help of imaginative supplementation, inference, and constructive thinking, which are all notoriously liable to error. To these aspects of perception we shall return later. Here we must observe certain further complications.

Suppose we restrict the use of the verbs to see, hear, and the like to objects which are only sense qualities, and say that we see colors and shapes, hear noises, smell odors, and so on. Do we, in the case of sight, see the *real* colors and shapes of objects? For the most part, we do not. We see the table top as a rhomboid and, if it shines, as white, whereas we affirm it to be rectangular and brown; we see a coin as elliptical, though we know it to be circular, and what is worse, these shapes and colors are constantly changing with our point of view and with changes of lighting, while we take the qualities of the material objects to remain constant, or at least relatively stable. Again, there seems good reason for Plato to allege that the senses do not and cannot give us knowledge of the reality, because what they do give us is constantly fluctuating, whereas the reality, if it is to be knowable in any precise way, must be unchanging or at least stable; and what the senses tell us is more often than not quite different from what we confidently take the reality to be.

There is, further, an even worse consequence of this disparity between the sensible and the real. Later philosophers, observing the facts we have just been describing, asserted that sense qualities did not belong to material things at all but were simply the effects they produced in us—in our minds—by interaction with our bodily sense organs.[4] Hence they called them "secondary qualities" in contrast to shape, size, number, and such "primary qualities" as were held to exist in material things themselves. If such a theory is true, it follows at once that the senses cannot give us the real truth about material objects and deceive us into believing they have a whole range of qualities they do not possess at all, but with which they are only subjectively arrayed in our minds.

---

[4] The first philosopher to propound this sort of theory was Democritus, who wrote: "By use there is sweet, by use there is bitter; by use there is warm, by use there is cold; by use there is color: but in truth there are atoms and the void." The theory was revived in modern times by Galileo and was restated by Descartes and Locke.

We shall have more to say about this theory at a later stage. Let us attend here to a slightly different, though related, question. Setting aside the so-called secondary qualities for the moment, consider the primary ones of size and shape. Even these appear to us through the senses in distorted form. Shape varies with position, size with distance. How do we discover what the real size and shape of bodies are? The answer at once springs to our minds that we do so by measurement.

Measurement, however, requires precise comparison of quantities, which we do not sense in any precise way. Further, mere comparison is not enough; we need to adopt precise units and to count them. So we must use numbers. But these are not objects of sense perception. The notion of unity is purely ideal. We can, no doubt, apply it to whatever sensible object we please — we may use any convenient quantity or thing as a unit (compare the way in which we teach children arithmetic). But what a unit is, as such, we can never show ostensively or perceive directly. Unity is purely conceptual. Similarly, and in consequence, numbers are ideas, not sensible things.

Shape and its precise determination involves the use of geometrical concepts such as point, line, angle, and curve, and though these can be sensibly represented, we never take the sensible diagram as more than an approximate illustration; nor, in fact, is it ever completely accurate (for deductive geometry we do not even require that it should be). The ideas of point, line, circle, and the rest are all ultimately *abstract* ideas, never strictly realized or realizable in material media.

It is at least arguable, therefore (and Plato argues with persistent emphasis), that to discover what things really are like, we can never rely upon sense perception alone, but must make use of "ideas" without which the deliverances of sense are merely bewildering and deceptive. The senses at best give us *appearances*, but can never penetrate to the reality that lies behind the appearance. That reality can be discerned only by the intellect making use of ideas which are not sensible objects at all. We shall later have occasion to discuss at some length the distinction between them. Plato, we shall find, drives to such lengths what is a necessary and important distinction that it becomes an unbridgeable and illegitimate separation, and consequently he finds himself in insuperable difficulties.

Plato's ethical theory, which is closely bound up with his theory of knowledge, reflects the sharp cleavage between these two aspects of experience: on the one hand, sensation, with the associated appetitive urges which motivate action and thinking, and on the other hand, the power of understanding and knowing to control and direct the appetites and passions. What he has to say about immortality is also intimately dependent upon both of these elements in his philosophy. This should become apparent as we proceed. We shall turn next to the proofs of immortality that are offered in the *Phaedo* and the doctrines of ideas and of reminiscence as the source of knowledge with which they are interlocked.

SUGGESTIONS FOR FURTHER READING

Plato, *Republic*, Books I–IV, London: University of Cambridge, paperback edition, 1966.
Protagoras, Charmides, Laches, Apology, and *Crito* in *Plato, Collected Dialogues* (E. Hamilton and H. Cairns, eds.), New York: Pantheon Books, Random House, 1961.

CHAPTER 4

Immortality

PHAEDO
(Continued)

When Socrates had finished, Cebes began to speak: I agree, Socrates, in the
70 greater part of what you say. But in what concerns the soul, men are apt to be
incredulous; they fear that when she has left the body her place may be
nowhere, and that on the very day of death she may perish and come to an end
immediately on her release from the body, issuing forth like smoke or breath,
dispersing and vanishing away into nothingness in her flight. If she could only
be collected into herself after she has obtained release from the evils of which
you were speaking, there would be much reason for the goodly hope, Socrates,
b that what you say is true. But surely it requires a great deal of persuasion and
proof to show that when the man is dead his soul yet exists, and has any force
or intelligence.

True, Cebes, said Socrates; and shall I suggest that we speculate a little
together concerning the probabilities of these things?

For my part, said Cebes, I should greatly like to know your opinion about
them.

I reckon, said Socrates, that no one who heard me now, not even if he were
c one of my old enemies, the comic poets, could accuse me of idle talking about
matters in which I have no concern: If you please, then, we will proceed with
the inquiry.

Suppose we consider the question whether the souls of men after death are or are not in the world below. There comes into my mind an ancient doctrine which affirms that they are there after they leave our world, and returning hither, are born again from the dead. Now if it be true that the living come
d from the dead, then our souls must exist in the other world, for if not, how could they have been born again? And this would be conclusive, if it were established that the living are born from the dead and have no other origin; but if this is not so, then other arguments will have to be adduced.

Very true, replied Cebes.

Then let us consider the whole question, not in relation to man only, but in relation to animals generally, and to plants, and to everything of which there is
e generation, and the proof will be easier. Are not all things which have opposites generated out of their opposites? I mean such things as the beautiful and the ugly, the just and the unjust — and there are innumerable other cases. Let us consider therefore whether it is necessary that a thing should come to be from its own opposite, if it has one, and from no other source: for example, anything which becomes greater must become greater after being less?

True.

And that which becomes less must have been once greater and then have
71 become less?

Yes.

And the weaker is generated from the stronger, and the swifter from the slower?

Very true.

And the worse is from the better, and the more just is from the more unjust?

Of course.

And is this true of all opposites? and are we convinced that all of them are generated out of opposites?

Yes.

And in this universal opposition of all things, are there not also two inter-
b mediate processes which are ever going on, from one to the other opposite, and back again; for example, where there is a greater and a less there is also the intermediate process of increase and diminution, and so a thing is said to increase or to diminish?

Yes, he said.

And there are many other processes, such as analysis and combination, cooling and heating, which equally involve a passage into and out of one another. And this necessarily holds of all opposites, even though not always expressed in words — they are really generated out of one another, and there is a passing or process from one to the other of them?

Very true, he replied.
c Well, and is there not an opposite of being alive, as sleep is the opposite of being awake?

True, he said.

And what is it?

Being dead, he answered.

And these, if they are opposites, are generated the one from the other, and have their two intermediate processes also?

Of course.

Now, said Socrates, I will analyse one of the two pairs of opposites which I

have mentioned to you, and also its intermediate processes, and you shall
analyse the other to me. The two members of the first pair are sleep and
d waking. The state of sleep is opposed to the state of waking, out of sleeping
waking is generated, and out of waking, sleeping; and the process of generation
is in the one case falling asleep, and in the other waking up. Do you agree?

I entirely agree.

Then, suppose that you analyse life and death to me in the same manner. Is
not the state of death opposed to that of life?

Yes.

And they are generated one from the other?

Yes.

What is generated from the living?

The dead.

And what from the dead?

I can only say in answer—the living.

Then the living, whether things or persons, Cebes, are generated from the
dead?

e   So it would seem, he replied.

Then the inference is that our souls exist in the world below?

It appears so.

And one of the two processes or generations is visible—for surely the act of
dying is visible?

Surely, he said.

What then is to be the result? Shall we exclude the opposite process? and
shall we suppose nature to be lame in this respect? Must we not rather assign
to the act of dying some corresponding process of generation?

Certainly, he replied.

And what is that?

Return to life.

And return to life, if there be such a thing, is the birth of the dead into the
72 number of the living?

Quite true.

Then here is a new way by which we arrive at the conclusion that the living
come from the dead, just as the dead come from the living; and we agreed that
this, if true, would be adequate proof that the souls of the dead must exist in
some place out of which they come again.

Yes, Socrates, he said; the conclusion seems to flow necessarily out of our
previous admissions.

And that these admissions were not wrong, Cebes, he said, may be shown, I
b think, as follows: If generation were in a straight line only, and there were no
compensation or circle in nature, no turn or return of elements into their
opposites, then you know that all things would at last have the same form and
suffer the same fate, and there would be no more generation of them.

What do you mean? he said.

A simple thing enough, which I will illustrate by the case of sleep, he replied.
You know that if there were no alternation of sleeping and waking, the tale of
c the sleeping Endymion would in the end have no point, because all other things
would be asleep too, and he would not be distinguishable from the rest. Or if
there were combination only, and no analysis of substances, then we should
soon have the chaos of Anaxagoras where 'all things were together'. And in

like manner, my dear Cebes, if all things which partook of life were to die, and after they were dead remained in the form of death, and did not come to life again, all would at last be dead, and nothing would be alive — what other result could there be? For if living things had some other origin, and living things died, must not all things at last be swallowed up in death?[1]

There is no escape, Socrates, said Cebes; and to me your argument seems to be absolutely true.

Yes, he said, Cebes, it is and must be so, in my opinion, and we have not been deluded in making these admissions; but I am confident that there truly is such a thing as living again, and that the living spring from the dead, and that the souls of the dead are in existence.

1. THE FIRST PROOF: PROCESS BETWEEN OPPOSITES

Anaximander is reputed to have written "And into that from which things originate they pass away once more, as is meet; for they make reparation and satisfaction to one another for their injustice according to the ordering of time." Heraclitus developed this idea and alleged that all things arose out of the cyclic flux of conflagration and passed into it again. "Fire lives the death of air," he wrote, "and air lives the death of fire; water lives the death of earth, earth that of water."[2] Later Empedocles put forward the theory that individual things, including man, came into being through the combining of the four elements and went out of existence as a result of their separation, the whole cosmic process being a periodic alternation between combination and dissipation.

Almost certainly Plato had these doctrines in his mind when he produced the theory of generation that is put forward in the *Phaedo*. He argues here that all things come into being out of their opposites, the warm from the cold, the wet from the dry, and vice versa. Whatever comes to be, comes to be from what it previously was not, and what passes away ceases to be what it formerly was. Death visibly supervenes upon the living state; if life were not regenerated from the dead, death would ultimately prevail; for if all living things died and no dead things came to life, the supply of living things would run out and all life would eventually cease. So he concludes that the living must come from the nonliving (or dead), in which case the soul (which is the principle of life) must wait in some other world for a rebirth after the death of the body.

The doctrine of generation from opposites was taken up again by

---

[1]Cf. *Republic* x, 611a.
[2]See page 18 above.

Aristotle who based his theories of movement and change upon it. It is of importance if only because it stimulates reflection upon the logical nature of opposition, as well as upon the causal and temporal relations of opposites in the process of becoming. Intriguing as these matters are, we cannot enter upon a discussion of them here. Let us now consider the force of Plato's argument.

At best it is a *non sequitur*. If the opposite of life is death and all things are generated from their opposites, then the living should be generated from the nonliving, the quick from the dead. This would be a theory of spontaneous generation of life from nonliving matter, a theory typical of the earlier philosophers whom we have quoted. But it is not what Plato believed or claims to have proved. He thought the soul was the essential living principle and all that was alive in us. The body is merely material and earthly and is not alive at all, except by virtue of the soul's infusion into it. What his argument should prove, if it were consistent, is that the soul arises out of the (dead) body and that the body passes away into soul. But what Plato claims to prove is that the soul does not change or die or pass away at all (except in a spatial sense) but merely leaves the husk of the body and departs to another place, until it enters a new and different body. This is not a process of generation between opposites at all and that doctrine of generation is really irrelevent to the conclusion drawn from it.

What Plato wants to argue is that nothing can really be alive without a soul, and that the soul, being the essential source of all life, cannot itself die or cease to be alive, but he introduces this argument only at a later stage (105c *et seq.*)

Phaedo
(Continued)

Yes, said Cebes interposing, your favourite doctrine, Socrates, that our learning is simply recollection, if true, also necessarily implies a previous time in which we have learned that which we now recollect. But this would be impossible unless our soul had been somewhere before existing in this form of man; here then is another proof of the soul's immortality.

But tell me, Cebes, interrupted Simmias, what arguments are urged in favour of this doctrine or recollection. I am not very sure at the moment that I remember them.

One excellent proof, said Cebes, is afforded by questions. If you put a question to a person properly, he will give a true answer of himself, but how could he do this unless there were knowledge and a right account of the matter b already in him? Again, this is most clearly shown when he is taken to a diagram or to anything of that sort.[3]

But if, said Socrates, you are still incredulous, Simmias, I would ask you whether you may not agree with me when you look at the matter in another way; I mean, if you are still incredulous as to whether what is called learning is recollection?

Incredulous I am not, said Simmias; but I want to have this doctrine of recollection brought to my own recollection, and, from what Cebes has started to say, I am beginning to recollect and be convinced: but I should still like to hear you develop your own argument.

c This is what I would say, he replied: We should agree, if I am not mistaken, that what a man is to recollect he must have known at some previous time.

Very true.

And do we also agree that knowledge obtained in the way I am about to describe is recollection? I mean to ask, Whether a person who, having seen or heard or in any way perceived anything, knows not only that, but also thinks of something else which is the subject not of the same but of some other kind of

d knowledge, may not be fairly said to recollect that of which he thinks?

How do you mean?

I mean what I may illustrate by the following instance: The knowledge of a lyre is not the same as the knowledge of a man?

Of course not.

And yet what is the feeling of lovers when they recognize a lyre, or a cloak, or anything else which the beloved has been in the habit of using? Do not they, from knowing the lyre, form in the mind's eye an image of the youth to whom the lyre belongs? And this is recollection. In like manner anyone who sees Simmias may often remember Cebes; and there are endless examples of the same thing.

Endless, indeed, replied Simmias.

e And is not this sort of thing a kind of recollection—though the word is most commonly applied to a process of recovering that which has been already forgotten through time and inattention?

Very true, he said.

Well; and may you not also from seeing the picture of a horse or a lyre recollect a man? and from the picture of Simmias, you may be led to recollect Cebes?

True.

Or you may also be led to the recollection of Simmias himself?

74 Quite so.

And in all these cases, the recollection may be derived from things either like or unlike?

It may be.

And when the recollection is derived from like things, then another consideration is sure to arise, which is—whether the likeness in any degree falls short or not of that which is recollected?

Certainly, he said.

Now consider this question. We affirm, do we not, that there is such a thing as equality, not of one piece of wood or stone or similar material thing with

---

[3] Cf. *Meno*, 83 foll.

another, but that, over and above this, there is absolute equality? Shall we say so?

b   Say so, yes, replied Simmias, and swear to it, with all the confidence in life.
And do we know the nature of this absolute existence?
To be sure, he said.
And whence did we obtain our knowledge? Did we not see equalities of material things, such as pieces of wood and stones, and conceive from them the idea of an equality which is different from them? For you will acknowledge that there is a difference? Or look at the matter in another way: Do not the same pieces of wood or stone appear to one man equal, and to another unequal?
That is certain.

c   But did pure equals ever appear to you unequal? or equality the same as inequality?
Never, Socrates.
Then these equal objects are not the same with the idea of equality?
I should say, clearly not, Socrates.
And yet from these equals, although differing from the idea of equality, you obtained the knowledge of that idea?
Very true, he said.
Which might be like, or might be unlike them?
Yes.
But that makes no difference: so long as from seeing one thing you conceive

d   another, whether like or unlike, there must surely have been an act of recollection?
Very true.
But what would you say of equal portions of wood or other material equals? and what is the impression produced by them? Are they equals in the same sense in which absolute equality is equal? or do they fall short of this perfect equality in a measure?
Yes, he said, in a very great measure too.
And must we not allow, that when a man, looking at any object, reflects "the

e   thing which I see aims at being like some other thing, but falls short of and cannot be like that other thing, and is inferior," he who so reflects must have had a previous knowledge of that to which the other, although similar, was inferior?
Certainly.
And has not this been our own case in the matter of equals and of absolute equality?
Precisely.
Then we must have known equality previously to the time when we first saw

75   the material equals, and reflected that they all strive to attain absolute equality, but fall short of it?
Very true.
And we recognize also that we have only derived this conception of absolute equality, and can only derive it, from sight or touch, or from some other of the senses, which are all alike in this respect?
Yes, Socrates, for the purposes of the present argument, one of them is the same as the other.

b   From the senses then is derived the conception that all sensible equals aim at an absolute equality of which they fall short?

Yes.

Then before we began to see or hear or perceive in any way, we must have had a knowledge of absolute equality, or we could not have referred to that standard the equals which are derived from the senses? – for to that they all aspire, and of that they fall short.

No other inference can be drawn from the previous statements.

And did we not begin to see and hear and have the use of our other senses as soon as we were born?

Certainly.

c   Then we must have acquired the knowledge of equality at some previous time?

Yes.

That is to say, before we were born, I suppose?

It seems so.

And if we acquired this knowledge before we were born, and were born having the use of it, then we also knew before we were born and at the instant of birth not only the equal or the greater or the less, but all other such ideas;

d   for we are not speaking only of equality, but of beauty, goodness, justice, holiness, and of all which we stamp with the name of absolute being in the dialectical process, both when we ask and when we answer questions. Of all this we affirm with certainty that we acquired the knowledge before birth?

We do.

But if, after having acquired, we have not on each occasion forgotten what we acquired, then we must always come into life having this knowledge, and shall have it always as long as life lasts – for knowing is the acquiring and retaining knowledge and not losing it. Is not the loss of knowledge, Simmias, just what we call forgetting?

e   Quite true, Socrates.

But if this knowledge which we acquired before birth was lost by us at birth, and if afterwards by the use of the senses we recovered what we previously knew, will not the process which we call learning be a recovering of knowledge which is natural to us, and may not this be rightly termed recollection?

Very true.

76   So much is clear – that when we perceive something, either by the help of sight, or hearing, or some other sense, that perception can lead us to think of some other thing like or unlike which is associated with it but has been forgotten. Whence, as I was saying, one of two alternatives follows: either we all have this knowledge at birth, and continue to know through life; or, after birth, those who are said to learn only recollect, and learning is simply recollection.

Yes, that is quite true, Socrates.

And which alternative, Simmias, do you prefer? Have we the knowledge at

b   our birth, or do we recollect afterwards things which we knew previously to our birth?

I cannot decide at the moment.

At any rate you can decide whether he who has knowledge will or will not be able to render an account of his knowledge? What do you say?

Certainly, he will.

But do you think that every man is able to give an account of the matters about which we were speaking a moment ago?

Would that they could, Socrates, but I much rather fear that tomorrow, at this time, there will no longer be anyone alive who is able to give an account of them such as ought to be given.

c   Then you are not of opinion, Simmias, that all men know these things?

Certainly not.

They are in process of recollecting that which they learned before?

Certainly.

But when did our souls acquire this knowledge? — clearly not since we were born as men?

Certainly not.

And therefore, previously?

Yes.

Then, Simmias, our souls must also have existed without bodies before they were in the form of man, and must have had intelligence.

Unless indeed you suppose, Socrates, that all such knowledge is given us at the very moment of birth; for this is the only time which remains.

d   Yes, my friend, but if so, when, pray, do we lose it? for it is not in us when we are born — that is admitted. Do we lose it at the moment of receiving it, or if not at what other time?

No, Socrates, I perceive that I was unconsciously talking nonsense.

Then may we not say, Simmias, that if there do exist these things of which we are always talking, absolute beauty and goodness, and all that class of realities; and if to this we refer all our sensations and with this compare them,

e   finding the realities to be pre-existent and our own possession — then just as surely as these exist, so surely must our souls have existed before our birth? Otherwise our whole argument would be worthless. By an equal compulsion we must believe both that these realities exist, and that our souls existed before our birth; and if not the realities, then not the souls.

Yes, Socrates; I am convinced that there is precisely the same necessity for

77 the one as for the other; and the argument finds a safe refuge in the position that the existence of the soul before birth cannot be separated from the existence of the reality of which you speak. For there is nothing which to my mind is so patent as that beauty, goodness, and the other realities of which you were just now speaking, exist in the fullest possible measure; and I am satisfied with the proof.

2. THE SECOND PROOF: RECOLLECTION

Although Cebes refers to the doctrine of *anamnesis* as one frequently taught by Socrates, it is part of the theory of knowledge usually held to be typically Platonic. The view is that our knowledge is for the most part recollection, for there are certain universal concepts essential to any knowledge which we could not possibly have derived from sense experience yet without which no sense experience would give us anything intelligible. If we cannot acquire these ideas through sensation, and we experience sensible objects from the time of our birth by the use of our bodily senses, our souls must have acquired the knowledge of the ideas before we were born, but must have forgotten them on entering their earthly bodies. Our sense experience, as we acquire it, then reminds us of the ideas, so that what we call learning is really only recollection.

The argument runs as follows:

First, we are given a definition of recollection as the experience in which something which we perceive causes us to think of something else that is either similar to it or somehow associated with it. Thus, when we see a musical instrument we are reminded of the musician who usually plays it, or when we see a picture of a person we think of the person himself.

Next, our attention is drawn to the fact that we have and use certain ideas, such as equality, but that what we precisely mean by them is never exactly exemplified in any of the sensible examples we observe. No two material objects are ever quite equal; even if we draw two lines as equal as we can, by the most careful measurement, we can never attain more than an approximation, however close. The idea of equality itself (absolute and unqualified) could not, therefore, have been de- rived from sense perception. We must have possessed it prior to any perception in which we recognize two things to be more or less equal, and our sensory experience, being similar to what we previously knew, reminds us of the absolute idea.

Once again the appeal is away from the merely sensible to the purely intelligible, and we must observe that to get from the perceived in- stances of equality to the "absolute" idea is not simply a matter of trying to extrapolate, or to imagine something more equal than any- thing we have ever perceived. To compare different instances of equality as more and less exact is itself possible only if we have some criterion of accuracy. But our criterion cannot be any instance of equality, sensed or imagined, for to accept any such as a standard we must be able to judge it more equal than any other example (or, at least, sufficiently equal for our purpose), and that itself involves a criterion. Only the conception of equality itself can serve as a criterion, not any perceived fact that something (A) is more or less equal to something else (B). Such a conception, however, cannot be derived from sense (so the argument runs) because any and every sensible instance of equality presupposes it.

Accordingly, as we have perceived examples of equal things from the time of our birth, and any such perception presupposes the knowledge of the concept, we must have had the concept prior to our birth. Simi- larly, the knowledge of quite complicated mathematical truths can be elicited from untutored pupils by judicious questioning. They can be made to "see" the implications of the perceived facts (for example, that the square on the diagonal is twice the size of a given square[4]). Thus, learning must be the recollection of something which we knew before and have forgotten, but which has later been recalled by the approximation (or likeness) to it of sensible things.

In later philosophy we shall meet a doctrine similar to this, held by some philosophers and denied by others. Descartes put forward the theory that certain ideas were innate — or at least self-evident — so that they had only to be presented to consciousness to be accepted. Locke denied this on the ground that the very young showed no evidence of possessing innate ideas. If, however, we think of the theory, not so much as an account of how we acquire knowledge, but as one of logical priorities among the elements of our knowledge, we are forced to the conclusion that to have any coherent experience of objects at all, certain conceptual principles (or categories) are involved from the outset. The doctrine reappears (as we shall find) in the philosophy of Kant, and it seems to be one side of the matter without the recognition of which no theory of knowledge can be adequate, although, as we shall see later, to press it too far to the exclusion of the other aspects of knowledge can be disastrous.

Perhaps it would be better to say that the conceptual element is implicit in all our perceptual knowledge and can be elicited from it by logical analysis than to say that we acquired it before we were born and are reminded of it by sensible objects. In any case, the conclusion which Plato seeks to draw from the epistemological analysis seems more dubious than the analysis itself. In order to be plausible the theory of recollection requires the prior demonstration of the preexistence of the soul and does not itself render that hypothesis more credible. If the soul existed before birth it would be reasonable to believe that we could remember what our senses in this life had not yet conveyed to us. But if we have no other evidence of preexistence, the possession of knowledge not derived from sense is hardly enough to establish preexistence, for the nonsensuous knowledge might be more plausibly explained in some other way.

Phaedo

(Continued)

Well, but is Cebes satisfied? for I must convince him too.

I think, said Simmias, that Cebes is satisfied: although he is the most incredulous of mortals, yet I believe that he is sufficiently convinced of the existence of

---

[4] Plato demonstrates at length in the *Meno* how an ignorant slave boy can be made to see this, without being given the information, but simply by being asked the right questions.

b the soul before birth. But that after death the soul will continue to exist is not yet proven even to my own satisfaction. I cannot get rid of the objection to which Cebes was referring—the common fear that at the moment when the man dies the soul is dispersed, and that this may be the end of her. For admitting that she may have come into being and been framed out of some unknown other elements, and was in existence before entering the human body, why after having entered in and gone out again may she not herself be destroyed and come to an end?

c Very true, Simmias, said Cebes; it appears that about half of what was required has been proven; to wit, that our souls existed before we were born; that the soul will exist after death as well as before birth is the other half of which the proof is still wanting, and has to be supplied; when that is given the demonstration will be complete.

But that proof, Simmias and Cebes, has been already given, said Socrates, if you put the two arguments together—I mean this and the former one, in which we agreed that everything living is born of the dead. For if the soul exists

d before birth, and in coming to life and being born can be born only from death and the state of death, must she not after death continue to exist, since she has to be born again? Surely the proof which you desire has been already furnished. Still I suspect that you and Simmias would be glad to probe the argument further. Like children, you are haunted with a fear that when the soul leaves the body, the wind may really blow her away and scatter her; especially if a

e man should happen to die in a great storm and not when the weather is calm.

Cebes answered with a smile: Then, Socrates, you must argue us out of our fears—and yet, strictly speaking, they are not our fears, but perhaps even in us men there is a child to whom death is a sort of hobgoblin: him too we must persuade not to be afraid.

Socrates said: Let the voice of the charmer be applied daily until you have charmed away the fear.

78 And where shall we find a good charmer of our fears, Socrates, now that you are abandoning us?

Hellas, he replied, is a large place, Cebes, and has good men, and there are barbarous races not a few: seek for him among them all, far and wide, sparing neither pains nor money; for there is no better way of spending your money. And you must seek yourselves too, along with one another; for perhaps you will not easily find others better able to do it.

The search, replied Cebes, shall certainly be made. And now, if you please,

b let us return to the point of the argument at which we digressed.

By all means, replied Socrates; what else should I please?

Very good.

Must we not, said Socrates, ask ourselves what kind of thing that is which is liable to be scattered, and for what kind of thing we ought to fear that fate? and what is that for which we need have no fear? And then we may proceed further to inquire to which of the two classes soul belongs—our hopes and fears as to our own souls will turn upon the answers to these questions.

Very true, he said.

c Now that which is compounded and is by nature composite may be supposed to be therefore capable, as of being compounded, so also of being dissolved; but that which is not composite, and that only, must be, if anything is, indissoluble.

Yes; I should imagine so, said Cebes.

And the non-composite may be assumed to be the same and unchanging, whereas the composite is always changing and never the same.

I agree, he said.

Then now let us return to the previous discussion. Is that reality of whose
d being we give account in the dialectical process — whether equality, beauty, or
anything else — are these realities, I say, liable at times to some degree of
change? or are they each of them always what they are, having the same
uniform self-existent and unchanging natures, not admitting of variation at all,
or in any way, or at any time?

They must be always the same, Socrates, replied Cebes.

And what would you say of the many beautiful, for instance, men or horses
e or garments or any other such things, or of the many equal, or generally of all
the things which are named by the same names as the realities — are they the
same always? May they not rather be described in exactly opposite terms, as
almost always changing and hardly ever the same either with themselves or
with one another?

The latter, replied Cebes; they are always in a state of change.

79   And these you can touch and see and perceive with the senses, but the
unchanging things you can only grasp with the mind — they are invisible and
are not seen?

That is very true, he said.

Well then, added Socrates, let us suppose that there are two sorts of existences — one seen, the other unseen.

Let us suppose them.

The seen is the changing, and the unseen is the unchanging?

That may be also supposed.

b   And, further, of ourselves is not one part body, another part soul?

To be sure.

And to which class is the body more alike and akin?

Clearly to the seen — no one can doubt that.

And is the soul seen or not seen?

Not by man, Socrates.

And what we mean by "seen" and "not seen" is that which is or is not visible
to the eye of man?

Yes, to the eye of man.

And is the soul seen or not seen?

Not seen.

Unseen then?

Yes.

Then the soul is more like to the unseen, and the body to the seen?

c   That follows necessarily, Socrates.

And were we not saying some time ago that the soul when using the body as
an instrument of perception, that is to say, when using the sense of sight or
hearing or some other sense (for the meaning of perceiving through the body is
perceiving through the senses) were we not saying that the soul too is then
dragged by the body into the region of the changeable, and wanders and is
confused; the world spins round her, and she is like a drunkard, when she
touches change?

Very true.

d   But when returning into herself she reflects, then she passes into the other
world, the region of purity, and eternity, and immortality, and unchangeable-
ness, which are her kindred, and with them she ever lives, when she is by

herself and is not let or hindered; then she ceases from her wandering, and being in contact with things unchanging is unchanging in relation to them. And this state of the soul is called wisdom?

That is well and truly said, Socrates, he replied.

And to which class is the soul more nearly alike and akin, as far as may be
e inferred from this argument, as well as from the preceding one?

I think, Socrates, that, in the opinion of everyone who follows the argument, the soul will be infinitely more like the unchangeable—even the most stupid person will not deny that.

And the body is more like the changing?

Yes.

Yet once more consider the matter in another light: When the soul and the
80 body are united, then nature orders the soul to rule and govern, and the body to obey and serve. Now which of these two functions is like to the divine? and which to the mortal? Does not the divine appear to you to be that which is formed to govern and command, and the mortal to be that which is by its nature subject and servant?

True.

And which does the soul resemble?

The soul resembles the divine, and the body the mortal—there can be no doubt of that, Socrates.

Then reflect, Cebes: of all which has been said is not this the conclu-
b sion?—that the soul is in the very likeness of the divine, and immortal, and rational, and uniform, and indissoluble, and unchangeable; and that the body is in the very likeness of the human, and mortal, and irrational, and multiform, and dissoluble, and changeable. Can we, my dear Cebes, find any possible ground for rejecting this conclusion?

We cannot.

But if it be true, then is not the body liable to speedy dissolution? and is not the soul almost or altogether indissoluble?
c Certainly.

And do you further observe, that after a man is dead, the body, or visible part of him, which is lying in the visible world, and is called a corpse, and would naturally be dissolved and decomposed and dissipated, is not dissolved or decomposed at once, but may remain for some time, nay even for a long time, if the constitution be sound at the time of death, and the season of the year favourable? For the body when shrunk and embalmed, as the manner is
d in Egypt, may remain almost entire for a prodigious time; and even in decay, there are still some portions, such as the bones and ligaments, which are practically indestructible: Do you agree?

Yes.

And is it likely that the soul, which is invisible, in passing to the place of the true Hades, which like her is invisible, and pure, and noble, and on her way to the good and wise God, whither, if God will, my soul is also soon to go—that the soul, I repeat, if this be her nature, is blown away and destroyed immediately
e on quitting the body, as the many say? That can never be, my dear Simmias and Cebes. The truth rather is that the soul which is pure at departing and draws after her no bodily taint, having never voluntarily during life had connexion with the body, which she is ever avoiding, herself gathered into herself, and making such abstraction her perpetual study—all this means that she has been a true disciple of philosophy; and therefore has in fact been always

practising how to die without complaint. For is not such a life the practice of
81 death?

Certainly.

That soul, I say, herself invisible, departs to the invisible world — to the divine
and immortal and rational: thither arriving, she is secure of bliss and is released from the error and folly of men, their fears and wild passions and all
other human ills, and for ever dwells, as they say of the initiated, in company
with the gods.[5] Is not this true, Cebes?

Yes, said Cebes, beyond a doubt.

b   But the soul which has been polluted, and is impure at the time of her departure, and is the companion and servant of the body always, and is in love with
and bewitched by the body and by the desires and pleasures of the body, until
she is led to believe that the truth only exists in a bodily form, which a man may
touch and see, and drink and eat, and use for the purposes of his lusts — the soul,
I mean, accustomed to hate and fear and avoid that which to the bodily eye is
dark and invisible, but is the object of mind and can be attained by philosophy;
c   do you suppose that such a soul will depart pure and unalloyed?

Impossible, he replied.

She is intermixed with the corporeal, which the continual association and constant care of the body have wrought into her nature.

Very true.

And this corporeal element, my friend, is burdensome and weighty and
earthy, and is visible; a soul thus hampered is depressed and dragged down
again into the visible world, because she is afraid of the invisible and of the
d   other world — prowling about tombs and sepulchres, near which, as they tell us,
are seen certain ghostly apparitions of souls, spectres emanating from souls
which have not departed pure, but still retain something of the visible element: which is why they can be seen.

That is very likely, Socrates.

Yes, that is very likely, Cebes; and these must be the souls, not of the good,
but of the evil, which are compelled to wander about such places in payment of
the penalty of their former evil way of life; and they continue to wander until
e   through the craving after their constant associate, the corporeal, they are imprisoned finally in another body. And they may be supposed to find their prisons
in natures of the same character as they have cultivated in their former lives.

What natures do you mean, Socrates?

What I mean is that men who have followed after gluttony, and wantonness,
and drunkenness, and have had no thought of avoiding them, would pass into
82 asses and animals of that sort. What do you think?

I think such an opinion to be exceedingly probable.

And those who have chosen the portion of injustice, and tyranny, and violence,
will pass into wolves, or into hawks and kites; whither else can we suppose them
to go?

Yes, said Cebes; into such creatures, beyond question.

And there is no difficulty, he said, in assigning to each class of them places
answering to their several natures and propensities?

There is not, he said.

Even among these, some are happier than others; and the happiest both in

---

[5] Cf. *Apology*, 40 e.

themselves and in the place to which they go are those who have practised the
virtues of the populace, the social virtues which are called by them temperance
b and justice, and are acquired by habit and practice without philosophy and
mind.[6]

Why are they the happiest?

Because they may be expected to pass into some gentle and social kind which
is like their own, such as bees or wasps or ants, or back again into the form of
man, and worthy men may be supposed to spring from them.

Very likely.

But to the company of the gods no one who has not studied philosophy and
c who is not entirely pure at the time of his departure is admitted, save only the
lover of knowledge. And this is the reason, Simmias and Cebes, why the true
votaries of philosophy abstain from all fleshly lusts, and hold out against them
and refuse to give themselves up to them — not because they fear poverty or the
ruin of their families, like the lovers of money, and the world in general; nor
like the lovers of power and honour, because they dread the dishonour or dis-
grace of evil deeds.

No, Socrates, that would not become them, said Cebes.

d No, indeed, he replied; and therefore they who have any care of their own
souls, and do not merely live for the body and its fashioning, say farewell to all
this; they will not walk in the ways of the blind: and when philosophy offers them
purification and release from evil, they feel that they ought not to resist her
influence, and whither she leads they turn and follow. ·

What do you mean, Socrates?

I will tell you, he said. The lovers of knowledge are conscious that the soul
e was simply fastened and glued to the body — until philosophy took her hand,
she could only view real existence through the bars of a prison, not in and
through herself, and she was wallowing in the mire of every sort of ignorance.
This was her original state; and then, as I was saying, and as the lovers of
83 knowledge are well aware, philosophy saw the ingenuity of her prison — a prison
built by lust so that a captive might be the principal accomplice in his own
captivity — and took her in hand, and gently comforted her and sought to release
her, pointing out that the eye and the ear and the other senses are full of deception, and persuading her to retire from them, and abstain from all but the necessary use of them, and be gathered up and collected into herself, bidding her
b trust only in herself and her own pure apprehension of pure existence, and to
mistrust whatever comes to her through other channels and is subject to variation; for such things are sensible and visible, but what she sees in her own nature
is of the mind and invisible. And the soul of the true philosopher thinks that she
ought not to resist this deliverance, and therefore abstains from pleasures and
desires and pains, as far as she is able; reflecting that when a man has great
joys or fears or desires, he suffers from them not merely the sort of evil which
c might be anticipated — as for example, the loss of his health or property which
he has sacrificed to his lusts — but an evil greater far, which is the greatest and
worst of all evils, and one of which he never thinks.

What is it, Socrates? said Cebes.

The evil is that when the feeling of pleasure or pain is most intense, every
soul of man imagines the objects of this intense feeling to be then plainest and

---

[6]Cf. *Republic* x, 619c. ·

truest, though they are not so. And the things of sight are the chief of these objects, are they not?

Yes.

d   And is not this the state in which the soul becomes most firmly gripped by the body?

How so?

Why, because each pleasure and pain is a sort of nail which nails and rivets the soul to the body, until she becomes like the body, and believes that to be true which the body affirms to be true; and from agreeing with the body and having the same delights she is obliged to have the same habits and haunts, and is not likely ever to be pure at her departure to the world below, but is always infected by the body; and so she sinks into another body and there

e   germinates and grows, and has therefore no part in the communion of the divine and pure and simple.

Most true, Socrates, answered Cebes.

And this, Cebes, is the reason why the true lovers of knowledge are temperate and brave; and not for the reason which the world gives.

84   Certainly not.

Certainly not! The soul of a philosopher will reason in quite another way; she will not ask philosophy to release her in order that in the very process of release she may deliver herself up again to the thraldom of pleasures and pains, doing a work only to be undone again, weaving and in turn unweaving her Penelope's web. But she will calm passion, and follow reason, and dwell always with her, contemplating the true and the divine and that which is

b   beyond appearance and opinion, and thence deriving nourishment. Thus she seeks to live while she lives, and after death she hopes to go to her own kindred and to that which is like her, and to be freed from human ills. Thus nurtured, Simmias and Cebes, a soul will never fear that at her departure from the body she will be scattered and blown away by the winds and be nowhere and nothing.

3. THE THIRD PROOF

Plato argues, next, that only what is composite is susceptible to corruption and dissolution, or decomposition. What is simple and uncompounded cannot be dissolved. Conversely, we may assume that what is always changing — coming to be and passing away — is composite in character, but what is always the same and does not change is not composite.

What is constantly undergoing change, Plato believes (and argues elsewhere, in the *Republic* and the *Theaetetus*), cannot be fully real, for the true reality must be eternal and unchanging. Such are the ideas themselves — equality, beauty, and goodness — to which we referred earlier. Sensible, unchangeable things at best approximate to the ideas. What we can see and touch, the material world around us, is composite, changeable, and corruptible, but the ideas are not sensible but only intelligible; they cannot be seen or touched; they do not change but are eternal and incorruptible.

Now, the body is part of and is akin to the sensible, corruptible world, but the soul is invisible and akin to the eternal ideas, among which it finds itself more at home. The association of the soul with the body forces it to make use of sense perception, but its primary function is thinking. When it thinks it abstracts from the sensible and dwells among ideas. Thus the soul is more akin to the eternal and the intelligible. Moreover, it is the soul that directs and rules over the body and is therefore more like the divine (and immortal).

Plato concludes that while the body is subject to corruption and dissolution, the soul is not, for it is elemental and uncompounded and hence, indestructible.

There follows a restatement of the moral theory, that the good of the soul consists in its seeking purity in philosophy and in withdrawal from bodily desires and pleasures. The penalty for indulgence of physical appetites is to become earthbound, a flitting ghost unable to find satisfaction and condemned to return into a new body. The pure soul, on the other hand, is freed to return to the blessed life of the gods.[7]

Let us now examine these arguments. (a) The argument from simplicity hardly seems conclusive. The simple is not susceptible to gradual changes, for that implies parts, some of which change while others remain the same. But it may be liable to instantaneous annihilation or substitution. If so, simplicity is no guarantee of immortality. (b) The argument from kinship to the intelligible is likewise inconclusive, for no claim is made that the soul is itself an idea but only that, being invisible, it is known through the intellect and so is akin to the ideas. But the ideas (or "forms" as they are also called) are not temporal and so are not strictly everlasting; they are eternal or timeless. If the soul were like the ideas, it might be intelligible but it still would not be an everlasting, substantial thing.

Again, does invisibility prove anything to the point? Suppose we altogether deny the existence of a soul, it would then be invisible, but not immortal on that account. Perhaps because it is invisible we have no right to postulate its existence at all, let alone its survival after the death of the body. But this denial is too glib; we cannot dispose of Plato's argument quite so easily. For how should we account for consciousness, intelligence, and what, in general, we call "the mind" in purely physical terms. Plato says in the *Philebus*, "Wisdom and mind without soul could not come into being." Is he on firm ground here or

---

[7]Cf. Pythagorean doctrine, chapter 2 above.

could it be demonstrated that wisdom and mind could be no more than bodily functions?

There is today a considerable body of argument which contends that consciousness is no more than a form of neurophysiological functioning. If this were true, Socrates' argument would be of no avail, because the invisibility of the soul would be evidence of nothing so much as its nonexistence. We cannot at this stage discuss the modern theory, which is generally known as the neural-identity theory, for to do so adequately would require careful consideration of psychological as well as neurophysiological facts and theories, and also much conceptual analysis. A not dissimilar theory, however, is shortly to be stated in the *Phaedo* itself, and we shall examine Plato's retort to it. What can be said here is that the common reason why we affirm the existence of a soul or mind at all is the undeniable existence of consciousness, especially the consciousness of our own agency in thinking, judging, making decisions, and initiating action. It is this that must be accounted for, whether as physiological activity or as the activity of some mysterious, immaterial entity. The attempt to account for it in either way is beset with difficulties.

It is to be noticed that awareness of one's body is on a par (for the most part) with awareness of other bodies. In all such cases the percept is objective to our minds as knowing subjects. The awareness of oneself, on the other hand, is not so objective to a knowing subject but is rather the subject's direct consciousness of its own activity, which is not presented to it as an "external" object (and so is "invisible"). The subjective element is present in both cases and it is this that must be explained. It is very unlikely that we could explain it successfully by reducing it to an object (such as physiological activity). For that object would again demand a subject if it were to be known. It is, moreover, difficult to understand how a merely physical entity or process could be aware of its own agency in judging and making decisions. However it is difficult, in any case, to understand what is involved in these activities.

Consciousness, whatever it may be, seems to have properties that are quite different from and incompatible with those of physical things. It is aware of spatiotemporal relations. How, then, could it be spatiotemporal itself—that is, how could it be restricted to certain points in space and time and yet be aware of their relation to other points, more remote? The conscious being represents to himself other things than himself and is at the same time aware of their relation to him. Could any merely physical entity do this? It seems improbable that we could give a satisfactory answer and we seem, in consequence, forced to make *some* distinction between mind and body, even if it is hard to clarify; and if we must do this we are entitled to try, as Socrates is made to try in the dialogue, to explain the difference between them. Nevertheless, we cannot be satisfied that Plato has, up to this point, given any finally convincing proof of immortality, and as the dialogue proceeds it is clear that he is himself aware of the fact and is not satisfied with what he has so far established.

Phaedo
(Continued)

c   When Socrates had done speaking, for a considerable time there was silence; he himself appeared to be meditating, as most of us were, on what had been said; only Cebes and Simmias spoke a few words to one another. And Socrates observing them asked what they thought of the argument, and whether there was anything wanting? For, said he, there are many points still open to suspicion and attack, if anyone were disposed to sift the matter thoroughly. Should you be considering some other matter I say no more, but if you feel any doubt on the present subject do not hesitate either to give us your own thoughts if you
d   have any improvement to suggest, or, if you think that you will make more progress with my assistance, allow me to help you.

*   Simmias said: I must confess, Socrates, that doubts do arise in our minds, and each of us has for some time been urging and inciting the other to put the question which we wanted to have answered but which neither of us liked to ask, fearing that our importunity might be troublesome at such a time.

Socrates replied with a smile: O Simmias, what are you saying? I am not very
e   likely to persuade other men that I do not regard my present situation as a misfortune if I cannot even persuade you, and find you afraid that I may be more irritable than I used to be. Will you not allow that I have as much of the spirit of prophecy in me as the swans? For they, when they perceive that they must die, having sung at times during their life, do then sing a longer and
85 lovelier song than ever, rejoicing in the thought that they are about to go away to the god whose ministers they are. But men, because they are themselves afraid of death, slanderously affirm of the swans that they sing a lament at the last, a cry of woe, not considering that no bird sings when cold, or hungry, or in pain, not even the nightingale, nor the swallow, nor yet the hoopoe; which are said indeed to tune a woeful lay, although I do not believe this to be true of
b   them any more than of the swans. But because they are sacred to Apollo, they have the gift of prophecy, and anticipate the good things of another world; wherefore they sing and rejoice in that day more than ever they did before. And I too, believing myself to be the consecrated servant of the same god, and the fellow servant of the swans, and thinking that I have received from my master gifts of prophecy which are not inferior to theirs, would not go out of life less merrily than the swans. Never mind then, if this be your only objection, but

speak and ask anything which you like, while the eleven magistrates of Athens allow.

Very good, Socrates, said Simmias; then I will tell you my difficulty, and
c Cebes will tell you his. I felt myself (and I dare say that you have the same feeling) that it is impossible or at least very hard to attain any certainty about questions such as these in the present life. And yet I should deem him a coward who did not prove what is said about them to the uttermost, not desisting until he had examined them on every side. For he should persevere until he has acheived one of these things: either he should discover, or be taught the truth about them; or, if this be impossible, I would have him take the best and most
d irrefragable of human theories, and let this be the raft upon which he sails through life – not without risk, as I admit, if he cannot find some word of God which will more surely and safely carry him. And now, as you bid me, I will venture to question you, and then I shall not have to reproach myself hereafter with not having said at the time what I think. For when I consider the matter, either alone or with Cebes, the argument does certainly appear to me, Socrates, to be not sufficient.

e   Socrates answered: I dare say, my friend, that you may be right, but I should like to know in what respect the argument is insufficient.

In this respect, replied Simmias: Suppose a person to use the same argument about harmony[8] and the lyre – might he not say that harmony is a thing invisi-
86 ble, incorporeal, perfect, divine, existing in the lyre which is harmonized, but that the lyre and the strings are matter and material, composite, earthy, and akin to mortality? And when someone breaks the lyre, or cuts and rends the strings, then he who takes this view would argue as you do, and on the same analogy, that the harmony survives, and has not perished – you cannot imagine, he would say, that the lyre without the strings, and the broken strings them-
b selves which are mortal remain, and yet that the harmony, which is of heavenly and immortal nature and kindred, has perished – perished before the mortal. The harmony must still be somewhere, and the wood and strings will decay before anything can happen to that. The thought, Socrates, must have occurred to your own mind that such is our conception of the soul; and that when the body is in a manner strung and held together by the elements of hot and cold,
c wet and dry, then the soul is the harmony or due proportionate admixture of them. But if so, whenever the strings of the body are unduly loosened or overstrained through disease or other injury, then the soul, though most divine, like other harmonies of music or of works of art, of course perishes at once; although the material remains of the body may last for a considerable time,
d until they are either decayed or burnt. And if any one maintains that the soul, being an admixture of the elements of the body, is first to perish in that which is called death, how shall we answer him?

Socrates looked fixedly at us as his manner was, and said with a smile:

---

[8]In Greek the word *harmonia* does not mean "harmony," if "harmony" conveys to us the concord of several sounds. The Greeks called that *symphonia*. *Harmonia* meant originally the orderly adjustment of parts in a complete fabric; then, in particular, the tuning of a musical instrument; and finally the musical scale, composed of several notes yielded by the tuned strings. (Cornford, *The Unwritten Philosophy and other Essays.* C.U.P., 1950, p. 19.)

Simmias has reason on his side; and why does not some one of you who is
better able than myself answer him? for there is force in his line of argument.
e But perhaps, before we answer him, we had better also hear what Cebes has
to say that we may gain time for reflection, and when they have both spoken,
we may either assent to them, if there is truth in their concord, or if not, then
we must fight our case. Please to tell me then, Cebes, he said, what was the
difficulty which troubled you?

Cebes said: I will tell you. My feeling is that the argument is where it was,
87 and open to the same objections which were urged before; for I am ready to
admit that the existence of the soul before entering into the bodily form has
been very ingeniously, and, if I may say so, quite sufficiently proven; but the
existence of the soul after death is in my judgement unproven. Now in spite of
Simmias' objections I am not disposed to deny that the soul is stronger and
more lasting than the body, being of opinion that in all such respects the soul
very far excels the body. Well then, says the argument to me, why do you remain unconvinced? When you see that the weaker continues in existence
after the man is dead, will you not admit that the more lasting must
b also survive during the same period of time? Now I will ask you to consider
whether the objection, which I think I must, like Simmias, express in a figure, is
of any weight. The analogy which I will adduce is that of an old weaver, who
dies, and after his death somebody says: He is not dead, he must be alive
somewhere; see, there is the coat which he himself wove and wore, surviving
c whole and unruined. And then he proceeds to ask of someone who is incredulous, whether a man lasts longer, or the coat which is in use and wear; and
when he is answered that a man lasts far longer, thinks that he has thus
certainly demonstrated the survival of the man, inasmuch as the less lasting has
not perished. But that, Simmias, as I would beg you to remark, is a mistake;
anyone would retort that he who talks thus is talking nonsense. For the truth is
that the weaver aforesaid, having woven and worn many such coats, outlived
d several of them, but was outlived by the last; yet a man is not therefore proved
to be slighter and weaker than a coat. Now the relation of the body to the soul
may be expressed in a similar figure; and anyone may very fairly say in like
manner that the soul is lasting, and the body weak and shortlived in comparison. He may argue that every soul wears out many bodies, expecially if a man
live many years. While he is alive the body deliquesces and decays, and the
e soul always weaves another garment and repairs the waste. But of course,
whenever the soul perishes, she must have on her last garment, and this will
survive her; and then at length, when the soul is dead, the body will show its
native weakness, and quickly decompose and pass away. I would therefore
rather not rely on the argument from superior strength to prove the continued
88 existence of the soul after death. For granting even more than you affirm to be
possible, and acknowledging not only that the soul existed before birth, but also
that the souls of some exist and will continue to exist after death, and will be
born and die again and again, and that there is a natural strength in the soul by
which she will hold out and be born many times—nevertheless, we may be still
inclined to think that she will weary in the labours of successive births, and
may at last succumb in one of her deaths and utterly perish; and this death and
b dissolution of the body which brings destruction to the soul may be unknown to
any of us, for no one of us can have had any experience of it: and if so, then I

maintain that he who is confident about death can have but a foolish confidence, unless he is able to prove that the soul is altogether immortal and imperishable. But if he cannot prove the soul's immortality, he who is about to die will always have reason to fear that when the body is disunited, the soul also may utterly perish.

c   All of us, as we afterwards remarked to one another, had an unpleasant feeling at hearing what they said. When we had been so firmly convinced before, now to have our faith shaken seemed to introduce a confusion and uncertainty, not only into the previous argument, but into any future one; either we were but poor judges, or the subject itself might prove to be such that certainty was impossible.

ECH. There I feel with you—by heaven I do, Phaedo, and when you were
d speaking, I was moved to ask myself the same question: What argument can I ever trust again? For what could be more convincing than the argument of Socrates, which has now fallen into discredit? That the soul is a kind of harmony is a doctrine which has always had a wonderful hold upon me, and, when mentioned, came back to me at once, as my own original conviction. And now I must begin again and find another argument which will assure me that when the man is dead the soul survives. Tell me, I implore you, how did Socrates
e pursue the argument? Did he appear to share the unpleasant feeling which you mention? or did he calmly meet the attack? And did he succeed in meeting it, or fail? Narrate what passed as exactly as you can.

PHAED. Often, Echecrates, I have wondered at Socrates, but never more than
89 on that occasion. That he should be able to answer was perhaps nothing, but what astonished me was, first, the gentle and pleasant and approving manner in which he received the words of the young men, and then his quick sense of the wound which had been inflicted on us by the argument, and the readiness with which he healed it. He might be compared to a general rallying his defeated and broken army, urging them to follow his lead and return to the field.

ECH. What followed?

PHAED. You shall hear, for I was close to him on his right hand, seated on a
b sort of stool, and he on a couch which was a good deal higher. He stroked my head, and pressed the hair upon my neck—he had a way of teasing me about my hair; and then he said: Tomorrow, Phaedo, I suppose that these fair locks of yours will be severed.

Yes, Socrates, I suppose that they will, I replied.

Not so, if you will take my advice.

What shall I do with them? I said.

Today, he replied, and not tomorrow, if this argument dies and we cannot
c bring it to life again, you and I will both cut off our hair: and if I were you, and the argument got away from me, and I could not hold my ground against Simmias and Cebes, I would myself take an oath, like the Argives, not to let my hair grow any more until I had renewed the conflict and defeated them.

Yes, I said; but Heracles himself is said not to be a match for two.

Summon me then, he said, and I will be your Iolaus until the sun goes down.

I summon you rather, I rejoined, not as Heracles summoning Iolaus, but as Iolaus might summon Heracles.

That will do as well, he said. But first let us take care that we avoid a danger.

Of what nature? I said.

d   Lest we become misologists, he replied: no worse thing can happen to a man than this. For as there are misanthropists or haters of mankind, there are also misologists or haters of argument, and both spring from the same cause, which is ignorance of the world. Misanthropy arises out of the too great confidence of inexperience; you trust a man and think him altogether true and sound and faithful, and then in a little while he turns out to be false and knavish; and then another and another, and when this has happened several times to a man,

e   especially when it happens among those whom he deems to be his own most trusted and familiar friends, after many disappointments he at last hates all men, and believes that no one has any good in him at all. You must have observed this process?

I have.

And is it not discreditable? Is it not obvious that such a one was attempting to deal with other men before he had acquired the art of human relationships? This art would have taught him the true state of the case, that few are the good

90 and few the evil, and that the great majority are in the interval between them.

What do you mean? I said.

I mean, he replied, as you might say of the very large and very small—that nothing is more uncommon than a very large or very small man; and this applies generally to all extremes, whether of great and small, or swift and slow, or fair and foul, or black and white: and whether the instances you select be men or dogs or anything else, very few are the extremes, but in the mean between them there is a countless multitude. Did you never observe this?

Yes, I said, I have.

b   And do you not imagine, he said, that if there were a competition in evil, even there the pre-eminent would be found to be very few?

That is very likely, I said.

Yes, that is very likely, he replied; although in this respect arguments are unlike men—there I was led on by you to say more than I had intended. The point of comparison was, that when a simple man who has no skill in dialectics believes an argument to be true which he afterwards imagines to be false whether really false or not, and then another and another,—and those espe-

c cially who have devoted themselves to the study of antinomies come, as you know, to think at last that they have grown to be the wisest of mankind, and that they alone perceive how unsound and unstable are things themselves and all our arguments about them, and how all existence, like the currents in the Euripus, hurries up and down in never-ceasing ebb and flow.

That is quite true, I said.

Yes, Phaedo, he replied, and if there be such a thing as truth or certainty or

d possibility of knowledge, how melancholy that a man should have lighted upon some argument or other which at first seemed true and then turned out to be false, and instead of blaming himself and his own want of wit, should at last out of sheer annoyance be only too glad to transfer the blame from himself to arguments in general: and for ever afterwards should hate and revile them, and lose truth and the knowledge of realities.

Yes, indeed, I said; that would be most melancholy.

Let us then, in the first place, he said, be careful of allowing or of admitting

e into our souls the notion that there may be no health or soundness in any arguments at all. Rather say that we have not yet attained to soundness in ourselves, and that we must struggle manfully and do our best to gain it — you and all other men having regard to the whole of your future life, and I myself in 91 the prospect of death. For at this moment I fear that I have not the temper of a philosopher; like the vulgar, I am only a partisan. Now the partisan, when he is engaged in a dispute, cares nothing about the rights of the question, but is anxious only to convince his hearers of his own assertions. And the difference between him and me at the present moment is merely this — that whereas he seeks to convince his hearers that what he says is true, I am rather seeking to convince myself; to convince my hearers is a secondary matter with me. And b do but see how I stand to gain either way by the argument. For if what I say is true, then I do well to be persuaded of the truth; but if there be nothing after death, still, during the short time that remains, I shall not distress my friends with lamentations, and my folly will not last, but will die very soon, and therefore no harm will be done. This is the state of mind, Simmias and Cebes, in which I approach the argument. And I would ask you to be thinking of the c truth and not of Socrates: agree with me, if I seem to you to be speaking the truth; or if not, withstand me might and main, that I may not deceive you as well as myself in my enthusiasm, and like the bee leave my sting in you before I die.

4. OBJECTIONS AND MISGIVINGS

The next section of the *Phaedo* is in many ways the most important, dramatically, historically, and philosophically. It has the character of a dramatic climax, heightening the suspense and expectation of the reader, after what has appeared to be a conclusive proof of Socrates' thesis, by a sudden subversion of the whole position, the telling statement of new objections, and the elaboration of a new theory of the soul. Plato introduces here a literary device which is very characteristic of his writing. He interrupts the argument with description or banter and interpolates a long introduction to its renewal, keeping the reader in suspense, just before some passage of special importance.

It is also to be observed that Plato adopts what is the special mark of sincere and competent philosophical method, the aim of which is not merely to make a case or win an argument (in the manner of the Sophists), but to discover the truth. Although the proofs already presented seem plausible enough, Plato now introduces new and more formidable objections, stated in the strongest possible manner. If he is to prove his point it will be by no easy shortcut, evading the most formidable difficulties, but in the only convincing way, in the face of the best statement of opposing views that can be mustered. One may compare this procedure with that adopted in *Republic* II, where, after complete discomfiture of Thrasymachus in Book I, Socrates is asked to prove his point all over again against a restatement of Thrasymachus' theory much more ably and cogently argued by Glaucon and Adeimantus (who, because they do not really believe it and only want to hear it refuted, have no axe to grind in its defense).

Simmias and Cebes, after some hesitation and private conference, express dissatisfaction with the proofs of immortality hitherto offered. Simmias states the theory, prevalent among the Pythagoreans of the day and attributed to Philolaus, that the soul is a harmony of activities of the body related to it as the harmony of the lyre is related to the vibration of its separate strings. This has all the attributes Socrates has been predicating of the soul (including invisibility) and is yet nothing substantial over and above the strings themselves. So the living body is a harmony or organization of numerous different physiological functions and the soul may be (probably is) no more than the unifying principle of the bodily functions which, so to speak, brings them to life, but which can neither precede nor outlast them.

Cebes declares that, even if it can be shown that the soul does outlive several bodies, it does not prove that it can outlive any given number and will not at some time come to an end itself, just as a man outlives any number of garments but, when he dies, will leave some behind which outlast him.

At this point the dramatic device of interrupting and holding up the dialogue is introduced before Socrates' reply. The original narrators, Phaedo and Echecrates, are reintroduced and then comes the touching digression about Socrates fondling the hair of his young friend's head and advising him not to cut it off in mourning for him, but to do so only if the argument for the soul's immortality cannot be saved from the formidable objections of Simmias and Cebes.

He then warns his hearers against the sin of "misology," a warning not altogether irrelevant in our own day. It is common especially among beginners in philosophy when they have followed arguments for and against several theories, only to find them each in turn refuted, and can discover none that seem immune from objection, that they reject reason altogether and despair of philosophy. This is a self-destructive scepticism which is less tolerable than the continual failure of new arguments. For to reject all theorizing and reflection as futile implies positive knowledge by reference to which we condemn the theories we reject, and to deny the possibility of any such knowledge would be to renounce our right to despise the fruits of reflection. Our best and only hope is to continue thinking and correcting our errors in the faith that there is a true theory, and that if we pursue the right method we shall steadily (if only slowly) progress toward it.

Phaedo

(continued)

And now let us proceed, he said. And first of all let me be sure that I have in my mind what you were saying. Simmias, if I remember rightly, has fears and misgivings whether the soul, although a fairer and diviner thing than the body, being as she is in the form of harmony may not perish first. On the other hand, Cebes appeared to grant that the soul was more lasting than the body, but he said that no one could know whether the soul, after having worn out many bodies, might not perish herself and leave her last body behind her; and that this might be death, the destruction not of the body but of the soul, for in the body the work of destruction is ever going on. Are not these, Simmias and Cebes, the points which we have to consider?

d

e   They both agreed to this statement of them.

He proceeded: And did you deny the force of the whole preceding argument, or of a part only?

Of a part only, they replied.

And what did you think, he said, of that part of the argument in which we said that learning was recollection, and hence inferred that the soul must have previously existed somewhere else before she was imprisoned in the body?

92

Cebes said that he had been wonderfully impressed by that part of the argument, and that his conviction remained absolutely unshaken. Simmias agreed, and added that he himself could hardly imagine the possibility of his ever thinking differently.

But, rejoined Socrates, you will have to think differently, my Theban friend, if you still maintain that harmony is a composite thing, and that the soul is a harmony which is made out of strings set in the frame of the body; for you will surely never allow yourself to say that a harmony is composed and exists prior to the elements necessary to its composition.

b

Never, Socrates

But do you not see that this is what you imply when you say both that the soul existed before she took the form and body of man, and that she was made up of elements which as yet had no existence? For harmony is not like that to which you are comparing it; but first the lyre, and the strings, and the sounds exist in a state of discord, and then harmony is made last of all, and perishes first. And how can such an account of the soul as this be in concord with your former statement?

c

Not at all, replied Simmias.

And yet, he said, there surely ought to be harmony in a discourse of which harmony is the theme?

There ought, replied Simmias.

But there is no harmony, he said, in the two propositions that learning is recollection, and that the soul is a harmony. Which of them will you retain?

I think, he replied, that I have a much stronger faith, Socrates, in the first of the two; of the latter I have had no demonstration at all, but derived it only from a specious analogy, which has commended it to most of its adherents. I know too well that these arguments from analogies are impostors, and unless great caution is observed in the use of them, they are very deceptive—in geometry, and in other things too. But the doctrine of learning and recollection derives its proof from a satisfactory postulate: and the proof was that the soul

d

must have existed before she came into the body, because to her belongs the reality of which the very name signifies existence. Having, as I am convinced,
e rightly accepted this postulate, and on sufficient grounds, I must, as I suppose, cease to argue or allow others to argue that the soul is a harmony.

Let me put the matter, Simmias, he said, in another point of view: Do you
93 imagine that a harmony or any other composition can be in a state other than that of the elements out of which it is compounded?

Certainly not.

Or do or suffer anything other than they do or suffer?

He agreed.

Then a harmony does not, properly speaking, lead the parts or elements which make up the harmony, but only follows them.

He assented.

So it is far from being possible that a harmony can have any motion, or sound, or other quality which is opposed to that of its parts.

Far indeed, he replied.

And does not the nature of every harmony depend upon the manner in which the elements are harmonized?

I do not understand you, he said.

I mean to say that a harmony is more of a harmony, and more completely a
b harmony, when more truly and fully harmonized, supposing such a thing is possible; and less of a harmony, and less completely a harmony, when less truly and fully harmonized.

True.

Now does the soul admit of degrees? or is one soul in the very least degree more or less, or more or less completely, a soul than another?

Not in the least.

Yet surely of two souls, one is said to have intelligence and virtue, and to be
c good, and the other to have folly and vice, and to be an evil soul: and this is said truly?

Yes, truly.

But what will those who maintain the soul to be a harmony say of this presence of virtue and vice in the soul? — will they say that here is another harmony, and another discord, and that the virtuous soul is harmonized, and herself being a harmony has another harmony within her, and that the vicious soul is both herself inharmonical and has no other harmony within her?

I cannot tell, replied Simmias; but clearly something of the sort would be asserted by those who say that the soul is a harmony.

d And we have already admitted that no soul is more a soul than another; which means admitting that one harmony is not more or less harmony, or more or less completely a harmony, than another?

Quite true.

And that which is not more or less a harmony is not more or less harmonized?

True.

And that which is not more or less harmonized cannot have more or less of harmony, but only an equal harmony?

Yes, an equal harmony.

Then one soul not being more or less completely a soul than another, is not
e more or less harmonized?

Exactly.

And therefore has neither more nor less of discord, nor yet of harmony?

She has not.

And having neither more nor less of harmony or of discord, one soul has no more vice or virtue than another, if vice be discord and virtue harmony?

Not at all more.

94 Or speaking more correctly, Simmias, the soul, if she is a harmony, will never have any vice; because a harmony, being entirely harmony, can have no part in the inharmonical.

No.

Nor, I presume, could a soul, being entirely soul have any part in vice?

How can she have, if the previous argument holds?

Then, if all souls are equally by their nature souls, all souls of all living creatures will be equally good?

I agree with you, Socrates, he said.

Well, can all this be true, think you? he said; and would such consequences b have followed if the assumption that the soul is harmony were correct?

It cannot be true.

Once more, he said, what ruler is there of the elements of human nature other than soul, and especially the wise soul? Do you know of any?

Indeed, I do not.

And is the soul in agreement with the affections of the body? or is she at variance with them? For example, when the body is hot and thirsty, does not the soul pull us away from drinking? and when the body is hungry, away from c eating? And this is only one instance out of ten thousand of the opposition of the soul to the things of the body.

Very true.

But we have already acknowledged that the soul, if she were a harmony, could never utter a note at variance with the tensions and relaxations and percussions and other affections of the strings out of which she is composed; she could only follow, she could not lead them?

It must be so, he replied.

And yet do we not now discover the soul to be doing the exact opposite — leading the elements of which she is believed to be composed; almost always d opposing and coercing them in all sorts of ways throughout life, sometimes more violently with the pains of medicine and gymnastic; then again more gently; now threatening, now admonishing the desires, passions, fears, as if talking to a thing which is not herself, as Homer in the Odyssey represents Odysseus doing in the words:

He beat his breast, and thus reproached his heart:
e   Endure, my heart; far worse hast thou endured!

Do you think that Homer wrote this under the idea that the soul is a harmony destined to be led by the affections of the body, and not rather of a nature which should lead and master them — herself far too divine a thing to be compared with any harmony?

Yes, Socrates, I quite think so.

Then, my friend, we can never be right in saying that the soul is a kind of har-
95 mony, for we should apparently contradict the divine Homer, and contradict ourselves.

True, he said.

Thus much, said Socrates, of Harmonia, your Theban goddess, who has graciously yielded to us; but what shall I say, Cebes, to her husband Cadmus, and how shall I make peace with him?

I think that you will discover a way of propitiating him, said Cebes; I am sure that you have put the argument with Harmonia in a manner that I could never
b have expected. For when Simmias was mentioning his difficulty, I quite imagined that no answer could be given to him, and therefore I was surprised at finding that his argument could not sustain the first onset of yours, and not impossibly the other, whom you call Cadmus, may share a similar fate.

Nay, my good friend, said Socrates, do not boast, lest some evil eye should blight the growing argument. That, however, may be left in the hands of those above; while we draw near the foe in Homeric fashion, and try the mettle of your words. Here lies the point: You want to have it proven to you that the soul
c is imperishable and immortal, for otherwise the philosopher, who meets death confidently in the belief that he will fare better in the world below than if he had led another sort of life, must be the dupe of a vain and foolish confidence: and you say that the demonstration of the strength and divinity of the soul, and of her existence prior to our becoming men, does not necessarily imply her immortality, but only that she is longlived, and has known and done much in a
d former state of immense duration. Still she is not on that account immortal; and her entrance into the human form may itself be a sort of disease which is the beginning of dissolution, and she may be sorely vexed during her earthly life, and sooner or later perish in that which is called death. And whether the soul enters into the body once only or many times, does not, so you say, make any difference in the fears of individuals. For any man who is not devoid of sense must fear, if he has no knowledge and can give no account of the soul's immortality. This, or something like this, I suspect to be your view, Cebes; and I have
e designedly repeated it more than once in order that nothing may escape us, and that you may, if you wish, add or subtract anything.

But, said Cebes, as far as I see at present, I have nothing to add or subtract; I mean what you say that I mean.

5. SOCRATES' REPLY

After a brief restatement of the objections, Socrates argues against the view that the soul is the harmony of the bodily elements:

(a) that if the theory of recollection (*anamnesis*) is true it proves the prior existence of the soul and is therefore incompatible with the harmony theory, for a harmony cannot exist prior to the elements of which it is the harmonizing.

(b) that harmony admits of degrees—the lyre may be more or less in tune and some notes harmonize better than others—but there are no degrees of soul.

(c) that the soul is virtuous or vicious in varying degrees and we usually consider virtue to be a harmonious condition of the soul and

vice an inharmonious condition.[9] If this be so, and the soul is a harmony, there must be a harmony of a harmony, which is absurd, or else
all souls must be equally virtuous and incapable of vice, which is palpably false.

In our comment upon the theory of recollection, however, we found
that even if it were the case that some elements of knowledge are not
traceable back to sense perception, it does not follow that they were
remembered from some former existence (in fact, we shall see that this
could not intelligibly be so) and that immortality is not proven by this
argument. Again, if the soul (or mind) is characterized by consciousness
it would be true to say that there can be degrees of it. Our awareness
and its organization does vary from the vague confusion of half sleep
(or waking) to the precision of clear and concentrated attention. A drug
or a blow on the head reduces the degree of consciousness enjoyed,
which may decline to the point of oblivion. Furthermore, virtue may
well be just a higher degree of organization than vice. To explain this in
detail would take us too long, but it is not outrageous or implausible to
suggest that intelligence is nothing else but a high degree of organization in consciousness and that intelligent action is just a high degree of
organization in behavior. If, then, virtue is rational action and vice
irrational (as Plato would want to maintain), a high degree of harmony
(or organization) is not at all absurd. Modern biology gives us innumerable examples of organized complexities, the elements of which are
already highly organized systems.

Socrates' argument presumes throughout that soul and body are and
must be separate entities. The theory of the soul as a harmony of
physiological elements, in effect, denies this, and no argument that the
dialogue contains conclusively proves that there are two such separate
entities in external relation. On the other hand, surely the significant
fact about a harmony is that it is something over and above the mere
collection or aggregation of the elements harmonized. The lyre is not
just a number of pieces of wood and cat-gut tied together, but an
organized structure. The sounds it produces are in harmony not when
it is struck at random but only when the strings are carefully tuned and
the notes sounded are precisely related to one another. A symphony is
not just a collection of noises; it is an organization of sound according to
strict rules of counterpoint and composition, and its total effect is
something more than can be derived from the separate effects of its
elements. Here we have an apt example of a complex in which the
whole is more than the sum of its parts. It is a complex in which the

---

[9]Cf. *Republic IV*, 443d–444b.

function performed in the total effect by each part is explicable only in terms of its special relations to the other parts, and those are determined by the principles of order that give the totality its special structure.

If, therefore, the soul were a harmony of some sort it could not be simply analysed away into the elements of which it was the harmony. Those elements simply thrown together would give rise to no soul. If it were the harmony of physiological functions, it could not be simply resolved into them, whether taken singly or as an aggregate all taken together. It would be some peculiar supervenient quality characterizing a special degree and kind of organization—possibly a high degree of very complex organization of already highly organized systems. So that *some* form of distinction between body (as the mere aggregate, or a less highly organized phase of physiological functionings) and mind (or soul) might still be justified, though it would not imply separate existence and would give no obvious support to any theory of immortality.

The reply to Cebes is more elaborate and leads to the final *denouement* of the argument. Its importance is emphasized by the long introduction with which it is prefaced, and we may treat it in three parts: (a) the autobiographical prologue, (b) the return to the theory of ideas or forms, and (c) the final proof of immortality.

There follows a typical example of Plato's myths, which he invents with great artistry and uses to recommend doctrines which he feels go beyond the capacity of man to demonstrate. The stories, he says, are not literally true, but he believes something like them to be true. We need not discuss the myth further for it follows upon the establishment of the immortality of the soul, without which its moral is entirely lost.

Phaedo

(continued)

Socrates paused for a long while, and seemed to be absorbed in reflection. At length he said: You are raising a tremendous question, Cebes, involving the whole nature and cause of coming into being and ceasing to be, about which, if you like, I will give you my own experience; and if anything which I say seems helpful to you, you may use it to overcome your difficulty.

I should very much like, said Cebes, to hear what you have to say.

Then I will tell you, said Socrates. When I was young, Cebes, I had a prodigious desire to know that department of philosophy which is called the investigation of nature; to know the causes of things, and why a thing is and is created

or destroyed, appeared to me to be a lofty profession; and I was always agitat-
b ing myself with the consideration of questions such as these: Is the growth of
animals the result of some putrefaction which the hot and the cold principle
suffer, as some have said? Is the blood the element with which we think, or the
air, or the fire? or perhaps nothing of the kind — but the brain may be the
originating power of the perceptions of hearing and sight and smell, and
memory and opinion may come from them, and knowledge from memory and
opinion when they have attained fixity. And then I went on to examine the
c corruptions of them, and then to the things of heaven and earth, and at last I
concluded myself to be utterly and absolutely incapable of these inquiries, as I
will satisfactorily prove to you. For I was fascinated by them to such a degree
that my eyes grew blind to things which I had seemed to myself, and also to
others, to know quite well; I unlearned what I had before thought self-evident
truths; e.g. such a fact as that the growth of man is the result of eating and
d drinking; for when by the digestion of food flesh is added to flesh and bone to
bone, and when by the same process each tissue has received its appropriate
accretion, then the lesser bulk becomes larger and so the small man becomes
big. Was not that a reasonable notion?

Yes, said Cebes, I think so.

Well; but let me tell you something more. There was a time when I thought
that I understood the meaning of greater and less pretty well; and when I saw
a big man standing by a little one, I fancied that one was taller than the other
e just by the head, and similarly with horses: and still more clearly did I seem to
perceive that ten is more than eight because it has two additional units, and
that two cubits are more than one because it is larger by a half of itself.

And what is now your notion of such matters? said Cebes.

I should be far enough from imagining, he replied, that I knew the cause of
any of them, by heaven I should; for I cannot satisfy myself that, when one is
97 added to one, either the one to which the addition is made or the one which is
added becomes two, or that the two units added together make two by reason
of the addition. I cannot understand how, when separated from the other, each
of them was one and not two, and now, when they are brought together, the
mere juxtaposition or meeting of them should be the cause of their becoming
two. Neither can I believe that the division of one is the way to make two; for
b then an opposite cause would produce the same effect — as in the former
instance the addition and juxtaposition of one to one was the cause of two, in
this the separation and subtraction of one from the other would be the cause.
Nor am I any longer satisfied that I understand how the unit comes into being
at all, or in short how anything else is either generated or destroyed or exists,
so long as this is the method of approach; but I have in my mind some confused
notion of a new method, and can never admit the other.
c   Then I heard someone reading, as he said, from a book of Anaxagoras, that
mind was the disposer and cause of all, and I was delighted at this notion,
which appeared quite admirable, and I said to myself: If mind is the disposer,
mind will dispose all for the best, and put each particular in the best place; and
I argued that if anyone desired to find out the cause of the generation or
destruction or existence of anything, he must find out what state of being or
d doing or suffering was best for that thing, and therefore a man had only to
consider what was best and most desirable both for the thing itself and for
other things, and then he must necessarily also know the worse, since the same

science comprehended both. Arguing in this way, I rejoiced to think that I had found in Anaxagoras a teacher of the causes of existence such as I desired, and I imagined that he would tell me first whether the earth is flat or round; and
e after telling me this, he would proceed to explain the cause and the necessity of this being so, starting from the greater good, and demonstrating that it is better for the earth to be such as it is; and if he said that the earth was in the centre, he would further explain that this position was the better, and I should be
98 satisfied with the explanation given, and not want any other sort of cause. And I thought that I would then go on and ask him about the sun and moon and stars, and that he would explain to me their comparative swiftness, and their returning and various states, active and passive, and in what way all of them were for the best. For I could not imagine that when he spoke of mind as the disposer of them, he would give any other account of their being as they are,
b except that this was best; and I thought that while explaining to me in detail the cause of each and the cause of all, he would also explain to me what was best for each and what was good for all. These hopes I would not have sold for a large sum of money, and I seized the books and started to read them as fast as I could in my eagerness to know the best and the worse.

How high were my hopes, and how quickly were they lost to me! As I proceeded, I found my philosopher altogether forsaking mind and making no appeal to any other principle of order, but having recourse to air, and ether,
c and water, and many other eccentricities. I might compare him to a person who began by maintaining generally that mind is the cause of the actions of Socrates, but who, when he endeavoured to explain the causes of my several actions in detail, went on to show that I sit here because my body is made up of bones and muscles; and the bones, as he would say, are hard and have joints
d which divide them, and the muscles are elastic, and they cover the bones, which have also a covering or environment of flesh and skin which contains them; and as the bones swing in their sockets, through the contraction or relaxation of the muscles I am able to bend my limbs, and this is why I am sitting here in a curved posture — that is what he would say; and he would have a similar explanation of my talking to you, which he would attribute to sound, and air, and hearing, and he would assign ten thousand other causes of the
e same sort, forgetting to mention the true cause, which is, that the Athenians have thought it better to condemn me, and accordingly I have thought it better
99 and more right to remain here and undergo my sentence; for I strongly suspect that these muscles and bones of mine would long ago have been in Megara or Boeotia, borne there by their own idea of what was best, if I did not think it more right and honourable to endure any penalty ordered by the state, instead of running away into exile. There is surely a strange confusion of causes and conditions in all this. It may be said, indeed, that without bones and muscles and the other parts of the body I cannot execute my purposes. But to say at the same time that I act from mind, and that I do as I do because of them and not
b from the choice of the best, is a very careless and idle mode of speaking. I wonder that they cannot distinguish the cause from the condition without which the cause would never be the cause; it is the latter, I think, which the many, feeling about in the dark, are always mistaking and misnaming "cause." And thus one man sets the earth within a cosmic whirling, and steadies it by the heaven; another gives the air as a support to the earth, which is a sort of
c broad trough. They never look for the power which in arranging them as they

are arranges them for the best; and instead of ascribing to it any superhuman strength, they rather expect to discover another Atlas who is stronger and more everlasting than this earthly Atlas, and better able to hold all things together. That it is really the good and the right which holds and binds things together, they never reflect. Such then is the principle of causation which I would fain learn if anyone would teach me. But as I have failed either to

d discover it myself, or to learn it of anyone else, I will exhibit to you, if you like, the method I have followed as the second best mode of inquiring into the cause.

I should very much like to hear, he replied.

Socrates proceeded: I thought that as I had failed in the study of material things, I ought to be careful that I did not lose the eye of my soul; as people may injure their bodily eye by observing and gazing on the sun during an eclipse, unless they take the precaution of only looking at the image reflected in

e the water, or in some similar medium. So in my own case, I was afraid that my soul might be blinded altogether if I looked at things with my eyes or tried to apprehend them by the help of particular senses. And I thought that I had better retreat to the domain of reasoning and seek there the truth of existence.

00 I dare say that the simile is not perfect—for I do not quite agree that he who contemplates things through the medium of thought, sees them only "through a glass darkly," more so than he who considers them in their material existence. However, this was the method which I adopted: I first assumed some proposition, which I judged to be the strongest, and then I affirmed as true whatever seemed to agree with this, whether relating to causation or to anything else; and that which disagreed I regarded as untrue. But I should like to explain my meaning more clearly, as I do not think that you as yet understand me.

No indeed, replied Cebes, not very well.

b There is nothing new, he said, in what I am about to tell you; but only what I have been always and everywhere repeating in the previous discussion and on other occasions: I shall try to show you the sort of causation which has occupied my thoughts. I shall have to go back to those familiar theories which are in the mouth of everyone, and first of all assume that there is an absolute beauty and goodness and greatness, and the like; grant me these and admit that they exist, and I hope to be able to show you the nature of cause, and to prove the immortality of the soul.

c Cebes said: You may proceed at once with the proof, for I grant you this.

Well, he said, then I should like to know whether you agree with me in the next step; for I cannot help thinking that if there be anything beautiful other than absolute beauty it is beautiful only in so far as it partakes of absolute beauty—and I should say the same of everything. Do you agree in this notion of the cause?

Yes, he said, I agree.

He proceeded: I no longer look for, nor can I understand, those other ingen-

d ious causes which are alleged; and if a person says to me that the bloom of colour, or form, or any such thing is a source of beauty, I dismiss all that, which is only confusing to me, and simply and singly, and perhaps foolishly, hold and am assured in my own mind that nothing makes a thing beautiful but the presence or participation of beauty in whatever way or manner obtained; for as to the manner I am uncertain, but I stoutly contend that by beauty all beautiful things become beautiful. This appears to me to be the safest answer which I can give, either to myself or to another, and to this I cling, in the persuasion that this principle will never be overthrown, and that to myself or to e anyone who asks the question, I may safely reply, That by beauty beautiful things become beautiful. Do you not agree with me?

I do.

And that by greatness great things become great and greater greater, and by smallness the less become less?

True.

Then if a person were to remark that A is taller by a head than B, and B less
101 by a head than A, you would refuse to admit his statement, and would stoutly contend that what you mean is only that the greater is greater by, and by reason of, greatness, and the less is less only by, and by reason of, smallness. I imagine you would be afraid of a counter-argument that if the greater is greater and the less less by the head, then, first, the greater is greater and the less less by the same thing; and, secondly, the greater man is greater by the head which is itself small, and so you get the monstrous absurdity that a man is
b great by something small. You would be afraid of this, would you not?

Indeed I should, said Cebes, laughing.

In like manner you would think it dangerous to say that ten exceeded eight by, and by reason of, two; but would say by, and by reason of, number; or you would say that two cubits exceed one cubit not by a half, but by magnitude? —for there is the same danger in all these cases.

Very true, he said.

Again, would you not be cautious of affirming that the addition of one to one,
c or the division of one, is the cause of two? And you would loudly asseverate that you know of no way in which anything comes into existence except by participation in the distinctive reality of that in which it participates, and consequently, as far as you know, the only cause of two is the participation in duality — this is the way to make two, and the participation in unity is the way to make one. You would say: "I will let alone all subtleties like these of division and addition — wiser heads than mine may answer them; inexperienced as I am, and
d ready to start, as the proverb says, at my own shadow, I cannot afford to give up the sure ground of the original postulate." And if anyone fastens on you there, you would not mind him, or answer him until you could see whether the consequences which follow agree with one another or not, and when you are further required to give an account of this postulate, you would give it in the same way, assuming some higher postulate which seemed to you to be the best founded,
e until you arrived at a satisfactory resting-place; but you would not jumble together the fundamental principle and the consequences in your reasoning, like the eristics — at least if you wanted to discover real existence. Not that this confusion signifies to them, who probably never care or think about the matter at all, for they have the wit to be well pleased with themselves however thorough may be the muddle of their ideas. But you, if you are a philosopher, will
102 certainly do as I say.

What you say is most true, said Simmias and Cebes, both speaking at once.

ECH. Yes, Phaedo; and I do not wonder at their assenting. Anyone who has the least sense will acknowledge the wonderful clearness of Socrates' reasoning.

PHAED. Certainly, Echecrates; and such was the feeling of the whole company at the time.

ECH. Yes, and equally of ourselves, who were not of the company, and are now listening to your recital. But what followed?

PHAED. After all this had been admitted, and they had agreed, that the forms b exist individually, and that other things participate in them and derive their names from them, Socrates, if I remember rightly, said:

This is your way of speaking; and yet when you say that Simmias is greater than Socrates and less than Phaedo, do you not predicate of Simmias both greatness and smallness?

Yes, I do.

But still, he continued, you allow that Simmias does not in fact exceed Socrates, as the words may seem to imply, essentially because he is Simmias,

c but by reason of the size which he happens to have; exactly as on the other hand he does not exceed Socrates because Socrates is Socrates, but because Socrates has smallness when compared with the greatness of Simmias?

True.

And if Phaedo exceeds him in size, this is not because Phaedo is Phaedo, but because Phaedo has greatness relatively to Simmias, who is comparatively smaller?

That is true.

And therefore Simmias is said to be small, and is also said to be great,

d because he is in a mean between them, submitting his smallness to be exceeded by the greatness of the one, and presenting his greatness to the other to exceed that other's smallness. He added, laughing, I am speaking like a book, but I believe that what I am saying is true.

Simmias assented.

I speak as I do because I want you to agree with me in thinking, not only that absolute greatness will never be simultaneously great and small, but also that the greatness in us will never admit the small or consent to be exceeded; instead of this, one of two things will happen, either it will fly and retire before

e its opposite, the small, or at the approach of its opposite it has already ceased to exist; but it refuses to become other than what it was staying and receiving smallness. For instance, I having received and admitted smallness remain as I was, and am the same person and small: but greatness has not condescended to

103 become small. In like manner the smallness in us refuses to be or become great; nor can any other opposite which remains the same ever be or become its own opposite, but either goes away or perishes in the change.

That, replied Cebes, is quite my notion.

Hereupon one of the company, though I do not exactly remember which of them, said: In heaven's name, is not this the direct contrary of what was admitted before—that out of the greater came the less and out of the less the greater, and that opposites were simply generated from opposites; but now this principle seems to be utterly denied.

Socrates turned his head to the speaker and listened. I like your courage, he

b said, in reminding us of this. But you do not observe that there is a difference in the two cases. For then we were saying that an opposite thing comes into being from its opposite; now, however, speaking of bare opposites, and taking them either as they are realized in us or as they exist in themselves, we say that one of them can never become the other: then, my friend, we were speaking of things in which opposites are inherent and which are called after them, but now about the opposites which are inherent in them and which give their name to them;

c and these essential opposites will never, as we maintain, admit of generation into or out of one another. At the same time, turning to Cebes, he said: Are you at all disconcerted, Cebes, at our friend's objection?

No, not by this one, said Cebes; and yet I cannot deny that I am often disturbed by objections.

Then we are agreed after all, said Socrates, that the opposite will never in any case be opposed to itself?

To that we are quite agreed, he replied.

Yet once more let me ask you to consider the question from another point of view, and see whether you agree with me: There is a thing which you term heat, and another thing which you term cold?

Certainly.

But are they the same as fire and snow?

Most assuredly not.

d   Heat is a thing different from fire, and cold is not the same with snow?

Yes.

And yet I fancy you agree that when snow receives heat (to use our previous phraseology), they will not remain snow and heat; but at the advance of the heat, the snow will either retire or perish?

Very true, he replied.

And the fire too at the advance of the cold will either retire or perish; but it will never receive the cold, and yet insist upon remaining what it was, and so be at once fire and cold.

e   That is true, he said.

And in some cases the name of the form is attached not only to the form in an eternal connexion; but something else which, not being the form, yet never exists without it, is also entitled to be called by that name. I will try to make this clearer by an example: The odd number is always called by the name of odd?

Very true.

104 But is this the only thing which is called odd? Here is my point. Are there not other things which have their own name, and yet must be called odd, because, although not the same as oddness, they are essentially never without oddness? I mean such a case as that of the number three, and there are many other examples. Take that case. Would you not say that three may be called by its proper name, and also be called odd, which is not the same with three? and this may be said not only of three but also of five, and of every alternate

b   number – each of them without being oddness is odd; and in the same way two and four, and the other series of alternate numbers, has every number even, without being evenness. Do you agree?

Of course.

Then now mark the point at which I am aiming: not only do essential opposites seem to exclude one another, but also concrete things, which, although not in themselves opposed, contain opposites; these, I say, likewise reject the form opposed to that which is contained in them, and when it approaches them they

c   either perish or withdraw. For example, will not the number three endure annihilation or anything sooner than be converted into an even number, while remaining three?

Very true, said Cebes.

And yet, he said, the number two is certainly not opposed to the number three?

It is not.

Then not only do opposite forms repel the advance of one another, but also there are other things which withdraw before the approach of opposites.

Very true, he said.

Suppose, he said, that we endeavour, if possible, to determine what these are.

By all means.

d   Are they not, Cebes, such as compel anything of which they have possession, not only to take their own form, but also the form of an opposite?

What do you mean?

I mean, as I was just now saying, and as I am sure that you know, that those things which are possessed by the form of the number three must not only be three in number, but must also be odd.

Quite true.

And such things will never suffer the intrusion of the form opposite to that which gives this impress?

No.

And this impress was given by the form of the odd?

Yes.

And to the odd is opposed the even?

True.

e   Then the form of the even number will never intrude on three?

No.

Then three has no part in the even?

None.

Then the triad or number three is uneven?

Very true.

To return then to my definition of things which are not opposite to one of a pair of opposites, and yet do not admit that opposite — as, in the instance given, three, although not opposed to the even, does not any the more admit of the even, but always brings the opposite into play on the other side, or as two does
105 not receive the odd, or fire the cold — from these examples (and there are many more of them) perhaps you may be able to arrive at the general conclusion, that not only opposites will not receive opposites, but also that nothing which brings an opposite will admit the opposite of that which it brings, in that to which it is brought. And here let me recapitulate — for there is no harm in repetition. The number five will not admit the form of the even, any more than ten, which is the double of five, will admit the form of the odd. The double has itself a different
b opposite, but nevertheless rejects the odd altogether. Nor similarly will parts in the ratio 3:2 admit the form of the whole, nor will the half or the one-third, or any such fraction: You will agree?

Yes, he said, I entirely agree and go along with you in that.

And now, he said, let us begin again; and do not you answer my question in the words in which I ask it, but follow my example: let me have not the old safe answer of which I spoke at first, but another equally safe, of which the truth will be inferred by you from what has been just said. If you ask me "what that is, of which the inherence makes the body hot," I shall reply not heat (this is
c what I call the safe and stupid answer), but fire, a far superior answer, which we are now in a condition to give. Or if you ask me "why a body is diseased," I shall not say from disease, but from fever; and instead of saying that oddness is the cause of odd numbers, I shall say that the monad is the cause of them: and so of things in general, as I dare say that you will understand sufficiently without my adducing any further examples.

Yes, he said, I quite understand you.

Tell me, then, what is that of which the inherence will render the body alive?

The soul, he replied.

d   And is this always the case?

Yes, he said, of course.

Then whatever the soul occupies, to that she comes bearing life?

Yes, certainly.

And is there any opposite to life?

There is, he said.

And what is that?

Death.

Then from our previous conclusion it follows that the soul will never admit the opposite of what she always brings.

Impossible, replied Cebes.

And now, he said, what did we just now call that which does not admit the form of the even?

Uneven.

e   And that which does not admit the musical or the just?

The unmusical, he said, and the unjust.

And what do we call that which does not admit death?

The immortal, he said.

And does the soul admit of death?

No.

Then the soul is immortal?

Yes, he said.

And may we say that this has been proven?

Yes, abundantly proven, Socrates, he replied.

Supposing that the odd were necessarily imperishable, must not three be
106   imperishable?

Of course.

And if that which is cold were necessarily imperishable, when heat came attacking the snow, must not the snow have retired whole and unmelted – for it could never have perished, nor again could it have remained and admitted the heat?

True, he said.

Again, if that which cannot be cooled were imperishable, the fire when assailed by cold would not have perished or have been extinguished, but would have gone away unaffected?

Certainly, he said.

b   And the same may be said of the immortal: if the immortal is also imperishable, the soul when attacked by death cannot perish; for the preceding argument shows that the soul will not admit death, or exist as dead, any more than three or the odd number will exist as even, or fire, or the heat in the fire, will be cold. Yet a person may say: "But although the odd will not become even at
c   the approach of the even, why may not the odd perish and the even take the place of the odd?" Now to him who makes this objection, we cannot answer that the odd is imperishable; for this is not the fact. If we had accepted it as a fact, there would have been no difficulty in contending that at the approach of the even the odd and the number three took their departure; and the same argument would have held good of fire and heat and any other thing.

Very true.

And the same may be said of the immortal: if we agree that the immortal is

also imperishable, then the soul will be imperishable as well as immortal; but if
d not, some other proof of her imperishableness will have to be given.

No other proof is needed, he said; for if the immortal, being eternal, is liable
to perish, then nothing is imperishable.

Yes, replied Socrates, and all men, I think, will agree that God, and the
essential form of life, and the immortal in general, will never perish.

Yes, all men, he said—that is true; and what is more, gods, if I am not mistaken, as well as men.

e Seeing then that the immortal is indestructible, must not the soul, if she is
immortal, be also imperishable?

Most certainly.

Then when death attacks a man, the mortal portion of him may be supposed
to die, but the immortal retires at the approach of death and is preserved safe
and indestructible?

Yes.

Then, Cebes, beyond question, the soul is immortal and imperishable, and
107 our souls will truly exist in another world!

I am convinced, Socrates, said Cebes, and have nothing more to object; but if
my friend Simmias, or anyone else, has any further objection to make, he had
better speak out, and not keep silence, since I do not know to what other season
he can defer the discussion if there is anything which he wants to say or to
have said.

But I too, replied Simmias, can give no reason for doubting the result of the
b argument. It is when I think of the greatness of the subject and the feebleness
of man that I still feel and cannot help feeling uncertain in my own mind.

Yes, Simmias, replied Socrates, that is well said: and I may add that our first
principles, even if they appear to you certain, should be closely examined; and
when they are satisfactorily analysed, then you will, I imagine, follow up the
argument as far as is humanly possible; and if you make sure you have done
so, there will be no need for any further inquiry.

Very true.

c But then, O my friends, he said, if the soul is really immortal, what care
should be taken of her, not only in respect of the portion of time allowed to
what is called life, but of eternity! And the danger of neglecting her from this
point of view does indeed now appear to be awful. If death had only been the
end of all, dying would have been a godsend to the wicked, for they would
have been happily quit not only of their body, but of their own evil together
with their souls. But now, inasmuch as the soul is manifestly immortal, there is
d for her no release or salvation from evil except the attainment of the highest
virtue and wisdom. For the soul when on her progress to the world below takes
nothing with her but nurture and education; and these are said greatly to
benefit or greatly to injure the departed, at the very beginning of his journey
thither.

For after death, as they say, each individual is led by the genius to whom he
had been allotted in life to a certain place in which the dead are gathered
together, whence after submitting to judgement they pass into the world below,
e following the guide who is appointed to conduct them from this world to the
other: and when they have received their due and remained their time, another guide brings them back again after many revolutions of ages. Now this
way to the other world is not, as Aeschylus says in the *Telephus*, a single and

108 straight path — if that were so no guide would be needed, for no one could miss it; but there are many partings of the road, and windings, as I infer from the rites and sacrifices which are offered to the gods below in places where three ways meet on earth. The wise and orderly soul follows her appointed guide and knows her surroundings; but the soul which desires the body, and which,

b as I was relating before, has long been fluttering about the lifeless frame and the world of sight, is after many struggles and many sufferings hardly and with violence carried away by her attendant genius; and when she arrives at the place where the other souls are gathered, if she be impure and have done impure deeds, whether foul murders or other crimes which are the brothers of these, and the works of brothers in crime — from that soul everyone flees and turns away; no one will be her companion, no one her guide, but alone she

c wanders in extremity of distress until certain times are fulfilled, and when they are fulfilled, she is borne irresistibly to her own fitting habitation; as every pure and just soul which has passed through life in the company and under the guidance of the gods has also her own proper home.

Now the earth has divers wonderful regions, and is indeed in nature and extent very unlike the notions of geographers, as I believe on the authority of one who shall be nameless.

d What do you mean, Socrates? said Simmias. I have myself heard many descriptions of the earth, but I do not know, and I should very much like to hear the account in which you put faith.

Well, Simmias, replied Socrates, it scarcely needs the art of Glaucus to give you a description; although I know not that the art of Glaucus could prove the truth of my tale, which I myself should perhaps never be able to prove, and even if I could, I fear, Simmias, that my life would come to an end before the augument was completed. I may describe to you, however, the form and

e regions of the earth according to my conception of them.

That, said Simmias, will be enough.

Well then, he said, my conviction is, that the earth is a round body in the

109 centre of the heavens, and therefore has no need of air or of any similar force to be a support, but is kept there and hindered from falling or inclining any way by the equability of the surrounding heaven and by her own equipoise. For that which, being in equipoise, is in the centre of that which is equably diffused, will not incline any way in any degree, but being similarly related to every extreme will remain unmoving, and not deviate. And this is my first belief.

Which is surely a correct one, said Simmias.

Also I believe that the earth is very vast, and that we who dwell in the region

b extending from the River Phasis to the Pillars of Heracles inhabit a small portion only about the sea, like ants and frogs about a marsh, and that there are many other inhabitants of many other like places; for everywhere on the surface of the earth there are hollows of various forms and sizes, into which the water and the mist and the lower air have collected. But the true earth is pure and situated in the pure heaven — there are the stars also; and it is the heaven

c which is commonly spoken of by most authorities as the ether, and of which those other things are the sediment gathering in the hollows beneath. We who live in these hollows are deceived into the notion that we are dwelling above on the surface of the earth; which is just as if a creature who lived at the bottom of the sea were to fancy that he was living on the surface of the water, and that the sea was the heaven through which he saw the sun and the other stars, he

having never come to the surface by reason of his feebleness and sluggishness,
d and having never lifted up his head and seen, nor ever heard from one who
had seen, how much purer and fairer the world above is than his own. And
such is exactly our case. We are dwelling in a hollow of the earth, and fancy
that we are on the surface; and the air we call the heaven, in which we imagine
e that the stars move. But the fact is that owing to our feebleness and sluggishness we are prevented from reaching the surface of the air: for if any man
could arrive at the exterior limit, or take the wings of a bird and come to the
top, then, like a fish who puts his head out of the water and sees this world, he
would see a world beyond; and, if the nature of man could sustain the sight, he
would acknowledge that this other world was the place of the true heaven and
110 the true light and the true earth. For our earth, and the stones, and the entire
region which surrounds us, are spoilt and corroded, as in the sea all things are
corroded by the brine, neither has the sea any notable or perfect growth, but
even where it meets earth it has only caverns, and sand, and an endless slough
of mud — in no wise to be compared to the fairer sights of our world. And still
b less is this our world to be compared with the other. If a myth is not to be despised, Simmias, I can tell you one that is well worth hearing about that upper
earth which is under the heaven.

And we, Socrates, replied Simmias, shall be charmed to listen to your myth.

The tale, my friend, he said, is as follows: In the first place, the true earth,
when looked at from above, is in appearance like one of those balls which are
made of twelve pieces of leather; it is variegated, a patchwork of different colours of which the colours used by painters on our earth are in a manner samples.
c But there the whole earth is made up of them, and they are brighter far and
clearer than ours; there is a purple of wonderful lustre, also the radiance of
gold, and the white which is in the earth is whiter than any chalk or snow. Of
these and other colours the earth is made up, and they are more in number and
fairer than the eye of man has ever seen; the very hollows (of which I was speaking) filled with air and water have a colour of their own, and are seen like light
d gleaming amid the diversity of the other colours, so that the whole presents a
single and continuous appearance of variety in unity. And in this fair region all
things which grow — trees, and flowers, and fruits — are in a like degree fairer than
any here; and there are hills, having stones in them in a like degree smoother,
and more transparent, and fairer in colour than our highly valued emeralds
e and cornelians and jaspers and other gems, which are but minute fragments of
them: for there all the stones are like our precious stones, and fairer still.[10] The
reason is that they are pure, and not, like our precious stones, corroded or de-
filed by the confluence of corrupt briny elements which breed foulness and disease both in earth and stones, as well as in animals and plants. They are the
111 jewels of the upper earth, which also shines with gold and silver and the like,
and they are set in the light of day and are large and abundant and in all places,
making the earth a sight to gladden the beholder's eye. And there are many animals and also men, some living inland, others dwelling about the air as we dwell
about the sea; others in islands which the air flows round, near the mainland;
b and in a word, the air is used by them as the water and the sea are by us, and the
ether is to them what the air is to us. Moreover, the temperament of their seasons is such that they have no disease, and live much longer than we do, and

---

[10] Cf. *Revelation*, esp. xxi. 18 foll.

have sight and hearing and intelligence and all the other faculties in far greater perfection, in the same proportion that air is purer than water or the ether than air. Also they have temples and sacred places in which the gods really dwell,
c and they hear their voices and receive their answers, and are conscious of them and hold converse with them face to face; and they see the sun, moon, and stars as they truly are, and their other blessedness is of a piece with this.

Such is the nature of the whole earth, and of the things which are around the earth; and there are divers regions in the hollows on the face of the globe everywhere, some of them deeper and more extended than that which we inhabit, others deeper but narrower, and some are shallower and also wider.
d All have numerous perforations, and there are passages broad and narrow in the interior of the earth, connecting them with one another; and there flows out of and into them, as into basins, a vast tide of water, and huge subterranean streams of perennial rivers, and springs hot and cold, and a great fire, and great rivers of fire, and streams of liquid mud, thin or thick (like the rivers of
e mud in Sicily, and the lava streams which follow them), and the regions about which they happen to flow are filled up with them. And there is a swinging or see-saw in the interior of the earth which moves all this up and down, and is due
112 to the following cause: There is a chasm which is the vastest of them all, and pierces right through the whole earth; this is that chasm which Homer describes in the words:

Far off, where is the inmost depth beneath the earth;

and which he in other places, and many other poets, have called Tartarus. And the see-saw is caused by the streams flowing into and out of this chasm, and they each have the nature of the soil through which they flow. And the reason why the streams are always flowing in and out, is that the watery element has
b no bed or bottom, but is swinging and surging up and down, and the surrounding wind and air do the same; they follow the water up and down, towards the further side of the earth and back again; and just as in the act of respiration the air is always in process of inhalation and exhalation, so the wind swinging with the water in and out produces fearful and irresistible blasts:
c when the waters retire into the regions below, as they are called, they flow into the streams on the further side of the earth, and fill them up like water raised by a pump, and then when they leave those regions and rush back hither, they again fill the streams here, and these being filled flow through subterranean channels and find their way to their appointed places, forming seas, and lakes,
d and rivers, and springs. Thence they again enter the earth, some of them making a long circuit into many lands, others going to a few places and not so distant; and again fall into Tartarus, some at a point a good deal lower than that at which they rose, and others not much lower, but all in some degree lower than the point from which they came; and some fall in on the opposite side, and some on the same side. Some wind round the earth with one or many folds like the coils
e of a serpent, and after descending as far as they can fall again into the chasm. The rivers flowing in either direction can descend only to the center and no further, for on either side of it their course would be uphill.

Now these rivers are many, and mighty, and diverse, and there are four principal ones, of which the greatest and outermost is that called Oceanus, which flows round in a circle; and diametrically opposite to it is Acheron,
113 which flows in the opposite direction and passes through desert places and

under the earth into the Acherusian lake: this is the lake to the shores of which the souls of the many go when they are dead, and after waiting an appointed time, which is to some a longer and to some a shorter time, they are sent back to be born again as animals. The third river passes out between the two, and near the place of outlet pours into a vast region of fire, and forms a lake larger than the Mediterranean Sea, boiling with water and mud; and proceeding b muddy and turbid, and coiling round inside the earth, comes, among other places, to the extremities of the Acherusian lake, but mingles not with the waters of the lake, and after making many coils about the earth plunges into Tartarus at a deeper level. This is that Pyriphlegethon, as the stream is called, which throws up jets of lava in different parts of the earth. The fourth river goes out on the opposite side, and falls first of all, it is said, into a savage and frightful region, which is all of a blue-grey colour, like lapis lazuli; and this is c that region which is called the Stygian, and the lake which the river forms by its influx is called Styx. After falling into the lake and receiving strange powers in the waters, it passes under the earth, winding round in the opposite direction to Pyriphlegethon, and meets it at the Acherusian lake from the opposite side. And the water of this river too mingles with no other, but flows round in a circle and falls into Tartarus over against Pyriphlegethon; and the name of the river, as the poets say, is Cocytus.

d   Such is the nature of the other world; and when the dead arrive at the place to which the genius of each severally guides them, first of all, they submit themselves to judgement, as they have lived well and piously or not. And those who appear to have lived neither well nor ill, go to the river Acheron, and embarking in the vessels which we may imagine they find there, are carried in them to the lake, and there they dwell and are purified of their evil deeds, and having suffered the penalty of the wrongs which they have done to others, they are absolved, and receive the rewards of their good deeds, each of them e according to his deserts. But those who appear to be incurable by reason of the greatness of their crimes — who have committed many and terrible deeds of sacrilege, many murders foul and violent, or the like — such are hurled into Tartarus which is their fitting destiny, and they never come out. Those again who have committed crimes, which, although great, are not irremediable — who in a moment of anger, for example, have done some violence to a father or a 114 mother, and have repented for the remainder of their lives, or who have taken the life of another under the like extenuating circumstances — these are plunged into Tartarus, the pains of which they are compelled to undergo for a year, but at the end of the year the wave casts them forth — mere homicides by way of Cocytus, parricides and matricides by Pyriphlegethon — and they are borne to the Acherusian lake, and there they lift up their voices and call upon the victims whom they have slain or wronged, to have pity on them, and to be b kind to them, and let them come out into the lake. And if they prevail, then they come forth and cease from their troubles; but if not, they are carried back again into Tartarus and from thence into the rivers unceasingly, until they obtain mercy from those whom they have wronged: for that is the sentence inflicted upon them by their judges. But those who have been pre-eminent for c holiness of life are released from this earthly prison, and go to their pure home which is above, and dwell on the true earth; and of these, such as have duly purified themselves with philosophy live henceforth altogether without the body, in mansions fairer still, which are not easily to be described, and of which the time now fails me to tell.

Wherefore, Simmias, seeing all these things, what ought not we to do that we
may obtain virtue and wisdom in this life? Fair is the prize, and the hope great!
d   A man of sense ought not to assert that the description which I have given of
the soul and her mansions is exactly true. But I do say that, inasmuch as the
soul is shown to be immortal, he may venture to think, not improperly or
unworthily, that something of the kind is true. The venture is a glorious one,
and he ought to comfort himself with words of power like these, which is the
e   reason why I lengthen out the tale. Wherefore, I say, let a man be of good
cheer about his soul, who having cast away the pleasures and ornaments of the
body as alien to him and working harm rather than good, has sought after the
pleasures of knowledge; and has arrayed the soul, not in some foreign attire,
but in her own proper jewels, temperance, and justice, and courage, and
115   nobility, and truth—in these adorned she is ready to go on her journey to the
world below. You, Simmias and Cebes, and you others, will depart at some
time or other. Me already, as a tragic poet would say, the voice of fate calls.
Soon I must drink the poison; and I think that I had better repair to the bath
first, in order that the women may not have the trouble of washing my body
after I am dead.

(a) AUTOBIOGRAPHICAL INTRODUCTION. Socrates points out that the
question of generation and decay is very difficult and important and
that a deeper consideration of the problem is needed. He offers to trace
the course of his own researches and then embarks upon a philosophical autobiography.

The question may be raised whether this passage gives us a true
historical account of Socrates' life and thought, or whether it is just a
device Plato uses to review rapidly and in highly condensed form a
number of difficult and complex philosophical ideas. It would not be
unreasonable to believe that it is historical, for who other than Plato,
who was Socrates' most brilliant pupil and the friend of his later years,
would have been better qualified to give an accurate account of his
philosophical development.

The passage begins (96b-e) with a brief reference to the views of
earlier philosophers which Socrates says he studied in his youth
—Heraclitus' notion that the soul (with which we think) is fire; the doctrine of Anaximenes and Diogenes of Apollonia that it is air;[11] Empedocles' view that it is the mixture in the blood of all the elements; and also
the various theories of the cosmos which Socrates says he studied until
in bewilderment he gave them up as unsatisfactory. His self-confessed
incapacity for this sort of speculation is illustrated by a reference to the
perplexities arising out of ideas of change and relativity. How does One
become Two, by addition or by division? The question is really one
about the subject of change. If One is added to One, which has become

[11]See pp. 15 and 18 above. Diogenes borrowed from several other thinkers, particularly
from Anaximenes.

Two? Or, if neither, how has Two come into being? The point being made is that neither has One changed into Two, nor has Two arisen out of One; the change is merely apparent. Socrates suggests that this method of consideration cannot solve the problem. But if we think of the numbers, One and Two, as immutable ideas, we may conceive of some changeable matter as somehow participating first in one of them and then in the other.

Socrates then encounters the theory of his immediate predecessor, Anaxagoras, who said that the cause of all things and all order is mind (*nous*), an idea that appealed to him, for he thought it would explain the generation of things in terms of "what it was best for them to be," because mind always seeks what is best. He was disappointed, however, because Anaxagoras never really made use of this idea in his exposition, but explained things, as before, by reference to air, water, and other physical principles.

The point of this passage is that the only satisfactory explanation of change would be a teleological one, for apart from considerations of what is better and worse there is no reason why things should be disposed one way rather than another. Thus, no merely physical (or "scientific") explanation can really be finally satisfactory. If to explain a particular change or event we point to a physical cause, that is just another physical change or event and is just as much in need of explanation as the first. To point to another physical cause is of no avail for it again would not really help us; it would simply lead into an infinite regress giving no proper explanation at all. Therefore we are apt to ask, "What is the point or purpose of all this incessant, apparently meaningless, change from event to event?" and thus we seek a teleological explanation in terms of purpose and value.

Many thinkers today reject teleological explanation as too anthropomorphic—that is, as an unjustifiable interpretation of all natural occurrences on the analogy of human thought and action. We behave purposively and do what we do for the sake of ends we consider good, but it by no means follows that everything that happens other than human action is for the sake of some purpose. Sometimes it is said that whatever happens happens for the best because it is brought about by God's will and fulfills his purposes, but this too is unsatisfactory as an explanation, for either God's purpose is to produce what is good in itself, or else what happens is good because it fulfills God's purpose. But if it is good in itself, its intrinsic goodness must be explained independently of God's will; and if God's will makes it good, then it remains inexplicable as long as the reason of God's action is not revealed. Accordingly, whether we attempt a physical, nonteleological ("causal") or a teleological explanation the search for intellectual satisfaction seems to be frustrated. This is a problem to which we shall return.

Some philosophers, however, maintain that once we work out an adequate value theory, we find principles of value involved in all forms of explanation, so that all explanation does ultimately turn out to be teleological in some sense. Plato is hinting at something of this sort in the present passage. The analogy between human action and other events is brought out by Socrates' protest against trying to explain his presence in prison by reference to the action of his muscles, bones, and sinews instead of through his intentions and what he judges to be right and wrong, good and bad. This, Plato thinks, must be the ultimate explanation, and the only satisfying one, of all things. So in *Charmides* he says that not even the knowledge of all the sciences will fully satisfy us without the science of good and evil (174c).

Here, however, Socrates puts aside this method of inquiry as too difficult and turns to what he describes as second best. This is a half-humorous, self-depreciating way of referring to what Plato considered to be of major importance as the correct method of philosophizing – the method which elsewhere he calls dialectic. It is to adopt as a hypothesis what seems to be the best available theory and to develop logically what follows from it. Whatever is in conformity with it one asserts as true, and what conflicts with it one rejects as false. But if one finds the consequences to be mutually inconsistent or in conflict with obvious facts, one must revise the original hypothesis and repeat the analytic examination of the new version. If no fault can be found with it, one then seeks a higher level hypothesis from which the first can be deduced, and so on, until and ultimate principle of explanation is reached which can be affirmed unconditionally.[12] Having briefly outlined the method, he proceeds to apply it.

(b) RETURN TO THE THEORY OF FORMS. The theory which Socrates says he has come to find most satisfactory is that there are certain absolute qualitative principles inherent in all things which are the actual source of the properties which the things possess. These were called forms. They are the absolute criteria which (we have seen) must be presupposed for any relative judgments to be possible. They are, says Socrates, the real causes or explanations of the nature of things, which come to be as they are by participation in the relevant forms.

As stated in the dialogue, this theory would appear to be a mere quibble or tautology. How, we may ask, does it help to say that a thing

---

[12] See *Republic* VI, 511b, and VII, 533c.

is beautiful because it partakes of, or participates in, Beauty (even though we spell it with a capital B)? How are we helped to understand anything by being told that Phaedo is taller than Simmias by virtue of Tallness, or that one and one make two by virtue of Duality? But Plato is not just quibbling; he is drawing attention to an aspect of our thinking which had never before been noticed and is struggling to understand it. This is the relation of what (as a result of Plato's work) Aristotle and later philosophers came to call "the universal" to "the particular."

The things we call beautiful all differ. Some are gorgeously colored, yet other things, because they are brightly colored, we say are garish and ugly. Other things we call beautiful because of their delicacy and faintness, others because of their shape. So none of these differences are what we mean by beauty, yet somehow all of them are relevant. What is it in all beautiful things by virtue of which we think them beautiful—how can we define Beauty (as such)? Likewise, with any quality we might name, we attribute it to all sorts of different *particular* things, and seemingly for different reasons, yet the quality itself is *universal* to all of them. What precisely is this universal concept (idea or form) and how is it related to the particular things which exemplify it?

When things change, their qualities come to be different from what they were before, yet something has remained the same (for instance, in the example of adding one to one to make two). What is it that changes and what is it that does not? The suggestion made here is that by participating in or partaking of the universal form the particular comes to be what it is, and when it changes it is by participating in another form. Thus, the sensible things can at different times admit of opposite predicates—tall, short, beautiful, ugly, and so on; but the forms themselves are absolute and unchanging. This is the hypothesis of which we must develop the consequences to see if it is self-consistent and from which we must try to proceed to a higher and ultimately indubitable principle (*vide* 101c-e). The relation which Plato suggests here between the forms and the sensible things is participation, but (at 100d) he also suggests that the form is a sort of goal or purpose toward which the changing thing is striving. In the next chapter we shall examine these suggestions and see how Plato develops from them the kind of teleological explanation mentioned above.

(c) THE FINAL PROOF OF IMMORTALITY. The final argument for immortality is a model of philosophical exposition. First it faces and removes what seems to be an obvious contradiction; then it proceeds point by point, in closely reasoned sequence, to apply the theory of forms to the relationship of opposition—first, in general terms, then by means of special examples, and finally to the specific matter in hand.

One of the audience points out that what has just been admitted — that the forms themselves cannot admit of opposite predicates — appears to be in flat contradiction with what was maintained in the first proof, that opposites are always generated from opposites. Socrates points out, however, that the former argument applied only to the sensible material things which do undergo change, so that they do in fact admit of opposite predicates whereas the present discussion is of forms which, being "absolute" and each precisely itself, cannot, without self-contradiction, become its opposite. That which is hot may become cold, but heat itself cannot become cold. That which by comparison with one standard is short, by reference to another may be tall (as Simmias is short by comparison with Phaedo but tall by comparison with Socrates), but tallness cannot become shortness or shortness tallness.

Nevertheless, some things are so typically characterized by one opposite that they cannot admit of or turn into the other without being altogether dissipated. For instance, snow is essentially cold and, though not itself the opposite of heat, cannot become hot and remain snow. If heated it is dissipated altogether. Three is essentially odd and, though not itself the opposite of even, can by no means become even without ceasing to be three. Further, whatever admits snow into its constitution must be cold, and whatever has a triadic character must be odd, and if any such thing admits the opposite quality, the snow, or the triadic character (as the case may be), will leave it.

So fire makes things hot because it partakes of the form of heat, and must be absent from anything which is cold for it cannot itself become cold. And similarly, what makes things live is the soul, which participates essentially in the form of life, so that if a being dies, the soul must leave it. But the soul itself cannot die, because it is what it is precisely by participating in, or being the principle of, life. It can no more partake of death than fire can of cold or two of oddness.

Although snow, being unable to admit heat, may be destroyed by being heated, the soul cannot be destroyed when what it quickens is killed, because the soul is essentially the principle of life, or essentially participates in the form of life. That which cannot admit of death (the opposite of life) is imperishable or immortal, and therefore the soul is immortal.

This cannot be said of the body, which can participate in both the opposite forms of life and death. It is a visible, sensible, material thing and can change from one opposite to another. But what makes it live cannot change into what makes it die and cannot itself become dead or admit of the opposite of life.

The validity of this proof depends entirely upon what the soul, which is said essentially to participate in the form of life, is taken to be. If, as we proposed before, we equate it with consciousness and thinking, there may be in the doctrine something of value and importance, which we shall examine in Chapter 6. But if the soul is regarded as some sort of substantial thing, like the body but differently constituted, neither this nor any other of the proofs in the *Phaedo* does anything to establish its existence, let alone its unending duration.

Having proved to the satisfaction of the company that the soul is immortal, Plato makes Socrates describe in a myth the destiny of the soul after the death of the body. This is a matter about which we can have no demonstrative knowledge, so he describes what he believes to be something like the truth. When this is done, Socrates retires to the bath, and then there follows the final moving scene of his leave-taking and death.

Phaedo

(continued)

b   When he had done speaking, Crito said: And have you any commands for us, Socrates — anything to say about your children, or any other matter in which we can serve you?

Nothing particular, Crito, he replied: only, as I have always told you, take care of yourselves; this is a service which you may be ever rendering to me and mine and to yourselves, whether you promise to do so or not. But if you have no thought for yourselves, and care not to walk in the path of life which I have shown you, not now for the first time, then however much and however c earnestly you may promise at the moment, it will be of no avail.

We will do our best, said Crito: And in what way shall we bury you?

In any way that you like; but you must first get hold of me, and take care that I do not run away from you. Then he turned to us, and added with a smile: I cannot make Crito believe that I am the same Socrates who have been talking and conducting the argument; he fancies that I am the other Socrates whom he d will soon see, a dead body — and indeed he asks, How shall he bury me? And though I have spoken many words in the endeavour to show that when I have drunk the poison I shall leave you and go to the joys of the blessed — these words of mine, with which I was comforting you and myself, have had, as I perceive, no effect upon Crito. And therefore I want you to be surety for me to him now, as at the trial he was surety to the judges for me: but let the promise be of another sort; for he was surety for me to the judges that I would remain, and you must be my surety to him that I shall not remain, but go away and e depart; and then he will suffer less at my death, and not be grieved when he sees my body being burned or buried. I would not have him sorrow at my hard

lot, or say at the burial, Thus we lay our Socrates, or, Thus we follow him to the grave or bury him; for be well assured, my dear Crito, that false words are not only evil in themselves, but they infect the soul with evil. Be of good cheer then and say that you are burying my body only, and do with that whatever is usual,
116 and what you think best.

When he had spoken these words, he arose and went into a chamber to bathe; Crito followed him and told us to wait. So we remained behind, talking and thinking of the subject of discourse, and also of the greatness of our loss; he was like a father of whom we were being bereaved, and we were about to
b pass the rest of our lives as orphans. When he had taken the bath his children were brought to him (he had two young sons and an elder one); and the women of his family also came, and he talked to them and gave them a few directions in the presence of Crito; then he dismissed them and returned to us.

Now the hour of sunset was near, for a good deal of time had passed while he was within. When he came out, he sat down with us again after his bath, but not much was said. Soon the jailer, who was the servant of the Eleven, entered
c and stood by him, saying: To you, Socrates, whom after your time here I know to be the noblest and gentlest and best of all who ever came to this place, I will not impute the angry feelings of other men, who rage and swear at me, when, in obedience to the authorities, I bid them drink the poison—indeed, I am sure that you are not angry with me; for others, as you are aware, and not I, are to
d blame. And so fare you well, and try to bear lightly what must needs be—you know my errand. Then bursting into tears he turned and started on his way out.

Socrates looked up at him and said: I return your good wishes, and will do as you bid. Then turning to us, he said, How charming the man is: since I have been in prison he has always been coming to see me, and at times he would talk to me, and was as good to me as could be, and now see how generously he sorrows on my account. We must do as he says, Crito; and therefore let the cup be brought, if the poison is prepared: if not, let the attendant prepare some.
e But, said Crito, the sun is still upon the hill-tops, and is not yet set. I know that many a one takes the draught quite a long time after the announcement has been made to him, when he has eaten and drunk to his satisfaction and enjoyed the society of his chosen friends; do not hurry—there is time enough.

Socrates said: Yes, Crito, and therein they of whom you speak act logically, for they think that they will be gainers by the delay; but I likewise act logically in not following their example, for I do not think that I should gain anything by
117 drinking the poison a little later; I should only be ridiculous in my own eyes for sparing and saving a life which is already down to its dregs. Please then to do as I say, and not to refuse me.

Crito made a sign to the servant, who was standing by; and he went out, and having been absent for some time, returned with the jailer carrying the cup of poison. Socrates said: You, my good friend, who are experienced in these matters, shall give me directions how I am to proceed. The man answered: You
b have only to walk about until your legs are heavy, and then to lie down, and the poison will act. At the same time he handed the cup to Socrates, who in the easiest and gentlest manner, without the least fear or change of colour or feature, and looking at the man sideways with the droll glance of his, took the cup and said: What do you say about making a libation out of this cup to any god?
c May I, or not? The man answered: We only prepare, Socrates, just so much as

we deem enough. I understand, he said: but a prayer to the gods I may and must offer, that they will prosper my journey from this to the other world — even so — and so be it according to my prayer. Then he held his breath and drank off the poison quite readily and cheerfully. And hitherto most of us had been fairly able to control our sorrow; but now when we saw him drinking, and saw too that he had finished the draught, we could no longer forbear, and in spite of myself my own tears were flowing fast; so that I covered my face and wept, not indeed
d for him, but at the thought of my own calamity in having to part from such a friend. Nor was I the first; for Crito, when he found himself unable to restrain his tears, had got up, and I followed; and at that moment, Apollodorus, who had been weeping all the time, burst out in a loud and passionate cry which broke us all down. Socrates alone retained his calmness: What is this strange outcry? he said. I sent away the women mainly in order that they might not misbehave
e in this fashion, for I have been told that a man should die in peace. Be quiet then, and bear yourselves with fortitude. When we heard his words we were ashamed, and refrained our tears; and he walked about until, as he said, his legs began to fail, and then he lay on his back, according to the directions, and the man who gave him the poison now and then looked at his feet and legs; and
118 after a while he pressed his foot hard, and asked him if he could feel; and he said, No; and then his leg, and so upwards and upwards, and showed us that he was becoming cold and stiff. And he felt them himself, and said: When the poison reaches the heart, that will be the end. He was beginning to grow cold about the groin, when he uncovered his face, for he had covered himself up, and said — they were his last words — he said: Crito, I owe a cock to Aesculapius; will you remember to pay the debt? The debt shall be paid, said Crito; is there anything else? There was no answer to this question; but in a minute or two a movement was heard, and the attendant uncovered him; his eyes were set, and Crito closed his eyes and mouth.

Such was the end, Echecrates, of our friend; concerning whom we may truly say that of all the men of his time whom we have known, he was the wisest and justest and best.

SUGGESTIONS FOR FURTHER READING

Plato, *Republic*, Books V – X. London: University of Cambridge, paperback edition, 1966.

————, *Meno*. New York: Liberal Arts Press, 1951.

A. E. Taylor, *Plato, the Man and His Work*. New York: Meridian Books, 1956.

————, *The Mind of Plato*. Ann Arbor, Mich.: University of Michigan, paperback edition, 1964.

CHAPTER 5

The Theory of Forms

1. KNOWLEDGE AND REALITY OF UNIVERSALS

Ever since Plato—or perhaps Socrates—became aware of the problem of universals it has been much discussed by philosophers. Socrates was probably the first to recognize the problem in his effort to understand the precise nature of the moral virtues and in his demand for exact definitions of them. If one succeeded in framing a definition, one would know what was universal to all instances of the virtue defined; one would grasp "the idea" of it, or its essential "form." For Plato this notion of idea or form was fundamental both for knowledge and for the structure of reality,[1] so that his epistemological and metaphysical theories are closely interdependent. Especially the theory of forms and the theory of the soul are mutually inseparable. It will, however, be easier and more convenient to discuss each separately and to explain their interconnection later. This chapter will be devoted to the theory of forms; in the next chapter we shall turn our attention to Plato's theory of the soul.

---

[1] Cf. the Pythagorean doctrine of numbers, pp. 15–18 above.

In *Republic* V, 476–477, Plato distinguishes between knowledge and opinion by insisting that knowledge is of the real, while opinion is of what only seems to be the case but is in some way doubtful, confused, or fluctuating, or all three together. We should generally agree that knowledge must be true, so that it seems natural enough to maintain that the proper object of knowledge is actual reality (or what the Greeks called Being). Plato then asks what would be the proper object of ignorance, and gives the obvious and natural answer that it would be nothing, or Nonbeing. He then makes the somewhat more startling assertion that the object of opinion is a combination of being and nonbeing, or Becoming. This can be explained in three mutually complementary ways:

(a) If we ask of an object, which is continuously changing, what it is, we have to give an ambiguous answer. We have to say that it is X and yet it is not X, because it has changed and become something different. For example, a seed is a tree, though it is not yet a tree; or a boy is a man, yet he is not a man but only a child. To give a precise account of anything that changes continuously we have to make seemingly contradictory statements about it. So, says Plato, it is a kind of mixture of what is and what is not, of being and not-being, because it is constantly *becoming* something other than it now is.

(b) Further, we tend to describe changeable objects by employing terms that are (as we say) purely relative. We say that one thing (B) is larger than another (A) but smaller than a third (C); or we take something as a unit and call two such things double the unit and the unit half the two; or we say one thing is better than another and worse than something else. But all these distinctions depend upon what we arbitrarily choose as our standard of comparison. B is thus both larger and smaller (according as we shift the standard). What we take to be half a certain quantity is also double another quantity (4 is half of 8 but double 2), and similarly, what is better can also be worse if compared with a different standard. Moreover our choice of standard is not fixed. There is no absolute standard of largeness (or size): a lake is large by comparison with a pond but small as compared with the sea, yet the pond is large by comparison with a puddle.

Again, what we take to be our unit when we count things is purely arbitrary. My hand has five fingers and each is one, yet each finger has three sections (separated by the knuckles); nevertheless it is all one hand. The arbitrariness of the choice of unit had been impressed upon the Pythagoreans by their discovery, in geometry, of incommensurables. The sides of an isosceles right-angled triangle cannot all be measured exactly with the same units of length, for whatever we put equal to 1 will fail to divide either the hypotenuse or the other two sides into an exact number of parts. Consequently, in all such relative matters, we are once more compelled to apply contradictory, or at least divergent, terms to the same object. It both is and is not large, or one, or double, or half, or many.

(c) Thirdly, if we make use of a general term to describe the property of a whole class of things, as for instance when we speak of triangularity or humanity, we can apply the term only ambiguously, or with qualifications to any of its instances. No given triangle is itself triangularity, for that covers all kinds of triangles, isosceles, equilateral, and scalene, and any given triangle can be only one of these. Nevertheless, any triangle is a case of triangularity. No human being adequately represents or embodies what we mean by humanity, yet everyone does in some way represent and embody what we mean by the term. So here again we tend to say "it is" and "it is not" of the same object.

In all such cases, Plato thought, the object of our awareness is imprecise, uncertain, and indeterminate. We cannot, therefore, really know what it is. We can have only opinions about it. The object of true knowledge cannot be susceptible of contradictory predicates, and as the object of true knowledge is reality, what is susceptible of contradictory predicates cannot be real. The object of opinion, then, is only apparent. Accordingly, whatever is changeable, whatever is relative, whatever is particular (a mere example of some general or universal character) is only appearance and not properly real. What is real must be unchanging, absolute, and universal.

Let us approach the matter in a slightly different way. How do we characterize any object that we seek to know? We specify its determinate attributes and properties. For example, let us consider how we seek to know a box or describe it accurately. First, we should specify its shape, its size, then its color, the material of which it is made, then the use for which it is intended (or its function), and so on. But the box itself would not be identical with each or any of these attributes for it has any one of them in common with many other things. For instance, if it is rectangular, so are many other things; if it is brown, other things too are brown which are not boxes; if it is used as a receptacle; there are other kinds of receptacles; and so forth. Each general term denoting a special attribute is common to many other kinds of objects. Each is a universal, yet the box is described by means of a number of different universals.

In order to know what the box is like we must know each of the universals we apply to it in description independently of, and prior to, knowing about the box itself. For we cannot say that it is rectangular unless and until we know what it is to be rectangular; or that it is brown, if we do not know what the color brown is; or that it is a receptacle, except as we understand what a receptacle is.

Secondly, there is a general character which a box shares with all other boxes, whether it be rectangular, square, or spherical; whether it be brown, green, or yellow; whether it is used to hold pins, cards, or bananas. We may, for convenience, call this common character of boxes "boxiness." Again, if we did not know what this was we could not recognize or identify boxes when we saw them. It is said that the people of a certain tribe of aborigines, when they first saw a horse, called it a pig, for they were familiar with pigs (or pigginess) but not with horses (or horsiness). At the same time, no individual box is *identical* with boxiness.

So of every individual thing we may say that it has (but is not identical with) numerous attributes which are common to many other things of different kinds, and that it exemplifies (but is not identical with) a special character which it has in common with all other things of the same kind. And all these common characters are universals, and they all must be known (so it would appear) *prior* to our being able to know, with any degree of accuracy, the individual things to which we apply them as descriptive terms.

These universals are what Plato calls ideas or forms, and they contrast sharply in several respects with the individual things which they qualify. The individual things, as we have explained, are complex entities involving several different forms, yet they exemplify any and all of them only approximately and imperfectly. They come to be, change, and pass away. But the universal forms are unchanging and constant, each is single and incomposite. They do not come to be or pass away and, so far as our analysis has shown, they seem to be prior, at least logically, and perhaps (so Plato thought) temporally, to the individual existents. Further, the individual things, their properties and qualities, are sensible and we come to know them through perception; but none of the ideas, properly speaking, can be perceived by means of the senses—they are only intelligible or thinkable. Not even universal ideas of color are sensed. What we see are color patches of differing hues, and each is variable according to lighting, contrast, and the condition of the eyes. No sensible exemplification of color, or of any particular color, is itself the color exemplified without qualification, still less is it color in general. No red patch is just red as such; there are always other shades and intensities—varieties of red from which this particular patch differs. But the idea of red (or redness) applies to them all equally and is understood (or conceived) but not imagined or perceived.

We must not, however, jump to the conclusion that Plato's forms are simply ideas "in our heads"—merely something subjective to our thinking. He explicitly and emphatically rejects any such notion,[2] because, so far as they are thoughts, they must be thoughts of something—they must have some objects. If these are not, as we have seen they are not, the sensible objects, they must be objects of some other kind. When Socrates is asked by the sage Parmenides in Plato's dialogue of that name:

"Is each form one of these thoughts and yet a thought of nothing?" he replies: "No, that is impossible."

"So it is a thought of something?"

"Yes."

"Of something that is or that is not?"

"Of something that is."

In fact, because the forms are single, unchanging, and in their very nature definite and precise, or absolute, Plato came to regard them as real *par excellence*, as the ultimate reality, and so the exact opposite of our fleeting and uncertain subjective ideas. Even the sensible objects which exemplify them approximately are, he thought, just appearances, that are made meaningful to us only by their relation to the intelligible forms. We make sense of the sensible only be referring it to the intelligible; or as Plato somewhat confusedly expresses it, the sense experience recalls the forms to our minds.

We may pause here briefly to point out (what we shall study more closely at a later stage) that this theory is precisely the reverse of the one most popular and widespread today, that nothing really makes sense unless it can be referred back to perceptible particulars from which alone all general concepts are and can be derived.

2. DIFFICULTIES OF THE THEORY OF FORMS

When one reads the opening passages of the *Parmenides*, one at once becomes aware that Plato realized the weaknesses of the theory of forms, and in some of his latter dialogues he tried to overcome them by modifying the theory and making it more complicated. The main difficulties are to explain how the forms are related to one another and to the sensible material things which exemplify them—or, if you will, how the "reality" is related to the "appearance," or knowledge to opinion. Plato is very vague on this matter and gives only occasional hints to guide us in the later dialogues. In *Republic* VI very little is said on the subject.

---

[2]See *Parmenides*, 132b-c.

(a) GENUS AND SPECIES. First, we must observe that the relation of universals to particulars is not simple and direct, because universals may be of different levels of generality. We have not only genera but species and also subspecies and higher genera. Which of these is to be *the* form, or are they all forms?

For example, any sensible object may be taken as one, exemplifying the form of unity; but one is also a number. Are we to say that Number is the form of Unity and Unity is the form of one? And is One the form exemplified by the sensible thing, or is it Unity or Number? Is each form related to the others or only directly to the particulars? If each is related to the others, are they still single and uncompounded? Does Number include Unity and One, and also Multiplicity and all the other numbers? Or are they all mutually exclusive? In either case, what are we to say about Even and Odd and their relation to Number and to One and to Two?

Or take the form (or idea) of Virtue. How is it related to the ideas of courage, temperance, and justice? Is not each of these a form related in some special way to particular acts of courage, temperance, and justice, as well as to the moral qualities (or dispositions) that go by these names in individual men and women? Is Virtue the form of all these or is it not? And what about special forms of (say) courage? There is physical courage and moral courage, rashness and cool, calculated fearlessness. Must each of these have a separate form as well as the more universal idea?

Plato never really faces this difficulty but tends to avoid it, keeping all forms mutually separate and making sensible things somehow participate in many different forms at the same time (cf. *Parmenides*, 129).

(b) INFIMAE SPECIES.[3] We may pursue this difficulty in another way. Consider animals. They all presumably participate in the form of "animality." But does not each of them also participate in the form of its own species—horse, dog, cat, man, *et cetera*? If so, will there not also be forms of sheepdog, alsatian, cairn, foxterrier, bulldog, and so on? But if there are also these subforms, why do we not go on until we can particularize completely and have a separate form for each individual thing? The young Socrates is shown, in the *Parmenides*, as eagerly advocating forms for abstract notions such as one, many, like, unlike, and for moral and aesthetic qualities, such as justice, beauty, and wisdom; but as hesitating over the forms of man, water, fire, and air, and as utterly rejecting the possibility of forms of hair, mud, dirt, and the like, "for fear," he says, "of tumbling into a bottomless pit of

---

[3]Lowest species.

nonsense." For this hesitation and resistance Parmenides chides him gently for not having the full courage of his convictions and pressing his theory to its final conclusion. A hint is given here that the solution of the difficulty may be that these crass material entities are wholly composite, constituted out of matter which is itself a compound of elements, each participating in various forms, for example, earth, air, fire, and water being compounds of hot, cold, wet, and dry in different permutations. Yet if universal forms are the unitary ideas covering a multiplicity of instances, should there not be a form for everything, even hair, mud, and dirt (for there are different varieties and instances of each of these)?

NOMINALISM. One attempt that has been made in the history of philosophy to solve this problem has been to say that the universal is no more than a word or name for a whole group of particular things, but that this name does not denote anything at all other than the particulars which fall under it. This doctrine is known as Nominalism and we shall meet it again later. The attempt fails, however, because we must have some means of deciding which individual things are included under the universal name and of recognizing any new instances which should be included. For this purpose we must somehow be able to indicate or define what distinguishing mark or character qualifies a particular to be brought under the universal, and if the name does not stand for any such distinguishing mark it will be of no help in description or explanation. Moreover, the individual things will fall under the universal only insofar as they possess the distinguishing character, otherwise they are just *not* what is denoted by the name. Yet every individual thing possesses other characters as well, which will therefore not be denoted by the universal name in question. If we say that it is only insofar as they do possess the special character that the universal name applies to them, either we identify the name with the character as universal, and so give up nominalism, or we identify it with the character as possessed by any one of the particular things, and that, as Plato well recognized, is impossible (for in each of them it is never exactly the same, nor in any precisely what the universal stands for). Moreover, in most cases of any interest, the number of instances falling under the universal is inexhaustible, so that we cannot delineate the precise group to which the universal name is supposed to apply, except by attributing to all its members (whatever they may be) some universal character. The attempt sometimes made to avoid this difficulty by saying that the universal name applies simply to this thing—pointing to one particular example—and to any others that are like it, will not do, because it is essential to indicate in what respect the other things must be similar to the one pointed out. For example, to say that "red" means simply a tomato, and any other thing resembling it, does not make clear whether all things of a certain color are meant, or all things of a certain (roughly spherical) shape; and in identifying the respect in which they are alike we are identifying the universal. Even apart from this difficulty, we should still be left with the notion of similarity or resemblance applied to the things denoted, which (as Bertrand Russell has pointed out)[4] remains universal in a sense which is not nominalistic.

(c) PARTICIPATION. Another difficulty in Plato's theory is to understand how things can participate in the forms. Is one to say that the form as a whole, or as such, is in each particular? Surely not, for the form is one and single, whereas the particulars are indefinitely many. If the form were, as a whole, in each particular, there would be as many copies or replicas of the form as there are particulars, like the endless series of mirror images obtained when two mirrors are placed opposite each other. Must we then say that each particular contains only a portion of the form? That would fragment the unity of the form into innumerable parts with no principle of differentiation to determine how it was divided. Neither can we break the form up into pieces, nor, if we could, would any piece be of any avail in defining the particular; for it is not a piece of Evenness that makes 2 an even number, but Evenness itself.

(d) IMITATION. Does it help to say that the particulars imitate or approximate to the form? If we say they do, we are alleging that the particulars are like the form in some way and in some degree. But again they are not similar to it in all respects (as we have seen). There must then be some special respect in which they are alike. But it is just because the particulars resemble each other in a special way that we bring them under the form, so should we not do likewise with the form and the particulars? If the relation between them is imitation or likeness, should we not postulate yet another form to cover the particulars (as one term of the relation of similarity) and the first form (as the other)? If so, we shall then be in need of yet another form to explain the relation of the first (and the particulars) to the second, and so on *ad infinitum*.

Again, if the form is like the particulars and their sole relationship is resemblance, any difference between particulars, or between them and the form, becomes irrelevant. Accordingly, either each particular (so far as relevant) is identical with the form—and this we have already

---

[4]Cf. *The Problems of Philosophy* (Oxford University Press, 1950), Chapter 9, p. 96. See pp. 368, 430–440 below.

rejected — or the form will be just another particular case of the common property, another particular. This, in effect, is Aristotle's criticism, commonly known as "the third man" argument: If the form of Man is what all men resemble, is it not just another man? If it is not, how can men resemble it?

(e) ASPIRATION OR NISUS TOWARD. The sense of "imitation" used above is purely passive. It is the sense in which *a* may be said to imitate *A* simply by being like *A*. But there is a more active sense, in which something imitates something else by trying to be or become more like it, as a boy imitates the man he admires by trying to act like him. It is in this sense that some commentators interpret Plato's view that the particulars imitate the forms. John Burnet interprets the passage in the *Phaedo*, 100d, in this way,[5] and R. G. Collingwood regards it as the most mature form of Plato's theory.[6] As we shall presently see, there is good reason to attribute the view to Plato that the forms are ideals which the things of the material world try to realize in the process of coming to be.

It is quite plausible to argue that, in the case of a human artifact, it comes to be as an attempt to realize an idea or an ideal, for human activity is purposive and the purpose is in various degrees preconceived, so that the idea of the end of the activity guides its course — the process by which the artifact comes into being. But is this account of the genesis of natural things, whether animate or inanimate, plausible? If it were to be proposed, what would be the force of attraction exercised by the form, which would direct the process of generation?[7] How and why do we, when we produce works of art or craft, aim at ideals or standards? Plato's answer to these questions is to be gleaned from his theory of the Good.

3. THE IDEA OF THE GOOD

(a) FUNCTION AS DEFINITIVE. Let us return to the task of understanding what a thing really is: One way of doing this is to discover what it does — its function. In *Republic* I, 352e, Plato adopts this method. What, he asks, is a pruning hook? It is a kind of cutting instrument for pruning trees; it is what prunes trees better than any other cutting instrument (for example, a sword or a dinner knife), and it can prune trees better

---

[5]*Greek Philosophy from Thales to Plato*, Chapter 9, pp. 124–127.
[6]*The Idea of Nature*, Part I, Chapter 2, p. 2 (viii).
[7]Cf. Aristotle, *Metaphysics*, 1080a.

than it can do anything else (for example, cut paper or meat). Its precise function defines it; and its function is what it is "good for."

But that which defines a thing—that which tells us what it is—is its "idea" or "form." So this must be the same as its function or what it is good for. Moreover, the special excellences or qualities of a thing are those which enable it to perform its proper function most adequately. A knife is at its best when it is sharp and strong and can cut well. We are apt to say that when it has these qualities it is most truly a knife—a real knife; but to the extent that it lacks them we are inclined to doubt this. Is a paper knife a "real" knife? Is a chipped stone used as a knife a real knife? We are apt to hesitate in such cases. But when the thing fulfills its purpose most adequately we do not hesitate, but tend to be quite emphatic and enthusiastic in saying "That's a real so-and-so" (knife, or whatever it may be).

(b) ARTIFACTS AND NATURAL OBJECTS. The functions of human artifacts are relative to human purposes, but this is not the case with natural things, which can therefore be subjected to this sort of analysis only so far as they are developing things, the development of which is governed by that which they are coming to be. For instance, what is a rose bud? Is it not *really* a rose? It is what it is just so far as it is becoming a rose and nothing else. The "form" of rose governs and determines the process of becoming.

But why could we not (you may object) say that *really* it is just a rose bud? Because if we did we should beg the question by the use of the name. What is a bud but an immature or potential flower, and a rose bud but a potential rose? What then would be the "function" of a rose bud? Plato would say it is what it can do best and do better than anything else can do it. In this case, that would be to produce, or become, a rose. (The function of the rose presumably would be to bloom and generate seeds and more roses.)

What a thing is, then, is what it does, and what it does is its function. It does it well when it is most fully what it is meant to be, when it realizes most fully its idea or form. So that in a sense everything is, as it were, trying to realize its proper form. And that coincides with its function—it is what it is good for—or is realized when its specific and appropriate excellence is realized. Thus, to understand what a thing really is, one must understand what makes it good of its kind, and so we are finally led, in our quest for knowledge of the nature of things, to the form or idea of the Good.

(c) THE GOOD AS SUCH. *Republic* VI, 505-509, is the only passage in which Plato tries to give any clear account of the Good. There we are told (1) that it is what makes all things intelligible and the mind intelligent; (2) that it is the object of all desire — what all things and persons strive after; and (3) that it is the creating and sustaining cause of all things.

The Good makes all things intelligible in the way that we have just explained. We understand them so far as we understand their function and what in them makes them perform it well — what they are good for and what being "good" is in their special case.

It makes the mind intelligent, first, because what the mind does best is to think, and it does it better than anything else can do it; and what makes it think well is its own peculiar virtue of wisdom. Its "good" is to be intelligent, thus the idea of the Good makes it so. Secondly, if we can grasp and fully understand the nature of value and goodness we have the key to the nature of all things; so to know the Good is to be intelligent and wise.

It is the creating cause of all things in the sense that it is the ultimate reason for their being — it is that (as Aristotle later said) "for the sake of which" all things come to be. And the Good is their sustaining cause because it (their value or function) is what makes (and keeps) things what they are. Their existence and self-maintenance is their effort to realize their form — or "what it is best for them to be."

Consequently, Plato says (in *Republic* VI, 505a) that all the forms are subordinate to the Good. We know them fully only if we know the form of goodness. So we know the nature of any of the virtues fully only so far as we know this. Whatever we desire we desire because it is in some sense good, and where goodness is concerned we will never be put off with mere imitations or substitutes. Consequently, the greatest good for man is to know the Good, for that knowledge is the source of all knowledge and of all virtue. And, as we have seen, we can come to know the form of the Good only if we are not misled by appearances, by what our senses suggest to us, and thus are not led astray in the pursuit of unnecessary pleasures and appetitive distractions. Ultimately the only way to wisdom is through virtue and the only way to virtue is through knowledge — of the Good.

4. THE DIVIDED LINE

Finally (*Republic* VI, 509–511), Plato represents knowledge and its relation to opinion by the diagram of a line divided into two main parts, each of which is again divided in two, as in the chart on page 112. The lowest portion represents mere guesswork or superstition and its objects are shadows, images, and reflections of things — the mere fleet-

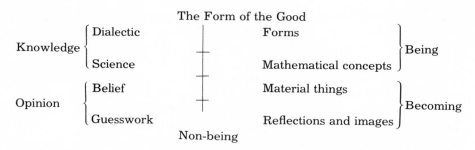

ing appearances with which our senses present us. The next represents our common-sense beliefs about material objects and the way they ordinarily behave. These two together comprise the sphere of opinion the object of which is Becoming. Next comes the realm of mathematics — scientific knowledge, which starts from unquestioned hypotheses and employs sensible objects (such as lines and figures) but which is not concerned with these for their own sakes but only with the ideas they represent. Finally, at the top is the science of dialectic which pursues knowledge of forms as such, critically examining all hypotheses and dispensing with the help of sensible representations altogether. These two sections constitute knowledge proper, whose object is Being or Reality, and which culminates in the knowledge of the Good.

Thus, the doctrine that virtue is knowledge is vindicated because in the end knowledge turns out to be that of the ultimate principle of value, and by seeking to know the Good man is doing what he can do better than anything else, and better than anything else can do it — he is fulfilling his true function, or being at his best. If this is possible only for the thinking soul in its purity and imperishable essence by emancipation from the distractions of the bodily appetites and the misrepresentations of the bodily senses, immortality is the ultimate realization of man's highest good. But that there is a soul apart from the human body and that it is immortal are different questions, which we shall now proceed to consider.

SUGGESTIONS FOR FURTHER READING

Plato, *Theatetus, Parmenides.* (*Plato's Theory of Knowledge, Plato and Parmenides*, F. M. Cornford) New York: Liberal Arts Press, 1957.

J. Burnet, *Greek Philosophy from Thales to Plato.* New York: Macmillan, 1960.

J. A. Stewart, *Plato's Doctrine of Ideas.* New York: Oxford University Press, 1909.

G. C. Field, *The Philosophy of Plato.* Oxford: H.U.L., 1956.

R. G. Collingwood, *The Idea of Nature* (Part I). New York: Oxford University Press, 1965.

E. E. Harris, *Nature, Mind and Modern Science*, Part I, Chapter 4. London: Allen and Unwin, 1954; New York: Humanities Press, 1954.

R. L. Nettleship, *Lectures on the Republic of Plato*. New York: Macmillan, 1958.

Bertrand Russell, *The Problems of Philosophy*. Oxford: Galaxy, H.U.L., 1959.

CHAPTER 6

Body and Soul

It should by now be apparent that Plato's theory of knowledge is inseparable from his theory of the soul, its relation to the body, and its immortality. Let us briefly retrace the steps of the argument.

Because the senses are deceptive and confusing and their objects are rendered intelligible only by reference to the forms, and because the forms are purely intelligible objects without which knowledge would be impossible, Plato argues that it is not through the instrumentality of the bodily sense organs that we come to know the real, but only through the thinking activity of the soul, that is, what the soul can do best and can do better than anything else can do it.

The whole trend of this argument is toward a complete separation of soul, as the agency of thinking, and body, as a material thing. Body does not know. What its senses deliver to the mind is a confused and bewildering flux of ephemeral qualities.[1] This process excites in us passions and desires (themselves bodily feelings) which distract and

---

[1] In the *Theaetetus* we learn that the senses are a sort of physiological process—a flux of material particles in the body which plays upon the external flux of the material world (a conscious and deliberate reference to the teachings of Heraclitus).

confuse the mind still further. Only so far as it is ruled and directed by reason is the body either virtuous in its conduct or sober and discriminating in its apprehension of facts. Reason is the activity of the soul alone and in its purity, and the body has no part in it, save through the soul's government and guidance. Similarly, except as it were by infection, the soul has no part in bodily functions. Although some question might be raised about sensation, Plato holds that the soul can and does think independently of the body and does so better for the absence of sensation, feeling, and appetite. It is, therefore, taken to be a separate entity from the body, merely housed within it — in effect, what Gilbert Ryle refers to as "the ghost in the machine."[2]

From this theory it seems to follow unquestionably that only in its "pure," unpolluted state, free of all connection with the body, can the soul function properly, and only in that state can it have a clear and unclouded knowledge of the forms. While associated with the body it is not in this condition but is hampered in its activity; and in its efforts to grasp the truth its objects are distorted and confused by sensuous contamination. Consequently, the body and its senses are not the source of, nor the means to, the soul's knowledge of forms; yet without that knowledge the deliverances of perception cannot be made intelligible. It follows that the soul must have acquired that knowledge from some other source, prior to its association with the body.

Further, soul is the source of life, is presupposed by generation, is simple and thus incorruptible, is invisible (not an object of sense perception) and so akin to the eternal forms. Therefore it must be immortal. If it were not (if it did not pre-exist), knowledge in this earthly life would be impossible, and the perfected knowledge, which is necessarily implied by the relative and partial knowledge we now enjoy, could never be attained.

Hence the body is one thing and the soul another, different thing. But the tacit assumption is that both are, as it were, on the same level of existence, just as two different bodies are separate and independent entities on the same level of existence. The soul is taken to be somehow "in" the body, as water might be in a can, or (a simile later used — and rejected — by Aristotle) like quicksilver which has been poured into a hollow statue. But when the body dies the soul is said to come out or withdraw, and as it is incorruptible it does not decay like the composite body but goes on existing indefinitely. Its immortality is an extended endurance in time.

---

[2]For Plato and the Greeks the body was not so much a machine as a flux of elemental substances, but this difference is of little importance here.

From all this three questions arise:
1. What is the relation of soul to body?
2. What is the relation of the soul to the forms in knowledge?
3. What is to be understood by the soul's immortality?

1. RELATION OF SOUL TO BODY[3]

Plato's explanation of the connection between soul and body is never precise. He expounds it almost invariably in the form of myth, indicating that he did not believe it possible to give any exact account of it, but only a pictorial one, "something like" the actual truth. In *Phaedrus* he explains the matter by the help of a beautiful poetic image of a charioteer driving two horses: a black and recalcitrant steed, and a white thoroughbred, docile, and obedient to direction. The black horse represents the desires and passions which resist the driver's whip and pull the chariot out of its true course; the white horse is the spirited element which follows the dictates of reason and helps to keep the black wanton under control. The driver himself is reason whose skill and foresight directs the chariot to the abode of the immortal gods beyond the outer sphere of the heaven, where the forms in their clear reality are to be seen.

Here, as in the fourth book of the *Republic*, all three parts or functions are represented as belonging to the soul, though reason is clearly its dominant characteristic. And elsewhere in *Phaedrus* Socrates is made to speak of the soul almost as if it were a body and had physical sensations, such as itches and tinglings, heat, and pain.[4] On the other hand, near the end of the *Republic*[5], Plato alleges that the "parts" of the soul are really the distortion imposed upon it by association with the body, and that properly speaking it is simple, without parts, as we have been told in *Phaedo*. In other passages, he seems to suggest that sensation and passion belong wholly to the body and are felt by the soul, as it were, by reflection, at secondhand.[6] In that case the vision of the bodily eye is, properly speaking, not a function of the soul at all. It is supposed only to "recall" a different kind of cognition — that of forms which the soul experienced at some earlier time elsewhere. The exact relationship is thus never made clear and is left always somewhat confused.

---

[3]Cf. Pythagorean and Orphic doctrines, pp. 7f. above.
[4]*Phaedrus*, 251b-c.
[5]*Republic*, X, 611.
[6]*Phaedo*, 83.

2. RELATION OF SOUL TO THE FORMS

Nevertheless, Plato frequently describes the soul's knowledge of the forms in terms of vision. The charioteer in the *Phaedrus*, who succeeds in getting his head above the heaven, "sees" the forms. In *Republic* VII, in another elaborate myth, Socrates compares ignorant humanity to prisoners chained in a cavern unable to see anything but shadows cast upon the wall, which accordingly they take for reality. The proper educational process, leading through the sciences to philosophy, is compared to the release of these prisoners and their being led up the rugged ascent out of the cave into the sunlight, where, when they become accustomed to the brightness, they can see the reality in its true form. This is the process of turning "the eye of the soul" toward the light.[7] These are all only metaphors, but, on this topic, Plato gives us little else to go upon; and they are puzzling metaphors, because we are also told that forms are not "visible" and we cannot see them, in the ordinary sense of "see"; and "the eye of the soul" is not the bodily eye. In what way, then, do we come to know the forms?

The best clue we are given is in *Republic* VI (511) in a brief account of dialectic. According to Plato, the only proper method of acquiring knowledge of purely intelligible objects is dialectic; it is an activity of reasoning which uses hypotheses (such as are necessary in the special sciences) only as provisional assumptions, which are later criticized and "removed" by reference to a principle which is real and not merely presupposed. As Spinoza said twenty centuries later, "demonstrations (and these alone) are the eyes with which the mind sees things."

If this is what Plato means, the forms must be principles of logical connection or necessitation—concepts to which the passage of time and the changing events of the world make no difference; which are eternally what they are, unaffected by the temporal variations that occur only in the sensible things that partially exemplify them.

But what is eternal is not immortal, in the sense of enduring for an indefinitely long time, because the eternal does not endure through time at all, but is strictly speaking timeless. A mathematical formula or concept is not subject to change. $\pi = 3.14159265 \ldots$ is an eternal truth. The changing quantities of physical things are irrelevant to it. Likewise, whatever may be the shapes assumed by mutable things in time, the circle and the dodecahedron never vary—not because they are made of indestructible material and so are ever-lasting, but because temporal pred-

---

[7]*Republic*, 518c–519b.

icates simply do not apply to them. They are not things or events or processes made up of events and are not subject to changes of state or quality.

3. THE NOTION OF IMMORTALITY

(a) ITS BEARING ON VIRTUE AND KNOWLEDGE. Accordingly, if the reason for thinking the soul immortal is that it is akin to the forms, immortality cannot be conceived as indefinite endurance. The ability to grasp an eternal, intelligible principle requires a sort of insight which is not, in itself, dependent on longevity. It may take time to acquire it (though even that can be questioned), but once acquired its exercise is not dependent on duration. Possibly, if the soul's true function is thinking, and this is hampered by the body (as Plato says), it might think more efficiently if it could be relieved of this obstruction, but the length of time for which it continues to exist should have no effect upon its capacity to grasp the forms. Further, as we shall presently see, it might not make sense to say that the soul (if that means the knowing subject) is in time at all.

Further, if longevity does not contribute anything to the capacity to apprehend eternal truths, it seems equally to contribute little or nothing to the practice of virtue. All the Platonic virtues, except knowledge itself, are exercised in restraining the desires and overcoming the weaknesses of the flesh, and knowledge itself is perfected only when these have been mastered. Again, then, to be relieved of the body might prove helpful to knowledge, but it removes at the same time all possibility of exercising the other virtues. A disembodied soul would have no occasion for temperance, and it is not easy to see against what dangers it need be courageous. Where earthly social functions concerned with the acquisition and exchange of material possessions are not performed, what could justice consist in? How then could continued existence without the body be of value either intellectually or morally?

(b) ITS RELATION TO SPACE AND TIME. Moreover, the release of the soul from the body which is supposed to be of such advantage for knowledge is, in the last analysis, only a change of spatial relations. The soul which was "in" the body is then "out" of it. But this implies that the soul itself is spatial and can have position. If it is not spatial it can be nowhere in space at any time, and so neither in the body nor out. If the soul were spatial, it would not be by virtue of its spatial character that it could think, so its being in, or out of, the body should not affect it.

Again, if its activity is hampered by the body, this implies that the body exerts some kind of physical effect upon it. But for an immaterial, nonspatial entity to be physically affected by a material entity is impossible.

A spatial entity would have parts, would thus be compound and so should be liable to change and corruptible. If not, it could not be "distorted" by association with a physical thing like the body.

A spatial entity would have size; but if we ever speak of a "great" soul or a "petty" one we speak only metaphorically in reference to its moral or artistic propensities. We do not mean that it is (for example) ten feet tall, or only three. These metaphors are evaluative, not quantitative.

If that which thinks, insofar as it thinks, is not in space, can it be in time? Does not thinking take time? As a psychological process it does, but whenever we try to account for thought in purely psychological terms we miss its essential character. Four examples are worth consideration:

(i) *The specious present.* Psychologists have tried to account for our awareness of the passage of time by postulating a series of successive momentary percepts in each of which there is some lapse or temporal diversity (that is, it is not a bare instant). Such a percept of what is going on now is called a "specious present." In the specious present we are aware, all at once, of a succession, but our awareness is not itself successive. But if this is so, our awareness cannot be an item of, or an event in, the successive series. It is not so much in time as time is in it (at least the succession contained in the specious present). Then, another difficulty arises in understanding how successive specious presents can succeed one another, for the specious present (at least for any one person) is alleged to have a definite, measurable, finite span. Does one specious present disappear before the next occurs or do successive specious presents overlap? And, in either case, how do we become aware of the succession of specious presents, for if they do not overlap we can never be aware of any two at once and so cannot grasp their successiveness. We should be aware only of a perpetual "now", and should be at a loss to account for the transition from one to the next. Yet, if they overlap, will not two (or more) of the successive moments within them have to coincide, which would contradict their successive character? For example, if one specious present covers *ABCD* and the next *EFGH*, they could overlap only if *D* and *E* (at least) were simultaneous, which they are not. But, if the specious present after *ABCD* were *BCDE*, then the specious present itself would have to be in flux, which is not supposed to be the case. It is supposed to be "all at once," an instantaneous awareness of successive items; and if it is, whatever alternative we espouse, we cannot account for the transition from one specious present to the next. Consequently, the attempt to resolve our awareness of the passage of time into a series of psychological presentations breaks down. The act of thought which apprehends temporal relations cannot be one of the related events. That which is aware of passage cannot itself be in passage.

(ii) *Perception of spatial coexistence.* This fact can be illustrated in a different way. The perception of any large-scale, spatial pattern is attainable only by successive perceptions of its parts, but we do not cognize (or think) the pattern as a succession of parts. We see a building successively from different points of view, but we conceive it as a coexistent whole which is nonsuccessive. Our thought of it is somehow mediated by the psychological series of successive percepts but it is not itself any one of them.

(iii). *Memory.* Psychologically, consciousness occurs as a stream of presentations, or states. Where and how does memory fit into this stream? To remember is to be aware now of something that was experienced before and, at the same time, to be aware of it as that *former* experience. It should be a particular state of consciousness in the stream. If so, what is its content? It cannot be simply a reproduction of the past experience, because that would be merely what one is now aware of—that is, it cannot simply be the repetition of some image or feeling, for that is simply something experienced now, and to be remembered it must also be referred to the past. What is visualized in remembering is not just a scene, but a scene known to have been seen in the past. How does this reference to the past appear in the present stream of consciousness, for whatever form it takes it would still be merely what is now being cognized. To recognize this imagined scene as the one I once saw, I must somehow be able to compare it with the original, but the original is past and gone, and its revival just *is* this present image. I do not recall two images of the past scene and compare them, and if I did, I should still not have what is needed. I cannot say that I "remember" this image to be like the past original, because remembering is the present act which we are trying to analyse and seeking to identify with this present image. What we remember is what we are *not* now experiencing, yet in remembering it, it is somehow present. The image is a sort of vehicle or tool used in remembering but cannot itself be the act of remembering.[8] This cannot be reduced simply to an item in the stream of consciousness, because in remembering we have somehow to review the course of the stream and identify the remembered item and its temporal relation to other items both before and after it. One item in the series cannot review the series as a whole and determine its own relation in time to other members.

(iv) *Awareness of space, as such.* I am aware of space as an expanse extending all around my body, behind as well as in front. In my awareness space is conceived as a whole—though indefinite in extent. But, if so, my act of awareness cannot be an event occurring at some particular point in the space which it conceives as a whole. The whole cannot be contained in one of its own parts.

Is this an equivocation? Is the space contained the same as the space in which it is contained? Consider a mirror. A whole room may be reflected in it, yet it may be in that room, and in only a small part of it. But what is in the mirror is the reflection of the room only, not the fact that it is a reflection of the room, which is "out there," and is not in the mirror at all. My awareness of space is not just something reflected in me (my body); it is an awareness of the spatial relations between me (my body) and the space which is "out there" and of the fact that it is out there. To be aware of "out-there-ness" my thought cannot be confined to the "here." To be aware of space I must somehow transcend space.

Now the stream of consciousness is alleged to take place "here," in me; and my awareness of space is always from the point of view of my body, where my consciousness is somehow taken to be located. Yet to be properly aware of all this, my awareness must transcend the "here" as well as the "now" and can never be simply reduced to it. Once again the psychological stream of consciousness proves inadequate to account for thought.

Some contemporary philosophers would try to avoid this conclusion by identifying consciousness with the neural process in the brain which is its indispensable condition. If we could do this, we could say that my awareness of space just was this neural process, and so was in my head. But how such a theory can make intelligible the reference of some process going on in my brain to something existing outside my body is not at all clear. This so-called neural-identity theory has to face all the problems we have discussed in a more acute form than was stated above.

---

[8]Some thinkers have said that in remembering we are directly aware of the past without any present intermediary. But, if so, our act of remembering can be neither present nor past and so not in the stream of consciousness.

In one way or another, they are all problems of reference, and how reference is to be reduced to a neural process is not easily apparent.

CONCLUSION

To return then to Plato, we can now see that his argument is on the right lines when he suggests that thinking, knowledge, reason, and intellect, like their intelligible objects, transcend time and space in some significant way. The subject of which they are activities is, therefore, not limited, like the body, to a finite time span. But it does not follow that it, therefore, continues to exist independently of the body for an infinite or indefinite time span. It seems somehow altogether independent of time and so to "exist" in some altogether different sense from that in which the body is said to "exist."

Plato is wrong so far as he suggests that the soul is a something, like the body, in that it has a spatiotemporal existence, though an existence that endures forever instead of coming to an end after a limited period. He is wrong so far as he suggests the existence of a soul that is "in" the body and at death comes "out" of the body to go on existing "elsewhere" for an indefinitely long time. None of his proofs really establish any of these allegations.

Our common use of the term immortality really refers more properly to the attainment of certain values — of a degree of sublimity — than to extended duration. When we speak of "the immortal bard" we do not think of Shakespeare's ghost, but rather of Hamlet's or Banquo's. We refer to the excellence of the poetry and the drama Shakespeare wrote, which is unaffected by time and change, and to his transfiguration of language to express truths and beautiful conceits which are equally eternal in their quality.

One speaks of Plato and Socrates in the same way — and also of Homer and Sophocles. We do not mean by this that they are not dead, but that their achievements are of a transcendent excellence undimmed and unaffected by time.

We do not describe the Pyramid of Cheops as immortal though it has lasted thousands of years and shows no sign of disintegrating.

Immortality, then, is best understood as a quality of being rather than as an indefinite prolongation of life, and, by careful siftings, we can learn this from Plato. If we embrace other conclusions (as he seems to have done himself) and interpret his arguments to support them, the arguments cease to be valid and we may be misled.

SUGGESTIONS FOR FURTHER READING

A. C. Ewing, *The Fundamental Questions of Philosophy*. London: Routledge and Kegan Paul, 1958.

A. E. Taylor, *Elements of Metaphysics*, Book IV. New York: Barnes and Noble, 1961.

William James, *Human Immortality, Two Supposed Objections*. Boston: Houghton Mifflin, 1898.

J. C. Smart, *Philosophy and Scientific Realism*. New York: Humanities Press, 1963.

PART II

Descartes
and
Rationalism

CHAPTER 7

The Ghost and the Machine

The next phase of our study will be directed to the attempts of certain thinkers of the seventeenth and eighteenth centuries to wrestle with problems akin to those which Plato discussed, but modified and changed in aspect as the result of new developments in science and the influence of medieval religious ideas. It will not be possible, nor (for our purpose) necessary, to go into the details of this intervening historical process, for we are not tracing the entire history of philosophy, nor could we, in a short course, study all the relevant texts. Nevertheless, a few words about the influences that impinged upon seventeenth-century thinkers may be admissible, to illuminate the sources out of which the problems of knowledge and of man's relation to God and the world arose anew.

The legacy of ancient philosophy may roughly be said to comprise two main streams of influence, Platonism and Aristotelianism. During the Middle Ages the influence of Plato was preserved only indirectly, through that of the Neo-Platonists (especially Plotinus). Augustine was strongly influenced by Platonic doctrines and, through him, these influences were also exerted upon Anselm (and, thus, in some measure, on all medieval thought).[1]

In the twelfth century the works of Aristotle, which had been temporarily lost in the West, but which had been preserved in Byzantium in the East and had become known to Arab scholars, were reintroduced into Western Europe with the Moorish incursions into Spain. At first the western Church rejected the Aristotelian doctrines as incompatible with the Christian faith; but later Thomas Aquinas studied the works of Aristotle intensively and commented upon them in great detail, arguing that they were not incompatible with the truth revealed in Christianity, so that the Church reversed its position and later accepted them so implicitly that the authority of Aristotle came almost to rank with that of the Scriptures and of the Fathers of the Church. Platonic influences accordingly fell into the background and became for the most part eclipsed.

Thinkers and teachers of the Middle Ages, who were associated with the schools originally set up by Charlemagne, from which the great medieval universities later developed, are generally known as the Schoolmen or Scholastics. They were all essentially clerics and theologians and treated every question as one of religion, or as arising out of religious doctrine. Even so, it would not be wrong to divide the most important issues with which they were concerned into three classes: (a) those arising directly from religious doctrine, such as the problem of evil (and how it could be reconciled with the existence of an omnipotent and infinitely beneficent God), the problem of God's existence itself, how it can be known and whether it can be proved, the freedom of the human will and its compatibility with God's omniscience, besides a number of others of lesser significance; (b) what we may call logical and epistemological questions, centering for the most part around the question whether universal concepts are real (as Plato thought) or merely names for classes of particulars — this was the debate between the so-called Realists and Nominalists; and (c) those concerned with difficulties arising out of the Aristotelian system of physics and cosmology, especially in connection with movement. We shall have occasion in examining Descartes' philosophy to make comparisons with some of the medieval discussions of the proof of God's existence, and we shall find some degree of analogy to the dispute between realists and nominalists in the different approaches of rationalists, like Descartes, and empiricists, like Hume, to the problem of universality.

------

[1]We shall have occasion shortly to refer to some of Anselm's arguments concerning the existence of God.

The last group of issues is directly related to the scientific development of the sixteenth century which gave rise to modern philosophy. A brief glance at the main problem will not come amiss. Aristotle had taught that the earth was the center of the universe and that the moon and heavenly bodies, each embedded in a crystalline sphere, revolved round the earth in roughly concentric circles. This circular motion (he said) was perpetual and "natural" to the heavens. Other bodies, according to the element of which they were made, each had its own natural place. Earth, the natural place of which was in the center, always moved naturally toward the center. The place of water was immediately above the earth, and it would move naturally into that position; air belonged naturally next above the water; and fire naturally moved upward to the outer perimeter of the sublunary sphere. Sublunary bodies normally rested each in its proper place and moved only if forcibly dislodged from where it belonged. Such motion was "violent" motion, and it was followed by the "natural" motion of the body as it strove to return to its natural place.

Thus, if a stone were thrown into the air, the violent motion bore it upward, and as this ceased (because of air resistance and the natural countervailing tendency of the stone to return toward the earth's center), it fell back by its natural motion. A problem arose, however, with respect to missiles propelled parallel to the earth's surface, such, for instance, as an arrow. While it was in contact with the bowstring it would, of course, be pushed forward; but why on leaving the bow did it not fall straight to the ground? Aristotle maintained that the air rushing in behind it to prevent the formation of a vacuum pushed it onward. But, if so, why did it ever stop? The answer given by the Aristotelians was that it was slowed down and eventually fell to earth because of the resistance of the air in front of it. But in that case the cause of its movement and the cause of its ceasing to move would be the same, which hardly seemed possible.

In the thirteenth century Jean Buridan of the University of Paris put forward the theory that the motion imparted to a body by an initial impulse gave it a property which he called "impetus," and which continued to carry it forward until the impetus gradually died out. For a time this enabled scholars to overcome some of the difficulties of the Aristotelian theory. Later, as a result of the work of Galileo, Kepler, and Descartes, Newton substituted the law of inertia for the principle of impetus: the law that bodies continued in a state of rest or uniform rectilinear motion unless they were diverted by the exercise upon them of some external force. So we come to what we generally call the modern period, which took its rise from the Renaissance, the revival of the works of the Ancients, not only of Plato, but also of the Greek atomists, along with the scientific works of Archimedes and Aristarchus.

1. THE NEW WORLD VIEW OF SCIENCE

The modern age was inaugurated by the great scientific revolution which began with Copernicus' revival of the heliocentric hypothesis in astronomy. The idea had first been suggested by Aristarchus of Samos in the third century B. C. but was not taken seriously until revived by Copernicus nineteen centuries later. The effect of Copernicus' hypothesis was to undermine the elaborate Aristotelian system of physics and cosmology which had been dominant throughout the later Middle Ages, and so to create a ferment in contemporary thinking out of which arose new philosophical problems (or old ones in a new form).

The Aristotelian universe (as we have noticed) had consisted of two main spheres, the celestial, which was incorruptible and moved perpetually with a circular motion around the earth as center, and the sublunary (or terrestrial), which was the sphere of change and corruption, of coming to be and passing away, and within which the motion of bodies was quite different from that of the heavenly bodies. For Aristotle, as for the Greeks generally, the world was a living creature with a soul, which gave birth to other living beings with souls, and the movement of bodies and changes of all kinds were explained (in the last resort) teleologically, in terms of "final causes" or desires on the part of the things concerned. In all this the influence of Plato is not lacking, but we must not digress by attempting to trace it here. What is important to note is that the Aristotelian system had become dominant throughout the later Middle Ages, and along with the consequences which flowed from it, came sharply into conflict with the Copernican hypothesis.

The significance of the Copernican change is not, as is so often alleged, that it removed the earth from the center where it had hitherto held pride of place, and reduced the importance of the heavens by making them subject to terrestrial laws. By removing the earth from the center and placing it among the planets, Copernicus (if anything) elevated the earth in importance by making it a heavenly body in its own right. Further, in order to explain why the earth's revolution round the sun produced no effect of parallax in our views of the fixed stars, he asserted that the sphere of the stars was immeasurably more distant from us than had ever before been contemplated. The heavens therefore came to be viewed as inflnitely vast and the object of even greater awe. Though succeeding astronomers, Tycho Brahe and Galileo, revealed changes in the heavenly bodies which ran counter to the Aristotelian idea.of their incorruptibility, nevertheless the new cosmology engendered a reverence for the greatness of the universe equally profound, to which Kant, two centuries later, bore witness when he declared, "There are two things which have always filled me with awe, the starry heavens above me and the moral low within."

The real importance of the Copernican revolution consisted in the fact that by placing the sun at the center and the earth among the planets, thus making the earth one of the heavenly bodies, the distinction between sublunary and celestial spheres was broken down. Further, the followers of Copernicus, Kepler, and Galileo discovered laws of motion governing the revolution of the planets (including the earth) as well as for bodies falling on to the earth's surface. Newton later was able to weld these into a comprehensive system of mechanics which applied to all bodies whatsoever, so that the whole physical universe came to be viewed as a single mechanical system. In short, the universe came to be conceived as a vast machine, the working of which was governed throughout by uniform laws which depended on nothing other than the mass and position of material bodies and their mathematical interrelations. Thus, to account for the behavior of any material bodies whatsoever, one need only apply laws derived from the observation and measurement of their masses, positions, and velocities at any given moment—the laws of mechanics. The machine was constructed originally by God, but once made and the laws of its working established, it would run automatically without further need of God's intervention.

This conception did not, however, have to wait for Newton and is already to be found in the thought of Descartes, who tried to work it out in an early treatise called *Le Monde*. Referring to what he had written there, he says, in Part V of the *Discourse on Method*:

I pointed out what are the laws of nature, and . . . tried . . . to show that they are of such a nature that even if God had created other worlds, He could not have created any in which these laws would fail to be observed. After that, I showed how the greatest part of the matter of which this chaos is constituted, must, in accordance with these laws, dispose and arrange itself in such a fashion as to render it similar to our heavens; and how meantime some of its parts must form an earth, some planets, some others a sun and fixed stars . . . so that I thought I had said enough to make it clear that there is nothing to be seen in the heavens and stars pertaining to our system which must not, or at least may not appear exactly the same in those of the system which I described.

In this way, although He had not, to begin with, given this world any other form than that of chaos, provided that the laws of nature had once been established and that He had lent His aid in order that its action should be according to its wont, we may well believe, without doing outrage to the miracle of creation, that by this means alone all things which are purely material might in course of time have become such as we observe them to be at present.[2]

2. PHILOSOPHICAL CONSEQUENCES

Scientifically this conception of the physical universe proved fruitful beyond the wildest expectation. Philosophically it gave rise to acute and difficult questions. The machine was, at least in part, knowable by man. Its structure was being triumphantly discovered and the laws of its working revealed. What, then, was man's mind? Was it part of the machine? If so, could one explain consciousness and knowledge on mechanical principles? But if the mind was not part of the machine, how was it related to it, as a whole, in knowledge, and to that piece of it, man's body, upon which it had obvious dependence? In short, how are we to conceive the relation of man's mind to the object of its knowledge in natural science?

There are three ways in which this problem may be approached. (a) We may deny all distinction between mind and machine and assert that the human body is an automaton and that knowing is a mechanical process performed by the brain. This is the position of materialism, which was adopted in the seventeenth century by men like Thomas Hobbes and Pierre Gassendi and was summed up in the famous dictum of the eighteenth-century materialist Baron d'Holbach: "The brain secretes thought as the liver secretes bile." Sensation and consciousness are regarded as mechanical, physiological processes; as Hobbes maintains:

All which qualities, called *Sensible*, are in the object that causeth them, but so many several motions of the matter, by which it presseth our organs diversely. Neither in us that are pressed, are they any thing else, but diverse motions; (for motion, produceth nothing but, motion). But their appearance to us is Fancy, the same waking, that dreaming.[3]

The materialist position is far from dead or outdated. Some modern

---

[2] *Discourse on Method*, Part V (Haldane and Ross, Vol. I, London, 1931), pp. 108–109.
[3] *Leviathan*, Part I, Chapter I.

physiologists, psychologists, and philosophers still try to explain conscious behavior in terms of mechanical devices, called servo-mechanisms, and to identify feeling and awareness unreservedly with brain processes and physiological activity. But one problem remains unsolved, which is latent in Hobbes' remark, ". . . their appearance to us is Fancy, the same waking that dreaming." In what conceivable sense can a motion of material particles constitute "an appearance" to anybody or anything? How can a brain process *be* an appearance of something else?

Accordingly, this method of approach fails, because it leaves unexplained the "appearances to us as Fancy," and this is the one factor the existence of which cannot be denied, for it is that of which we are directly aware. We cannot deny the existence of consciousness, for to deny it we must be conscious, and thus the denial is itself evidence of the existence of consciousness.

(b) The second approach to the problem is to separate the mind rigidly and completely from the machine and so exclude it from the material universe altogether. This is not difficult in the case of God's mind, the creator of the world, for His mind can remain outside. The world is the world of nature and God's mind is super-natural. God's knowledge would thus be accountable as the eternal act of awareness which is the source of the world's existence and which maintains it in being.

But the mind of man presents difficulties because it is part of God's creation yet, apparently, not part of the great cosmic machine. Man's body is part of the material world and his mind is obviously very specially related to that part and in numerous ways closely dependent upon it. It seems to be so dependent even for its knowledge of the world, for is it not through the bodily organs of sense that we learn about external objects? How, then, is this nonmechanical, nonmaterial mind (or soul) related to the material body? And how through that relationship does it come to be related in knowledge to the rest of the material world?

This, in the main, is the approach of Descartes, and we can see that it places him in a position similar in many ways to Plato's. But Plato takes much for granted that Descartes seeks to prove on rational grounds; Plato's problem had a different, if not altogether unrelated, source. His primary question was "How ought one to live?" and from that he was led to ask "How and what do we know?" Descartes begins by asking the latter question and leaves the former to others.

If we assume a separation between mind and the material objects which it knows, we can attempt to account for knowledge in either of two ways: (i) We may begin from the mind and the contents of its consciousness, its percepts, imaginings, feelings, and the like, and we may ask how far they represent anything which exists independently of the mind. So far as they do, we say they are true and call them knowledge. So far as they do not, we say they are false and call them illusion or fantasy. In order to make this distinction we need some criterion, so that the primary question of epistemology becomes, What is the criterion of truth? This, we shall find, is the procedure adopted by Descartes and it is characteristic of the type of philosophy usually called Rationalism, because the criterion, on this view, must obviously have its source in the mind's capacity for thinking or reflection, and so would be a "rational" criterion. (ii) Or we may begin at the other end by considering how external bodies affect our bodies and trace these effects through the sense organs and nervous system to the brain. We may then try to account for knowledge in terms of these processes by building it up out of their end products, which are taken to be the data of sense. This is the procedure of John Locke and represents the approach in philosophy known as Empiricism.

Both these methods of dealing with the problem, though mutually in contrast, are natural consequences of the new world view which arose from the scientific revolution of the seventeenth century. If the world is conceived as a machine, which consists entirely of matter and motion and works according to mechanical laws, consciousness, feeling, thinking, and knowing are excluded from it. Mind, in consequence, is conceived as separate from the machine, and in order to know the machine, mind must, as it were, approach the world from outside and inspect it from afar through the sense organs, like an astronomer in an observatory viewing the heavens through a telescope.

We must observe that this sharp dichotomy of mind from external object is not necessary except as a consequence of a special world view, and if, as we shall find it does, it gives rise to insuperable philosophical difficulties, the fault may lie in the initial premises of the reasoning rather than elsewhere.

(c) The third approach to the problem is to deny the existence of matter altogether and to regard the entire spectacle of the physical world as a complex of ideas in an infinite mind. The finite human mind then has somehow to participate in the infinite, and the precise relationship remains obscure. This position is called Idealism.

CHAPTER 8

Descartes's Method

1. INITIAL PRESUPPOSITIONS

To judge from his own account, in *Rules for the Direction of the Mind* and the *Discourse on Method*, Descartes's approach to the problem of knowledge sprang originally from a critical review of the state of contemporary learning and science as he had become acquainted with it in the very thorough training he had received in traditional disciplines during his years as a student at the Jesuit college of La Flèche. Typical of his age, he refused to accept anything as true merely on authority and determined to credit only what his own judgement told him was reliable. This attitude immediately committed him to two presuppositions: (a) that his reason (and so, by generalization, human reason as such) was capable of attaining truth by its own unaided operation; and (b) that there is available to such reason a criterion for deciding between true and false, reliable and unreliable, opinions.

The first of these presuppositions is an indispensable condition and an incontrovertible assumption of all knowledge, and Descartes asserts it at the outset:

Good sense is of all things in the world the most equally distributed, for everybody thinks himself so abundantly provided with it, that even those most difficult to please in all other matters do not commonly desire more of it than they already possess. It is unlikely that this is an error on their part; it seems rather to be evidence in support of the view that the power of forming a good judgment and of distinguishing the true from the false, which is properly speaking what is called good sense or reason, is by nature equal in all men.[1]

Descartes's first presupposition is indispensable because, without it, no theory based on reasoned argument can be given any weight, and rational reflection cannot therefore begin without making this assumption. It is incontrovertible because any denial of the competence of reason must, to be considerable, rest upon evidence and argument which only reason or "good sense" is competent to judge.

The second assumption requires further investigation. That we claim to distinguish between true and false opinions is undoubtedly the case, but it is not obvious on what criterion we do so (or if we always do so by reference to the same criterion). The best way to prove that we have such a criterion is to produce it, and Descartes almost at once sets himself to look for and identify such a criterion.

First, however, he states his reasons for refusing to rely upon the accepted learning of his time.

2. DESCARTES'S CRITIQUE OF CURRENT LEARNING

(a) Descartes sets aside the study of languages and literature as giving us no scientific knowledge but only art of a kind that, for the most part, requires special gifts not universal in all men.

(b) Mathematics he finds more reliable, but maintains that no proper use has been made of the science, which he considered to be in need of reform. This reform he himself undertook with notable and spectacular results. What especially impressed him about mathematics was the "simplicity" of its objects and the clarity and cogency of its proofs, so that it became for him (as it had been for the Pythagoreans and in large measure for Plato) a model for all science.

(c) Of philosophy all Descartes can say is that despite its cultivation for so many centuries by the best minds, "nevertheless no single thing is to be found in it that is not subject of dispute."[2] Later in the Dis-

---

[1]Discourse, Part I. (Haldane and Ross edition, London, 1931), p. 81.
[2]Discourse, Part I, pp. 85-86.

course he is even less flattering: "There is nothing imaginable," he says, "so strange and so little credible that it has not been maintained by one philosopher or another."[3] These are complaints which have frequently been repeated since Descartes's time in spite of what he thought he could do to improve matters.

3. RULES OF PROCEDURE

Accordingly, while professing disapproval of any private attempt to reform the established sciences, he decides (as he puts it) to reject all his own former opinions and to rebuild his knowledge according to a strict method of his own, the first rule of which is:

> to accept nothing as true which I did not clearly recognize to be so: that is to say, carefully to avoid precipitation and prejudice in judgments and to accept in them nothing more than what was presented to my mind so clearly and distinctly that I could have no occasion to doubt it.[4]

The crucial question here is just how do we see things to be true without possibility of doubt? Descartes will shortly address himself to this question which he recognizes as central.

The last three rules of the method as stated in the *Discourse*, Part II, though methodologically very important, are epistemologically less vital than the first. They concern the best way to proceed in acquiring knowledge rather than the principles on which the very existence and possibility of knowledge depend.

> The second was to divide up each of the difficulties which I examined into as many parts as possible, and as seemed requisite in order that it might be resolved in the best manner possible.[5]

The assumption here is that what is most simple is most easily understood. In his earlier, unfinished treatise, *Rules for the Direction of the Mind*, Descartes maintained that there are certain "simple natures" into which all complex objects can be analyzed (or divided) and which can be grasped by the mind, without possibility of error, each in a single act of immediate intuition.

Once the ultimate simples have been reached, there is a proper

---

[3]*Discourse*, Part II, p. 90.
[4]*Discourse*, Part II, p. 92.
[5]*Discourse*, Part II, p. 92.

order in which they can be successively combined, by a process of "illation" or deduction, to constitute the complex objects which have to be explained. If this correct order is followed, Descartes believed, each step would be as evident and infallible as the intuition of the original simples. So the third rule, as given in the *Discourse* reads:

> The third was to carry on my reflections in due order, commencing with objects that were the most simple and easy to understand, in order to rise little by little, or by degrees, to knowledge of the most complex, assuming an order, even if a fictitious one, among those which do not follow a natural sequence relatively to one another.[6]

The fourth is a kind of *aide-mémoire* to see that each step in the reasoning is correct and that none have been missed.

> The last was in all cases to make enumerations so complete and reviews so general that I should be certain of having omitted nothing.[7]

These are useful and important precepts, but they presuppose a theory of knowledge and reasoning which does not withstand the test of criticism. It depends, in the last resort, on the possibility of infallible apprehension of simple objects, but we shall not discuss it until we have considered more fully Descartes's account of the criterion of truth.

Meditations on the First Philosophy, in Which the Existence of God, and the Real Distinction of Mind and Body, are Demonstrated[8]

MEDITATION I: OF THE THINGS OF WHICH WE MAY DOUBT

Several years have now elapsed since I first became aware that I had accepted, even from my youth, many false opinions for true, and that consequently what I afterwards based on such principles was highly doubtful; and from that time I was convinced of the necessity of undertaking once in my life to rid myself of all the opinions I had adopted, and of commencing anew the work of building from the foundation, if I desired to establish a firm and abiding superstructure in the sciences. But as this enterprise appeared to me to

---

[6]*Discourse*, Part II, *ibid.*
[7]*Discourse*, Part II, *ibid.*
[8]The translation is by John Vietch.

be one of great magnitude, I waited until I had attained an age so mature as to leave me no hope that at any stage of life more advanced I should be better able to execute my design. On this account, I have delayed so long that I should henceforth consider I was doing wrong were I still to consume in deliberation any of the time that now remains for action. To-day, then, since I have opportunely freed my mind from all cares, [and am happily disturbed by no passions], and since I am in the secure possession of leisure in a peaceable retirement, I will at length apply myself earnestly and freely to the general overthrow of all my former opinions. But, to this end, it will not be necessary for me to show that the whole of these are false — a point, perhaps, which I shall never reach; but as even now my reason convinces me that I ought not the less carefully to withhold belief from what is not entirely certain and indubitable, than from what is manifestly false, it will be sufficient to justify the rejection of the whole if I shall find in each some ground for doubt. Nor for this purpose will it be necessary even to deal with each belief individually, which would be truly an endless labour; but, as the removal from below of the foundation necessarily involves the downfall of the whole edifice, I will at once approach the criticism of the principles on which all my former beliefs rested.

All that I have, up to this moment, accepted as possessed of the highest truth and certainty, I received either from or through the senses. I observed, however, that these sometimes misled us; and it is the part of prudence not to place absolute confidence in that by which we have even once been deceived.

But it may be said, perhaps, that, although the senses occasionally mislead us respecting minute objects, and such as are so far removed from us as to be beyond the reach of close observation, there are yet many other of their informations (presentations), of the truth of which it is manifestly impossible to doubt; as for example, that I am in this place, seated by the fire, clothed in a winter dressing-gown, that I hold in my hands this piece of paper, with other intimations of the same nature. But how could I deny that I possess these hands and this body, and withal escape being classed with persons in a state of insanity, whose brains are so disordered and clouded by dark bilious vapours as to cause them pertinaciously to assert that they are monarchs when they are in the greatest poverty; or clothed [in gold] and purple when destitute of any covering; or that their head is made of clay, their body of glass, or that they are gourds? I should certainly be not less insane than they, were I to regulate my procedure according to examples so extravagant.

Though this be true, I must nevertheless here consider that I am a man, and that, consequently, I am in the habit of sleeping, and representing to myself in dreams those same things, or even sometimes others less probable, which the insane think are presented to them in their waking moments. How often have I dreamt that I was in these familiar circumstances — that I was dressed, and occupied this place by the fire, when I was lying undressed in bed? At the present moment, however, I certainly look upon this paper with eyes wide awake; the head which I now move is not asleep; I extend this hand consciously and with express purpose, and I perceive it; the occurrences in sleep are not so distinct as all this. But I cannot forget that, at other times, I have been deceived in sleep by similar illusions; and, attentively considering those cases, I perceive so clearly that there exist no certain marks by which the state of waking can ever be distinguished from sleep, that I feel greatly astonished; and in amazement I almost persuade myself that I am now dreaming.

Let us suppose, then, that we are dreaming, and that all these particulars — namely, the opening of the eyes, the motion of the head, the forth-putting of the hands — are merely illusions; and even that we really possess neither an entire body nor hands such as we see. Nevertheless, it must be admitted at least that the objects which appear to us in sleep are, as it were, painted representations which could not have been formed unless in the likeness of realities; and, therefore, that those general objects, at all events — namely, eyes, a head, hands, and an entire body — are not simply imaginary, but really existent. For, in truth, painters themselves, even when they study to represent sirens and satyrs by forms the most fantastic and extraordinary, cannot bestow upon them natures absolutely new, but can only make a certain medley of the members of different animals; or if they chance to imagine something so novel that nothing at all similar has ever been seen before, and such as is, therefore, purely fictitious and absolutely false, it is at least certain that the colours of which this is composed are real.

And on the same principle, although these general objects, viz. [a body], eyes, a head, hands, and the like, be imaginary, we are nevertheless absolutely necessitated to admit the reality at least of some other objects still more simple and universal than these, of which, just as of certain real colours, all those images of things, whether true and real, or false and fantastic, that are found in our consciousness (*cogitatio*), are formed.

To this class of objects seem to belong corporeal nature in general and its extension; the figure of extended things, their quantity or magnitude, and their number, as also the place in, and the time during, which they exist, and other things of the same sort. We will not, therefore, perhaps reason illegitimately if we conclude from this that Physics, Astronomy, Medicine, and all the other sciences that have for their end the consideration of composite objects, are indeed of a doubtful character; but that Arithmetic, Geometry, and the other sciences of the same class, which regard merely the simplest and most general objects, and scarcely inquire whether or not these are really existent, contain somewhat that is certain and indubitable: for whether I am awake or dreaming, it remains true that two and three make five, and that a square has but four sides; nor does it seem possible that truths so apparent can ever fall under a suspicion of falsity [or incertitude].

Nevertheless, the belief that there is a God who is all-powerful, and who created me, such as I am, has, for a long time, obtained steady possession of my mind. How, then, do I know that he has not arranged that there should be neither earth, nor sky, nor any extended thing, nor figure, nor magnitude, nor place, providing at the same time, however, for [the rise in me of the perceptions of all these objects, and] the persuasion that these do not exist otherwise than as I perceive them? And further, as I sometimes think that others are in error respecting matters of which they believe themselves to possess a perfect knowledge, how do I know that I am not also deceived each time I add together two and three, or number the sides of a square, or form some judgment still more simple, if more simple indeed can be imagined? But perhaps Deity has not been willing that I should be thus deceived, for He is said to be supremely good. If, however, it were repugnant to the goodness of Deity to have created me subject to constant deception, it would seem likewise to be contrary to his goodness to allow me to be occasionally deceived; and yet it is clear that this is permitted. Some, indeed, might perhaps be found who would be disposed rather to deny the existence of a Being so powerful than to believe that there is nothing certain. But let us for the present refrain from opposing this

opinion, and grant that all which is here said of a Deity is fabulous: nevertheless in whatever way it be supposed that I reached the state in which I exist,
whether by fate, or chance, or by an endless series of antecedents and conse-
quents, or by any other means, it is clear (since to be deceived and to err is a
certain defect) that the probability of my being so imperfect as to be the constant victim of deception, will be increased exactly in proportion as the power
possessed by the cause, to which they assign my origin, is lessened. To these
reasonings I have assuredly nothing to reply, but am constrained at last to
avow that there is nothing of all that I formerly believed to be true of which it is
impossible to doubt, and that not through thoughtlessness or levity, but from
cogent and maturely considered reasons; so that henceforward, if I desire to
discover anything certain, I ought not the less carefully to refrain from assenting to those same opinions than to what might be shown to be manifestly
false.

But it is not sufficient to have made these observations; care must be taken
likewise to keep them in remembrance. For those old and customary opinions
perpetually recur — long and familiar usage giving them the right of occupying
my mind, even almost against my will, and subduing my belief; nor will I lose
the habit of deferring to them and confiding in them so long as I shall consider
them to be what in truth they are, viz., opinions to some extent doubtful, as I
have already shown, but still highly probable, and such as it is much more
reasonable to believe than deny. It is for this reason I am persuaded that I shall
not be doing wrong, if, taking an opposite judgment of deliberate design, I
become my own deceiver, by supposing, for a time, that all those opinions are
entirely false and imaginary, until at length, having thus balanced my old by my
new prejudices, my judgment shall no longer be turned aside by perverted
usage from the path that may conduct to the perception of truth. For I am
assured that, meanwhile, there will arise neither peril nor error from this
course, and that I cannot for the present yield too much to distrust, since the
end I now seek is not action but knowledge.

I will suppose, then, not that Deity, who is sovereignly good and the fountain
of truth, but that some malignant demon, who is at once exceedingly potent and
deceitful, has employed all his artifice to deceive me: I will suppose that the
sky, the air, the earth, colours, figures, sounds, and all external things, are
nothing better than the illusions of dreams, by means of which this being has
laid snares for my credulity; I will consider myself as without hands, eyes, flesh,
blood, or any of the senses, and as falsely believing that I am possessed of
these; I will continue resolutely fixed in this belief, and if indeed by this means
it be not in my power to arrive at the knowledge of truth, I shall at least do
what is in my power, viz., [suspend my judgment], and guard with settled
purpose against giving my assent to what is false, and being imposed upon by
this deceiver, whatever be his power and artifice.

But this undertaking is arduous, and a certain indolence insensibly leads me
back to my ordinary course of life; and just as the captive, who, perchance, was
enjoying in his dreams an imaginary liberty, when he begins to suspect that it is
but a vision, dreads awakening, and conspires with the agreeable illusions that
the deception may be prolonged; so I, of my own accord, fall back into the train
of my former beliefs, and fear to arouse myself from my slumber, lest the time
of laborious wakefulness that would succeed this quiet rest, in place of bringing
any light of day, should prove inadequate to dispel the darkness that will arise
from the difficulties that have now been raised.

4. THE METHOD OF DOUBT

Dissatisfaction with current learning induces Descartes to reject all his former opinions, but in following his resolution to accept nothing which is not clearly recognizable as true he goes much further and determines, at least provisionally and for the purpose of discovering a solid foundation on which to build, to reject any proposition which is in any way susceptible of doubt. In Meditation I he therefore examines all categories of knowledge to see whether any assertion in any one of them is free from doubt on any possible grounds. The fact that some of the reasons for doubt which he offers are extraordinary and even fantastic is not to the point. He is not here maintaining that the doubtful opinions are in fact false and must be rejected — on the contrary, he is later to reinstate many of them — but only that we ought, at least once in our lives, to consider all possible grounds for doubting our opinions, and in this instance the aim is to find out whether some proposition may not be impregnable and free from all uncertainty.

He rejects both the deliverances of the senses and the conclusions of reason, in both cases because he can point to some occasions on which we are deceived by them. He does not deny that on some (possibly many) occasions they may be reliable; but if on any occasions, while we are still using the same means of ascertaining the truth, we find ourselves in error, how are we to know that we are not actually in error on those occasions when we think we are right? What we must constantly bear in mind here is that Descartes's object is to discover the criterion by which we distinguish the true from the false, not to decide when we are deceived or whether we are deceived more or less often than not.

Consequently, Descartes observes that, however plain and forceful our sense perception may be, it is not this characteristic of it that can guarantee its truth, for this characteristic belongs to it even in dreams, which are readily admitted to be illusions. What then can guarantee its truth? How do you know when you are dreaming and when you are awake? How do you know that you are not dreaming now, seeing that when you do dream (and while you are dreaming) you usually believe yourself to be awake and to be having an experience of the real world? Even in the most fantastic and inconsequent dreams we seldom believe *at the time* that our experience is illusory.

Note that when I ask: How do I know whether or not I am dreaming now? I am not asserting that I do not know, or that I could not or never do know. I am asking *how* I know; I am asking, if and when I do know, by what criterion I distinguish dreams from waking consciousness.

So likewise with reasonings, mathematical and scientific, they do not always seem to be infallible for we occasionally make mistakes. Might we not then be in error also when we think we have made no mistake, for commonly when we are in error we believe that we are not? Descartes, however, goes even beyond this argument. He supposes (what is not absolutely impossible even if farfetched) that some evil genius might be systematically causing him to see as mathematically rigorous what is actually fallacious—and, after all, we do frequently commit fallacies in reasoning while believing ourselves to be thinking validly. So he concludes, the mere fact that *we think* an argument valid is not in itself sufficient to guarantee the truth of its conclusion. (We all know that, for a conclusion to be true, not only must the argument be valid, but the premises must also be true. What then is the source of our knowledge of the premises and what guarantees their truth?)

5. MISPLACED CRITICISM OF DESCARTES'S METHOD OF DOUBT

Several contemporary philosophers have raised objections to arguing in the way that Descartes does. They say that to doubt all opinions in this way is not only unwarranted but impossible, because if we are aware of the fact that we are often in error or sometimes suffer from illusion, this is only because most of the time we are not deceived, and it is only by contrast with true and reliable knowledge that we come to recognize our mistakes. If we were always deceived we should never know it because we should never be able to distinguish between truth and falsity at all. But we do distinguish and we do occasionaly find ourselves in error, which is thus evidence in itself that we cannot always be deceived.[9] Descartes uses the fact that we know ourselves to be deceived sometimes as a ground for asserting (or assuming for the purposes of argument) that we may always be in error. In so doing, these critics allege, he is arguing fallaciously, for the conclusion (if only entertained as a hypothesis) does not follow. What does follow is its contradictory.

Except for the final indictment of Descartes, all this is true enough. To know that I am sometimes in error implies that I can distinguish error from truth and that I know equally that I am often right. If I did not know the latter I could not know the former. But the question at issue—and this is Descartes's question—is, *how* do I know and *how* do I distinguish?—by what criterion? It is therefore beside the point to object that if I make the distinction I must have a criterion and could not otherwise ever know that I was deceived. We have to discover what

---

[9]Cf. Gilbert Ryle, *Dilemmas* (Cambridge University Press, 1954), pp. 94ff., where a similar argument is applied to doubts about the reliability of perception.

the criterion is, not just that there must be one.

Descartes is not asserting or even assuming that we always are deceived, he is simply setting on one side every kind of opinion and belief which for any conceivable reason could be false in the hope of discovering something which could on no account be doubted. For if he succeeds in discovering something altogether indubitable, he ought (so he thinks) by examining this to be able to find out by what criterion its truth is guaranteed.

6. PHILOSOPHICAL AND SCEPTICAL DOUBT

Accordingly Descartes's doubting is not sceptical. That is to say, he is not by his doubting seeking to deny the existence of any truth or of any criterion. On the contrary, he is attempting to discover and establish such a criterion. The sceptic refuses to accept any belief because he asserts dogmatically that there is no truth and no way of determining whether any proffered theory is true or false — that there is no criterion. But this sceptical position is self-contradictory, because it is itself a position asserted as true, presumably on some grounds which the sceptic will, on request, produce. If he cannot produce grounds, his position has no claim to be considered, much less to be believed. Yet what it asserts is that no grounds can ever be given because no assertion can ever claim truth. The sceptical assertion likewise, therefore, can claim no truth and so cannot be made. As Spinoza says, the consistent sceptic must be dumb.

Descartes does not adopt this position, but rather the truly philosophical attitude that no proposition, hypothesis, or doctrine is immune from questioning, and therefore it is requisite at some stage to doubt — or to call in question — every belief. This doubt is not final and dogmatic like the sceptic's, but provisional and explorative (heuristic); its aim is to examine and criticize beliefs in order to discover truth, not to deny it absolutely (which is incompatible with any inquiry). Descartes seeks to discover what is true and how he knows it to be so.[10] He presupposes from the first that there is a criterion. What he endeavors to do is to identify it, and when he has done this, to his own satisfaction, he proceeds to rebuild his knowledge systematically on what he takes to be a firm and reliable foundation.

---

[10]Cf. Reply to Objection II (Haldane and Ross, vol. II) p. 31. This objective is clearly stated in Meditation II.

CHAPTER 9

I Think, Therefore I Am

MEDITATION II: OF THE NATURE OF THE HUMAN MIND; AND THAT IT
IS MORE EASILY KNOWN THAN THE BODY

The Meditation of yesterday has filled my mind with so many doubts, that
it is no longer in my power to forget them. Nor do I see, meanwhile, any principle on which they can be resolved; and, just as if I had fallen all of a sudden
into very deep water, I am so greatly disconcerted as to be unable either to
plant my feet firmly on the bottom or sustain myself by swimming on the surface. I will, nevertheless, make an effort, and try anew the same path on which
I had entered yesterday, that is, proceed by casting aside all that admits of
the slightest doubt, not less than if I had discovered it to be absolutely false;
and I will continue always in this track until I shall find something that is
certain, or at least, if I can do nothing more, until I shall know with certainty
that there is nothing certain. Archimedes, that he might transport the entire
globe from the place it occupied to another, demanded only a point that was
firm and immovable; so also, I shall be entitled to entertain the highest expectations, if I am fortunate enough to discover only one thing that is certain
and indubitable.

I suppose, accordingly, that all the things which I see are false (fictitious); I
believe that none of those objects which my fallacious memory represents ever
existed; I suppose that I possess no senses; I believe that body, figure, extension, motion, and place are merely fictions of my mind. What is there, then, that

145

can be esteemed true? Perhaps this only, that there is absolutely nothing certain.

But how do I know that there is not something different altogether from the objects I have now enumerated, of which it is impossible to entertain the slightest doubt? Is there not a God, or some being, by whatever name I may designate him, who causes these thoughts to arise in my mind? But why suppose such a being, for it may be I myself am capable of producing them? Am I, then, at least not something? But I before denied that I possessed senses or a body; I hesitate, however, for what follows from that? Am I so dependent on the body and the senses that without these I cannot exist? But I had the persuasion that there was absolutely nothing in the world, that there was no sky and no earth, neither minds nor bodies; was I not, therefore, at the same time, persuaded that I did not exist? Far from it; I assuredly existed, since I was persuaded. But there is I know not what being, who is possessed at once of the highest power and the deepest cunning, who is constantly employing all his ingenuity in deceiving me. Doubtless, then, I exist, since I am deceived; and, let him deceive me as he may, he can never bring it about that I am nothing, so long as I shall be conscious that I am something. So that it must, in fine, be maintained, all things being maturely and carefully considered, that this proposition (*pronunciatum*) I am, I exist, is necessarily true each time it is expressed by me, or conceived in my mind.

But I do not yet know with sufficient clearness what I am, though assured that I am; and hence, in the next place, I must take care, lest perchance I inconsiderately substitute some other object in room of what is properly myself, and thus wander from truth, even in that knowledge (cognition) which I hold to be of all others the most certain and evident. For this reason, I will now consider anew what I formerly believed myself to be, before I entered on the present train of thought; and of my previous opinion I will retrench all that can in the least be invalidated by the grounds of doubt I have adduced, in order that there may at length remain nothing but what is certain and indubitable. What then did I formerly think I was? Undoubtedly I judged that I was a man. But what is a man? Shall I say a rational animal? Assuredly not; for it would be necessary forthwith to inquire into what is meant by animal, and what by rational, and thus, from a single question, I should insensibly glide into others, and these more difficult than the first; nor do I now possess enough of leisure to warrant me in wasting my time amid subtleties of this sort. I prefer here to attend to the thoughts that sprung up of themselves in my mind, and were inspired by my own nature alone, when I applied myself to the consideration of what I was. In the first place, then, I thought that I possessed a countenance, hands, arms, and all the fabric of members that appears in a corpse, and which I called by the name of body. It further occurred to me that I was nourished, that I walked, perceived, and thought, and all those actions I referred to the soul; but what the soul itself was I either did not stay to consider, or, if I did, I imagined that it was something extremely rare and subtile, like wind, or flame, or ether, spread through my grosser parts. As regarded the body, I did not even doubt of its nature, but thought I distinctly knew it, and if I had wished to describe it according to the notions I then entertained, I should have explained myself in this manner: By body I understand all that can be terminated by a certain figure; that can be comprised in a certain place, and so fill a certain space as therefrom to exclude every other body; that can be perceived either by touch, sight, hearing, taste, or smell; that can be moved in different ways, not indeed of itself, but by something foreign to it by which it is touched [and from which it receives the impression]; for the power of self-motion, as likewise that of perceiving and thinking, I held as by no means pertaining to the nature of body; on the contrary, I was somewhat astonished to find such faculties existing in some bodies.

But [as to myself, what can I now say that I am], since I suppose there exists an extremely powerful, and, if I may so speak, malignant being, whose whole endeavours are directed towards deceiving me? Can I affirm that I possess any one of all those attributes of which I have lately spoken as belonging to the nature of body? After attentively considering them in my own mind, I find none of them that can properly be said to belong to myself. To recount them were idle and tedious. Let us pass, then, to the attributes of the soul. The first mentioned were the powers of nutrition and walking; but, if it be true that I have no body, it is true likewise that I am capable neither of walking nor of being nourished. Perception is another attribute of the soul; but perception too is impossible without the body: besides, I have frequently, during sleep, believed that I perceived objects which I afterwards observed I did not in reality perceive. Thinking is another attribute of the soul; and here I discover what properly belongs to myself. This alone is inseparable from me. I am—I exist: this is certain; but how often? As often as I think; for perhaps it would even happen, if I should wholly cease to think, that I should at the same time altogether cease to be. I now admit nothing that is not necessarily true: I am therefore, precisely speaking, only a thinking thing, that is, a mind (*mens sive animus*), understanding, or reason—terms whose signification was before unknown to me. I am, however, a real thing, and really existent; but what thing? The answer was, a thinking thing. The question now arises, am I aught besides? I will stimulate my imagination with a view to discover whether I am not still something more than a thinking being. Now it is plain I am not the assemblage of members called the human body; I am not a thin and penetrating air diffused through all these members, or wind, or flame, or vapour, or breath, or any of all the things I can imagine; for I supposed that all these were not, and, without changing the supposition, I find that I still feel assured of my existence.

But it is true, perhaps, that those very things which I suppose to be nonexistent, because they are unknown to me, are not in truth different from myself whom I know. This is a point I cannot determine, and do not now enter into any dispute regarding it. I can only judge of things that are known to me: I am conscious that I exist, and I who know that I exist inquire into what I am. It is, however, perfectly certain that the knowledge of my existence, thus precisely taken, is not dependent on things, the existence of which is as yet unknown to me: and consequently it is not dependent on any of the things I can feign in imagination. Moreover, the phrase itself, I frame an image (*effingo*), reminds me of my error; for I should in truth frame one if I were to imagine myself to be anything, since to imagine is nothing more than to contemplate the figure or image of a corporeal thing; but I already know that I exist, and that it is possible at the same time that all those images, and in general all that relates to the nature of body, are merely dreams [or chimeras]. From this I discover that it is not more reasonable to say, I will excite my imagination that I may know more distinctly what I am, than to express myself as follows: I am now awake, and perceive something real; but because my perception is not sufficiently clear, I will of express purpose go to sleep that my dreams may represent to me the object of my perception with more truth and clearness. And, therefore, I know that nothing of all that I can embrace in imagination belongs to the knowledge which I have of myself, and that there is need to recall with the utmost care the mind from this mode of thinking, that it may be able to know its own nature with perfect distinctness.

But what, then, am I? A thinking thing, it has been said. But what is a thinking thing? It is a thing that doubts, understands, [conceives], affirms, denies, wills, refuses, that imagines also, and perceives. Assuredly it is not little, if all these properties belong to my nature. But why should they not belong to it? Am I not that very being who now doubts of almost everything; who, for all that, understands and conceives certain things; who affirms one alone as true, and denies the others; who desires to know more of them, and does not wish to be deceived; who imagines many things, sometimes even despite his will; and is likewise percipient of many, as if through the medium of the senses? Is there nothing of all this as true as that I am, even although I should be always dreaming, and although he who gave me being employed all his ingenuity to deceive me? Is there also any one of these attributes that can be properly distinguished from my thought, or that can be said to be separate from myself? For it is of itself so evident that it is I who doubt, I who understand, and I who desire, that it is here unnecessary to add anything by way of rendering it more clear. And I am as certainly the same being who imagines; for, although it may be (as I before supposed) that nothing I imagine is true, still the power of imagination does not cease really to exist in me and to form part of my thought. In fine, I am the same being who perceives, that is, who apprehends certain objects as by the organs of sense, since, in truth, I see light, hear a noise, and feel heat. But it will be said that these presentations are false, and that I am dreaming. Let it be so. At all events it is certain that I seem to see light, hear a noise, and feel heat; this cannot be false, and this is what in me is properly called perceiving (*sentire*), which is nothing else than thinking. From this I begin to know what I am with somewhat greater clearness and distinctness than heretofore.

But, nevertheless, it still seems to me, and I cannot help believing, that corporeal things, whose images are formed by thought, [which fall under the senses], and are examined by the same, are known with much greater distinctness than that I know not what part of myself which is not imaginable; although, in truth, it may seem strange to say that I know and comprehend with greater distinctness things whose existence appears to me doubtful, that are unknown, and do not belong to me, than others of whose reality I am persuaded, that are known to me, and appertain to my proper nature; in a word, than myself. But I see clearly what is the state of the case. My mind is apt to wander, and will not yet submit to be restrained within the limits of truth. Let us therefore leave the mind to itself once more, and, according to it every kind of liberty, [permit it to consider the objects that appear to it from without], in order that, having afterwards withdrawn it from these gently and opportunely, [and fixed it on the consideration of its being and the properties it finds in itself], it may then be the more easily controlled.

Let us now accordingly consider the objects that are commonly thought to be [the most easily, and likewise] the most distinctly known, viz., the bodies we touch and see; not, indeed, bodies in general, for these general notions are usually somewhat more confused, but one body in particular. Take, for example, this piece of wax; it is quite fresh, having been but recently taken from the bee-hive; it has not yet lost the sweetness of the honey it contained, it still retains somewhat of the odour of the flowers from which it was gathered; its colour, figure, size, are apparent (to the sight); it is hard, cold, easily handled; and sounds when struck upon with the finger. In fine, all that contributes to make a body as distinctly known as possible, is found in the one before us. But, while I am speaking, let it be placed near the fire — what remained of the taste exhales, the smell evaporates, the colour changes, its figure is destroyed, its size increases, it becomes liquid, it grows hot, it can hardly be handled, and, although struck upon, it emits no sound. Does the same wax still remain after this change? It must be admitted that it does remain; no one doubts it, or judges otherwise. What, then, was it I knew with so much distinctness in the piece of wax? Assuredly, it could be nothing of all that I observed by means of the senses, since all the things that fell under taste, smell, sight, touch, and hearing are changed, and yet the same wax remains. It was perhaps what I now think, viz., that this wax was neither the sweetness of honey, the pleasant odour of flowers, the whiteness, the figure, nor the sound, but only a body that a little before appeared to me conspicuous under these forms, and which is now perceived under others. But, to speak precisely, what is it that I imagine when I think of it in this way? Let it be attentively considered, and, retrenching all that does not belong to the wax, let us see what remains. There certainly remains nothing, except something extended, flexible, and movable. But what is meant by flexible and movable? Is it not that I imagine that the piece of wax, being round, is capable of becoming square, or of passing from a square into a triangular figure? Assuredly such is not the case, because I conceive that it admits of an infinity of similar changes; and I am, moreover, unable to compass this infinity by imagination, and consequently this conception which I have of the wax is not the product of the faculty of imagination. But what now is this extension? Is it not also unknown? for it becomes greater when the wax is melted, greater when it is boiled, and greater still when the heat increases; and I should not conceive [clearly and] according to truth, the wax as it is, if I did not suppose that the piece we are considering admitted even of a wider variety of extension than I ever imagined. I must, therefore, admit that I cannot even comprehend by imagination what the piece of wax is, and that it is the mind alone (*mens*, Lat., *entendement*, F.) which perceives it. I speak of one piece in particular; for, as to wax in general, this is still more evident. But what is the piece of wax that can be perceived only by the [understanding or] mind? It is certainly the same which I see, touch, imagine; and, in fine, it is the same which, from the beginning, I believed it to be. But (and this it is of moment to observe) the perception of it is neither an act of sight, of touch, nor of imagination, and never was either of these, though it might formerly seem so, but is simply an intuition (*inspectio*) of the mind, which may be imperfect and confused, as it formerly was, or very clear and distinct, as it is at present, according as the attention is more or less directed to the elements which it contains, and of which it is composed.

But, meanwhile, I feel greatly astonished when I observe [the weakness of my mind, and] its proneness to error. For although, without at all giving expression to what I think, I consider all this in my own mind, words yet occasionally impede my progress, and I am almost led into error by the terms of ordinary language. We say, for example, that we see the same wax when it is before us, and not that we judge it to be the same from its retaining the same colour and figure: whence I should forthwith be disposed to conclude that the wax is known by the act of sight, and not by the intuition of the mind alone, were it not for the analogous instance of human beings passing on in the street below, as observed from a window. In this case I do not fail to say that I see the men themselves, just as I say that I see the wax; and yet what do I see from the window beyond hats and cloaks that might cover artificial machines, whose motions might be determined by springs? But I judge that there are human beings from these appearances, and thus I comprehend, by the faculty of judgment alone which is in the mind, what I believed I saw with my eyes.

The man who makes it his aim to rise to knowledge superior to the common, ought to be ashamed to seek occasions of doubting from the vulgar forms of speech: instead, therefore, of doing this, I shall proceed with the matter in hand, and inquire whether I had a clearer and more perfect perception of the piece of wax when I first saw it, and when I thought I knew it by means of the external sense itself, or, at all events, by the common sense (*sensus communis*), as it is called, that is, by the imaginative faculty; or whether I rather apprehend it more clearly at present, after having examined with greater care, both what it is, and in what way it can be known. It would certainly be ridiculous to entertain any doubt on this point. For what, in that first perception, was there distinct? What did I perceive which any animal might not have perceived? But when I distinguish the wax from its exterior forms, and when, as if I had stripped it of its vestments, I consider it quite naked, it is certain, although some error may still be found in my judgment, that I cannot, nevertheless, thus apprehend it without possessing a human mind.

But, finally, what shall I say of the mind itself, that is, myself? for as yet I do not admit that I am anything but mind. What, then! I who seem to possess so distinct an apprehension of the piece of wax—do I not know myself, both with greater truth and certitude, and also much more distinctly and clearly? For if I judge that the wax exists because I see it, it assuredly follows, much more evidently, that I myself am or exist, for the same reason: for it is possible that what I see may not in truth be wax, and that I do not even possess eyes with which to see anything; but it cannot be that when I see, or, which comes to the same thing, when I think I see, I myself who think am nothing. So likewise, if I judge that the wax exists because I touch it, it will still also follow that I am; and if I determine that my imagination, or any other cause, whatever it be, persuades me of the existence of the wax, I will still draw the same conclusion. And what is here remarked of the piece of wax, is applicable to all the other things that are external to me. And further, if the [notion or] perception of wax appeared to me more precise and distinct, after that not only sight and touch, but many other causes besides, rendered it manifest to my apprehension, with how much greater distinctness must I now know myself, since all the reasons that contribute to the knowledge of the nature of wax, or of any body whatever, manifest still better the nature of my mind? And there are besides so many other things in the mind itself that contribute to the illustration of its nature, that those dependent on the body, to which I have here referred, scarcely merit to be taken into account.

But, in conclusion, I find I have insensibly reverted to the point I desired; for, since it is now manifest to me that bodies themselves are not properly perceived by the senses nor by the faculty of imagination, but by the intellect alone; and since they are not perceived because they are seen and touched, but only because they are understood [or rightly comprehended by thought], I readily discover that there is nothing more easily or clearly apprehended than my own mind. But because it is difficult to rid one's self so promptly of an opinion to which one has been long accustomed, it will be desirable to tarry for some time at this stage, that, by long continued meditation, I may more deeply impress upon my memory this new knowledge.

In Part IV of the *Discourse* Descartes enunciates the famous dictum on the strength of which he proceeds to rebuild the edifice of knowledge. To doubt, or to think all opinions false, necessitates the existence of the doubter. If I doubt, I think; if I think, then I exist — *cogito ergo sum*.

Doubt what or howsoever I may, I cannot do so without thinking and to think I must be something. I cannot doubt that I exist, for to do so I must exist. I cannot doubt that I think, because to doubt is to think. Here, then, is a proposition which is indubitable. This not only can, but must, be taken as true, and from it Descartes proceeds to deduce all such knowledge as he considers dependable. So he rebuilds, on what he takes to be a surer foundation, what his method of doubt provisionally demolished.

Before discussing the implications of this important dictum and of the argument by which it is reached, we must observe that Descartes meant by "thinking" not only reasoning or calculation, but any sort of cognition or awareness.[1] He does not consider the possibility of a nonconscious, calculating machine, nor would this be relevent; for no such machine could significantly refer to itself as "I." Only a conscious subject can do that.

1. HOW MUCH DOES THIS ARGUMENT PROVE?

(a) It is clear that the argument establishes, beyond cavil, the occurrence of one's own conscious awareness. The existence of some consciousness cannot be denied without self-refutation — behaviorists notwithstanding. For he who denies it must himself be conscious; and he who is conscious cannot but know himself to be so and cannot consistently deny it. An unconscious robot (a computer, for instance) might be made to produce a symbol which could be interpreted as meaning *cogito ergo sum*; but it would be the interpreter and not the robot to whom alone the statement could refer. Or again, the robot

---

[1]Cf. *Principles of Philosophy*, Part I, ix: "By the word thought I understand all that of which we are conscious as operating in us. And that is why not alone understanding, willing, imagining, but also feeling, are here the same thing as thought."

might produce a symbol which, being interpreted, says *non cogito*; but this would be a self-contradiction, because if true (in reference to the robot) it could not be significantly asserted in the first person, and if it were again referred to the interpreter, who must think in order to interpret, it would be false.

(b) If I cannot doubt or deny that I think and thus exist, does this prove more than that there is some consciousness now occurring? What is the "I" which thinks? Is it the same "I" each time I assert it? Is it, as Descartes goes on to maintain, "a thinking thing" (*res cogitans*) – is it a "substance" or a self?

Let us take the last question first. Thinking is going on. What is "thinking"? Presumably it is some sort of activity. Can an activity go on without an agent? Or should we say that thinking is just a sort of natural process like the *aurora borealis* or soil erosion? Even here we should seek a cause or agency which produced the action (solar radiation or water pressure), but these, one might allege, are either prior events and processes or are generalized ideas of such events. Could thinking be just some such process caused by other prior processes?

If thinking is conscious and self-aware, so that it can express itself in the first person, it must be something more than just a natural process, unless we are to regard all natural processes as conscious of themselves – for which, to say the least, there is no clear evidence. That which says "I", and claims the activity as its own, must surely *be* an agent – that which thinks. This again is undeniable, for to claim agency is to *do* something, and so to be an agent. If then I claim that *I* am because *I* think, I must be the agent that does both the claiming and the thinking.

(c) Is it always the same subject – the same I? Let us for a moment assume that it is not. Yet the second time I assert it I am aware that it is the second time. In other words I am aware, not only of thinking, but of thinking twice, so that I can raise the question whether, in both cases, the "I" is the same subject. Thus I am aware that both occurrences of thinking belong to the same time series, that one comes before the other; and I am aware of them as two that can be contrasted and compared, each as an act of an agent who may be the same or different. We saw earlier, in discussing Plato's theory of the soul, that awareness of succession in time, and of terms in relations of identity and difference, is possible only if both occurrences (or terms) related are the objects of (or are in some sense "present to") a single unitary subject, which must be one and the same throughout the succession. The "I" must therefore refer to the same subject on each occasion that I judge.

Descartes does not set out any such argument. He simply assumes its conclusion. He accepts its truth without working out any proof of self-identity. But the conclusion establishes itself as soon as the criticism is made — which often is made — that he took too much for granted in assuming that *cogito ergo sum* proved self-identity.

He did assert that the thinking thing was a substance, but, if he was wrong, it was not through lack of cogency in the argument that supported the existence of a thinking subject, or because the identity and persistence of the subject did not follow from it. If Descartes was wrong, his error lay in his conception of substance, a question of considerable difficulty and obscurity which we cannot profitably discuss at this stage.

2. SEPARATION OF BODY AND MIND

By his method of doubt Descartes succeeds in establishing the existence of consciousness and the thinking subject, but in the course of doing so he has assumed the nonexistence — or possible nonexistence — of material entities, including his own body. He has provisionally discounted the apparent existence of all sensible objects as independent of his consciousness. That appearance might be a mere phantasmagoria, yet, if it were, the thinking subject would still exist.

Note that Descartes does not deny the occurrence of sensory experiences. It is immediate consciousness of these (among other forms of awareness) that assures him of his own existence. So the occurrence of sensory experiences cannot be denied. All he rejects (provisionally) is any judgment as to what they represent. Until he can prove it satisfactorily, he refuses to take these experiences, as we commonly do, to be evidence of the existence of material bodies, though he admits that he had previously done so without question.[2] Nevertheless, even presuming the nonexistence of material things, and actually by doing so, he is assured of his own existence as a thinking thing.

Descartes argues, in consequence, that the mind (*res cogitans*) exists whether or not any bodies whatsoever (including his own) exist, and concludes that it must be an entirely separate and independent entity, or substance.[3] In the *Principles of Philosophy*, Part I, he says:

---

[2]Meditation II, p. 148 above, and Meditation III, p. 156 below.

[3]This characteristic of being independently existent, of depending for existence on nothing but itself, is taken as the definition of substance. Descartes later admits that the thinking thing, like all else, is dependent for its existence upon God, so that, strictly speaking, God is the only substance. But he is prepared to call other things created substances, in a kind of secondary sense, if their existence depends only upon God and nothing else. He finally decides that there are two, and only two, created substances: thinking substance and extended substance.

This notion of thought precedes that of all corporeal things and is the most certain, since we still doubt that there are any other things in the world, while we already perceive that we think.[4]

The total separation of mind from body confronts Descartes with a problem which he never really solves, that of discovering the precise relation between the human soul and its body and of accounting for their influence upon one another. It remains as great a difficulty for him as it was for Plato.

---

[4]Cf. also Meditation IV (below).

CHAPTER 10

The Criterion of Truth

I will now close my eyes, I will stop my ears, I will turn away my senses from their objects, I will even efface from my consciousness all the images of corporeal things; or at least, because this can hardly be accomplished, I will consider them as empty and false; and thus, holding converse only with myself, and closely examining my nature, I will endeavour to obtain by degrees a more intimate and familiar knowledge of myself. I am a thinking (conscious) thing, that is, a being who doubts, affirms, denies, knows a few objects, and is ignorant of many, — [who loves, hates], wills, refuses, — who imagines likewise, and perceives; for, as I before remarked, although the things which I perceive or imagine are perhaps nothing at all apart from me [and in themselves], I am nevertheless assured that those modes of consciousness which I call perceptions and imaginations, in as far only as they are modes of consciousness, exist in me. And in the little I have said I think I have summed up all that I really know, or at least all that up to this time I was aware I knew. Now, as I am endeavouring to extend my knowledge more widely, I will use circumspection, and consider with care whether I can still discover in myself anything further which I have not yet hitherto observed. I am certain that I am a thinking thing; but do I not therefore likewise know what is required to render me certain of a truth? In this first knowledge, doubtless, there is nothing that gives me assurance of its truth except the clear and distinct perception of what I affirm, which

155

would not indeed be sufficient to give me the assurance that what I say is true, if it could ever happen that anything I thus clearly and distinctly perceived should prove false; and accordingly it seems to me that I may now take as a general rule, that all that is very clearly and distinctly apprehended (conceived) is true.

Nevertheless I before received and admitted many things as wholly certain and manifest, which yet I afterwards found to be doubtful. What, then, were those? They were the earth, the sky, the stars, and all the other objects which I was in the habit of perceiving by the senses. But what was it that I clearly [and distinctly] perceived in them? Nothing more than that the ideas and the thoughts of those objects were presented to my mind. And even now I do not deny that these ideas are found in my mind. But there was yet another thing which I affirmed, and which, from having been accustomed to believe it, I thought I clearly perceived, although, in truth, I did not perceive it at all; I mean the existence of objects external to me, from which those ideas proceeded, and to which they had a perfect resemblance; and it was here I was mistaken, or if I judged correctly, this assuredly was not to be traced to any knowledge I possessed (the force of my perception, Lat.).

But when I considered any matter in arithmetic and geometry, that was very simple and easy, as, for example, that two and three added together make five, and things of this sort, did I not view them with at least sufficient clearness to warrant me in affirming their truth? Indeed, if I afterwards judged that we ought to doubt of these things, it was for no other reason than because it occurred to me that a God might perhaps have given me such a nature as that I should be deceived, even respecting the matters that appeared to me the most evidently true. But as often as this preconceived opinion of the sovereign power of a God presents itself to my mind, I am constrained to admit that it is easy for him, if he wishes it, to cause me to err, even in matters where I think I possess the highest evidence; and, on the other hand, as often as I direct my attention to things which I think I apprehend with great clearness, I am so persuaded of their truth that I naturally break out into expressions such as these: Deceive me who may, no one will yet ever be able to bring it about that I am not, so long as I shall be conscious that I am, or at any future time cause it to be true that I have never been, it being now true that I am, or make two and three more or less than five, in supposing which, and other like absurdities, I discover a manifest contradiction.

And in truth, as I have no ground for believing that Deity is deceitful, and as, indeed, I have not even considered the reasons by which the existence of a Deity of any kind is established, the ground of doubt that rests only on this supposition is very slight, and, so to speak, metaphysical. But, that I may be able wholly to remove it, I must inquire whether there is a God, as soon as an opportunity of doing so shall present itself; and if I find that there is a God, I must examine likewise whether he can be a deceiver; for, without the knowledge of these two truths, I do not see that I can ever be certain of anything. And that I may be enabled to examine this without interrupting the order of meditation I have proposed to myself [which is, to pass by degrees from the notions that I shall find first in my mind to those I shall afterwards discover in it], it is necessary at this stage to divide all my thoughts into certain classes, and to consider in which of these classes truth and error are, strictly speaking, to be found.

Of my thoughts some are, as it were, images of things, and to these alone properly belongs the name *idea;* as when I think [represent to my mind] a man, a chimera, the sky, an angel, or God. Others, again, have certain other forms; as when I will, fear, affirm, or deny, I always, indeed, apprehend something as the object of my thought, but I also embrace in thought something more than the representation of the object; and of this class of thoughts some are called volitions or affections, and others judgments.

Now, with respect to ideas, if these are considered only in themselves, and are not referred to any object beyond them, they cannot, properly speaking, be false; for, whether I imagine a goat or a chimera, it is not less true that I imagine the one than the other. Nor need we fear that falsity may exist in the will or affections; for, although I may desire objects that are wrong, and even that never existed, it is still true that I desire them. There thus only remain our judgments, in which we must take diligent heed that we be not deceived. But the chief and most ordinary error that arises in them consists in judging that the ideas which are in us are like or conformed to the things that are external to us; for assuredly, if we but considered the ideas themselves as certain modes of our thought (consciousness), without referring them to anything beyond, they would hardly afford any occasion of error.

But, among these ideas, some appear to me to be innate, others adventitious, and others to be made by myself (factitious); for, as I have the power of conceiving what is called a thing, or a truth, or a thought, it seems to me that I hold this power from no other source than my own nature; but if I now hear a noise, if I see the sun, or if I feel heat, I have all along judged that these sensations proceeded from certain objects existing out of myself; and, in fine, it appears to me that sirens, hippogryphs, and the like, are inventions of my own mind. But I may even perhaps come to be of opinion that all my ideas are of the class which I call adventitious, or that they are all innate, or that they are all factitious, for I have not yet clearly discovered their true origin; and what I have here principally to do is to consider, with reference to those that appear to come from certain objects without me, what grounds there are for thinking them like these objects.

The first of these grounds is that it seems to me I am so taught by nature; and the second that I am conscious that those ideas are not dependent on my will, and therefore not on myself, for they are frequently presented to me against my will—as at present, whether I will or not, I feel heat; and I am thus persuaded that this sensation or idea (*sensum vel ideam*) of heat is produced in me by something different from myself, viz., by the heat of the fire by which I sit. And it is very reasonable to suppose that this object impresses me with its own likeness rather than any other thing.

But I must consider whether these reasons are sufficiently strong and convincing. When I speak of being taught by nature in this matter, I understand by the word nature only a certain spontaneous impetus that impels me to believe in a resemblance between ideas and their objects, and not a natural light that affords a knowledge of its truth. But these two things are widely different; for what the natural light shows to be true can be in no degree doubtful, as, for example, that I am because I doubt, and other truths of the like kind: inasmuch as I possess no other faculty whereby to distinguish truth from error, which can teach me the falsity of what the natural light declares to be true, and which is equally trustworthy; but with respect to [seemingly] natural impulses, I have observed, when the question related to the choice of right or wrong in action, that they frequently led me to take the worse part; nor do I see that I have any better ground for following them in what relates to truth and error. Then, with respect to the other reason, which is that because these ideas do not depend on my will, they must arise from objects existing without me, I do not find it more convincing than the former; for, just as those natural impulses, of which I have lately spoken, are found in me, notwithstanding that they are not always in harmony with my will, so likewise it may be that I possess some power not sufficiently known to myself capable of producing ideas without the aid of external objects, and, indeed, it has always hitherto appeared to me that they are formed during sleep, by some power of this nature, without the aid of aught external. And, in fine, although I should grant that they proceeded from those objects, it is not a necessary consequence that they must be like them. On the contrary, I have observed, in a number of instances, that there was a great difference between the object and its idea. Thus, for example, I find in my mind two wholly diverse ideas of the sun; the one, by which it appears to me extremely small, draws its origin from the senses, and should be placed in the class of adventitious ideas; the other, by which it seems to be many times larger than the whole earth, is taken up on astronomical grounds, that is, elicited from certain notions born with me, or is framed by myself in some other manner. These two ideas cannot certainly both resemble the same sun; and reason teaches me that the one which seems to have immediately emanated from it is the most unlike. And these things sufficiently prove that hitherto it has not been from a certain and deliberate judgment, but only from a sort of blind impulse, that I believed in the existence of certain things different from myself, which, by the organs of sense, or by whatever other means it might be, conveyed their ideas or images into my mind [and impressed it with their likenesses].

The certainty of his own existence so long as he is conscious provides Descartes with a truth differing from his other opinions in that it is not susceptible of doubt. By scrutinizing the indubitable proposition (*cogito ergo sum*) can he now determine the mark or characteristic which distinguishes it from the doubtful and the false? Descartes asserts that its distinguishing mark is its clearness and distinctness to his mind.[1]

1. WHAT DOES DESCARTES MEAN BY "CLEAR AND DISTINCT"?

Descartes is quite emphatic, not only in the *Meditations*, but also in the *Rules for the Direction of the Mind* and in the *Principles of Philosophy*, that by "clear and distinct" he does not mean the kind of vividness and sharpness of outline which is characteristic of sensory experience when we describe it as clear and distinct. Clear and distinct ideas are not, for him, well defined and easily describable sense data.

In the *Rules* (III) we find the following passage:

By *intuition* I understand not the fluctuating testimony (*fidem*) of the senses, nor the misleading judgment that proceeds from the blundering constructions of imagination, but the conception which an unclouded and attentive mind

---

[1]Cf. *Discourse,* Part IV (Haldane and Ross), p. 102.

gives us so readily and distinctly that we are wholly freed from doubt about
that which we understand.

What he calls "intuition" in this passage is what in the *Meditations* he
calls "the natural light;" it is what gives us clear and distinct ideas and
is not to be confused with the "testimony of the senses."

The same point may be extracted from the passage in Meditation II
about the wax. Sense qualities, for all their apparent clarity and force-
fulness, do not give clear and distinct *understanding*. They vary and
fluctuate and, after the wax has melted, they leave us bewildered by
the question "Is it still the same wax?" The same applies to the imagination. Descartes, accordingly, concludes "that it is my mind alone
which perceives" that the wax is still the same body.

Thus "perception" is denied of the senses and imagination and
attributed solely to the mind, or faculty of thinking. What in the *Rules*
he calls "intuition," in this passage he calls "inspection of the mind"
(*inspectio mentis*). We are reminded of Plato's contrast between the
bodily eye and the eye of the soul. Inquiry into the essential nature of
the wax (*what* it essentially is) leads to a pure abstraction — extension — an idea conceived by the intellect, not perceived by the senses or
figured in the imagination, but properly understood only in terms of
geometry. What then, we may ask, is there about geometry and mathematics generally which gives us so much more confidence in their truth
than in other forms of knowledge? Is it not something they have in
common with *cogito ergo sum*? What assures us of this truth, we have
been told, is clearness and distinctness. If this is what also assures us of
the truths of mathematics we have a clue to Descartes's meaning, for
what is characteristic of mathematical truths is their logical necessity — the impossibility, without becoming involved in self-contradiction,
of denying them.

We shall find this suggestion corroborated when Descartes turns to
the proof of God's existence, for he argues that existence is implied in
the conception of God in the same necessary way as the equality of the
sum of its angles to two right angles is undeniably involved in the
conception of a triangle.[2] The "clearness and distinctness" in both
cases consists in nothing other than logical necessity.

What else Descartes could mean is difficult to see. In the *Rules* he

---

[2]*Cf. Discourse*, Part IV, pp. 103f. "For, to take an example, I saw very well that if we
suppose a triangle to be given, the three angles must certainly be equal to two right
angles; but for all that I saw no reason to be assured that there was any such triangle in
existence, while on the contrary, on reverting to the examination of the idea which I had
of a Perfect Being I found that in this case existence was implied in it in the same manner
in which the equality of its three angles to two right angles is implied in the idea of a triangle."

does speak of "intuition" as grasping simple truths with certainty and he seems to contemplate a kind of self-evidence belonging to what he terms "simple natures," but when he gives examples of them they are by no means homogeneous. Some are abstract ideas, like figure, extension, and motion; others state a logical nexus between two ideas, like $2 + 2 = 4$, of the same kind as we have in the geometrical example and in *cogito ergo sum*.

If it is the case that Descartes's criterion of truth is logical necessity, modern logicians are likely to tell us that it reduces all certain knowledge to triviality, for according to current logical doctrine, logical necessity (or entailment) belongs only to so-called analytic statements which tell us only what is meant by their subject term and which are therefore strictly tautological. Thus, "A bachelor is an unmarried man" is a logically necessary truth because "unmarried man" is what "bachelor" means, but as soon as we go beyond the meaning of the subject term and make the statement "synthetic" it ceases to be necessarily (or *logically*) true. Thus, "A bachelor has more freedom than a married man" may be true, but not of necessity, or indubitably. Consequently, all necessary (or logical) truths being tautological, none can tell us anything new about the world; they can at most explicate the meanings of words.

This doctrine, however persistent and widely held, is highly questionable. "I think, therefore I exist" is (as we have seen) certainly true, and logically necessary, for to deny it involves self-contradiction. But it is not a tautology, to think and to exist do not mean the same. The same thing holds for the following statements:

If anything is colored it is extended.

Whatever has shape has size.

An integer is either odd or even.

A circle encloses a larger area than any other figure of equal circumference.

None of these propositions can plausibly be regarded as tautological and all of them are logically necessary.

It will be important to bear this in mind when we come to examine Descartes's argument for the existence of God, because to assert the existence of something is to assert a synthetic proposition (or what may be called "a matter of fact"), and if tautologies, which are never matters of *fact* but only of conventional definition, are the only kind of proposition that can be logically necessary, existence can never be proved on purely logical grounds. What, in that case, becomes of *cogito ergo sum*?

2. DESCARTES'S METHOD RECONSIDERED

But, to return from this digression to Descartes's criterion of truth. If it is seen to be logical necessity, it will follow that all knowledge which, for him, would be worthy of the name, would have to be either self-evident or rigorously deducible from premises which were self-evident. It seems clear that Descartes took logical necessity and self-evidence to be the same thing. In the *Rules* (III) he says that intuition possesses "immediately presented evidence" (*praesens evidentia*) and he describes its object in that treatise as "something known through itself" (*res per se nota*). Likewise, elsewhere, he insists that *cogito ergo sum* is not a syllogism or conclusion drawn from a major premise, "Whatever thinks, exists," for it does not follow from this statement that there is anything that thinks, and in the very act of considering it I must myself think, so that my own existence is self-evident without the major premise, and is more certainly known than if it had been deduced from it.

Descartes rejected the syllogism as a mode of scientific discovery. He says it is more suitable for stating what is already known than for eliciting new knowledge. For him the only sound scientific procedure is to begin from self-evident certainties, and then, by intuiting necessary logical connections between them, to proceed by necessary steps (each in itself equally self-evident) to determinate conclusions. He believed that it was possible to derive all knowledge in this way and only what answered to this pattern did he regard as reliable. This is the theory elaborated in the *Rules for the Direction of the Mind,* and reflected in the four rules stated in *Discourse,* Part II:

(a)   We accept to begin with nothing that is not self-evidently true — clearly and distinctly seen to be so.

(b)   If we divide the problem into its simplest parts we shall be able to grasp each by intuition, clearly and distinctly, and shall similarly be able to perceive their self-evident logical interconnections.

(c)   If we then go from one logical implication to the next by self-evident steps, we shall necessarily follow the right order from simple to complex. This is the process called deduction (*deductio*).

(d)   To be sure that we overlook nothing relevant, we conduct as complete an enumeration as possible of self-evident truths and the steps of the deduction from them (as a mathematician numbers the steps of a proof). This Descartes calls "induction" or "enumeration," and he says it is especially necessary where the chains of reasoning become unduly long and steps therefore liable to be forgotten or omitted. Just what is the logical significance of this process he never makes clear and seems himself to be uncertain.[3]

This theory shows the essential character of the Cartesian method and it is to this that we chiefly refer when we speak of Descartes as a Rationalist. Unfortunately the underlying assumptions are unsound. There do not seem, even on Descartes's showing, to be any self-evident, simple truths upon which such a deductive system could be based. The *cogito* itself is established by Descartes by means of an elaborate argument and, as we have seen, requires defense before it can be pronounced indubitable. Its certainty depends wholly on the cogency of the argument that supports it and not upon any immediate intuition of its truth. Apart from this fact, *cogito ergo sum* is not simple. It is a logical nexus between two concepts, self-awareness and existence, which are distinguished within it and connected together. Most of the examples given in the *Rules* are of this type and none, even those of the abstract idea variety, can be shown to be absolutely simple. *A fortiori* no step in a deduction from premises to conclusion can be represented as simple even if it is claimed as self-evident. The conception of knowledge which Descartes adopts is therefore in need of revision.

It does not follow that he has given us nothing of any value in this account of the structure of scientific knowledge. For anything worthy of the name "science" is an effort to organize material systematically so that its conclusions follow logically from its fundamental principles, and we do seek adequate assurance of their truth, even if we sometimes despair of absolute certainty. A criterion by which we can distinguish sound doctrine from unsound is also desirable, and logical cogency is at the very least an essential part of it. But to say all this still leaves much to be explained.

---

[3]Cf. *Rules for the Direction of the Mind*, Part VII, pp. 19–22.

CHAPTER 11

The Existence of God

But there is still another way of inquiring whether, of the objects whose ideas are in my mind, there are any that exist out of me. If ideas are taken in so far only as they are certain modes of consciousness, I do not remark any difference or inequality among them, and all seem, in the same manner, to proceed from myself; but, considering them as images, of which one represents one thing and another a different, it is evident that a great diversity obtains among them. For, without doubt, those that represent substances are something more, and contain in themselves, so to speak, more objective reality [that is, participate by representation in higher degrees of being or perfection], than those that represent only modes or accidents; and again, the idea by which I conceive a God [sovereign], eternal, infinite, [immutable], all-knowing, all-powerful, and the creator of all things that are out of himself—this, I say, has certainly in it more objective reality than those ideas by which finite substances are represented.

Now, it is manifest by the natural light that there must at least be as much reality in the efficient and total cause as in its effect; for whence can the effect draw its reality if not from its cause? and how could the cause communicate to it this reality unless it possessed it in itself? And hence it follows, not only that what is cannot be produced by what is not, but likewise that the more perfect—in other words, that which contains in itself more reality—cannot be the effect of the less perfect: and this is not only evidently true of those effects, whose reality

163

is actual or formal, but likewise of ideas, whose reality is only considered as objective. Thus, for example, the stone that is not yet in existence, not only cannot now commence to be, unless it be produced by that which possesses in itself, formally or eminently, all that enters into its composition, [in other words, by that which contains in itself the same properties that are in the stone, or others superior to them]; and heat can only be produced in a subject that was before devoid of it, by a cause that is of an order [degree or kind], at least as perfect as heat; and so of the others. But further, even the idea of the heat, or of the stone, cannot exist in me unless it be put there by a cause that contains, at least, as much reality as I conceive existent in the heat or in the stone: for, although that cause may not transmit into my idea anything of its actual or formal reality, we ought not on this account to imagine that it is less real; but we ought to consider that, [as every idea is a work of the mind], its nature is such as of itself to demand no other formal reality than that which it borrows from our consciousness, of which it is but a mode, [that is, a manner or way of thinking]. But in order that an idea may contain this objective reality rather than that, it must doubtless derive it from some cause in which is found at least as much formal reality as the idea contains of objective; for, if we suppose that there is found in an idea anything which was not in its cause, it must of course derive this from nothing. But, however imperfect may be the mode of existence by which a thing is objectively [or by representation] in the understanding by its idea, we certainly cannot, for all that, allege that this mode of existence is nothing, nor, consequently, that the idea owes its origin to nothing. Nor must it be imagined that, since the reality which is considered in these ideas is only objective, the same reality need not be formally (actually) in the causes of these ideas, but only objectively: for, just as the mode of existing objectively belongs to ideas by their peculiar nature, so likewise the mode of existing formally appertains to the causes of these ideas (at least to the first and principal), by their peculiar nature. And although an idea may give rise to another idea, this regress cannot, nevertheless, be infinite; we must in the end reach a first idea, the cause of which is, as it were, the archetype in which all the reality [or perfection] that is found objectively [or by representation] in these ideas is contained formally [and in act]. I am thus clearly taught by the natural light that ideas exist in me as pictures or images, which may in truth readily fall short of the perfection of the objects from which they are taken, but can never contain anything greater or more perfect.

And in proportion to the time and care with which I examine all those matters, the conviction of their truth brightens and becomes distinct. But, to sum up, what conclusion shall I draw from it all? It is this: if the objective reality [or perfection] of any one of my ideas be such as clearly to convince me, that this same reality exists in me neither formally nor eminently, and if, as follows from this, I myself cannot be the cause of it, it is a necessary consequence that I am not alone in the world, but that there is besides myself some other being who exists as the cause of that idea; while, on the contrary, if no such idea be found in my mind, I shall have no sufficient ground of assurance of the existence of any other being besides myself; for, after a most careful search, I have, up to this moment, been unable to discover any other ground.

But, among these, my ideas, besides that which represent myself, respecting which there can be here no difficulty, there is one that represents a God; others that represent corporeal and inanimate things; others angels; others animals; and, finally, there are some that represent men like myself. But with respect to

the ideas that represent other men, or animals, or angels, I can easily suppose
that they were formed by the mingling and composition of the other ideas
which I have of myself, of corporeal things, and of God, although there were,
apart from myself, neither men, animals, nor angels. And with regard to the
ideas of corporeal objects, I never discovered in them anything so great or
excellent which I myself did not appear capable of originating; for, by considering these ideas closely and scrutinising them individually, in the same way
that I yesterday examined the idea of wax, I find that there is but little in them
that is clearly and distinctly perceived. As belonging to the class of things that
are clearly apprehended, I recognise the following, viz., magnitude or extension in length, breadth, and depth; figure, which results from the termination of
extension; situation, which bodies of diverse figures preserve with reference to
each other; and motion or the change of situation; to which may be added
substance, duration, and number. But with regard to light, colours, sounds,
odours, tastes, heat, cold, and the other tactile qualities, they are thought with
so much obscurity and confusion, that I cannot determine even whether they
are true or false; in other words, whether or not the ideas I have of these
qualities are in truth the ideas of real objects. For although I before remarked
that it is only in judgments that formal falsity, or falsity properly so called, can
be met with, there may nevertheless be found in ideas a certain material falsity,
which arises when they represent what is nothing as if it were something.
Thus, for example, the ideas I have of cold and heat are so far from being clear
and distinct, that I am unable from them to discover whether cold is only the
privation of heat, or heat the privation of cold; or whether they are not real
qualities: and since, ideas being as it were images, there can be none that does
not seem to us to represent some object, the idea which represents cold as
something real and positive will not improperly be called false, if it be correct to
say that cold is nothing but a privation of heat; and so in other cases. To ideas
of this kind, indeed, it is not necessary that I should assign any author besides
myself: for if they are false, that is, represent objects that are unreal, the natural light teaches me that they proceed from nothing; in other words, that
they are in me only because something is wanting to the perfection of my
nature; but if these ideas are true, yet because they exhibit to me so little
reality that I cannot even distinguish the object represented from non-being, I
do not see why I should not be the author of them.

With reference to those ideas of corporeal things that are clear and distinct,
there are some which, as appears to me, might have been taken from the idea I
have of myself, as those of substance, duration, number, and the like. For when
I think that a stone is a substance, or a thing capable of existing of itself, and
that I am likewise a substance, although I conceive that I am a thinking and non-
extended thing, and that the stone, on the contrary, is extended and unconscious, there being thus the greatest diversity between the two concepts—yet
these two ideas seem to have this in common that they both represent substances. In the same way, when I think of myself as now existing, and recollect
besides that I existed some time ago, and when I am conscious of various
thoughts whose number I know, I then acquire the ideas of duration and
number, which I can afterwards transfer to as many objects as I please. With
respect to the other qualities that go to make up the ideas of corporeal objects, viz., extension, figure, situation, and motion, it is true that they are not
formally in me, since I am merely a thinking being; but because they are only

certain modes of substance, and because I myself am a substance, it seems possible that they may be contained in me eminently.

There only remains, therefore, the idea of God, in which I must consider whether there is anything that cannot be supposed to originate with myself. By the name God, I understand a substance infinite, [eternal, immutable], independent, all-knowing, all-powerful, and by which I myself, and every other thing that exists, if any such there be, were created. But these properties are so great and excellent, that the more attentively I consider them the less I feel persuaded that the idea I have of them owes its origin to myself alone. And thus it is absolutely necessary to conclude, from all that I have before said, that God exists: for though the idea of substance be in my mind owing to this that I myself am a substance, I should not, however, have the idea of an infinite substance, seeing I am a finite being, unless it were given me by some substance in reality infinite.

And I must not imagine that I do not apprehend the infinite by a true idea, but only by the negation of the finite, in the same way that I comprehend repose and darkness by the negation of motion and light: since, on the contrary, I clearly perceive that there is more reality in the infinite substance than in the finite, and therefore that in some way I possess the perception (notion) of the infinite before that of the finite, that is, the perception of God before that of myself, for how could I know that I doubt, desire, or that something is wanting to me, and that I am not wholly perfect, if I possessed no idea of a being more perfect than myself, by comparison of which I knew the deficiencies of my nature?

And it cannot be said that this idea of God is perhaps materially false, and consequently that it may have arisen from nothing, [in other words, that it may exist in me from my imperfection], as I before said of the ideas of heat and cold, and the like: for, on the contrary, as this idea is very clear and distinct, and contains in itself more objective reality than any other, there can be no one of itself more true, or less open to the suspicion of falsity.

The idea, I say, of a being supremely perfect, and infinite, is in the highest degree true; for although, perhaps, we may imagine that such a being does not exist, we cannot, nevertheless, suppose that his idea represents nothing real, as I have already said of the idea of cold. It is likewise clear and distinct in the highest degree, since whatever the mind clearly and distinctly conceives as real or true, and as implying any perfection, is contained entire in this idea. And this is true, nevertheless, although I do not comprehend the infinite, and although there may be in God an infinity of things that I cannot comprehend, nor perhaps even compass by thought in any way; for it is of the nature of the infinite that it should not be comprehended by the finite; and it is enough that I rightly understand this, and judge that all which I clearly perceive, and in which I know there is some perfection, and perhaps also an infinity of properties of which I am ignorant, are formally or eminently in God, in order that the idea I have of him may become the most true, clear, and distinct of all the ideas in my mind.

But perhaps I am something more than I suppose myself to be, and it may be that all those perfections which I attribute to God, in some way exist potentially in me, although they do not yet show themselves, and are not reduced to act. Indeed, I am already conscious that my knowledge is being increased [and perfected] by degrees; and I see nothing to prevent it from thus gradually increasing to infinity, nor any reason why, after such increase and perfection, I should not be able thereby to acquire all the other perfections of the Divine nature; nor, in fine, why the power I possess of acquiring those perfections, if it really now exist in me, should not be sufficient to produce the ideas of them. Yet, on looking more closely into the matter, I discover that this cannot be; for, in the first place, although it were true that my knowledge daily acquired new degrees of perfection, and although there were potentially in my nature much that was not as yet actually in it, still all these excellences make not the slightest approach to the idea I have of the Deity, in whom there is no perfection merely potentially [but all actually] existent; for it is even an unmistakeable token of imperfection in my knowledge, that it is augmented by degrees. Further, although my knowledge increase more and more, nevertheless I am not, therefore, induced to think that it will ever be actually infinite, since it can never reach that point beyond which it shall be incapable of further increase. But I conceive God as actually infinite, so that nothing can be added to his perfection. And, in fine, I readily perceive that the objective being of an idea cannot be produced by a being that is merely potentially existent, which, properly speaking, is nothing, but only by a being existing formally or actually.

And, truly, I see nothing in all that I have now said which it is not easy for any one, who shall carefully consider it, to discern by the natural light; but when I allow my attention in some degree to relax, the vision of my mind being obscured, and, as it were, blinded by the images of sensible objects, I do not readily remember the reason why the idea of a being more perfect than myself, must of necessity have proceeded from a being in reality more perfect. On this account I am here desirous to inquire further, whether I, who possess this idea of God, could exist supposing there were no God. And I ask, from whom could I, in that case, derive my existence? Perhaps from myself, or from my parents, or from some other causes less perfect than God; for anything more perfect, or even equal to God, cannot be thought or imagined. But if I [were independent of every other existence, and] were myself the author of my being, I should doubt of nothing, I should desire nothing, and, in fine, no perfection would be awanting to me; for I should have bestowed upon myself every perfection of which I possess the idea, and I should thus be God. And it must not be imagined that what is now wanting to me is perhaps of more difficult acquisition than that of which I am already possessed; for, on the contrary, it is quite manifest that it was a matter of much higher difficulty that I, a thinking being, should arise from nothing, than it would be for me to acquire the knowledge of many things of which I am ignorant, and which are merely the accidents of a thinking substance; and certainly, if I possessed of myself the greater perfection of which I have now spoken, [in other words, if I were the author of my own existence], I would not at least have denied to myself things that may be more easily obtained, [as that infinite variety of knowledge of which I am at present destitute]. I could not, indeed, have denied to myself any property which I perceive is contained in the idea of God, because there is none of these that seems to me to be more difficult to make or acquire; and if there were any that should happen to be more difficult to acquire, they would certainly appear so to me (supposing that I myself were the source of the other things I possess), because I should discover in them a limit to my power. And though I were to suppose that I always was as I now am, I should not, on this ground, escape the force of these reasonings, since it would not follow, even on this supposition, that no author of my existence needed to be sought after. For the whole time of my life may be divided into an infinity of parts, each of which is in no way dependent on any other; and, accordingly, because I was in existence a short time ago, it does not follow that I must now exist, unless in this moment some cause create me anew as it were—that is, conserve me. In truth, it is perfectly clear and evident to all who will attentively consider the nature of duration, that the conservation of a substance, in each moment of its duration, requires the same power and act that would be necessary to create it, supposing it were not yet in existence; so that it is manifestly a dictate of the natural light that conservation and creation differ merely in respect of our mode of thinking [and not in reality]. All that is here required, therefore, is that I interrogate myself to discover whether I possess any power by means of which I can bring it about that I, who now am, shall exist a moment afterwards; for, since I am merely a thinking thing (or since, at least, the precise question, in the meantime, is only of that part of myself), if such a power resided in me, I should, without doubt, be conscious of it; but I am conscious of no such power, and thereby I manifestly know that I am dependent upon some being different from myself.

But perhaps the being upon whom I am dependent, is not God, and I have been produced either by my parents, or by some causes less perfect than Deity. This cannot be: for, as I before said, it is perfectly evident that there must at least be as much reality in the cause as in its effect; and accordingly, since I am a thinking thing, and possess in myself an idea of God, whatever in the end be the cause of my existence, it must of necessity be admitted that it is likewise a thinking being, and that it possess in itself the idea and all the perfections I attribute to Deity. Then it may again be inquired whether this cause owes its origin and existence to itself, or to some other cause. For if it be self-existent, it follows, from what I have before laid down, that this cause is God; for, since it possesses the perfection of self-existence, it must likewise, without doubt, have the power of actually possessing every perfection of which it has the idea—in other words, all the perfections I conceive to belong to God. But if it owe its existence to another cause than itself, we demand again, for a similar reason, whether this second cause exists of itself or through some other, until, from stage to stage, we at length arrive at an ultimate cause, which will be God. And it is quite manifest that in this matter there can be no infinite regress of causes, seeing that the question raised respects not so much the cause which once produced me, as that by which I am at this present moment conserved.

Nor can it be supposed that several causes concurred in my production, and that from one I received the idea of one of the perfections I attribute to Deity, and from another the idea of some other, and thus that all those perfections are indeed found somewhere in the universe, but do not all exist together in a single being who is God; for, on the contrary, the unity, the simplicity or inseparability of all the properties of Deity, is one of the chief perfections I conceive him to possess; and the idea of this unity of all the perfections of Deity could certainly not be put into my mind by any cause from which I did not likewise receive the ideas of all the other perfections; for no power could enable me to embrace them in an inseparable unity, without at the same time giving me the knowledge of what they were [and of their existence in a particular mode].

Finally, with regard to my parents [from whom it appears I sprung], although all that I believed respecting them be true, it does not, nevertheless, follow that I am conserved by them, or even that I was produced by them, in so far as I am a thinking being. All that, at the most, they contributed to my origin was the giving of certain dispositions (modifications) to the matter in which I have hitherto judged that I or my mind, which is what alone I now consider to be myself, is enclosed; and thus there can here be no difficulty with respect to them, and it is absolutely necessary to conclude from this alone that I am, and possess the idea of a being absolutely perfect, that is, of God, that his existence is most clearly demonstrated.

There remains only the inquiry as to the way in which I received this idea from God; for I have not drawn it from the senses, nor is it even presented to me unexpectedly, as is usual with the ideas of sensible objects, when these are presented or appear to be presented to the external organs of the senses; it is not even a pure production or fiction of my mind, for it is not in my power to take from or add to it; and consequently there but remains the alternative that it is innate, in the same way as is the idea of myself. And, in truth, it is not to be wondered at that God, at my creation, implanted this idea in me, that it might serve, as it were, for the mark of the workman impressed on his work; and it is not also necessary that the mark should be something different from the work itself; but considering only that God is my creator, it is highly probable that he in some way fashioned me after his own image and likeness, and that I perceive this likeness, in which is contained the idea of God, by the same faculty by which I apprehend myself—in other words, when I make myself the object of reflection, I not only find that I am an incomplete, [imperfect] and dependent being, and one who unceasingly aspires after something better and greater than he is; but, at the same time, I am assured likewise that he upon whom I am dependent possesses in himself all the goods after which I aspire, [and the ideas of which I find in my mind], and that not merely indefinitely and potentially, but infinitely and actually, and that he is thus God. And the whole force of the argument of which I have here availed myself to establish the existence of God, consists in this, that I perceive I could not possibly be of such a nature as I am, and yet have in my mind the idea of a God, if God did not in reality exist—this same God, I say, whose idea is in my mind—that is, a being who possesses all those lofty perfections, of which the mind may have some slight conception, without, however, being able fully to comprehend them—and who is wholly superior to all defect, [and has nothing that marks imperfection]: whence it is sufficiently manifest that he cannot be a deceiver, since it is a dictate of the natural light that all fraud and deception spring from some defect.

But before I examine this with more attention, and pass on to the consideration of other truths that may be evolved out of it, I think it proper to remain here for some time in the contemplation of God himself—that I may ponder at leisure his marvellous attributes—and behold, admire, and adore the beauty of this light so unspeakably great, as far, at least, as the strength of my mind, which is to some degree dazzled by the sight, will permit. For just as we learn by faith that the supreme felicity of another life consists in the contemplation of the Divine majesty alone, so even now we learn from experience that a like meditation, though incomparably less perfect, is the source of the highest satisfaction of which we are susceptible in this life.

1. TRANSITION TO THE PROOF OF GOD'S EXISTENCE

Discussing the criterion of truth, clearness, and distinctness, and considering to what it properly applies, Descartes asserts that our ideas and perceptions are not themselves true or false but only our judg-

ments, and he briefly reviews once more the reasons on which he has
judged in the past of the existence of external things. We shall return to
this topic in the next chapter for Descartes does not bring the matter to
any conclusion until he has settled a more important question, which he
thinks is prior to any unassailable belief about the material world – that
is, the existence of God.

The transition from the existence of the self to the existence of God is
made strictly in accordance with the prescribed method by deductive
steps. The argument runs as follows:

(a) I am aware that I think – the content of my thought being bewilder-
     ment because of frequent errors and doubt about the truth of my
     opinions.
(b) Therefore, I must exist – for otherwise I cannot even be deceived.
(c) I am, in consequence, a thinking being.
(d) Doubt and error are, however, defects; therefore, *qua* thinking
     thing, I am not perfect. I am limited and finite.
     i.   The idea of finitude and limitation is relative to some stand-
          ard of completeness and perfection.
     ii. A finite and imperfect being cannot be dependent only upon
          itself for its existence. If it were self-dependent and self-
          creative it would be perfect, for it could remedy its own
          defects.
(e) Therefore the *idea* of myself as a finite, imperfect, and limited being
     implies the idea of a perfect, complete, and self-dependent being.
     (This leads on to the proof of God's existence given in Meditation V,
     known as the Ontological Proof).
(f) The *existence* of a dependent, finite being implies the existence of
     a perfect and infinite God as the source and sustainer of the exist-
     ence of the dependent being. (This is the proof given in Medita-
     tion III.)

Throughout the long history of philosophy few topics have raised so
much and such sustained discussion as the validity of the proofs of
God's existence. They are usually divided into three main types:

(a) such as proceed directly from the idea of God to His existence
     (Ontological);
(b) such as proceed from the existence of the contingent to that of the
     necessary (Cosomological);
(c) such as proceed from the evidence of design in the world to the
     existence of a designer (Teleological).

Descartes does not make use of the third, but it is not unconnected with
one form of the second type, which he does use. The evidence of
design in the world is never complete, but because its very incomplete-

ness and imperfection point to a completeness and perfection, it furnishes a pretext for an argument for God's existence. Furthermore, in the world there is evidence in the realm of life and human affairs of a striving toward greater perfection — a teleological process — which can be taken as evidence of a goal or perfection toward which this striving is directed. These arguments might therefore be assimilated to the teleological and Descartes, as we shall see, frequently argues from imperfection to an ultimate standard of value or perfection.

The type of proof given in Meditation III is of the cosmological kind. The ontological argument is reserved until later.

2. DESCARTES'S FIRST PROOF OF GOD'S EXISTENCE

As we have seen, doubt and error presuppose a standard of truth. The standard offered by Descartes does not seem to require omniscience because that would involve complete freedom from all error and doubt (even suspended judgment) and from all ignorance. I may be confident about such of my ideas as are clear and distinct without omniscience. On the other hand, to be aware that I am ignorant of anything, to remain in doubt about anything, to know that I have ideas which are not clear and distinct, is to be aware of my shortcomings, and I can be so aware only if I presume some standard of perfect knowledge or omniscience with which I (openly or implicitly) compare my own. Hence, the very awareness of the imperfections of my knowledge implies the *idea* of perfect and complete truth. This is not the possession of perfect knowledge, only the presumption of the existence of a standard of perfection of which I judge myself to fall short.

We may say, then, that imperfect knowledge implies perfect knowledge. But can we go on to say that perfect knowledge implies a perfect knower? The answer will depend upon whether knowledge and knowing can legitimately be separated. Without discussing this question at length, let us consider an example. What could be meant by saying that the Pythagorean theorem in geometry would be knowledge independently of anybody's knowing it? Fermat claimed that he had a proof of the Great Theorem,[1] but he never divulged it. Nobody else has ever succeeded in finding one. Is the proof of the Great Theorem (if there is one) knowledge? We should be inclined to say no, not unless somebody knew what it was — or, at least, it would be right to say that

---

[1] If n is a natural number greater than 2, there cannot be three natural numbers such that $x^n + y^n = z^n$.

its being knowledge implies the *idea* of somebody's knowing it. Consequently, we are on safe ground if we argue that the idea of perfect
knowledge implies the idea of a perfect knower and that this is all
implicit in the awareness of the imperfection of our own knowledge.

Descartes moves from this knowledge of imperfection to the assertion
of dependence for existence on something more perfect. But he gives
the argument an interesting twist. He does not go directly from his own
existence to that of God as the source of his being, but from the existence of the idea of God in his mind (which, as we have seen, is well
established) to the existence of an adequate cause of the idea. He
argues that he could not himself be the cause of it, because the cause of
any idea must contain at least as much reality, "formally" or "eminently," as the idea itself contains "objectively."

The technical terms require explanation. What an idea contains
objectively is what it presents to the mind, what we might call its content; and "reality" is taken by Descartes to mean much the same as
perfection or completeness, what we might prefer to call "concreteness." "Objective reality" of an idea is therefore the degree of completeness or perfection of that which is presented in an idea to the
mind. "Formal reality" is the degree of completeness or perfection which
anything has in itself—what is essentially involved in its nature; and
what a thing contains "eminently" is what it has the power to produce.
Descartes argues that "it is manifest by the natural light"—that is,
self-evident—that what can produce something, X, or bring it into existence, must contain either eminently or formally at least as much reality
as X, because if it did not, something would have been produced out
of nothing. It was a long established principle of medieval philosophy
that nothing can come out of nothing—*ex nihilo nihil fit*—and Descartes
is simply restating this principle here.

The argument for God's existence, following upon this principle, is
that the idea of a Perfect Being which is in the mind in consequence of
the knowledge of one's own imperfection contains "objectively" more
reality than any imperfect being and so could not be caused or produced by anything as imperfect as the human mind. What produces it
in our minds must, therefore, be a being containing formally at least as
much perfection as the idea contains objectively.

Descartes seeks next to support this argument by reverting to its
alternative form: by asking whether he himself, an imperfect being,
could exist if God did not exist. The principle of the argument is the
same, *ex nihilo nihil fit*. Whatever exists must have some cause of
existence which is at least as real as the effect. What lacks nothing in its
own nature which is necessary to its own existence is self-existent cause

of itself (*causa sui*); but what is finite, does lack something necessary to its own existence, otherwise, as has been said, it would be capable of repairing its own deficiencies and would not be finite.[2] Consequently its existence must be referred to some extraneous cause. To be finite is precisely to be insufficient, or incomplete, in itself — to point beyond itself for completion to that which is not included in itself, but which is implied or required for self-completion. So a finite entity, so far as it is not self-sufficient, requires a cause for its existence which cannot be itself but must lie outside, or go beyond, its own limits. If this is some other finite entity, we are forced beyond that again to seek another cause, and so on, either *ad infinitum*, or until we reach a self-sufficient, self-complete, self-dependent entity which can account at once for its own existence and that of everything else. A regress *ad infinitum* leaves us with no ultimate ground for the existence of anything, so we are led to assert the existence of an absolute, or perfect, or self-complete and self-sufficient being, namely God.

In essence and foundation this argument is of the same kind as those given by St. Thomas Aquinas in the first four of his five ways of proving the existence of God.[3] Proofs of this type may be described as arguments from the finitude or contingency of things (*argumenta e contingentia mundi*) and they have been criticized (especially by Kant) as presupposing the ontological proof which we are shortly to consider. The criticism is damaging only if the critique concurrently offered against the validity of the ontological proof is sound, but that the ontological argument is implicit in other proofs we shall indeed find to be the case.

Possible objections to the argument may be considered.

a. The idea of a perfect being might be constructed simply by thinking of something more perfect than myself and then something more perfect than that and so, by extrapolation, arriving at a fictitious idea of a perfect being. Why, it might be asked, should this require the actual existence of any cause more perfect than my own mind? Descartes has dealt implicitly with this objection. In effect, it is not possible to produce the idea of a perfect being in the manner suggested, by progressively augmenting my own attributes, unless I already have ideas of the various perfections which I lack. The suggested process presupposes the idea of a standard of perfection. And the contention is that to have

---

[2] A living organism has in some measure the capacity to repair its own physical defects, but only in limited measure and only some of its deficiencies.

[3] See *Summa Theologica* I, *Quaestio* II, 10.

these perfections in idea, though I do not possess them in fact, is
evidence that I could not myself be their originating cause, because I
do not possess formally or eminently as much reality as they possess
objectively.

b. One might reach the notion of an infinite being simply as the
negative of a finite one. This Descartes also rejects, and rightly; because the negative conception here is finiteness, not its opposite. A
finite being is one which has prescribable limits and is in definite ways
restricted. These limitations and restrictions are negations of further
qualities and capacities. It is by removing the negations that we proceed to the infinite, which, as Descartes maintains, has more positive
content, not less, than the finite. Moreover the infinite is that by reference to which the limitations of the finite are recognized, for it is the
criterion of perfection. It is therefore logically prior to the finite. Accordingly Descartes claims that he possesses the notion of the infinite
before that of the finite — meaning that it is presupposed by the idea of
the finite. This is much the same sort of argument as is used by Plato to
prove that the idea of perfect equality is presupposed by our ability to
recognize equality, however approximate, in sensible objects.

c. But Descartes claims that his idea of God is "very clear and distinct" and that for this reason it cannot be a false or illusory idea. Some
might object that it is quite the contrary. Because of our finitude we
cannot form a clear and distinct idea of infinite perfection and such
vague and confused ideas of it as we do have may, on that account, be
altogether false and illusory. We must remember, however, that "clear
and distinct" does not mean well-defined and detailed; it means necessary. What Descartes is claiming then is that this idea of God, or infinite
perfection, is inescapably implied by his ideas of his own imperfect
being. It is unavoidable. He admits that God's infinite nature is not
comprehensible. He has no precise idea of what God in his complete
and detailed totality is like. But the idea of something infinite and
perfect he cannot dispense with because without it he would not be
aware of his own imperfection.

d. Descartes also rejects the possibility that the idea of God might be
a composite of ideas of various mutually independent perfections,
simply collated by the human mind. For the chief perfection of God is
unity correlating and ordering all perfections inseparably in a single
whole. Descartes states this point briefly and dogmatically, but it is a
very vital and significant truth. A mere collection of qualities or properties, however admirable singly, is strictly meaningless, for the value
or "perfection" of any quality depends upon function in some intelligible system. And this, to be intelligible, must be ordered according to

some single principle. The perfection of God is the sort of perfection requisite in a criterion or standard – something by reference to which we judge. It must, therefore, be at least intelligible (if also much more, for example, beneficent, omnipotent, and so on). To be intelligible it must be systematic and unitary and must therefore bring all its various perfections or qualities into mutual correlation and unity. This unity is its most important characteristic; and it cannot, therefore, be a mere colligation of fortuitous qualities.

e. The entire argument, however, might be denied. An objector might say that we need no idea of an infinitely perfect being in order to be and be aware of imperfection and finitude. All we need is the idea of something slightly better and somewhat more complete than ourselves and the ideas we have of other things. But this idea of something better makes exactly the demand to which Descartes is drawing attention. I can know what is better than X only if I have an idea of a best. Only if I have such an idea can I know in what direction to move in order to improve upon X. Of any two ideas, X and Y, I could not know which was better, or more complete, without some (at least implicit) conception of an ultimate criterion of goodness and completion (or perfection).[4] I may, indeed, know that 5 is more than 3 without having any idea of a greatest number or quantity, but that is only because I have an idea of progression or generation in the number series – strictly the idea of number (or quantity) as such – and this is no specific number (or quantity) and cannot itself be augmented, for it is itself complete and adequate (like a Platonic idea). So even a notion of augmentation of value or excellence implies an idea of value or excellence, as such, which is another way of indicating an idea of perfection, what Plato would have called the Idea of the Good.

Descartes's conclusion, therefore, seems well-founded that this idea of perfect being is one that we simply cannot dispense with, and one that is logically prior to all finite and imperfect ideas. This truth we shall find intimately involved in the forthcoming ontological argument for God's existence.

---

[4]Strictly the two words mean the same: *perficere* = to make thoroughly (or completely).

CHAPTER 12

JUDGMENT AND WILL

MEDITATION IV: OF TRUTH AND ERROR

I have been habituated these bygone days to detach my mind from the senses, and I have accurately observed that there is exceedingly little which is known with certainty respecting corporeal objects—that we know much more of the human mind, and still more of God himself. I am thus able now without difficulty to abstract my mind from the contemplation of [sensible or] imaginable objects, and apply it to those which, as disengaged from all matter, are purely intelligible. And certainly the idea I have of the human mind in so far as it is a thinking thing, and not extended in length, breadth, and depth, and participating in none of the properties of body, is incomparably more distinct than the idea of any corporeal object; and when I consider that I doubt, in other words, that I am an incomplete and dependent being, the idea of a complete and independent being, that is to say of God, occurs to my mind with so much clearness and distinctness —and from the fact alone that this idea is found in me, or that I who possess it exist, the conclusions that God exists, and that my own existence, each moment of its continuance, is absolutely dependent upon him, are so manifest—as to lead me to believe it impossible that the human mind can know anything with more clearness and certitude. And now I seem to discover a path that will conduct us from the contemplation of the true God, in whom are contained all the treasures of science and wisdom, to the knowledge of the other things in the universe.

176

For, in the first place, I discover that it is impossible for him ever to deceive me, for in all fraud and deceit there is a certain imperfection: and although it may seem that the ability to deceive is a mark of subtlety or power, yet the will testifies without doubt of malice and weakness; and such, accordingly, cannot be found in God. In the next place, I am conscious that I possess a certain faculty of judging [or discerning truth from error], which I doubtless received from God, along with whatever else is mine; and since it is impossible that he should will to deceive me, it is likewise certain that he has not given me a faculty that will ever lead me into error, provided I use it aright.

And there would remain no doubt on this head, did it not seem to follow from this, that I can never therefore be deceived; for if all I possess be from God, and if he planted in me no faculty that is deceitful, it seems to follow that I can never fall into error. Accordingly, it is true that when I think only of God (when I look upon myself as coming from God, Fr.), and turn wholly to him, I discover [in myself] no cause of error or falsity: but immediately thereafter, recurring to myself, experience assures me that I am nevertheless subject to innumerable errors. When I come to inquire into the cause of these, I observe that there is not only present to my consciousness a real and positive idea of God, or of a being supremely perfect, but also, so to speak, a certain negative idea of nothing — in other words, of that which is at an infinite distance from every sort of perfection, and that I am, as it were, a mean between God and nothing, or placed in such a way between absolute existence and non-existence, that there is in truth nothing in me to lead me into error, in so far as an absolute being is my creator; but that, on the other hand, as I thus likewise participate in some degree of nothing or of non-being, in other words, as I am not myself the supreme Being, and as I am wanting in many perfections, it is not surprising I should fall into error. And I hence discern that error, so far as error, is not something real, which depends for its existence on God, but is simply defect; and therefore that, in order to fall into it, it is not necessary God should have given me a faculty expressly for this end, but that my being deceived arises from the circumstance that the power which God has given me of discerning truth from error is not infinite.

Nevertheless this is not yet quite satisfactory; for error is not a pure negation, [in other words, it is not the simple deficiency or want of some knowledge which is not due], but the privation or want of some knowledge which it would seem I ought to possess. But, on considering the nature of God, it seems impossible that he should have planted in his creature any faculty not perfect in its kind, that is, wanting in some perfection due to it: for if it be true, that in proportion to the skill of the maker the perfection of his work is greater, what thing can have been produced by the supreme Creator of the universe that is not absolutely perfect in all its parts? And assuredly there is no doubt that God could have created me such as that I should never be deceived; it is certain, likewise, that he always wills what is best; is it better, then, that I should be capable of being deceived than that I should not?

Considering this more attentively, the first thing that occurs to me is the reflection that I must not be surprised if I am not always capable of comprehending the reasons why God acts as he does; nor must I doubt of his existence because I find, perhaps, that there are several other things besides the present respecting which I understand neither why nor how they were created by him; for, knowing already that my nature is extremely weak and limited, and that the nature of God, on the other hand, is immense, incomprehensible, and infinite, I have no longer any difficulty in discerning that there is an infinity of things in his power whose causes transcend the grasp of my mind: and this consideration alone is sufficient to convince me, that the whole class of final causes is of no avail in physical [or natural] things; for it appears to me that I cannot, without exposing myself to the charge of temerity, seek to discover the [impenetrable] ends of Deity.

It further occurs to me that we must not consider only one creature apart from the others, if we wish to determine the perfection of the works of Deity, but generally all his creatures together; for the same object that might perhaps, with some show of reason, be deemed highly imperfect if it were alone in the world, may for all that be the most perfect possible, considered as forming part of the whole universe: and although, as it was my purpose to doubt of everything, I only as yet know with certainty my own existence and that of God, nevertheless, after having remarked the infinite power of Deity, I cannot deny that he may have produced many other objects, or at least that he is able to produce them, so that I may occupy a place in the relation of a part to the great whole of his creatures.

Whereupon, regarding myself more closely, and considering what my errors are (which alone testify to the existence of imperfection in me), I observe that these depend on the concurrence of two causes, viz., the faculty of cognition which I possess, and that of election or the power of free choice – in other words, the understanding and the will. For by the understanding alone, I [neither affirm nor deny anything, but] merely apprehend (*percipio*) the ideas regarding which I may form a judgment; nor is any error, properly so called, found in it thus accurately taken. And although there are perhaps innumerable objects in the world of which I have no idea in my understanding, it cannot, on that account, be said that I am deprived of those ideas [as of something that is due to my nature], but simply that I do not possess them, because, in truth, there is no ground to prove that Deity ought to have endowed me with a larger faculty of cognition than he has actually bestowed upon me; and however skilful a workman I suppose him to be, I have no reason, on that account, to think that it was obligatory on him to give to each of his works all the perfections he is able to bestow upon some. Nor, moreover, can I complain that God has not given me freedom of choice, or a will sufficiently ample and perfect, since, in truth, I am conscious of will so ample and extended as to be superior to all limits. And what appears to me here to be highly remarkable is that, of all the other properties I possess, there is none so great and perfect as that I do not clearly discern it could be still greater and more perfect. For, to take an example, if I consider the faculty of understanding which I possess, I find that it is of very small extent, and greatly limited, and at the same time I form the idea of another faculty of the same nature, much more ample and even infinite; and seeing that I can frame the idea of it, I discover, from this circumstance alone, that it pertains to the nature of God. In the same way, if I examine the faculty of memory or imagination, or any other faculty I possess, I find none that is not small and circumscribed, and in God immense [and infinite]. It is the faculty of will only, or freedom of choice, which I experience to be so great that I am unable to conceive the idea of another that shall be more ample and extended; so that it is chiefly my will which leads me to discern that I bear a certain image and similitude of Deity.

For although the faculty of will is incomparably greater in God than in myself, as well in respect of the knowledge and power that are conjoined with it, and that render it stronger and more efficacious, as in respect of the object, since in him it extends to a greater number of things, it does not, nevertheless, appear to me greater, considered in itself formally and precisely: for the power of will consists only in this, that we are able to do or not to do the same thing (that is, to affirm or deny, to pursue or shun it), or rather in this alone, that in affirming or denying, pursuing or shunning, what is proposed to us by the understanding, we so act that we are not conscious of being determined to a particular action by any external force. For, to the possession of freedom, it is not necessary that I be alike indifferent towards each of two contraries; but, on the contrary, the more I am inclined towards the one, whether because I clearly know that in it there is the reason of truth and goodness, or because God thus internally disposes my thought, the more freely do I choose and embrace it; and assuredly divine grace and natural knowledge, very far from diminishing liberty, rather augment and fortify it. But the indifference of which I am conscious when I am not impelled to one side rather than to another for want of a reason, is the lowest grade of liberty, and manifests defect or negation of knowledge rather than perfection of will; for if I always clearly knew what was true and good, I should never have any difficulty in determining what judgment I ought to come to, and what choice I ought to make, and I should thus be entirely free without ever being indifferent.

From all this I discover, however, that neither the power of willing, which I have received from God, is of itself the source of my errors, for it is exceedingly ample and perfect in its kind; nor even the power of understanding, for as I conceive no object unless by means of the faculty that God bestowed upon me, all that I conceive is doubtless rightly conceived by me, and it is impossible for me to be deceived in it.

Whence, then, spring my errors? They arise from this cause alone, that I do not restrain the will, which is of much wider range than the understanding, within the same limits, but extend it even to things I do not understand, and as the will is of itself indifferent to such, it readily falls into error and sin by choosing the false in room of the true, and evil instead of good.

For example, when I lately considered whether aught really existed in the world, and found that because I considered this question, it very manifestly followed that I myself existed, I could not but judge that what I so clearly conceived was true, not that I was forced to this judgment by any external cause, but simply because great clearness of the understanding was succeeded by strong inclination in the will; and I believed this the more freely and spontaneously in proportion as I was less indifferent with respect to it. But now I not only know that I exist, in so far as I am a thinking being, but there is likewise presented to my mind a certain idea of corporeal nature; hence I am in doubt as to whether the thinking nature which is in me, or rather which I myself am, is different from that corporeal nature, or whether both are merely one and the same thing, and I here suppose that I am as yet ignorant of any reason that would determine me to adopt the one belief in preference to the other: whence it happens that it is a matter of perfect indifference to me which of the two suppositions I affirm or deny, or whether I form any judgment at all in the matter.

This indifference, moreover, extends not only to things of which the understanding has no knowledge at all, but in general also to all those which it does not discover with perfect clearness at the moment the will is deliberating upon them; for, however probable the conjectures may be that dispose me to form a judgment in a particular matter, the simple knowledge that these are merely conjectures, and not certain and indubitable reasons, is sufficient to lead me to form one that is directly the opposite. Of this I lately had abundant experience, when I laid aside as false all that I had before held for true, on the single ground that I could in some degree doubt of it. But if I abstain from judging of a thing when I do not conceive it with sufficient clearness and distinctness, it is plain that I act rightly, and am not deceived; but if I resolve to deny or affirm, I then do not make a right use of my free will; and if I affirm what is false, it is evident that I am deceived: moreover, even although I judge according to truth, I stumble upon it by chance, and do not therefore escape the imputation of a wrong use of my freedom; for it is a dictate of the natural light, that the knowledge of the understanding ought always to precede the determination of the will.

And it is this wrong use of the freedom of the will in which is found the privation that constitutes the form of error. Privation, I say, is found in the act, in so far as it proceeds from myself, but it does not exist in the faculty which I received from God, nor even in the act, in so far as it depends on him; for I have assuredly no reason to complain that God has not given me a greater power of intelligence or more perfect natural light than he has actually bestowed, since it is of the nature of a finite understanding not to comprehend many things, and of the nature of a created understanding to be finite; on the contrary, I have every reason to render thanks to God, who owed me nothing, for having given me all the perfections I possess, and I should be far from thinking that he has unjustly deprived me of, or kept back, the other perfections which he has not bestowed upon me.

I have no reason, moreover, to complain because he has given me a will more ample than my understanding, since, as the will consists only of a single element, and that indivisible, it would appear that this faculty is of such a nature that nothing could be taken from it [without destroying it]; and certainly, the more extensive it is, the more cause I have to thank the goodness of him who bestowed it upon me.

And, finally, I ought not also to complain that God concurs with me in forming the acts of this will, or the judgments in which I am deceived, because those acts are wholly true and good, in so far as they depend on God; and the ability to form them is a higher degree of perfection in my nature than the want of it would be. With regard to privation, in which alone consists the formal reason of error and sin, this does not require the concurrence of Deity, because it is not a thing [or existence], and if it be referred to God as to its cause, it ought not to be called privation, but negation, [according to the signification of these words in the schools]. For in truth it is no imperfection in Deity that he has accorded to me the power of giving or withholding my assent from certain things of which he has not put a clear and distinct knowledge in my understanding; but it is doubtless an imperfection in me that I do not use my freedom aright, and readily give my judgment on matters which I only obscurely and confusedly conceive.

I perceive, nevertheless, that it was easy for Deity so to have constituted me as that I should never be deceived, although I still remained free and possessed of a limited knowledge, viz., by implanting in my understanding a clear and dis-

tinct knowledge of all the objects respecting which I should ever have to deliberate; or simply by so deeply engraving on my memory the resolution to judge
of nothing without previously possessing a clear and distinct conception of it,
that I should never forget it. And I easily understand that, in so far as I consider
myself as a single whole, without reference to any other being in the universe,
I should have been much more perfect than I now am, had Deity created me
superior to error; but I cannot therefore deny that it is not somehow a greater
perfection in the universe, that certain of its parts are not exempt from defect,
as others are, than if they were all perfectly alike.

And I have no right to complain because God, who placed me in the world,
was not willing that I should sustain that character which of all others is the chief
and most perfect; I have even good reason to remain satisfied on the ground
that, if he has not given me the perfection of being superior to error by the first
means I have pointed out above, which depends on a clear and evident knowledge of all the matters regarding which I can deliberate, he has at least left in my
power the other means, which is, firmly to retain the resolution never to judge
where the truth is not clearly known to me: for, although I am conscious of the
weakness of not being able to keep my mind continually fixed on the same
thought, I can nevertheless, by attentive and oft-repeated meditation, impress
it so strongly on my memory that I shall never fail to recollect it as often as I
require it, and I can acquire in this way the habitude of not erring; and since it is
in the being superior to error that the highest and chief perfection of man consists, I deem that I have not gained little by this day's meditation, in having discovered the source of error and falsity.

And certainly this can be no other than what I have now explained: for as
often as I so restrain my will within the limits of my knowledge, that it forms no
judgment except regarding objects which are clearly and distinctly represented
to it by the understanding, I can never be deceived; because every clear and
distinct conception is doubtless something, and as such cannot owe its origin to
nothing, but must of necessity have God for its author — God, I say, who, as supremely perfect, cannot, without a contradiction, be the cause of any error;
and consequently it is necessary to conclude that every such conception [or
judgment] is true. Nor have I merely learned to-day what I must avoid to escape
error, but also what I must do to arrive at the knowledge of truth; for I will
assuredly reach truth if I only fix my attention sufficiently on all the things I
conceive perfectly, and separate these from others which I conceive more confusedly and obscurely: to which for the future I shall give diligent heed.

1. THE SOURCE OF ERROR

Once the existence of God has been established, Descartes moves on
to the assertion that it is impossible for a perfect being to deceive His
own creature or to make anything defective, for to do either would be a
mark of imperfection. Accordingly, we may be confident that whatever
we clearly and distinctly perceive is true. As we shall see later, this
move is important for the proof of the existence of material things, but

it sets Descartes the immediate problem of explaining the existence of that very finite and imperfect character in himself which led him to the idea of God. What a perfect creator makes ought to be faultless, but faultless entities are themselves perfect and so would either reduplicate or be identical with God himself. It is not difficult to see that two absolutely perfect beings cannot exist, because either they would have different powers and properties, each lacking what the other possessed, in which case neither would be complete and perfect in itself; or each would have exactly the same powers and properties so that they would be indistinguishable and would coincide. God's creatures must therefore, to exist at all, be finite, yet if so, how can God be a perfect creator?

Descartes answers by saying that, subject to our limitations (and consequent inability to comprehend God's immensity and inscrutable purposes), we must realize that God's creation constitutes one single whole, the perfection of which, as a whole, nevertheless permits of finiteness in the parts (for, after all, they are only parts). In fact, defects in the parts may even be a condition of the greater perfection of the whole.

Secondly, even the deficiencies in man may not be imputed to God's workmanship. There are two kinds of defect: (a) the deprivation of something properly belonging to one's nature and (b) the lack of attributes which are no proper part of one's own nature but lie beyond its limits. The latter Descartes calls "negation," as distinct from "privation," which is the former.

Now God has given man an intellect which is perfect in its kind, because intuition can never err. In apprehending what is clear and distinct it knows with certainty. So, says Descartes, as long as the intellect is rightly used it cannot fall into error, and it is rightly used if only what is clear and distinct is asserted. The intellect, therefore, suffers no privation. It is not however conversant with all truth and is often presented with matters which are not clear and distinct; thus it is limited and subject to negation, but this is not necessarily an imperfection in God's creation as a whole.

How then do errors ever arise? Only judgment is subject to error, as we have seen, not mere perception. But judgment, Descartes alleges, is an act of will — of giving assent. Our will, moreover, is also perfect as a faculty, its perfection consisting in its complete freedom. Further, it is unlimited, ranging wherever it will. Thus the will is larger in scope than the intellect and we are able to give assent to much that is not clear and distinct to our intellect. When we do this we fall into error — not through any fault of God's creation, which is perfect both in intellectual insight and in the freedom and limitless scope of its will, but through our own fault in judging when we ought to suspend judgment.

2. IS DESCARTES GUILTY OF CIRCULAR ARGUMENT?

There is more in this argument than we can properly undertake to discuss here. First, critics have accused Descartes of introducing circularity into his argument by claiming that because God's perfection precludes His being a deceiver we may be certain of all that is clear and distinct. For, if the foundation of certainty is God's veracity (and Descartes frequently speaks in this way), then the proof of God's existence itself must depend on God's goodness and truthfulness. But our knowledge of God's existence must be prior to our confidence in His truthfulness (for if He did not exist, we should have nothing in which to be confident). We cannot make the proof of God's existence depend on our reliance upon God's veracity.

But this criticism is not fairly applicable to Descartes. He does not really claim that the truth of clear and distinct ideas depends on God's veracity. The clarity and distinctness is the very mark of truth. What he claims is that because God is perfect he gave man a faultless intelligence capable of infallibility in that what it clearly and distinctly intuits is indubitably true. The fact that we have this natural light is the result of God's goodness, not the truth of what it reveals, which shines by its own illumination. God's existence, therefore, as established by the proofs, is knowable, because clear and distinct, independently and prior to our knowing that He does not deceive us—though this also follows from His nature.

Descartes, however, is himself responsible for the confusion; for he introduced at the start the hypothesis of the evil genius who might deceive him even when he was most convinced that he was right (for example, in mathematics). Might not this evil genius deceive one into believing something to be clear and distinct which was actually false? If so, it would seem, an appeal to God's veracity might be needed to remove this hazard. Yet how could it, unless we assume also that God's goodness must necessarily protect us from evil demons who might make us believe that He existed though there were no God? Any such assumption would obviously be circular and fallacious.

However, Descartes is not really in this dilemma. His earlier argument about the evil genius is intended merely to emphasize that, even in mathematics we can be wrong though we believe ourselves to be right, and that if this is possible at all it might be possible always. But that is when, and because, we do not know the criterion of truth. Once we have discovered an indubitable truth and find its indubitability to lie in its clarity and distinctness, we know without fail that what is clear and distinct is true, and can then defy the evil demon; and we discover it when we see that no evil demon can possibly deceive us about our own existence.

The veracity of God is needed for the proof of the existence of material things in Meditation VI, and there no circular argument is involved.

3. THE RELATION OF INTELLECT AND WILL

The next question is whether the intellect is as indifferent to affirmation in judgment as Descartes seems to imply, and if this latter can properly be regarded as an act of will.

Descartes is here relying on a sort of "faculty" psychology which has long passed out of date. Even so, his own doctrine militates against his separation of affirmation, or assent, from the understanding. If I understand the meaning of *cogito ergo sum* I must assent to it. What is self-evidently true cannot be significantly denied. But it is the intellect that apprehends the logical nexus and it is to the intellect that the truth is evident. What need, then, is there of the will to affirm what is already seen to be true? This is not to say, however, that thinking is passive reception of self-evident data. It is an activity—for the most part the very activity of affirming and denying that Descartes attributes to the will.

The product of confused thinking is just as much a matter of affirming and denying as are clear and distinct ideas. That a sensed color patch is the surface of a material object is not a self-evident truth, but no color patch is ever barely sensed; it is always perceived as something; that is, the seeing is itself at least an inchoate judgment. To exclaim "How hot!" is at once to feel and to judge. How can we distinguish here between understanding (or sense) and will?

What then is the function of the will, even if, like Descartes, we speak in terms of faculties? It is, surely, to make decisions. But, blind impulse apart, we cannot make a decision except on the basis of some judgment. If I decide to assert that all men are mortal it can only be because I have judged it to be the case, just as I must have made a number of pertinent judgments before I decide to cross a busy street. The decision simply is the issue of the complex judgment. Will and intellect are not two faculties but two aspects of a complex mental activity.

4. THE FREEDOM OF THE WILL

Descartes does not question the freedom of the will or discuss it as in any way problematical, though his immediate successor, Spinoza, denies it altogether. In view of the mechanistic view taken by Descartes of the body and its action his belief in freedom might be more surprising than Spinoza's denial of it. Descartes, however, separated the soul completely from the body and attributed will to the former, and Spinoza, having denied freedom in one sense proceeds to reintroduce it at a later stage of his argument in a somewhat different sense, making it dependent upon intelligence, or adequate ideas.

More recent discussions of freedom have arisen from the causal influences on human action alleged by the sciences of physiology and psychology, more in reference to ethics than to epistemology. For we ask whether people should, or can, be held morally responsible for their actions unless they are free to choose. Interesting and important as the topic is, we cannot enter into a full discussion of it here, but a few remarks may be made.

First, it is difficult to make sense of the idea of a principle of action which is in no way influenced or determined by anything whatsoever, for how then could it act at all? How could I decide to cross a street if nothing influenced me — not a desire to get to the other side, nor a lull in the traffic, nor someone beckoning to me to cross, nor anything else?

A principle which acted in disregard of all influences, relevant or irrelevant, would not be so much free as fortuitous — a mere chance occurrence acting on no principle whatever. No such principle could support or account for human moral responsibility.

Secondly, deliberate human action, which is the sort we are concerned with in morals, and which Descartes is also concerned with in judgment, requires the activity at once of both intellect and will, and is more responsible the more it is subject to rational direction. It would be a truer description of it to reverse Descartes's order and to say that will is the enactment of an intellectual decision or judgment rather than an affirmation of what the intellect may or may not approve. Will is rather reason in action. Moreover, what we hail as its freedom is the degree of its adherence to rational judgment. Descartes recognizes this when he says:

> For to the possession of freedom, it is not necessary that I be alike indifferent toward each of two contraries; but, on the contrary, the more I am inclined toward the one, whether because I clearly know that in it there is the reason of truth and goodness, or because God thus internally disposes my thought, the more freely do I choose and embrace it; and assuredly divine grace and natural knowledge, very far from diminishing liberty, rather augment and fortify it.

Properly speaking, what is free in the last resort is the intellect and the so-called freedom of the will is derived from it (so far as will is just intelligence in action). Judgment must be free if there is to be any such thing as true judgment, for truth and falsity do not apply to movements, or events, merely mechanically determined. The movements of a clock are not true or false, only the interpretation *we* give to the position of its hands as indicating time, and that is judgment. If our own judgment were similarly determined, to call it true or false would be nonsense, even if what the judgment stated agreed or coincided with some factual state of affairs in the world.

First, it is not the marks on paper or the noises made when a person talks that are the judgment, but the meaning given to them; and it is only this meaning that can be said to correspond with some factual state of affairs. But the meaning is nothing more nor less than an intellectual grasp of the *fact that* the state of affairs is such and such — it is the awareness of the state of affairs itself. If this were something mechanical like the movement of the clock hands, it would not be a judgment but just another state of affairs requiring interpretation before it could be said to agree, correspond, or coincide with anything else. Even if we think of it as an image or picture this would be so, for no image or picture is a likeness to anything except when *recognized* as such.

Further, if it is said that our judgments are physiologically and psychologically determined, meaning that they are the product of our innate dispositions, our glandular secretions, and the like, then again to say that they are true or false is meaningless. No glandular secretion, nor any of its consequences, can sensibly be said to be either. Likewise, if they are the product of subconscious, repressed, emotional urges, they are only effects of causes, not judgments properly speaking at all. But suppose that this were the case and what we take for judgment and think to be true (or otherwise) is only a blind event caused by other blind events. Then, first, it would be a contradiction to say that we *take* such events for judgments and *think* them to be true, for that taking and thinking would be judging (even though false). And, secondly, it would have to be true of all so-called judgments, including the physiological and psychological theories on the basis of which we say that judgments are merely determined events. So that these theories themselves, and the denial of freedom they prompt, would not be judgments and would have no truth value. In short, judgment must be free; to judge otherwise is to contradict oneself. And the will is free so far as it follows judgment, or is judgment in action.

But this is a digression from our discussion of Descartes, to which we must return.

CHAPTER 13

The Ontological Argument

MEDITATION V: OF THE ESSENCE OF MATERIAL THINGS;
AND, AGAIN, OF GOD; THAT HE EXISTS

Several other questions remain for consideration respecting the attributes of God and my own nature or mind. I will, however, on some other occasion perhaps resume the investigation of these. Meanwhile, as I have discovered what must be done and what avoided to arrive at the knowledge of truth, what I have chiefly to do is to essay to emerge from the state of doubt in which I have for some time been, and to discover whether anything can be known with certainty regarding material objects. But before considering whether such objects as I conceive exist without me, I must examine their ideas in so far as these are to be found in my consciousness, and discover which of them are distinct and which confused.

In the first place, I distinctly imagine that quantity which the philosophers commonly call continuous, or the extension in length, breadth, and depth that is in this quantity, or rather in the object to which it is attributed. Further, I can enumerate in it many diverse parts, and attribute to each of these all sorts of sizes, figures, situations, and local motions; and, in fine, I can assign to each of these motions all degrees of duration. And I not only distinctly know these things when I thus consider them in general; but besides, by a little attention, I discover innumerable particulars respecting figures, numbers, motion, and the like, which are so evidently true, and so accordant with my nature, that when I now discover them I do not so much appear to learn anything new, as to call to remembrance what I before knew, or for the first time to remark what was before in my mind, but to which I had not hitherto directed my attention. And what I here find of most importance is, that I discover in my mind innumerable ideas of certain objects, which cannot be esteemed pure negations, although perhaps they possess no reality beyond my thought, and which are not framed by me though it may be in my power to think, or not to think them, but possess true and immutable natures of their own. As, for example, when I imagine a triangle, although there is not perhaps and never was in any place in the universe apart from my thought one such figure, it remains true nevertheless that this figure possesses a certain determinate nature, form, or essence, which is immutable and eternal, and not framed by me, nor in any degree dependent on my thought; as appears from the circumstance, that diverse properties of the triangle may be demonstrated, viz., that its three angles are equal to two right, that its greatest side is subtended by its greatest angle, and the like, which, whether I will or not, I now clearly discern to belong to it, although before I did not at all think of them, when, for the first time, I imagined a triangle, and which accordingly cannot be said to have been invented by me. Nor is it a valid objection to allege, that perhaps this idea of a triangle came into my mind by the medium of the senses, through my having seen bodies of a triangular figure; for I am able to form in thought an innumerable variety of figures with regard to which it cannot be supposed that they were ever objects of sense, and I can nevertheless demonstrate diverse properties of their nature no less than of the triangle, all of which are assuredly true since I clearly conceive them: and they are therefore something, and not mere negations; for it is highly evident that all that is true is something, [truth being identical with existence]; and I have already fully shown the truth of the principle, that whatever is clearly and distinctly known is true. And although this had not been demonstrated, yet the nature of my mind is such as to compel me to assent to what I clearly conceive while I so conceive it; and I recollect that even when I still strongly adhered to the objects of sense, I reckoned among the number of the most certain truths those I clearly conceived relating to figures, numbers, and other matters that pertain to arithmetic and geometry, and in general to the pure mathematics.

But now if because I can draw from my thought the idea of an object, it follows that all I clearly and distinctly apprehend to pertain to this object, does in truth belong to it, may I not from this derive an argument for the existence of God? It is certain that I no less find the idea of a God in my consciousness, that is, the idea of a being supremely perfect, than that of any figure or number whatever: and I know with not less clearness and distinctness that an [actual and] eternal existence pertains to his nature than that all which is demonstrable of any figure or number really belongs to the nature of that figure or number; and, therefore, although all the conclusions of the preceding Meditations were false, the existence of God would pass with me for a truth at least as certain as I ever judged any truth of mathematics to be, although indeed such a doctrine may at first sight appear to contain more sophistry than truth. For, as I have been accustomed in every other matter to distinguish between existence and essence, I easily believe that the existence can be separated from the essence of God, and that thus God may be conceived as not actually existing. But, nevertheless, when I think of it more attentively, it appears that the existence can no more be separated from the essence of God, than the idea of a mountain from that of a valley, or the equality of its three angles to two right angles, from the essence of a [rectilineal] triangle; so that it is not less impossible to conceive a God, that is, a being supremely perfect, to whom existence is awanting, or who is devoid of a certain perfection, than to conceive a mountain without a valley.

But though, in truth, I cannot conceive a God unless as existing, any more than I can a mountain without a valley, yet, just as it does not follow that there is any mountain in the world merely because I conceive a mountain with a valley, so likewise, though I conceive God as existing, it does not seem to follow on that account that God exists; for my thought imposes no necessity on things; and as I may imagine a winged horse, though there be none such, so I could perhaps attribute existence to God, though no God existed. But the cases are not analogous, and a fallacy lurks under the semblance of this objection: for because I cannot conceive a mountain without a valley, it does not follow that there is any mountain or valley in existence, but simply that the mountain or valley, whether they do or do not exist, are inseparable from each other; whereas, on the other hand, because I cannot conceive God unless as existing, it follows that existence is inseparable from him, and therefore that he really exists: not that this is brought about by my thought, or that it imposes any necessity on things, but, on the contrary, the necessity which lies in the thing itself, that is, the necessity of the existence of God, determines me to think in this way: for it is not in my power to conceive a God without existence, that is, a being supremely perfect, and yet devoid of an absolute perfection, as I am free to imagine a horse with or without wings.

Nor must it be alleged here as an objection, that it is in truth necessary to admit that God exists, after having supposed him to possess all perfections, since existence is one of them, but that my original supposition was not necessary; just as it is not necessary to think that all quadrilateral figures can be inscribed in the circle, since, if I supposed this, I should be constrained to admit that the rhombus, being a figure of four sides, can be therein inscribed, which, however, is manifestly false. This objection is, I say, incompetent; for although it may not be necessary that I shall at any time entertain the notion of Deity, yet each time I happen to think of a first and sovereign being, and to draw, so to speak, the idea of him from the storehouse of the mind, I am necessitated to attribute to him all kinds of perfections, though I may not then enumerate them all, nor think of each of them in particular. And this necessity is sufficient, as soon as I discover that existence is a perfection, to cause me to infer the existence of this first and sovereign being: just as it is not necessary that I should ever imagine any triangle, but whenever I am desirous of considering a rectilineal figure composed of only three angles, it is absolutely necessary to attribute those properties to it from which it is correctly inferred that its three angles are not greater than two right angles, although perhaps I may not then advert to this relation in particular. But when I consider what figures are capable of being inscribed in the circle, it is by no means necessary to hold that all quadrilateral figures are of this number; on the contrary, I cannot even imagine such to be the case, so long as I shall be unwilling to accept in thought aught that I do not clearly and distinctly conceive: and consequently there is a vast difference between false suppositions, as is the one in question, and the true ideas that were born with me, the first and chief of which is the idea of God.

For indeed I discern on many grounds that this idea is not factitious, depending simply on my thought, but that it is the representation of a true and immutable nature: in the first place, because I can conceive no other being, except God, to whose essence existence necessarily. pertains; in the second, because it is impossible to conceive two or more Gods of this kind; and it being supposed that one such God exists, I clearly see that he must have existed from all eternity, and will exist to all eternity; and finally, because I apprehend many other properties in God, none of which I can either diminish or change.

But, indeed, whatever mode of probation I in the end adopt, it always returns to this, that it is only the things I clearly and distinctly conceive which have the power of completely persuading me. And although, of the objects I conceive in this manner, some, indeed, are obvious to every one, while others are only discovered after close and careful investigation; nevertheless, after they are once discovered, the latter are not esteemed less certain than the former. Thus, for example, to take the case of a right-angled triangle, although it is not so manifest at first that the square of the base is equal to the squares of the other two sides, as that the base is opposite to the greatest angle; nevertheless, after it is once apprehended, we are as firmly persuaded of the truth of the former as of the latter. And, with respect to God, if I were not pre-occupied by prejudices, and my thought beset on all sides by the continual presence of the images of sensible objects, I should know nothing sooner or more easily than the fact of his being. For is there any truth more clear than the existence of a Supreme Being, or of God, seeing it is to his essence alone that necessary and eternal. existence pertains? And although the right conception of this truth has cost me much close thinking, nevertheless at present I feel not only as assured of it as of what I deem most certain, but I remark further that the certitude of all other truths is so absolutely dependent on it, that without this knowledge it is impossible ever to know anything perfectly.

For although I am of such a nature as to be unable, while I possess a very clear and distinct apprehension of a matter, to resist the conviction of its truth, yet because my constitution is also such as to incapacitate me from keeping my mind continually fixed on the same object, and as I frequently recollect a past judgment without at the same time being able to recall the grounds of it, it may happen meanwhile that other reasons are presented to me which would readily cause me to change my opinion, if I did not know that God existed; and thus I should possess no true and certain knowledge, but merely vague and vacillating opinions. Thus, for example, when I consider the nature of the [rectilineal] triangle, it most clearly appears to me, who have been instructed in the principles of geometry, that its three angles are equal to two right angles, and I find it impossible to believe otherwise, while I apply my mind to the demonstration; but as soon as I cease from attending to the process of proof, although I still remember that I had a clear comprehension of it, yet I may readily come to doubt of the truth demonstrated, if I do not know that there is a God: for I may persuade myself that I have been so constituted by nature as to be sometimes deceived, even in matters which I think I apprehend with the greatest evidence and certitude, especially when I recollect that I frequently considered many things to be true and certain which other reasons afterwards constrained me to reckon as wholly false.

But after I have discovered that God exists, seeing I also at the same time observed that all things depend on him, and that he is no deceiver, and thence inferred that all which I clearly and distinctly perceive is of necessity true: although I no longer attend to the grounds of a judgment, no opposite reason can be alleged sufficient to lead me to doubt of its truth, provided only I remember that I once possessed a clear and distinct comprehension of it. My knowledge of it thus becomes true and certain. And this same knowledge extends likewise to whatever I remember to have formerly demonstrated, as the truths of geometry and the like: for what can be alleged against them to lead me to doubt of them? Will it be that my nature is such that I may be frequently deceived? But I already know that I cannot be deceived in judgments of the grounds of which I possess a clear knowledge. Will it be that I formerly deemed things to be true and certain which I afterwards discovered to be false? But I had no clear and distinct knowledge of any of those things, and, being as yet ignorant of the rule by which I am assured of the truth of a judgment, I was led to give my assent to them on grounds which I afterwards discovered were less strong than at the time I imagined them to be. What further objection, then, is there? Will it be said that perhaps I am dreaming (an objection I lately myself raised), or that all the thoughts of which I am now conscious have no more truth than the reveries of my dreams? But although, in truth, I should be dreaming, the rule still holds that all which is clearly presented to my intellect is indisputably true.

And thus I very clearly see that the certitude and truth of all science depends on the knowledge alone of the true God, insomuch that, before I knew him, I could have no perfect knowledge of any other thing. And now that I know him, I possess the means of acquiring a perfect knowledge respecting innumerable matters, as well relative to God himself and other intellectual objects as to corporeal nature, in so far as it is the object of pure mathematics [which do not consider whether it exists or not].

1. DESCARTES'S VERSION OF THE ARGUMENT

The second argument for God's existence is set out in full in Meditation V, though a very brief statement of the central nexus is also given in the *Discourse*.

The argument in the Meditation may be summarized as follows: Just as in my mind I have ideas of geometrical figures and numbers (many of which I could not possibly have acquired through sense—for instance, a chiliogon), and to which I clearly and distinctly perceive certain properties necessarily to pertain, so also I have in my mind an idea of a perfect being which contains in its essence all perfections. It follows inevitably that such a being must exist, for otherwise it would lack a perfection, namely existence. As it is of the essence of God to possess all perfections, he cannot lack existence any more than any other perfection; it is involved in his essence. To think of a perfect being as nonexistent is to contradict myself.

God can no more be conceived without existence than a mountain can be conceived without a declivity or a triangle the sum of the internal angles of which is not equal to 180°.

Descartes, however, issues a caveat. Though I cannot conceive a mountain without a valley, it does not follow that either exists. That the sum of the internal angles of any triangle is 180° says nothing about the existence of triangles. The statement expressing the necessity of the connection between the ideas is purely hypothetical. It might thus be argued that the same is true of God—in fact, through the centuries since Descartes wrote, this argument has persistently been raised against him. It is important to observe that he anticipated it and rejected it as sophistical. For what is hypothetically asserted is not the existence of the necessary connection but only the existence of the entities and properties between which it is being categorically asserted. To say "If a triangle exists, the sum of its angles will be 180°" is to say categorically that there is a necessary logical connection between triangularity and this property. Likewise, to say of God that his perfection necessarily includes existence is to state categorically that existence is logically inseparable from his nature or essence—that he cannot but exist. We shall consider presently whether this rebuttal is valid.

2. ANSELM'S VERSION

First, let us note that the argument does not originate with Descartes but was first stated and elaborated by Anselm in the twelfth century. Its origins might well be traced back much further to Plato, but an historical excursus is not our purpose here. It would be instructive, however, to compare Anselm's statement with Descartes's.

Anselm defines God as "that than which nothing greater can be conceived." He then argues that he can understand what this definition means; therefore he has in his understanding the idea of an object than which nothing greater is conceivable. If, however, this object existed only in the understanding and not in reality, he could conceive of something greater—a corresponding object which exists both in the intellect and in reality. Consequently, that which exists only in the intellect is not that than which a greater cannot be conceived. Therefore, God, that than which nothing greater is conceivable, must exist in reality. To think otherwise is to contradict oneself. It is only the fool who hath said in his heart "There is no God"—that is why he is a fool.

Controversy about the validity of this argument has raged ever since Anselm propounded it. Gaunilo claimed to refute it. Aquinas rejected it, but Descartes revived it. Kant again refuted it, but Hegel reinstated it.

In contemporary philosophy it has been defended by Collingwood, opposed by Gilbert Ryle, restated by Charles Hartshorne, re-refuted by A. N. Prior, J. J. C. Smart (with some wavering), and J. N. Findlay (who uses a similar argument to prove the nonexistence of God), only to be revived once more by Norman Malcolm whose new defense of Anselm has excited a new spate of opposition[1] Whatever may be alleged of God, this argument is far from dead.

3. FORMAL REFUTATION OF THE ARGUMENT

There are two main props to the common refutation of the ontological proof: the first is that logical necessity is possible only for a connection between two attributes of a subject and cannot apply to the existence of the subject itself; the second is that existence is not logically a "predicate," that is, it does not predicate anything (any attribute) of any subject, and so is not included among the "perfections" attributed to God.

a. A deductive proof can establish connections only between concepts and the conclusion is always hypothetical. The conception of a triangle entails the conception of its having three angles together equal to two right angles. But this proves the existence of nothing. If anything is a triangle it will be such that it has this property, but that anything is a triangle is another matter.

Likewise, if God is conceived as perfect he must be conceived as existing, but that something is *conceived* as existing does not entail that it exists. We may say that if there is a perfect being then existence will belong to it, but that is only a hypothetical statement. So the monk, Gaunilo, argued against Anselm that one might conceive an island to be perfect but it would not follow that a perfect island existed. Aquinas argued that though we mean by the name "God" that than which we can conceive nothing greater, and though this includes existence, it does not follow that anything exists answering to the concept which we so form, or to what we mean by the name.[2]

b. The objection that existence is not a predicate was first put forward by Kant. If I have an idea of anything I can predicate of it whatever is appropriate. If I conceive a triangle I predicate of it three sides and three angles and the various properties that go along with these

---

[1] See the bibliography at the end of the chapter.

[2] Cf. *Summa Theological*, Quaestio II, 1. These arguments were repeated by Jean Cater (Caterus) in response to Descartes. See *Objections*, I.

attributes. But if I then say that what I conceive exists, I add no further attribute to my conception of it. A triangle in idea is in all respects the same, so far as predicable attributes are concerned, as an existing triangle. My idea of a hundred dollars has the same content as a hundred dollars in my pocket. The existence of the latter is not an additional attribute. The ontological argument is therefore invalid because from the attribute of a conceived object one can deduce only other implied attributes and existence can never be one of these, for it is not an attribute at all. So Kant repeats the charge that the conclusion of any such argument can only be hypothetical at best. Even if we treat existence as if it were a predicate, it would allow us to conclude only that if there were a God, he would exist of necessity, not that there is one.

Gilbert Ryle and the modern critics in effect repeat these arguments or state variants of them. Their demand is for "empirical premises" in any proof of existence. Existence, they say, is always a particular matter of fact and that can be established only from premises at least one of which states a matter of fact—that is, something directly experienced. To know that X exists I must either have had direct acquaintance with X (I must have seen, heard, or otherwise contacted X), or I must have had direct acquaintance with something else which I know to be causally connected with X.

The presupposition of all such arguments is that knowledge of factual matters is always and can only be derived from sense perception. This is a special kind of philosophical theory called Empiricism, which we are to discuss at length in the next section, so that, strictly speaking, the validity of this refutation of the ontological proof depends in the last resort on the truth of empiricism. If that proves not to be a tenable doctrine it would be rash to base any argument on it. Leaving the question open for the present whether empiricism is or is not sound, let us consider the arguments as they stand and as they affect the position of Anselm and Descartes. In essence, all the objections come down to the contention that it is never legitimate to conclude from mere idea to fact, from universal to particular, from essence to existence.

4. DEFENSE OF THE ARGUMENT

Both St. Anselm and Descartes admit the principle in general that essence does not imply existence, but they make God the single exception to this principle. Anselm, in his reply to Gaunilo, says: "Whatever at any place or at any time does not exist as a whole, even if it is existent, can be conceived not to exist." And: "The real existence of a being which is said to be greater than all other beings cannot be demonstrated in the same way as the real existence of one that is said to be *a being* than which a greater cannot be conceived."[3]

Descartes, similarly, in the *Discourse*, admits that he has no assurance of the existence of things such as triangles, whereas "on examination of the idea . . . of a Perfect Being . . . in this case existence was implied in it . . . ."[4] And again in the Meditation: "For being accustomed in all other things to make a distinction between existence and essence, I easily persuade myself that the existence can be separated from the essence of God."[5]

It is because God alone is infinite and perfect that His essence involves existence. No other essence is in the same case. A perfect island is really a contradiction in terms for by the very fact that something is an island, it follows that it is limited and in various ways defective (for example, it is limited in space, destructible, subject to variable conditions of weather—however pleasant—and so forth); it cannot therefore be a self-complete and self-dependent entity such that nothing greater is conceivable.

It is also admitted that to have the idea of a perfect being is not necessarily to know in detail everything that pertains to its nature (that would involve having complete and perfect knowledge or omniscience, and actually being God). To conceive of a perfect being is no more than to understand what is involved in the idea of perfection. We are not, therefore, dealing only with the name "God" or with the phrase "perfect being" but with what the adequate concept of perfection or self-completeness involves. It is argued that it must involve existence or it would not be adequate; but if an adequate *concept* of perfection involves existence, does this mean more than a *concept* of existence (the idea of an existing perfect being), and is the idea of an existent God the same as, or does it necessarily involve, an actually existent God?

The empiricist denies that it does on the ground that the existence of anything can be proved only by producing empirical evidence, that is, observational or sense-given evidence. But a philosopher, who, like Descartes (and Plato before him), denies the efficacy and reliability of sense in the provision of any sound evidence of existence and insists that, even in the case of material things, we know them—whether and

---

[3]See *St. Anselm* (Open Court, La Salle, Ill., 1962), pp. 156, 161–162.
[4]*Discourse*, Haldane and Ross, p. 104.
[5]See page 189, above.

what they are — only by the exercise of the intellect (compare the case of the wax), is not likely to disqualify the proof of existence of a perfect being properly conceived because of the absence of empirical premises.

The nub of the argument (though never stated in this way by Descartes) is that any final proof of existence depends on an adequate intellectual grasp of the nature of the thing concerned and the conditions of its existence. This is strictly possible only if the grounds (or conditions) of existence of any being whatsoever are either known or presupposed. In other words, in any proof of existence we presuppose the existence of a ground of being which is self-guaranteed or necessary. This must be a being that is by nature self-dependent and self-complete, the conditions of whose existence are already given in the conception of its essence, for it is its own condition of existence (*causa sui*). If adequately conceived, therefore, it is understood necessarily to exist because to assert the opposite would be to contradict the essence, and incidentally to invalidate any proof of existence of anything whatsoever.

This may not be obvious at first sight, but though normally we assume the existence of objects we perceive by means of the senses, it is clear that merely sensing them is not enough to assure us of their existence; and if we admit that sense perception gives no absolute proof of their reality, then we must seek that proof elsewhere. If, as Descartes does, we seek it in intellectual insight or logical cogency, we must investigate the source of such cogency. Descartes never really succeeds in showing what this is (for clarity and distinctness are ambiguous terms which partly evade the issue). Later philosophers, of whom Spinoza and Hegel are perhaps the most important, traced such cogency to systematic completeness, or absolute concreteness of conception[6] to which all adequate proof must ultimately lead. To know fully that an object of my experience really exists I must be able to assemble a body of evidence which is not limited to what I sense but which includes all science and philosophy and would ultimately go beyond all the knowledge I possess. It therefore presupposes a structure or system of being and knowledge which is transcendent or perfect and the ground of all being and all knowledge.

The establishment of the "existence" or reality of anything, therefore, is not just the addition to the concept of that thing of another predicate (Hegel scornfully declares that to say of God that He exists is to say the least possible about Him), and we may well agree that exist-

---

[6]Spinoza called this "an adequate idea of the formal essence of certain attributes of God." For Hegel it is the "Absolute Idea."

ence adds nothing and is not a predicate. To establish reality we have to develop the idea of the thing and its conditions into a self-supporting system or totality of being and show that it is an ineradicable ingredient in that totality. To deny the existence of the totality itself would thus be self-refuting and ludicrous.

Such a being exists of necessity. Its very concept implies existence, because logically prior to the concept (or meaning) of existence as such. To see this is, at the same time, to see that the existence of the perfect being is presupposed by the existence of anything and everything, so that the ontological and the cosmological arguments are really only two different aspects of the same proof. Their basis is the same. Similarly, Descartes's two proofs are mutually implicated. The reason why the idea of God in a finite mind is evidence of His existence is that the "objective essence" of the idea, what it presents to the mind, is a being which is the ground of existence not only of the idea itself but equally of the mind in which it is entertained. Because it is a being which guarantees its own existence, the idea is direct evidence that it is produced by such a being and nothing less. If there were no God, man could not conceive of God—or of anything else (because in all other conceptions this ultimate ground of the being of their object is presupposed).

Though this is the foundation of Descartes's proof, it is never clearly developed by Descartes. Consequently, his position seems to be assailable by the argument that the idea alone can never establish the existence of its object. The true position is that the nature of the object guarantees the validity of the idea, and its existence is established by its priority to all existence. In like manner, Descartes should have identified the idea of God as the ultimate criterion of truth. He is vaguely aware of this and so vacillates continually between the self-evidence of intuition and the necessary veracity of God as the source of assurance.

A persistent critic might claim that different entities have different grounds of existence and that there is no one ultimate ground of all existence. At least, there is no need to assume any such thing. If one does assume that there is an ultimate ground, it does not follow from this idea that its object exists in fact. This is superficially a plausible argument, and if the objector were pressed to say what sort of grounds of existence different entities had, he would probably refer to scientific evidence. He would probably also hold that scientific evidence is, in the last resort, necessarily empirical. Again we are confronted with an empiricist opponent, so the validity of the argument will depend on the truth of an empiricist theory of knowledge, into which we must shortly inquire. Meanwhile, we can only state somewhat dogmatically that no empirical evidence in science is acceptable unless it has been tested in the light of accepted scientific knowledge. If I claim to see a flying saucer, this is not scientific evidence until what I describe can be fitted into a scientific (theoretical) context. It must be shown that what I saw was not an illusion, or merely the effect of light on clouds; that I had not mistaken a conventional airplane or a weather balloon for some out-landish flying object. If the object I saw can be identified, what is already scientifically known about it must be explored before we can say just what evidence it provides and of what it is evidence. In short, established scientific theories must be brought to bear upon the empir-ical facts before their worth as evidence can be evaluated. Observation and theory in science are mutually dependent and only that ranks as observation which is scientifically warranted, which competent scien-tists approve and have submitted to numerous and varied tests, all of which are grounded in theory.

The grounds for the existence of any entity which science can pro-vide, therefore, are rooted in the system of scientific theory as a co-herent body of knowledge. But this itself rests upon the unstated assumption in the minds of all scientists that an intelligible account can ultimately be given of the things and events subject to investigation. If it could not, the aim of science would be frustrated *ab initio*. The ultimate presupposition of all science is, in other words, that there is an ultimate ground of existence.

The claim of our captious objector is thus based on inadequate analysis of the nature of scientific grounds and of scientific evidence, which, if more thoroughly pursued, would lead back to a position supporting, rather than denying, the validity of the ontological argu-ment.

SUGGESTIONS FOR FURTHER READING

Anselm, *Proslogion; Basic Writings.* La Salle, Ill.: Open Court Publishing Co., 1962.

Aquinas, *Summa Theologica,* I., Q. II. New York: Random House, Modern Li-brary edition, 1948.

B. Bosanquet, *The Meeting of Extremes in Contemporary Philosophy,* Chapter 3. New York: Macmillan, 1924.

R. G. Collingwood, *An Essay on Philosophical Method,* Chapter 6. New York: Oxford University Press, 1962.

————, *An Essay on Metaphysics,* Chapters 20 and 21. New York: Oxford University Press, 1940.

Descartes, Replies to Objections, *Philosophical Writings* (Haldane and Ross, eds.). New York: Dover Books, 1955.

A. Flew and A. MacIntyre (eds.), *New Essays in Philosophical Theology.* London: Student Christian Movement Press, 1963.

E. E. Harris, *Revelation through Reason.* New Haven, Conn.: Yale University Press, 1958.

————, "Mr. Ryle and the Ontological Argument," *Mind,* **65**, 1936.

John Hick and A. C. McGill (eds.), *The Many Faced Argument.* New York: Macmillan, 1967.

W. E. Hocking, *The Meaning of God in Human Experience,* Chapter 22. New Haven, Conn.: Yale University Press, 1912.

I. Kant, *Critique of Pure Reason,* Transcendental Dialectic, Book II, Chapter 3, Kemp Smith translation. New York: Macmillan, 1950.

N. Malcolm, "Anselm's Ontological Arguments," *The Philosophical Review,* **69**, 1960.

A. Plantinga (ed.), *The Ontological Argument.* New York: Doubleday, Anchor Books, 1965.

Gilbert Ryle, "Mr. Collingwood and the Ontological Argument," *Mind,* **64**, 1935.

————, "Back to the Ontological Argument," *Mind,* **66**, 1937.

CHAPTER 14

The Existence
of Material Things

MEDITATION VI: OF THE EXISTENCE OF MATERIAL THINGS AND OF
THE REAL DISTINCTION BETWEEN THE MIND AND BODY OF MAN

There now only remains the inquiry as to whether material things exist. With
regard to this question, I at least know with certainty that such things may
exist, in as far as they constitute the object of the pure mathematics, since,
regarding them in this aspect, I can conceive them clearly and distinctly. For
there can be no doubt that God possesses the power of producing all the
objects I am able distinctly to conceive, and I never considered anything
impossible to him, unless when I experienced a contradiction in the attempt to
conceive it aright. Further, the faculty of imagination which I possess, and of
which I am conscious that I make use when I apply myself to the consideration
of material things, is sufficient to persuade me of their existence: for, when I
attentively consider what imagination is, I find that it is simply a certain application of the cognitive faculty (*facultas cognoscitiva*) to a body which is
immediately present to it, and which therefore exists.

And to render this quite clear, I remark, in the first place, the difference that
subsists between imagination and pure intellection [or conception]. For example, when I imagine a triangle I not only conceive (*intelligo*) that it is a figure
comprehended by three lines, but at the same time also I look upon (*intueor*)
these three lines as present by the power and internal application of my mind
(*acie mentis*), and this is what I call imagining. But if I desire to think of a

chiliogon, I indeed rightly conceive that it is a figure composed of a thousand sides, as easily as I conceive that a triangle is a figure composed of only three sides; but I cannot imagine the thousand sides of a chiliogon as I do the three sides of a triangle, nor, so to speak, view them as present [with the eyes of my mind]. And although, in accordance with the habit I have of always imagining something when I think of corporeal things, it may happen that, in conceiving a chiliogon, I confusedly represent some figure to myself, yet it is quite evident that this is not a chiliogon, since it in no wise differs from that which I would represent to myself, if I were to think of a myriogon, or any other figure of many sides; nor would this representation be of any use in discovering and unfolding the properties that constitute the difference between a chiliogon and other polygons. But if the question turns on a pentagon, it is quite true that I can conceive its figure, as well as that of a chiliogon, without the aid of imagination; but I can likewise imagine it by applying the attention of my mind to its five sides, and at the same time to the area which they contain. Thus I observe that a special effort of mind is necessary to the act of imagination, which is not required to conceiving or understanding (*ad intelligendum*); and this special exertion of mind clearly shows the difference between imagination and pure intellection (*imaginatio et intellectio pura*). I remark, besides, that this power of imagination which I possess, in as far as it differs from the power of conceiving, is in no way necessary to my [nature or] essence, that is, to the essence of my mind; for although I did not possess it, I should still remain the same that I now am, from which it seems we may conclude that it depends on something different from the mind. And I easily understand that, if some body exists, with which my mind is so conjoined and united as to be able, as it were, to consider it when it chooses, it may thus imagine corporeal objects; so that this mode of thinking differs from pure intellection only in this respect, that the mind in conceiving turns in some way upon itself, and considers some one of the ideas it possesses within itself; but in imagining it turns towards the body, and contemplates in it some object conformed to the idea which it either of itself conceived or apprehended by sense. I easily understand, I say, that imagination may be thus formed, if it is true that there are bodies; and because I find no other obvious mode of explaining it. I thence, with probability, conjecture that they exist, but only with probability, and although I carefully examine all things, nevertheless I do not find that, from the distinct idea of corporeal nature I have in my imagination, I can necessarily infer the existence of any body.

But I am accustomed to imagine many other objects besides that corporeal nature which is the object of the pure mathematics, as, for example, colours, sounds, tastes, pain, and the like, although with less distinctness; and, inasmuch as I perceive these objects much better by the senses, through the medium of which and of memory, they seem to have reached the imagination, I believe that, in order the more advantageously to examine them, it is proper I should at the same time examine what sense-perception is, and inquire whether from those ideas that are apprehended by this mode of thinking (consciousness), I cannot obtain a certain proof of the existence of corporeal objects.

And, in the first place, I will recall to my mind the things I have hitherto held as true, because perceived by the senses, and the foundations upon which my belief in their truth rested; I will, in the second place, examine the reasons that afterwards constrained me to doubt of them; and, finally, I will consider what of them I ought now to believe.

Firstly, then, I perceived that I had a head, hands, feet, and other members composing that body which I considered as part, or perhaps even as a whole, of myself. I perceived further, that that body was placed among many others, by which it was capable of being affected in diverse ways, both beneficial and hurtful; and what was beneficial I remarked by a certain sensation of pleasure, and what was hurtful by a sensation of pain. And, besides this pleasure and pain, I was likewise conscious of hunger, thirst, and other appetites, as well as certain corporeal inclinations towards joy, sadness, anger, and similar passions. And, out of myself, besides the extension, figure, and motions of bodies, I likewise perceived in them hardness, heat, and the other tactile qualities, and, in addition, light, colours, odours, tastes, and sounds, the variety of which gave me the means of distinguishing the sky, the earth, the sea, and generally all the other bodies, from one another. And certainly, considering the ideas of all these qualities, which were presented to my mind, and which alone I properly and immediately perceived, it was not without reason that I thought I perceived certain objects wholly different from my thought, namely, bodies from which those ideas proceeded; for I was conscious that the ideas were presented to me without my consent being required, so that I could not perceive any object, however desirous I might be, unless it were present to the organ of sense; and it was wholly out of my power not to perceive it when it was thus present. And because the ideas I perceived by the senses were much more lively and clear, and even in their own way, more distinct than any of those I could of myself frame by meditation, or which I found impressed on my memory, it seemed that they could not have proceeded from myself, and must therefore have been caused in me by some other objects; and as of those objects I had no knowledge beyond what the ideas themselves gave me, nothing was so likely to occur to my mind as the supposition that the objects were similar to the ideas which they caused. And because I recollected also that I had formerly trusted to the senses, rather than to reason, and that the ideas which I myself formed were not so clear as those I perceived by sense, and that they were even for the most part composed of the latter, I was readily persuaded that I had no idea in my intellect which had not formerly passed through the senses. Nor was I altogether wrong in likewise believing that that body which, by a special right, I called my own, pertained to me more properly and strictly than any of the others; for in truth, I could never be separated from it as from other bodies: I felt in it and on account of it all my appetites and affections, and in fine I was affected in its parts by pain and the titillation of pleasure, and not in the parts of the other bodies that were separated from it. But when I inquired into the reason why, from this I know not what sensation of pain, sadness of mind should follow, and why from the sensation of pleasure joy should arise, or why this indescribable twitching of the stomach, which I call hunger, should put me in mind of taking food, and the parchedness of the throat of drink, and so in other cases, I was unable to give any explanation, unless that I was so taught by nature; for there is assuredly no affinity, at least none that I am able to comprehend, between this irritation of the stomach and the desire of food, any more than between the perception of an object that causes pain and the consciousness of sadness which springs from the perception. And in the same way it seemed to me that all the other judgments I had formed regarding the objects of sense, were dictates of nature; because I remarked that those judgments were formed in me, before I had leisure to weigh and consider the reasons that might constrain me to form them.

But, afterwards, a wide experience by degrees sapped the faith I had re-
posed in my senses; for I frequently observed that towers, which at a distance
seemed round, appeared square when more closely viewed, and that colossal
figures, raised on the summits of these towers, looked like small statues, when
viewed from the bottom of them; and, in other instances without number, I also
discovered error in judgments founded on the external senses; and not only in
those founded on the external, but even in those that rested on the internal
senses; for is there aught more internal than pain? and yet I have sometimes
been informed by parties whose arm or leg had been amputated, that they still
occasionally seemed to feel pain in that part of the body which they had lost—a
circumstance that led me to think that I could not be quite certain even that
any one of my members was affected when I felt pain in it. And to these
grounds of doubt I shortly afterwards also added two others of very wide
generality: the first of them was that I believed I never perceived anything
when awake which I could not occasionally think I also perceived when asleep,
and as I do not believe that the ideas I seem to perceive in my sleep proceed
from objects external to me, I did not any more observe any ground for believing this of such as I seem to perceive when awake; the second was that
since I was as yet ignorant of the author of my being, or at least supposed
myself to be so, I saw nothing to prevent my having been so constituted by
nature as that I should be deceived even in matters that appeared to me to
possess the greatest truth. And, with respect to the grounds on which I had
before been persuaded of the existence of sensible objects, I had no great
difficulty in finding suitable answers to them; for as nature seemed to incline
me to many things from which reason made me averse, I thought that I ought
not to confide much in its teachings. And although the perceptions of the senses
were not dependent on my will, I did not think that I ought on that ground to
conclude that they proceeded from things different from myself, since perhaps
there might be found in me some faculty, though hitherto unknown to me,
which produced them.

But now that I begin to know myself better, and to discover more clearly the
author of my being, I do not, indeed, think that I ought rashly to admit all which
the senses seem to teach, nor, on the other hand, is it my conviction that I ought
to doubt in general of their teachings.

And, firstly, because I know that all which I clearly and distinctly conceive
can be produced by God exactly as I conceive it, it is sufficient that I am able
clearly and distinctly to conceive one thing apart from another, in order to be
certain that the one is different from the other, seeing they may at least be
made to exist separately, by the omnipotence of God; and it matters not by
what power this separation is made, in order to be compelled to judge them
different; and, therefore, merely because I know with certitude that I exist, and
because, in the meantime, I do not observe that aught necessarily belongs to
my nature or essence beyond my being a thinking thing, I rightly conclude that
my essence consists only in my being a thinking thing, [or a substance whose
whole essence or nature is merely thinking]. And although I may, or rather, as
I will shortly say, although I certainly do possess a body with which I am very
closely conjoined; nevertheless, because, on the one hand, I have a clear and
distinct idea of myself, in as far as I am only a thinking and unextended thing,
and as, on the other hand, I possess a distinct idea of body, in as far as it is only
an extended and unthinking thing, it is certain that I, [that is, my mind, by

which I am what I am], is entirely and truly distinct from my body, and may exist without it.

Moreover, I find in myself diverse faculties of thinking that have each their special mode: for example, I find I possess the faculties of imagining and perceiving, without which I can indeed clearly and distinctly conceive myself as entire, but I cannot reciprocally conceive them without conceiving myself, that is to say, without an intelligent substance in which they reside, for [in the notion we have of them, or to use the terms of the schools] in their formal concept, they comprise some sort of intellection; whence I perceive that they are distinct from myself as modes are from things. I remark likewise certain other faculties, as the power of changing place, of assuming diverse figures, and the like, that cannot be conceived and cannot therefore exist, any more than the preceding, apart from a substance in which they inhere. It is very evident, however, that these faculties, if they really exist, must belong to some corporeal or extended substance, since in their clear and distinct concept there is contained some sort of extension, but no intellection at all. Farther, I cannot doubt but that there is in me a certain passive faculty of perception, that is, of receiving and taking knowledge of the ideas of sensible things; but this would be useless to me, if there did not also exist in me, or in some other thing, another active faculty capable of forming and producing those ideas. But this active faculty cannot be in me [in as far as I am but a thinking thing], seeing that it does not presuppose thought, and also that those ideas are frequently produced in my mind without my contributing to it in any way, and even frequently contrary to my will. This faculty must therefore exist in some substance different from me, in which all the objective reality of the ideas that are produced by this faculty, is contained formally or eminently, as I before remarked; and this substance is either a body, that is to say, a corporeal nature in which is contained formally [and in effect] all that is objectively [and by representation] in those ideas; or it is God himself, or some other creature, of a rank superior to body, in which the same is contained eminently. But as God is no deceiver, it is manifest that he does not of himself and immediately communicate those ideas to me, nor even by the intervention of any creature in which their objective reality is not formally, but only eminently, contained. For as he has given me no faculty whereby I can discover this to be the case, but, on the contrary, a very strong inclination to believe that those ideas arise from corporeal objects, I do not see how he could be vindicated from the charge of deceit, if in truth they proceeded from any other source, or were produced by other causes than corporeal things: and accordingly it must be concluded, that corporeal objects exist. Nevertheless they are not perhaps exactly such as we perceive by the senses, for their comprehension by the senses is, in many instances, very obscure and confused; but it is at least necessary to admit that all which I clearly and distinctly conceive as in them, that is, generally speaking, all that is comprehended in the object of speculative geometry, really exists external to me.

But with respect to other things which are either only particular, as, for example, that the sun is of such a size and figure, etc., or are conceived with less clearness and distinctness, as light, sound, pain, and the like, although they are highly dubious and uncertain, nevertheless on the ground alone that God is no deceiver, and that consequently he has permitted no falsity in my opinions which he has not likewise given me a faculty of correcting, I think I may with safety conclude that I possess in myself the means of arriving at the truth. And, in the first place, it cannot be doubted that in each of the dictates of nature there is some truth: for by nature, considered in general, I now understand nothing more than God himself, or the order and disposition established by God in created things; and by my nature in particular I understand the assemblage of all that God has given me.

But there is nothing which that nature teaches me more expressly [or more sensibly] than that I have a body which is ill affected when I feel pain, and stands in need of food and drink when I experience the sensations of hunger and thirst, etc. And therefore I ought not to doubt but that there is some truth in these informations.

Nature likewise teaches me by these sensations of pain, hunger, thirst, etc., that I am not only lodged in my body as a pilot in a vessel, but that I am besides so intimately conjoined, and as it were intermixed with it, that my mind and body compose a certain unity. For if this were not the case, I should not feel pain when my body is hurt, seeing I am merely a thinking thing, but should perceive the wound by the understanding alone, just as a pilot perceives by sight when any part of his vessel is damaged; and when my body has need of food or drink, I should have a clear knowledge of this, and not be made aware of it by the confused sensations of hunger and thirst: for, in truth, all these sensations of hunger, thirst, pain, etc., are nothing more than certain confused modes of thinking, arising from the union and apparent fusion of mind and body.

Besides this, nature teaches me that my own body is surrounded by many other bodies, some of which I have to seek after, and others to shun. And indeed, as I perceive different sorts of colours, sounds, odours, tastes, heat, hardness, etc., I safely conclude that there are in the bodies from which the diverse perceptions of the senses proceed, certain varieties corresponding to them, although, perhaps, not in reality like them; and since, among these diverse perceptions of the senses, some are agreeable, and others disagreeable, there can be no doubt that my body, or rather my entire self, in as far as I am composed of body and mind, may be variously affected, both beneficially and hurtfully, by surrounding bodies.

But there are many other beliefs which, though seemingly the teaching of nature, are not in reality so, but which obtained a place in my mind through a habit of judging inconsiderately of things. It may thus easily happen that such judgments shall contain error: thus, for example, the opinion I have that all space in which there is nothing to affect [or make an impression on] my senses is void; that in a hot body there is something in every respect similar to the idea of heat in my mind; that in a white or green body there is the same whiteness or greenness which I perceive; that in a bitter or sweet body there is the same taste, and so in other instances; that the stars, towers, and all distant bodies, are of the same size and figure as they appear to our eyes, etc. But that I may avoid everything like indistinctness of conception, I must accurately define what I properly understand by being taught by nature. For nature is here taken in a narrower sense than when it signifies the sum of all the things which God has given me; seeing that in the meaning the notion comprehends much that belongs only to the mind [to which I am not here to be understood as referring when I use the term nature]; as, for example, the notion I have of the truth, that what is done cannot be undone, and all the other truths I discern by the natural light [without the aid of the body]; and seeing that it comprehends likewise much besides that belongs only to body, and is not here any more contained under the name nature, as the quality of heaviness, and the like, of which I do not speak—the term being reserved exclusively to designate the things which God has given to me as a being composed of mind and body. But nature, taking the term in the sense explained, teaches me to shun what causes in me the sensation of pain, and to pursue what affords me the sensation of pleasure, and other things of this sort; but I do not discover that it teaches me, in addition to this, from these diverse perceptions of the senses, to draw any conclusions respecting external objects without a previous [careful and mature] consideration of them by the mind; for it is, as appears to me, the office of the mind alone, and not of the composite whole of mind and body, to discern the truth in those matters. Thus, although the impression a star makes on my eye is not larger than that from the flame of a candle, I do not, nevertheless, experience any real or positive impulse determining me to believe that the star is not greater than the flame; the true account of the matter being merely that I have so judged from my youth without any rational ground. And, though on approaching the fire I feel heat, and even pain on approaching it too closely, I have, however, from this no ground for holding that something resembling the heat I feel is in the fire, any more than that there is something similar to the pain; all that I have ground for believing is, that there is something in it, whatever it may be, which excites in me those sensations of heat or pain. So also, although there are spaces in which I find nothing to excite and affect my senses, I must not therefore conclude that those spaces contain in them no body; for I see that in this, as in many other similar matters, I have been accustomed to pervert the order of nature, because these perceptions of the senses, although given me by nature merely to signify to my mind what things are beneficial and hurtful to the composite whole of which it is a part, and being sufficiently clear and distinct for that purpose, are nevertheless used by me as infallible rules by which to determine immediately the essence of the bodies that exist out of me, of which they can of course afford me only the most obscure and confused knowledge.

But I have already sufficiently considered how it happens that, notwithstanding the supreme goodness of God, there is falsity in my judgments. A difficulty, however, here presents itself, respecting the things which I am taught by nature must be pursued or avoided, and also respecting the internal sensations in which I seem to have occasionally detected error, [and thus to be directly deceived by nature]: thus, for example, I may be so deceived by the agreeable taste of some viand with which poison has been mixed, as to be induced to take the poison. In this case, however, nature may be excused, for it simply leads me to desire the viand for its agreeable taste, and not the poison, which is unknown to it; and thus we can infer nothing from this circumstance beyond that our nature is not omniscient; at which there is assuredly no ground for surprise, since, man being of a finite nature, his knowledge must likewise be of limited perfection. But we also not infrequently err in that to which we are directly impelled by nature, as is the case with invalids who desire drink or food that would be hurtful to them. It will here, perhaps, be alleged that the reason why such persons are deceived is that their nature is corrupted; but this leaves the difficulty untouched, for a sick man is not less really the creature of God than a man who is in full health; and therefore it is as repugnant to the goodness of God that the nature of the former should be deceitful as it is for that of the latter to be so. And, as a clock, composed of wheels and counter weights, observes not the less accurately all the laws of nature when it is ill made, and points out the hours incorrectly, than when it satisfies the desire of the maker in every respect; so likewise if the body of man be considered as a kind of machine, so made up and composed of bones, nerves, muscles, veins, blood, and skin, that although there were in it no mind, it would still exhibit the same motions which it at present manifests involuntarily, and therefore without the aid of the mind, [and simply by the dispositions of its organs], I easily discern that it would also be as natural for such a body, supposing it dropsical, for example, to experience the parchedness of the throat that is usually accompanied in the mind by the sensation of thirst, and to be disposed by this parchedness to move its nerves and its other parts in the way required for drinking, and thus increase its malady and do itself harm, as it is natural for it, when it is not indisposed to be stimulated to drink for its good by a similar cause; and although looking to the use for which a clock was destined by its maker, I may say that it is deflected from its proper nature when it incorrectly indicates the hours, and on the same principle, considering the machine of the human body as having been formed by God for the sake of the motions which it usually manifests, although I may likewise have ground for thinking that it does not follow the order of its nature when the throat is parched and drink does not tend to its preservation, nevertheless I yet plainly discern that this latter acceptation of the term nature is very different from the other; for this is nothing more than a certain denomination, depending entirely on my thought, and hence called extrinsic, by which I compare a sick man and an imperfectly constructed clock with the idea I have of a man in good health and a well made clock; while by the other acceptation of nature is understood something which is truly found in things, and therefore possessed of some truth.

But certainly, although in respect of a dropsical body, it is only by way of exterior denomination that we say its nature is corrupted, when, without requiring drink, the throat is parched; yet, in respect of the composite whole, that is, of the mind in its union with the body, it is not a pure denomination, but really an error of nature, for it to feel thirst when drink would be hurtful to it: and, accordingly, it still remains to be considered why it is that the goodness of God does not prevent the nature of man thus taken from being fallacious.

To commence this examination accordingly, I here remark, in the first place, that there is a vast difference between mind and body, in respect that body, from its nature, is always divisible, and that mind is entirely indivisible. For in truth, when I consider the mind, that is, when I consider myself in so far only as I am a thinking thing, I can distinguish in myself no parts, but I very clearly discern that I am somewhat absolutely one and entire; and although the whole mind seems to be united to the whole body, yet, when a foot, an arm, or any other part is cut off, I am conscious that nothing has been taken from my mind; nor can the faculties of willing, perceiving, conceiving, etc., properly be called its parts, for it is the same mind that is exercised [all entire] in willing, in perceiving, and in conceiving, etc. But quite the opposite holds in corporeal or extended things; for I cannot imagine any one of them [how small soever it may be], which I cannot easily sunder in thought, and which, therefore, I do not know to be divisible. This would be sufficient to teach me that the mind or soul of man is entirely different from the body, if I had not already been apprised of it on other grounds.

I remark, in the next place, that the mind does not immediately receive the impression from all the parts of the body, but only from the brain, or perhaps even from one small part of it, viz., that in which the common sense (*sensus communis*) is said to be, which as often as it is affected in the same way, gives rise to the same perception in the mind, although meanwhile the other parts of the body may be diversely disposed, as is proved by innumerable experiments, which it is unnecessary here to enumerate.

I remark, besides, that the nature of body is such that none of its parts can be moved by another part a little removed from the other, which cannot likewise be moved in the same way by any one of the parts that lie between those two, although the most remote part does not act at all. As, for example, in the cord A, B, C, D, [which is in tension], if its last part D, be pulled, the first part A, will not be moved in a different way than it would be were one of the intermediate parts B or C to be pulled, and the last part D meanwhile to remain fixed. And in the same way, when I feel pain in the foot, the science of physics teaches me that this sensation is experienced by means of the nerves dispersed over the foot, which, extending like cords from it to the brain, when they are contracted in the foot, contract at the same time the inmost parts of the brain in which they have their origin, and excite in these parts a certain motion appointed by nature to cause in the mind a sensation of pain, as if existing in the foot: but as these nerves must pass through the tibia, the leg, the loins, the back, and neck, in order to reach the brain, it may happen that although their extremities in the foot are not affected, but only certain of their parts that pass through the loins or neck, the same movements, nevertheless, are excited in the brain by this motion as would have been caused there by a hurt received in the foot, and hence the mind will necessarily feel pain in the foot, just as if it had been hurt; and the same is true of all the other perceptions of our senses.

I remark, finally, that as each of the movements that are made in the part of the brain by which the mind is immediately affected, impresses it with but a single sensation, the most likely supposition in the circumstances is, that this movement causes the mind to experience, among all the sensations which it is capable of impressing upon it, that one which is the best fitted, and generally the most useful for the preservation of the human body when it is in full health. But experience shows us that all the perceptions which nature has given us are of such a kind as I have mentioned; and accordingly, there is nothing found in them that does not manifest the power and goodness of God. Thus, for example, when the nerves of the foot are violently or more than usually shaken, the motion passing through the medulla of the spine to the innermost parts of the brain affords a sign to the mind on which it experiences a sensation, viz., of pain, as if it were in the foot, by which the mind is admonished and excited to do its utmost to remove the cause of it as dangerous and hurtful to the foot. It is true that God could have so constituted the nature of man as that the same motion in the brain would have informed the mind of something altogether different: the motion might, for example, have been the occasion on which the mind became conscious of itself, in so far as it is in the brain, or in so far as it is in some place intermediate between the foot and the brain, or, finally, the occasion on which it perceived some other object quite different, whatever that might be; but nothing of all this would have so well contributed to the preservation of the body as that which the mind actually feels. In the same way, when we stand in need of drink, there arises from this want a certain parchedness in the throat that moves its nerves, and by means of them the internal parts of the brain; and this movement affects the mind with the sensation of thirst because there is nothing on that occasion which is more useful for us than to be made aware that we have need of drink for the preservation of our health; and so in other instances.

Whence it is quite manifest that, notwithstanding the sovereign goodness of God, the nature of man, in so far as it is composed of mind and body, cannot but be sometimes fallacious. For, if there is any cause which excites, not in the foot, but in some one of the parts of the nerves that stretch from the foot to the brain, or even in the brain itself, the same movement that is ordinarily created when the foot is ill affected, pain will be felt, as it were, in the foot, and the sense will thus be naturally deceived; for as the same movement in the brain can but impress the mind with the same sensation, and as this sensation is much more frequently excited by a cause which hurts the foot than by one acting in a different quarter, it is reasonable that it should lead the mind to feel pain in the foot rather than in any other part of the body. And if it sometimes happens that the parchedness of the throat does not arise, as is usual, from drink being necessary for the health of the body, but from quite the opposite cause, as is the case with the dropsical, yet it is much better that it should be deceitful in that instance, than if, on the contrary, it were continually fallacious when the body is well-disposed; and the same holds true in other cases.

And certainly this consideration is of great service, not only in enabling me to recognize the errors to which my nature is liable, but likewise in rendering it more easy to avoid or correct them: for, knowing that all my senses more usually indicate to me what is true than what is false, in matters relating to the advantage of the body, and being able almost always to make use of more than a single sense in examining the same object, and besides this, being able to use my memory in connecting present with past knowledge, and my understanding which has already discovered all the causes of my errors, I ought no longer to fear that falsity may be met with in what is daily presented to me by the senses. And I ought to reject all the doubts of those bygone days, as hyperbolical and ridiculous, especially the general uncertainty respecting sleep, which I could not distinguish from the waking state: for I now find a very marked difference between the two states, in respect that our memory can never connect our dreams with each other and with the course of life, in the way it is in the habit of doing with events that occur when we are awake. And, in truth, if some one, when I am awake, appeared to me all of a sudden and as suddenly disappeared, as do the images I see in sleep, so that I could not observe either whence he came or whither he went, I should not without reason esteem it either a spectre or phantom formed in my brain, rather than a real man. But when I perceive objects with regard to which I can distinctly determine both the place whence they come, and that in which they are, and the time at which they appear to me, and when, without interruption, I can connect the perception I have of them with the whole of the other parts of my life, I am perfectly sure that what I thus perceive occurs while I am awake and not during sleep. And I ought not in the least degree to doubt of the truth of those presentations, if, after having called together all my senses, my memory, and my understanding for the purpose of examining them, no deliverance is given by any one of these faculties which is repugnant to that of any other: for since God is no deceiver, it necessarily follows that I am not herein deceived. But because the necessities of action frequently oblige us to come to a determination before we have had leisure for so careful an examination, it must be confessed that the life of man is frequently obnoxious to error with respect to individual objects; and we must, in conclusion, acknowledge the weakness of our nature.

1. THOUGHT AND EXTENSION – SOUL AND BODY

In Meditation III Descartes remarks that before he embarked upon his method of doubt he had believed that the ideas of material objects perceived by means of the senses proceeded from material things and were entirely similar to the things which caused them. But, he asserts, he did not in fact perceive this at all. What he really perceived was only "that the ideas and thoughts of those objects were presented to his mind." This was not to be denied, but what the source of these ideas could be remains to be investigated, and in the last Meditation he seeks the answer to that question.

First, he recapitulates the considerations which supported his former beliefs in the existence of his own and other bodies. These include the fact that sense perceptions come to him without his concurrence and even against his will, that they are stronger and more definite than ideas of the memory or the imagination, and that the latter are for the most part constituted of fragmentary revivals of sensuously experienced objects. But all these reasons he had rejected after reflection upon the various deceptive appearances presented by the senses (changes of apparent size and shape in objects seen from nearby and from afar, the illusions of phantom limbs described by the victims of amputation, the difficulty of distinguishing between dream and waking consciousness, and similar bewildering experiences).

In this review of experience Descartes makes a sharp distinction between ideas formed by the intellect, which may be clearly and distinctly perceived, like the mathematical conceptions of geometrical figures, and mental images produced by imagination. As Plato distinguished between geometrical concepts and the more or less rough diagrams by means of which we help ourselves to the study of them, so Descartes distinguishes between such concepts and the vague and imprecise images we may form of them. We can, for instance, deduce precisely the mathematical properties of a thousand-sided figure (a chiliogon), but cannot clearly envisage it in imagination. The image we form of it may be indistinguishable from the image we form of some other figure (equally hard to imagine) which has quite different, yet clearly conceived, mathematical properties.

Descartes believed that the imagination, like the senses, belonged to the body and that imaginary ideas were produced in a bodily organ, as sensory ideas are produced in the sense organs. He thought they were a kind of impression made by the sensory ideas on a part of the brain which he called the phantasia, as an impression is made in wax by a signet. There they were retained for later inspection by the mind. So he says that the mind "in imagining . . . turns toward the body and contemplates in it some object conformed to the idea which it either conceived or apprehended by sense."

These doctrines are consequent upon Descartes's sharp separation of the mind from the body which is strongly reminiscent of, though in many respects more definite and precise than, Plato's theory. Plato was led to separate soul from body in part by the influence of the Orphic and Pythagorean tradition concerning purification of the soul, and in part by his own theory of knowledge and the difficulty of relating the flux of sensation to the universal ideas essential to systematic knowledge. The historical background of Descartes's dichotomy is the seventeenth-century scientific presupposition of a mechanical world of which the body is a part and which has no place in it for consciousness and thought. Accordingly, for him, the thinking thing, which has no properties pertaining to extension, is not part of the mechanical world and is altogether distinct from extended things. So Descartes came eventually to divide reality into two created substances, each dependent for its existence directly upon God: Thought and Extension.

The soul is a thinking thing; the body is an extended, material thing. How are they so intimately related in each of us that, as Descartes says, "I could never be separated from it as from other bodies"? In Meditation VI he tells us that the soul somehow pervades the whole body, so that we feel sensations wherever our bodies are affected, and is not lodged in it "as a pilot in a vessel." Yet elsewhere[1] he entertains the hypothesis that the seat of the soul is the pineal gland situated in the center of the brain where numerous nerve fibers appear to converge and where impulses from all over the body could be collected and correlated.

As we have seen, Descartes thought that the imagination (phantasia) was a bodily organ, situated presumably in the brain, in which physical impressions derived from the senses were stored. He also believed that there was an organ in the brain in which sensations from all the various senses came together and where impressions (of some unexplained

---

[1]See *Principles of Philosophy*, Part IV, cxcvi, and *The Passions of the Soul*, Part I, Arts. xxxi and xxxii.

sort) were made of their common qualities. This he called the common sense (*sensus communis*), following Aristotle and the Schoolmen.

All these belong to the extended, material body. The mind (or soul) becomes aware of them, as it were, by simply inspecting them. But how this "inspection" (*intuere*) conveys to the soul the contents of the bodily organs or their relation to external bodies, which it must know if it is to understand their significance and interpret them aright, remains a mystery. The whole theory, as we shall see, raises serious difficulties with respect to perception, which Descartes escapes only by his appeal to God's veracity. Before we explore these difficulties, however, we must return to the argument by which Descartes establishes the existence of material bodies, that has been taken for granted in the theory outlined above.

He says that all his former beliefs in the reality of bodies were more or less instinctive — the "dictates of nature," as he calls them — acquired before he undertook to examine and reflect upon them philosophically. That reflection gave rise to doubts, which he now proceeds to dispel by an argument resting upon the truths he has hitherto discovered: his own indubitable existence as a thinker, the existence of God, and the knowledge that God, being perfect, cannot deceive him.

2. THE ARGUMENT FOR THE EXISTENCE OF MATERIAL THINGS

The cause of any idea, we have learned by now, must contain, either formally or eminently, as much reality as the idea contains objectively.[2] But I (the *ego*) am a thinking thing and, as such, have no spatial or material properties. Thus I do not contain formally in my (thinking) self the "reality" which the ideas of material things have objectively. Likewise, I do not contain that reality eminently for I have not the power to produce the ideas at will; they come to me whenever my senses function, without my concurrence or cooperation and regardless of my wishes. They must therefore be produced either by God, who contains their reality eminently (that is, is able to produce them), or by some other reality (material things themselves) which contain it formally (that is, have the same form and character).

If they were produced by God alone and not by material things, and if no such material things existed, God would be causing me to think

---

[2]It must be remembered that for Descartes this means what is presented to the mind, not what exists independently of the mind, in our modern sense of the word.

what was not true (that material things exist), and so He would be deceiving me. But that we have seen to be impossible. Therefore, the ideas must be caused by material substances which contain formally the reality which the ideas contain objectively.

We should, however, not be justified in accepting as true of such material substances everything which appears to us through the senses, but only what we conceive of them clearly and distinctly; for what the senses impart is often confused and obscure—as we noted in the case of the wax and its persistence through bewildering changes. And what do we conceive of material substances that is clear and distinct? Only their mathematical properties, that is, their extended and quantitative character. Yet we need not be deceived even by the other qualities which they appear to have because we know how to discover the truth about them. Descartes thereupon proceeds to explain the more deceptive appearances in terms of what in the various sciences (of physics and physiology) is clearly and distinctly conceived.

3. DESCARTES'S THEORY OF PERCEPTION

Relying on the fact that God does not deceive him, Descartes accepts the existence of bodies as actual, first his own and then others, on the ground that there must be some truth "in all things which nature teaches." From his examples this phrase seems to mean little more than what he is inclined by instinct to believe. He does not say that this is all clear and distinct—far from it—but that it must contain some truth. He then proceeds to sift the grain from the chaff. The mathematical, or "primary," qualities of bodies we can understand to be real, because God can create whatever we clearly and distinctly conceive exactly as we conceive it. What belongs peculiarly to the mind, however, does not belong to nature apart from the mind. The colors, sounds, scents, and tastes of things (what came to be called "secondary qualities") are not so much qualities in the things themselves as ways in which they affect us so as to incline us toward what is beneficial to our health and avert us from what is harmful. But here the constitution of our bodies is such that we may be misled, because other things affect us in ways which may produce reactions in our brains that are normally produced otherwise; so we misplace pains and suffer various other kinds of illusion. To the question how we decide which sensations are misleading and which are not Descartes gives the sort of answer we shall find specially important and shall elaborate later. What we can connect together consecutively and coherently we take to be real, what we cannot we take to be imaginary or illusory. But Descartes makes no appeal here to self-evidence, only, in the last resort, to God's truthfulness.

Descartes sketches a theory of the way in which we receive sensations from external things through the effects they have on our sense organs, which are conveyed along the nerves to the brain, which in turn excites ideas in the mind. But, as we noticed above, he gives no clear account of how the soul's "inspection" of the bodily impressions communicates to it either their character or the relations between them and the external world which enables it to interpret them (as Descartes himself, in this Meditation, has explained and interpreted them). He does not seem to notice that a second theory of perception is needed to explain how the soul perceives the body. Setting that aside, there are still further difficulties. If the soul can grasp immediately by inspection the forms and qualities of the bodily organs (in the brain or elsewhere), why could it not similarly apprehend by immediate intuition the existence and nature of other (external) bodies? Why is the mediation of its own body with its sense organs necessary? And if it is necessary, because for some unstated reason the soul can only inspect the organs of its own body, how does it discover from the end results of the physical and physiological processes which Descartes alleges, what these processes in their entirety have been, and what the causal connection is between the impressions in the *sensus communis* and the *phantasia* and the outside world? This must be known before the soul can tell that these impressions in any way represent external objects, for it is from these impressions alone that its ideas of other material bodies are derived.

In order to know that the impressions of sense and imagination are made by transmission from external things the soul would have to inspect both the external things directly and the impressions, as well as the process from one to the other. But if it could know (form ideas of) the outer reality by inspecting it directly, it would have no need of ideas derived from the intermediary impressions; while if it could not, the latter would be insufficient to convey to the mind what Descartes claims they do convey or what he claims to know about them.

But Descartes never asserts that it is from the intrinsic character of these ideas, or because of the causal processes in our bodies which he describes, that the mind discovers its own ideas to have been so produced. On the contrary, we know this because we can rely on God's veracity. Our knowledge of the process is subsequent to our belief in the existence of bodies, and this is reliable because revealed by God ("taught by nature") and, since the natural belief in itself is not clear and distinct, in no other way. Thus, he avoids what would otherwise be an insuperable obstacle to our knowledge of an external world.

Such a view seems to be an odd reversal of the normal order of things in which our common knowledge of the world is taken to depend directly on sense perception and only supernatural truths are divinely revealed. Consequently, later thinkers, who were disinclined to appeal to divine revelation for our ordinary knowledge of the world around us, attempted to reverse Descartes's order and to explain our knowledge of material objects in terms of the causal process by which effects are produced in the brain. This is the course taken by Locke, but, so far from being more enlightening, we shall find that it leads only to disaster.

4. CRITICISM OF DESCARTES'S THEORY

At least part of the problem originally posed by the separation of the mind from material bodies was to explain how the mind comes to know the material world. This, it will be remembered, is the problem arising out of conception of the world as a machine, which can nevertheless be known by the scientist — the question latent in the reflections of Descartes and his contemporaries. This is not simply a question of how the ideas of material bodies get into our minds (though it is partly that), but also of how we know which of the ideas appearing to be of real things are trustworthy.

Descartes was primarily interested in the second part of the problem. He stresses the notion of knowledge as what is true. To know the world is to know the truth about it. What elements in our experience, then, can we rely on as true of the world? To what criterion of truth can we refer? This was Descartes's original approach when he refused to credit at their face value the ideas he had of material things, because he found reason to believe that some of them (for example, dreams) were deceptive. His question was, in effect, how (by what criterion) do we distinguish illusory perceptions from veridical.

Has Descartes provided any satisfactory answer to this question?

The criterion of truth he has given us is clearness and distinctness, but he explicitly excludes from this the force and sharpness of outline of sensory percepts, asserting that these are no necessary mark of truth. The criterion is intellectual clarity only and seems to be restricted to logical cogency. Can this help us to discriminate between illusory and veridical sense perception — between dream and waking, for example?

It would seem not. Descartes does not argue that our percepts contain in themselves any evidence that they correspond to, or represent, or are caused by eternal things. In fact, in Meditation III he explicitly denies this: "In truth," he says, "I did not perceive it at all." He deduces these relations between our percepts and the external entities only from the veracity of God. Even so, only what is intellectually clear and distinct about material bodies can be accepted as true, only their mathematical properties. But these are common both to illusions and to veridical percepts. Even dream triangles must have three angles totaling 180°. What is mathematically clear and distinct (in Descartes's sense) about sensuous perception is not what enables us to distinguish the imaginary from the real—and it must be noticed in passing that sensory clarity and distinctness are equally unavailing for this purpose, for dreams, hallucinations, and many illusions may be very vivid while veridical perception is often vague and dim.

We can as little appeal to God's veracity in this predicament, because, according to Descartes's argument, that assures us only that there are external objects from which our ideas proceed; it does not tell us whether the ideas represent them correctly or, if any do, which they are. And, as it was declared at the outset that we know ourselves to be deceived sometimes, it is essential to discover how we know this and what enables us to distinguish those sensuous experiences which are not deceptive. As it stands, the argument from God's veracity could apply equally to dreams and hallucinations, for they come to us without our own concurrence and could not be produced by God without deception. It does not help to say that the "confusion" involved in dreams and hallucinations are the source of their falsity, because veridical perception is not always clear, and illusions are often sensorily very sharp and vivid. The confusion, if it is to be relevant, must be confusion of judgment, and unless we know the criterion by which to judge, we have no sure way to avoid confusion.

Let us return to an earlier clue offered by Descartes. He reminds us that perception in itself, whatever it is, is never false. That we have the experience is indubitable, and that it is what it is in our minds. All that is true or false is what we judge about it—for example, that there exists a material thing corresponding to it. What could make such a judgment—a judgment of fact—logically cogent (clear and distinct)?

If logical necessity were purely a result of tautology it could never apply to judgments of fact, but it could no more do so if it were, as Descartes alleges, a matter of pure intellectual intuition, for factual matters of the sort under discussion (that there is a table here, that our percepts are caused by bodies which they resemble, and so forth) are never self-evident; nor is it obvious that they could be deduced from any propositions which are self-evident. But if logical cogency is somehow related to systematic interconnection and mutual corroboration of evidence, then it would seem possible to make at least some judgments of fact with assurance.

Now systematic corroboration of evidence is precisely what we do use to distinguish illusion from fact, dream from waking. If a line drawn across radiating transversals looks curved, but when tested with a straight edge coincides with it, I conclude that the first appearance was illusory. If you object that the straightness of the edge with which I tested might have been illusory, I test that again in as many different ways as I can. If they all give me the same result, I am apt to say it *must* be straight. (For instance, if I measure the angles the edge makes with each one of the transversals and find that the sum of the adjacent angles is always 180°, I should regard the proof as cogent.) A persistent objector might say that the perceptions involved in measuring could have been illusory. But then I should appeal to the systematic corroboration of a whole body of evidence that I had found: direct contact tests, measurements of lengths and angles, different appearances from different viewpoints which fit together geometrically, and so on, and I should say that the extent and the coherence of the evidence make it impossible for me to doubt all of it, because to believe in the existence of a world at all is neither more nor less than to believe in just such a coherent, systematic interconnection of objects and their mutual relations. And when I have accumulated a body of systematically corroborative evidence, because it *is* all systematically interrelated, I cannot deny any one item without denying the whole system.

Descartes's argument, whatever its shortcomings may be, would preclude our denying the entire body of evidence, for then we could give no account whatsoever of our experiences. Their occurrence and nature would be sheer mystery. In fact, the situation would be still more serious, as we can see if we retrace briefly the steps of the reasoning. Descartes bases his belief in the existence of an external world of at least some sort upon the veracity of God, and if we understand God in the sense required for the validation of the proofs of His existence, He is the ground of all being of whatever sort. The indubitable existence of a finite ego cannot account for the contents of its own experience; they must then be referred to some other existent which is

---

[3]Observe that recognizing God as the ground of all existence is the same thing as not being deceived by God as to the existence of things. God's existence and His veracity coincide.

grounded in the being of God.[3] To deny this would be equivalent to denying the existence of any ground. But to do that would be to destroy the basis of all belief and to embrace scepticism; and that is impossible without self-contradiction, because it destroys equally the basis of any reason for denial.

If, however, we refrain from this intellectual suicide and follow the direction of Descartes's argument, we must acknowledge the existence of something other than ourselves—some sort of external world which is the source of our sensory experience. If this is to be at all intelligible, its parts must be related in some systematic manner. If, therefore, the factual evidence before us for the reality of this or that object—evidence derived from sense perception—is extensive, systematic, and coherent so that to deny the existence of the object would be to contradict the systematic character of the world we experience, we have all we need or can desire. The cogency of the factual proof, then, amounts to this, that the evidence is such—is so extensive and systematic—that we must either accept the conclusion or abandon all basis for belief in an intelligible world; and that amounts to saying that the acceptance is epistemologically, if not logically, necessary and the proof of existence is compelling.

But to adopt a criterion of this sort would be to hold a different theory about logic and truth from Descartes, and would involve the rejection of self-evidence as the final test and the ultimate source of all truth.

SUGGESTIONS FOR FURTHER READING

René Descartes, *Discourse on Method. Rules for the Direction of the Mind. Principles of Philosophy.* In *Philosophical Works* (E. S. Haldane and G. Ross, eds.). New York: Dover, 1955.

N. Kemp Smith, *New Studies in the Philosophy of Descartes.* New York: Macmillan, 1963.

Mahaffy, Sir John, *Descartes.* London: Blackwood, 1896.

A. Boyce-Gibson, *The Philosophy of Descartes.* London: Methuen, 1932.

R. G. Collingwood, *The Idea of Nature.* New York: Oxford University Press, 1965.

E. E. Harris, *Nature, Mind and Modern Science.* Chapter 6. London: Allen and Unwin, 1954; New York: Humanities Press, 1954.

H. H. Joachim, *Descartes's Rules for the Direction of the Mind.* New York: Barnes & Noble, 1957.

S. V. Keeling, *Descartes.* New York: Oxford University Press, 1934.

J. Maritain, *The Dream of Descartes.* New York: Philosophical Library, 1944.

PART III

Empiricism: Locke,
Berkeley, and Hume

CHAPTER 15

John Locke and the Way
of Ideas

As we have said, the main problem of the seventeenth century was How is the knowledge which man acquires through the sciences related to the mechanical universe which those sciences discover? A different approach from that of Descartes is made by John Locke in his great *Essay Concerning Human Understanding*. This work is too long for us to examine all of it here and we shall look only at those chapters which are essential to Locke's position. We shall omit his arguments rejecting innate ideas and also his discussion (in Book III) of language and confine ourselves to the main contentions by which his position stands or falls.

The great merit of Locke's work (and that of the empirical school in general) is that it broke, once and for all, with an effete tradition, refused to accept doctrines on authority, and appealed directly to experience for the validation of beliefs. Descartes had concentrated so much upon the power of reason that his theory had the effect of playing down the importance of what we learn by experience. But without experience reason would have no material to work upon, and though we shall later find that the sharp separation of thought from sense leads to disaster, the neglect of either is equally fatal. What rationalism tends to

overlook, empiricism stresses (often to excess). In so doing, it redresses
the balance upset by the opposite one-sidedness of theories such as
those we have so far considered.

An Essay Concerning Human Understanding

INTRODUCTION

(Book I, Chapter 1)

1. *An inquiry into the understanding, pleasant and useful.* Since it is the
understanding that sets man above the rest of sensible beings, and gives him all
the advantage and dominion which he has over them, it is certainly a subject,
even for its nobleness, worth our labour to inquire into. The understanding,
like the eye, whilst it makes us see and perceive all other things, takes no
notice of itself; and it requires art and pains to set it at a distance, and make it
its own object. But whatever be the difficulties that lie in the way of this inquiry, whatever it be that keeps us so much in the dark to ourselves, sure I am
that all the light we can let in upon our own minds, all the acquaintance we can
make with our own understandings, will not only be very pleasant, but bring us
great advantage in directing our thoughts in the search of other things.

2. *Design.* This therefore being my purpose, to inquire into the original, certainty, and extent of human knowledge, together with the grounds and degrees
of belief, opinion and assent, I shall not at present meddle with the physical
consideration of the mind, or trouble myself to examine wherein its essence
consists, or by what motions of our spirits or alterations of our bodies, we come
to have any sensation by our organs, or any ideas in our understandings; and
whether those ideas do, in their formation, any or all of them, depend on matter or no: these are speculations which, however curious and entertaining, I
shall decline, as lying out of my way in the design I am now upon. It shall suffice to my present purpose, to consider the discerning faculties of a man as they
are employed about the objects which they have to do with; and I shall imagine
I have not wholly misemployed myself in the thoughts I shall have on this occasion, if, in this historical, plain method, I can give any account of the ways
whereby our understandings come to attain those notions of things we have, and
can set down any measures of the certainty of our knowledge, or the grounds
of those persuasions which are to be found amongst men, so various, different,
and wholly contradictory; and yet asserted somewhere or other with such assurance, and confidence, that he that shall take a view of the opinions of mankind, observe their opposition, and at the same time consider the fondness and
devotion wherewith they are embraced, the resolution and eagerness wherewith they are maintained, may perhaps have reason to suspect that either there
is no such thing as truth at all, or that mankind hath no sufficient means to attain
a certain knowledge of it.

3. *Method.* It is therefore worth while to search out the bounds between opinion and knowledge, and examine by what measures, in things whereof we have no certain knowledge, we ought to regulate our assent, and moderate our persuasions. In order whereunto, I shall pursue this following method:

First. I shall inquire into the original of those ideas, notions, or whatever else you please to call them, which a man observes, and is conscious to himself he has in his mind, and the ways whereby the understanding comes to be furnished with them.

Secondly. I shall endeavour to show what knowledge the understanding hath by those ideas, and the certainty, evidence, and extent of it.

Thirdly. I shall make some inquiry into the nature and grounds of faith or opinion; whereby I mean, that assent which we give to any proposition as true; of whose truth yet we have no certain knowledge: and here we shall have occasion to examine the reasons and degrees of assent.

4. *Useful to know the extent of our comprehension.* If by this inquiry into the nature of the understanding, I can discover the powers thereof, how far they reach, to what things they are in any degree proportionate, and where they fail us, I suppose it may be of use to prevail with the busy mind of man to be more cautious in meddling with things exceeding its comprehension, to stop when it is at the utmost extent of its tether, and to sit down in a quiet ignorance of those things which, upon examination, are found to be beyond the reach of our capacities. We should not then, perhaps, be so forward, out of an affectation of an universal knowledge, to raise questions, and perplex ourselves and others with disputes, about things to which our understandings are not suited, and of which we cannot frame in our minds any clear or distinct perceptions, or whereof (as it has, perhaps, too often happened) we have not any notions at all. If we can find out how far the understanding can extend its view, how far it has faculties to attain certainty, and in what cases it can only judge and guess, we may learn to content ourselves with what is attainable by us in this state.

6. *Knowledge of our capacity a cure of scepticism and idleness.* When we know our own strength, we shall the better know what to undertake with hopes of success; and when we have well surveyed the powers of our own minds, and made some estimate what we may expect from them, we shall not be inclined either to sit still, and not set our thoughts on work at all, in despair of knowing anything; nor, on the other side, question everything, and disclaim all knowledge, because some things are not to be understood. It is of great use to the sailor to know the length of his line, though he cannot with it fathom all the depths of the ocean; it is well he knows that it is long enough to reach the bottom at such places as are necessary to direct his voyage, and caution him against running upon shoals that may ruin him. Our business here is not to know all things, but those which concern our conduct. If we can find out those measures whereby, a rational creature, put in that state which man is in in this world, may and ought to govern his opinions and actions depending thereon, we need not be troubled that some other things escape our knowledge.

7. *Occasion of this Essay.* This was that which gave the first rise to this Essay concerning the Understanding. For I thought that the first step towards satisfying several inquiries the mind of man was very apt to run into, was, to take a survey of our own understandings, examine our own powers, and see to what things they were adapted. Till that was done, I suspected we began at the wrong end, and in vain sought for satisfaction in a quiet and sure possession of truths

that most concerned us, whilst we let loose our thoughts into the vast ocean of being; as if all that boundless extent were the natural and undoubted possession of our understandings, wherein there was nothing exempt from its decisions, or that escaped its comprehension. Thus men, extending their inquiries beyond their capacities, and letting their thoughts wander into those depths where they can find no sure footing, it is no wonder that they raise questions and multiply disputes, which, never coming to any clear resolution, are proper only to continue and increase their doubts, and to confirm them at last in perfect scepticism. Whereas, were the capacities of our understandings well considered, the extent of our knowledge once discovered, and the horizon found which sets the bounds between the enlightened and dark parts of things — between what is and what is not comprehensible by us — men would, perhaps, with less scruple, acquiesce in the avowed ignorance of the one, and employ their thoughts and discourse with more advantage and satisfaction in the other.

8. *What "idea" stands for.* Thus much I thought necessary to say concerning the occasion of this inquiry into human understanding. But, before I proceed on to what I have thought on this subject, I must here, in the entrance, beg pardon of my reader for the frequent use of the word "idea" which he will find in the following treatise. It being that term which, I think, serves best to stand for whatsoever is the object of the understanding when a man thinks, I have used it to express whatever is meant by phantasm, notion, species, or whatever it is which the mind can be employed about in thinking; and I could not avoid frequently using it.

I presume it will be easily granted me, that there are such *ideas* in men's minds. Every one is conscious of them in himself; and men's words and actions will satisfy him that they are in others.

Our first inquiry, then, shall be, how they come into the mind.

OF IDEAS IN GENERAL, AND THEIR ORIGINAL

(Book II, Chapter 1)

1. *Idea is the object of thinking.* Every man being conscious to himself, that he thinks, and that which his mind is applied about, whilst thinking, being the ideas that are there, it is past doubt that men have in their mind several ideas, such as are those expressed by the words, "whiteness," "hardness," "sweetness," "thinking," "motion," "man," "elephant," "army," "drunkenness," and others. It is in the first place then to be inquired, How he comes by them? I know it is a received doctrine, that men have native ideas and original characters stamped upon their minds in their very first being. This opinion I have at large examined already; and, I suppose, what I have said in the foregoing book will be much more easily admitted, when I have shown whence the understanding may get all the ideas it has, and by what ways and degrees they may come into the mind; for which I shall appeal to every one's own observation and experience.

2. *All ideas come from sensation or reflection.* Let us then suppose the mind to be, as we say, white paper, void of all characters, without any ideas; how comes it to be furnished? Whence comes it by that vast store, which the busy and boundless fancy of man has painted on it with an almost endless variety? Whence has it all the materials of reason and knowledge? To this I answer, in

one word, From experience: in that all our knowledge is founded, and from
that it ultimately derives itself. Our observation, employed either about external sensible objects, or about the internal operations of our minds, perceived
and reflected on by ourselves, is that which supplies our understandings with
all the materials of thinking. These two are the foundations of knowledge, from
whence all the ideas we have, or can naturally have, do spring.

3. *The object of sensation one source of ideas.* First. Our senses, conversant
about particular sensible objects, do convey into the mind several distinct
perceptions of things, according to those various ways wherein those objects do
affect them; and thus we come by those ideas we have of yellow, white, heat,
cold, soft, hard, bitter, sweet, and all those which we call sensible qualities;
which when I say the senses convey into the mind, I mean, they from external
objects convey into the mind what produces there those perceptions. This great
source of most of the ideas we have, depending wholly upon our senses, and
derived by them to the understanding, I call "sensation."

4. *The operations of our minds the other source of them.* Secondly. The other
fountain, from which experience furnisheth the understanding with ideas, is
the perception of the operations of our own minds within us, as it is employed
about the ideas it has got; which operations, when the soul comes to reflect on
and consider, do furnish the understanding with another set of ideas which
could not be had from things without; and such are perception, thinking,
doubting, believing, reasoning, knowing, willing, and all the different actings of
our own minds; which we, being conscious of, and observing in ourselves, do
from these receive into our understanding as distinct ideas, as we do from
bodies affecting our senses. This source of ideas every man has wholly in
himself; and though it be not sense as having nothing to do with external
objects, yet it is very like it, and might properly enough be called "internal
sense." But as I call the other "sensation," so I call this "reflection," the ideas it
affords being such only as the mind gets by reflecting on its own operations
within itself. By reflection, then, in the following part of this discourse, I would
be understood to mean that notice which the mind takes of its own operations,
and the manner of them, by reason whereof there come to be ideas of these
operations in the understanding. These two, I say, viz., external material things
as the objects of sensation, and the operations of our own minds within as the
objects of reflection, are, to me, the only originals from whence all our ideas
take their beginnings. The term "operations" here, I use in a large sense, as
comprehending not barely the actions of the mind about its ideas, but some sort
of passions arising sometimes from them, such as is the satisfaction or uneasiness arising from any thought.

5. *All our ideas are of the one or the other of these.* The understanding seems
to me not to have the least glimmering of any ideas which it doth not receive
from one of these two. External objects furnish the mind with the ideas of
sensible qualities, which are all those different perceptions they produce in us;
and the mind furnishes the understanding with ideas of its own operations.

These, when we have taken a full survey of them, and their several modes,
combinations, and relations, we shall find to contain all our whole stock of
ideas; and that we have nothing in our minds which did not come in one of
these two ways. Let any one examine his own thoughts, and thoroughly search
into his understanding, and then let him tell me, whether all the original ideas
he has there, are any other than of the objects of his senses, or of the opera-

tions of his mind considered as objects of his reflection; and how great a mass of knowledge soever he imagines to be lodged there, he will, upon taking a strict view, see that he has not any idea in his mind but what one of these two hath imprinted, though perhaps with infinite variety compounded and enlarged by the understanding, as we shall see hereafter.

6. *Observable in children.* He that attentively considers the state of a child at his first coming into the world, will have little reason to think him stored with plenty of ideas that are to be the matter of his future knowledge. It is by degrees he comes to be furnished with them; and though the ideas of obvious and familiar qualities imprint themselves before the memory begins to keep a register of time and order, yet it is often so late before some unusual qualities come in the way, that there are few men that cannot recollect the beginning of their acquaintance with them; and, if it were worth while, no doubt a child might be so ordered as to have but a very few even of the ordinary ideas till he were grown up to a man. But all that are born into the world being surrounded with bodies that perpetually and diversely affect them, variety of ideas, whether care be taken about it, or no, are imprinted on the minds of children. Light and colours are busy at hand everywhere when the eye is but open; sounds and some tangible qualities fail not to solicit their proper senses, and force an entrance to the mind; but yet I think it will be granted easily, that if a child were kept in a place where he never saw any other but black and white till he were a man, he would have no more ideas of scarlet or green, than he that from his childhood never tasted an oyster or a pine-apple has of those particular relishes.

7. *Men are differently furnished with these according to the different objects they converse with.* Men then come to be furnished with fewer or more simple ideas from without, according as the objects they converse with afford greater or less variety; and from the operations of their minds within, according as they more or less reflect on them. For, though he that contemplates the operations of his mind cannot but have plain and clear ideas of them; yet, unless he turn his thoughts that way, and considers them attentively, he will no more have clear and distinct ideas of all the operations of his mind, and all that may be observed therein, than he will have all the particular ideas of any landscape, or of the parts and motions of a clock, who will not turn his eyes to it, and with attention heed all the parts of it. The picture or clock may be so placed that they may come in his way every day; but yet he will have but a confused idea of all the parts they are made of, till he applies himself with attention to consider them each in particular.

8. *Ideas of reflection later, because they need attention.* And hence we see the reason why it is pretty late before most children get ideas of the operations of their own minds; and some have not any very clear or perfect ideas of the greatest part of them all their lives: — because, though they pass there continually, yet like floating visions, they make not deep impressions enough to leave in the mind clear, distinct, lasting ideas, till the understanding turns inwards upon itself, reflects on its own operations, and makes them the object of its own contemplation.

9. *The soul begins to have ideas when it begins to perceive.* To ask, at what time a man has first any ideas, is to ask when he begins to perceive; having ideas, and perception, being the same thing. I know it is an opinion, that the

soul always thinks; and that it has the actual perception of ideas within itself constantly, as long as it exists; and that actual thinking is as inseparable from the soul, as actual extension is from the body: which, if true, to inquire after the beginning of a man's ideas is the same as to inquire after the beginning of his soul. For, by this account, soul and its ideas, as body and its extension, will begin to exist both at the same time.

10. *The soul thinks not always; for this wants proofs.* But whether the soul be supposed to exist antecedent to, or coeval with, or some time after, the first rudiments or organisation, or the beginnings of life in the body, I leave to be disputed by those who have better thought of that matter. I confess myself to have one of those dull souls that doth not perceive itself always to contemplate ideas; nor can it conceive it any more necessary for the soul always to think, than for the body always to move.

18. *How knows anyone that the soul always thinks? For if it be not a self-evident proposition, it needs proof.* I would be glad also to learn from these men, who so confidently pronounce that the human soul, or, which is all one, that a man, always thinks, how they come to know it; nay, how they come to know that they themselves think, when they themselves do not perceive it? This, I am afraid, is to be sure without proofs, and to know without perceiving. It is, I suspect, a confused notion taken up to serve an hypothesis; and none of those clear truths that either their own evidence forces us to admit, or common experience makes it impudence to deny. For the most that can be said of it is, that it is possible the soul may always think, but not always retain it in memory; and I say, it is as possible that the soul may not always think, and much more probable that it should sometimes not think, than that it should often think, and that a long while together, and not be conscious to itself, the next moment after, that it had thought.

23. If it shall be demanded, then, when a man begins to have any ideas? I think, the true answer is, When he first has any sensation. For since there appear not to be any ideas in the mind before the senses have conveyed any in, I conceive that ideas in the understanding are coeval with sensation; which is such an impression or motion made in some part of the body as produces some perception in the understanding. It is about these impressions made on our senses by outward objects, that the mind seems first to employ itself in such operations as we call "perception," "remembering," "consideration," "reasoning," etc.

24. *The original of all our knowledge.* In time the mind comes to reflect on its own operations about the ideas got by sensation, and thereby stores itself with a new set of ideas, which I call "ideas of reflection." These — the impressions that are made on our senses by outward objects, and its own operations, proceeding from powers intrinsical and proper to itself, which, when reflected on by itself, become also objects of its contemplation — are, as I have said, the original of all knowledge. Thus the first capacity of human intellect is, that the mind is fitted to receive the impressions made on it, either through the senses by outward objects, or by its own operations when it reflects on them. This is the first step a man makes towards the discovery of anything, and the groundwork whereon to build all those notions which ever he shall have naturally in this world. All those sublime thoughts which tower above the clouds, and reach as high as heaven itself, take their rise and footing from here: in all that great

extent wherein the mind wanders in those remote speculations it may seem to be elevated with, it stirs not one jot beyond those ideas which *sense* or *reflection* have offered for its contemplation.

25. *In the reception of simple ideas, the understanding is for the most part passive.* In this part the understanding is merely passive; and whether or not it will have these beginnings and, as it were, materials of knowledge, is not in its own power. For the objects of our senses do many of them obtrude their particular ideas upon our minds, whether we will or no; and the operations of our minds will not let us be without at least some obscure notions of them. No man can be wholly ignorant of what he does when he thinks. These simple ideas, when offered to the mind, the understanding can no more refuse to have, nor alter when they are imprinted, nor blot them out and make new ones itself, than a mirror can refuse, alter or obliterate the images or ideas, which the objects set before it do therein produce. As the bodies that surround us do diversely affect our organs, the mind is forced to receive the impressions, and cannot avoid the perception of those ideas that are annexed to them.

OF SIMPLE IDEAS

(Book II, Chapter 2)

1. *Uncompounded appearances.* The better to understand the nature, manner, and extent of our knowledge, one thing is carefully to be observed concerning the ideas we have; and that is, that some of them are simple, and some complex.

Though the qualities that affect our senses are, in the things themselves, so united and blended that there is no separation, no distance between them; yet it is plain the ideas they produce in the mind enter by the senses simple and unmixed. For though the sight and touch often take in from the same object at the same time different ideas — as a man sees at once motion and colour, the hand feels softness and warmth in the same piece of wax — yet the simple ideas thus united in the same subject are as perfectly distinct as those that come in by different senses; the coldness and hardness which a man feels in a piece of ice being as distinct ideas in the mind as the smell and whiteness of a lily, or as the taste of sugar and smell of a rose: and there is nothing can be plainer to a man than the clear and distinct perception he has of those simple ideas; which, being each it itself uncompounded, contains in it nothing but one uniform appearance or conception in the mind, and is not distinguishable into different ideas.

2. *The mind can neither make nor destroy them.* These simple ideas, the materials of all our knowledge, are suggested and furnished to the mind only by those two ways above mentioned, viz., sensation and reflection. When the understanding is once stored with these simple ideas, it has the power to repeat, compare, and unite them, even to an almost infinite variety, and so can make at pleasure new complex ideas. But it is not in the power of the most exalted wit or enlarged understanding, by any quickness or variety of thoughts, to invent or frame one new simple idea in the mind, not taken in by the ways before mentioned; nor can any force of the understanding destroy those that

are there. The same inability will everyone find in himself, who shall go about to fashion in his understanding any simple idea not received in by his senses from external objects, or by reflection from the operations of his own mind about them.

3. I think it is not possible for anyone to imagine any other qualities in bodies, howsoever constituted, whereby they can be taken notice of, besides sounds, tastes, smells, visible and tangible qualities. And had mankind been made with but four senses, the qualities then, which are the objects of the fifth sense, had been as far from our notice, imagination, and conception, as now any belonging to a sixth, seventh, or eighth sense, can possibly be. I have here followed the common opinion of man's having but five senses, though perhaps there may be justly counted more; but either supposition serves equally to my present purpose.

OF IDEAS OF ONE SENSE

(Book II, Chapter 3)

1. *Division of simple ideas.* The better to conceive the ideas we receive from sensation, it may not be amiss for us to consider them in reference to the different ways whereby they make their approaches to our minds, and make themselves perceivable by us.

First, then, there are some which come into our minds by one sense only.

Secondly. There are others that convey themselves into the mind by more senses than one.

Thirdly. Others that are had from reflection only.

Fourthly. There are some that make themselves way, and are suggested to the mind, by all the ways of sensation and reflection.

We shall consider them apart under these several heads.

1. There are some ideas which have admittance only through one sense, which is peculiarly adapted to receive them. Thus light and colours, as white, red, yellow, blue, with their several degrees or shades and mixtures, as green, scarlet, purple, sea-green, and the rest, come in only by the eyes; all kinds of noises, sounds, and tones, only by the ears; the several tastes and smells, by the nose and palate. And if these organs, or the nerves which are the conduits to convey them from without to their audience in the brain, the mind's presence-room (as I may so call it), are, any of them, so disordered as not to perform their functions, they have no postern to be admitted by, no other way to bring themselves into view, and be received by the understanding.

The most considerable of those belonging to the touch are heat, and cold, and solidity; all the rest — consisting almost wholly in the sensible configuration, as smooth and rough; or else more or less firm adhesion of the parts, as hard and soft, tough and brittle — are obvious enough.

2. I think it will be needless to enumerate all the particular simple ideas belonging to each sense. Nor indeed is it possible if we would, there being a great many more of them belonging to most of the senses than we have names for. I shall therefore, in the account of simple ideas I am here giving, content myself to set down only such as are most material to our present purpose, or are in themselves less apt to be taken notice of, though they are very frequent-

ly the ingredients of our complex ideas; amongst which I think I may well account "solidity," which therefore I shall treat of in the next chapter.

OF SIMPLE IDEAS OF REFLECTION

(Book II, Chapter 6)

1. *Simple ideas of reflection are the operations of the mind about its other ideas.* The mind, receiving the ideas mentioned in the foregoing chapters from without, when it turns its view inward upon itself, and observes its own actions about those ideas it has, takes from thence other ideas, which are as capable to be the object of its contemplation as any of those it received from foreign things.

2. *The idea of perception, and idea of willing, we have from reflection.* The two great and principal actions of the mind, which are most frequently considered, and which are so frequent that everyone that pleases may take notice of them in himself, are these two: perception or thinking, and volition or willing. The power of thinking is called "the understanding," and the power of volition is called "the will"; and these two powers or abilities in the mind are denominated "faculties." Of some of the modes of these simple ideas of reflection, such as are remembrance, discerning, reasoning, judging, knowledge, faith, etc., I shall have occasion to speak hereafter.

1. THE SOURCE AND NATURE OF IDEAS

The position developed by Locke is important because it is closely akin to the account of knowledge which would normally be given by a non-philosopher who might be brought to reflect on the question how we come to know about the objects in the world around us. And it is instructive because the consequences to which it leads are incoherent. In the last analysis, Locke's theory is question-begging, inconsistent, and impossible, but until we see why this is so we are very liable to fall into similar errors; and even philosophers who know the difficulties of Locke's position have tried to revive it, and have hoped that, by a little juggling, they can somehow make it work.

Locke is more concerned with how we get knowledge than with the criterion of truth, though he does finally address himself — with questionable success — to that matter also. His first and constant assertion is that all knowledge comes from experience, and none of it is innate in the mind. But just what Locke means by experience is not obvious, and we shall have to determine this from the way in which he develops his theory.

He completely rejects the doctrine that the mind brings with it any innate ideas. To begin with, it is "formless and void," like the world in the second verse of the Book of Genesis. It is like a blank tablet, "white paper, void of all characters," an empty cabinet, or a dark room. We begin to know only when we first begin to have "ideas" and these we acquire through the senses, in the first instance, and, in the second, from reflection upon the operations of our mind, which, without "ideas of sensation", it could not perform.

How, then, do we acquire ideas by means of the senses? Locke describes the process without adducing evidence or argument. He does so only briefly, in one passage, and he does not dwell upon or elaborate the hypothesis, perhaps because, as he says in the Introduction, he does not wish "to meddle with physical considerations of the mind." Nevertheless, this hypothesis is central to his whole theory and the source of its incoherence. In Chapter 8 of the *Essay* (see below, p. 238) he writes:

> If, then, external objects be not united to our minds when they produce ideas in it, and yet we perceive these original qualities in such of them as singly fall under our senses, it is evident that some motion must be thence continued by our nerves or animal spirits, by some parts of our bodies, to the brains or the seat of sensation, there to produce in our minds the particular ideas we have of them.[1]

Ideas are thus the end results of physical and physiological processes which convey certain "motions" from external objects to our brains, that somehow produce effects in our minds (or consciousness).

This, however, is not how Locke defines ideas. They are, he says, "whatsoever is the object of the understanding when a man thinks" (Book I, Chapter 1, 8), or "that which the mind is applied about, whilst thinking" (Book II, Chapter 1, 1), or "the immediate object of perception, thought, or understanding" (Book II, Chapter 8, 8). These definitions are very wide and clearly are meant to include all possible objects of consciousness, but the ultimate origin of all these objects of thinking is for Locke sensation (for even ideas of reflection presuppose those of sensation as that upon which the mind operates), and ideas of sensation are produced in our minds in the manner described above. However that may be, once we have them, they are essentially objects of perception, "that which the mind is applied about, whilst thinking," and when not perceived (Locke tells us) they are nothing at all.[2]

---

[1]We are reminded of Hobbes' remark, "Neither in us . . . are they anything else, but diverse motions (for motion produceth nothing but motion). But its appearance to us is Fancy the same waking that dreaming." (*Leviathan*, Chapter I)

[2]*Essay*, Book II, Chapter 10, 2. "But our ideas being nothing but actual perceptions in the mind, which cease to be anything when there is no perception of them . . . "

The end results of the physico-physiological process are "ideas of sensation," reflection on the operation of the mind upon these produces "ideas of reflection" and both kinds may be either simple or complex, the latter being combinations of the former. But how the transition is effected — or could be — between the physiological process and the mental Locke never considers. Yet, even if we raise no question or demur on this score, the theory leads to insurmountable difficulties.

2. THE FIRST BEGINNINGS OF KNOWLEDGE

(a) SIMPLE IDEAS OF SENSATION. What Locke says in some places about simple ideas of sensation is inconsistent with what he says of them in others, and the examples he gives of them are so various that it is not immediately clear what they are supposed to be. Sometimes he speaks of them as if they are what modern philosophers call sense data: for example, patches of color, sounds, scents, and the like; sometimes he refers to the qualities of objects as simple ideas; sometimes they seem to be abstract ideas of color or other qualities. In Book II, Chapter 1, 3, he speaks of "yellow, white, heat, cold, soft, hard, bitter, sweet" as "sensible qualities," and though it is not yet specified whether or not they are simple ideas, they are said to be the objects of sensation and to be conveyed into the mind by the senses (we have already seen that immediate objects of perception, and that which the mind is applied about when thinking, are ideas), and we are left with the strong impression that these are examples of simple ideas of sensation.

In the following chapter he mentions "softness and warmth," "coldness and hardness" as distinct ideas, under the heading of simple, and also the "smell of a rose," "the taste of sugar," and "the whiteness of a lily." To all of these he refers as simple ideas. But "yellow" and "white" are the general names of certain colors; "softness," "warmth," "coldness," "hardness" and "whiteness" are abstract nouns; "the smell of a rose," if meant to be a particular scent, is, like "the taste of sugar," a sense datum. On the other hand, if the last two are meant as general descriptions, they are universal ideas. Nevertheless, in spite of Locke's imprecision there is little doubt that what he really intends is simple sense data like a color patch, a whiff of scent, a tang of taste, and so forth. And he insists that each one of them is *a particular existent*. This should be remembered, as it will later be seen to have important consequences.

Locke tells us further (Book II, Chapter 2) that though in the things themselves the qualities that affect our senses are "so united and blended that there is no separation, no distance between them," the ideas they produce in the mind are distinct and separate, simple and unmixed:

The coldness and hardness which a man feels in a piece of ice being as distinct ideas in the mind as the smell and whiteness of a lily, or as the taste of sugar and the smell of a rose.

(b) SIMPLE IDEAS OF REFLECTION. These must not be confused with reflection upon ideas — or ideas derived from reflection upon experience. They are not abstract, or philosophical, or theoretical ideas as opposed to immediate experience. What Locke means by reflection is better indicated by the word reflex. Ideas of reflection, for him, are the product of introspection — that is, the awareness of the workings of our own minds. They are the mind's ideas of its own operation "as it is employed about the ideas it has got" (by sensation).

These reflex ideas are just as immediate as are the ideas of sensation and Locke calls this form of apprehension "internal sense" (Book II, Chapter 1, 4). Ideas of reflection are no less primitive or primary than ideas of sensation, except that before the mind has acquired any of the latter, it does not begin to be employed about anything, or to operate, and so there are no objects for ideas of reflection. Thus ideas of sensation are prior in time and their existence is a necessary condition of our having ideas of reflection, but in other respects the two types of idea are coordinate and, for Locke, are the original materials of all our knowledge.

These two kinds of idea are said to be the original source and the first beginnings of knowledge. They comprise "our whole stock of ideas" and out of them (as out of a stock of building bricks) all our knowledge is constructed.

Nor let any one think these too narrow bounds for the capacious mind of man to expatiate in, which takes its flight farther than the stars, and cannot be confined by the limits of the world. I grant all this, but desire any one to assign any simple idea which is not received from one of those inlets before mentioned, nor any complex idea not made out of those simple ones.

3. PASSIVITY AND ACTIVITY OF THE MIND

In the receipt of these simple ideas the mind is wholly passive. It cannot make or destroy them at will or alter them as they come to it, any more than a mirror can reject or alter or obliterate the images of the objects it reflects. But the mind can operate in various ways with simple ideas it has already received. It can repeat or recall them (or most of them) after they have passed away, it can separate or combine them in infinite permutations, different from the order and combinations in which they come to it.

The results of these operations are (a) complex ideas—combinations of simple ones; (b) ideas of relation or comparison, and (c) abstract ideas, that is, ideas separated from others which normally accompany them, as when we think of a color apart from its shape, or a shape without considering what color it may be or what material it may have.

4. AMBIGUITY OF LOCKE'S USE OF "IDEA"

The account Locke gives of ideas contains a radical ambiguity which later proves fatal to his theory of knowledge.

First, he describes them as coming to us from external objects—as the end product of a causal process; but also, secondly, he says that they are immediate objects of perception "which cease to be anything when there is no perception of them." Their being imprinted on the understanding is nothing but "the making of them to be perceived." In ideas as such—as immediate objects of perception—there is nothing to suggest the alleged manner of their production. We do not perceive the causal process by which some "motion" is transmitted from an external object to our organ of sense and thence, through the nerves, to the brain, or the brain's generation of an idea in our mind. We perceive only the idea (or immediate object, which ceases to be anything when not perceived). Later we find Locke insisting that ideas are totally unlike their causes, so different, he says, that no two ideas can be more so.[3] It is, therefore, not in or through the perception of the ideas themselves that we learn how they are produced in us by external things. We shall find it hard, on the basis of Locke's theory, to explain how we can ever discover this process.

But whichever way we understand the word "idea," whether as the product of a causal process originating externally, or as an immediate object of awareness affording no evidence of its external source, it is clear that ideas are and can only be "in the mind." The end product of

---

[3]*Essay*, Book III, Chapter 4, 10: "For the cause of any sensation, and the sensation itself, in all simple ideas of one sense, are two ideas; and two ideas so different and distant one from another, that no two can be more so."

the causal chain is the idea in the mind and, likewise, the immediate object of perception is the idea in the mind, which ceases to be anything at all when it is not perceived.[4]

As for the mind, its whole furniture and all its contents are constituted by ideas, without which it is altogether empty and blank, and the only sources from which ideas can be originally obtained are sensation and reflection.

How, we must ask, does the mind acquire the idea of the causal process by which its ideas of sensation are produced in it? This is the crucial question for Locke, though he never explicitly raises it and postpones as long as possible the duty of facing the problem of how we know which ideas are so produced, and that they are so produced. Yet, upon the possibility of solving this problem his whole theory of knowledge eventually has to depend.

---

[4]We shall find Berkeley deriving far-reaching consequences from this contention.

CHAPTER 16

Primary and Secondary Qualities

SOME FARTHER CONSIDERATIONS CONCERNING OUR SIMPLE IDEAS

(Book II, Chapter 8)

1. *Positive ideas from privative causes.* Concerning the simple ideas of sensation it is to be considered, that whatsoever is so constituted in nature as to be able by affecting our senses to cause any perception in the mind, doth thereby produce in the understanding a simple idea; which, whatever be the external cause of it, when it comes to be taken notice of by our discerning faculty, it is by the mind looked on and considered there to be a real positive idea in the understanding, as much as any other whatsoever; though perhaps the cause of it be but a privation in the subject.

2. Thus the ideas of heat and cold, light and darkness, white and black, motion and rest, are equally clear and positive ideas in the mind; though perhaps some of the causes which produce them are barely privations in those subjects from whence our senses derive those ideas.

7. *Ideas in the mind, qualities in bodies.* To discover the nature of our ideas the better, and to discourse of them intelligibly, it will be convenient to distinguish them, as they are ideas or perceptions in our minds, and as they are modifications of matter in the bodies that cause such perceptions in us; that so we may not think (as perhaps usually is done) that they are exactly the images and resemblances of something inherent in the subject; most of those of sensation being in the mind no more the likeness of something existing without us

than the names that stand for them are the likeness of our ideas, which yet upon hearing they are apt to excite in us.

8. Whatsoever the mind perceives in itself, or is the immediate object of perception, thought, or understanding, that I call "idea"; and the power to produce any idea in our mind, I call "quality" of the subject wherein that power is. Thus a snowball having the power to produce in us the ideas of white, cold, and round, the powers to produce those ideas in us as they are in the snowball, I call "qualities"; as they are sensations or perceptions in our understandings, I call them "ideas"; which ideas, if I speak of them sometimes as in the things themselves, I would be understood to mean those qualities in the objects which produce them in us.

9. *Primary qualities.* Qualities thus considered in bodies are, First, such as are utterly inseparable from the body, in what estate soever it be; such as, in all the alterations and changes it suffers, all the force can be used upon it, it constantly keeps; and such as sense constantly finds in every particle of matter which has bulk enough to be perceived, and the mind finds inseparable from every particle of matter, though less than to make itself singly be perceived by our senses; *v.g.*, take a grain of wheat, divide it into two parts, each part has still solidity, extension, figure, and mobility; divide it again, and it retains still the same qualities; and so divide it on till the parts become insensible, they must retain still each of them all those qualities. For, division (which is all that a mill or pestle or any other body does upon another, in reducing it to insensible parts) can never take away either solidity, extension, figure, or mobility from any body, but only makes two or more distinct separate masses of matter of that which was but one before; all which distinct masses, reckoned as so many distinct bodies, after division, make a certain number. These I call *original* or *primary* qualities of body, which I think we may observe to produce simple ideas in us, viz., solidity, extension, figure, motion or rest, and number.

10. *Secondary qualities.* Secondly. Such qualities, which in truth are nothing in the objects themselves, but powers to produce various sensations in us by their primary qualities, *i.e.*, by the bulk, figure, texture, and motion of their insensible parts, as colours, sounds, tastes, etc., these I call *secondary* qualities. To these might be added a third sort, which are allowed to be barely powers, though they are as much real qualities in the subject as those which I, to comply with the common way of speaking, call qualities, but, for distinction, *secondary* qualities. For, the power in fire to produce a new colour or consistence in wax or clay by its primary qualities, is as much a quality in fire as the power it has to produce in me a new idea or sensation of warmth or burning, which I felt not before, by the same primary qualities, viz., the bulk, texture, and motion of its insensible parts.

11. *How primary qualities produce their ideas.* The next thing to be considered is, how bodies produce ideas in us; and that is manifestly by impulse, the only way which we can conceive bodies operate in.

12. If, then, external objects be not united to our minds when they produce ideas in it, and yet we perceive these original qualities in such of them as singly fall under our senses, it is evident that some motion must be thence continued by our nerves or animal spirits, by some parts of our bodies, to the brain or the seat of sensation, there to produce in our minds the particular ideas we have of them. And since the extension, figure, number, and motion of bodies of an observable bigness, may be perceived at a distance by the sight, it is evident

some singly imperceptible bodies must come from them to the eyes, and thereby convey to the brain some motion which produces these ideas which we have of them in us.

13. *How secondary.* After the same manner that the ideas of these original qualities are produced in us, we may conceive that the ideas of secondary qualities are also produced, viz., by the operation of insensible particles on our senses. For it being manifest that there are bodies, and good store of bodies, each whereof are so small that we cannot by any of our senses discover either their bulk, figure, or motion (as is evident in the particles of the air and water, and other extremely smaller than those, perhaps as much smaller than the particles of air or water as the particles of air or water are smaller than pease or hailstones): let us suppose at present that the different motions and figures, bulk and number, of such particles, affecting the several organs of our senses, produce in us those different sensations which we have from the colours and smells of bodies, *v. g.*, that a violet, by the impulse of such insensible particles of matter of peculiar figures and bulks, and in different degrees and modifications of their motions, causes the ideas of the blue colour and sweet scent of that flower to be produced in our minds; it being no more impossible to conceive that God should annex such ideas to such motions with which they have no similitude, than that He should annex the idea of pain to the motion of a piece of steel dividing our flesh, with which that idea hath no resemblance.

14. What I have said concerning colours and smells may be understood also of tastes and sounds, and other the like sensible qualities; which, whatever reality we by mistake attribute to them, are in truth nothing in the objects themselves, but powers to produce various sensations in us, and depend on those primary qualities, viz., bulk, figure, texture, and motion of parts, as I have said.

15. *Ideas of primary qualities are resemblances; of secondary, not.* From whence I think it is easy to draw this observation, that the ideas of primary qualities of bodies are resemblances of them, and their patterns do really exist in the bodies themselves; but the ideas produced in us by these secondary qualities have no resemblance of them at all. There is nothing like our ideas existing in the bodies themselves. They are, in the bodies we denominate from them, only a power to produce those sensations in us; and what is sweet, blue, or warm in idea, is but the certain bulk, figure, and motion of the insensible parts in the bodies themselves, which we call so.

16. Flame is denominated *hot* and *light*; snow, *white* and *cold*, and manna, *white* and *sweet*, from the ideas they produce in us, which qualities are commonly thought to be the same in those bodies that those ideas are in us, the one the perfect resemblance of the other, as they are in a mirror, and it would by most men be judged very extravagant, if one should say otherwise. And yet he that will consider that the same fire that at one distance produces in us the sensation of warmth, does at a nearer approach produce in us the far different sensation of pain, ought to bethink himself what reason he has to say, that his idea of warmth which was produced in him by the fire, is actually in the fire, and his idea of pain which the same fire produced in him the same way is not in the fire. Why is whiteness and coldness in snow and pain not, when it produces the one and the other idea in us, and can do neither but by the bulk, figure, number, and motion of its solid parts?

17. The particular bulk, number, figure, and motion of the parts of fire or snow are really in them, whether anyone's senses perceive them or no; and

therefore they may be called *real* qualities, because they really exist in those bodies. But light, heat, whiteness, or coldness, are no more really in them than sickness or pain is in manna. Take away the sensation of them; let not the eyes see light or colours, nor the ears hear sounds; let the palate not taste, nor the nose smell; and all colours, tastes, odours and sounds, as they are such particular ideas, vanish and cease, and are reduced to their causes, *i. e.*, bulk, figure, and motion of parts.

18. A piece of manna of a sensible bulk is apt to produce in us the idea of a round or square figure; and, by being removed from one place to another, the idea of motion. This idea of motion represents it as it really is in the manna moving; a circle or square are the same, whether in idea or existence, in the mind or in the manna; and this both motion and figure are really in the manna, whether we take notice of them or no: this everybody is ready to agree to. Besides, manna, by the bulk, figure, texture, and motion of its parts, has a power to produce the sensations of sickness, and sometimes of acute pains or gripings, in us. That these ideas of sickness and pain are not in the manna, but effects of its operations on us, and are nowhere when we feel them not; this also everyone agrees to. And yet men are hardly to be brought to think that sweetness and whiteness are not really in manna, which are but the effects of the operations of manna by the motion, size and figure of its particles on the eyes and palate; as the pain and sickness caused by manna, are confessedly nothing but the effects of its operations on the stomach and guts by the size, motion, and figure of its insensible parts (for by nothing else can a body operate, as has been proved).

22. I have, in what just goes before, been engaged in physical inquiries a little farther than perhaps I intended. But it being necessary to make the nature of sensation a little understood, and to make the difference between the qualities in bodies and the ideas produced by them in the mind to be distinctly conceived, without which it were impossible to discourse intelligibly of them, I hope I shall be pardoned this little excursion into natural philosophy, it being necessary in our present inquiry to distinguish the primary and real qualities of bodies, which are always in them (viz., solidity, extension, figure, number, and motion or rest, and are sometimes perceived by us, viz., when the bodies they are in are big enough singly to be discerned), from those secondary and imputed qualities, which are but the powers of several combinations of those primary ones, when they operate without being distinctly discerned; whereby we also may come to know what ideas are, and what are not, resemblances of something really existing in the bodies we denominate from them.

23. *Three sorts of qualities in bodies.* The qualities then that are in bodies, rightly considered, are of three sorts:

First. The bulk, figure, number, situation, and motion or rest of their solid parts; those are in them, whether we perceive them or no; and when they are of that size that we can discover them, we have by these an idea of the thing as it is in itself, as is plain in artificial things. These I call *primary* qualities.

Secondly. The power that is in any body by reason of its insensible primary qualities, to operate after a peculiar manner on any of our senses, and thereby produce in us the different ideas of several colours, sounds, smells, tastes, etc. These are usually called *sensible* qualities.

Thirdly. The power that is in any body, by reason of the particular constitution of its primary qualities, to make such a change in the bulk, figure, texture, and motion of another body, as to make it operate on our senses differently from what it did before. Thus the sun has a power to make wax white, and fire, to make lead fluid. These are usually called "powers."

The first of these, as has been said, I think may be properly called real, original, or primary qualities, because they are in the things themselves, whether they are perceived or no; and upon their different modifications it is that the secondary qualities depend.

The other two are only powers to act differently upon other things, which powers result from the different modifications of those primary qualities.

24. *The first are resemblances; the second thought resemblances, but are not; the third neither are, nor are thought so.* But though these two latter sorts of qualities are powers barely, and nothing but powers, relating to several other bodies, and resulting from the different modifications of the original qualities, yet they are generally otherwise thought of. For the second sort, viz., the powers to produce several ideas in us by our senses, are looked upon as real qualities in the things thus affecting us; but the third sort are called and esteemed barely powers. *V. g.*, the idea of heat or light which we receive by our eyes or touch from the sun, are commonly thought real qualities existing in the sun, and something more than mere powers in it. But when we consider the sun in reference to wax, which it melts or blanches, we look upon the whiteness and softness produced in the wax, not as qualities in the sun, but effects produced by powers in it: whereas, if rightly considered, these qualities of light and warmth, which are perceptions in me when I am warmed or enlightened by the sun, are no otherwise in the sun than the changes made in the wax, when it is blanched or melted, are in the sun. They are all of them equally powers in the sun, depending on its primary qualities, whereby it is able in the one case so to alter the bulk, figure, texture, or motion of some of the insensible parts of my eyes or hands as thereby to produce in me the idea of light or heat, and in the other it is able so to alter the bulk, figure, texture, or motion of the insensible parts of the wax as to make them fit to produce in me the distinct ideas of white and fluid.

25. The reason why the one are ordinarily taken for real qualities, and the other only for bare powers, seems to be because the ideas we have of distinct colours, sounds, etc., containing nothing at all in them of bulk, figure, or motion, we are not apt to think them the effects of these primary qualities which appear not to our senses to operate in their production, and with which they have not any apparent congruity, or conceivable connection. Hence it is that we are so forward to imagine that those ideas are the resemblances of something really existing in the objects themselves, since sensation discovers nothing of bulk, figure, or motion of parts, in their production, nor can reason show how bodies by their bulk, figure, and motion, should produce in the mind the ideas of blue or yellow, etc. But, in the other case, in the operations of bodies changing the qualities one of another, we plainly discover that the quality produced hath commonly no resemblance with anything in the thing producing it; wherefore we look on it as a bare effect of power. For though, receiving the idea of heat or light from the sun, we are apt to think it is a perception and resemblance of such a quality in the sun, yet when we see wax or a fair face receive change of colour from the sun, we cannot imagine that to be the perception or resemblance of anything in the sun, because we find not those different colours in the sun itself: for, our senses being able to observe a likeness or unlikeness of sensible qualities in two different external objects, we forwardly enough conclude the production of any sensible quality in any subject to be an effect of bare power, and not the communication of any quality which

was really in the efficient, when we find no such sensible quality in the thing that produced it. But our senses not being able to discover any unlikeness between the idea produced in us and the quality of the object producing it, we are apt to imagine that our ideas are resemblances of something in the objects, and not the effects of certain powers placed in the modification of their primary qualities, with which primary qualities the ideas produced in us have no resemblance.

26. *Secondary qualities twofold: first, immediately perceivable; secondly, mediately perceivable.* To conclude: Besides those before-mentioned primary qualities in bodies, viz., bulk, figure, extension, number, and motion of their solid parts, all the rest whereby we take notice of bodies, and distinguish them one from another, are nothing else but several powers in them depending on those primary qualities, whereby they are fitted, either by immediately operating on our bodies, to produce several different ideas in us; or else by operating on other bodies, so to change their primary qualities as to render them capable of producing ideas in us different from what before they did. The former of these, I think, may be called secondary qualities immediately perceivable; the latter, secondary qualities mediately perceivable.

1. IDEAS IN OUR MINDS AND QUALITIES IN BODIES

Locke distinguishes between ideas "as they are perceptions in our minds" and "as they are modifications of matter in the bodies which cause perceptions in us." This implies, or should imply, that, as ideas are in our minds, so far as modifications of matter in the bodies are ideas, these must also be in our minds. Of course, Locke does not intend to say that they are, but what he does intend is not consistent with his account of ideas. For if the modifications of matter are not in our minds they cannot be ideas in any sense, but at most, causes of them. Yet we have already noted, and shall soon find even more distressingly, that the causal relation is difficult to explain and a source of considerable epistemological perplexity.

In us, however, the ideas are perceptions. In the bodies they are said to be qualities, or powers to produce ideas in us.

Such qualities are of two, or even of three, kinds:

(a) PRIMARY QUALITIES. Those which are "utterly inseparable from body in what state so-ever it may be," for example, figure, extension, number, mobility, and solidity, are called primary qualities. If a body could be deprived of these qualities it would no longer be a body, and whatever can be called a body possesses them all.

Notice that these are the measurable properties of things, in virtue of which they may be described quantitatively. They are those aspects of things which can be treated mathematically — what Descartes commended to our notice as the ideas of external bodies which are, or can be made, clear and distinct. These were the properties to the investigation of which the new science was exclusively devoted and were the foundation of its mechanistic conception of the world.

Ideas of these qualities, Locke says, are resemblances of the actual qualities as they really exist in the things. "Their patterns do really exist in the bodies themselves." They represent the qualities precisely as they are in the bodies. This gives us what we shall call a *representative theory* of perception, according to which the idea is a sort of copy or picture of the object.

(b) SECONDARY QUALITIES. Other qualities such as colors, sounds, odors, tastes and tactual qualities like heat and cold are produced in us by the action upon our sense organs of the "bulk, figure, texture, and motion" of the insensible particles of bodies impinging upon them. These are all the qualitative aspects of things which cannot be treated mathematically (even though they may be correlated with primary qualities which can).

Locke denies that the ideas of these qualities resemble anything at all in the bodies themselves and so they are merely secondary qualities. The ideas of them, however, do correspond to powers in the bodies to produce effects in us. With respect to secondary qualities, therefore, Locke gives what we may call a *causal* or *correspondence theory* of perception.[1]

The secondary qualities are in the bodies at all only as causal properties and, Locke says, they in no way differ from other causal powers which a body may have. For instance, the power of fire to cause a sensation of heat in us is of the same kind as its power to melt wax. Locke actually classifies these other powers as a third sort of quality, but he regards them as on a par with secondary for they are all just various powers to produce various effects.

2. THE DISTINCTION AND DIVERGENCE
OF CAUSE AND EFFECT

What we must especially note is that our ideas of secondary qualities are quite unlike their causes, which reside in the bulk, figure, texture, and motion of the *insensible* parts of bodies. Being insensible, we can (presumably) have no ideas of sensation depicting these minute particles. They are not perceived at all and so, as Locke admits, our ideas

[1]As we have seen, the distinction of primary and secondary qualities is also to be found in the Sixth Meditation of Descartes and it had previously been made by Galileo. It did not originate even with him but can be traced back to the ancient Atomists, in particular to Democritus.

contain "nothing of them" and "they appear not to our senses to operate in their production" (Book II, Chapter 8, 25). But that such ideas as
we have of secondary qualities should be associated with such causes,
which are totally unlike the ideas, Locke thinks no more impossible
than that pain should be associated with the dividing of flesh by a
sword (Book II, Chapter 8, 13). It does not occur to him that his example is no less puzzling than that which it is meant to elucidate. That we
feel pain when our flesh is lacerated is no more intelligible than that we
see colors when light falls upon our eyes, or hear sounds when vibrations enter our ears. We can explain or understand any one of these
phenomena as little or as much as any other.

Strictly speaking, we should not attribute secondary qualities, as we
perceive them, to bodies at all, and Locke does so (he says) only "to
comply with the common way of speaking." We habitually do attribute
them to bodies only because *we do not perceive their causes.* There is
no difference in principle between things causing ideas in us and their
causing changes in one another, yet when the fire melts the wax we do
not attribute the liquidity of the wax to the fire, though when it produces a sensation of heat or brightness in us we do attribute these
qualities to it. Nevertheless, Locke assures us, the power to produce
the change is a real property of the thing which causes it.

The significant feature of the causal theory of perception offered
here is that it excludes representation. The idea is said to correspond to
a power in the object which causes it, but it does not in any way represent or reveal that cause, which appears not to our senses to operate.
Serious and insurmountable difficulties follow from this position.

3. CONSEQUENCES OF THE DOCTRINE

If all this is as Locke says, how do we come to know it? He insisted at
the beginning that the original and only source of our knowledge was
ideas, all derived in the first instance from simple ideas of sensation
and reflection. What does not appear to our senses, therefore, is not
among our simple ideas and so is no part of our knowledge. The causes
of our ideas of sensation are not (or at least are not held to be) simply
the operations of our minds, so we cannot have any ideas of reflection
which reveal them to us. How then do we discover what they are? Can
we in any way infer from alleged effects, which are ideas, to causes,
which are not ideas, and if we cannot, how can we acquire any ideas of
the causes at all? Let us consider these questions.

In Chapter 23 of Book II Locke tells us that "had we senses acute
enough to discern the minute particles of bodies, and the real constitu-

tion on which their sensible qualities depend . . . they would produce quite different ideas in us" (see p. 251 below). How, we may ask, would these ideas be different, Would they not be ideas of secondary qualities and, if not, then of what would they be ideas?

If we had such acute senses, Locke suggests, the yellow color of gold would disappear and we should see only "an admirable texture of parts of a certain size and figure." But how should we see these if they had no color of any sort? Locke failed to realize, as Berkeley later did not, that without ideas of secondary qualities we should have no sensible ideas of bodies at all, and so, according to his theory, no knowledge of them whatsoever.

Yet secondary qualities, as we perceive them, are not resemblances of anything, and their causes do not appear in them. How then can we discover these causes, ideas of which Locke provides no means of obtaining? Could we infer from our perception of the causes by some objects of effects in others that our ideas of secondary qualities are similar effects of similar causes? It would hardly seem so because the conclusion would not follow from the premise. That B is caused by A is no evidence that D is caused by C. Moreover, when we perceive A causing B, we have ideas of both and of the relation between them, but the ideas themselves are not similarly related in our experience to anything else, and Locke is quite clear and specific on this point. Moreover, in the first case both cause (A) and effect (B) are ideas, but in the second the cause is not an idea at all and we have none of it and no means of obtaining any. How, then, is it possible to infer from ideas to a relation between those ideas and things which are not, and of which we have no, ideas? The belief that we can do this legitimately, or in any way, is a persistent and prevalent belief, but it has no ground or foundation whatever.

This being so, the whole of Locke's theory is put in jeopardy, for he claims to know that our ideas are caused in the way he describes and that there are bodies in the external world which cause them, which possess powers to produce ideas of secondary qualities, and also primary qualities of which the ideas are resemblances. Yet, if we all acquire knowledge by acquiring ideas in this manner, the theorist (Locke) himself must have acquired his own knowledge of all these facts in the same way, and the account he gives of the ideas is such that it provides no means of discovering the facts he claims to know. This result is reinforced and the predicament intensifies as Locke proceeds, so let us pass on to the next main feature of his .doctrine which contributes to the central problem he is bound to face if his theory of knowledge is to succeed. This next feature is Locke's theory of substance.

CHAPTER 17

The Idea of Substance

OF OUR COMPLEX IDEAS OF SUBSTANCES

(Book II, Chapter 23)

1. *Ideas of substances, how made.* The mind being, as I have declared, furnished with a great number of the simple ideas conveyed in by the senses, as they are found in exterior things, or by reflection on its own operations, takes notice, also, that a certain number of these simple ideas go constantly together; which being presumed to belong to one thing, and words being suited to common apprehensions, and made use of for quick despatch, are called, so united in one subject, by one name; which, by inadvertency, we are apt afterward to talk of and consider as one simple idea, which indeed is a complication of many ideas together: because, as I have said, not imagining how these simple ideas can subsist by themselves, we accustom ourselves to suppose some *substratum* wherein they do subsist, and from which they do result; which therefore we call "substance."

2. *Our idea of substance in general.* So that if anyone will examine himself concerning his notion of pure substance in general, he will find he has no other idea of it at all, but only a supposition of he knows not what support of such qualities which are capable of producing simple ideas in us; which qualities are commonly called "accidents." If anyone should be asked, "What is the subject wherein colour or weight inheres?" he would have nothing to say but, "The solid extended parts." And if he were demanded "What is it that solidity and

extension inhere in?" he would not be in a much better case than the Indian before mentioned, who, saying that the world was supported by a great elephant, was asked, what the elephant rested on? to which his answer was, "A great tortoise": but being again pressed to know what gave support to the broad-backed tortoise, replied — something, he knew not what. And thus here, as in all other cases where we use words without having clear and distinct ideas, we talk like children; who, being questioned what such a thing is which they know not readily, give this satisfactory answer — that it is something; which in truth signified no more, when so used, either by children or men, but that they know not what; and that the thing they pretend to know and talk of, is what they have no distinct idea of at all, and so are perfectly ignorant of it, and in the dark. The idea, then, we have, to which we give the general name "substance", being nothing but the supposed, but unknown, support of those qualities we find existing, which we imagine cannot subsist *sine re substante*, "without something to support them", we call that support *substantia*; which, according to the true import of the word, is, in plain English, "standing under", or "upholding".

3. *Of the sorts of substances.* An obscure and relative idea of substance in general being thus made, we come to have the ideas of particular sorts of substances, by collecting such combinations of simple ideas as are by experience and observation of men's senses taken notice of to exist together, and are therefore supposed to flow from the particular internal constitution or unknown essence of that substance. Thus we come to have the ideas of a man, horse, gold, water, etc., of which substances, whether anyone has any other clear idea, farther than of certain simple ideas co-existing together, I appeal to everyone's own experience. It is the ordinary qualities observable in iron or a diamond, put together, that make the true complex idea of those substances, which a smith or a jeweller commonly knows better than a philosopher; who, whatever substantial forms he may talk of, has no other idea of those substances than what is framed by a collection of those simple ideas which are to be found in them. Only we must take notice, that our complex ideas of substances, besides all these simple ideas they are made up of, have always the confused idea of something to which they belong and in which they subsist: and therefore, when we speak of any sort of substance we say it is a thing having such or such qualities; as, body is a thing that is extended, figured, and capable of motion; spirit, a thing capable of thinking; and so hardness, friability, and power to draw iron we say, are qualities to be found in a loadstone. These and the like fashions of speaking, intimate that the substance is supposed always something, besides the extension, figure, solidity, motion, thinking, or other observable ideas, though we know not what it is.

4. *No clear idea of substance in general.* Hence, when we talk or think of any particular sort of corporeal substances, as horse, stone, etc., though the idea we have of either of them be but the complication or collection of those several simple ideas of sensible qualities which we used to find united in the thing called "horse" or "stone"; yet because we cannot conceive how they should subsist alone, nor one in another, we suppose them existing in, and supported by, some common subject; which support we denote by the name "substance," though it be certain we have no clear or distinct idea of that thing we suppose a support.

5. *As clear an idea of spirit as body.* The same happens concerning the

operations of the mind; viz., thinking, reasoning, fearing, etc., which we concluding not to subsist of themselves, nor apprehending how they can belong to
body, or be produced by it, we are apt to think these the actions of some other
substance, which we call "spirit"; whereby yet it is evident that, having no
other idea or notion of matter, but something wherein those many sensible
qualities which affect our senses do subsist; by supposing a substance wherein
thinking, knowing, doubting, and a power of moving, etc., do subsist; we have as
clear a notion of the substance of spirit as we have of body; the one being
supposed to be (without knowing what it is) the *substratum* to those simple
ideas we have from without; and the other supposed (with a like ignorance of
what it is) to be the *substratum* to those operations which we experiment in
ourselves within. It is plain, then, that the idea of corporeal substance in matter
is as remote from our conceptions and apprehensions as that of spiritual
substance, or spirit; and therefore, from our not having any notion of the
substance of spirit, we can no more conclude its non-existence than we can, for
the same reason, deny the existence of body: it being as rational to affirm there
is no body, because we have no clear and distinct idea of the substance of
matter, as to say there is no spirit, because we have no clear and distinct idea
of the substance of a spirit.

6. *Of the sorts of substances.* Whatever therefore be the secret and abstract
nature of substance in general, all the ideas we have of particular, distinct sorts
of substances, are nothing but several combinations of simple ideas co-existing
in such, though unknown, cause of their union, as makes the whole subsist of
itself. It is by such combinations of simple ideas, and nothing else, that we
represent particular sorts of substances to ourselves; such are the ideas we
have of their several species in our minds; and such only do we, by their
specific names, signify to others; *v. g.*, man, horse, sun, water, iron: upon
hearing which words everyone, who understands the language, frames in his
mind a combination of those several simple ideas which he has usually observed or fancied to exist together under that denomination; all which he
supposes to rest in, and be, as it were, adherent to, that unknown common
subject, which inheres not in anything else; though in the meantime it be
manifest, and everyone upon inquiry into his own thoughts will find, that he
has no other idea of any substance, *v. g.*, let it be gold, horse, iron, man, vitriol,
bread, but what he has barely of those sensible qualities which he supposes to
adhere, with a supposition of such a *substratum* as gives, as it were, a support
to those qualities, or simple ideas, which he has observed to exist united
together. Thus, the idea of the sun, what is it but an aggregate of those several
simple ideas—bright, hot, roundish, having a constant regular motion, at a
certain distance from us—and perhaps some other? as he who thinks and
discourses of the sun has been more or less accurate in observing those sensi-
qualities, ideas, or properties which are in that thing which he calls the "sun."

7. *Their active and passive powers, a great part of our complex ideas of
substances.* For he has the perfectest idea of any of the particular sorts of
substances who has gathered and put together most of those simple ideas
which do exist in it, among which are to be reckoned its active powers and
passive capacities; which, though not simple ideas, yet in this respect, for
brevity's sake, may conveniently enough be reckoned amongst them. Thus, the
power of drawing iron is one of the ideas of the complex one of that substance
we call a "loadstone," and a power to be so drawn is a part of the complex one

we call "iron"; which powers pass for inherent qualities in those subjects: because every subject being as apt, by the powers we observe in it, to change some sensible qualities in other subjects, as it is to produce in us those simple ideas which we receive immediately from it, does, by those new sensible qualities introduced into other subjects, discover to us those powers which do thereby mediately affect our senses as regularly as its sensible qualities do it immediately; v. g., we immediately by our senses perceive in fire its heat and colour; which are, if rightly considered, nothing but powers in it to produce those ideas in us: we also by our senses perceive the colour and brittleness of charcoal, whereby we come by the knowledge of another power in fire, which it has to change the colour and consistency of wood. By the former, fire immediately, by the latter it mediately, discovers to us these several powers, which therefore we look upon to be a part of the qualities of fire, and so make them a part of the complex ideas of it.

8. *And why.* Nor are we to wonder that powers make a great part of our complex ideas of substances, since their secondary qualities are those which, in most of them, serve principally to distinguish substances one from another, and commonly make a considerable part of the complex idea of the several sorts of them. For, our senses failing us in the discovery of the bulk, texture, and figure of the minute parts of bodies, on which their real constitutions and differences depend, we are fain to make use of their secondary qualities, as the characteristical notes and marks whereby to frame ideas of them in our minds, and distinguish them one from another. All which secondary qualities, as has been shown, are nothing but bare powers. For the colour and taste of opium are, as well as its soporific or anodyne virtues, mere powers depending on its primary qualities, whereby it is fitted to produce different operations on different parts of our bodies.

9. *Three sorts of ideas make our complex ones of substances.* The ideas that make our complex ones of corporeal substances are of these three sorts. First. The ideas of the primary qualities of things which are discovered by our senses, and are in them even when we perceive them not: such are the bulk, figure, number, situation, and motion of the parts of bodies, which are really in them, whether we take notice of them or no. Secondly. The sensible secondary qualities which, depending on these, are nothing but the powers those substances have to produce several ideas in us by our senses; which ideas are not in the things themselves otherwise than as anything is in its cause. Thirdly. The aptness we consider in any substance to give or receive such alterations of primary qualities as that the substance so altered should produce in us different ideas from what it did before; these are called "active and passive powers": all which powers, as far as we have any notice or notion of them, terminate only in sensible simple ideas. For, whatever alteration a loadstone has the power to make in the minute particles of iron, we should have no notion of any power it had at all to operate on iron, did not its sensible motion discover it; and I doubt not but there are a thousand changes that bodies we daily handle have a power to cause in one another, which we never suspect, because they never appear in sensible effects.

10. *Powers make a great part of our complex idea of substances.* Powers therefore justly make a great part of our complex ideas of substances. He that will examine his complex idea of gold, will find several of its ideas that make it up to be only powers: as the power of being melted, but of not spending itself in

the fire, of being dissolved in *aqua regia*, are ideas as necessary to make up our complex idea of gold, as its colour and weight: which, if duly considered, are also nothing but different powers. For, to speak truly, yellowness is not actually in gold; but is a power in gold to produce that idea in us by our eyes, when placed in a due light: and the heat which we cannot leave out of our idea of the sun, is no more really in the sun than the white colour it introduces into wax. These are both equally powers in the sun, operating, by the motion and figure of its insensible parts, so on a man as to make him have the idea of heat; and so on wax as to make it capable to produce in a man the idea of white.

11. *The now secondary qualities of bodies would disappear, if we could dis-cover the primary ones of their minute parts.* Had we senses acute enough to discern the minute particles of bodies, and the real constitution on which their sensible qualities depend, I doubt not but they would produce quite different ideas in us, and that which is now the yellow colour of gold would then disappear and instead of it we should see an admirable texture of parts of a certain size and figure. This microscopes plainly discover to us; for, what to our naked eyes produces a certain colour is, by thus augmenting the acuteness of our senses, discovered to be quite a different thing; and the thus altering, as it were, the proportion of the bulk of the minute parts of a coloured object to our usual sight, produces different ideas from what it did before. Thus sand or pounded glass, which is opaque and white to the naked eye, is pellucid in a microscope; and a hair seen this way loses its former colour, and is in a great measure pellucid, with a mixture of some bright sparkling colours, such as appear from the refraction of diamonds and other pellucid bodies. Blood to the naked eye appears all red; but by a good microscope, wherein its lesser parts appear, shows only some few globules of red, swimming in a pellucid liquor; and how these red globules will appear, if glasses could be found that yet could magnify them one thousand or ten thousand times more, is uncertain.

14. *Specific ideas of substances.* The ideas we have of substances, and the way come by them; I say, Our specific ideas of substances are nothing else but a collection of a certain number of simple ideas, considered as united in one thing. These ideas of substances, though they are commonly called "simple apprehen-sions," and the names of them "simple terms"; yet, in effect, are complex and compounded. Thus the idea which an Englishman signifies by the name "swan," is white colour, long neck, red beak, black legs, and whole feet, and all these of a certain size, with a power of swimming in the water, and making a certain kind of noise; and perhaps to a man who has long observed those kind of birds, some other properties, which all terminate in sensible simple ideas, all united in one common subject.

15. *Idea of spiritual substances as clear as of bodily substances.* Besides the complex ideas we have of material sensible substances, of which I have last spoken, by the simple ideas we have taken from those operations of our own minds, which we experiment daily in ourselves, as thinking, understanding, will-ing, knowing, and power of beginning motion, etc., co-existing in some sub-stance, we are able to frame the complex idea of an immaterial spirit. And thus, by putting together the ideas of thinking, perceiving, liberty, and power of mov-ing themselves and other things, we have as clear a perception and notion of im-material substances as we have of material. For putting together the ideas of thinking and willing, or the power of moving or quieting corporeal motion, joined to substance, of which we have no distinct idea, we have the idea of an

immaterial spirit, and by putting together the ideas of coherent solid parts, and a power of being moved, joined with substance, of which, likewise, we have no positive idea, we have the idea of matter. The one is as clear and distinct an idea as the other; the idea of thinking and moving a body being as clear and distinct ideas as the ideas of extension, solidity, and being moved. For our idea of substance is equally obscure, or none at all, in both; it is but a supposed I-know-not-what, to support those ideas we call "accidents." It is for want of reflection that we are apt to think that our senses show us nothing but material things. Every act of sensation, when duly considered, gives us an equal view of both parts of nature, the corporeal and spiritual. For, whilst I know, by seeing or hearing, etc., that there is some corporeal being without me, the object of that sensation, I can more certainly know that there is some spiritual being within me that sees and hears. This I must be convinced cannot be the action of bare insensible matter, nor even could be without an immaterial thinking being.

16. *No idea of abstract substance.* By the complex idea of extended, figured, coloured, and all other sensible qualities which is all that we know of it we are as far from the idea of the substance of body as if we knew nothing at all: nor, after all the acquaintance and familiarity which we imagine we have with matter, and the many qualities men assure themselves they perceive and know in bodies, will it, perhaps, upon examination be found, that they have any more or clearer primary ideas belonging to body than they have belonging to immaterial spirit. . . .

1. SUBSTANCE IN GENERAL

Locke tells us that the mind is "furnished with a great number of the simple ideas conveyed in by the senses, as they are found in exterior things." He does not tell us by what means they are found in exterior things. They are indeed in our minds, but how we know that as they are in our minds so they are in external things is a matter for further investigation.

Meanwhile, our attention is drawn to the fact that a certain number of these simple ideas "go constantly together" and are called by one name. Thus the frequent association of rotundity, redness, hardness, and taste of a certain kind cause us to attribute them all to one object — which we give the name "apple" — and we come to regard that as the name of one simple idea, as Locke says, "by inadvertency," though it is really complex. Then, because we cannot imagine how the simple ideas going constantly together could subsist by themselves, we presume an object of the supposed simple idea — a substratum, holding all the members of the complex together, a substance in which all the different qualities inhere.

What is this substance, or substratum? We cannot say. We have no other idea of it than a vague supposition of something, "we know not what," to support the various qualities which we call its accidents.

Locke might also have argued from the changes we experience as occurring in things which we still regard as persisting through the changes. The alterations occur in the "accidents" (or qualities) of the thing, but the thing itself, we usually assume, remains the same thing — that is, its substance remains identical with itself. Once again, what is this permanent substance persisting through changes of, and among, its accidental qualities? — something, we know not what.

In an instructive passage Locke writes:

> If anyone should be asked, what is the subject wherein colour or weight inheres, he would have nothing to say, but the solid extended parts: and if he were demanded, what is that that solidity and extension inhere in, he would not be in a much better case than the Indian . . . who saying that the world was supported by a great elephant, was asked, what the elephant rested on; to which his answer was, "a great tortoise": but being again pressed to know what gave support to the broad-backed tortoise, replied, something, he knew not what.

This is how children (and some adults) respond when pressed to specify some matter which they claim to know, but of which they are really ignorant. They say it is "something," and then relapse into silence.

This passage suggests that (a) secondary qualities, ideas of which are in the mind only and copy nothing in reality, and which are thus in a sense illusory, are supported (or caused) by, or inhere in (b) primary qualities, ideas of which are resemblances of real qualities; but (c) these are not self-subsistent and must inhere in substances. What substance is, however, we do not know. We say it is "something," which, Locke tells us, is as much as to say we have no idea of it at all.

Yet he persists that we thus make "an obscure and relative idea of *substance in general*," which he is still prepared to entertain. It is apparently a simple idea, but it can hardly be an idea of sensation, nor yet one of reflection. Strictly speaking, therefore, Locke should not admit to its existence, but he has so healthy a respect for "experience," and it is so patent a fact that we do (or, at least, people in Locke's day did) speak and think of substances, that he cannot but allow that we must have some idea of it. Where would we get such an idea? In this chapter Locke is trying to answer that question, and though he is led to a position which should make it obvious that neither of the two sources of ideas which alone he is prepared to acknowledge could produce the idea of substance in general, he refuses either to modify his original view of the origins of our ideas, or to give up the idea of substance, preferring to be inconsistent in order, as he feels, to be faithful to experience.

Berkeley, we shall find, is much more thoroughgoing and consistent in his empiricism. He loses no time in disposing of this embarassing
idea.

2. COMPLEX IDEAS OF SUBSTANCES

On Locke's theory, the groups of ideas that go constantly together in
our experience are combined to make complex ideas of things or
particular substances. The word "substance" here is not being used as it
usually is today to refer to chemical substances, or the matter out of
which something is made. Nor is it used to denote elements, either
chemical elements in the modern sense, or in the ancient sense of
"element" as it was applied to earth, water, air, and fire. What Locke
means by a particular substance is a particular material thing, such as a
block of marble, a lump of wax, or an apple. But along with such
examples, Locke also includes general terms such as gold, water, and
iron. This is a habit he has of including class names along with examples of class members, but it is fairly clear that what he means here is
the objects that belong to these classes.

In any such thing (particular substance) the various simple ideas
(sometimes called its "accidents") which go together to make the complex idea are held together by what Locke refers to as its *internal
constitution*. This also determines which accidents belong to a given substance. But he tells us that the internal constitution of any substance is
unknown to us, and, it would seem, undiscoverable.

What the medieval and Aristotelian philosophers called "substantial
forms," Locke scoffs at. We have no ideas, he thinks, of any such things
and they are purely fictitious. Our actual ideas include only groups of
simple, sensed qualities combined into complex ideas of things, plus the
confused idea of something in which they inhere — the idea of substance
in general.

3. IDEAS OF SPIRITS AND OF BODIES

Just as we collect together simple ideas of sensation and suppose that
they inhere in bodily substance, so we combine ideas of reflection, such
as perceiving, reasoning, imagining, fearing, into a complex idea of a
spiritual substance. We cannot imagine bodies performing these mental
operations, so we postulate spirits (or souls) as their subjects. Consequently our idea of a spiritual substance is just as clear, or as obscure,

as our idea of material substance. And just as we shall find Berkeley abandoning the former, so we shall find Hume subsequently abandoning the latter as well.

4. ABSTRACT SUBSTANCE

Finally, however many and various our complex ideas of substances may be, whether of material or of spiritual substances, they bring us no nearer to the idea of substance as such. Strictly speaking, Locke admits, we have no abstract idea of substance.

5. CONSEQUENCES FOR KNOWLEDGE

Our knowledge, then, is restricted to simple ideas of sensation and reflection and the complex ideas of bodies and souls which we compose out of them. To attend for the moment only to bodies, as they are the furniture of the external world which is accessible to our senses, we have of them only ideas of primary and secondary qualities, but strictly no idea of that substance in which they adhere. The secondaries are not resemblances of anything but must be referred to the primaries. Yet it is not so much the primary qualities of the bodies as wholes that are the causes of the secondary qualities; it is the primary qualities of their insensible particles, which we do not perceive, and their internal constitution, which we have no means of knowing. Moreover, if we had no ideas of secondary qualities, we should have none of primary qualities either. This is a point that Locke misses, but it is not far to seek. Figure and size are conveyed to us by extended colors and by tactual sensations of pressure, warmth, and cold, as is any idea of solidity. Number implies something to count and the numerical properties of things cannot be ascertained unless they can be distinguished as unitary objects, which is possible only by means of their secondary qualities. The same is true of motion, which can be perceived only in moving bodies and changes of position in their secondary qualities. For us, therefore, if Locke is right, ideas of secondary qualities are the indispensable condition of all knowledge of material things.

But secondary qualities do not resemble anything in the external world and give only some unspecified sort of indication of external causes to which they correspond. Yet these external causes are inaccessible to us; we have no ideas of them and no means of getting any, for they reside in the insensible, imperceptible particles, and in the unknown internal constitution—presumably, in the substance as such, of which we have no idea and no knowledge. But, surely, what in our knowledge of the actual external thing should be nearest to it would be the idea of that thing stripped of all additions supplied by the mind. That would be the substance of the thing itself in which the primary and most real qualities inhere most closely.

Without primaries the thing cannot exist. Can the primaries exist without the substance? It would hardly seem so. We know the substance via the primaries and the primaries via the secondaries, yet secondaries do not belong to the thing, properly speaking, and do not resemble it.

They are *caused* by it—but by what? By its real internal constitution—of which we have no idea at all. How then do we know—or could we know—that they are so caused, unless of course we have an innate idea of the necessity of causation (which Locke would have denied), and even that could not take us far.

From the beginnings of knowledge, which Locke admits and which he insists are the sole sources of experience, without which we do not so much as begin to think, the external world cannot be reached. The reality itself recedes at each approach Locke makes to it. It is not in the ideas of secondary qualities, which are most accessible to us; the ideas of the primary qualities which are said to resemble their objects are accessible only through those of secondary qualities and the source of both primary and secondary qualities is totally obscure and inaccessible. As he himself says, at the conclusion of Book II, Chapter 23:[1]

> Most of the simple ideas that make up our complex ideas of substances, when truly considered, are only powers; however we are apt to take them for positive qualities . . . and are not really in the [thing] considered barely in itself, though they depend on those real and primary qualities of its internal constitution, whereby it has a fitness differently to operate and be operated on by several other substances.

But this internal constitution, we have been told, is not and cannot be known to us, and the primary qualities on which the powers depend are said to belong to insensible particles, of which, because insensible, we can have no ideas.

We shall follow up this line of argument in the following chapter and see how Locke's theory of knowledge is swamped by it.

---

[1]Omitted from the text above.

CHAPTER 18

Knowledge of the Real

OF KNOWLEDGE IN GENERAL

(Book IV, Chapter 1)

1. *Our knowledge conversant about our ideas.* Since the mind, in all its thoughts and reasonings, hath no other immediate object but its own ideas, which it alone does or can contemplate, it is evident that our knowledge is only conversant about them.

2. *Knowledge is the perception of the agreement or disagreement of two ideas.* Knowledge then seems to me to be nothing but the perception of the connection and agreement, or disagreement and repugnancy, of any of our ideas. In this alone it consists. Where this perception is, there is knowledge; and where it is not, there, though we may fancy, guess, or believe, yet we always come short of knowledge. For, when we know that white is not black, what do we else but perceive that these two ideas do not agree? When we possess ourselves with the utmost security of the demonstration that the three angles of a triangle are equal to two right ones, what do we more but perceive, that equality to two right ones does necessarily agree to, and is inseparable from, the three angles of a triangle?

3. *This agreement fourfold.* But, to understand a little more distinctly, wherein this agreement or disagreement consists, I think we may reduce it all to these four sorts: (1). Identity, or diversity. (2). Relation. (3). Co-existence, or necessary connection. (4). Real existence.

4. *First, Of identity or diversity.* First, As to the first sort of agreement or disagreement, viz., identity or diversity. It is the first act of the mind, when it

has any sentiments or ideas at all, to perceive its ideas, and, so far as it perceives them, to know that one is not another. This is so absolutely necessary, that without it there could be no knowledge, no reasoning, no imagination, no distinct thoughts at all. By this the mind clearly and infallibly perceives each idea to agree with itself, and to be what it is; and all distinct ideas to disagree, *i. e.*, the one not to be the other: and this it does without pains, labour, or deduction, but at first view, by its natural power of perception and distinction.

5. *Secondly, Relative.* Secondly, The next sort of agreement or disagreement the mind perceives in any of its ideas may, I think, be called "relative", and is nothing but the perception of the relation between any two ideas, of what kind soever, whether substances, modes, or any other. For, since all distinct ideas must eternally be known not to be the same, and so be universally and constantly denied one of another: there could be no room for any positive knowledge at all, if we could not perceive any relation between our ideas, and find out the agreement or disagreement they have one with another, in several ways the mind takes of comparing them.

6. *Thirdly, Of co-existence.* Thirdly, The third sort of agreement or disagreement to be found in our ideas, which the perception of the mind is employed about, is co-existence, or non-co-existence in the same subject: and this belongs particularly to substances. Thus when we pronounce concerning "gold" that it is fixed, our knowledge of this truth amounts to no more but this, that fixedness, or a power to remain in the fire unconsumed, is an idea that always accompanies and is joined with that particular sort of yellowness, weight, fusibility, malleableness and solubility in *aqua regia*, which make our complex idea, signified by the word "gold".

7. *Fourthly, Of real existence.* Fourthly, The fourth and last sort is that of actual real existence agreeing to any idea. Within these four sorts of agreement or disagreement is, I suppose, contained all the knowledge we have or are capable of; for, all the inquiries that we can make concerning any of our ideas, all that we know or can affirm concerning any of them, is that it is or is not the same with some other; that it does or does not always co-exist with some other idea in the same subject; that it has this or that relation to some other idea; or that it has a real existence without the mind. Thus, "Blue is not yellow," is of identity. "Two triangles upon equal bases between two parallels are equal," is of relation. "Iron is susceptible of magnetical impressions," is of co-existence. "God is," is of real existence. Though identity and co-existence are truly nothing but relations, yet they are so peculiar ways of agreement or disagreement of our ideas, that they deserve well to be considered as distinct heads, and not under relation in general; since they are so different grounds of affirmation and negation, as will easily appear to any one who will but reflect on what is said in several places of this Essay.

OF THE REALITY OF HUMAN KNOWLEDGE

(Book IV, Chapter 4)

1. *Objection. Knowledge placed in ideas may be all bare vision.* I doubt not but my reader by this time may be apt to think that I have been all this while only building a castle in the air; and be ready to say to me, "To what purpose

all this stir? 'Knowledge,' say you, 'is only the perception of the agreement or disagreement of our own ideas'; but who knows what those ideas may be? Is there any thing so extravagant as the imaginations of men's brains? Where is the head that has no chimeras in it? Or if there be a sober and a wise man, what difference will there be, by your rules, between his knowledge, and that of the most extravagant fancy in the world? They both have their ideas, and perceive their agreement and disagreement one with another. If there be any difference between them, the advantage will be on the warm-headed man's side, as having the more ideas, and the more lively. And so, by your rules, he will be the more knowing. If it be true, that all knowledge lies only in the perception of the agreement or disagreement of our own ideas, the visions of an enthusiast, and the reasonings of a sober man, will be equally certain. It is no matter how things are: so a man observe but the agreement of his own imaginations, and talk conformably, it is all truth, all certainty. Such castles in the air will be as strongholds of truth as the demonstrations of Euclid. That an harpy is not a centaur, is by this way as certain knowledge, and as much a truth, as that a square is not a circle.

"But of what use is all this fine knowledge of men's own imaginations to a man that inquires after the reality of things? It matters not what men's fancies are, it is the knowledge of things that is only to be prized: it is this alone gives a value to our reasonings, and preference to one man's knowledge over another's, that it is of things as they really are, and not of dreams and fancies."

2. *Answer. Not so where ideas agree with things.* To which I answer, That if our knowledge of our ideas terminate in them, and reach no farther, where there is something farther intended, our most serious thoughts will be of little more use than the reveries of a crazy brain: and the truths built thereon of no more weight than the discourses of a man who sees things clearly in a dream, and with great assurance utters them. But I hope before I have done to make it evident that this way of certainty, by the knowledge of our own ideas, goes a little farther than bare imagination; and I believe it will appear, that all the certainty of general truths a man has lies in nothing else.

3. It is evident the mind knows not things immediately, but only by the intervention of the ideas it has of them. Our knowledge therefore is real only so far as there is a conformity between our ideas and the reality of things. But what shall be here the criterion? How shall the mind, when it perceives nothing but its own ideas, know that they agree with things themselves? This, though it seems not to want difficulty, yet I think there be two sorts of ideas that we may be assured agree with things.

4. *As, First, all simple ideas do.* First, The first are simple ideas, which since the mind, as has been showed, can by no means make to itself, must necessarily be the product of things operating on the mind in a natural way, and producing therein those perceptions which by the wisdom and will of our Maker they are ordained and adapted to. From whence it follows, that simple ideas are not fictions of our fancies, but the natural and regular productions of things without us really operating upon us; and so carry with them all the conformity which is intended, or which our state requires; for they represent to us things under those appearances which they are fitted to produce in us, whereby we are enabled to distinguish the sorts of particular substances, to discern the states they are in, and so to take them for our necessities, and apply them to our uses. Thus the idea of whiteness or bitterness, as it is in the mind, exactly

answering that power which is in any body to produce it there, has all the real conformity it can or ought to have with things without us. And this conformity between our simple ideas and the existence of things is sufficient for real knowledge.

5. *Secondly, All complex ideas except of substances.* Secondly, All our complex ideas except those of substances being archetypes of the mind's own making, not intended to be the copies of any thing, nor referred to the existence of any thing, as to their originals, cannot want any conformity necessary to real knowledge. For that which is not designed to represent any thing but itself, can never be capable of a wrong representation, nor mislead us from the true apprehension of any thing by its dislikeness to it; and such, excepting those of substances, are all our complex ideas: which, as I have showed in another place, are combinations of ideas which the mind by its free choice puts together without considering any connection they have in nature. And hence it is, that in all these sorts the ideas themselves are considered as the archetypes, and things no otherwise regarded but as they are conformable to them. So that we cannot but be infallibly certain, that all the knowledge we attain concerning these ideas is real, and reaches things themselves; because in all our thoughts, reasonings, and discourses of this kind, we intend things no farther than as they are conformable to our ideas. So that in these we cannot miss of a certain and undoubted reality.

6. *Hence the reality of mathematical knowledge.* I doubt not but it will be easily granted that the knowledge we have of mathematical truths, is not only certain but real knowledge; and not the bare empty vision of vain, insignificant chimeras of the brain: and yet, if we will consider, we shall find that it is only of our own ideas. The mathematician considers the truth and properties belonging to a rectangle or circle, only as they are an idea in his own mind. For it is possible he never found either of them existing mathematically, *i. e.*, precisely true, in his life. But yet the knowledge he has of any truths or properties belonging to a circle, or any other mathematical figure, are never the less true and certain even of real things existing: because real things are no farther concerned, nor intended to be meant by any such propositions, than as things really agree to those archetypes in his mind. Is it true of the idea of a triangle, that its three angles are equal to two right ones? It is true also of a triangle wherever it really exists.

7. *And of moral.* And hence it follows that moral knowledge is as capable of real certainty as mathematics. For, certainty being but the perception of the agreement or disagreement of our ideas, and demonstration nothing but the perception of such agreement by the intervention of other ideas or mediums, our moral ideas as well as mathematical being archetypes themselves, and so adequate and complete ideas, all the agreement or disagreement which we shall find in them will produce real knowledge, as well as in mathematical figures.

11. *Ideas of substances have their archetypes without us.* Thirdly, There is another sort of complex ideas, which being referred to archetypes without us may differ from them, and so our knowledge about them may come short of being real. Such are our ideas of substances, which consisting of a collection of simple ideas, supposed taken from the works of nature, may yet vary from them, by having more or different ideas united in them that are to be found

united in the things themselves: from whence it comes to pass, that they may and often do fail of being exactly conformable to things themselves.

12. Whatever ideas we have, the agreement we find they have with others will still be knowledge. If those ideas be abstract, it will be general knowledge. But to make it real concerning substances, the ideas must be taken from the real existence of things. Whatever simple ideas have been found to co-exist in any substance, these we may with confidence join together again, and so make abstract ideas of substances. For whatever have once had an union in nature, may be united again.

18. *Recapitulation.* Wherever we perceive the agreement or disagreement of any of our ideas, there is certain knowledge: and wherever we are sure those ideas agree with the reality of things, there is certain real knowledge. Of which agreement of our ideas with the reality of things having here given the marks, I think I have shown wherein it is that certainty, real certainty, consists. Which, whatever it was to others, was, I confess, to me heretofore one of those *desiderata* which I found great want of.

1. TRUE AND FALSE

What Locke professes to do in the *Essay* is to explain how we acquire knowledge, and to assess its extent and limits. But knowledge implies distinctions between true and false, illusory and veridical, apparent and real. So far all Locke has given us is an account of "ideas" alleged to have been acquired in the way described. All these ideas are apparent, they are the contents of our awareness, but as such the question of truth or falsity does not automatically arise. As Descartes said, our perceptions are not in themselves true or false but only the judgments we pass concerning them when we refer them to the real world. The most important question to raise therefore is how we distinguish among our ideas, between those which apprise us of the real world and those that do not.

Here we may confine ourselves to this crucial question, leaving aside those details of what Locke says about the general nature of knowledge, its degrees and extent, such as do not bear directly upon it.

That not all of our ideas convey to us the actual nature of things in the world Locke freely admits, though it is only when we refer them to extraneous things that they can properly be said to be true or false; for instance, (a) when one refers an idea to what other people have in their minds answering to a common name, such as temperance or justice, or (b) when one refers one's idea to an external reality (for example, a man or a centaur), or (c) when one refers it to the real constitution or essence of something (for example, in the case of ideas of substance). In this last category our judgments, Locke maintains, are always false.

2. ADEQUATE AND INADEQUATE IDEAS

In the thirty-first chapter of Book II of the *Essay* Locke says that of our real ideas those are adequate "which perfectly represent those archetypes which the mind supposes them taken from." It is not clear at this stage whether by "adequate" he means "true," though he speaks of "our real ideas," by which phrase it later transpires he means our ideas of the real. Nevertheless, in this context he maintains only that ideas are adequate if they perfectly represent what the mind *intends* them to stand for. He does not say that the mind need be right in its supposition of their origin, nor does he say that what it intends them to stand for need be anything real.

On these terms Locke is prepared first to vouch for all simple ideas, because, he says, they cannot but be correspondent and adequate to those powers in things which produce the sensations in us (Book II, Chapter 31, 2). However, we may merely be making the supposition that they are so caused. If they are, they will inevitably be adequate. But we must remember that simple ideas of secondary qualities are not resemblances of anything in things and we are given no precise account of how they correspond to their causes. Without ideas of secondary qualities we could have none of primary qualities, which are said to resemble the actual properties of things. But here, again, we are not told what in the things have these properties. If it is only their insensible particles, which we do not perceive, it is not easy to understand how they resemble them — still less, how we know that they do. Further, these qualities are supposed to inhere in substances, of which we have no proper idea at all. Yet we suppose, and Locke makes no scruple to assert, that substances do cause our ideas, though we are not told whether or how we can be assured that this is the case. So far it has simply been stipulated.

Secondly, Locke is equally prepared to vouch for our ideas of what he calls "modes," a term he uses to refer to complex ideas of abstract qualities, chiefly moral, such as justice, murder, benevolence, and the like. These are ideas we construct ourselves and define by convention. They are, he says, archetypes of the mind's own making; consequently, they cannot but be adequate, or represent that which the mind intends them to stand for.

Our complex ideas of substances, on the other hand, are never wholly adequate, because we intend them to represent things as they really exist. But however many simple ideas we may combine in any one complex idea of a substance, we can never be sure that they fully correspond to everything that is in the substance — rather the contrary.

Moreover, however many ideas we may have of the powers, or secondary qualities, of a substance, we still know nothing (Locke is here quite specific[1]) of its essence or real internal constitution from which these qualities flow and on which they depend. "Besides," he says, "a man has no idea of substance in general, nor knows what substance is in itself."[2]

But clearly nothing we are told here is a sufficient theory of knowledge, of how we know, if we do know, what the world is like. For though we may suppose our ideas to be caused by external things, to answer to their powers to produce sensations in us and to resemble their primary qualities, how can we test this supposition? Is it true? Though we may *intend* our ideas to represent things in the world, how do we know that they do? If we could not answer these questions we could never tell whether we had any real knowledge of the world as opposed to mere speculative guess-work. Locke is, as we shall see, quite definite on this point, yet it is not until we come to the fourth chapter of Book IV in the *Essay* that we find Locke facing these questions squarely and attempting to answer them. We must consider the adequacy of his answers.

3. KNOWLEDGE

We must note first that Locke insists that the mind has no other immediate object than its own ideas and that therefore our knowledge "is only conversant about them" (Book IV, Chapter 1, 1). He makes this statement also in other contexts; there is nothing inadvertent about it. In Book IV, Chapter 4, 3, he says, "It is evident the mind knows not things immediately, but only by the intervention of the ideas it has of them." Nor could he have held anything else consistently with the account he has given of ideas and the ways in which they are produced.

This being so, knowledge is (and, it would seem, could only be) the perception of the agreement or disagreement of our ideas, of which Locke distinguishes four kinds: identity or diversity, relation, coexistence or necessary connection, and real existence.

As Locke explains the first three of these kinds of knowledge, it is clear that they are but matters of agreement and disagreement (or comparison) between our ideas, but the fourth kind requires something

---

[1]Book II, Chapter 31, 13.
[2]Book II, Chapter 31, 13.

more. It demands agreement between our ideas and external things. To be assured of this we must be able to compare our ideas with things, which are not ideas. How, we may ask, is this possible if our knowledge is conversant only about our ideas?

Moreover, the first three types of agreement do not really amount to knowledge proper, as Locke says: "If our knowledge of our ideas terminate in them, and reach no farther, where something farther is intended, our most serious thoughts are of little more use than the reveries of a crazy brain; and the truths built thereon of no more weight than the discourses of a man who sees things clearly in a dream, and with great assurance utters them" (Book IV, Chapter 4, 2). Everything, therefore, depends upon the fourth variety and the vital question to be faced, as Locke himself poses it, is "How shall the mind, when it perceives nothing but its own ideas, know that they agree with things themselves?" By what criterion can we tell which ideas (if any) do so agree and which do not? We shall find that Locke offers only one test, and one that is bogus and unavailing.

4. THE CRITERION OF TRUTH

Though "the mind knows not things immediately, but by the intervention of the ideas it has of them," nevertheless Locke holds that our knowledge is real (or true) if there is conformity between the ideas and the things. How, then, can we discover if and when this is so? By what criterion can we tell which ideas conform and which do not? Locke honestly raises the question and in answer gives us three criteria, all of which reduce to the first.

(a) SIMPLE IDEAS. Locke says simple ideas must conform to things because we cannot produce them at will. Therefore "they must necessarily be the product of things operating on the mind." He says (Book IV, Chapter 2, 14) that we have knowledge of particular external objects "by that perception and consciousness we have of the actual entrance of ideas from them."

But this, surely, is what we have no consciousness or perception of. Locke himself has told us that the causes of our ideas "appear not to our senses to operate in their production". We are never aware of the action upon our nerves, or animal spirits, or upon our brains, of external causes; we are aware only of what are alleged (by Locke) to be their effects. To these awkward facts we must return; let us look next at the other criteria Locke offers.

(b) COMPLEX IDEAS OF MODES. As complex ideas of modes are "archetypes of the mind's own making," as they are more or less conventional in character and are subsumed under conventional definitions, they "cannot want any conformity necessary to real knowledge." But whether anything in the real world corresponds to them is another matter. For instance, I may define justice as the equitable distribution of material goods, and nothing can prevent my idea from conforming to my definition, but nothing in the real world may correspond to it. Or I may define a triangle as a plane figure bounded by three straight lines, and on that basis produce a whole science of geometry. Yet there need not be any such thing in existence as a triangle so defined. Locke therefore adds that if anything does exist in nature which answers to the idea, then the idea will constitute real knowledge. If there are triangles in the world our geometry will be true of the world; and the same applies to moral concepts.

But how are we to discover whether there are things in the world which conform to our complex ideas of modes? On this question Locke is silent.

(c) COMPLEX IDEAS OF SUBSTANCES. These are true of the real so far as the simple ideas conjoined in them are put together as the actual qualities occur in nature. Again we ask, how do we discover whether or not this is the case? What means have we of investigating nature apart from our ideas to ascertain whether our ideas are conjoined as the qualities (or powers) which produce them occur in nature?

The only answer to this question, or the parallel one about modes, which we can derive from Locke's theory is that simple ideas themselves are the means by which we discover what exists in the external world, so far as we are conscious of and perceive their actual entrance from external things. This is ultimately the one and only criterion of truth he makes available to us. Simple ideas will inform us whether anything exists answering to our ideas of modes, and whether the qualities of material bodies occur in nature as we conjoin them in ideas.

5. FAILURE OF LOCKE'S CRITERION

But it is clear that Locke's criterion of truth will not serve. There are no good grounds for the contention that simple ideas of sensation are "adequate" in Locke's sense, or that they conform to their archetypes. Just what Locke means by conformity is never explained. So far as ideas of secondary qualities are concerned, it certainly cannot mean resemblance, for we are explicitly told that they do not resemble external things. In what way they could conform to their causes is wholly obscure. What their causes are does not appear in them, so we could not know the relation between them and the causes, whatever it might be, which constitutes conformity. Moreover, they are notoriously unreliable. We frequently see colors where there are no colored objects (for example, in the rainbow) and we suffer all kinds of visual illusions. The illusory "ideas" do not differ in quality from those which are not illusory, so they cannot themselves serve as criteria for distinguishing between illusory and veridical.

Ideas of primary qualities are no better, for, though they are said to be resemblances of qualities of external things, our experience shows us that many of them are not. Rectangles seen obliquely look rhomboid, circular objects frequently appear oval, receding parallels appear to meet. The criterion by which we distinguish between the appearances which are, and those which are not, faithful to the external things cannot be the simple ideas themselves.

We are variously subject to sensory illusion. We dream, we imagine, we see mirages, we feel pains where we have no hurt. All these illusions are made up of sensory data which are exactly like those we experience when we suspect no illusion and claim that we know the object before us to be real. Is there any mark intrinsic to the ideas which can serve as a criterion of distinction between the true and the false?

There is not. Strength or vividness is not enough, for our dreams and delusions are often as strong and vivid as any ideas we have. Are the facts, alleged by Locke, that our simple ideas come to us whether we will or no, and that we cannot produce them ourselves, sufficient to mark the true from the illusory? No, because they are not facts. We can and do call up (in imagination) simple and complex ideas and these can sometimes be so vivid that we cannot distinguish them from perception. Again, perception can at times be so vague and dim that we cannot be sure it is not just imagination. Under the influence of shock vivid visual or auditory (or other sensory) images may plague us against our will and beyond our control, but that does not make them real. Furthermore, that an idea comes to me against my will or without my concurrence is no evidence that it conforms in any way to anything else.

Finally we have seen that, on Locke's theory and by his own argument, we do not and cannot know the causes of our simple ideas; and it is an actual fact of experience that in themselves they give no evidence of their sources or of the process by which they are produced in us. If they did, we never could be mistaken or deluded about them.

Accordingly, Locke's theory of knowledge collapses, because the crux upon which it (like any theory of knowledge) depends is the criterion it offers for distinguishing true ideas from false, by means of which we can definitely know which of our experiences actually do convey to us the nature of the real world about us. Locke, strictly speaking, can offer us no criterion. The simple ideas of sensation which he installs in the judgment seat are themselves what have to be judged, and it is through them alone that we are supposed to judge between the real and the merely subjective in complex ideas.

Yet Locke's own confidence in these simple ideas is unshakable: "I ask anyone, whether he be not invincibly conscious to himself of a different perception when he looks on the sun by day, and thinks on it by night; when he actually tastes wormwood, or smells a rose, or only thinks on that savour or odour?" No doubt, but substitute the word "dreams" for "thinks" and the matter is not so easily settled.

CHAPTER 19

The Representative Theory of Perception

1. REVIEW

The theories of knowledge offered by Descartes and Locke, although in spirit diametrically opposed, have many features in common, which reflect their origin in the seventeenth-century world view initiated by the new science. Descartes, it is true, tries to deduce everything from first principles and believes knowledge to depend entirely on intellectual insight, while Locke considers all concepts derivative from sense and all deduction only a matter of comparing ideas derived from sensation and reflection.

Nevertheless, both philosophers find the source of all reliable knowledge in simple ideas, though for each of them these simples are of a very different kind. For Descartes they are self-evidently intelligible; for Locke they are evident primarily to the senses. Descartes builds knowledge out of simples by deduction; Locke by combination derived from experience—a process later to be called induction. For both, external objects are the causes of our sense percepts, and for both it is their primary or mathematical properties that convey to us the most reliable indications of their real structure. But Descartes does not find the actual truth of these ideas, as conveying to us knowledge of the existence of things, in the content of the ideas themselves. What can be intuited in and deduced from them is at best hypothetical. He relies in the last resort on faith in God's veracity to assure him of the existence of a material world.

Locke, on the other hand, though to some extent he also takes the ideas to give only hypothetical knowledge (for instance, our complex ideas of modes), believes that we know directly from inspection of simple ideas that they are caused by, and in some respects (primary qualities) resemble, external objects.

Both philosophers, therefore, offer what may be called a causal and a representative theory of perception of the external material world. This involves three factors:

(a)   ideas in the mind;

(b)   external bodies to which they are held to refer, and

(c)   a double relation between (a) and (b) of resemblance (or representation) and between (b) and (a) of causation.

The view of the world as a machine, which resulted from the new science, more or less forced such theories upon philosophers. If the machine was to be known (as it obviously was known by the scientists), some sort of representation or replica of its parts and their mutual relations had to get into the mind of the knower. As the human mind was (somehow) lodged in the human body, and as that, being part of the material world, was also a machine, what entered the mind had to be (somehow) the result of a (mechanical) causal process from external bodies to our own bodies ("for motion begets nothing but motion"), and if the effects of external causes are to inform us about the world they must somehow represent their causes. Each in his own way, Descartes and Locke, tried to work out a theory of knowledge conforming to these conditions.

The theory which resulted had a persistent appeal and was repeated with modifications by later thinkers, in spite of formidable difficulties (some of which have already become apparent). Even in the twentieth century it has been revived in highly sophisticated forms by Bertrand Russell and Ludwig Wittgenstein and it is still tacitly held by many scientists, whose knowledge of the external world in the light of contemporary science ought to have given them better insight. For this reason it will repay us to consider the theory in some detail.

2. THE SOURCE OF THE PROBLEM OF PERCEPTION

As Descartes made very clear, the central question concerns the criterion of truth (or, in perception, veridicality).

(a) NAÏVE REALISM. Common sense tends to believe that what we perceive by sight, hearing, and touch is the external object itself, directly, as it actually is. The color which I see is the real color of the flower before me and I perceive it immediately; the sound which I hear is the sound of the flute itself resulting from the passage of air through it and the vibrations it makes, and so on. This approach is called naïve realism, the theory that our percepts are the actual qualities or parts of the objects, if not the objects themselves, as they actually present themselves to us — as if somehow the senses transported the objects intact into our brains.

One has only to put the matter in that way to make it seem ridiculous, and indeed, on reflection, the view breaks down for the following reasons, together known as the argument from illusion.

(b) THE ARGUMENT FROM ILLUSION. First, there are notorious occasions when the senses present us with percepts which are by no means external objects. In jaundice we see things yellow which are not in fact yellow. Patients who lose limbs by amputation report that they still feel pains and other sensations in the absent limb. Drugs induce visual illusions. The toper sees double, the inveterate alcoholic sees pink elephants and all manner of things. Mescalin produces illusory perceptions as vivid as any that are normal.

Secondly, in less exceptional circumstances, we experience perceptions which are illusory. The example cited *ad nauseam* is the stick half-immersed in water that appears bent. There are images in mirrors which look real but show objects where they are not and with left and right reversed. There are mirages; and still more common, there are dreams.

Thirdly, and more important than all these, there is what may be called normal illusion. Shapes of objects are perspectivally distorted in virtually all visual perception. Colors are modified by contrast, by reflected and changing light, by distance, by refraction, and by all kinds of vicarious influences. Much the same is true of distorting influences on sounds and tastes, though over a smaller range of variety and contrast.

These common experiences make naïve realism untenable, because they make it obvious that the immediately perceived objects, the sense qualities and their groupings, are seldom, if ever, the actual parts of external things. Sometimes they occur when no relevant external things are present at all; sometimes they distort and diverge from the qualities we take the external things to have. The circumstances in which we have evidence of any kind that our percepts are exactly like what we take ourselves to be perceiving in the external world are rare and exceptional.

Though philosophers have sometimes drawn the conclusion, these facts do not show that our percepts are or may be always illusory. That cannot follow from the facts because in every case the recognition of the fact depends on our making a distinction between the true and the false. We make a distinction between dream and waking, and only on that condition could we claim to know that in dreams the apparent objects are not physically present. We claim to know that the stick half-immersed in water is straight although it looks bent. If we did not, we could not recognize the experience as an illusion.

But the facts are evidence that the percepts are not identical with external objects, as naïve realism wants to maintain, and yet they do not reveal to us the criterion by which we make the distinction between the illusory (or merely apparent) and the veridical (the real). This is the situation that raises the problem of the criterion of perceptual truth (and of truth in general).

Descartes seeks and offers a rational criterion — logical cogency; Locke an empirical one — correspondence between ideas and external things. For Descartes such correspondence also holds, but he deduces it *a priori* from the veracity of God and finds it only where clear and distinct reasoning leads him to believe in it. Locke, on the other hand, asserts dogmatically (and as we have seen, falsely) that such correspondence must obtain between our simple ideas and their external objects, when and because we are "invincibly conscious" of it.

3. REPRESENTATIVE IDEAS

The argument from illusion and the failure of naïve realism lead to the postulation of an intermediary between external objects and our perception of them. The percepts of which we are immediately aware are now taken to be only representative of external things. They are thought to be the effects produced by the action of those things upon our sense organs and to copy, in some way, the sources from which they originate. As a mirror reflects objects in front of it, or as a camera produces likenesses inside itself of objects outside, so the mind is thought to mirror the world or to form copies or representations of external things, with the help of the mechanisms of the sense organs, the nerves, and the brain. Our ideas are thus taken to be pictures of external objects which may or may not be accurate likenesses, and only those are true which correctly correspond to their external causes.

But now intractable difficulties arise about the criterion by which we judge which ideas do correspond to external things. How are we to discover such correspondence? If the account of perception and knowledge so far given were correct, it would follow immediately and inescapably that all our awareness must be restricted to ideas in the mind. The alleged representations are all that can ever be available to us. But to know whether or not they resemble, represent, correspond to, or are caused by, external things we must somehow know the existence and nature of those things independently of the supposed representations, in order to compare the two and decide whether and to what extent they are alike, and what other relations, if any, obtain between them.

If we have no means, except perception and its consequent representations, of knowing the external things, we cannot tell whether our percepts are representations of anything at all, whether they are caused as we imagine they are, whether they resemble anything other than themselves, or what, if anything, they correspond to.

This conclusion seems to be reinforced by the theory itself. Physiologists tell us that stimulation of certain regions of the brain causes a patient to experience percepts exactly similar to those experienced in the presence of external objects. Dreams and some delusions (such as phantom limbs mentioned above) are explained in this way. Further, it is obvious that if the representative theory of perception were true, whatever produced the final ideas, or at least the same brain states as are supposed to cause them, the effects in the mind would be the same as if they had been caused by external objects. Might it not then be true after all that our belief in the external world, as a whole, is a delusion? Could Descartes's supposition not be true that no material bodies exist but that our apparent awareness of them is produced in some other way, altogether unknown to and unknowable by us?

Disconcerting as this thought may be, it does not of course follow from the foregoing argument, but, if taken as a hypothetical conclusion from the premises stated, it contradicts them. For the argument begins by assuming an external world causing activity in our sense organs and nervous system which results in percepts; it then alleges that the effects could be produced by other causes; and then concludes that there might not be any external world or any sense organs or brain in which it could cause effects. But if that were so, the first premise would have been demolished.

4. THE EPISTEMOLOGIST'S FALLACY

The reason for this debacle is that a fallacy has been committed which is frequently committed by epistemologists and proves fatal to the majority of theories of knowledge. This is the fallacy of giving an account of knowledge which could be given only by someone whose own knowledge was an exception to the theory proposed. In order to know that ideas were generated as Locke maintains, that they did or did not represent external bodies, in what respects they resembled their objects and in what respects they did not, it would be necessary for the theorist to have access to the external objects by some other means than the ideas themselves, as well as through their mediation, so that he could determine these relationships. It would not be sufficient to have ideas of material things external and causally related to other people's bodies, even if one also had ideas which appeared to communicate what those people were at the same time experiencing; for it is the validity of all such ideas that is in question. But knowledge acquired through access to external objects by other means independent of ideas would be an exception to the theory—which asserts that human beings have no other means. The theorist who claims to know all this would therefore have to be more than human.

The epistemologist's fallacy is that of propounding a theory of knowledge which, if generally true so that it included the theorist's own knowledge, is one which he could not possibly know or discover. Or to put it another way, it is the fallacy of presupposing that one has access to facts the possibility of which one's theory of knowledge excludes.

This is the fallacy inherent in the representative theory of knowledge. If it were true, it could, strictly speaking, be known only to God, who might presumably have access to the facts from which we were inevitably barred. In that case Descartes is at least consistent in relying for the knowledge of the theory only on divine revelation. In this way alone he escapes the fallacy. But Locke falls headlong into the trap. He sets out to discover the limits of human knowledge, gives an account of it which limits it to ideas in the mind, and then confidently asserts a knowledge of the relations between ideas in the mind and things outside the mind, which he could have only if he were not subject to the limitations he has himself imposed.

Neither theory is, however, satisfactory, for neither can give a workable criterion of factual truth. Descartes's criterion should make us infallible, not only with respect to clear and distinct ideas, but also with respect to veridical and illusory sense qualities. Locke's criterion fails because simple ideas, on which he relies, may themselves be either veridical or (like after-images) illusory; they cannot, therefore, function as a test for making this distinction.

5. POSSIBLE DEFENSE OF THE THEORY

As the representative theory, in one form or another, reappears so often in attempts to deal with the problem of knowledge, we must consider possible arguments in its favor. Is there not, perhaps, some way out of the *impasse* we have described above?

(1) Could we not infer from the experiences we have to causes in the external world, which are admittedly beyond and outside the closed circle of the experiences themselves?

Inference from effect to cause is possible only on one or both of two conditions: (a) if we know a causal law connecting A and B such that we can infer from the occurrence of B that A caused it and must have occurred prior to or concurrently with it; (b) if we have previously been acquainted with both A and B, and have examined the relation between them so as to discover a causal connection.

But in the case of percepts of which we are conscious, we know no causal law connecting the consciousness with brain states. We do commonly assume a connection but we have no idea what it could be. We have no clear conception of how brain states could cause conscious states. Some philosophers identify the two unreservedly, saying that the conscious states are nothing but states of the brain. This, however, is a dubious supposition for we do not directly experience our own brain states at all, and our problem is to correlate what we do directly experience with them. Moreover, what physiologists tell us about the activity of the brain gives no ground for thinking that it has any characters in common with consciousness, except possibly that they occur simultaneously. The neural concomitant of a seen color seems to be a pattern of electrical discharges, quite different in configuration from that of the color seen; and that of a heard sound which has no assignable shape is, apparently, also a spatial pattern of electrical discharges in the brain. The two brain states differ, so far as anybody knows, only in spatial disposition; but the two states of consciousness are different beyond description. What can it possibly mean, then, to say that the brain states and the percepts are identical?[1]

In the case of Locke's theory, it would be impossible to discover any causal law connecting simple ideas with external things, because we are supposed to start with blank minds and derive all knowledge from the subsequently experienced ideas, among which no causal laws revealing the origin of those ideas are included. We might discover causal laws linking some ideas with other ideas, but not linking ideas with external bodies. According to Locke we have no innate ideas of anything — causal laws included; so the first condition could not be fulfilled. Hume, as we shall see, developed the implications of this position with devastating results.

The second condition is equally unattainable for *by hypothesis* we never experience anything except ideas — or in other words we can have had no acquaintance with anything except percepts, so we have never had the opportunity to investigate the relation between them and their alleged causes. Consequently, we lack the premises from which we could infer from percepts, of which we are aware, to causes, of which we are not.

(2) A similar argument applies even more obviously and more cogently to the suggestion that we might be able to infer from the appearances which we experience to the character of the things of which they are held to be appearances. The presumption now is that there is some sort of likeness between the two. But unless we have experienced *both*, this cannot possibly be inferred. If we had had the opportunity to make the comparison even in some few cases, we might argue by analogy to others; but in the nature of the case we could never have perceived anything but the appearances, and could there-fore not tell whether they resembled other things we had never expe-rienced. I may admire a portrait for any number of reasons, but I cannot judge it to be a good likeness unless I have also seen the original model. This, when it comes to the archetypes of my immediately cog-nized percepts, is ruled out by the theory itself.

(3) Finally, let us consider the consequences of adopting a causal and representative theory merely as an hypothesis to see if it will help us understand how our experience of the world is possible.

When a scientist adopts an hypothesis in order to test its truth, he de-

---

[1] For further and more detailed discussion see E. E. Harris, "The Neural-Identity Theory and the Person," *International Philosophical Quarterly* Vol. VI, 4, December 1966. Other references are listed at the end of the chapter.

duces consequences from it to see whether they agree with other
established theories, with common experience, or with the results of
new experiments and observations. In this case we cannot experiment,
and no special observations are relevant. Common experience is all we
can go by. Now, our common experience is of a more or less orderly
world of objects related to ourselves in space and time and in various other ways. Do the consequences that follow from the causal-
representative theory of perception agree with this? Hardly. For if it
were true, all we could possibly be aware of would be the end results
of an alleged (or hypothesized) causal process. These end results give no
indication of their origins, and from them no experience of an external
world could be derived.

First, if our ideas of things were merely results of the effects in the
brain of motions conveyed along the nerves from the sense organs,
they would occur in the same haphazard order as the impulses impinging
upon our receptors. This, in fact, is how sensations do occur. As I
turn my head I experience a kaleidoscopic succession of colors and
shapes. All kinds of sounds assail me in all sorts of orders. A host of
various tactual sensations are always present to me. None of these "go
constantly together." What go together sometimes occur separately at
others. My attention wanders among these experiences at will; now
picking out one, now another. If the occurrence of these data, as they
come to me, were all I had to go upon, I could never construct from
them any orderly world at all. To do that I need some principles of
order and relationship. But nothing of that sort comes to me as a sensation. If I had no innate knowledge of such principles, I should not have
the sort of knowledge of an external world that I now enjoy.

But suppose I did have innate knowledge of such principles. I could
then construct a world of objects from the data I received, but I should
still have no means of knowing that my way of putting them together
corresponded with anything in the real world, and the hypothesis that
it might so correspond could not be substantiated. But then the original
hypothesis would already have been vitiated by the presumption of
innate principles; because according to that hypothesis, the order of my
percepts is supposed to be the consequence of their having been
caused by external things, and not the result of subjective organization.

Again, it follows from the hypothesis that our percepts themselves
would give no indication of their original causes, and we should not
therefore have reason to suspect or assume that there were material
things causally related to them. In that case, the very temptation to
assume the hypothesis would be inexplicable. Further, the percepts
themselves could give no evidence that they bore any similarity to

external things. In fact, on the strength of the hypothesis, the great probability would be to the contrary, for brain processes have a minimum of resemblance to trees, buildings, hills, and rocks, and there is no apparent way in which they could give rise to ideas which do, and no obvious reason why they should.

So, if we adopt the hypothesis we find that it does not account for or agree with our normal experience, nor does it help us to find corroborative evidence in its own support; on the contrary, the consequences we deduce from it only reduce it to absurdity. We should, therefore, reject it.

Finally, we can only say of the causal-representative theory of perception that if it were true we could not possibly know it; and if we could know it, it could not be true. In this unpromising situation Berkeley and Hume made heroic efforts to develop a consistent theory from Locke's empiricist beginnings. Berkeley, in effect, accepts the first alternative. The external world, which does not appear to operate in the production of ideas, he rejects as a fiction. Hume proceeds to show that we are then left with no properly reliable criterion of objective truth.

It is of the utmost importance for students of philosophy to follow out the critique of Locke's theory by subsequent thinkers and their efforts to construct a self-consistent system upon Locke's original assumptions. Neither Berkeley nor Hume calls into question the presupposition that the original source of our knowledge is what comes to us through the senses and that everything we know can and must be traced back, or related in some way, to sense-given particulars. And this, after all, is what we normally assume in our unphilosophical moments. We believe ourselves to be, in some way, lodged inside our heads, and we naturally assume that we learn about the outside world (as well as about our own bodies) by receiving sense percepts of them through our sense organs. All this seems obviously true. It is mere common sense. But if it is true, how do we know that it is? As soon as we take it seriously it leads us directly to some form of causal or representative theory of perception, or both, and the task of maintaining any such theory consistently proves difficult in the extreme. Yet it has been repeatedly attempted, and there are still philosophers today who try to rehabilitate it and make it coherent. There are still more who maintain theories of knowledge which tacitly presuppose a representative theory, while their authors seem totally unaware of its pitfalls and difficulties.

Berkeley and Hume were acutely aware of the difficulties of Locke's position, but they accepted his starting point (as most of us do in our unreflective moments, and some of us even after long reflection). Their theories are the results of efforts to produce a coherent account of experience and knowledge without abandoning what seems to be so obvious a truth, the premise that all our knowledge begins with sense perception. The careful study of these philosophers, therefore, will make us aware of the consequences implicit in our common assumptions, which should put us on our guard against errors into which it is all too easy to fall.

SUGGESTIONS FOR FURTHER READING

J. Locke, *Essay Concerning the Human Understanding.* New York: Macmillan, paperback edition, 1965.

R. I. Aaron, *John Locke.* New York: Oxford University Press, 1955.

D. J. O'Connor, *John Locke.* New York: Dover, 1967.

A. Sinclair, *An Introduction to Philosophy.* New York: Oxford University Press, 1944.

————, *The Conditions of Knowing.* New York: Harcourt, 1951.

N. Kemp-Smith, *Prolegomena to an Idealist Theory of Knowledge.* New York: Macmillan, 1924.

E. E. Harris, *Nature, Mind and Modern Science,* Chapter 6. New York: Humanities Press, 1954.

S. Hook (Ed.), *Dimensions of Mind.* New York: Crowell-Collier and Macmillan, Inc., 1961.

R. J. Swartz (Ed.), *Perceiving, Sensing, Knowing.* New York: Doubleday & Company, Inc., 1965.

CHAPTER 20

Bishop Berkeley's Idealism

1. SOLIPSISM

We have said that if the representative theory of knowledge were true we could not possibly know that it was true, because our knowledge would be restricted inevitably to ideas in our minds and the relations between them and things which are not in our minds would be excluded from it. Each of us should then, strictly speaking, be imprisoned in a closed circle of ideas; each should have his own picture of his own world, with no possiblity of knowing what, if anything, it corresponded to. Even the existence of other persons with their minds and knowledge would have to be mediated for me through my ideas (for you, through yours) and so the knowledge of the actual existence of other persons independently of representations in my mind would be inaccessible to me. Consequently no appeal to others, no agreement or disagreement with them as to what they perceived and believed about the world could remedy the predicament.

An extreme theory based on this conclusion is that I alone exist and the rest of the world is only my idea. This is called solipsism (from the Latin, *solus ipse*, myself alone). It is a direct consequence of the comfortable, common-sensical presumptions with which Locke began that we learn about the world through the effects that things produce on our sense organs and that without these effects we have no ideas from which to start.

2. REMOVING INCONSISTENCIES

If the theory is wrong, what is wrong with it? Berkeley maintained that the error was simply the belief in an unperceived material world corresponding to our ideas. That these come to us from the senses is obvious, but why not be content with that? Why need we postulate anything external which causes them? The world is what we perceive (not what we don't perceive) and all we perceive are ideas; what need is there, then, to suppose the existence of anything else? Berkeley, however, is no solipsist and just how he avoids that extreme conclusion we shall see as we proceed.

Berkeley's theory follows naturally and logically from Locke's differing from his mainly by preserving consistency where Locke holds incompatible positions.

a. If knowledge is, as Locke said, merely agreement or disagreement among our ideas, the external world plays no part in it and contributes nothing.

Why then need we appeal to it?

b. Locke's account of real knowledge proves disastrous. He provides no adequate criterion of correspondence between ideas and real things. To make his theory consistent, therefore, our knowledge must, after all, "terminate in [ideas], and reach no further." Accordingly, the assumption that "there is something further intended" is treated by Berkeley as "of little more use than the reveries of a crazy brain" (cf. Locke's *Essay*, Book IV, Chapter 4, 2).

c. According to Locke (*Essay*, Book III, Chapter 3, 1 and 6; Book IV, Chapter 17, 8), all ideas are particular existences. Berkeley concludes that there can be no abstract ideas, and in the Introduction to his *Treatise Concerning the Principles of Human Knowledge*, Berkeley argues at length against Locke on this point. He maintains that the capacity of framing abstract ideas, which Locke attributed to the mind, does not exist. Men, no more than animals, Berkeley declares, can form such ideas, because they are really inconceivable. One can recall objects previously experienced, and one can separate and rearrange them in imagination. One can imagine a man with two heads or a hippogryph, or a hand, or nose, without the rest of the body. But one cannot think of a man who is neither tall nor short, nor yet of middle height, who is neither dark nor fair, strong nor weak; or who has no *particular* or definite properties. One cannot therefore frame an abstract idea of humanity or of man, as such. What is central and crucial to Plato's philosophy and is essential to all forms of rationalism, Berkeley flatly denies to be possible at all.

Similarly, one cannot conceive of motion without something moving, or of extension without shape or size, or for that matter quality of some kind. Abstract ideas of motion, figure, number, and the like, so Berkeley argues, we just never have at all. There is no idea of a triangle which has no size, is not isosceles or equilateral or scalene, but is just triangular.

What Locke calls abstract ideas, he maintains, are simply particular ones — and, after all, Locke himself has told us that *all* ideas are particular — which we use as signs to represent others which resemble them in certain specific ways.

d. Our simple ideas of sensation, Locke has told us, are immediate objects of sense. They are "actual perceptions in the mind, which cease to be anything when there is no perception of them." To be objects of sense they must (obviously) be sensible. If they were not they would not be objects to the senses. So Berkeley argues that the immediate objects of sense are the sensible qualities and nothing else; and as they cease to be anything when not perceived, their *esse* is *percipi*; that is, their very being is to be perceived.

e. Locke asserts that all knowledge consists of simple ideas and the compounds into which we build them. Berkeley contends that their *esse* is *percipi*. It follows that everything we can possibly know exists only so far as it is perceived.[1]

The use of the word "perceived," however, is somewhat different from our modern use. It is nearer to our use of "cognized."[2] To perceive something, for Berkeley, is to be aware of it in any way at all. So to imagine, or conceive, or think of anything whatsoever is, for him, to perceive it. The senses need not necessarily be involved; and if by that we mean the sense organs, Berkeley might well deny that they could be involved, for the sense organs are material objects and, as we shall see, for him these are simply collections of perceived ideas. Perception, therefore, must be prior to any ideas of sense organs. Nevertheless,

---

[1] Though this would be the logical conclusion from Locke's premise, we shall see that Berkeley modifies it somewhat at a later stage.

[2] This applies both to Descartes and to Berkeley — in fact, generally in the eighteenth century.

following Locke, Berkeley held all ideas (properly so called) to be sensible in kind. Even ideas of reflection were a sort of inner sense. Imaginations are a variety of sensible images and, as we have just noted, he takes "abstract" ideas to be particular (sense) images used to stand for groups of others.

Once having stated his main position, Berkeley devotes himself to the refutation in detail of the arguments for Lockean realism—that is, for belief in the existence of a material world external to the mind. To attempt to escape his criticism (as some philosophers have done)[3] simply by reasserting Locke's position is futile. For that simply re-establishes the paradoxes we have shown Locke's position to involve; and Berkeley's theory results from the direct attempt to remove those paradoxes. We may feel that he creates new ones; but, if so, we must discover what they are and criticize them in the proper place. It is no reply to Berkeley simply to restate the Lockean theory he is attempting to correct.

Three Dialogues between Hylas and Philonous, in Opposition to Sceptics and Atheists

THE FIRST DIALOGUE

PHILONOUS. Good morrow, Hylas: I did not expect to find you abroad so early.

HYLAS. It is indeed something unusual; but my thoughts were so taken up with a subject I was discoursing of last night, that finding I could not sleep, I resolved to rise and take a turn in the garden.

PHIL. It happened well, to let you see what innocent and agreeable pleasures you lose every morning. Can there be a pleasanter time of the day, or a more delightful season of the year? That purple sky, those wild but sweet notes of birds, the fragrant bloom upon the trees and flowers, the gentle influence of the rising sun, these and a thousand nameless beauties of nature inspire the soul with secret transports; its faculties too being at this time fresh and lively, are fit for those meditations, which the solitude of a garden and tranquillity of the morning naturally dispose us to. But I am afraid I interrupt your thoughts: for you seemed very intent on something.

HYL. It is true, I was, and shall be obliged to you if you will permit me to go on in the same vein; not that I would by any means deprive myself of your company, for my thoughts always flow more easily in conversation with a

---

[3]See *Nature, Mind and Modern Science*, Chapter 7.

friend, than when I am alone: but my request is, that you would suffer me to impart my reflexions to you.

PHIL. With all my heart, it is what I should have requested myself if you had not prevented me.

HYL. I was considering the odd fate of those men who have in all ages, through an affectation of being distinguished from the vulgar, or some unaccountable turn of thought, pretended either to believe nothing at all, or to believe the most extravagant things in the world. This however might be borne, if their paradoxes and scepticism did not draw after them some consequences of general disadvantage to mankind. But the mischief lieth here; that when men of less leisure see them who are supposed to have spent their whole time in the pursuits of knowledge professing an entire ignorance of all things, or advancing such notions as are repugnant to plain and commonly received principles, they will be tempted to entertain suspicions concerning the most important truths, which they had hitherto held sacred and unquestionable.[4]

PHIL. I entirely agree with you, as to the ill tendency of the affected doubts of some philosophers, and fantastical conceits of others. I am even so far gone of late in this way of thinking, that I have quitted several of the sublime notions I had got in their schools for vulgar opinions. And I give it you on my word; since this revolt from metaphysical notions to the plain dictates of nature and common sense, I find my understanding strangely enlightened, so that I can now easily comprehend a great many things which before were all mystery and riddle.

HYL. I am glad to find there was nothing in the accounts I heard of you.

PHIL. Pray, what were those?

HYL. You were represented, in last night's conversation, as one who maintained the most extravagant opinion that ever entered into the mind of man, to wit, that there is no such thing as *material substance* in the world.

PHIL. That there is no such thing as what *philosophers* call *material substance*, I am seriously persuaded: but, if I were made to see anything absurd or sceptical in this, I should then have the same reason to renounce this that I imagine I have now to reject the contrary opinion.

HYL. What! can anything be more fantastical, more repugnant to Common Sense, or a more manifest piece of Scepticism, than to believe there is no such thing as *matter*?

PHIL. Softly, good Hylas. What if it should prove that you, who hold there is, are, by virtue of that opinion, a greater sceptic, and maintain more paradoxes and repugnances to Common Sense, than I who believe no such thing?

HYL. You may as soon persuade me, the part is greater than the whole, as that, in order to avoid absurdity and Scepticism, I should ever be obliged to give up my opinion in this point.

PHIL. Well then, are you content to admit that opinion for true, which upon examination shall appear most agreeable to Common Sense, and remote from Scepticism?

HYL. With all my heart. Since you are for raising disputes about the plainest things in nature, I am content for once to hear what you have to say.

PHIL. Pray, Hylas, what do you mean by a *sceptic*?

---

[4]Cf. *Principles*, Introduction, section 1.

HYL. I mean what all men mean—one that doubts of everything.

PHIL. He then who entertains no doubt concerning some particular point, with regard to that point cannot be thought a sceptic.

HYL. I agree with you.

PHIL. Whether doth doubting consist in embracing the affirmative or negative side of a question?

HYL. In neither; for whoever understands English cannot but know that *doubting* signifies a suspense between both.

PHIL. He then that denies any point, can no more be said to doubt it, than he who affirmeth it with the same degree of assurance.

HYL. True.

PHIL. And, consequently, for such his denial no more to be esteemed a sceptic than the other.

HYL. I acknowledge it.

PHIL. How cometh it to pass then, Hylas, that you pronounce me a *sceptic*, because I deny what you affirm, to wit, the existence of Matter? Since, for aught you can tell, I am as peremptory in my denial, as you in you affirmation.

HYL. Hold, Philonous, I have been a little out in my definition; but every false step a man makes in discourse is not to be insisted on. I said indeed that a *sceptic* was one who doubted of everything; but I should have added, or who denies the reality and truth of things.

PHIL. What things? Do you mean the principles and theorems of sciences? But these you know are universal intellectual notions, and consequently independent of Matter. The denial therefore of this doth not imply the denying them.

HYL. I grant it. But are there no other things? What think you of distrusting the senses, of denying the real existence of sensible things, or pretending to know nothing of them. Is not this sufficient to denominate a man a *sceptic*?

PHIL. Shall we therefore examine which of us it is that denies the reality of sensible things, or professes the greatest ignorance of them; since, if I take you rightly, he is to be esteemed the greatest *sceptic*?

HYL. That is what I desire.

PHIL. What mean you by Sensible Things?

HYL. Those things which are perceived by the senses. Can you imagine that I mean anything else?

PHIL. Pardon me, Hylas, if I am desirous clearly to apprehend your notions, since this may much shorten our inquiry. Suffer me then to ask you this farther question. Are those things only perceived by the senses which are perceived immediately? Or, may those things properly be said to be *sensible* which are perceived mediately, or not without the intervention of others?

HYL. I do not sufficiently understand you.

PHIL. In reading a book, what I immediately perceive are the the letters; but mediately, or by means of these, are suggested to my mind the notions of God, virtue, truth, &c. Now, that the letters are truly sensible things, or perceived by sense, there is no doubt: but I would know whether you take the things suggested by them to be so too.

HYL. No, certainly: it were absurd to think *God* or *virtue* sensible things; though they may be signified and suggested to the mind by sensible marks, with which they have an arbitrary connexion.

PHIL. It seems then, that by *sensible things* you mean those only which can be perceived *immediately* by sense?

HYL. Right.

PHIL. Doth it not follow from this, that though I see one part of the sky red, and another blue, and that my reason doth thence evidently conclude there must be some cause of that diversity of colours, yet that cause cannot be said to be a sensible thing, or perceived by the sense of seeing?

HYL. It doth.

PHIL. In like manner, though I hear variety of sounds, yet I cannot be said to hear the causes of those sounds?

HYL. You cannot.

PHIL. And when by my touch I perceive a thing to be hot and heavy, I cannot say, with any truth or propriety, that I feel the cause of its heat or weight?

HYL. To prevent any more questions of this kind, I tell you once for all, that by *sensible things* I mean those only which are perceived by sense; and that in truth the senses perceive nothing which they do not perceive *immediately*: for they make no inferences. The deducing therefore of causes or occasions from effects and appearances, which alone are perceived by sense, entirely relates to reason.[5]

PHIL. This point then is agreed between us — That *sensible things are those only which are immediately perceived by sense.* You will farther inform me, whether we immediately perceive by sight anything beside light, and colours, and figures; or by hearing, anything but sounds; by the palate, anything beside tastes; by the smell, beside odours; or by the touch, more than tangible qualities.

HYL. We do not.

PHIL. It seems, therefore, that if you take away all sensible qualities, there remains nothing sensible?

HYL. I grant it.

PHIL. Sensible things therefore are nothing else but so many sensible qualities, or combinations of sensible qualities?

HYL. Nothing else.

PHIL. *Heat* then is a sensible thing?

HYL. Certainly.

PHIL. Doth the *reality* of sensible things consist in being perceived? or, is it something distinct from their being perceived, and that bears no relation to the mind?

HYL. To *exist* is one thing, and to be *perceived* is another.

PHIL. I speak with regard to sensible things only. And of these I ask, whether by their real existence you mean a subsistence exterior to the mind, and distinct from their being perceived?

HYL. I mean a real absolute being, distinct from, and without any relation to, their being perceived.

PHIL. Heat therefore, if it be allowed a real being, must exist without the mind?

HYL. It must.

PHIL. Tell me, Hylas, is this real existence equally compatible to all degrees of heat, which we perceive; or is there any reason why we should attribute it to some, and deny it to others? And if there be, pray let me know that reason.

HYL. Whatever degree of heat we perceive by sense, we may be sure the same exists in the object that occasions it.

---

[5]Cf. *Theory of Vision Vindicated*, section 42.

PHIL. What! the greatest as well as the least?

HYL. I tell you, the reason is plainly the same in respect of both. They are both perceived by sense; nay, the greater degree of heat is more sensibly perceived; and consequently, if there is any difference, we are more certain of its real existence than we can be of the reality of a lesser degree.

PHIL. But is not the most vehement and intense degree of heat a very great pain?

HYL. No one can deny it.

PHIL. And is any unperceiving thing capable of pain or pleasure?

HYL. No, certainly.

PHIL. Is your material substance a senseless being, or a being endowed with sense and perception?

HYL. It is senseless without doubt.

PHIL. It cannot therefore be the subject of pain?

HYL. By no means.

PHIL. Nor consequently of the greatest heat perceived by sense, since you acknowledge this to be no small pain?

HYL. I grant it.

PHIL. What shall we say then of your external object; is it a material Substance, or no?

HYL. It is a material substance with the sensible qualities inhering in it.

PHIL. How then can a great heat exist in it, since you own it cannot in a material substance? I desire you would clear this point.

HYL. Hold, Philonous, I fear I was out in yielding intense heat to be a pain. It should seem rather, that pain is something distinct from heat, and the consequence or effect of it.

PHIL. Upon putting your hand near the fire, do you perceive one simple uniform sensation, or two distinct sensations?

HYL. But one simple sensation.

PHIL. Is not the heat immediately perceived?

HYL. It is.

PHIL. And the pain?

HYL. True.

PHIL. Seeing therefore they are both immediately perceived at the same time, and the fire affects you only with one simple or uncompounded idea, it follows that this same simple idea is both the intense heat immediately perceived, and the pain; and, consequently, that the intense heat immediately perceived is nothing distinct from a particular sort of pain.

HYL. It seems so.

PHIL. Again, try in your thoughts, Hylas, if you can conceive a vehement sensation to be without pain or pleasure.

HYL. I cannot.

PHIL. Or can you frame to yourself an idea of sensible pain or pleasure in general, abstracted from every particular idea of heat, cold, tastes, smells? &c.

HYL. I do not find that I can.

PHIL. Doth it not therefore follow, that sensible pain is nothing distinct from those sensations or ideas, in an intense degree?

HYL. It is undeniable; and, to speak the truth, I begin to suspect a very great heat cannot exist but in a mind perceiving it.

PHIL. What! are you then in that sceptical state of suspense, between affirming and denying?

HYL. I think I may be positive in the point. A very violent and painful heat cannot exist without the mind.

PHIL. It hath not therefore, according to you, any *real* being?

HYL. I own it.

PHIL. Is it therefore certain, that there is no body in nature really hot?

HYL. I have not denied there is any real heat in bodies. I only say, there is no such thing as an intense real heat.

PHIL. But, did you not say before that all degrees of heat were equally real; or, if there was any difference, that the greater were more undoubtedly real than the lesser?

HYL. True: but it was because I did not then consider the ground there is for distinguishing between them, which I now plainly see. And it is this: because intense heat is nothing else but a particular kind of painful sensation; and pain cannot exist but in a perceiving being; it follows that no intense heat can really exist in an unperceiving corporeal substance. But this is no reason why we should deny heat in an inferior degree to exist in such a substance.

PHIL. But how shall we be able to discern those degrees of heat which exist only in the mind from those which exist without it?

HYL. That is no difficult matter. You know the least pain cannot exist unperceived; whatever, therefore, degree of heat is a pain exists only in the mind. But, as for all other degrees of heat, nothing obliges us to think the same of them.

PHIL. I think you granted before that no unperceiving being was capable of pleasure, any more than of pain.

HYL. I did.

PHIL. And is not warmth, or a more gentle degree of heat than what causes uneasiness, a pleasure?

HYL. What then?

PHIL. Consequently, it cannot exist without the mind in an unperceiving substance, or body.

HYL. So it seems.

PHIL. Since, therefore, as well those degrees of heat that are not painful, as those that are, can exist only in a thinking substance; may we not conclude that external bodies are absolutely incapable of any degree of heat whatsoever?

HYL. On second thoughts, I do not think it so evident that warmth is a pleasure as that a great degree of heat is a pain.

PHIL. I do not pretend that warmth is as great a pleasure as heat is a pain. But, if you grant it to be even a small pleasure, it serves to make good my conclusion.

HYL. I could rather call it an *indolence*. It seems to be nothing more than a privation of both pain and pleasure. And that such a quality or state as this may agree to an unthinking substance, I hope you will not deny.

PHIL. If you are resolved to maintain that warmth, or a gentle degree of heat, is no pleasure, I know not how to convince you otherwise than by appealing to your own sense. But what think you of cold?

HYL. The same that I do of heat. An intense degree of cold is a pain; for to feel a very great cold, is to perceive a great uneasiness: it cannot therefore exist without the mind; but a lesser degree of cold may, as well as a lesser degree of heat.

PHIL. Those bodies, therefore, upon whose application to our own, we perceive a moderate degree of heat, must be concluded to have a moderate degree of heat or warmth in them; and those, upon whose application we feel a like degree of cold, must be thought to have cold in them.

HYL. They must.

PHIL. Can any doctrine be true that necessarily leads a man into an absurdity?

HYL. Without doubt it cannot.

PHIL. Is it not an absurdity to think that the same thing should be at the same time both cold and warm?

HYL. It is.

PHIL. Suppose now one of your hands hot, and the other cold, and that they are both at once put into the same vessel of water, in an intermediate state; will not the water seem cold to one hand, and warm to the other?[6]

HYL. It will.

PHIL. Ought we not therefore, by your principles, to conclude it is really both cold and warm at the same time, that is, according to your own concession, to believe an absurdity?

HYL. I confess it seems so.

PHIL. Consequently, the principles themselves are false, since you have granted that no true principle leads to an absurdity.

HYL. But, after all, can anything be more absurd than to say, *there is no heat in the fire*?

PHIL. To make the point still clearer; tell me whether, in two cases exactly alike, we ought not to make the same judgment?

HYL. We ought.

PHIL. When a pin pricks your finger, doth it not rend and divide the fibres of your flesh?

HYL. It doth.

PHIL. And when a coal burns your finger, doth it any more?

HYL. It doth not.

PHIL. Since, therefore, you neither judge the sensation itself occasioned by the pin, nor anything like it to be in the pin; you should not, conformably to what you have now granted, judge the sensation occasioned by the fire, or anything like it, to be in the fire.

HYL. Well, since it must be so, I am content to yield this point, and acknowledge that heat and cold are only sensations existing in our minds. But there still remain qualities enough to secure the reality of external things.

PHIL. But what will you say, Hylas, if it shall appear that the case is the same with regard to all other sensible qualities,[7] and that they can no more be supposed to exist without the mind, than heat and cold?

HYL. Then indeed you will have done something to the purpose; but that is what I despair of seeing proved.

PHIL. Let us examine them in order. What think you of *tastes* — do they exist without the mind, or no?

---

[6]Cf. *Principles*, section 14.

[7]Cf. *Principles*, sections 14 and 15.

HYL. Can any man in his senses doubt whether sugar is sweet, or wormwood bitter?

PHIL. Inform me, Hylas. Is a sweet taste a particular kind of pleasure or pleasant sensation, or is it not?

HYL. It is.

PHIL. And is not bitterness some kind of uneasiness or pain?

HYL. I grant it.

PHIL. If therefore sugar and wormwood are unthinking corporeal substances existing without the mind, how can sweetness and bitterness, that is, pleasure and pain, agree to them?

HYL. Hold, Philonous, I now see what it was deluded me all this time. You asked whether heat and cold, sweetness and bitterness, were not particular sorts of pleasure and pain; to which I answered simply, that they were. Whereas I should have thus distinguished: those qualities, as perceived by us, are pleasures or pains; but not as existing in the external objects. We must not therefore conclude absolutely, that there is no heat in the fire, or sweetness in the sugar, but only that heat or sweetness, as perceived by us, are not in the fire or sugar. What say you to this?

PHIL. I say it is nothing to the purpose. Our discourse proceeded altogether concerning sensible things, which you defined to be, *the things we immediately perceive by our senses*. Whatever other qualities, therefore, you speak of, as distinct from these; I know nothing of them, neither do they at all belong to the point in dispute. You may, indeed, pretend to have discovered certain qualities which you do not perceive, and assert those insensible qualities exist in fire and sugar. But what use can be made of this to your present purpose, I am at a loss to conceive. Tell me then once more, do you acknowledge that heat and cold, sweetness and bitterness (meaning those qualities which are perceived by the senses), do not exist without the mind?

HYL. I see it is to no purpose to hold out, so I give up the cause as to those mentioned qualities. Though I profess it sounds oddly, to say that sugar is not sweet.

PHIL. But, for your farther satisfaction, take this along with you: that which at other times seems sweet, shall, to a distempered palate, appear bitter. And, nothing can be plainer than that divers persons perceive different tastes in the same food; since that which one man delights in, another abhors. And how could this be, if the taste was something really inherent in the food?

HYL. I acknowledge I know not how.

PHIL. In the next place, *odours* are to be considered. And, with regard to these, I would fain know whether what hath been said of tastes doth not exactly agree to them? Are they not so many pleasing or displeasing sensations?

HYL. They are.

PHIL. Can you then conceive it possible that they should exist in an unperceiving thing?

HYL. I cannot.

PHIL. Or, can you imagine that filth and ordure affect those brute animals that feed on them out of choice, with the same smells which we perceive in them?

HYL. By no means.

PHIL. May we not therefore conclude of smells, as of the other forementioned qualities, that they cannot exist in any but a perceiving substance or mind?

HYL. I think so.

PHIL. Then as to *sounds*, what must we think of them: are they accidents really inherent in external bodies, or not?

HYL. That they inhere not in the sonorous bodies is plain from hence: because a bell struck in the exhausted receiver of an air-pump sends forth no sound. The air, therefore, must be thought the subject of sound.

PHIL. What reason is there for that, Hylas?

HYL. Because, when any motion is raised in the air, we perceive a sound greater or lesser, according to the air's motion; but without some motion in the air, we never hear any sound at all.

PHIL. And granting that we never hear a sound but when some motion is produced in the air, yet I do not see how you can infer from thence, that the sound itself is in the air.

HYL. It is this very motion in the external air that produces in the mind the sensation of *sound*. For, striking on the drum of the ear, it causeth a vibration, which by the auditory nerves being communicated to the brain, the soul is thereupon affected with the sensation called *sound*.

PHIL. What! is sound then a sensation?

HYL. I tell you, as perceived by us, it is a particular sensation in the mind.

PHIL. And can any sensation exist without the mind?

HYL. No, certainly.

PHIL. How then can sound, being a sensation, exist in the air, if by the *air* you mean a senseless substance existing without the mind?

HYL. You must distinguish, Philonous, between sound as it is perceived by us, and as it is in itself; or (which is the same thing) between the sound we immediately perceive, and that which exists without us. The former, indeed, is a particular kind of sensation, but the latter is merely a vibrative or undulatory motion in the air.

PHIL. I thought I had already obviated that distinction, by the answer I gave when you were applying it in a like case before. But, to say no more of that, are you sure then that sound is really nothing but motion?

HYL. I am.

PHIL. Whatever therefore agrees to real sound, may with truth be attributed to motion?

HYL. It may.

PHIL. It is then good sense to speak of *motion* as of a thing that is *loud, sweet, acute, or grave.*

HYL. I see you are resolved not to understand me. Is it not evident those accidents or modes belong only to sensible sound, or *sound* in the common acceptation of the word, but not to *sound* in the real and philosophic sense; which, as I just now told you, is nothing but a certain motion of the air?

PHIL. It seems then there are two sorts of sound—the one vulgar, or that which is heard, the other philosophical and real?

HYL. Even so.

PHIL. And the latter consists in motion?

HYL. I told you so before.

PHIL. Tell me, Hylas, to which of the senses, think you, the idea of motion belongs? to the hearing?

HYL. No, certainly; but to the sight and touch.

PHIL. It should follow then, that, according to you, real sounds may possibly be *seen* or *felt*, but never *heard*.

HYL. Look you, Philonous, you may, if you please, make a jest of my opinion, but that will not alter the truth of things. I own, indeed, the inferences you draw me into sound something oddly; but common language, you know, is framed by, and for the use of the vulgar: we must not therefore wonder if expressions adapted to exact philosophic notions seem uncouth and out of the way.

PHIL. Is it come to that? I assure you, I imagine myself to have gained no small point, since you make so light of departing from common phrases and opinions; it being a main part of our inquiry, to examine whose notions are widest of the common road, and most repugnant to the general sense of the world. But, can you think it no more than a philosophical paradox, to say that *real sounds are never heard*, and that the idea of them is obtained by some other sense? And is there nothing in this contrary to nature and the truth of things?

HYL. To deal ingenuously, I do not like it. And, after the concessions already made, I had as well grant that sounds too have no real being without the mind.

PHIL. And I hope you will make no difficulty to acknowledge the same of *colours*.

HYL. Pardon me: the case of colours is very different. Can anything be plainer than that we see them on the objects?

PHIL. The objects you speak of are, I suppose, corporeal Substances existing without the mind?

HYL. They are.

PHIL. And have true and real colours inhering in them?

HYL. Each visible object hath that colour which we see in it.

PHIL. How! is there anything visible but what we perceive by sight?

HYL. There is not.

PHIL. And, do we perceive anything by sense which we do not perceive immediately?

HYL. How often must I be obliged to repeat the same thing? I tell you, we do not.

PHIL. Have patience, good Hylas; and tell me once more, whether there is anything immediately perceived by the senses, except sensible qualities. I know you asserted there was not; but I would now be informed, whether you still persist in the same opinion.

HYL. I do.

PHIL. Pray, is your corporeal substance either a sensible quality, or made up of sensible qualities?

HYL. What a question that is! who ever thought it was?

PHIL. My reason for asking was, because in saying, *each visible object hath that colour which we see in it*, you make visible objects to be corporeal substances; which implies either that corporeal substances are sensible qualities, or else that there is something beside sensible qualities perceived by sight: but, as this point was formerly agreed between us, and is still maintained by you, it is a clear consequence, that your *corporeal substance* is nothing distinct from *sensible qualities*.

HYL. You may draw as many absurd consequences as you please, and endeavour to perplex the plainest things; but you shall never persuade me out of my senses. I clearly understand my own meaning.

PHIL. I wish you would make me understand it too. But, since you are unwilling to have your notion of corporeal substance examined, I shall urge that point no farther. Only be pleased to let me know, whether the same colours which we see exist in external bodies, or some other.

HYL. The very same.

PHIL. What! are then the beautiful red and purple we see on yonder clouds really in them? Or do you imagine they have in themselves any other form than that of a dark mist or vapour?

HYL. I must own, Philonous, those colours are not really in the clouds as they seem to be at this distance. They are only apparent colours.

PHIL. *Apparent* call you them? how shall we distinguish these apparent colours from real?

HYL. Very easily. Those are to be thought apparent which, appearing only at a distance, vanish upon a nearer approach.

PHIL. And those, I suppose, are to be thought real which are discovered by the most near and exact survey.

HYL. Right.

PHIL. Is the nearest and exactest survey made by the help of a microscope, or by the naked eye?

HYL. By a microscope, doubtless.

PHIL. But a microscope often discovers colours in an object different from those perceived by the unassisted sight. And, in case we had microscopes magnifying to any assigned degree, it is certain that no object whatsoever, viewed through them, would appear in the same colour which it exhibits to the naked eye.

HYL. And what will you conclude from all this? You cannot argue that there are really and naturally no colours on objects: because by artificial managements they may be altered, or made to vanish.

PHIL. I think it may evidently be concluded from your own concessions, that all the colours we see with our naked eyes are only apparent as those on the clouds, since they vanish upon a more close and accurate inspection which is afforded us by a microscope. Then, as to what you say by way of prevention: I ask you whether the real and natural state of an object is better discovered by a very sharp and piercing sight, or by one which is less sharp?

HYL. By the former without doubt.

PHIL. Is it not plain from *Dioptrics* that microscopes make the sight more penetrating, and represent objects as they would appear to the eye in case it were naturally endowed with a most exquisite sharpness?

HYL. It is.

PHIL. Consequently the microscopical representation is to be thought that which best sets forth the real nature of the thing, or what it is in itself. The colours, therefore, by it perceived are more genuine and real than those perceived otherwise.

HYL. I confess there is something in what you say.

PHIL. Besides; it is not only possible but manifest, that there actually are animals whose eyes are by nature framed to perceive those things which by reason of their minuteness escape our sight. What think you of those inconceivably small animals perceived by glasses? must we suppose they are all stark blind? Or, in case they see, can it be imagined their sight hath not the same use in preserving their bodies from injuries, which appears in that of all other animals? And if it hath, is it not evident they must see particles less than their own bodies; which will present them with a far different view in each object from that which strikes our senses?[8] Even our own eyes do not always represent objects to us after the same manner. In the jaundice every one knows that all things seem yellow. Is it not therefore highly probable those animals in whose eyes we discern a very different texture from that of ours and whose bodies abound with different humors, do not see the same colours in every object that we do? From all which, should it not seem to follow that all colours are equally apparent, and that none of those which we perceive are really inherent in any outward object?

HYL. It should.

PHIL. The point will be past all doubt, if you consider that, in case colours were real properties or affections inherent in external bodies, they could admit of no alteration without some change wrought in the very bodies themselves: but, is it not evident from what hath been said that, upon the use of microscopes, upon a change happening in the humours of the eye, or a variation of distance, without any manner of real alteration in the thing itself, the colours of any object are either changed, or totally disappear? Nay, all other circumstances remaining the same, change but the situation of some objects, and they shall present different colours to the eye. The same thing happens upon viewing an object in various degrees of light. And what is more known than that the same bodies appear differently coloured by candle-light from what they do in the open day? Add to these the experiment of a prism which, separating the heterogeneous rays of light, alters the colour of any object, and will cause the whitest to appear of a deep blue or red to the naked eye. And now tell me whether you are still of opinion that every body hath its true real colour inhering in it; and, if you think it hath, I would fain know farther from you, what certain distance and position of the object, what peculiar texture and formation of the eye, what degree or kind of light is necessary for ascertaining that true colour, and distinguishing it from apparent ones.

HYL. I own myself entirely satisfied, that they are all equally apparent, and that there is no such thing as colour really inhering in external bodies, but that it is altogether in the light. And what confirms me in this opinion is, that in proportion to the light colours are still more or less vivid; and if there be no light, then are there no colours perceived. Besides, allowing there are colours on external objects, yet, how is it possible for us to perceive them? For no external body affects the mind, unless it acts first on our organs of sense. But the only action of bodies is motion; and motion cannot be communicated otherwise than by impulse. A distant object therefore cannot act on the eye; nor consequently make itself or its properties perceivable to the soul. Whence it plainly follows that it is immediately some contiguous substance, which, operating on the eye, occasions a perception of colours: and such is light.

PHIL. How! is light then a substance?

HYL. I tell you, Philonous, external light is nothing but a thin fluid substance, whose minute particles being agitated with a brisk motion, and in various manners reflected from the different surfaces of outward objects to the eyes, communicate different motions to the optic nerves; which, being propagated to the brain, cause therein various impressions; and these are attended with the sensations of red, blue, yellow, &c.

PHIL. It seems then the light doth no more than shake the optic nerves.

---

[8]Cf. *New Theory of Vision*, sections 80–86.

HYL. Nothing else.

PHIL. And consequent to each particular motion of the nerves, the mind is affected with a sensation, which is some particular colour.

HYL. Right.

PHIL. And these sensations have no existence without the mind.

HYL. They have not.

PHIL. How then do you affirm that colours are in the light; since by *light* you understand a corporeal substance external to the mind?

HYL. Light and colours, as immediately perceived by us, I grant cannot exist without the mind. But in themselves they are only the motions and configurations of certain insensible particles of matter.

PHIL. Colours then, in the vulgar sense, or taken for the immediate objects of sight, cannot agree to any but a perceiving substance.

HYL. That is what I say.

PHIL. Well then, since you give up the point as to those sensible qualities which are alone thought colours by all mankind beside, you may hold what you please with regard to those invisible ones of the philosophers. It is not my business to dispute about *them*; only I would advise you to bethink yourself, whether, considering the inquiry we are upon, it be prudent for you to affirm — *the red and blue which we see are not real colours, but certain unknown motions and figures which no man ever did or can see are truly so*. Are not these shocking notions, and are not they subject to as many ridiculous inferences, as those you were obliged to renounce before in the case of sounds?

HYL. I frankly own, Philonous, that it is in vain to stand out any longer. Colours, sounds, tastes, in a word all those termed *secondary qualities*, have certainly no existence without the mind. But by this acknowledgment I must not be supposed to derogate anything from the reality of Matter, or external objects; seeing it is no more than several philosophers maintain, who nevertheless are the farthest imaginable from denying Matter. For the clearer understanding of this, you must know sensible qualities are by philosophers divided into *Primary* and *Secondary*.[9] The former are Extension, Figure, Solidity, Gravity, Motion, and Rest; and these they hold exist really in bodies. The latter are those above enumerated; or, briefly, *all sensible qualities beside the Primary*; which they assert are only so many sensations or ideas existing nowhere but in the mind. But all this, I doubt not, you are apprised of. For my part, I have been a long time sensible there was such an opinion current among philosophers, but was never thoroughly convinced of its truth until now.

PHIL. You are still then of opinion that *extension* and *figures* are inherent in external unthinking substances?

HYL. I am.

PHIL. But what if the same arguments which are brought against Secondary Qualities will hold good against these also?

HYL. Why then I shall be obliged to think, they too exist only in the mind.

PHIL. Is it your opinion the very figure and extension which you perceive by sense exist in the outward object or material substance?

---

[9]Cf. *Principles*, sections 9–15. See also Descartes, *Meditations*, III, and Locke's *Essay*, Book II, Chapter 8.

HYL. It is.

PHIL. Have all other animals as good grounds to think the same of the figure and extension which they see and feel?

HYL. Without doubt, if they have any thought at all.

PHIL. Answer me, Hylas. Think you the senses were bestowed upon all animals for their preservation and well-being in life? or were they given to men alone for this end?

HYL. I make no question but they have the same use in all other animals.

PHIL. If so, is it not necessary they should be enabled by them to perceive their own limbs, and those bodies which are capable of harming them?

HYL. Certainly.

PHIL. A mite therefore must be supposed to see his own foot, and things equal or even less than it, as bodies of some considerable dimension; though at the same time they appear to you scarce discernible, or at best as so many visible points?[10]

HYL. I cannot deny it.

PHIL. And to creatures less than the mite they will seem yet larger?

HYL. They will.

PHIL. Insomuch that what you can hardly discern will to another extremely minute animal appear as some huge mountain?

HYL. All this I grant.

PHIL. Can one and the same thing be at the same time in itself of different dimensions?

HYL. That were absurd to imagine.

PHIL. But, from what you have laid down it follows that both the extension by you perceived, and that perceived by the mite itself, as likewise all those perceived by lesser animals, are each of them the true extension of the mite's foot; that is to say, by your own principles you are led into an absurdity.

HYL. There seems to be some difficulty in the point.

PHIL. Again, have you not acknowledged that no real inherent property of any object can be changed without some change in the thing itself?

HYL. I have.

PHIL. But, as we approach to or recede from an object, the visible extension varies, being at one distance ten or a hundred times greater than at another. Doth it not therefore follow from hence likewise that it is not really inherent in the object?

HYL. I own I am at a loss what to think.

PHIL. Your judgment will soon be determined, if you will venture to think as freely concerning this quality as you have done concerning the rest. Was it not admitted as a good argument, that neither heat nor cold was in the water, because it seemed warm to one hand and cold to the other?

HYL. It was.

PHIL. Is it not the very same reasoning to conclude, there is no extension or figure in an object, because to one eye it shall seem little, smooth, and round, when at the same time it appears to the other, great, uneven, and angular?

HYL. The very same. But does this latter fact ever happen?

PHIL. You may at any time make the experiment, by looking with one eye bare, and with the other through a microscope.

---

[10]Cf. *New Theory of Vision*, section 80.

HYL. I know not how to maintain it; and yet I am loath to give up *extension*, I see so many odd consequences following upon such a concession.

PHIL. Odd, say you? After the concessions already made, I hope you will stick at nothing for its oddness. But, on the other hand, should it not seem very odd, if the general reasoning which includes all other sensible qualities did not also include extension? If it be allowed that no idea, nor anything like an idea, can exist in an unperceiving substance, then surely it follows that no figure, or mode of extension, which we can either perceive, or imagine, or have any idea of, can be really inherent in Matter; not to mention the peculiar difficulty there must be in conceiving a material substance, prior to and distinct from extension, to be the *substratum* of extension. Be the sensible quality what it will — figure, or sound, or colour, it seems alike impossible it should subsist in that which doth not perceive it.

HYL. I give up the point for the present, reserving still a right to retract my opinion, in case I shall hereafter discover any false step in my progress to it.

PHIL. That is a right you cannot be denied. Figures and extension being despatched, we proceed next to *motion*. Can a real motion in any external body be at the same time both very swift and very slow?

HYL. It cannot.

PHIL. Is not the motion of a body swift in a reciprocal proportion to the time it takes up in describing any given space? Thus a body that describes a mile in an hour moves three times faster than it would in case it described only a mile in three hours.

HYL. I agree with you.

PHIL. And is not time measured by the succession of ideas in our minds?

HYL. It is.

PHIL. And is it not possible ideas should succeed one another twice as fast in your mind as they do in mine, or in that of some spirit of another kind?

HYL. I own it.

PHIL. Consequently the same body may to another seem to perform its motion over any space in half the time that it doth to you. And the same reasoning will hold as to any other proportion: that is to say, according to your principles (since the motions perceived are both really in the object) it is possible one and the same body shall be really moved the same way at once, both very swift and very slow. How is this consistent either with common sense, or with what you just now granted?

HYL. I have nothing to say to it.

PHIL. Then as for *solidity*; either you do not mean any sensible quality by that word, and so it is beside our inquiry: or if you do, it must be either hardness or resistance. But both the one and the other are plainly relative to our senses: it being evident that what seems hard to one animal may appear soft to another, who hath greater force and firmness of limbs. Nor is it less plain that the resistance I feel is not in the body.

HYL. I own the very *sensation* of resistance, which is all you immediately perceive, is not in the body; but the *cause* of that sensation is.

PHIL. But the causes of our sensations are not things immediately perceived, and therefore are not sensible. This point I thought had been already determined.

HYL. I own it was; but you will pardon me if I seem a little embarrassed: I know not how to quit my old notions.

PHIL. To help you out, do but consider that if *extension* be once acknowledged to have no existence without the mind, the same must necessarily be granted of motion, solidity, and gravity; since they all evidently suppose extension. It is therefore superfluous to inquire particularly concerning each of them. In denying extension, you have denied them all to have any real existence.

HYL. I wonder, Philonous, if what you say be true, why those philosophers who deny the Secondary Qualities any real existence should yet attribute it to the Primary. If there is no difference between them, how can this be accounted for?

PHIL. It is not my business to account for every opinion of the philosophers. But, among other reasons which may be assigned for this, it seems probable that pleasure and pain being rather annexed to the former than the latter may be one. Heat and cold, tastes and smells, have something more vividly pleasing or disagreeable than the ideas of extension, figure, and motion affect us with. And, it being too visibly absurd to hold that pain or pleasure can be in an unperceiving Substance, men are more easily weaned from believing the external existence of the Secondary than the Primary Qualities. You will be satisfied there is something in this, if you recollect the difference you made between an intense and more moderate degree of heat; allowing the one a real existence, while you denied it to the other. But, after all, there is no rational ground for that distinction; for, surely an indifferent sensation is as truly *a sensation* as one more pleasing or painful; and consequently should not any more than they be supposed to exist in an unthinking subject.

HYL. It is just come into my head, Philonous, that I have somewhere heard of a distinction between absolute and sensible extension.[11] Now, though it be acknowledged that *great* and *small*, consisting merely in the relation which other extended beings have to the parts of our own bodies, do not really inhere in the substances themselves; yet nothing obliges us to hold the same with regard to *absolute extension*, which is something abstracted from *great* and *small*, from this or that particular magnitude or figure. So likewise as to motion; *swift* and *slow* are altogether relative to the succession of ideas in our own minds. But, it doth not follow, because those modifications of motion exist not without the mind, that therefore absolute motion abstracted from them doth not.

PHIL. Pray what is it that distinguishes one motion, or one part of extension, from another? Is it not something sensible, as some degree of swiftness or slowness, some certain magnitude or figure peculiar to each?

HYL. I think so.

PHIL. These qualities, therefore, stripped of all sensible properties, are without all specific and numerical differences, as the schools call them.

HYL. They are.

PHIL. That is to say, they are extension in general, and motion in general.

HYL. Let it be so.

PHIL. But it is a universally received maxim that *Everything which exists is particular*.[12] How then can motion in general or extension in general, exist in any corporeal substance?

---

[11]Cf. *New Theory of Vision*, section 122–126; *Principles*, section 123; and *Siris*, section 270.

[12]Cf. *Principles*, Introduction, section 15.

HYL. I will take time to solve your difficulty.

PHIL. But I think the point may be speedily decided. Without doubt you can tell whether you are able to frame this or that idea. Now I am content to put our dispute on this issue. If you can frame in your thoughts a distinct *abstract idea* of motion or extension, divested of all those sensible modes, as swift and slow, great and small, round and square, and the like, which are acknowledged to exist only in the mind, I will then yield the point you contend for. But if you cannot, it will be unreasonable on your side to insist any longer upon what you have no notion of.

HYL. To confess ingenuously, I cannot.

PHIL. Can you even separate the ideas of extension and motion from the ideas of all those qualities which they who make the distinction term *secondary*?

HYL. What! is it not an easy matter to consider extension and motion by themselves, abstracted from all other sensible qualities? Pray how do the mathematicians treat of them?

PHIL. I acknowledge, Hylas, it is not difficult to form general propositions and reasonings about those qualities, without mentioning any other; and, in this sense, to consider or treat of them abstractedly.[13] But, how doth it follow that, because I can pronounce the word *motion* by itself, I can form the idea of it in my mind exclusive of body? or, because theorems may be made of extension and figures, without any mention of *great* or *small*, or any other sensible mode or quality, that therefore it is possible such an abstract idea of extension, without any particular size or figure, or sensible quality, should be distinctly formed, and apprehended by the mind? Mathematicians treat of quantity, without regarding what other sensible qualities it is attended with, as being altogether indifferent to their demonstrations. But, when laying aside the words, they contemplate the bare ideas, I believe you will find, they are not the pure abstracted ideas of extension.

HYL. But what say you to *pure intellect*? May not abstracted ideas be framed by that faculty?

PHIL. Since I cannot frame abstract ideas at all, it is plain I cannot frame them by the help of *pure intellect*; whatsoever faculty you understand by those words. Besides, not to inquire into the nature of pure intellect and its spiritual objects, as *virtue, reason, God,* or the like, thus much seems manifest—that sensible things are only to be perceived by sense, or presented by the imagination. Figures, therefore, and extension, being originally perceived by sense, do not belong to pure intellect: but, for your farther satisfaction, try if you can frame the idea of any figure, abstracted from all particularities of size, or even from other sensible qualities.

HYL. Let me think a little—I do not find that I can.

PHIL. And can you think it possible that should really exist in nature which implies a repugnancy in its conception?

HYL. By no means.

PHIL. Since therefore it is impossible even for the mind to disunite the ideas of extension and motion from all other sensible qualities, doth it not follow, that where the one exist there necessarily the other exist likewise?

HYL. It should seem so.

---

[13]Cf. *Principles*, Introduction, section 16.

PHIL. Consequently, the very same arguments which you admitted as conclusive against the Secondary Qualities are, without any farther application of force, against the Primary too. Besides, if you will trust your senses, is it not plain all sensible qualities coexist, or to them appear as being in the same place? Do they ever represent a motion, or figure, as being divested of all other visible and tangible qualities?

HYL. You need say no more on this head. I am free to own, if there be no secret error or oversight in our proceedings hitherto, that *all* sensible qualities are alike to be denied existence without the mind. But, my fear is that I have been too liberal in my former concessions, or overlooked some fallacy or other. In short, I did not take time to think.

PHIL. For that matter, Hylas, you may take what time you please in reviewing the progress of our inquiry. You are at liberty to recover any slips you might have made, or offer whatever you have omitted which makes for your first opinion.

HYL. One great oversight I take to be this—that I did not sufficiently distinguish the *object* from the *sensation*.[14] Now, though this latter may not exist without the mind, yet it will not thence follow that the former cannot.

PHIL. What object do you mean? the object of the senses?

HYL. The same.

PHIL. It is then immediately perceived?

HYL. Right.

PHIL. Make me to understand the difference between what is immediately perceived and a sensation.

HYL. The sensation I take to be an act of the mind perceiving; besides which, there is something perceived; and this I call the *object*. For example, there is red and yellow on that tulip. But then the act of perceiving those colours is in me only, and not in the tulip.

PHIL. What tulip do you speak of? Is it that which you see?

HYL. The same.

PHIL. And what do you see beside colour, figure, and extension?[15]

HYL. Nothing.

PHIL. What you would say then is that the red and yellow are coexistent with the extension; is it not?

HYL. That is not all; I would say they have a real existence without the mind, in some unthinking substance.

PHIL. That the colours are really in the tulip which I see is manifest. Neither can it be denied that this tulip may exist independent of your mind or mine; but, that any immediate object of the senses—that is, any idea, or combination of ideas—should exist in an unthinking substance, or exterior to *all* minds, is in itself an evident contradiction. Nor can I imagine how this follows from what you said just now, to wit, that the red and yellow were on the tulip *you saw*, since you do not pretend to *see* that unthinking substance.

HYL. You have an artful way, Philonous, of diverting our inquiry from the subject.

PHIL. I see you have no mind to be pressed that way. To return then to your

[14]Cf. *New Theory of Vision Vindicated*, section 8.
[15]Cf. *New Theory of Vision*, section 43.

distinction between *sensation* and *object*; if I take you right, you distinguish in every perception two things, the one an action of the mind, the other not.

HYL. True.

PHIL. And this action cannot exist in, or belong to, any unthinking thing,[16] but, whatever beside is implied in a perception may?

HYL. That is my meaning.

PHIL. So that if there was a perception without any act of the mind, it were possible such a perception should exist in an unthinking substance?

HYL. I grant it. But it is impossible there should be such a perception.

PHIL. When is the mind said to be active?

HYL. When it produces, puts an end to, or changes, anything.

PHIL. Can the mind produce, discontinue, or change anything, but by an act of the will?

HYL. It cannot.

PHIL. The mind therefore is to be accounted *active* in its perceptions so far forth as *volition* is included in them?

HYL. It is.

PHIL. In plucking this flower I am active; because I do it by the motion of my hand, which was consequent upon my volition; so likewise in applying it to my nose. But is either of these smelling?

HYL. No.

PHIL. I act too in drawing the air through my nose; because my breathing so rather than otherwise is the effect of my volition. But neither can this be called *smelling*: for, if it were, I should smell every time I breathed in that manner?

HYL. True.

PHIL. Smelling then is somewhat consequent to all this?

HYL. It is.

PHIL. But I do not find my will concerned any farther. Whatever more there is—as that I perceive such a particular smell, or any smell at all—this is independent of my will, and therein I am altogether passive. Do you find it otherwise with you, Hylas?

HYL. No, the very same.

PHIL. Then, as to seeing, is it not in your power to open your eyes, or keep them shut; to turn them this or that way?

HYL. Without doubt.

PHIL. But, doth it in like manner depend on *your* will that in looking on this flower you perceive *white* rather than any other colour? Or directing your open eyes towards yonder part of the heaven, can you avoid seeing the sun? Or is light or darkness the effect of your volition?

HYL. No, certainly.

PHIL. You are then in these respects altogether passive?

HYL. I am.

PHIL. Tell me now, whether *seeing* consists in perceiving light and colours, or in opening and turning the eyes?

HYL. Without doubt, in the former.

PHIL. Since therefore you are in the very perception of light and colours altogether passive, what is become of that action you were speaking of as an

---

[16]Cf. *Principles*, sections 25 and 26.

ingredient in every sensation? And, doth it not follow from your own concessions, that the perception of light and colours, including no action in it, may exist in an unperceiving substance? And is not this a plain contradiction?

HYL. I know not what to think of it.

PHIL. Besides, since you distinguish the *active* and *passive* in every perception, you must do it in that of pain. But how is it possible that pain, be it as little active as you please, should exist in an unperceiving substance? In short, do but consider the point, and then confess ingenuously, whether light and colours, tastes, sounds, &c. are not all equally passions or sensations in the soul. You may indeed call them *external objects*, and give them in words what subsistence you please. But, examine your own thoughts, and then tell me whether it be not as I say?

HYL. I acknowledge, Philonous, that, upon a fair observation of what passes in my mind, I can discover nothing else but that I am a thinking being, affected with variety of sensations; neither is it possible to conceive how a sensation should exist in an unperceiving substance. But then, on the other hand, when I look on sensible things in a different view, considering them as so many modes and qualities, I find it necessary to suppose a *material substratum*, without which they cannot be conceived to exist.

PHIL. *Material substratum* call you it? Pray, by which of your senses came you acquainted with that being?

HYL. It is not itself sensible; its modes and qualities only being perceived by the senses.

PHIL. I presume then it was by reflection and reason you obtained the idea of it?

HYL. I do not pretend to any proper positive *idea* of it. However, I conclude it exists, because qualities cannot be conceived to exist without a support.

PHIL. It seems then you have only a relative *notion* of it, or that you conceive it not otherwise than by conceiving the relation it bears to sensible qualities?

HYL. Right.

PHIL. Be pleased therefore to let me know wherein that relation consists.

HYL. Is it not sufficiently expressed in the term *substratum*, or *substance*?

PHIL. If so, the word *substratum* should import that it is spread under the sensible qualities or accidents?

HYL. True.

PHIL. And consequently under extension?

HYL. I own it.

PHIL. It is therefore somewhat in its own nature entirely distinct from extension?

HYL. I tell you, extension is only a mode, and Matter is something that supports modes. And is it not evident the thing supported is different from the thing supporting?

PHIL. So that something distinct from, and exclusive of, extension is supposed to be the *substratum* of extension?

HYL. Just so.

PHIL. Answer me, Hylas. Can a thing be spread without extension? or is not the idea of extension necessarily included in *spreading*?

HYL. It is.

PHIL. Whatsoever therefore you suppose spread under anything must have in itself an extension distinct from the extension of that thing under which it is spread?

HYL. It must.

PHIL. Consequently, every corporeal substance, being the *substratum* of extension, must have in itself another extension, by which it is qualified to be a *substratum*: and so on to infinity? And I ask whether this be not absurd in itself, and repugnant to what you granted just now, to wit, that the *substratum* was something distinct from and exclusive of extension?

HYL. Aye but, Philonous, you take me wrong. I do not mean that Matter is *spread* in a gross literal sense under extension. The word *substratum* is used only to express in general the same thing with *substance*.

PHIL. Well then, let us examine the relation implied in the term *substance*. Is it not that it stands under accidents?

HYL. The very same.

PHIL. But, that one thing may stand under or support another, must it not be extended?

HYL. It must.

PHIL. Is not therefore this supposition liable to the same absurdity with the former?

HYL. You still take things in a strict literal sense. That is not fair, Philonous.

PHIL. I am not for imposing any sense on your words: you are at liberty to explain them as you please. Only, I beseech you, make me understand something by them. You tell me Matter supports or stands under accidents. How! is it as your legs support your body?

HYL. No; that is the literal sense.

PHIL. Pray let me know any sense, literal or not literal, that you understand it in. How long must I wait for an answer, Hylas?

HYL. I declare I know not what to say. I once thought I understood well enough what was meant by Matter's supporting accidents. But now, the more I think on it the less can I comprehend it: in short I find that I know nothing of it.

PHIL. It seems then you have no idea at all, neither relative nor positive, of Matter; you know neither what it is in itself, nor what relation it bears to accidents?

HYL. I acknowledge it.

PHIL. And yet you asserted that you could not conceive how qualities or accidents should really exist, without conceiving at the same time a material support of them?

HYL. I did.

PHIL. That is to say, when you conceive the *real* existence of qualities, you do withal conceive Something which you cannot conceive?

HYL. It was wrong, I own. But still I fear there is some fallacy or other. Pray what think you of this? It is just come into my head that the ground of all our mistake lies in your treating of each quality by itself. Now, I grant that each quality cannot singly subsist without the mind. Colour cannot without extension, neither can figure without some other sensible quality. But, as the several qualities united or blended together form entire sensible things, nothing hinders why such things may not be supposed to exist without the mind.

PHIL. Either, Hylas, you are jesting, or have a very bad memory. Though indeed we went through all the qualities by name one after another, yet my arguments, or rather your concessions, nowhere tended to prove that the

Secondary Qualities did not subsist each alone by itself; but, that they were not *at all* without the mind. Indeed, in treating of figure and motion we concluded they could not exist without the mind, because it was impossible even in thought to separate them from all secondary qualities, so as to conceive them existing by themselves. But then this was not the only argument made use of upon that occasion. But (to pass by all that hath been hitherto said, and reckon it for nothing, if you will have it so) I am content to put the whole upon this issue. If you can conceive it possible for any mixture or combination of qualities, or any sensible object whatever, to exist without the mind, then I will grant it actually to be so.

HYL. If it comes to that the point will soon be decided. What more easy than to conceive a tree or house existing by itself, independent of, and unperceived by, any mind whatsoever? I do at this present time conceive them existing after that manner.

PHIL. How say you, Hylas, can you see a thing which is at the same time unseen?

HYL. No, that were a contradiction.

PHIL. Is it not as great a contradiction to talk of *conceiving* a thing which is *unconceived*?

HYL. It is.

PHIL. The tree or house therefore which you think of is conceived by you?

HYL. How should it be otherwise?

PHIL. And what is conceived is surely in the mind?

HYL. Without question, that which is conceived is in the mind.

PHIL. How then came you to say, you conceived a house or tree existing independent and out of all minds whatsoever?

HYL. That was I own an oversight; but stay, let me consider what led me into it. It is a pleasant mistake enough. As I was thinking of a tree in a solitary place, where no one was present to see it, methought that was to conceive a tree as existing unperceived or unthought of; not considering that I myself conceived it all the while. But now I plainly see that all I can do is to frame ideas in my own mind. I may indeed conceive in my own thoughts the idea of a tree, or a house, or a mountain, but that is all. And this is far from proving that I can conceive them *existing out of the minds of all Spirits*.

PHIL. You acknowledge then that you cannot possibly conceive how any one corporeal sensible thing should exist otherwise than in a mind?

HYL. I do.

PHIL. And yet you will earnestly contend for the truth of that which you cannot so much as conceive?

HYL. I profess I know not what to think; but still there are some scruples remain with me. Is it not certain I *see things at a distance*? Do we not perceive the stars and moon, for example, to be a great way off? Is not this, I say, manifest to the senses?

PHIL. Do you not in a dream too perceive those or the like objects?

HYL. I do.

PHIL. And have they not then the same appearance of being distant?

HYL. They have.

PHIL. But you do not thence conclude the apparitions in a dream to be without the mind?

HYL. By no means.

PHIL. You ought not therefore to conclude that sensible objects are without the mind, from their appearance, or manner wherein they are perceived.

HYL. I acknowledge it. But doth not my sense deceive me in those cases?

PHIL. By no means. The idea or thing which you immediately perceive, neither sense nor reason informs you that *it* actually exists without the mind. By sense you only know that you are affected with such certain sensations of light and colours, &c. And these you will not say are without the mind.

HYL. True: but, beside all that, do you not think the sight suggests something of *outness* or *distance*?

PHIL. Upon approaching a distant object, do the visible size and figure change perpetually, or do they appear the same at all distances?

HYL. They are in a continual change.

PHIL. Sight therefore doth not suggest, or any way inform you, that the visible object you immediately perceive exists at a distance,[17] or will be perceived when you advance farther onward; there being a continued series of visible objects succeeding each other during the whole time of your approach.

HYL. It doth not; but still I know, upon seeing an object, what object I shall perceive after having passed over a certain distance: no matter whether it be exactly the same or no: there is still something of distance suggested in the case.

PHIL. Good Hylas, do but reflect a little on the point, and then tell me whether there be any more in it than this: From the ideas you actually perceive by sight, you have by experience learned to collect what other ideas you will (according to the standing order of nature) be affected with, after such a certain succession of time and motion.

HYL. Upon the whole, I take it to be nothing else.

PHIL. Now, is it not plain that if we suppose a man born blind was on a sudden made to see, he could at first have no experience of what may be *suggested* by sight?

HYL. It is.

PHIL. He would not then, according to you, have any notion of distance annexed to the things he saw; but would take them for a new set of sensations, existing only in his mind?

HYL. It is undeniable.

PHIL. But, to make it still more plain: is not *distance* a line turned endwise to the eye?[18]

HYL. It is.

PHIL. And can a line so situated be perceived by sight?

HYL. It cannot.

PHIL. Doth it not therefore follow that distance is not properly and immediately perceived by sight?

HYL. It should seem so.

PHIL. Again, is it your opinion that colours are at a distance?[19]

---

[17]See the *Essay towards a New Theory of Vision*, and its *Vindication*. Note by the Author in the 1734 edition.

[18]Cf. *Essay on Vision*, section 2.

[19]Cf. *Essay on Vision*, section 43.

HYL. It must be acknowledged they are only in the mind.

PHIL. But do not colours appear to the eye as coexisting in the same place with extension and figures?

HYL. They do.

PHIL. How can you then conclude from sight that figures exist without, when you acknowledge colours do not; the sensible appearance being the very same with regard to both?

HYL. I know not what to answer.

PHIL. But, allowing that distance was truly and immediately perceived by the mind, yet it would not thence follow it existed out of the mind. For, whatever is immediately perceived is an idea: and can any idea exist out of the mind?

HYL. To suppose that were absurd: but, inform me, Philonous, can we perceive or know nothing beside our ideas?

PHIL. As for the rational deducing of causes from effects, that is beside our inquiry. And, by the senses you can best tell whether you perceive anything which is not immediately perceived. And I ask you, whether the things immediately perceived are other than your own sensations or ideas? You have indeed more than once, in the course of this conversation, declared yourself on those points; but you seem, by this last question, to have departed from what you then thought.

HYL. To speak the truth, Philonous, I think there are two kinds of objects: the one perceived immediately, which are likewise called *ideas*; the other are real things or external objects, perceived by the mediation of ideas, which are their images and representations. Now, I own ideas do not exist without the mind; but the latter sort of objects do. I am sorry I did not think of this distinction sooner; it would probably have cut short your discourse.

PHIL. Are those external objects perceived by sense, or by some other faculty?

HYL. They are perceived by sense.

PHIL. How! Is there anything perceived by sense which is not immediately perceived?

HYL. Yes, Philonous, in some sort there is. For example, when I look on a picture or statue of Julius Cæsar, I may be said after a manner to perceive him (though not immediately) by my senses.

PHIL. It seems then you will have our ideas, which alone are immediately perceived, to be pictures of external things: and that these also are perceived by sense, inasmuch as they have a conformity or resemblance to our ideas?

HYL. That is my meaning.

PHIL. And, in the same way that Julius Cæsar, in himself invisible, is nevertheless perceived by sight; real things, in themselves imperceptible, are perceived by sense.

HYL. In the very same.

PHIL. Tell me, Hylas, when you behold the picture of Julius Cæsar, do you see with your eyes any more than some colours and figures, with a certain symmetry and composition of the whole?

HYL. Nothing else.

PHIL. And would not a man who had never known anything of Julius Cæsar see as much?

HYL. He would.

PHIL. Consequently he hath his sight, and the use of it, in as perfect degree as you?

HYL. I agree with you.

PHIL. Whence comes it then that your thoughts are directed to the Roman emperor, and his are not? This cannot proceed from the sensations or ideas of sense by you then perceived; since you acknowledge you have no advantage over him in that respect. It should seem therefore to proceed from reason and memory: should it not?

HYL. It should.

PHIL. Consequently, it will not follow from that instance that anything is perceived by sense which is not immediately perceived. Though I grant we may, in one acceptation, be said to perceive sensible things mediately by sense: that is, when, from a frequently perceived connexion, the immediate perception of ideas by one sense *suggests* to the mind others, perhaps belonging to another sense, which are wont to be connected with them. For instance, when I hear a coach drive along the streets, immediately I perceive only the sound; but, from the experience I have had that such a sound is connected with a coach, I am said to hear the coach. It is nevertheless evident that, in truth and strictness, nothing can be *heard* but *sound*; and the coach is not then properly perceived by sense, but suggested from experience. So likewise when we are said to see a red-hot bar of iron; the solidity and heat of the iron are not the objects of sight, but suggested to the imagination by the colour and figure which are properly perceived by that sense. In short, those things alone are actually and strictly perceived by any sense, which would have been perceived in case that same sense had been first conferred on us. As for other things, it is plain they are only suggested to the mind by experience, grounded on former perceptions. But, to return to your comparison of Cæsar's picture, it is plain, if you keep to that, you must hold the real things, or archetypes of our ideas, are not perceived by sense, but by some internal faculty of the soul, as reason or memory. I would therefore fain know what arguments you can draw from reason for the existence of what you call *real things* or *material objects*. Or, whether you remember to have seen them formerly as they are in themselves; or, if you have heard or read of any one that did.

HYL. I see, Philonous, you are disposed to raillery; but that will never convince me.

PHIL. My aim is only to learn from you the way to come at the knowledge of *material beings*. Whatever we perceive is perceived immediately or mediately: by sense, or by reason and reflexion. But, as you have excluded sense, pray shew me what reason you have to believe their existence; or what *medium* you can possibly make use of to prove it, either to mine or your own understanding.

HYL. To deal ingenuously, Philonous, now I consider the point, I do not find I can give you any good reason for it. But, thus much seems pretty plain, that it is at least possible such things may really exist. And, as long as there is no absurdity in supposing them, I am resolved to believe as I did, till you bring good reasons to the contrary.

PHIL. What! Is it come to this, that you only *believe* the existence of material objects, and that your belief is founded barely on the possibility of its being true? Then you will have me bring reasons against it: though another would think it reasonable the proof should lie on him who holds the affirmative. And, after all, this very point which you are now resolved to maintain, without any reason, is in effect what you have more than once during this discourse seen good reason to give up. But, to pass over all this; if I understand you rightly, you say our ideas do not exist without the mind, but that they are copies, images, or representations, of certain originals that do?

HYL. You take me right.

PHIL. They are then like external things?[20]

HYL. They are.

PHIL. Have those things a stable and permanent nature, independent of our senses; or are they in a perpetual change, upon our producing any motions in our bodies — suspending, exerting, or altering, our faculties or organs of sense?

HYL. Real things, it is plain, have a fixed and real nature, which remains the same notwithstanding any change in our senses, or in the posture and motion of our bodies; which indeed may affect the ideas in our minds, but it were absurd to think they had the same effect on things existing without the mind.

PHIL. How then is it possible that things perpetually fleeting and variable as our ideas should be copies or images of anything fixed and constant? Or, in other words, since all sensible qualities, as size, figure, colour, &c., that is, our ideas, are continually changing, upon every alteration in the distance, medium, or instruments of sensation; how can any determinate material objects be properly represented or painted forth by several distinct things, each of which is so different from and unlike the rest? Or, if you say it resembles some one only of our ideas, how shall we be able to distinguish the true copy from all the false ones?

HYL. I profess, Philonous, I am at a loss. I know not what to say to this.

PHIL. But neither is this all. Which are material objects in themselves — perceptible or imperceptible?

HYL. Properly and immediately nothing can be perceived but ideas. All material things, therefore, are in themselves insensible, and to be perceived only by our ideas.

PHIL. Ideas then are sensible, and their archetypes or originals insensible?

HYL. Right.

PHIL. But how can that which is sensible be *like* that which is insensible? Can a real thing, in itself *invisible*, be like a *colour*; or a real thing, which is not *audible*, be like a *sound*? In a word, can anything be like a sensation or idea, but another sensation or idea?

HYL. I must own, I think not.

PHIL. Is it possible there should be any doubt on the point? Do you not perfectly know your own ideas?

HYL. I know them perfectly; since what I do not perceive or know can be no part of my idea.[21]

PHIL. Consider, therefore, and examine them, and then tell me if there be anything in them which can exist without the mind: or if you can conceive anything like them existing without the mind.

HYL. Upon inquiry, I find it is impossible for me to conceive or understand how anything but an idea can be like an idea. And it is most evident that *no idea can exist without the mind*.

PHIL. You are therefore, by your principles, forced to deny the *reality* of sensible things; since you made it to consist in an absolute existence exterior to

---

[20]Cf. *Principles*, section 8.

[21]Cf. *Principles*, section 25 and 26.

the mind. That is to say, you are a downright sceptic. So I have gained my point, which was to shew your principles led to Scepticism.

HYL. For the present I am, if not entirely convinced, at least silenced.

PHIL. I would fain know what more you would require in order to a perfect conviction. Have you not had the liberty of explaining yourself all manner of ways? Were any little slips in discourse laid hold and insisted on? Or were you not allowed to retract or reinforce anything you had offered, as best served your purpose? Hath not everything you could say been heard and examined with all the fairness imaginable? In a word, have you not in every point been convinced out of your own mouth? And, if you can at present discover any flaw in any of your former concessions, or think of any remaining subterfuge, any new distinction, colour, or comment whatsoever, why do you not produce it?

HYL. A little patience, Philonous. I am at present so amazed to see myself ensnared, and as it were imprisoned in the labyrinths you have drawn me into, that on the sudden it cannot be expected I should find my way out. You must give me time to look about me and recollect myself.

PHIL. Hark; is not this the college bell?

HYL. It rings for prayers.

PHIL. We will go in then, if you please, and meet here again to-morrow morning. In the meantime, you may employ your thoughts on this morning's discourse, and try if you can find any fallacy in it, or invent any new means to extricate yourself.

HYL. Agreed.

CHAPTER 21

Refutation of Realism

1. IMMEDIATE OBJECTS OF SENSE

Berkeley begins by establishing the dependence on the mind of all sensible objects. He draws attention to the fact that the sensation of pain is always thought of as mind-dependent and is never attributed to the thing causing it, as are other sensible qualities. Thus fire burns us, but we attribute to the fire only color and heat, not pain. Yet our own sensation of the pain is identical with our sensation of extreme heat. When not painful we attribute it to the fire, but when painful we do not. Is this a consistent proceeding? As the pain, being immediately felt, is acknowledged to be a modification of consciousness and nothing more, so should the other sensible qualities be recognized as modifications of consciousness only. They are immediate objects of sense.

2. EXTERNAL CAUSES

This, however, is conceded by Hylas, in the dialogue, who for the most part presents Locke's arguments. The secondary qualities *are* mind-dependent; but not their causes. Similarly, in seeking to refute

309

Berkeley, Bertrand Russell[1] maintains that instead of identifying the heat with the pain, we should recognize that the heat causes the pain. But what then is the heat? Is it a sensible object immediately perceived or something else? If, as Locke hinted, it is a movement of insensible particles, it is no object of perception at all, and if not that, we have no idea of it and so cannot know that it exists, or causes pain or anything else. If it is an immediate object of sense, so says Berkeley, it must be sensible and so can exist only as sensed — its being, in short, is to be perceived — it is mind-dependent.

But, you may say, we do know, from physics, that the sensation of heat is caused by the motion of molecules (insensible particles). These, however, are either sensible objects visible by means of such instruments as the electron microscope, or are theoretical concepts which are inferred from such sensible objects and are still dependent on our thinking. Philosophers who follow Locke insist that they are derived from our immediate sense percepts, or observations, of macroscopic objects, and Berkeley argues that these are all of necessity mind-dependent. If they are, so must be the theoretical concepts.

Hylas frequently appeals to these supposed causes of our sensations, the physical processes to which scientists testify and which Locke postulated. The sound we hear may be mind-dependent, he argues, but not the vibrations in the air; the colors we see may be only apparent but not the real motions of insensible particles. But Berkeley (Philonous) argues that we cannot hear undulations in the air, only sounds; and it is not true, nor is it maintained by anybody, that we *see* the sound vibrations. We might feel them (as when a deep organ note is sounded), but that feeling is only another mind-dependent sensation. The motion of imperceptible particles is something nobody experiences or could experience. All that is ever apparent is color, sound, and the like, and all of these qualities *are* apparent and nothing else. What does not appear to the senses is nothing real (so Berkeley maintains), and all that ever appear are sense qualities. It is therefore futile to speak, as Locke did, of causes "which appear not to operate."

Thus Berkeley disposes of what some philosophers have called unsensed *sensibilia* — what J. S. Mill called "permanent possibilities of sensation." A *sensibile* (that is, a possible object of sense) is what can only exist as sensed — a color, a sound, a taste, some sensible quality. But these qualities, we have been told by Locke, are not in external bodies (except as "powers" which are altogether imperceptible), nor do they resemble anything in external bodies. They have been called secondary and are admittedly dependent on the mind. The scientist

---

[1]*The History of Western Philosophy* (London, Thomas Nelson and Sons, 1946), p. 679.

does not attribute them to physical things but speaks only of "insensible particles" (or, today, of electromagnetic waves), or vibrations of chemical processes, which are alleged to cause, but not to be, sensible qualities (*sensibilia*). But if a *sensibile* is not actually sensed, what can it be? Unsensed it is nothing. Unsensed sensibilia is a contradiction in terms. There can be no colors, sounds, tastes, and the like, floating about perceived by nobody at all.

3. PRIMARY QUALITIES

What, then, of primary qualities? Are they not real? Hylas declares that they are. Berkeley, however, makes Philonous show that the very reasons which persuade us of the mind-dependence of secondary qualities apply equally to primary. They fluctuate with the conditions of perception, they are relative to one another and to our point of view. This is true of them all—shape, size, position, motion, and number. In the case of the last, the number of any sensible aggregate depends on what is taken as the unit, and that is a matter of arbitrary choice. Is a hand one thing or five (fingers)? Is a finger one thing or three (knuckles)? Is a wood one thing or a hundred? Is a tree one thing or a million? —and so on.

Moreover, the primary qualities (as we have already noted) are perceptible only because and by means of the secondaries. No spatial shape is perceptible unless it has some color, no tactual shape unless it has some "feel." Size and position depend on the boundaries between perceived secondary qualities, and so does the number of any perceptible aggregate of things. If we wish to count apples we must see each of them as an individual object by means of its color, or feel it to be such by its tactual qualities. Without secondary qualities, which are conceded by Hylas (and Locke) to be mind-dependent, there could be no primaries. So the primaries must be at least as much dependent on the mind.

In fact, they are more so.

It is often maintained in support of Locke[2] that the fluctuating appearances of primary qualities can be corrected, or counteracted, by measurement, which informs us precisely of the real qualities of the object. But we have already learned from our study of Plato and Descartes that measurement is an appeal from sensible qualities to intelligible concepts all closely related to numbers. If these are to be admitted at all, they are all obviously mind-dependent—the products of

---

[2]Cf. G. J. Warnock, *Berkeley* (Penguin Books, 1953), p. 99.

pure thought. But Berkeley would not have admitted them. For him they would be abstract ideas, of which he denies the existence. All he will admit are particular ideas, some of which may be used as signs or symbols of others. But apart from this, as Plato showed, the empirical measurement of any material object is never precise. In sense perception we never come across perfect equality, which is the presumed basis of all measurement—the coincidence or congruence of equal quantities. What we sense is, again, the fluctuating secondary qualities, and only by comparison of these can we measure what is perceptible. We cannot, therefore, *sense* the exact equality of our measuring unit, or any multiple of it, with the measured object. Further, the measurement of distant objects (like the moon in Berkeley's example) is largely a matter of mathematical calculation, not of immediate perception. It is, in fact, essentially a product of ideal construction and thinking, no mere reflection of external properties. Not even measurement, therefore, helps us to establish independence of the mind's sensing and thinking of the measured object. In fact it makes it still more dependent upon thinking than we might at first have imagined.

4. MATERIAL SUBSTANCE AND ABSTRACT IDEAS

No more successful is Hylas' appeal to abstract notions, motion-in-general, extension-in-general, and the like. Philonous shows that there can be no idea of a motion which is neither fast nor slow, nor up, nor down, nor left, nor right. There can be no motion which lacks all particular determinations. The same would be true of extension that has neither shape nor size. So abstract ideas are disposed of, and with them the abstract idea of matter-in-general.

So we eventually come to substance, that in which qualities inhere, and Berkeley dispenses with this as easily as with the rest of the abstracta and imperceptibles (unobservables). Thus, all the points at which Locke's theory showed inconsistency and signs of breakdown have been removed: the distinction of primary from secondary qualities, the postulation of external causes of our ideas, the idea of substance in general—of something, we know not what.

5. IDEAS AS RESEMBLANCES

After many fruitless twists and turns Hylas resorts to a representative theory, asking whether our mind-dependent ideas may not, after all, be pictures, as it were, of external things. To this the reply, in brief, is "an idea can be like nothing but an idea."[3] How, asks Philonous, can our fleeting, changing, variable ideas resemble what is alleged to be stable, definite, and enduring? How can what is perceptible resemble what is in principle imperceptible? How can qualities that can exist only in the mind (in being perceived) resemble qualities which exist only in inert senseless substance — only as not perceived? The objector (Hylas) asks if this is not conceivable but has already conceded that it is inconceivable and self-contradictory. What, in short, can we possibly mean here by resemblance?

6. "OUTNESS"

The appearance of things at a distance is the next consideration to which Hylas appeals in his desire to avoid the conclusion that all we know is our own ideas and that they are all and only in the mind. (Note that this is Locke's own stipulation, yet it conflicts with the realism he wishes to maintain.) This appearance of "outness" is what modern psychologists call visual depth. It is well-known that as a direct sensory appearance it is limited to relatively short distances. Perceptual appearances of larger distances are mediated by experience, association, and imaginative supplementation of direct perception. Be that as it may, visual depth itself is an appearance to the sense and, as such, all Berkeley's arguments for mind-dependence apply to it. It is an appearance of a certain (spatial) relation between sensed objects, not of a relation between sensed objects and unsensed external entities. Moreover, one of the sensed objects is the body of the perceiver, the status of which is to be discussed in the next dialogue, and which is perceived in much the same way as are other bodies. Here Berkeley's argument, based largely on the conclusions of an earlier treatise, *A New Theory of Vision*, is to the effect that our awareness of distance is always a construction out of immediately sensed percepts and never itself an immediate awareness.

7. CONCEPTION AND PERCEPTION

Finally, can we not conceive of a tree, or a rock, or some such thing, existing where nobody perceives it? Of course we can, but not without either imagining it or conceiving it. I may imagine a lonely tree or one in the depth of a forest. But then my imagination is an idea and is

---

[3]Cf. *The Principles of Human Knowledge*, section 8.

mind-dependent. The tree I merely imagine may, however, not exist at
all, and what is being argued is that there can be an actual unperceived
tree. So there may be. But it will be either one I have perceived at
some time and am now remembering; that is, my awareness of it is still
an idea and I know nothing of the tree or its existence without some
such idea; or else, it is a tree which I have never seen, and perhaps
nobody has ever seen. Yet in speaking of such a tree I conceive its
existence and my concept is still mind-dependent. No reference can be
made to anything unconceived. There are no unconceived concepts
just as there are no unsensed *sensibilia*. If so, there are no unconceived entities; for in alleging that there may be (or are) we at once
conceive of at least their existence. Again we should note that, for
Berkeley, to perceive something is to be aware of it in any way, not only
to perceive it as sensibly present. It does not then make sense to speak
of unknown entities not perceived or conceived by anybody, for any
reference to them at all is already conception of them.

8. BERKELEY AS CRITIC OF LOCKE

The cogency and unanswerableness of Berkeley's arguments depend upon the fact that they are levelled against Locke's palpably
untenable position. Hylas puts Locke's position and uses Locke's
supporting arguments, and what Philonous is made to do is, first, to
show their inconsistency ("manifest repugnance") and, secondly, to
remove the contradictions so as to make Locke's theory self-consistent.
If you begin with the assumption that ideas of sense and reflection are
the only source of knowledge and that these are essentially "in the mind"
(as they must be), Berkeley's conclusions are inescapable. The failure
of Hylas' arguments, like those of some modern philosophers (eminently Bertrand Russell) is due to their attempt to reinstate Locke's
main position. From that point of view Berkeley is unassailable, but we
shall see presently that his theory also is unsatisfactory and that it can
be successfully criticized from its own presuppositions.

In effect, such criticism is implicit in Hume's development of Berkeley's position, which is a still further effort to render self-consistent the
radically empiricist theory of knowledge introduced by Locke.

THE SECOND DIALOGUE

HYLAS. I beg your pardon, Philonous, for not meeting you sooner. All this
morning my head was so filled with our late conversation that I had not leisure
to think of the time of the day, or indeed of anything else.

PHILONOUS. I am glad you were so intent upon it, in hopes if there were any mistakes in your concessions, or fallacies in my reasonings from them, you will now discover them to me.

HYL. I assure you I have done nothing ever since I saw you but search after mistakes and fallacies, and, with that view, have minutely examined the whole series of yesterday's discourse: but all in vain, for the notions it led me into, upon review, appear still more clear and evident; and, the more I consider them, the more irresistibly do they force my assent.

PHIL. And is not this, think you, a sign that they are genuine, that they proceed from nature, and are conformable to right reason? Truth and beauty are in this alike, that the strictest survey sets them both off to advantage; while the false lustre of error and disguise cannot endure being reviewed, or too nearly inspected.

HYL. I own there is a great deal in what you say. Nor can any one be more entirely satisfied of the truth of those odd consequences, so long as I have in view the reasonings that lead to them. But when these are out of my thoughts, there seems, on the other hand, something so satisfactory, so natural and intelligible, in the modern way of explaining things that, I profess, I know not how to reject it.

PHIL. I know not what way you mean.

HYL. I mean the way of accounting for our sensations or ideas.

PHIL. How is that?

HYL. It is supposed the soul makes her residence in some part of the brain, from which the nerves take their rise, and are thence extended to all parts of the body; and that outward objects, by the different impressions they make on the organs of sense, communicate certain vibrative motions to the nerves; and these being filled with spirits propagate them to the brain or seat of the soul, which, according to the various impressions or traces thereby made in the brain, is variously affected with ideas.

PHIL. And call you this an explication of the manner whereby we are affected with ideas?

HYL. Why not, Philonous? Have you anything to object against it?

PHIL. I would first know whether I rightly understand your hypothesis. You make certain traces in the brain to be the causes or occasions of our ideas. Pray tell me whether by the *brain* you mean any sensible thing.

HYL. What else think you I could mean?

PHIL. Sensible things are all immediately perceivable; and those things which are immediately perceivable are ideas; and these exist only in the mind. Thus much you have, if I mistake not, long since agreed to.

HYL. I do not deny it.

PHIL. The brain therefore you speak of, being a sensible thing, exists only in the mind. Now, I would fain know whether you think it reasonable to suppose that one idea or thing existing in the mind occasions all other ideas. And, if you think so, pray how do you account for the origin of that primary idea or brain itself?

HYL. I do not explain the origin of our ideas by that brain which is perceivable to sense—this being itself only a combination of sensible ideas—but by another which I imagine.

PHIL. But are not things imagined as truly *in the mind* as things perceived?

HYL. I must confess they are.

PHIL. It comes, therefore, to the same thing; and you have been all this while accounting for ideas by certain motions or impressions of the brain; that is, by some alterations in an idea, whether sensible or imaginable it matters not.

HYL. I begin to suspect my hypothesis.

PHIL. Besides spirits, all that we know or conceive are our own ideas. When, therefore, you say all ideas are occasioned by impressions in the brain, do you conceive this brain or no? If you do, then you talk of ideas imprinted in an idea causing that same idea, which is absurd. If you do not conceive it, you talk unintelligibly, instead of forming a reasonable hypothesis.

HYL. I now clearly see it was a mere dream. There is nothing in it.

PHIL. You need not be much concerned at it; for after all, this way of explaining things, as you called it, could never have satisfied any reasonable man. What connexion is there between a motion in the nerves, and the sensations of sound or colour in the mind? Or how is it possible these should be the effect of that?

HYL. But I could never think it had so little in it as now it seems to have.

9. PHYSIOLOGICAL IDEALISM

It is often thought that Berkeley, by the above argument, claims or attempts to establish that material things are nothing but ideas in our heads; but this is a gross misinterpretation which he himself anticipates and dispels. It was some such misunderstanding that led Samuel Johnson to declare that by kicking a stone he could refute Berkeley's theory. The notion that ideas are in our heads springs directly from the kind of account which Locke gives of their causation, which is precisely repeated by Hylas at the beginning of the second dialogue. Such an account, whichever way you try to develop it, leads to absurdity.

First, if one takes it at its face value, it leads necessarily to the conclusion that all the mind can know is the end result of the physiological process by which impulses on the sense organs made by external things are conveyed to the brain. The situation of the soul, as described by Hylas, has been compared to that of a housemaid sitting in the back kitchen of a house watching a set of indicators which are operated by persons in the various parts of the house by pressing a bell-push. The bell sounds in the kitchen and the indicator shows in which part of the house it was rung. But the maid is locked in the kitchen and can respond to these signals only by pushing other buttons which communicate with the outside. In such a situation (especially as she must be assumed never to have been out of the kitchen) she has no real means of knowing that the indicator really is connected with the room it indicates, or, for that matter, whether there are any other rooms in the house. In a situation of this kind, the soul would have "ideas" but could not know how they were produced, could have no knowledge of sense organs, nerves, or brains connected with itself. This sort of account of perception has been called physiological idealism.

Secondly, if you treat the physiological description as Berkeley does, you must say that bodies, sense organs, and brains are all sensible objects — in Locke's terminology, "complex ideas of substances" — made up of simple ideas of sensation. All such ideas exist only in being perceived and so are "in the mind" or mind-dependent. Bodies, nerves, and brains, therefore, cannot be the causal agents producing ideas, for they are themselves ideas to which the mind (or seat of the alleged effects) is prior.

Material things, accordingly, are not "in our heads" because our heads (with the rest of our bodies) are themselves among the ideas of material things said to be "in the mind." According to Berkeley, Dr. Johnson's foot along with the stone he kicked was equally in his mind, and his action contradicted nothing that the theory maintained, because it consisted of nothing other than the sensible movements of sensible objects. For Berkeley, the whole sensible world is "in our minds" and all that exists is a multitude of minds or spirits, enjoying ideas.

CHAPTER 22

God and Reality

THE SECOND DIALOGUE (Continued)

PHIL. Well then, are you at length satisfied that no sensible things have a real existence; and that you are in truth an arrant sceptic?

HYL. It is too plain to be denied.

PHIL. Look! are not the fields covered with a delightful verdure? Is there not something in the woods and groves, in the rivers and clear springs, that soothes, that delights, that transports the soul? At the prospect of the wide and deep ocean, or some huge mountain whose top is lost in the clouds, or of an old gloomy forest, are not our minds filled with a pleasing horror? Even in rocks and deserts is there not an agreeable wildness? How sincere a pleasure is it to behold the natural beauties of the earth! To preserve and renew our relish for them, is not the veil of night alternately drawn over her face, and doth she not change her dress with the seasons? How aptly are the elements disposed! What variety and use in the meanest productions of nature! What delicacy, what beauty, what contrivance, in animal and vegetable bodies! How exquisitely are all things suited, as well to their particular ends, as to constitute opposite parts of the whole! And, while they mutually aid and support, do they not also set off and illustrate each other? Raise now your thoughts from this ball of earth to all those glorious luminaries that adorn the high arch of heaven. The motion and situation of the planets, are they not admirable for use and order? Were those (miscalled *erratic*) globes once known to stray, in their repeated journeys through the pathless void? Do they not measure areas round the sun ever proportioned to the times? So fixed, so immutable are the laws by which the unseen Author of nature actuates the universe. How vivid and radiant is the lustre of the fixed stars! How magnificent and rich that negligent profusion with which they appear to be scattered throughout the whole azure vault! Yet, if you take the telescope, it brings into your sight a new host of stars that escape the naked eye. Here they seem contiguous and minute, but to a nearer view immense orbs of light at various distances, far sunk in the abyss of space. Now you must call imagination to your aid. The feeble narrow sense cannot descry innumerable worlds revolving round the central fires; and in those worlds the energy of an all-perfect Mind displayed in endless forms. But, neither sense nor imagination are big enough to comprehend the boundless extent, with all its glittering furniture. Though the labouring mind exert and strain each power to its utmost reach, there still stands out ungrasped a surplusage immeasurable. Yet all the vast bodies that compose this mighty frame, how distant and remote soever, are by some secret mechanism, some Divine art and force, linked in a mutual dependence and intercourse with each other; even with this earth, which was almost slipt from my thoughts and lost in the crowd of worlds. Is not the whole system immense, beautiful, glorious beyond expression and beyond thought! What treatment, then, do those philosophers deserve, who would deprive these noble and delightful scenes of all *reality*? How should those Principles be entertained that lead us to think all the visible beauty of the creation a false imaginary glare? To be plain, can you expect this Scepticism of yours will not be thought extravagantly absurd by all men of sense?

HYL. Other men may think as they please; but for your part you have nothing to reproach me with. My comfort is, you are as much a sceptic as I am.

PHIL. There, Hylas, I must beg leave to differ from you.

HYL. What! Have you all along agreed to the premises, and do you now deny the conclusion, and leave me to maintain those paradoxes by myself which you led me into? This surely is not fair.

PHIL. I deny that I agreed with you in those notions that led to Scepticism. You indeed said the *reality* of sensible things consisted in an *absolute existence out of the minds of spirits*, or distinct from their being perceived. And pursuant to this notion of reality, *you* are obliged to deny sensible things any real existence: that is, according to your own definition, you profess yourself a sceptic. But I neither said nor thought the reality of sensible things was to be defined after that manner. To me it is evident, for the reasons you allow of, that sensible things cannot exist otherwise than in a mind or spirit. Whence I conclude, not that they have no real existence, but that, seeing they depend not on my thought, and have an existence distinct from being perceived by me, *there must be some other Mind wherein they exist*. As sure, therefore, as the sensible world really exists, so sure is there an infinite omnipresent Spirit who contains and supports it.

HYL. What! This is no more than I and all Christians hold; nay, and all others too who believe there is a God, and that He knows and comprehends all things.

PHIL. Aye, but here lies the difference. Men commonly believe that all things are known or perceived by God, because they believe the being of a God: whereas I, on the other side, immediately and necessarily conclude the being of a God, because all sensible things must be perceived by Him.

HYL. But, so long as we all believe the same thing, what matter is it how we come by that belief?

PHIL. But neither do we agree in the same opinion. For philosophers, though they acknowledge all corporeal beings to be perceived by God, yet they attribute to them an absolute subsistence distinct from their being perceived by any mind whatever; which I do not. Besides, is there no difference between saying, *There is a God, therefore He perceives all things;* and saying, *Sensible things do really exist; and, if they really exist, they are necessarily perceived by an infinite Mind: therefore there is an infinite Mind, or God?*[1] This furnishes you with a direct and immediate demonstration, from a most evident principle, of the *being of a God.* Divines and philosophers had proved beyond all controversy, from the beauty and usefulness of the several parts of the creation, that it was the workmanship of God. But that—setting aside all help of astronomy and natural philosophy, all contemplation of the contrivance, order, and adjustment of things—an infinite Mind should be necessarily inferred from the bare *existence of the sensible world,* is an advantage to them only who have made this easy reflexion: That the sensible world is that which we perceive by our several senses; and that nothing is perceived by the senses beside ideas; and that no idea or archetype of an idea can exist otherwise than in a mind. You may now, without any laborious search into the sciences, without any subtlety of reason, or tedious length of discourse, oppose and baffle the most strenuous advocate for Atheism. Those miserable refuges, whether in an eternal succession of unthinking causes and effects, or in a fortuitous concourse of atoms; those wild imaginations of Vanini, Hobbes, and Spinoza: in a word, the whole system of Atheism, is it not entirely overthrown, by this single reflexion on the repugnancy included in supposing the whole, or any part, even the most rude and shapeless, of the visible world, to exist without a Mind? Let any one of those abettors of impiety but look into his own thoughts, and there try if he can conceive how so much as a rock, a desert, a chaos, or confused jumble of atoms; how anything at all, either sensible or imaginable, can exist independent of a Mind, and he need go no farther to be convinced of his folly. Can anything be fairer than to put a dispute on such an issue, and leave it to a man himself to s . ? if he can conceive, even in thought, what he holds to be true in fact, and from a notional to allow it a real existence? . . . .

HYL. I think I understand you very clearly; and own the proof you give of a Deity seems no less evident than it is surprising. But, allowing that God is the supreme and universal Cause of all things, yet, may there not be still a Third Nature besides Spirits and Ideas? May we not admit a subordinate and limited cause of our ideas? In a word, may there not for all that be *Matter*?

PHIL. How often must I inculcate the same thing? You allow the things immediately perceived by sense to exist nowhere without the mind; but there is nothing perceived by sense which is not perceived immediately: therefore there is nothing sensible that exists without the mind. The Matter, therefore, which you still insist on is something intelligible, I suppose; something that may be discovered by reason, and not by sense.

HYL. You are in the right.

PHIL. Pray let me know what reasoning your belief of Matter is grounded on; and what this Matter is, in your present sense of it.

HYL. I find myself affected with various ideas, whereof I know I am not the

---

[1]Cf. *Principles,* section 90.

cause; neither are they the cause of themselves, or of one another, or capable of subsisting by themselves, as being altogether inactive, fleeting, dependent beings. They have therefore *some* cause distinct from me and them: of which I pretend to know no more than that it is *the cause of my ideas*. And this thing, whatever it be, I call Matter.

PHIL. Tell me, Hylas, hath every one a liberty to change the current proper signification attached to a common name in any language? For example, suppose a traveller should tell you that in a certain country men pass unhurt through the fire; and, upon explaining himself, you found he meant by the word *fire* that which others call *water*. Or, if he should assert that there are trees that walk upon two legs, meaning men by the term *trees*. Would you think this reasonable?

HYL. No; I should think it very absurd. Common custom is the standard of propriety in language. And for any man to affect speaking improperly is to pervert the use of speech, and can never serve to a better purpose than to protract and multiply disputes where there is no difference in opinion.

PHIL. And doth not *Matter*, in the common current acceptation of the word, signify an extended, solid, moveable, unthinking, inactive Substance?

HYL. It doth.

PHIL. And, hath it not been made evident that no *such* substance can possibly exist? And, though it should be allowed to exist, yet how can that which is *inactive* be a *cause*; or that which is *unthinking* be a *cause of thought*? You may, indeed, if you please, annex to the word *Matter* a contrary meaning to what is vulgarly received; and tell me you understand by it, an unextended, thinking, active being, which is the cause of our ideas. But what else is this than to play with words, and run into that very fault you just now condemned with so much reason? I do by no means find fault with your reasoning, in that you collect *a* cause from the *phenomena*: but I deny that *the* cause deducible by reason can properly be termed Matter.

HYL. There is indeed something in what you say. But I am afraid you do not thoroughly comprehend my meaning. I would by no means be thought to deny that God, or an infinite Spirit, is the Supreme Cause of all things. All I contend for is, that, subordinate to the Supreme Agent, there is a cause of a limited and inferior nature, which *concurs* in the production of our ideas, not by any act of will, or spiritual efficiency, but by that kind of action which belongs to Matter, viz. *motion*.

PHIL. I find you are at every turn relapsing into your old exploded conceit, of a movable, and consequently an extended, substance, existing without the mind. What! Have you already forgotten you were convinced; or are you willing I should repeat what has been said on that head? In truth this is not fair dealing in you, still to suppose the being of that which you have so often acknowledged to have no being. But, not to insist farther on what has been so largely handled, I ask whether all your ideas are not perfectly passive and inert, including nothing of action in them.[2]

HYL. They are.

PHIL. And are sensible qualities anything else but ideas?

HYL. How often have I acknowledged that they are not.

PHIL. But is not *motion* a sensible quality?

HYL. It is.

---

[2] Cf. *Principles*, sections 25 and 26.

PHIL. Consequently it is no action?

HYL. I agree with you. And indeed it is very plain that when I stir my finger, it remains passive; but my will which produced the motion is active.

PHIL. Now, I desire to know, in the first place, whether, motion being allowed to be no action, you can conceive any action besides volition: and, in the second place, whether to say something and conceive nothing be not to talk nonsense: and, lastly, whether, having considered the premises, you do not perceive that to suppose any efficient or active Cause of our ideas, other than *Spirit*, is highly absurd and unreasonable?

HYL. I give up the point entirely. But, though Matter may not be a cause, yet what hinders its being an *instrument*, subservient to the supreme Agent in the production of our ideas?

PHIL. An instrument say you; pray what may be the figure, springs, wheels, and motions, of that instrument?

HYL. Those I pretend to determine nothing of, both the substance and its qualities entirely unknown to me.

PHIL. What? You are then of opinion it is made up of unknown parts, that it hath unknown motions, and an unknown shape?

HYL. I do not believe that it hath any figure or motion at all, being already convinced, that no sensible qualities can exist in an unperceiving substance.

PHIL. But what notion is it possible to frame of an instrument void of all sensible qualities, even extension itself?

HYL. I do not pretend to have any notion of it.

PHIL. And what reason have you to think this unknown, this inconceivable Somewhat doth exist? Is it that you imagine God cannot act as well without it; or that you find by experience the use of some such thing, when you form ideas in your own mind?

HYL. You are always teasing me for reasons of my belief. Pray what reasons have you not to believe it?

PHIL. It is to me a sufficient reason not to believe the existence of anything, if I see no reason for believing it. But, not to insist on reasons for believing, you will not so much as let me know *what it is* you would have me believe; since you say you have no manner of notion of it. After all, let me entreat you to consider whether it be like a philosopher, or even like a man of common sense, to pretend to believe you know not what, and you know not why.

HYL. Hold, Philonous. When I tell you Matter is an *instrument*, I do not mean altogether nothing. It is true I know not the particular kind of instrument; but, however, I have some notion of *instrument in general*, which I apply to it.

PHIL. But what if it should prove that there is something, even in the most general notion of *instrument*, as taken in a distinct sense from *cause*, which makes the use of it inconsistent with the Divine attributes?

HYL. Make that appear and I shall give up the point.

PHIL. What mean you by the general nature or notion of *instrument*?

HYL. That which is common to all particular instruments composeth the general notion.

PHIL. Is it not common to all instruments, that they are applied to the doing those things only which cannot be performed by the mere act of our wills? Thus, for instance, I never use an instrument to move my finger, because it is done by a volition. But I should use one if I were to remove part of a rock, or tear up a tree by the roots. Are you of the same mind? Or, can you shew any example where an instrument is made use of in producing an effect *immedi-ately* depending on the will of the agent?

HYL. I own I cannot.

PHIL. How therefore can you suppose that an All-perfect Spirit, on whose Will all things have an absolute and immediate dependence, should need an instrument in his operations, or, not needing it, make use of it? Thus it seems to me that you are obliged to own the use of a lifeless inactive instrument to be incompatible with the infinite perfection of God; that is, by your own confession, to give up the point.

HYL. It doth not readily occur what I can answer you.

PHIL. But, methinks you should be ready to own the truth, when it has been fairly proved to you. We indeed, who are beings of finite powers, are forced to make use of instruments. And the use of an instrument sheweth the agent to be limited by rules of another's prescription, and that he cannot obtain his end but in such a way, and by such conditions. Whence it seems a clear consequence, that the supreme unlimited Agent useth no tool or instrument at all. The will of an Omnipotent Spirit is no sooner exerted than executed, without the application of means; which, if they are employed by inferior agents, it is not upon account of any real efficacy that is in them, or necessary aptitude to produce any effect, but merely in compliance with the laws of nature, or those conditions prescribed to them by the First Cause, who is Himself above all limitation or prescription whatsoever.

HYL. I will no longer maintain that Matter is an instrument. However, I would not be understood to give up its existence neither; since, notwithstanding what hath been said, it may still be an *occasion*.[3]

PHIL. How many shapes is your Matter to take? Or, how often must it be proved not to exist, before you are content to part with it? But, to say no more of this (though by all the laws of disputation I may justly blame you for so frequently changing the signification of the principal term)—I would fain know what you mean by affirming that matter is an occasion, having already denied it to be a cause. And, when you have shewn in what sense you understand *occasion*, pray, in the next place, be pleased to shew me what reason induceth you to believe there is such an occasion of our ideas?

HYL. As to the first point: by *occasion* I mean an inactive unthinking being, at the presence whereof God excites ideas in our minds.

PHIL. And what may be the nature of that inactive unthinking being?

HYL. I know nothing of its nature.

PHIL. Proceed then to the second point, and assign some reason why we should allow an existence to this inactive, unthinking, unknown thing.

HYL. When we see ideas produced in our minds, after an orderly and constant manner, it is natural to think they have some fixed and regular occasions, at the presence of which they are excited.

PHIL. You acknowledge then God alone to be the cause of our ideas, and that He causes them at the presence of those occasions.

HYL. That is my opinion.

PHIL. Those things which you say are present to God, without doubt He perceives.

HYL. Certainly; otherwise they could not be to Him an occasion of acting.

---

[3]Cf. *Principles*, sections 68

PHIL. Not to insist now on your making sense of this hypothesis, or answering all the puzzling questions and difficulties it is liable to: I only ask whether the order and regularity observable in the series of our ideas, or the course of nature, be not sufficiently accounted for by the wisdom and power of God; and whether it doth not derogate from those attributes, to suppose He is influenced, directed, or put in mind, when and what He is to act, by an unthinking substance? And, lastly, whether, in case I granted all you contend for, it would make anything to your purpose; it not being easy to conceive how the external or absolute existence of any unthinking substance, distinct from its being perceived, can be inferred from my allowing that there are certain things perceived by the mind of God, which are to Him the occasion of producing ideas in us?

HYL. I am perfectly at a loss what to think, this notion of *occasion* seeming now altogether as groundless as the rest.

PHIL. Do you not at length perceive that in all these different acceptations of *Matter*, you have been only supposing you know not what, for no manner of reason, and to no kind of use?

1. TRUTH AND SCEPTICISM

The rejection by Berkeley of the existence of material substance is not to be understood as a rejection of the reality of sensible objects. Scepticism, he says, is the result of concocting an idea of an insensible, unknowable matter, and then, finding it to be inconceivable, of denying the reality of sensible objects. Such scepticism Berkeley utterly condemns, for he claims that his argument establishes the reality of sensible objects. Their being sensed constitutes their reality. He inveighs against the suggestion that all the beauty, system, and complexity of the visible world is "a false imaginary glare." It is not the mere appearance of something else which lies concealed behind it but which is in itself imperceptible. What we perceive by sense is itself the reality and its reality is manifest in its being sensed.

But here two obvious difficulties arise. (a) If all sensible objects were real there would be no illusion. How are we to distinguish the true from the false? Once more we face the question of the criterion of truth. (b) If all sensible objects are real and all equally mind-dependent, what becomes of perceived objects, such as chairs and tables, when we are not perceiving them? Do they spring into existence whenever we sense them and cease to exist as soon as we turn our attention elsewhere?

To answer these questions Berkeley, like Descartes, but in a rather different manner, resorts to the existence of God.

2. THE PERSISTENCE OF SENSIBLE OBJECTS

Because we cannot create and suppress sensible ideas at will, nor control what affects our senses in the normal course of events, Berkeley concedes that sensible objects do not depend for their existence simply on our individual human minds. They do therefore persist when we are not aware of them. But because they cannot exist independently of some mind, they must, when we are not perceiving them, exist in some other mind. The limitation of human minds and their inability to control their percepts is equally applicable to all of them. Consequently, the persistence of sensible objects when not perceived by men must be due to their existence in a mind which is eternal and infinite — God's.

This is the doctrine which inspired the much quoted limericks:

> There was a young man who said, "God
> Must think it exceedingly odd
> That this jolly old tree
> Simply ceases to be
> When there's no one about in the quad."

And the reply:

> Dear Sir, your astonishment's odd.
> I am always about in the quad,
> and that's why the tree
> Continues to be,
> Since observed by Yours faithfully, God.

The argument as it is first introduced by Berkeley is really gratuitous, for he has already shown that all ideas — all objects of thought — are mind-dependent. Why then do we need to assume that any of them ever exist when nobody is experiencing them? The fact that some of them come to us whether we will or not does not show that they exist unperceived. Why then should we need to assume an eternal and infinite mind to keep them in existence when we are not perceiving them? Elsewhere Berkeley argues that we can and do produce some of our ideas at will; therefore the cause of all ideas must be volition — the act of a spiritual substance — as it cannot be an inert, unintelligent, and unintelligible material substance. Those ideas which come to us involuntarily, therefore, must be produced by some other will, and as one human being cannot produce ideas directly in the minds of other people, the will which produces ideas in our minds, such as we passively receive, must be God's.

In this form the argument is more consistent with Berkeley's general doctrine. However, it does not directly account for the possibility of trees existing in the quad when there is nobody about. For that, God has to perceive them. But Berkeley denies that God perceives as we do. He has understanding, but no senses; for he is in no way passive. In some obscure way, then, God actively understands or knows that there is a tree in the quad when nobody perceives it sensorily. This is hardly an appealing argument, as it suggests that God is in some sort of error: He understands that something exists unperceived which Berkeley has claimed to prove cannot exist unperceived (for its *esse* is *percipi*). All God could properly understand, in that case, would be how the tree could be perceived by men on the proper occasions, that is, when He should produce the appropriate ideas in their minds.

3. THE ORDER OF NATURE

But even if this did explain the existence (in some sense) of trees unperceived by men, it would not give a criterion for distinguishing those of men's ideas which are of real things and those which are merely imaginary, illusory, or in other ways false. This Berkeley explains by alleging (a)   that imaginary ideas are feebler than those of the real; (b)   that they are, in large measure, subject to our volition; and (c)   when they are not so subject (as in dreams) we can distinguish them from ideas of real things by their incoherence, both among themselves and with our waking consciousness. The last of these criteria is the most important and again depends on God, for He it is who produces true ideas in our minds. We know them as such because He produces them in a regular order, according to the settled laws of nature.[4] This, then, is the real and surest criterion of truth—that the ideas occur according to the settled order of nature; though, Berkeley maintains, God is always capable of producing ideas contrary to that order if He wishes, in which case He would be producing a miracle.

We learn the order of nature and the laws according to which it is subject from experience. It is nothing other than a system of regularities in the occurrence of our ideas. These ideas, Berkeley insists, cannot be causes, because they are inert and passive, and we perceive among them no necessary connections. In the *Principles of Human Knowledge* (31) he writes:

---

[4]Cf. *Principles of Human Knowledge*, sections 30–33.

That food nourishes, sleep refreshes, and fire warms us, that to sow in the seed-time is the way to reap in the harvest, and, in general, that to obtain such and such ends, such and such means are conducive, all this we know, not by discovering any necessary connection between our ideas, but only by observation of the settled Laws of Nature, without which we should be all in uncertainty and confusion . . .

He says that the connection of our ideas implies only the occurrence of certain of them as marks or signs of the occurrence of others, as a word serves as a sign of the object it signifies. Our sense experience is thus a kind of divine language through which God conveys to us the nature of the real; and the grammatical rules, by the help of which it is to be understood, are the Laws of Nature.

Berkeley's dependence on God for the reality and truth of ideas is quite different from Descartes's; in fact he virtually reverses Descartes's position and argument. Descartes maintained that, though God could produce in our minds ideas of material things in the absence of any such objects, He did not do so, because if He did He would be deceiving us. Therefore, as we could not produce them ourselves, they must be caused by objects "formally" as real as the ideas are "objectively." Berkeley, on the other hand, maintains that as God can produce the ideas in our minds, he has no need of material objects to prompt Him; and to assume their existence as the occasion of God's action is to derogate from His dignity and power. As He produces the ideas in a settled order according to laws which He himself has ordained, there can be no question of deception. We are not deceived so long as we expect only what the laws of nature prescribe, and act accordingly.

Another reversal of Descartes's procedure by Berkeley is in the relation between the proof of God's existence and that of material things. Descartes first proves that there is a God and makes the knowledge of material objects depend on His veracity. Berkeley makes the existence of material things, independently of his own finite perception, the premise for the proof of God's existence. Because things are not produced by finite minds and could exist only in an infinite mind, there must be a God. In this way, Berkeley claims, not only scepticism but also atheism is refuted.

The rest of the second dialogue (which we have omitted) is devoted to vain attempts by Hylas to rehabilitate the conception of matter as a cause or background of perceived entities, all of which Philonous defeats by showing that, apart from the ideas already admitted to exist only in the mind, the term which Hylas so jealously clings to has no meaning whatever for himself or for anybody else.

THE THIRD DIALOGUE

PHILONOUS. Tell me, Hylas, what are the fruits of yesterday's meditation? Has it confirmed you in the same mind you were in at parting? or have you since seen cause to change your opinion?

HYLAS. Truly my opinion is that all our opinions are alike vain and uncertain. What we approve to-day, we condemn to-morrow. We keep a stir about knowledge, and spend our lives in the pursuit of it, when, alas! we know nothing all the while: nor do I think it possible for us ever to know anything in this life. Our faculties are too narrow and too few. Nature certainly never intended us for speculation.

PHIL. What! Say you we can know nothing, Hylas?

HYL. There is not that single thing in the world whereof we can know the real nature, or what it is in itself.

PHIL. Will you tell me I do not really know what fire or water is?

HYL. You may indeed know that fire appears hot, and water fluid; but this is no more than knowing what sensations are produced in your own mind, upon the application of fire and water to your organs of sense. Their internal constitution, their true and real nature, you are utterly in the dark as to *that*.

PHIL. Do I not know this to be a real stone that I stand on, and that which I see before my eyes to be a real tree?

HYL. *Know?* No, it is impossible you or any man alive should know it. All you know is, that you have such a certain idea or appearance in your own mind. But what is this to the real tree or stone? I tell you that colour, figure, and hardness, which you perceive, are not the real natures of those things, or in the least like them. The same may be said of all other real things, or corporeal substances, which compose the world. They have none of them anything of themselves, like those sensible qualities by us perceived. We should not therefore pretend to affirm or know anything of them, as they are in their own nature.

PHIL. But surely, Hylas, I can distinguish gold, for example, from iron: and how could this be, if I knew not what either truly was?

HYL. Believe me, Philonous, you can only distinguish between your own ideas. That yellowness, that weight, and other sensible qualities, think you they are really in the gold? They are only relative to the senses, and have no absolute existence in nature. And in pretending to distinguish the species of real things, by the appearances in your mind, you may perhaps act as wisely as he that should conclude two men were of a different species, because their clothes were not of the same colour.

PHIL. It seems, then, we are altogether put off with the appearances of things, and those false ones too. The very meat I eat, and the cloth I wear, have nothing in them like what I see and feel.

HYL. Even so.

PHIL. But is it not strange the whole world should be thus imposed on, and so foolish as to believe their senses? And yet I know not how it is, but men eat, and drink, and sleep, and perform all the offices of life, as comfortably and conveniently as if they really knew the things they are conversant about.

HYL. They do so: but you know ordinary practice does not require a nicety of speculative knowledge. Hence the vulgar retain their mistakes, and for all that make a shift to bustle through the affairs of life. But philosophers know better things.

PHIL. You mean, they *know* that they *know nothing.*

HYL. That is the very top and perfection of human knowledge.

PHIL. But are you all this while in earnest, Hylas; and are you seriously persuaded that you know nothing real in the world? Suppose you are going to write, would you not call for pen, ink, and paper, like another man; and do you not know what it is you call for?

HYL. How often must I tell you, that I know not the real nature of any one thing in the universe? I may indeed upon occasion make use of pen, ink, and paper. But what any one of them is in its own true nature, I declare positively I know not. And the same is true with regard to every other corporeal thing. And, what is more, we are not only ignorant of the true and real nature of things, but even of their existence. It cannot be denied that we perceive such certain appearances or ideas; but it cannot be concluded from thence that bodies really exist. Nay, now I think on it, I must, agreeably to my former concessions, farther declare that it is impossible any *real* corporeal thing should exist in nature.

PHIL. You amaze me. Was ever anything more wild and extravagant than the notions you now maintain: and is it not evident you are led into all these extravagances by the belief of *material substance?* This makes you dream of those unknown natures in everything. It is this occasions your distinguishing between the reality and sensible appearances of things. It is to this you are indebted for being ignorant of what everybody else knows perfectly well. Nor is this all: you are not only ignorant of the true nature of everything, but you know not whether anything really exists, or whether there are any true natures at all; forasmuch as you attribute to your material beings an absolute or external existence wherein you suppose their reality consists. And, as you are forced in the end to acknowledge such an existence means either a direct repugnancy, or nothing at all, it follows that you are obliged to pull down your own hypothesis of material Substance, and positively to deny the real existence of any part of the universe. And so you are plunged into the deepest and most deplorable scepticism that ever man was. Tell me, Hylas, is it not as I say?

HYL. I agree with you. *Material substance* was no more than an hypothesis; and a false and groundless one too. I will no longer spend my breath in defence of it. But whatever hypothesis you advance, or whatsoever scheme of things you introduce in its stead, I doubt not it will appear every whit as false: let me but be allowed to question you upon it. That is, suffer me to serve you in your own kind, and I warrant it shall conduct you through as many perplexities and contradictions, to the very same state of scepticism that I myself am in at present.

PHIL. I assure you, Hylas, I do not pretend to frame any hypothesis at all. I am of a vulgar cast, simple enough to believe my senses, and leave things as I find them. To be plain, it is my opinion that the real things are those very things I see, and to feel, and perceive by my senses. These I know; and, finding they answer all the necessities and purposes of life, have no reason to be solicitous about any other unknown beings. A piece of sensible bread, for instance, would stay my stomach better than ten thousand times as much of that insensible, unintelligible, real bread you speak of. It is likewise my opinion that colours and other sensible qualities are on the objects. I cannot for my life help thinking that snow is white, and fire hot. You indeed, who by *snow* and *fire* mean certain external, unperceived, unperceiving substances, are in the right to deny whiteness or heat to be affections inherent in *them*. But I, who understand by those words the things I see and feel, am obliged to think like other folks. And, as I am no sceptic with regard to the nature of things, so neither am I as to their existence. That a thing should be really perceived by my senses, and at the same time not really exist, is to me a plain contradiction; since I cannot prescind or abstract, even in thought, the existence of a sensible thing from its being perceived. Wood, stones, fire, water, flesh, iron, and the like things, which I name and discourse of, are things that I know. And I should not have known them but that I perceived them by my senses; and things perceived by the senses are immediately perceived; and things immediately perceived are ideas; and ideas cannot exist without the mind; their existence therefore consists in being perceived; when, therefore, they are actually perceived there can be no doubt of their existence. Away then with all that scepticism, all those ridiculous philosophical doubts. What a jest is it for a philosopher to question the existence of sensible things, till he hath it proved to him from the veracity of God; or to pretend our knowledge in this point falls short of intuition or demonstration! I might as well doubt of my own being, as of the being of those things I actually see and feel.

HYL. Not so fast, Philonous: you say you cannot conceive how sensible things should exist without the mind. Do you not?

PHIL. I do.

HYL. Supposing you were annihilated, cannot you conceive it possible that things perceivable by sense may still exist?[5]

PHIL. I can; but then it must be in another mind. When I deny sensible things an existence out of the mind, I do not mean my mind in particular, but all minds. Now, it is plain they have an existence exterior to my mind; since I find them by experience to be independent of it. There is therefore some other Mind wherein they exist, during the intervals between the times of my perceiving them: as likewise they did before my birth, and would do after my supposed annihilation. And, as the same is true with regard to all other finite created spirits, it necessarily follows there is an *omnipresent eternal Mind*, which knows and comprehends all things, and according to such rules, as He Himself hath ordained, and are by us termed the *laws of nature*.

HYL. Answer me, Philonous. Are all our ideas perfectly inert beings? Or have they any agency included in them?

PHIL. They are altogether passive and inert.[6]

HYL. And is not God an agent, a being purely active?

PHIL. I acknowledge it.

HYL. No idea therefore can be like unto, or represent the nature of God?

PHIL. It cannot.

HYL. Since therefore you have no *idea* of the mind of God, how can you conceive it possible that things should exist in His mind? Or, if you can conceive the mind of God, without having an idea of it, why may not I be allowed to conceive the existence of Matter, notwithstanding I have no idea of it?

---

[5]Cf. *Principles of Human Knowledge*, 45–48.

[6]Cf. *Principles*, sections 25 and 26.

PHIL. As to your first question: I own I have properly no *idea*, either of God or any other spirit; for these being active, cannot be represented by things perfectly inert, as our ideas are. I do nevertheless know that I, who am a spirit or thinking substance, exist as certainly as I know my ideas exist.[7] Farther, I know what I mean by the terms *I* and *myself*; and I know this immediately or intuitively, though I do not perceive it as I perceive a triangle, a colour, or a sound. The Mind, Spirit, or Soul is that indivisible unextended thing which thinks, acts, and perceives. I say *indivisible*, because unextended; and *unextended*, because extended, figured, movable things are ideas; and that which perceives ideas, which thinks and wills, is plainly itself no idea, nor like an idea. Ideas are things inactive, and perceived. And Spirits a sort of beings altogether different from them. I do not therefore say my soul is an idea, or like an idea. However, taking the word *idea* in a large sense, my soul may be said to furnish me with an idea, that is, an image or likeness of God—though indeed extremely inadequate. For, all the notion I have of God is obtained by reflecting on my own soul, heightening its powers, and removing its imperfections. I have, therefore, though not an inactive idea, yet in *myself* some sort of an active thinking image of the Deity. And, though I perceive Him not by sense, yet I have a notion of Him, or know Him by reflexion and reasoning. My own mind and my own ideas I have an immediate knowledge of; and, by the help of these, do mediately apprehend the possibility of the existence of other spirits and ideas. Farther, from my own being, and from the dependency I find in myself and my ideas, I do, by an act of reason, necessarily infer the existence of a God, and of all created things in the mind of God. So much for your first question. For the second: I suppose by this time you can answer it yourself. For you neither perceive Matter[8] objectively, as you do an inactive being or idea; nor know it, as you do yourself, by a reflex act; neither do you mediately apprehend it by similitude of the one or the other;[9] nor yet collect it by reasoning from that which you know immediately.[10] All which makes the case of *Matter* widely different from that of the *Deity*.

HYL. You say your own soul supplies you with some sort of an idea or image of God. But, at the same time, you acknowledge you have, properly speaking, no *idea* of your own soul. You even affirm that spirits are a sort of beings altogether different from ideas. Consequently that no idea can be like a spirit. We have therefore no idea of any spirit. You admit nevertheless that there is spiritual Substance, although you have no idea of it; while you deny there can be such a thing as material Substance, because you have no notion or idea of it. Is this fair dealing? To act consistently, you must either admit Matter or reject Spirit. What say you to this?

PHIL. I say, in the first place, that I do not deny the existence of material substance, merely because I have no notion of it, but because the notion of it is inconsistent; or, in other words, because it is repugnant that there should be a notion of it. Many things, for aught I know, may exist, whereof neither I nor any other man hath or can have any idea or notion whatsoever. But then those things must be possible, that is, nothing inconsistent must be included in their

---

[7]Cf. *Principles*, sections 2,27,135, and 142.

[8]Cf. *Principles*, section 2.

[9]Cf. *Principles*, section 8.

[10]Cf. *Principles*, section 20.

definition. I say, secondly, that, although we believe things to exist which we do not perceive, yet we may not believe that any particular thing exists, without some reason for such belief: but I have no reason for believing the existence of Matter. I have no immediate intuition thereof: neither can I immediately from my sensations, ideas, notions, actions, or passions, infer an unthinking, unperceiving, inactive Substance — either by probable deduction, or necessary consequence. Whereas the being of my Self, that is, my own soul, mind, or thinking principle, I evidently know by reflexion. You will forgive me if I repeat the same things in answer to the same objections. In the very notion or definition of *material Substance*, there is included a manifest repugnance and inconsistency. But this cannot be said of the notion of Spirit. That ideas should exist in what doth not perceive, or be produced by what doth not act, is repugnant. But, it is no repugnancy to say that a perceiving thing should be the subject of ideas, or an active thing the cause of them. It is granted we have neither an immediate evidence nor a demonstrative knowledge of the existence of other finite spirits; but it will not thence follow that such spirits are on a foot with material substances: if to suppose the one be inconsistent, and it be not inconsistent to suppose the other; if the one can be inferred by no argument, and there is a probability for the other; if we see signs and effects indicating distinct finite agents like ourselves, and see no sign or symptom whatever that leads to a rational belief of Matter. I say, lastly, that I have a notion of Spirit, though I have not, strictly speaking, an idea of it.[11] I do not perceive it as an idea, or by means of an idea, but know it by reflexion.

HYL. Notwithstanding all you have said, to me it seems that, according to your own way of thinking, and in consequence of your own principles, it should follow that *you* are only a system of floating ideas, without any substance to support them. Words are not to be used without a meaning. And, as there is no more meaning in *spiritual Substance* than in *material Substance*, the one is to be exploded as well as the other.

PHIL. How often must I repeat, that I know or am conscious of my own being; and that *I myself* am not my ideas, but somewhat else,[12] a thinking, active principle that perceives, knows, wills, and operates about ideas. I know that I, one and the same self, perceive both colours and sounds: that a colour cannot perceive a sound, nor a sound a colour: that I am therefore one individual principle, distinct from colour and sound; and, for the same reason, from all other sensible things and inert ideas. But, I am not in like manner conscious either of the existence or essence of Matter. On the contrary, I know that nothing inconsistent can exist and that the existence of Matter implies an inconsistency. Further, I know what I mean when I affirm that there is a spiritual substance or support of ideas, that is, that a spirit knows and perceives ideas. But, I do not know what is meant when it is said that an unperceiving substance hath inherent in it and supports either ideas or the archetypes of ideas. There is therefore upon the whole no parity of case between Spirit and Matter.

HYL. I own myself satisfied in this point. But, do you in earnest think the real existence of sensible things consists in their being actually perceived? If so,

---

[11]Cf. *Principles*, section 142.
[12]Cf. *Principles*, section 2.

how comes it that all mankind distinguish between them? Ask the first man you meet, and he shall tell you, *to be perceived* is one thing, and *to exist* is another.

PHIL. I am content, Hylas, to appeal to the common sense of the world for the truth of my notion. Ask the gardener why he thinks yonder cherry-tree exists in the garden, and he shall tell you, because he sees and feels it; in a word, because he perceives it by his senses. Ask him why he thinks an orange-tree not to be there, and he shall tell you, because he does not perceive it. What he perceives by sense, that he terms a real being, and saith it *is* or exists; but, that which is not perceivable, the same, he saith, hath no being.

HYL. Yes, Philonous, I grant the existence of a sensible thing consists in being perceivable, but not in being actually perceived.

PHIL. And what is perceivable but an idea? And can an idea exist without being actually perceived? These are points long since agreed between us.

HYL. But, be your opinion never so true, yet surely you will not deny it is shocking, and contrary to the common sense of men.[13] Ask the fellow whether yonder tree hath an existence out of his mind: what answer think you he would make?

PHIL. The same that I should myself, to wit, that it doth exist out of his mind. But then to a Christian it cannot surely be shocking to say, the real tree, existing without his mind, is truly known and comprehended by (that is *exists in*) the infinite mind of God. Probably he may not at first glance be aware of the direct and immediate proof there is of this; inasmuch as the very being of a tree, or any other sensible thing, implies a mind wherein it is. But the point itself he cannot deny. The question between the Materialists and me is not, whether things have a *real* existence out of the mind of this or that person, but, whether they have an *absolute* existence, distinct from being perceived by God, and exterior to *all* minds. This indeed some heathens and philosophers have affirmed, but whoever entertains notions of the Deity suitable to the Holy Scriptures will be of another opinion.

HYL. But, according to your notions, what difference is there between real things, and chimeras formed by the imagination, or the visions of a dream —since they are all equally in the mind?[14]

PHIL. The ideas formed by the imagination are faint and indistinct; they have, besides, an entire dependence on the will. But the ideas perceived by sense, that is, real things, are more vivid and clear; and, being imprinted on the mind by a spirit distinct from us, have not the like dependence on our will. There is therefore no danger of confounding these with the foregoing: and there is as little of confounding them with the visions of a dream, which are dim, irregular, and confused. And, though they should happen to be never so lively and natural, yet, by their not being connected, and of a piece with the preceding and subsequent transactions of our lives, they might easily be distinguished from realities. In short, by whatever method you distinguish *things* from *chimeras* on your scheme, the same, it is evident, will hold also upon mine. For, it must be, I presume, by some perceived difference; and I am not for depriving you of any one thing that you perceive.

---

[13]Cf. *Principles*, sections 54–57.

[14]Cf. *Principles*, sections 29–41.

HYL. But still, Philonous, you hold, there is nothing in the world but spirits and ideas. And this, you must needs acknowledge, sounds very oddly.

PHIL. I own the word *idea*, not being commonly used for *thing*, sounds something out of the way. My reason for using it was, because a necessary relation to the mind is understood to be implied by that term; and it is now commonly used by philosophers to denote the immediate objects of the understanding. But, however oddly the proposition may sound in words, yet it includes nothing so very strange or shocking in its sense; which in effect amounts to no more than this, to wit, that there are only things perceiving, and things perceived; or that every unthinking being is necessarily, and from the very nature of its existence, perceived by some mind; if not by a finite created mind, yet certainly by the infinite mind of God, in whom 'we live, and move, and have our being.' Is this as strange as to say, the sensible qualities are not on the objects: or that we cannot be sure of the existence of things, or know anything of their real natures—though we both see and feel them, and perceive them by all our senses?

HYL. And, in consequence of this, must we not think there are no such things as physical or corporeal causes; but that a Spirit is the immediate cause of all the phenomena in nature? Can there be anything more extravagant than this?

PHIL. Yes, it is infinitely more extravagant to say—a thing which is inert operates on the mind, and which is unperceiving is the cause of our perceptions, without any regard either to consistency, or the old known axiom, *Nothing can give to another that which it hath not itself.* Besides, that which to you, I know not for what reason, seems so extravagant is no more than the Holy Scriptures assert in a hundred places. In them God is represented as the sole and immediate Author of all those effects which some heathens and philosophers are wont to ascribe to Nature, Matter, Fate, or the like unthinking principle. This is so much the constant language of Scripture that it were needless to confirm it by citations.

HYL. You are not aware, Philonous, that, in making God the immediate Author of all the motions in nature, you make Him the Author of murder, sacrilege, adultery, and the like heinous sins.

PHIL. In answer to that, I observe, first, that the imputation of guilt is the same, whether a person commits an action with or without an instrument. In case therefore you suppose God to act by the mediation of an instrument, or occasion, called *Matter*, you as truly make Him the author of sin as I, who think Him the immediate agent in all those operations vulgarly ascribed to Nature. I farther observe that sin or moral turpitude doth not consist in the outward physical action or motion, but in the internal deviation of the will from the laws of reason and religion. This is plain, in that the killing an enemy in a battle, or putting a criminal legally to death, is not thought sinful; though the outward act be the very same with that in the case of murder. Since, therefore, sin doth not consist in the physical action, the making God an immediate cause of all such actions is not making Him the Author of sin. Lastly, I have nowhere said that God is the only agent who produces all the motions in bodies. It is true I have denied there are any other agents besides spirits; but this is very consistent with allowing to thinking rational beings, in the production of motions, the use of limited powers, ultimately indeed derived from God, but immediately under the direction of their own wills, which is sufficient to entitle them to all the guilt of their actions.

HYL. But the denying Matter, Philonous, or corporeal Substance; there is the point. You can never persuade me that this is not repugnant to the universal sense of mankind. Were our dispute to be determined by most voices, I am confident you would give up the point, without gathering the votes.

PHIL. I wish both our opinions were fairly stated and submitted to the judgment of men who had plain common sense, without the prejudices of a learned education. Let me be represented as one who trusts his senses, who thinks he knows the things he sees and feels, and entertains no doubts of their existence; and you fairly set forth with all your doubts, your paradoxes, and your scepticism about you, and I shall willingly acquiesce in the determination of any indifferent person. That there is no substance wherein ideas can exist beside spirit is to me evident. And that the objects immediately perceived are ideas, is on all hands agreed. And that sensible qualities are objects immediately perceived no one can deny. It is therefore evident there can be no *substratum* of those qualities but spirit; *in* which they exist, not by way of mode or property, but as a thing perceived in that which perceives it.[15] I deny therefore that there is any unthinking *substratum* of the objects of sense, and *in that acceptation* that there is any material substance. But if by *material substance* is meant only *sensible body* — that which is seen and felt (and the unphilosophical part of the world, I dare say, mean no more) — then I am more certain of matter's existence than you or any other philosopher pretend to be. If there be anything which makes the generality of mankind averse from the notions I espouse: it is a misapprehension that I deny the reality of sensible things. But, as it is you who are guilty of that, and not I, it follows that in truth their aversion is against your notions and not mine. I do therefore assert that I am as certain as of my own being, that there are bodies or corporeal substances (meaning the things I perceive by my senses); and that, granting this, the bulk of mankind will take no thought about, nor think themselves at all concerned in the fate of those unknown natures, and philosophical quiddities, which some men are so fond of.

HYL. What say you to this? Since, according to you, men judge of the reality of things by their senses, how can a man be mistaken in thinking the moon a plain lucid surface, about a foot in diameter; or a square tower, seen at a distance, round; or an oar, with one end in the water, crooked?

PHIL. He is not mistaken with regard to the ideas he actually perceives, but in the inferences he makes from his present perceptions. Thus, in the case of the oar, what he immediately perceives by sight is certainly crooked; and so far he is in the right. But if he thence conclude that upon taking the oar out of the water he shall perceive the same crookedness; or that it would affect his touch as crooked things are wont to do: in that he is mistaken. In like manner, if he shall conclude from what he perceives in one station, that, in case he advances towards the moon or tower, he should still be affected with the like ideas, he is mistaken. But his mistake lies not in what he perceives immediately, and at present, (it being a manifest contradiction to suppose he should err in respect of that) but in the wrong judgment he makes concerning the ideas he apprehends to be connected with those immediately perceived: or, concerning the ideas that, from what he perceives at present, he imagines would be perceived in other circumstances. The case is the same with regard to the Copernican sys-

---

[15]Cf. *Principles*, section 49.

tem. We do not here perceive any motion of the earth: but it were erroneous thence to conclude, that, in case we were placed at as great a distance from that as we are now from the other planets, we should not then perceive its motion.[16]

HYL. I understand you; and must needs own you say things plausible enough. But, give me leave to put you in mind of one thing. Pray, Philonous, were you not formerly as positive that Matter existed, as you are now that it does not?

PHIL. I was. But here lies the difference. Before, my positiveness was founded, without examination, upon prejudice; but now, after inquiry, upon evidence.

HYL. After all, it seems our dispute is rather about words than things. We agree in the thing, but differ in the name. That we are affected with ideas *from without* is evident; and it is no less evident that there must be (I will not say archetypes, but) Powers without the mind, corresponding to those ideas. And, as these Powers cannot subsist by themselves, there is some subject of them necessarily to be admitted; which I call *Matter*, and you call *Spirit*. This is all the difference.

PHIL. Pray, Hylas, is that powerful Being, or subject of powers, extended?

HYL. It hath not extension; but it hath the power to raise in you the idea of extension.

PHIL. It is therefore itself unextended?

HYL. I grant it.

PHIL. Is it not also active?

HYL. Without doubt. Otherwise, how could we attribute powers to it?

PHIL. Now let me ask you two questions: *First*, Whether it be agreeable to the usage either of philosophers or others to give the name *Matter* to an unextended active being? And, *Secondly*, Whether it be not ridiculously absurd to misapply names contrary to the common use of language?

HYL. Well then, let it not be called Matter, since you will have it so, but some *Third Nature* distinct from Matter and Spirit. For what reason is there why you should call it Spirit? Does not the notion of spirit imply that it is thinking, as well as active and unextended?

PHIL. My reason is this: because I have a mind to have some notion of meaning in what I say: but I have no notion of any action distinct from volition, neither can I conceive volition to be anywhere but in a spirit: therefore, when I speak of an active being, I am obliged to mean a Spirit. Beside, what can be plainer than that a thing which hath no ideas in itself cannot impart them to me; and, if it hath ideas, surely it must be a Spirit. To make you comprehend the point still more clearly if it be possible. I assert as well as you that, since we are affected from without, we must allow Powers to be without, in a Being distinct from ourselves. So far we are agreed. But then we differ as to the kind of this powerful Being. I will have it to be Spirit, you Matter, or I know not what (I may add too, you know not what) Third Nature. Thus, I prove it to be Spirit. From the effects I see produced, I conclude there are actions; and, because actions, volitions; and, because there are volitions, there must be a *will*. Again, the things I perceive must have an existence, they or their archetypes, out of *my* mind: but, being ideas, neither they nor their archetypes can exist otherwise than in an understanding; there is therefore an *understanding*. But will and understanding constitute in the strictest sense a mind or spirit. The powerful cause, therefore, of my ideas is in strict propriety of speech a *Spirit*.

---

[16]Cf. *Principles*, section 58.

HYL. And now I warrant you think you have made the point very clear, little suspecting that what you advance leads directly to a contradiction. Is it not an absurdity to imagine any imperfection in God?

PHIL. Without a doubt.

HYL. To suffer pain is an imperfection?

PHIL. It is.

HYL. Are we not sometimes affected with pain and uneasiness by some other Being?

PHIL. We are.

HYL. And have you not said that Being is a Spirit, and is not that Spirit God?

PHIL. I grant it.

HYL. But you have asserted that whatever ideas we perceive from without are in the mind which affects us. The ideas, therefore, of pain and uneasiness are in God; or, in other words, God suffers pain: that is to say, there is an imperfection in the Divine nature: which, you acknowledged was absurd. So you are caught in a plain contradiction.

PHIL. That God knows or understands all things, and that He knows, among other things, what pain is, even every sort of painful sensation, and what it is for His creatures to suffer pain, I make no question. But, that God, though He knows and sometimes causes painful sensations in us, can Himself suffer pain, I positively deny. We, who are limited and dependent spirits, are liable to impressions of sense, the effects of an external Agent, which, being produced against our wills, are sometimes painful and uneasy. But God, whom no external being can affect, who perceives nothing by sense as we do; whose will is absolute and independent, causing all things, and liable to be thwarted or resisted by nothing: it is evident, such a Being as this can suffer nothing, nor be affected with any painful sensation, or indeed any sensation at all. We are chained to a body: that is to say, our perceptions are connected with corporeal motions. By the law of our nature, we are affected upon every alteration in the nervous parts of our sensible body; which sensible body, rightly considered, is nothing but a complexion of such qualities or ideas as have no existence distinct from being perceived by a mind. So that this connexion of sensations with corporeal motions means no more than a correspondence in the order of nature, between two sets of ideas, or things immediately perceivable. But God is a Pure Spirit, disengaged from all such sympathy, or natural ties. No corporeal motions are attended with the sensations of pain or pleasure in His mind. To know everything knowable, is certainly a perfection; but to endure, or suffer, or feel anything by sense, is an imperfection. The former, I say, agrees to God, but not the latter. God knows, or hath ideas; but His ideas are not conveyed to Him by sense, as ours are. Your not distinguishing, where there is so manifest a difference, makes you fancy you see an absurdity where there is none. . . .

HYL. I shall insist no longer on that point. Do you think, however, you shall persuade me the natural philosophers have been dreaming all this while? Pray what becomes of all their hypotheses and explications of the phenomena, which suppose the existence of Matter?[17]

PHIL. What mean you, Hylas, by the *phenomena*?

HYL. I mean the appearances which I perceive by my senses.

PHIL. And the appearances perceived by sense, are they not ideas?

---

[17]Cf. *Principles*, section 58.

HYL. I have told you so a hundred times.

PHIL. Therefore, to explain the phenomena is, to shew how we come to be affected with ideas, in that manner and order wherein they are imprinted on our senses. Is it not?

HYL. It is.

PHIL. Now, if you can prove that any philosopher has explained the production of any one idea in our minds by the help of *Matter*, I shall for ever acquiesce, and look on all that hath been said against it as nothing; but, if you cannot, it is vain to urge the explication of phenomena. That a Being endowed with knowledge and will should produce or exhibit ideas is easily understood. But that a Being which is utterly destitute of these faculties should be able to produce ideas, or in any sort to affect an intelligence, this I can never understand. This I say, though we had some positive conception of Matter, though we knew its qualities, and could comprehend its existence, would yet be so far from explaining things, that it is itself the most inexplicable thing in the world. And yet, for all this, it will not follow that Philosophers have been doing nothing; for, by observing and reasoning upon the connexion of ideas, they discover the laws and methods of nature, which is a part of knowledge both useful and entertaining.

HYL. After all, can it be supposed God would deceive all mankind? Do you imagine He would have induced the whole world to believe the being of Matter, if there was no such thing?

PHIL. That every epidemical opinion, arising from prejudice, or passion, or thoughtlessness, may be imputed to God, as the Author of it, I believe you will not affirm. Whatsoever opinion we father on Him, it must be either because He has discovered it to us by supernatural revelation; or because it is so evident to our natural faculties, which were framed and given us by God, that it is impossible we should withhold our assent from it. But where is the revelation? or where is the evidence that extorts the belief of Matter? Nay, how does it appear, that Matter, *taken for something distinct from what we perceive by our senses*, is thought to exist by all mankind; or, indeed, by any except a few philosophers, who do not know what they would be at? Your question supposes these points are clear; and, when you have cleared them, I shall think myself obliged to give you another answer. In the meantime, let it suffice that I tell you, I do not suppose God has deceived mankind at all. . . .

HYL. As for the difficulties other opinions may be liable to, those are out of the question. It is your business to defend your own opinion. Can anything be plainer than that you are for changing all things into ideas? You, I say, who are not ashamed to charge me with *scepticism*. This is so plain, there is no denying it.

PHIL. You mistake me. I am not for changing things into ideas, but rather ideas into things;[18] since those immediate objects of perception, which, according to you, are only appearances of things, I take to be the real things themselves.

HYL. Things! You may pretend what you please; but it is certain you leave us nothing but the empty forms of things, the outside only which strikes the senses.

---

[18]Cf. *Principles*, section 38.

PHIL. What you call the empty forms and outside of things seem to me the very things themselves. Nor are they empty or incomplete, otherwise than upon your supposition—that Matter is an essential part of all corporeal things. We both, therefore, agree in this, that we perceive only sensible forms: but herein we differ—you will have them to be empty appearances, I real beings. In short, you do not trust your senses, I do.

HYL. You say you believe your senses; and seem to applaud yourself that in this you agree with the vulgar. According to you, therefore, the true nature of a thing is discovered by the senses. If so, whence comes that disagreement? Why is not the same figure, and other sensible qualities, perceived all manner of ways? and why should we use a microscope the better to discover the true nature of a body, if it were discoverable to the naked eye?

PHIL. Strickly speaking, Hylas, we do not see the same object that we feel[19] neither is the same object perceived by the microscope which was by the naked eye.[20] But, in case every variation was thought sufficient to constitute a new kind of individual, the endless number or confusion of names would render language impracticable. Therefore, to avoid this, as well as other inconveniences which are obvious upon a little thought, men combine together several ideas, apprehended by divers senses, or by the same sense at different times, or in different circumstances, but observed, however, to have some connexion in nature, either with respect to co-existence or succession; all which they refer to one name, and consider as one thing. Hence it follows that when I examine, by my other senses, a thing I have seen, it is not in order to understand better the same object which I had perceived by sight, the object of one sense not being perceived by the other senses. And, when I look through a microscope, it is not that I may perceive more clearly what I perceived already with my bare eyes; the object perceived by the glass being quite different from the former. But, in both cases, my aim is only to know what ideas are connected together; and the more a man knows of the connexion of ideas, the more he is said to know of the nature of things. What, therefore, if our ideas are variable; what if our senses are not in all circumstances affected with the same appearances? It will not thence follow they are not to be trusted; or that they are inconsistent either with themselves or anything else: except it be with your preconceived notion of (I know not what) one single, unchanged, unperceivable, real Nature, marked by each name. Which prejudice seems to have taken its rise from not rightly understanding the common language of men, speaking of several distinct ideas as united into one thing by the mind. And, indeed, there is cause to suspect several erroneous conceits of the philosophers are owing to the same original: while they began to build their schemes not so much on notions as on words, which were framed by the vulgar, merely for conveniency and dispatch in the common actions of life, without any regard to speculation. . . .[21]

HYL. I acknowledge it.

But, after all, Philonous, when I consider the substance of what you advance

---

[19]Cf. *New Theory of Vision*, section 49; and *New Theory of Vision Vindicated*, sections 9, 10, and 15.

[20]Cf. *New Theory of Vision*, section 84–86.

[21]Cf. *Principles*, Introduction, sections 23–25.

against *Scepticism*, it amounts to no more than this:—We are sure that we really see, hear, feel; in a word, that we are affected with sensible impressions.

PHIL. And how are *we* concerned any farther? I see this cherry, I feel it, I taste it: and I am sure *nothing* cannot be seen, or felt, or tasted: it is therefore *real*. Take away the sensations of softness, moisture, redness, tartness, and you take away the cherry, since it is not a being distinct from sensations. A cherry, I say, is nothing but a congeries of sensible impressions, or ideas perceived by various senses: which ideas are united into one thing (or have one name given them) by the mind, because they are observed to attend each other. Thus, when the palate is affected with such a particular taste, the sight is affected with a red colour, the touch with roundness, softness, &c Hence, when I see, and feel, and taste, in such sundry certain manners, I am sure the cherry exists, or is real; its reality being in my opinion nothing abstracted from those sensations. But if by the word *cherry* you mean an unknown nature, distinct from all those sensible qualities, and by its *existence* something distinct from its being perceived; then, indeed, I own, neither you nor I, nor any one else, can be sure it exists.

HYL. But, what would you say, Philonous, if I should bring the very same reasons against the existence of sensible things *in a mind*, which you have offered against their existing *in a material substratum*?

PHIL. When I see your reasons, you shall hear what I have to say to them.

HYL. Is the mind extended or unextended?

PHIL. Unextended, without doubt.

HYL. Do you say the things you perceive are in your mind?

PHIL. They are.

HYL. Again, have I not heard you speak of sensible impressions?

PHIL. I believe you may.

HYL. Explain to me now, O Philonous! how it is possible there should be room for all those trees and houses to exist in your mind. Can extended things be contained in that which is unextended? Or, are we to imagine impressions made on a thing void of all solidity? You cannot say objects are in your mind, as books in your study: or that things are imprinted on it, as the figure of a seal upon wax. In what sense, therefore, are we to understand those expressions? Explain me this if you can: and I shall then be able to answer all those queries you formerly put to me about my *substratum*.

PHIL. Look you, Hylas, when I speak of objects as existing in the mind, or imprinted on the senses, I would not be understood in the gross literal sense; as when bodies are said to exist in a place, or a seal to make an impression upon wax. My meaning is only that the mind comprehends or perceives them; and that it is affected from without, or by some being distinct from itself. This is my explication of your difficulty; and how it can serve to make your tenet of an unperceiving material *substratum* intelligible, I would fain know.

HYL. Nay, if that be all, I confess I do not see what use can be made of it. But are you not guilty of some abuse of language in this?

PHIL. None at all. It is no more than common custom, which you know is the rule of language, hath authorised: nothing being more usual, than for philosophers to speak of the immediate objects of the understanding as things existing in the mind. Nor is there anything in this but what is conformable to the general analogy of language; most part of the mental operations being signified by words borrowed from sensible things; as is plain in the terms *comprehend*, *reflect, discourse, &c.*, which, being applied to the mind, must not be taken in their gross, original sense. . . .

HYL. I confess it seems to be as you say.

PHIL. As a balance, therefore, to this weight of prejudice, let us throw into the scale the great advantages[22] that arise from the belief of Immaterialism, both in regard to religion and human learning. The being of a God, and incorruptibility of the soul, those great articles of religion, are they not proved with the clearest and most immediate evidence? When I say the being of a God, I do not mean an obscure general Cause of things, whereof we have no conception, but God, in the strict and proper sense of the word. A Being whose spirituality, omnipresence, providence, omniscience, infinite power and goodness, are as conspicuous as the existence of sensible things, of which (notwithstanding the fallacious pretences and affected scruples of Sceptics) there is no more reason to doubt than of our own being. Then, with relation to human sciences. In Natural Philosophy, what intricacies, what obscurities, what contradictions hath the belief of Matter led men into! To say nothing of the numberless disputes about its extent, continuity, homogeneity, gravity, divisibility, &c. – do they not pretend to explain all things by bodies operating on bodies, according to the laws of motion? and yet, are they able to comprehend how one body should move another? Nay, admitting there was no difficulty in reconciling the notion of an inert being with a cause, or in conceiving how an accident might pass from one body to another; yet, by all their strained thoughts and extravagant suppositions, have they been able to reach the *mechanical* production of any one animal or vegetable body? Can they account, by the laws of motion, for sounds, tastes, smells, or colours; or for the regular course of things? Have they accounted, by physical principles, for the aptitude and contrivance even of the most inconsiderable parts of the universe? But, laying aside Matter and corporeal causes, and admitting only the efficiency of an All-perfect Mind, are not all the effects of nature easy and intelligible? If the *phenomena* are nothing else but *ideas*; God is a *spirit*, but Matter an unintelligent, unperceiving being. If they demonstrate an unlimited power in their cause; God is active and omnipotent, but Matter an inert mass. If the order, regularity, and usefulness of them can never be sufficiently admired; God is infinitely wise and provident, but Matter destitute of all contrivance and design. These surely are great advantages in *Physics*. Not to mention that the apprehension of a distant Deity naturally disposes men to a negligence in their moral actions; which they would be more cautious of, in case they thought Him immediately present, and acting on their minds, without the interposition of Matter, or unthinking second causes. Then in *Metaphysics*: what difficulties concerning entity in abstract, substantial forms, hylarchic principles, plastic natures, substance and accident, principle of individuation, possibility of Matter's thinking, origin of ideas, the manner how two independent substances so widely different as *Spirit* and *Matter*, should mutually operate on each other? what difficulties, I say, and endless disquisitions, concerning these and innumerable other the like points, do we escape, by supposing only Spirits and ideas? Even the *Mathematics* themselves, if we take away the absolute existence of extended things, become much more clear and easy; the most shocking paradoxes and intricate speculations in those sciences depending on the infinite divisibility of finite extension;

---

[22]Cf. *Principles*, sections 85 – 156.

which depends on that supposition. But what need is there to insist on the particular sciences? Is not that opposition to all science whatsoever, that frenzy of the ancient and modern Sceptics, built on the same foundation? Or can you produce so much as one argument against the reality of corporeal things, or in behalf of that avowed utter ignorance of their natures, which doth not suppose their reality to consist in an external absolute existence? Upon this supposition, indeed, the objections from the change of colours in a pigeon's neck, or the appearance of the broken oar in the water, must be allowed to have weight. But these and the like objections vanish, if we do not maintain the being of absolute external originals, but place the reality of things in ideas, fleeting indeed, and changeable; however, not changed at random, but according to the fixed order of nature. For, herein consists that constancy and truth of things which secures all the concerns of life, and distinguishes that which is *real* from the *irregular visions* of the fancy.[23]

HYL. I agree to all you have now said, and must own that nothing can incline me to embrace your opinion more than the advantages I see it is attended with. I am by nature lazy; and this would be a mighty abridgment in knowledge. What doubts, what hypotheses, what labyrinths of amusement, what fields of disputation, what an ocean of false learning, may be avoided by that single notion of *Immaterialism*!

4. ACTIVITY AND PASSIVITY

Berkeley considers himself to have disposed finally and incontrovertibly of both the idea and the existence of material substance. Our knowledge of the world consists entirely of ideas the existence of which consists entirely in their being perceived, and the only prerequisite of *percipi* is a mind which perceives. This, however, is a logical presupposition of perception, not an idea. We have no more idea of a mind (as Hylas reminds Philonous) than we have of material substance. This point was later taken up by Hume with results that we shall examine below.

The rejoinder which Berkeley makes is to agree: We have no ideas of ourselves and none of spirits. But he does not conclude from this that we have no knowledge of them, still less that they do not exist. That ideas are perceived is direct evidence of the existence of the perceiving subject. Without a perceiver no perception could occur — my direct awareness of the percept is itself evidence of my existence — *cogito ergo sum*. Of course, Berkeley does not use Descartes's dictum, but, in effect, both he, and Locke before him,[24] accept the Cartesian argument for the existence of the self.

---

[23]Cf. *Principles*, sections 28–42. In *Siris*, sections 294–297, 300–318, 335, and 359–365.
[24]Cf. Locke, *Essay*, Book IV, Chapter 9, 3.

We have no idea of the self because ideas, without exception, are passive and inert; they simply occur, or appear to us; they do nothing, effect nothing, have no causal properties but are simply successive appearances to a mind. (This again is to be built upon by Hume with far-reaching results.) But that which perceives is active. Like Descartes, Berkeley takes as indubitable the *agency* of the mind in thinking and concludes to its existence as a necessary condition of the occurrence of percepts.

Of activity, however, there are no ideas (= percepts); yet we are aware of ourselves as active. One might have thought that our awareness of mental activity would come to us as ideas of reflection; but, though Berkeley at first seems to adopt that position, in endorsing Locke's classification of ideas, he later at least qualifies it. Ideas of reflection are strictly what we perceive when we introspect, and they seem to comprise feelings and emotions of various kinds, what in general could be called passions. But our awareness of our own activity is the sort of thing we experience in volition and this is no passion, nor according to Berkeley, an idea. Yet we are somehow aware of it, "immediately or intuitively," Berkeley says (though both these terms apply equally to ideas). So he maintains that we have some *notion* of ourselves as thinking substances[25] (what Descartes called *res cogitantes*).

5. SELF AND OTHERS

By analogy with my own experience I can conclude to the existence of other spirits like myself and similarly have notions of them. When I have ideas of bodies like my own and observe their movements, which are similar to the movements which I am aware of causing by volition in my own body, I conclude to the existence of agents similar to myself, who cause these other movements in the other human bodies I perceive. Such movements include speech and my linguistic communication with other people is additional evidence of agents producing the language I use and understand in the same way as I produce it myself when I speak.

This is the *argument from analogy* for the existence of other minds.[26] One great difficulty of the idealistic position adopted by Berkeley is, as we saw earlier, the apparent impossibility not only of explaining, if all

[25]Cf. *Principles of Human Knowledge*, section 139.

[26]Cf. *Principles of Human Knowledge*, section 145.

we can know is ideas in our own minds, how we become aware of a world of external bodies (to say nothing of our own), but also of explaining or of finding grounds for the existence of other persons. The denial of all these leads to solipsism; but this Berkeley avoids by invoking the argument from analogy to establish the existence of other spirits, as well as the argument from the persistence of percepts and our inability to create and destroy them at will, to establish the existence of God. But God, who produces passive ideas in us, does not himself suffer passions. He only acts and so, strictly speaking, has not ideas (or percepts) of His own.

6. VOLITION AND MOVEMENT

When I will to move my hand, all I do, in effect, is cause myself and others, through the intermediary act of God, to experience certain ideas (of my hand moving). So others become aware of the movement as an effect of my willing and so can acquire the notion, on the analogy of their own experience of willing similar movements, of me as a person, soul, or spiritual substance. But why could I not directly produce the idea in your mind? Does not God's intervention (a) make Him responsible for my act, and (b) make His action subject to my volition?

Berkeley denies both of these suggestions. God gives men free will and limited responsibility so that they are responsible for the effects they voluntarily cause, and God has no further responsibility for men's actions than is implied in His having given them free will. Moreover, responsibility depends upon intention and not merely on movement, but men's acts follow from their own intentions, not God's. He *permits* the acts; He does not commit them. Secondly, God is responsible for the laws of nature and for maintaining the order of ideas in all minds according to those laws. His collaboration in men's actions, therefore, consists only in producing ideas according to the settled order when men will. Thus I cannot will to move mountains with my little finger, or to walk on water, because that would violate the order of nature. But if I will to move my hand, God simply produces the ideas which the laws of nature demand when I so will. If He did not, my will would be inoperative —I should not have free will.

Arguments of this kind are similarly used to reconcile Berkeley's idealistic doctrine with the teachings of the Scriptures. These, he maintains, use the ordinary language of common sense, with which his own doctrine is in full accord, because common sense believes in the reality of what the senses perceive. The rest, he claims, follows naturally.

7. UBIQUITOUS EVIDENCE OF GOD'S EXISTENCE

Finally, the whole spectacle of the universe, as it consists entirely of ideas whose *esse* is *percipi*, is direct evidence of God's being, for ideas cannot exist without a mind and our minds cannot account for more than a very few.

"Some truths," says Berkely, "there are so near and obvious to the mind that a man need only open his eyes to see them. Such I take this important one to be, viz. that all the choir of heaven and furniture of earth, in a word all those bodies which compose the mighty frame of the world, have not any substance without a mind; that their *being* is to be perceived or known; that consequently so long as they are not actually perceived by me, or do not exist in my mind, or that of any other created spirit, they must either have no existence at all, or else subsist in the mind of some Eternal Spirit. . ."[27]

Consequently, as we are conscious of our own inability to conceive "all the choir of heaven and furniture of earth" by any act of our own volition, and as the perceptions of them come to us without our concurrence or cooperation, they are direct and open evidence of the existence of a divine mind.

This argument for the existence of God is not ontological. It does not proceed from the idea of God's perfection to His existence. It is cosmological, yet with a difference. The cosmological argument goes from the finiteness, contingency, and dependency of everything in the experienced world to the existence of an infinite and self-dependent, necessary being. But Berkeley argues not simply from the contingency of our perceptions but from their necessary dependence on some mind. That they come to us without our will simply shows that we do not produce them ourselves. They are not themselves causes and we do not cause them, so they must be caused in us by something else. Descartes argued similarly for the existence of material bodies, but that, Berkeley holds, is a meaningless concept. Inert matter could not be a cause of ideas and ideas are not such as to give any sort of evidence of

---

[27]*Principles of Human Knowledge,* Section 6.

it. Their *esse* is *percipi*. But now, it seems, *percipi* is not a sufficient ground for *esse;* volition is needed as well.[28] But it is not our own volition. Therefore it must be God's. The evidence is the dependency of ideas for existence on something not themselves — on some cause — but the premise of the argument is not the dependence of all contingent existences on a prior cause (which, if itself contingent, points to another, and so on). It is the dependence only of ideas on some adequate cause for their existence. A sufficient cause is a mind; but not only a mind which perceives them. It must be a mind which actively produces them. As that is no finite mind like our own, it must be God's.

Further, there is a kinship in Berkeley's thought with the teleological argument also. For he appeals to the settled order of nature as evidence of those ideas produced by God, in contradistinction to those which our fancy produces arbitrarily. The settled order is a design, and, as Berkeley describes it, mainly purposive,[29] and it is presented as evidence that a mind, presumably beneficent, yet obviously not our own, produced it.

The difference of Berkeley's arguments from the traditional forms of proof are due to his stalwart empiricism. The only evidence which really weighs with him is the sensible evidence provided by "ideas" (in Locke's meaning of that term). In all the traditional proofs there is an element of *a priori* reasoning. This is obvious in the ontological proof. In the cosmological proof the *a priori* postulate is that every effect must have a cause which is an ultimate ground of its existence. The teleological proof assumes that the appearance of design and purpose cannot be the result of mere chance. These presuppositions, though present in Berkeley's thought, are not what he mainly relies on. He restricts himself (and us) firmly to the evidence of the senses. Percepts reveal themselves directly as immediate objects, the nature of which is such that they can be nothing but sensible objects. When not sensed they are nothing — we do not have them. There is no evidence without them of

---

[28]Cf. Berkeley's *Commonplace Book*: "Why may we not conceive it possible for God to create things out of nothing? Certainly we ourselves create in some wise whenever we imagine.

"'Ex nihilo nihil fit.' This and the like are called veritates oeternae, because 'nullam fidem habent extra mentem.' To make the axiom have a positive signification, one should express it thus: Every idea has a cause, i. e. is produced by a Will." (*Berkeley's Complete Works*, Vol. I; A. C. Fraser, ed., p. 53)

[29]"That food nourishes, sleep refreshes and fire warms us, that to sow in seed-time is the way to reap in the harvest, and, in general, that to obtain such and such ends, such and such means are conducive, all this we know . . . only by observation of the settled Laws of Nature. . . ." (*Principles*, Section 31).

anything at all. But what is sensed is sensed, and can only be sensed, by a conscious mind. Thus sensible percepts are at once evidence for their own existence and (as that is the same as *percipi*) for the existence of a perceiver. They are not, however, direct evidence for any causes, except that, so far as they are inert, they cannot themselves be causes and so, *a fortiori*, not causes of themselves. We are directly aware of causing some of them (in imagination), but equally we are aware that we do not cause the majority of them. The conclusion follows by analogy: there must be another mind which causes our ideas — and of this they are, for the reasons given, indirect evidence.

CHAPTER 23

Failure of Subjective Idealism

1. DISTINCTION OF APPEARANCE FROM REALITY

Berkeley, having taken over the initial empiricist presuppositions of Locke, that knowledge originates in simple ideas and consists of nothing beyond what can be derived from them by combination or separation, attempts to make the position self-consistent by remaining resolutely within the closed circle of ideas. The only exceptions he allows are the "notions" that seem to follow from the necessary conditions of the existence of ideas; notions of minds to which ideas are objects and which are aware of themselves as conscious agents.

In so attempting to keep the empiricist position self-consistent, Berkeley declares that he has retained the distinction between truth and falsehood, reality and illusion, and has preserved the attitude of common sense. Common sense, however, does not normally deny the existence of a material world external to and independent of the mind. Nor, Berkeley claims, does he, if the mind in question is man's. He has simply given a philosophical analysis of our experience of that world and of the meaning we attach to terms like existence. Common sense relies on the evidence of the senses for its belief in the existence of material things. Berkeley takes that as final.

But we have seen that the crucial problem of perceptual knowledge is to know by what criterion we distinguish between sensuous experiences which are veridical and apprise us of realities and those which are illusory or delusive; for, as overtly presented to us, they seem not to differ. Here Berkeley's answer is to resort to the settled order of occurrence of some ideas as opposed to others and to attribute the former to God. What is real is what exists in the mind of God, whether or not it exists in any other mind, and what is illusory is what exists only in human minds, is produced only by them, and is evanescent and transitory, having no existence at all when it is not experienced by men. The true ideas are produced by God in the minds of men according to laws He has ordained; false ideas are our own concoctions.

Berkeley thus offers us several criteria of truth:

(a) What is in God's mind, as opposed to what is not;
(b) What God produces in man's mind, as opposed to what man by his own volition invents;
(c) What occurs according to a settled order, as opposed to what occurs haphazardly and is incoherent either with the settled order, or with itself, or both;

And, for good measure, he adds (d) that fictitious and illusory ideas are less vivid and clear than those of real things.

2. FAILURE OF THE CRITERIA OF TRUTH

A criterion of truth, however, is valid only if available for making actual judgments between true and false ideas by the person who has the ideas. We must not commit the epistemologist's fallacy. No doubt God can distinguish between what He produces in our minds and what He does not, but can we do this? God knows what exists in His mind when nothing exists in ours but we do not. We should be able to distinguish orderly ideas from disorderly, but to do this we need a criterion of order—at least, if the order is to be regular or "settled," there must be some settled connection between the items which occur in it. No doubt, again, God knows what laws He has ordained and what ideas produced by Him in our minds obey them, but, without direct divine revelation, we cannot know this except by experience. If the criteria could be used only by God, for us to claim knowledge of them at all would be to commit the epistemologist's fallacy. Let us consider each of them in turn, therefore, to see whether or not the fallacy can be avoided.

(a) WHAT IS IN GOD'S MIND. Berkeley tells us that strictly speaking

God has no ideas, because an idea is inert and is passively received, but God is pure activity, is impassable, and does not "suffer." If this is so, our ideas of a tree, for example, cannot exist in God's mind when no sentient creature is perceiving them. Berkeley's proof of the persistence of nonsentient beings when they are not perceived by finite minds will not work therefore, and the second of the satirical limericks is inept, because a purely active God would not *observe* (or perceive); He would only create. But the persistence unperceived of sensible objects is, perhaps, not necessary to establish the reality of our ideas of them. It may be sufficient that they are produced in us by God, whenever they occur. This is the second criterion of truth.

(b) VOLUNTARY AND INVOLUNTARY PERCEPTION. How then can we know which ideas God produces in us? Berkeley asserts that what comes to us independently of our own volition is produced in our minds by God. But sensory illusions and all delusions (including dreams) occur without our concurrence. We see mirages in the desert as involuntarily as trees in the park, sticks half-submerged in water look bent as unavoidably as when not so submerged they look straight. We do not dream what we will to dream and we often dream what we do not want to experience in waking life. The fantasies that we deliberately arouse are a minority among ideas of the unreal; they are those by which we are least deceived (for we know them to be mere fantasy), and they are among the nearest to reality.

Moreover, if we adhere strictly to Berkeley's theory, we must hold that we often voluntarily produce ideas of real things, for whenever we act deliberately to produce changes in our surroundings, for instance, when I move a book on my desk, my volition causes new ideas to occur of something *real*.

Berkeley has two answers to this criticism. First, he says that illusory ideas are not in themselves false, for there is no doubt that we experience them and that they are what they appear to be. The falsity resides only in our judgments about them, especially about what other ideas we may expect to follow them. My view of the water in the desert is an illusion only because I anticipate drinking it. Its failure to persist as I approach proves *my hopes* false, not the appearance, for there really was an appearance of water. On Berkeley's principles there can be only ideas: the appearance of water persisting as other ideas occur associated with my approach to the apparent place where the water is and followed by yet other ideas associated with my drinking, and so forth. If some of these ideas are expected and do not occur, the error lies in the expectation, not in the ideas. This is really an appeal to the settled order of nature, the legitimacy of which we shall shortly examine.

Secondly, Berkeley would claim that voluntary acts produce ideas only through God's mediation. But the question to be faced is how we know when this is so, and if the book really has been moved, or if, Walter Mitty-like, I have not just imagined or dreamed that I have carried out my intention. God does not inform us directly of His collaboration. If we have no direct way of recognizing it we cannot use it to distinguish the real from the apparent without committing the epistemologist's fallacy.

(c) THE SETTLED ORDER OF NATURE. But ideas that God produces, we are told, occur in a settled order according to the laws of nature. This, perhaps, we can recognize directly. Some delusions and dreams do follow a familiar order, but they do not correlate regularly with that continuing experience of the natural order which we call sane and waking life, and so we can identify them as delusions.

The settled order of nature, however, can be known only through knowledge of its laws, and these can be discovered only by experience. But experience reveals no necessary connections between ideas — "That food nourishes, sleep refreshes, and fire warms us . . . we know, not by discovering any *necessary connexion* between our ideas, but only by the observation of the *settled laws* of nature. . . ." Moreover, what is usually overlooked, our ideas do not in fact come to us in any settled order, but entirely fortuitously. Visual presentations depend on a hundred and one different vicissitudes: when I open and when I close my eyes, whether and how my vision may be obstructed, the direction in which I look and how I may change it, the degree and direction of attention, and so forth. The same applies to all the other senses. If experience reveals no necessary (or "real") connections between ideas, what is the source of the settled order?

The only way in which we could become aware of any such order would be to discover what ideas, as Locke said, go constantly together. But actually none do. If we could discover connections between them which were necessary and universal we should know which to associate as belonging to the natural order, but Berkeley tells us that no necessary connections are revealed to us. If we know the laws of nature we can recognize the settled order; but the laws can be discovered only by experience, yet we cannot discover the laws of nature even by experience if we do not experience any necessary connections, for without them there is nothing to tie one idea to any other. It is true that when I look up from my desk to the window and see a tree outside, I do not associate the tree with the desk, as I do associate the appearance of the top of the desk with its side when I see them in succession. On what principles, then, do I collect together some ideas and attribute them to the desk and others which I attribute to the tree? I cannot appeal to the settled order of nature, first, because the ideas occur in no settled order and, secondly, because until I have learned how to collect ideas together and attribute them to the right objects I cannot discover any settled order. Accordingly, to become aware of, and recognize, the regularities among the events which we do indeed experience, more is needed than Berkeley has provided, and we are once more constrained to appeal for God's help in revealing to us the laws He has ordained.[1]

(d) CLARITY AND VIVIDNESS. The hope that we could do better by resorting to the last criterion is indeed forlorn. Clarity and vividness are by no means the exclusive prerogative of true ideas or of veridical perceptions. Illusions and errors are often much more forceful in their appeal, and reality at times reveals itself to us in the dimmest shapes. It is, in short, notorious that no intrinsic character of the experiences themselves can serve to differentiate indubitably imaginary objects from the perception of things physically present. And that only our most vivid ideas are those which belong to the settled order of nature is too implausible to be seriously entertained.

Berkeley's subjective idealism thus fails to provide a satisfactory theory of knowledge, because it fails to distinguish successfully between what is objective and what is subjective in our experience. Its failure is made more conclusively obvious by Hume's further development of it and his resolute determination to be more consistent in the adherence to empiricist principles than was Berkeley.

3. BERKELEY'S ABIDING CONTRIBUTION

But this ultimate failure of Berkeley's theory must not lead us to overlook the important advances and contributions that his philosophy makes. In the first place, we learn as much from the errors of great

---

[1]An interesting aside may be interpolated here. If we could accept Berkeley's criterion, and knew that the only ideas which were real were those that conformed to the settled laws of nature, we could never believe in miracles, as Berkeley contends we may; and if God were to perform any miracles they could have no efficacy in confirming belief. Berkeley allows that God may produce ideas in violation of the settled order, when there is need to shock us out of our indolence and unbelief. But if our only criterion of reality were the settled order, we should of necessity regard all such departures from it as delusory. In that case, the faith-producing function of miracles would be nullified. But a miracle, if any occurs, is by definition a real occurrence which violates the laws of nature, and on the theory Berkeley is offering that should be a contradiction in terms.

thinkers as we do from their insights, if not more; and from Berkeley we discover the paradoxes and difficulties into which we are led by the alluring realism of Locke. Locke's empiricism seems so sensible and sound that, when it breaks down in the attempt to discover how we can check the validity of our sense-given ideas, we are constrained to try to trim away its inconsistencies and construct a coherent theory on the same foundations. This is what Berkeley does, but his efforts lead us only deeper into the perplexity with which Locke left us. So we learn that the remedy for Locke's shortcomings does not lie in the direction in which Berkeley moves.

At the same time, his doctrine of the settled order of nature is very helpful and suggestive. The way in which we do check perceptual appearances about which any question is raised is to find whether they fit in with other perceptual deliverances and form, with them, a systematic structure according to definite and pervasive laws of interconnection. We constantly strive to understand and explain phenomena (that is, perceptual appearances) in the light of systematic theories which find a place for the phenomena in question in a regular and orderly framework. This sort of explanation we call scientific, and the more successful we are in accomplishing it, the more confident we feel about the reality of the objects and events so explained and of the validity of the experiences by which we became aware of them.

But how we come to discover the laws and principles of order which supply the framework for such scientific theories is a problem that remains. Berkeley assumes that we acquire our knowledge of these from experience, and yet he is aware that experience reveals to us no necessary connections. Is the assumption consistent with the insight? Much may depend upon the force given to the word necessary. Possibly experience reveals connections but no necessity. Then we must ask what kind of connection it is that is purely contingent, and whether a connection which, on different occasions, may or may not hold between perceived events is sufficient to constitute a law of nature and support a settled order.

These are problems which will become central in the theories of Hume and Kant and we shall pay further attention to them in what follows.

SUGGESTIONS FOR FURTHER READING

George Berkeley, *Principles of Human Knowledge*. Indianapolis, Ind.: Liberal Arts Press, 1965.

————, *A New Theory of Vision* (T. E. Jessop, ed.). New York: Nelson, 1952.

G. J. Warnock, *Berkeley*. London: Harmondsworth, Penguin Books, 1953.

A. A. Luce, *Berkeley's Immaterialism*. Toronto and Edinburgh: Nelson, 1945.

G. A. Johnston, *The Development of Berkeley's Philosophy*. New York: Atheneum Press, 1965.

W. E. Steinkraus (ed.), *New Studies in Berkeley's Philosophy*. New York: Holt, Rinehart and Winston, 1966.

J. O. Wisdom, *The Unconscious Origins of Berkeley's Philosophy*. London: Hogarth Press, 1953.

E. E. Harris, *Nature, Mind and Modern Science*, Chapter 7. New York: Humanities Press, 1954.

R. G. Collingwood, *The Idea of Nature*, Part II. New York: Oxford University Press, 1965.

G. Dawes Hicks, *Berkeley*. London: Benn, 1932.

John Wild, *George Berkeley*. Cambridge, Mass: Harvard University Press, 1961.

CHAPTER 24

Hume's Psychological Atomism

Hume picked up the torch almost exactly as Berkeley passed it on, but he dropped those elements of the theory which still seemed inconsistent with its main principles. As Berkeley abandoned the material substance which Locke failed to find beneath the ideas of sensation, so Hume abandoned the spiritual substance that Berkeley claimed to find behind ideas of reflection. The great power of Hume's mind is his fearless and relentless consistency – his firm determination to follow the argument wherever it may lead (as Plato had enjoined) and however unpalatable the consequences. In this he is like a rationalist – or rather, let us say, he is a true philosopher. But he is equally determined not to depart one iota from the deliverances of experience. What cannot be traced back to direct experience is to him no part of knowledge, is at best verbiage, and must be treated as worthless. He ends his shorter *Enquiry concerning Human Understanding* with this passage:

When we run over our libraries, persuaded of these principles, what havoc must we make? If we take in our hand any volume; of divinity or school metaphysics, for instance; let us ask, *Does it contain any abstract reasoning concerning quantity or number?* No. *Does it contain any experimental reasoning concerning matter of fact and existence?* No. Commit it then to the flames: for it can contain nothing but sophistry and illusion.

A Treatise of Human Nature

OF THE ORIGIN OF OUR IDEAS

(Book I, Part I, Section 1)

All the perceptions of the human mind resolve themselves into two distinct kinds, which I shall call *impressions* and *ideas*. The difference betwixt these consists in the degrees of force and liveliness, with which they strike upon the mind, and make their way into our thought or consciousness. Those perceptions which enter with most force and violence, we may name *impressions*; and, under this name, I comprehend all our sensations, passions, and emotions, as they make their first appearance in the soul. By *ideas*, I mean the faint images of these in thinking and reasoning; such as, for instance, are all the perceptions excited by the present discourse, excepting only those which arise from the sight and touch, and excepting the immediate pleasure or uneasiness it may occasion. I believe it will not be very necessary to employ many words in explaining this distinction. Every one of himself will readily perceive the difference betwixt feeling and thinking. The common degrees of these are easily distinguished; though it is not impossible but, in particular instances, they may very nearly approach to each other. Thus, in sleep, in a fever, in madness, or in any very violent emotions of soul, our ideas may approach to our impressions: as, on the other hand, it sometimes happens, that our impressions are so faint and low that we cannot distinguish them from our ideas. But, notwithstanding this near resemblance in a few instances, they are in general so very different, that no one can make a scruple to rank them under distinct heads, and assign to each a peculiar name to mark the difference.[1]

There is another division of our perceptions, which it will be convenient to observe, and which extends itself both to our impressions and ideas. This division is into *simple* and *complex*. Simple perceptions, or impressions and ideas, are such as admit of no distinction nor separation. The complex are the contrary to these, and may be distinguished into parts. Though a particular colour, taste, and smell, are qualities all united together in this apple, it is easy to perceive they are not the same, but are at least distinguishable from each other.

Having, by these divisions, given an order and arrangement to our objects, we may now apply ourselves to consider, with the more accuracy, their qualities and relations. The first circumstance that strikes my eye, is the great

---

[1] I here make use of these terms, *impression* and *idea*, in a sense different from what is usual, and I hope this liberty will be allowed me. Perhaps I rather restore the word idea to its original sense, from which Mr. Locke had perverted it, in making it stand for all our perceptions. By the term of impression, I would not be understood to express the manner in which our lively perceptions are produced in the soul, but merely the perceptions themselves; for which there is no particular name, either in the English or any other language that I know of.

resemblence betwixt our impressions and ideas in every other particular, except their degree of force and vivacity. The one seems to be, in a manner, the reflection of the other; so that all the perceptions of the mind are double, and appear both as impressions and ideas. When I shut my eyes, and think of my chamber, the ideas I form are exact representations of the impressions I felt; nor is there any circumstance of the one, which is not to be found in the other. In running over my other perceptions, I find still the same resemblance and representation. Ideas and impressions appear always to correspond to each other. This circumstance seems to me remarkable, and engages my attention for a moment.

Upon a more accurate survey I find I have been carried away too far by the first appearance, and that I must make use of the distinction of perceptions into *simple* and *complex*, to limit this general decision, *that all our ideas and impressions are resembling*. I observe that many of our complex ideas never had impressions that corresponded to them, and that many of our complex impressions never are exactly copied in ideas. I can imagine to myself such a city as the New Jerusalem, whose pavement is gold, and walls are rubies, though I never saw any such. I have seen Paris; but shall I affirm I can form such an idea of that city, as will perfectly represent all its streets and houses in their real and just proportions?

I perceive, therefore, that though there is, in general, a great resemblance betwixt our *complex* impressions and ideas, yet the rule is not universally true, that they are exact copies of each other. We may next consider, how the case stands with our *simple* perceptions. After the most accurate examination of which I am capable, I venture to affirm, that the rule here holds without any exception, and that every simple idea has a simple impression, which resembles it, and every simple impression a correspondent idea. That idea of red, which we form in the dark, and that impression which strikes our eyes in sunshine, differ only in degree, not in nature. That the case is the same with all our simple impressions and ideas, it is impossible to prove by a particular enumeration of them. Every one may satisfy himself in this point by running over as many as he pleases. But if any one should deny this universal resemblance, I know no way of convincing him, but by desiring him to show a simple impression that has not a correspondent idea, or a simple idea that has not a correspondent impression. If he does not answer this challenge, as it is certain he cannot, we may, from his silence and our own observation, establish our conclusion.

Thus we find, that all simple ideas and impressions resemble each other; and, as the complex are formed from them, we may affirm in general, that these two species of perception are exactly correspondent. Having discovered this relation, which requires no further examination, I am curious to find some other of their qualities. Let us consider, how they stand with regard to their existence, and which of the impressions and ideas are causes, and which effects.

The full examination of this question is the subject of the present treatise; and, therefore, we shall here content ourselves with establishing one general proposition, *That all our simple ideas in their first appearance, are derived from simple impressions, which are correspondent to them, and which they exactly represent.*

DIVISION OF THE SUBJECT

(Book I, Part I, Section 2)

Since it appears, that our simple impressions are prior to their correspondent ideas, and that the exceptions are very rare, method seems to require we should examine our impressions before we consider our ideas. Impressions may be divided into two kinds, those of *sensation*, and those of *reflection*. The first kind arises in the soul originally, from unknown causes. The second is derived, in a great measure, from our ideas, and that in the following order. An impression first strikes upon the senses, and makes us perceive heat or cold, thirst or hunger, pleasure or pain, of some kind or other. Of this impression there is a copy taken by the mind, which remains after the impression-ceases; and this we call an idea. This idea of pleasure or pain, when it returns upon the soul, produces the new impressions of desire and aversion, hope and fear, which may properly be called impressions of reflection, because derived from it. These again are copied by the memory and imagination, and become ideas: which, perhaps, in their turn, give rise to other impressions and ideas; so that the impressions of reflection are not only antecedent to their correspondent ideas, but posterior to those of sensation, and derived from them. The examination of our sensations belongs more to anatomists and natural philosophers than to moral; and, therefore, shall not at present be entered upon. And, as the impressions of reflection, viz., pasions, desires, and emotions, which principally deserve our attention, arise mostly from ideas, it will be necessary to reverse that method, which at first sight seems most natural; and, in order to explain the nature and principles of the human mind, give a particular account of ideas, before we proceed to impressions. For this reason, I have here chosen to begin with ideas.

OF THE IDEAS OF THE MEMORY AND IMAGINATION

(Book I, Part I, Section 3)

We find, by experience, that when any impression has been present with the mind, it again makes its appearance there as an idea; and this it may do after two different ways: either when, in its new appearance, it retains a considerable degree of its first vivacity, and is somewhat intermediate betwixt an impression and an idea; or when it entirely loses that vivacity, and is a perfect idea. The faculty by which we repeat our impressions in the first manner, is called the *memory*, and the other the *imagination*. It is evident, at first sight, that the ideas of the memory are much more lively and strong than those of the imagination, and that the former faculty paints its objects in more distinct colours than any which are employed by the latter. When we remember any past event, the idea of it flows in upon the mind in a forcible manner; whereas, in the imagination, the perception is faint and languid, and cannot, without difficulty, be preserved by the mind steady and uniform for any considerable time. Here, then, is a sensible difference betwixt one species of ideas and another. But of this more fully hereafter.[2]

---

[2]Part III, section 5.

There is another difference betwixt these two kinds of ideas, which is no less evident, namely, that though neither the ideas of the memory nor imagination, neither the lively nor faint ideas, can make their appearance in the mind, unless their correspondent impressions have gone before to prepare the way for them, yet the imagination is not restrained to the same order and form with the original impressions; while the memory is in a manner tied down in that respect, without any power of variation.

It is evident, that the memory preserves the original form in which its objects were presented, and that wherever we depart from it in recollecting anything, it proceeds from some defect or imperfection in that faculty. An historian may, perhaps, for the more convenient carrying on of his narration, relate an event before another to which it was in fact posterior; but then, he takes notice of this disorder, if he be exact; and, by that means, replaces the idea in its due position. It is the same case in our recollection of those places and persons, with which we were formerly acquainted. The chief exercise of the memory is not to preserve the simple ideas, but their order and position. In short, this principle is supported by such a number of common and vulgar phenomena, that we may spare ourselves the trouble of insisting on it any further.

The same evidence follows us in our second principle, *of the liberty of the imagination to transpose and change its ideas.* The fables we meet with in poems and romances put this entirely out of question. Nature there is totally confounded, and nothing mentioned but winged horses, fiery dragons, and monstrous giants. Nor will this liberty of the fancy appear strange, when we consider that all our ideas are copied from our impressions, and that there are not any two impressions which are perfectly inseparable. Not to mention, that this is an evident consequence of the division of ideas into simple and complex. Wherever the imagination perceives a difference among ideas, it can easily produce a separation.

OF THE CONNECTION OR ASSOCIATION OF IDEAS

(Book I, Part I, Section 4)

As all simple ideas may be separated by the imagination, and may be united again in what form it pleases, nothing would be more unaccountable than the operations of that faculty, were it not guided by some universal principles, which render it, in some measure, uniform with itself in all times and places. Were ideas entirely loose and unconnected, chance alone would join them; and it is impossible the same simple ideas should fall regularly into complex ones (as they commonly do), without some bond of union among them, some associating quality, by which one idea naturally introduces another. This uniting principle among ideas is not to be considered as an inseparable connection; for that has been already excluded from the imagination: nor yet are we to conclude that without it the mind cannot join two ideas; for nothing is more free than that faculty: but we are only to regard it as a gentle force, which commonly prevails, and is the cause why, among other things, languages so nearly correspond to each other; Nature, in a manner, pointing out to every one those simple ideas, which are most proper to be united into a complex one. The qualities, from which this association arises, and by which the mind is, after this manner, conveyed from one idea to another, are three, viz., *resemblance*, *contiguity* in time or place, and *cause* and *effect*.

I believe it will not be very necessary to prove, that these qualities produce an association among ideas, and, upon the appearance of one idea, naturally introduce another. It is plain, that, in the course of our thinking, and in the constant revolution of our ideas, our imagination runs easily from one idea to any other that *resembles* it, and that this quality alone is to the fancy a sufficient bond and association. It is likewise evident, that as the senses, in changing their objects, are necessitated to change them regularly, and take them as they lie *contiguous* to each other, the imagination must, by long custom, acquire the same method of thinking, and run along the parts of space and time in conceiving its objects. As to the connection that is made by the relation of *cause and effect*, we shall have occasion afterwards to examine it to the bottom, and therefore shall not at present insist upon it. It is sufficient to observe, that there is no relation, which produces a stronger connection in the fancy, and makes one idea more readily recall another, than the relation of cause and effect betwixt their objects.

That we may understand the full extent of these relations, we must consider, that two objects are connected together in the imagination, not only when the one is immediately resembling, contiguous to, or the cause of the other, but also when there is interposed betwixt them a third object, which bears to both of them any of these relations. This may be carried on to a great length; though, at the same time we may observe, that each remove considerably weakens the relation. Cousins in the fourth degree are connected by *causation*, if I may be allowed to use that term; but not so closely as brothers, much less as child and parent. In general, we may observe, that all the relations of blood depend upon cause and effect, and are esteemed near or remote, according to the number of connecting causes interposed betwixt the persons.

Of the three relations above mentioned, this of causation is the most extensive. Two objects may be considered as placed in this relation, as well when one is the cause of any of the actions or motions of the other, as when the former is the cause of the existence of the latter. For as that action or motion is nothing but the object itself, considered in a certain light, and as the object continues the same in all its different situations, it is easy to imagine how such an influence of objects upon one another may connect them in the imagination.

We may carry this further, and remark, not only that two objects are connected by the relation of cause and effect, when the one produces a motion or any action in the other, but also when it has a power of producing it. And this we may observe to be the source of all the relations of interest and duty, by which men influence each other in society, and are placed in the ties of government and subordination. A master is such a one as, by his situation, arising either from force or agreement, has a power of directing in certain particulars the actions of another, whom we call servant. A judge is one, who, in all disputed cases, can fix by his opinion the possession or property of anything betwixt any members of the society. When a person is possessed of any power, there is no more required to convert it into action, but the exertion of the will; and *that* in every case is considered as possible, and in many as probable; especially in the case of authority, where the obedience of the subject is a pleasure and advantage to the superior.

These are, therefore the principles of union or cohesion among our simple ideas, and in the imagination supply the place of that inseparable connection, by which they are united in our memory. Here is a kind of *attraction*, which in the mental world will be found to have as extraordinary effects as in the natural, and to show itself in as man and as various forms. Its effects are everywhere conspicuous; but, as to its causes, they are mostly unknown, and must be resolved into *original* qualities of human nature, which I pretend not to explain. Nothing is more requisite for a true philosopher, than to restrain the intemperate desire of searching into causes; and, having established any doctrine upon a sufficient number of experiments, rest contented with that, when he sees a further examination would lead him into obscure and uncertain speculations. In that case his inquiry would be much better employed in examining the effects than the causes of his principle. . . .

OF ABSTRACT IDEAS

(Book I, Part I, Section 7)

A very material question has been started concerning *abstract* or *general* ideas, *whether they be general or particular in the mind's conception of them*. A great philosopher[3] has disputed the received opinion in this particular, and has asserted, that all general ideas are nothing but particular ones annexed to a certain term, which gives them a more extensive signification, and makes them recall upon occasion other individuals, which are similar to them. As I look upon this to be one of the greatest and most valuable discoveries that has been made of late years in the republic of letters, I shall here endeavour to confirm it by some arguments, which I hope will put it beyond all doubt and controversy.

It is evident, that, in forming most of our general ideas, if not all of them, we abstract from every particular degree of quantity and quality, and that an object ceases not to be of any particular species on account of every small alternation in its extension, duration, and other properties. It may, therefore, be thought, that here is a plain dilemma, that decides concerning the nature of those abstract ideas, which have afforded so much speculation to philosophers. The abstract idea of a man represents men of all sizes and all qualities, which it is concluded it cannot do, but either by representing at once all possible sizes and all possible qualities, or by representing no particular one at all. Now, it having been esteemed absurd to defend the former proposition, as implying an infinite capacity in the mind, it has been commonly inferred in favour of the latter; and our abstract ideas have been supposed to represent no particular degree either of quantity or quality. But that this inference is erroneous, I shall endeavour to make appear, *first*, by proving, that it is utterly impossible to conceive any quantity or quality, without forming a precise notion of its degrees; and, *secondly*, by showing, that though the capacity of the mind be not infinite, yet we can at once form a notion of all possible degrees of quantity and quality, in such a manner at least, as, however imperfect, may serve all the purposes of reflection and conversation.

To begin with the first proposition, *that the mind cannot form any notion of quantity or quality without forming a precise notion of degrees of each*, we may

---

[3]Dr. Berkeley.

prove this by the three following arguments. First, we have observed, that whatever objects are different are distinguishable, and that whatever objects are distinguishable are separable by the thought and imagination. And we may here add, that these propositions are equally true in the *inverse*, and that whatever objects are separable are also distinguishable, and that whatever objects are distinguishable are also different. For how is it possible we can separate what is not distinguishable, or distinguish what is not different? In order, therefore, to know whether abstraction implies a separation, we need only consider it in this view, and examine, whether all the circumstances, which we abstract from in our general ideas, be such as are distinguishable and different from those, which we retain as essential parts of them. But it is evident at first sight, that the precise length of a line is not different nor distinguishable from the line itself; nor the precise degree of any quality from the quality. These ideas, therefore, admit no more of separation than they do of distinction and difference. They are, consequently, conjoined with each other in the conception; and the general idea of a line, notwithstanding all our abstractions and refinements, has, in its appearance in the mind, a precise degree of quantity and quality; however it may be made to represent others which have different degrees of both.

Secondly, it is confessed, that no object can appear to the senses; or in other words, that no impression can become present to the mind, without being determined in its degrees both of quantity and quality. The confusion, in which impressions are sometimes involved, proceeds only from their faintness and unsteadiness, not from any capacity in the mind to receive any impression, which in its real existence has no particular degree nor proportion. That is a contradiction in terms, viz., that it is possible for the same thing both to be and not to be.

Now, since all ideas are derived from impressions, and are nothing but copies and representations of them, whatever is true of the one must be acknowledged concerning the other. Impressions and ideas differ only in their strength and vivacity. The foregoing conclusion is not founded on any particular degree of vivacity. It cannot, therefore, be affected by any variation in that particular. An idea is a weaker impression; and, as a strong impression must necessarily have a determinate quantity and quality, the case must be the same with its copy or representative.

Thirdly, it is a principle generally received in philosophy, that everything in nature is individual, and that it is utterly absurd to suppose a triangle really existent, which has no precise proportion of sides and angles. If this, therefore, be absurd in *fact and reality*, it must also be absurd *in idea*; since nothing of which we can form a clear and distinct idea is absurd and impossible. But to form the idea of an object, and to form an idea simply, is the same thing; the reference of the idea to an object being an extraneous denomination, of which in itself it bears no mark or character. Now, as it is impossible to form an idea of an object that is possessed of quantity and quality, and yet is possessed of no precise degree of either, it follows, that there is an equal impossibility of forming an idea, that is not limited and confined in both these particulars. Abstract ideas are, therefore, in themselves individual, however they may become general in their representation. The image in the mind is only that of a particular object, though the application of it in our reasoning be the same as if it were universal.

This application of ideas, beyond their nature, proceeds from our collecting all their possible degrees of quantity and quality in such an imperfect manner as may serve the purposes of life, which is the second proposition I proposed to explain. When we have found a resemblance[4] among several objects, that often occur to us, we apply the same name to all of them, whatever differences we may observe in the degrees of their quantity and quality, and whatever other differences may appear among them. After we have acquired a custom of this kind, the hearing of that name revives the idea of one of these objects, and makes the imagination conceive it with all its particular circumstances and proportions. But as the same word is supposed to have been frequently applied to other individuals, that are different in many respects from that idea, which is immediately present to the mind; the word not being able to revive the idea of all these individuals, only touches the soul, if I may be allowed so to speak, and revives that custom, which we have acquired by surveying them. They are not really and in fact present to the mind, but only in power; nor do we draw them all out distinctly in the imagination, but keep ourselves in a readiness to survey any of them, as we may be prompted by a present design or necessity. The word raises up an individual idea, along with a certain custom, and that custom produces any other individual one, for which we may have occasion. But as the production of all the ideas, to which the name may be applied, is in the most cases impossible, we abridge that work by a more partial consideration, and find but few inconveniences to arise in our reasoning from that abridgment.

For this is one of the most extraordinary circumstances in the present affair, that after the mind has produced an individual idea, upon which we reason, the attendant custom, revived by the general or abstract term, readily suggests any other individual, if by chance we form any reasoning that agrees not with it. Thus, should we mention the word triangle, and form the idea of a particular equilateral one to correspond to it, and should we afterwards assert, *that the three angles of a triangle are equal to each other*, the other individuals of a scalenum and isosceles, which we overlooked at first, immediately crowd in upon us, and make us perceive the falsehood of this proposition, though it be true with relation to that idea which we had formed. If the mind suggests not always these ideas upon occasion, it proceeds from some imperfection in its faculties; and such a one as is often the source of false reasoning and sophistry. But this is principally the case with those ideas which are abstruse and com-

---

[4]It is evident, that even different simple ideas may have a similarity or resemblance to each other; nor is it necessary, that the point or circumstance of resemblance should be distinct or separable from that in which they differ. *Blue* and *green* are different simple ideas, but are more resembling than *blue* and *scarlet*; though their perfect simplicity excludes all possibility of separation or distinction. It is the same case with particular sounds, and tastes, and smells. These admit of infinite resemblances upon the general appearance and comparison, without having any common circumstance the same. And of this we may be certain, even from the very abstract terms *simple idea*. They comprehend all simple ideas under them. These resemble each other in their simplicity. And yet from their very nature, which excludes all composition, this circumstance, in which they resemble, is not distinguishable or separate from the rest. It is the same case with all the degrees in any quality. They are all resembling, and yet the quality, in any individual, is not distinct from the degree.

pounded. On other occasions the custom is more entire, and it is seldom that we run into such errors.

Nay so entire is the custom, that the very same idea may be annexed to several different words, and may be employed in different reasonings, without any danger of mistake. Thus the idea of an equilateral triangle of an inch perpendicular may serve us in talking of a figure, of a rectilineal figure, of a regular figure, of a triangle, and of an equilateral triangle. All these terms, therefore, are in this case attended with the same idea; but as they are wont to be applied in a greater or lesser compass, they excite their particular habits, and thereby keep the mind in a readiness to observe, that no conclusion be formed contrary to any ideas, which are usually comprised under them.

Before those habits have become entirely perfect, perhaps the mind may not be content with forming the idea of only one individual, but may run over several, in order to make itself comprehend its own meaning, and the compass of that collection, which it intends to express by the general term. That we may fix the meaning of the word, figure, we may revolve in our mind the ideas of circles, squares, parallelograms, triangles of different sizes and proportions, and may not rest on one image or idea. However this may be, it is certain *that we form the idea of individuals whenever we use any general term; that we seldom or never can exhaust these individuals; and that those which remain, are only represented by means of that habit by which we recall them, whenever any present occasion requires it*. This then is the nature of our abstract ideas and general terms; and it is after this manner we account for the foregoing paradox, *that some ideas are particular in their nature, but general in their representation*. A particular idea becomes general by being annexed to a general term; that is, to a term which, from a customary conjunction, has a relation to many other particular ideas, and readily recalls them in the imagination.

The only difficulty that can remain on this subject, must be with regard to that custom, which so readily recalls every particular idea for which we may have occasion, and is excited by any word or sound to which we commonly annex it. The most proper method, in my opinion, of giving a satisfactory explication of this act of the mind, is by producing other instances which are analogous to it, and other principles which facilitate its operation. To explain the ultimate causes of our mental actions is impossible. It is sufficient if we can give any satisfactory account of them from experience and analogy. . . .

Before I leave this subject, I shall employ the same principles to explain that *distinction of reason*, which is so much talked of, and is so little understood in the schools. Of this kind is the distinction betwixt figure and the body figured; motion and the body moved. The difficulty of explaining this distinction arises from the principle above explained, *that all ideas which are different are separable*. For it follows from thence, that if the figure be different from the body, their ideas must be separable as well as distinguishable; if they be not different, their ideas can neither be separable nor distinguishable. What then is meant by a distinction of reason, since it implies neither a difference nor separation?

To remove this difficulty, we must have recourse to the foregoing explication of abstract ideas. It is certain that the mind would never have dreamed of distinguishing a figure from the body figured, as being in reality neither distinguishable, nor different, nor separable, did it not observe, that even in this simplicity there might be contained many different resemblances and relations. Thus, when a globe of white marble is presented, we receive only the impression of a white colour disposed in a certain form, nor are we able to separate and distinguish the colour from the form. But observing afterwards a globe of black marble and a cube of white, and comparing them with our former object, we find two separate resemblances, in what formerly seemed, and really is, perfectly inseparable. After a little more practice of this kind, we begin to distinguish the figure from the colour by a *distinction of reason*; that is, we consider the figure and colour together, since they are, in effect, the same and undistinguishable; but still view them in different aspects, according to the resemblances of which they are susceptible. When we would consider only the figure of the globe of white marble, we form in reality an idea both of the figure and colour, but tacitly carry our eye to its resemblance with the globe of black marble: and in the same manner, when we would consider its colour only, we turn our view to its resemblance with the cube of white marble. By this means we accompany our ideas with a kind of reflection, of which custom renders us, in a great measure, insensible. A person who desires us to consider the figure of a globe of white marble without thinking on its colour, desires an impossibility; but his meaning is, that we should consider the colour and figure together, but still keep in our eye the resemblance to the globe of black marble, or that to any other globe of whatever colour or substance. . . .

OF THE IDEAS OF EXISTENCE, AND OF EXTERNAL EXISTENCE

(Book I, Part II, Section 6)

It may not be amiss, before we leave this subject, to explain the ideas of *existence* and of *external existence*; which have their difficulties, as well as the ideas of space and time. By this means we shall be the better prepared for the examination of knowledge and probability, when we understand perfectly all those particular ideas, which may enter into our reasoning.

There is no impression nor idea of any kind, of which we have any consciousness or memory, that is not conceived as existent; and it is evident that, from this consciousness, the most perfect idea and assurance of *being* is derived. From hence we may form a dilemma, the most clear and conclusive that can be imagined, viz., that since we never remember any idea or impression without attributing existence to it, the idea of existence must either be derived from a distinct impression, conjoined with every perception or object of our thought, or must be the very same with the idea of the perception or object.

As this dilemma is an evident consequence of the principle, that every idea arises from a similar impression, so our decision betwixt the propositions of the dilemma is no more doubtful. So far from there being any distinct impression attending every impression and every idea, that I do not think there are any two distinct impressions which are inseparably conjoined. Though certain sensations may at one time be united, we quickly find they admit of a separation, and may be presented apart. And thus, though every impression and idea we remember be considered as existent, the idea of existence is not derived from any particular impression.

The idea of existence, then, is the very same with the idea of what we conceive to be existent. To reflect on anything simply, and to reflect on it as existent, are nothing different from each other. That idea, when conjoined with the idea of any object, makes no addition to it. Whatever we conceive, we conceive to be existent. Any idea we please to form is the idea of a being; and the idea of a being is any idea we please to form.

Whoever opposes this, must necessarily point out that distinct impression, from which the idea of entity is derived, and must prove, that this impression is inseparable from every perception we believe to be existent. This we may without hesitation conclude to be impossible.

Our foregoing reasoning[5] concerning the *distinction* of ideas, without any real *difference*, will not here serve us in any stead. That kind of distinction is founded on the different resemblances, which the same simple idea may have to several different ideas. But no object can be presented resembling some object with respect to its existence, and different from others in the same particular; since every object that is presented, must necessarily be existent.

A like reasoning will account for the idea of *external existence*. We may observe, that it is universally allowed by philosophers, and is besides pretty obvious of itself, that nothing is ever really present with the mind but its perceptions or impressions and ideas, and that external objects become known to us only by those perceptions they occasion. To hate, to love, to think, to feel, to see; all this is nothing but to perceive.

Now since nothing is ever present to the mind but perceptions, and since all ideas are derived from something antecedently present to the mind; it follows, that it is impossible for us so much as to conceive or form an idea of anything specifically different from ideas and impressions. Let us fix our attention out of ourselves as much as possible; let us chase our imagination to the heavens, or to the utmost limits of the universe; we never really advance a step beyond ourselves, nor can conceive any kind of existence, but those perceptions, which have appeared in that narrow compass. This is the universe of the imagination, nor have we any idea but what is there produced.

The furthest we can go towards a conception of external objects, when supposed *specifically* different from our perceptions, is to form a relative idea of them, without pretending to comprehend the related objects. Generally speaking, we do not suppose them specifically different; but only attribute to them different relations, connections, and durations. But of this more fully hereafter.[6]

1. IMPRESSIONS AND IDEAS

The main essentials of the position laid down by Locke and developed by Berkeley are taken over intact by Hume, who makes one addition of his own. Locke's classification of ideas into simple and complex is retained, and likewise the distinction between ideas of sensation and those of reflection. But Hume adds a further distinction

---

[5]Part I, section 7.
[6]Part IV, section 2.

between impressions and ideas, impressions being the immediately apprehended presentations, and ideas the "paler copies" of these revived in memory and imagination and in all forms of thinking. Impressions are, as it were, consciousness of the first degree and ideas consciousness of the second degree, being ideas of the impressions. Between them they constitute all the materials of knowledge — "all the percepts of the human mind." The only difference between impressions and the corresponding ideas is one of force and liveliness; the impressions are more vivid and forceful, the ideas paler and less distinct.

But Hume is in no danger of falling into Locke's error of referring our ideas to archetypes beyond the reach of the mind. The causes of our impressions are, he says, unknown, and we shall find him denying emphatically any possible knowledge of external existence (*Treatise*, Book I, Part II, section 6, and Part IV, section 2).

Without impressions no ideas can exist and every idea derives from some original impression. In order to establish that we really do have some particular idea, therefore, we must be able to trace it back to an original impression. This principle enables Hume to dispose of several notions that he considers spurious; for example, the idea of substance (alleged by Locke) is one of which there is no impression, hence we have no idea of it. A substance is nothing but a collection of simple ideas to which we apply a particular name. Similarly, abstract ideas are dispensed with, due credit and admiration being given to Berkeley for disposing of them, while Hume offers additional reasons as confirmation of his teaching, and further explanation of how particular words come to be given a general reference.

2. NOMINALISM

In this last connection Hume produces the typical and only consistent theory of universals open to strict empiricism. Locke had asserted that the only source of knowledge was ideas, all of which were particular existences; but he had wrestled with the problem of universal concepts by trying to reduce them to simple ideas of the general character of a number or class of objects having something in common; or again by alleging the capacity of the mind to separate from a complex idea certain simples usually associated, each of which might be common to several complexes. Thus, of a number of colored objects, one color may be common to one subgroup and one shape to another. Some may be red (but variously shaped); some may be triangular (but variously colored). So we abstract the simple idea of the color and hold it as common to many things, or of the shape, as the case may be. But when the common property is simply shape (to take one possible example) what idea do we have which is a shape but not specially triangular, or square, or circular, or anything in particular? Locke tried to maintain the existence of such abstract ideas, but in doing so he was merely indulging his propensity for inconsistency. Hence Berkeley would have none of them and denied that they were possible. He substitutes for them particular ideas which serve as signs for the members of a group of similars. So we might define redness as the color of all things which are similar in hue to a tomato.

Hume goes one step further. He argues that, just as what can be distinguished can be separated, so what cannot be distinguished cannot be separated and therefore must be one. Shape, size, and color cannot be separated and so cannot really be distinguished. They are united in one idea and we can have no idea of shape which is not some definite shape, has not some definite size, and is not in some way colored. We can, however, make what Hume calls distinctions of reason, by noticing that one single object has different *resemblances* to other objects. For example, a block of marble may be white and square and so resemble other white things in one way and other square things in another. So we may give names to these resemblances (or, as Hume calls them, general characters). Then, when we use the name, the mind has a propensity to call up any idea among those which have the resembling quality; and if perchance we make a statement about the general character which is not true of all the objects sharing it, our minds readily recall the contrary cases and so enable us to correct the error.

On this view there are no universal ideas, only names designating general characters, or resemblances between members of a group of particular objects. This doctrine is known as nominalism, and it suffers from the difficulty that resemblance itself is the name for a general character, about which it would not be easy to give a similar account. For one can hardly say that resemblance applies to all such objects as resemble one another in the respect that they are alike (or resemble one another). This would be a flagrantly and a viciously circular definition. As Bertrand Russell points out,[7] there must be at least one universal, and that is resemblance. Again, Hume simply accepts, as a fact, the propensity of the mind to recall the appropriate particulars as required when the general name is applied. But how the mind succeeds in doing this appropriately he does not investigate. He says it is a matter of custom, but how is the habit acquired, unless the mind has

[7]*The Problems of Philosophy*, Chapter 9.

some capacity to recognize a universal whenever it is exemplified, an idea of something which really is in some way common to many particulars, yet not itself specified as a particular? What else, after all, is a resemblance? All triangles resemble one another in being triangular and no other property is common to them *all*. Yet so far as it is common to all, it is not scalene, or equilateral, or isoceles, or right-angled, or acute-angled, or obtuse. It is not particular but it is universal. We shall see later that Hume's refusal to admit this is really fatal to his whole theory of experience.

3. TWO KINDS OF KNOWLEDGE

According to Hume there are two (and only two) kinds of knowledge: (a) knowledge about matters of fact, and (b) knowledge of the relations between immediately presented ideas and impressions. This distinction is derived directly from Locke.

The second variety reveals to us relations of resemblance, contrariety, degree of quality, and proportion in quantity and number. These we can directly apprehend or can deduce by demonstrative reasoning from what we do directly apprehend, so that this kind of knowledge may be intuitive and certain, though we shall find later that its certainty is subject to such severe qualification as to make it far from reliable. Even so, its scope is very restricted and extends no further than mathematics and not even to all of that, but only to arithmetic and algebra, for geometry Hume regards as an approximate science, alleging that none of our experienced ideas of space exactly correspond to its theorems, as we have no precise criterion of spatial equality. This we may remember was one of the reasons which persuaded Plato of the existence of nonsensuous ideas — an argument which Hume could never accept, for he maintains that we can have no ideas which are not derived from, and are not exact resemblances of, impressions; and all our impressions of spatial quantity are approximate and limited in precision. Exact comparison between them would depend on our comparing the number of *minima sensibilia* (smallest possible sensible parts) which they contain, which we neither can nor ever do.[8]

The first kind of knowledge — that of matters of fact — goes beyond what is immediately presented and infers to absent things and events. We can make such inferences only by using the relation of cause and effect, from a knowledge of which we reason from a presented idea (or

---

[8] See *Treatise of Human Nature*, Book I, Part II.

impression) to others which either have caused it or are the effects which we expect to follow it.

All such factual knowledge is only probable, and most of our knowledge, Hume thought, was of this kind.[9] He spends much of his time, therefore, discussing the nature of probability, the belief founded upon it, and the relations between ideas which it involves, and he finds only one such relation of fundamental importance — that between cause and effect.

4. PSYCHOLOGICAL ATOMISM

The cornerstone of Hume's theory of knowledge is the principle which he lays down that "whatever objects are different are distinguishable, and whatever objects are distinguishable are separable by the thought and imagination." Indeed, there are no two impressions, he declares, which are perfectly inseparable. He goes so far as to say that what are separable in thought are separate existences,[10] which would follow naturally from Berkeley's assertion (following Locke) that every idea is a particular existence.

Our percepts thus become separate atoms of experience, whether they be impressions or ideas copied from them. Consequently, associations between them turn out to be contingent, and connections entirely loose. This analysis of experience into ultimate separable atomic presentations is what may be called psychological atomism.

The main, if not the only, principles of linkage between ideas and impressions which Hume offers are those of association of ideas: resemblance, contiguity, and causality. Ideas and impressions, he says, which have once, or several times, stood in these relations are apt to recall one another in the mind, so that when one of them is experienced the other tends to be repeated with it. This is the source of our complex ideas, which are simple ideas linked together as the result of this kind of association.

It will be observed that Hume tolerates no form of experience other than sensory impressions and mental imagery either of memory or imagination. Concepts, pure intelligibles, such as Plato and Descartes thought so important, he throws out as pure fictions. Either particular images or mere words are made to replace them and perform their function in knowledge.

---

[9]Later it turns out that all our knowledge is at best probable. See pages 397–398 below.
[10]Cf. Appendix to the *Treatise of Human Nature*.

From these foundations Hume elaborates two main doctrines the effect of which is to reduce empiricism to scepticism by undermining the distinction between scientific knowledge, on the one hand, and prejudice or sentiment on the other. These two doctrines are his analysis of cause and effect, with the accompanying theory of necessary connection, and his account of belief.

CHAPTER 25

Cause and Effect

A Treatise of Human Nature

OF KNOWLEDGE

(Book I, Part III, Section 1)

There are seven different kinds of philosophical relation,[1] viz., *resemblance, identity, relations of time and place, proportion in quantity or number, degrees in any quality, contrariety, and causation.* These relations may be divided into two classes; into such as depend entirely on the ideas, which we compare together, and such as may be changed without any change in the ideas. It is from the idea of a triangle, that we discover the relation of equality, which its three angles bear to two right ones; and this relation is invariable, as long as our idea remains the same. On the contrary, the relations of *contiguity* and *distance* betwixt two objects may be changed merely by an alternation of their place, without any change on the objects themselves or on their ideas, and the place depends on a hundred different accidents, which cannot be foreseen by the mind. It is the same case with *identity* and *causation.* Two objects, though perfectly resembling each other, and even appearing in the same place at different times, may be numerically different: and as the power, by which one object produces another, is never discoverable merely from their idea, it is

---

[1] Part I, section 5.

372

evident *cause* and *effect* are relations, of which we receive information from experience, and not from any abstract reasoning or reflection. There is no single phenomenon, even the most simple, which can be accounted for from the qualities of the objects, as they appear to us; or which we could foresee without the help of our memory and experience.

It appears therefore that of these seven philosophical relations, there remain only four, which depending solely upon ideas, can be the objects of knowledge and certainty. These four are *resemblance, contrariety, degrees in quality, and proportions in quantity or number*. Three of these relations are discoverable at first sight, and fall more properly under the province of intuition than demonstration. When any objects *resemble* each other, the resemblance will at first strike the eye, or rather the mind; and seldom requires a second examination. The case is the same with *contrariety*, and with the *degrees* of any *quality*. No one can once doubt but existence and non-existence destroy each other, and are perfectly incompatible and contrary. And though it be impossible to judge exactly of the degrees of any quality, such as colour, taste, heat, cold, when the difference betwixt them is very small; yet it is easy to decide, that any of them is superior or inferior to another, when their difference is considerable. And this decision we always pronounce at first sight, without any inquiry or reasoning.

We might proceed, after the same manner, in fixing the *proportions* of *quantity* or *number*, and might at one view observe a superiority, or inferiority betwixt any numbers, or figures; especially where the difference is very great and remarkable. As to equality or any exact proportion, we can only guess at it from a single consideration; except in very short numbers, or very limited portions of extension; which are comprehended in an instant, and where we perceive an impossibility of falling into any considerable error. In all other cases we must settle the proportions with some liberty, or proceed in a more *artificial* manner.

I already observed, that geometry, or the *art* by which we fix the proportions of figures; though it much excels both in universality and exactness, the loose judgments of the senses and imagination; yet never attains a perfect precision and exactness. Its first principles are still drawn from the general appearance of the objects; and that appearance can never afford us any security, when we examine the prodigious minuteness of which nature is susceptible. Our ideas seem to give a perfect assurance, that no two right lines can have a common segment; but if we consider these ideas, we shall find, that they always suppose a sensible inclination of the two lines, and that where the angle they form is extremely small, we have no standard of a right line so precise as to assure us of the truth of this proposition. It is the same case with most of the primary decisions of the mathematics.

There remain therefore algebra and arithmetic as the only sciences, in which we can carry on a chain of reasoning to any degree of intricacy, and yet preserve a perfect exactness and certainty. We are possessed of a precise standard, by which we can judge of the equality and proportion of numbers; and according as they correspond or not to that standard, we determine their relations, without any possibility of error. When two numbers are so combined, as that the one has always an unit answering to every unit of the other, we pronounce them equal; and it is for want of such a standard of equality in extension, that geometry can scarce be esteemed a perfect and infallible science.

But here it may not be amiss to obviate a difficulty, which may arise from my asserting, that though geometry falls short of that perfect precision and certainty, which are peculiar to arithmetic and algebra, yet it excels the imperfect judgments of our senses and imagination. The reason why I impute any defect to geometry is, because its original and fundamental principles are derived merely from appearances; and it may perhaps be imagined, that this defect must always attend it, and keep it from ever reaching a greater exactness in the comparison of objects or ideas, than what our eye or imagination alone is able to attain. I own that this defect so far attends it, as to keep it from ever aspiring to a full certainty: but since these fundamental principles depend on the easiest and least deceitful appearances, they bestow on their consequences a degree of exactness, of which these consequences are singly incapable. It is impossible for the eye to determine the angles of a chiliagon to be equal to 1996 right angles, or make any conjecture, that approaches this proportion; but when it determines, that right lines cannot concur; that we cannot draw more than one right line between two given points; its mistakes can never be of any consequence. And this is the nature and use of geometry, to run us up to such appearances, as, by reason of their simplicity, cannot lead us into any considerable error.

I shall here take occasion to propose a second observation concerning our demonstrative reasonings, which is suggested by the same object of the mathematics. It is usual with mathematicians to pretend, that those ideas, which are their objects, are of so refined and spiritual a nature, that they fall not under the conception of the fancy, but must be comprehended by a pure and intellectual view, of which the superior faculties of the soul are alone capable. The same notion runs through most parts of philosophy, and is principally made use of to explain our abstract ideas, and to show how we can form an idea of a triangle, for instance, which shall neither be an isosceles nor scalenum, nor be confined to any particular length and proportion of sides. It is easy to see why philosophers are so fond of this notion of some spiritual and refined perceptions; since by that means they cover many of their absurdities, and may refuse to submit to the decisions of clear ideas, by appealing to such as are obscure and uncertain. But to destroy this artifice, we need but reflect on that principle so oft insisted on, *that all our ideas are copied from our impressions.* For from thence we may immediately conclude, that since all impressions are clear and precise, the ideas, which are copied from them, must be of the same nature, and can never, but from our fault, contain anything so dark and intricate. An idea is by its very nature weaker and fainter than an impression; but being in every other respect the same, cannot imply any very great mystery. If its weakness render it obscure, it is our business to remedy that defect, as much as possible, by keeping the idea steady and precise; and till we have done so, it is in vain to pretend to reasoning and philosophy.

OF PROBABILITY, AND OF THE IDEA OF CAUSE AND EFFECT

(Book I, Part III, Section 2)

This is all I think necessary to observe concerning those four relations, which are the foundation of science; but as to the other three, which depend not upon the idea, and may be absent or present even while *that* remains the same, it will be proper to explain them more particularly. These three relations are *identity, the situations in time and place, and causation.*

All kinds of reasoning consist in nothing but a *comparison*, and a discovery of those relations, either constant or inconstant, which two or more objects bear to each other. This comparison we may make, either when both the objects are present to the senses, or when neither of them is present, or when only one. When both the objects are present to the senses along with the relation, we call *this* perception rather than reasoning; nor is there in this case any exercise of the thought, or any action, properly speaking, but a mere passive admission of the impressions through the organs of sensation. According to this way of thinking, we ought not to receive as reasoning any of the observations we may make concerning *identity* and the *relations of time* and *place*; since in none of them can the mind can go beyond what is immediately present to the senses, either to discover the real existence or the relations of objects. It is only *causation*, which produces such a connection, as to give us assurance from the existence or action of one object, that it was followed or preceded by any other exist-ence or action; nor can the other two relations ever be made use of in reason-ing, except so far as they either affect or are affected by it. There is nothing in any objects to persuade us, that they are either always *remote* or always *contiguous*; and when from experience and observation we discover, that their relation in this particular is in invariable, we always conclude there is some secret *cause* which separates or unites them. The same reasoning ex-tends to *identity*. We readily suppose an object may continue individually the same, though several times absent from and present to the senses; and ascribe to it an identity, notwithstanding the interruption of the perception, whenever we conclude, that if we had kept our eye or hand constantly upon it, it would have conveyed an invariable and uninterrupted perception. But this conclusion beyond the impressions of our senses can be founded only on the connection of *cause and effect*; nor can we otherwise have any security that the object is not changed upon us, however much the new object may resemble that which was formerly present to the senses. Whenever we discover such a perfect resem-blance, we consider whether it be common in that species of objects; whether possibly or probably any cause could operate in producing the change and resemblance; and according as we determine concerning these causes and effects, we form our judgment concerning the identity of the object.

Here then it appears, that of those three relations, which depend not upon the mere ideas, the only one that can be traced beyond our senses, and informs us of existences and objects, which we do not see or feel, is *causation*. This relation therefore we shall endeavour to explain fully before we leave the sub-ject of the understanding.

To begin regularly, we must consider the idea of *causation*, and see from what origin it is derived. It is impossible to reason justly, without understanding perfectly the idea concerning which we reason; and it is impossible perfectly to understand any idea, without tracing it up to its origin, and examining that primary impression, from which it arises. The examination of the impression bestows a clearness on the idea; and the examination of the idea bestows a like clearness on all our reasoning.

Let us therefore cast our eye on any two objects, which we call cause and effect, and turn them on all sides, in order to find that impression, which produces an idea of such prodigious consequence. At first sight I perceive, that I must not search for it in any of the particular *qualities* of the objects; since, whichever of these qualities I pitch on, I find some object that is not possessed of it, and yet falls under the denomination of cause or effect. And indeed there is nothing existent, either externally or internally, which is not to be considered either as a cause or an effect; though it is plain there is no one quality which universally belongs to all beings, and gives them a title to that denomination.

The idea then of causation must be derived from some *relation* among objects; and that relation we must now endeavour to discover. I find in the first place, that whatever objects are considered as causes or effects, are *contiguous*; and that nothing can operate in a time or place, which is ever so little removed from those of its existence. Though distant objects may sometimes seem productive of each other, they are commonly found upon examination to be linked by a chain of causes, which are contiguous among themselves, and to the distant objects; and when in any particular instance we cannot discover this connection, we still presume it to exist. We may therefore consider the relation of *contiguity* as essential to that of causation; at least may suppose it such, according to the general opinion, till we can find a more proper occasion[2] to clear up this matter, by examining what objects are or are not susceptible of juxtaposition and conjunction.

The second relation I shall observe as essential to causes and effects, is not so universally acknowledged, but is liable to some controversy. It is that of *priority* of time in the cause before the effect. Some pretend that it is not absolutely necessary, a cause should precede its effect; but that any object or action, in the very first moment of its existence, may exert its productive quality, and give rise to another object or action, perfectly contemporary with itself. But beside that experience in most instances seems to contradict this opinion, we may establish the relation of priority by a kind of inference or reasoning. It is an established maxim, both in natural and moral philosophy, that an object which exists for any time in its full perfection without producing another, is not its sole cause; but is assisted by some other principle which pushes it from its state of inactivity, and makes it exert that energy, of which it was secretly possessed. Now if any cause may be perfectly contemporary with its effect, it is certain, according to this maxim, that they must all of them be so; since any one of them, which retards its operation for a single moment, exerts not itself at that very individual time, in which it might have operated; and therefore is no proper cause. The consequence of this would be no less than the destruction of that succession of causes, which we observe in the world; and indeed the utter annihilation of time. For if one cause were contemporary with its effect, and this effect with *its* effect, and so on, it is plain there would be no such thing as succession, and all objects must be coexistent.

If this argument appear satisfactory, it is well. If not, I beg the reader to allow me the same liberty, which I have used in the preceding case, of supposing it such. For he shall find, that the affair is of no great importance.

Having thus discovered or supposed the two relations of *contiguity* and *succession* to be essential to causes and effects, I find I am stopped short, and can proceed no further in considering any single instance of cause and effect. Motion in one body is regarded upon impulse as the cause of motion in another.

---

[2]Part IV, section 5.

When we consider these objects with the utmost attention, we find only that the one body approaches the other; and that the motion of it precedes that of the other, but without any sensible interval. It is in vain to rack ourselves with *further* thought and reflection upon this subject. We can go no *further* in considering this particular instance.

Should any one leave this instance, and pretend to define a cause, by saying it is something productive of another, it is evident he would say nothing. For what does he mean by *production*? Can he give any definition of it, that will not be the same with that of causation? If he can, I desire it may be produced. If he cannot, he here runs in a circle, and gives a synonymous term instead of a definition.

Shall we then rest contented with these two relations of contiguity and succession, as affording a complete idea of causation? By no means. An object may be contiguous and prior to another, without being considered as its cause. There is a *necessary connection* to be taken into consideration; and that relation is of much greater importance, than any of the other two above mentioned.

Here again I turn the object on all sides, in order to discover the nature of this necessary connection, and find the impression, or impressions, from which its idea may be derived. When I cast my eye on the *known qualities* of objects, I immediately discover that the relation of cause and effect depends not in the least on *them*. When I consider their *relations*, I can find none but those of contiguity and succession; which I have already regarded as imperfect and unsatisfactory. Shall the despair of success make me assert, that I am here possessed of an idea, which is not preceded by any similar impression? This would be too strong a proof of levity and inconstancy; since the contrary principle has been already so firmly established, as to admit of no further doubt; at least, till we have more fully examined the present difficulty.

We must therefore proceed like those who, being in search of anything that lies concealed from them, and not finding it in the place they expected, beat about all the neighbouring fields, without any certain view or design, in hopes their good fortune will at last guide them to what they search for. It is necessary for us to leave the direct survey of this question concerning the nature of that *necessary connection*, which enters into our idea of cause and effect; and endeavour to find some other questions, the examination of which will perhaps afford a hint, that may serve to clear up the present difficulty. Of these questions there occur two, which I shall proceed to examine, viz.,

First, for what reason we pronounce it *necessary*, that everything whose existence has a beginning, should also have a cause?

Secondly, why we conclude, that such particular causes must *necessarily* have such particular effects; and what is the nature of that *inference* we draw from the one to the other, and of the *belief* we repose in it?

I shall only observe before I proceed any further, that though the ideas of cause and effect be derived from the impressions of reflection as well as from those of sensation, yet for brevity's sake, I commonly mention only the latter as the origin of these ideas; though I desire that, whatsoever I say of them, may also extend to the former. Passions are connected with their objects and with one another; no less than external bodies are connected together. The same relation then of cause and effect, which belongs to one, must be common to all of them. . . .

OF THE INFERENCE FROM THE IMPRESSION TO THE IDEA

(Book I, Part III, Section 6)

It is easy to observe, that in tracing this relation, the inference we draw from cause to effect, is not derived merely from a survey of these particular objects, and from such a penetration into their essences as may discover the dependence of the one upon the other. There is no object which implies the existence of any other, if we consider these objects in themselves, and never look beyond the ideas which we form of them. Such an inference would amount to knowledge, and would imply the absolute contradiction and impossibility of conceiving anything different. But as all distinct ideas are separable, it is evident there can be no impossibility of that kind. When we pass from a present impression to the idea of any object, we might possibly have separated the idea from the impression, and have substituted any other idea in its room.

It is therefore by *experience* only that we can infer the existence of one object from that of another. The nature of experience is this. We remember to have had frequent instances of the existence of one species of objects; and also remember, that the individuals of another species of objects have always attended them, and have existed in a regular order of contiguity and succession with regard to them. Thus we remember to have seen that species of object we call *flame*, and to have felt that species of sensation we call *heat*. We likewise call to mind their constant conjunction in all past instances. Without any further ceremony, we call the one *cause*, and the other *effect*, and infer the existence of the one from that of the other. In all those instances from which we learn the conjunction of particular causes and effects, both the causes and effects have been perceived by the senses, and are remembered: but in all cases, wherein we reason concerning them, there is only one perceived or remembered, and the other is supplied in conformity to our past experience.

Thus, in advancing, we have insensibly discovered a new relation betwixt cause and effect when we least expected it, and were entirely employed upon another subject. This relation is their *constant conjunction*. Contiguity and succession are not sufficient to make us pronounce any two objects to be cause and effect, unless we perceive that these two relations are preserved in several instances. We may now see the advantage of quitting the direct survey of this relation, in order to discover the nature of that *necessary connection* which makes so essential a part of it. There are hopes, that by this means we may at last arrive at our proposed end; though, to tell the truth, this new-discovered relation of a constant conjunction seems to advance us but very little in our way. For it implies no more than this, that like objects have always been placed in like relations of contiguity and succession; and it seems evident, at least at first sight, that by this means we can never discover any new idea, and can only multiply, but not enlarge, the objects of our mind. It may be thought, that what we learn not from one object, we can never learn from a hundred, which are all of the same kind, and are perfectly resembling in every circumstance. As our senses show us in one instance two bodies, or motions, or qualities, in certain relations of succession and contiguity, so our memory presents us only with a multitude of instances wherein we always find like bodies, motions, or qualities, in like relations. From the mere repetition of any past impression, even to infinity, there never will arise any new original idea, such as that of a necessary connection; and the number of impressions has in this case no more effect than if we confined ourselves to one only. But though this reasoning seems just and obvious, yet, as it would be folly to despair too soon, we shall continue the thread of our discourse; and having found, that after the discovery of the constant conjunction of any objects, we always draw an inference from one object to another, we shall now examine the nature of that inference, and of the transition from the impression to the idea. Perhaps it will appear in the end, that the necessary connection depends on the inference, instead of the inference's depending on the necessary connection.

Since it appears, that the transition from an impression present to the memory or senses to the idea of an object, which we call cause or effect, is founded on past *experience*, and on our remembrance of their *constant conjunction*, the next question is, whether experience produces the idea by means of the understanding or imagination; whether we are determined by reason to make the transition, or by a certain association and relation of perceptions. If reason determined us, it would proceed upon that principle, *that instances, of which we have had no experience, must resemble those of which we have had experience, and that the course of nature continues always uniformly the same.* In order, therefore, to clear up this matter, let us consider all the arguments upon which such a proposition may be supposed to be founded; and as these must be derived either from *knowledge* or *probability*, let us cast our eye on each of these degrees of evidence, and see whether they afford any just conclusion of this nature.

Our foregoing method of reasoning will easily convince us, that there can be no *demonstrative* arguments to prove, *that those instances of which we have had no experience resemble those of which we have had experience.* We can at least conceive a change in the course of nature; which sufficiently proves that such a change is not absolutely impossible. To form a clear idea of anything is an undeniable argument for its possibility, and is alone a refutation of any pretended demonstration against it.

Probability, as it discovers not the relations of ideas, considered as such, but only those of objects, must, in some respects, be founded on the impressions of our memory and senses, and in some respects on our ideas. Were there no mixture of any impression in our probable reasonings, the conclusion would be entirely chimerical: and were there no mixture of ideas, the action of the mind, in observing the relation, would, properly speaking, be sensation, not reasoning. It is, therefore, necessary, that in all probable reasonings there be something present to the mind, either seen or remembered; and that from this we infer something connected with it, which is not seen nor remembered.

The only connection or relation of objects, which can lead us beyond the immediate impressions of our memory and senses, is that of cause and effect; and that because it is the only one, on which we can found a just inference from one object to another. The idea of cause and effect is derived from *experience*, which informs us, that such particular objects, in all past instances, have been constantly conjoined with each other: and as an object similar to one of these is supposed to be immediately present in its impression, we thence presume on the existence of one similar to its usual attendant. According to this account of things, which is, I think, in every point unquestionable, probability is founded on the presumption of a resemblance betwixt those objects of which we have had experience, and those of which we have had none; and, therefore, it is impossible this presumption can arise from probability. The same principle cannot be both the cause and effect of another; and this is, perhaps, the only proposition concerning that relation, which is either intuitively or demonstratively certain.

Should any one think to elude this argument; and without determining whether our reasoning on this subject be derived from demonstration or probability, pretend that all conclusions from causes and effects are built on solid reasoning: I can only desire that this reasoning may be produced, in order to be exposed to our examination. It may perhaps be said, that after experience of the constant conjunction of certain objects, we reason in the following manner. Such an object is always found to produce another. It is impossible it could have this effect, if it was not endowed with a power of production. The power necessarily implies the effect; and therefore there is a just foundation for drawing a conclusion from the existence of one object to that of its usual attendant. The past production implies a power: the power implies a new production: and the new production is what we infer from the power and the past production.

It were easy for me to show the weakness of this reasoning, were I willing to make use of those observations I have already made, that the idea of *production* is the same with that of *causation*, and that no existence certainly and demonstratively implies a power in any other object; or were it proper to anticipate what I shall have occasion to remark afterwards concerning the idea we form of *power* and *efficacy*. But as such a method of proceeding may seem either to weaken my system, by resting one part of it on another, I shall endeavour to maintain my present assertion without any such assistance.

It shall therefore be allowed for a moment, that the production of one object by another in any one instance implies a power; and that this power is connected with its effect. But it having been already proved, that the power lies not in the sensible qualities of the cause; and there being nothing but the sensible qualities present to us; I ask, why in other instances you presume that the same power still exists, merely upon the appearance of these qualities? Your appeal to past experience decides nothing in the present case; and at the utmost can only prove, that that very object, which produced any other, was at that very instant endowed with such a power; but can never prove, that the same power must continue in the same object or collection of sensible qualities; much less, that a like power is always conjoined with like sensible qualities. Should it be said, that we have experience, that the same power continues united with the same object, and that like objects are endowed with like powers, I would renew my question, *why from this experience we form any conclusion beyond those past instances, of which we have had experience?* If you answer this question in the same manner as the preceding, your answer gives still occasion to a new question of the same kind, even *in infinitum*; which clearly proves, that the foregoing reasoning had no just foundation.

Thus, not only our reason fails us in the discovery of the *ultimate connection* of causes and effects, but even after experience has informed us of their *constant conjunction*, it is impossible for us to satisfy ourselves by our reason, why we should extend that experience beyond those particular instances which have fallen under our observation. We suppose, but are never able to prove, that there must be a resemblance betwixt those objects, of which we have had experience, and those which lie beyond the reach of our discovery.

We have already taken notice of certain relations, which make us pass from one object to another, even though there be no reason to determine us to that transition; and this we may establish for a general rule, that wherever the mind constantly and uniformly makes a transition without any reason, it is influenced by these relations. Now, this is exactly the present case. Reason can never show us the connection of one object with another, though aided by experience, and the observation of their constant conjunction in all past instances. When the mind therefore passes from the idea or impression of one object to the idea or belief of another, it is not determined by reason, but by certain principles, which associate together the ideas of these objects, and unite them in the imagination. Had ideas no more union in the fancy, than objects seem to have to the understanding, we could never draw any inference from causes to effects, nor repose belief in any matter of fact. The inference therefore depends solely on the union of ideas.

The principles of union among ideas, I have reduced to three general ones, and have asserted, that the idea or impression of any object naturally introduces the idea of any other object, that is resembling, contiguous to, or connected with it. These principles I allow to be neither the *infallible* nor the *sole* causes of a union among ideas. They are not the infallible causes. For one may fix his attention during some time on any one object without looking further. They are not the sole causes. For the thought has evidently a very irregular motion in running along its objects, and may leap from the heavens to the earth, from one end of the creation to the other, without any certain method or order. But though I allow this weakness in these three relations, and this irregularity in the imagination; yet I assert, that the only *general* principles which associate ideas, are resemblance, contiguity, and causation.

There is indeed a principle of union among ideas, which at first sight may be esteemed different from any of these, but will be found at the bottom to depend on the same origin. When every individual of any species of objects is found by experience to be constantly united with an individual of another species, the appearance of any new individual of either species naturally conveys the thought to its usual attendant. Thus, because such a particular idea is commonly annexed to such a particular word, nothing is required but the hearing of that word to produce the correspondent idea; and it will scarce be possible for the mind, by its utmost efforts, to prevent that transition. In this case it is not absolutely necessary, that upon hearing such a particular sound, we should reflect on any past experience, and consider what idea has been usually connected with the sound. The imagination of itself supplies the place of this reflection, and is so accustomed to pass from the word to the idea, that it interposes not a moment's delay betwixt the hearing of the one, and the conception of the other.

But though I acknowledge this to be a true principle of association among ideas, I assert it to be the very same with that betwixt the ideas of cause and effect, and to be an essential part in all our reasonings from that relation. We have no other notion of cause and effect, but that of certain objects, which have been *always conjoined* together, and which in all past instances have been found inseparable. We cannot penetrate into the reason of the conjunction. We only observe the thing itself, and always find that, from the constant conjunction, the objects acquire a union in the imagination. When the impression of one becomes present to us, we immediately form an idea of its usual attendant; and consequently we may establish this as one part of the definition of an opinion or belief, that it is *an idea related to or associated with a present impression.*

Thus, though causation be a *philosophical* relation, as implying contiguity, succession, and constant conjunction, yet it is only so far as it is a *natural* relation, and produces a union among our ideas, that we are able to reason upon it, or draw any inference from it.

OF THE NATURE OF THE IDEA OR BELIEF

(Book I, Part III, Section 7)

The idea of an object is an essential part of the belief of it, but not the whole. We conceive many things which we do not believe. In order, then, to discover more fully the nature of belief, or the qualities of those ideas we assent to, let us weigh the following considerations.

It is evident, that all reasonings from causes or effects terminate in conclusions concerning matter of fact; that is, concerning the existence of objects or of their qualities. It is also evident, that the idea of existence is nothing different from the idea of any object, and that when after the simple conception of anything we would conceive it as existent, we in reality make no addition to or alteration on our first idea. Thus, when we affirm that God is existent, we simply form the idea of such a Being as he is represented to us: nor is the existence, which we attribute to him, conceived by a particular idea, which we join to the idea of his other qualities, and can again separate and distinguish from them. But I go further; and, not content with asserting, that the conception of the existence of any object is no addition to the simple conception of it, I likewise maintain, that the belief of the existence joins no new ideas to those, which compose the idea of the object. When I think of God, when I think of him as existent, and when I believe him to be existent, my idea of him neither increases nor diminishes. But as it is certain there is a great difference betwixt the simple conception of the existence of an object, and the belief of it, and as this difference lies not in the parts or composition of the idea which we conceive; it follows, that it must lie in the *manner* in which we conceive it.

Suppose a person present with me, who advances propositions, to which I do not assent, *that Cæsar died in his bed, that silver is more fusible than lead, or mercury heavier than gold*; it is evident that, notwithstanding my incredulity, I clearly understand his meaning, and form all the same ideas which he forms. My imagination is endowed with the same powers as his; nor is it possible for him to conceive any idea, which I cannot conceive; or conjoin any, which I cannot conjoin. I therefore ask, wherein consists the difference betwixt believing and disbelieving any proposition? The answer is easy with regard to propositions, that are proved by intuition or demonstration. In that case, the person who assents not only conceives the ideas according to the proposition, but is necessarily determined to conceive them in that particular manner, either immediately, or by the interposition of other ideas. Whatever is absurd is unintelligible; nor is it possible for the imagination to conceive anything contrary to a demonstration. But as, in reasonings from causation, and concerning matters of fact, this absolute necessity cannot take place, and the imagination is free to conceive both sides of the question, I still ask, *wherein consists the difference betwixt incredulity and belief*? since, in both cases the conception of the idea is equally possible and requisite.

It will not be a satisfactory answer to say, that a person, who does not assent to a proposition you advance; after having conceived the object in the same manner with you, immediately conceives it in a different manner, and has different ideas of it. This answer is unsatisfactory; not because it contains any falsehood, but because it discovers not all the truth. It is confessed that, in all cases wherein we dissent from any person, we conceive both sides of the question; but as we can believe only one, it evidently follows, that the belief must make some difference betwixt that conception to which we assent, and that from which we dissent. We may mingle, and unite, and separate, and confound, and vary our ideas in a hundred different ways; but until there appears some principle, which fixes one of these different situations, we have in reality no opinion: and this principle, as it plainly makes no addition to our precedent ideas, can only change the *manner* of our conceiving them.

All the perceptions of the mind are of two kinds, viz., impressions and ideas, which differ from each other only in their different degrees of force and vivacity. Our ideas are copied from our impressions, and represent them in all their parts. When you would any way vary the idea of a particular object, you can only increase or diminish its force and vivacity. If you make any other change on it, it represents a different object or impression. The case is the same as in colours. A particular shade of any colour may acquire a new degree of liveliness or brightness without any other variation. But when you produce any other variation, it is no longer the same shade or colour; so that as belief does nothing but vary the manner in which we conceive any object, it can only bestow on our ideas an additional force and vivacity. An opinion, therefore, or belief, may be most accurately defined, *a lively idea related to or associated with a present impression.*[3]

Here are the heads of those arguments, which lead us to this conclusion.

---

[3]We may here take occasion to observe a very remarkable error, which, being frequently inculcated in the schools, has become a kind of established maxim, and is universally received by all logicians. This error consists in the vulgar division of the acts of the understanding into *conception, judgment,* and *reasoning,* and in the definitions we give of them. Conception is defined to be the simple survey of one or more ideas: judgment to be the separating or uniting of different ideas: reasoning to be the separating or uniting of different ideas by the interposition of others, which show the relation they bear to each other. But these distinctions and definitions are faulty in very considerable articles. For, *first,* it is far from being true, that, in every judgment which we form, we unite two different ideas; since in that proposition, *God is,* or indeed, any other, which regards existence, the idea of existence is no distinct idea, which we unite with that of the object, and which is capable of forming a compound idea by the union. *Secondly,* as we can thus form a proposition, which contains only one idea, so we may exert our reason without employing more than two ideas, and without having recourse to a third to serve as a medium betwixt them. We infer a cause immediately from its effect; and this inference is not only a true species of reasoning, but the strongest of all others, and more convincing than when we interpose another idea to connect the two extremes. What we may in general affirm concerning these three acts of the understanding is, that taking them in a proper light, they all resolve themselves into the first, and are nothing but particular ways of conceiving our objects. Whether we consider a single object or several; whether we dwell on these objects, or run from them to others; and in whatever form or order we survey them, the act of the mind exceeds not a simple conception; and the only remarkable difference, which occurs on this occasion, is, when we join belief to the conception, and are persuaded of the truth of what we conceive. This act of the mind has never yet been explained by any philosopher; and therefore I am at liberty to propose my hypothesis concerning it; which is, that it is only a strong and steady conception of any idea, and such as approaches in some measure to an immediate impression.

When we infer the existence of an object from that of others, some object must always be present either to the memory or senses, in order to be the foundation of our reasoning; since the mind cannot run up with its inferences *in infinitum*. Reason can never satisfy us that the existence of any one object does ever imply that of another; so that when we pass from the impression of one to the idea or belief of another, we are not determined by reason, but by custom, or a principle of association. But belief is somewhat more than a simple idea. It is a particular manner of forming an idea; and as the same idea can only be varied by a variation of its degrees of force and vivacity; it follows upon the whole, that belief is a lively idea produced by a relation to a present impression, according to the foregoing definition.

This operation of the mind, which forms the belief of any matter of fact, seems hitherto to have been one of the greatest mysteries of philosophy; though no one has so much as suspected, that there was any difficulty in explaining it. For my part, I must own, that I find a considerable difficulty in the case; and that even when I think I understand the subject perfectly, I am at a loss for terms to express my meaning. I conclude, by an induction which seems to me very evident, that an opinion or belief is nothing but an idea, that is different from a fiction, not in the nature, or the order of its parts, but in the *manner* of its being conceived. But when I would explain this *manner*, I scarce find any word that fully answers the case, but am obliged to have recourse to every one's feeling, in order to give him a perfect notion of this operation of the mind. An idea assented to *feels* different from a fictitious idea, that the fancy alone presents to us: and this different feeling I endeavour to explain by calling it a superior *force*, or *vivacity*, or *solidity*, or *firmness*, or *steadiness*. This variety of terms, which may seem so unphilosophical, is intended only to express that act of the mind, which renders realities more present to us than fictions, causes them to weigh more in the thought, and gives them a superior influence on the passions and imagination. Provided we agree about the thing, it is needless to dispute about the terms. The imagination has the command over all its ideas, and can join, and mix, and vary them in all the ways possible. It may conceive objects with all the circumstances of place and time. It may set them, in a manner, before our eyes in their true colours, just as they might have existed. But as it is impossible that that faculty can ever of itself reach belief, it is evident, that belief consists not in the nature and order of our ideas, but in the manner of their conception, and in their feeling to the mind. I confess, that it is impossible to explain perfectly this feeling or manner of conception. We may make use of words that express something near it. But its true and proper name is *belief*, which is a term that every one sufficiently understands in common life. And in philosophy, we can go no further than assert, that it is something *felt* by the mind, which distinguishes the ideas of the judgment from the fictions of the imagination. It gives them more force and influence; makes them appear of greater importance; infixes them in the mind; and renders them the governing principles of all our actions.

This definition will also be found to be entirely conformable to every one's feeling and experience. Nothing is more evident, than that those ideas, to which we assent, are more strong, firm, and vivid, than the loose reveries of a castle-builder. If one person sits down to read a book as a romance, and another as a true history, they plainly receive the same ideas, and in the same order; nor does the incredulity of the one, and the belief of the other, hinder them from putting the very same upon their author. His words produce the same ideas in both;

though his testimony has not the same influence on them. The latter has a more lively conception of all the incidents. He enters deeper into the concerns of the persons: represents to himself their actions, and characters, and friendships, and person. While the former, who gives no credit to the testimony of the author, has a more faint and languid conception of all these particulars, and except on account of the style and ingenuity of the composition, can receive little entertainment from it. . . .

OF THE IDEA OF NECESSARY CONNECTION[4]

(Book I, Part III, Section 14)

Having thus explained the manner *in which we reason beyond our immediate impressions, and conclude that such particular causes must have such particular effects*; we must now return upon our footsteps to examine that question[5] which first occurred to us, and which we dropped in our way, viz., *What is our idea of necessity, when we say that two objects are necessarily connected together?* Upon this head I repeat, what I have often had occasion to observe, that as we have no idea that is not derived from an impression, we must find some impression that gives rise to this idea of necessity, if we assert we have really such an idea. In order to this, I consider in what objects necessity is commonly supposed to lie; and, finding that it is always ascribed to causes and effects, I turn my eye to two objects supposed to be placed in that relation, and examine them in all the situations of which they are susceptible. I immediately perceive that they are *contiguous* in time and place, and that the object we call cause *precedes* the other we call effect. In no one instance can I go any further, nor is it possible for me to discover any third relation betwixt these objects. I therefore enlarge my view to comprehend several instances, where I find like objects always existing in like relations of contiguity and succession. At first sight this seems to serve but little to my purpose. The reflection on several instances only repeats the same objects; and therefore can never give rise to a new idea. But upon further inquiry I find that the repetition is not in every particular the same, but produces a new impression, and by that means the idea which I at present examine. For, after a frequent repetition, I find that upon the appearance of one of the objects the mind is *determined* by custom to consider its usual attendant, and to consider it in a stronger light upon account of its relation to the first object. It is this impression, then, or *determination*, which affords me the idea of necessity. . . .

There is no question which, on account of its importance, as well as difficulty, has caused more disputes both among ancient and modern philosophers, than this concerning the efficacy of causes, or that quality which makes them be followed by their effects. But before they entered upon these disputes, methinks it would not have been improper to have examined what idea we have of that efficacy, which is the subject of the controversy. This is what I find principally wanting in their reasonings, and what I shall here endeavour to supply.

---

[4]See also *Enquiry*, Part I, section 7, p. 509.

[5]Section 2.

I begin with observing that the terms of *efficacy, agency, power, force, energy, necessity, connection,* and *productive quality,* are all nearly synonymous; and therefore it is an absurdity to employ any of them in defining the rest. By this observation we reject at once all the vulgar definitions which philosophers have given of power and efficacy; and instead of searching for the ideas in these definitions, must look for it in the impressions from which it is originally derived. If it be a compound idea, it must arise from compound impressions. If simple, from simple impressions.

I believe the most general and most popular explication of this matter, is to say,[6] that finding from experience that there are several new productions in matter, such as the motions and variations of body, and concluding that there must somewhere be a power capable of producing them, we arrive at last by this reasoning at the idea of power and efficacy. But to be convinced that this explication is more popular than philosophical, we need but reflect on two very obvious principles. *First,* that reason alone can never give rise to any original idea; and, *secondly,* that reason, as distinguished from experience, can never make us conclude that a cause or productive quality is absolutely requisite to every beginning of existence. Both these considerations have been sufficiently explained; and therefore shall not at present be any further insisted on.

I shall only infer from them, that since reason can never give rise to the idea of efficacy, that idea must be derived from experience, and from some particular instances of this efficacy, which make their passage into the mind by the common channels of sensation or reflection. Ideas always represent their objects or impressions; and *vice versa*, there are some objects necessary to give rise to every idea. If we pretend, therefore, to have any just idea of this efficacy, we must produce some instance wherein the efficacy is plainly discoverable to the mind, and its operations obvious to our consciousness or sensation. By the refusal of this, we acknowledge that the idea is impossible and imaginary; since the principle of innate ideas, which alone can save us from this dilemma, has been already refuted, and is now almost universally rejected in the learned world. Our present business, then, must be to find some natural production, where the operation and efficacy of a cause can be clearly conceived and comprehended by the mind, without any danger of obscurity or mistake. . . .

Suppose two objects to be presented to us, of which the one is the cause and the other the effect; it is plain that, from the simple consideration of one or both these objects, we never shall perceive the tie by which they are united, or be able certainly to pronounce, that there is a connection betwixt them. It is not, therefore, from any one instance, that we arrive at the idea of cause and effect, of a necessary connection of power, of force, of energy, and of efficacy. Did we never see any but particular conjunctions of objects, entirely different from each other, we should never be able to form any such ideas.

But, again, suppose we observe instances in which the same objects are always conjoined together, we immediately conceive a connection betwixt them, and begin to draw an inference from one to another. This multiplicity of resembling instances, therefore, constitutes the very essence of power or connection, and is the source from which the idea of it arises. In order, then, to understand the idea of power, we must consider that multiplicity; nor do I ask more to give a solution of that difficulty which has so long perplexed us. For

---

[6]See Mr. Locke; chapter of Power.

thus I reason. The repetition of perfectly similar instances can never *alone* give rise to an original idea, different from what is to be found in any particular instance, as has been observed, and as evidently follows from our fundamental principle, *that all ideas are copied from impressions*. Since, therefore, the idea of power is a new original idea, not to be found in any one instance, and which yet arises from the repetition of several instances, it follows that the repetition *alone* has not that effect, but must either *discover* or *produce* something new, which is the source of that idea. Did the repetition neither discover nor produce anything new, our ideas might be multiplied by it, but would not be enlarged above what they are upon the observation of one single instance. Every enlargement, therefore (such as the idea of power or connection), which arises from the multiplicity of similar instances, is copied from some effects of the multiplicity, and will be perfectly understood by understanding these effects. Wherever we find anything new to be discovered or produced by the repetition, there we must place the power, and must never look for it in any other object.

But it is evident, in the first place, that the repetition of like objects in like relations of succession and contiguity, *discovers* nothing new in any one of them; since we can draw no inference from it, nor make it a subject either of our demonstrative or probable reasonings; as has been already proved.[7] Nay, suppose we could draw an inference, it would be of no consequence in the present case; since no kind of reasoning can give rise to a new idea, such as this of power is; but wherever we reason, we must antecedently be possessed of clear ideas, which may be the objects of our reasoning. The conception always precedes the understanding; and where the one is obscure, the other is uncertain; where the one fails, the other must fail also.

Secondly, it is certain that this repetition of similar objects in similar situations, *produces* nothing new either in these objects, or in any external body. For it will readily be allowed, that the several instances we have of the conjunction of resembling causes and effects, are in themselves entirely independent, and that the communication of motion, which I see result at present from the shock of two billiard balls, is totally distinct from that which I saw result from such an impulse a twelvemonth ago. These impulses have no influence on each other. They are entirely divided by time and place; and the one might have existed and communicated motion, though the other never had been in being.

There is, then, nothing new either discovered or produced in any objects by their constant conjunction, and by the uninterrupted resemblance of their relations of succession and contiguity. But it is from this resemblance that the ideas of necessity, of power, and of efficacy, are derived. These ideas, therefore, represent not anything that does or can belong to the objects which are constantly conjoined. This is an argument which, in every view we can examine it, will be found perfectly unanswerable. Similar instances are still the first source of our idea of power or necessity; at the same time that they have no influence by their similarity either on each other, or on any external object. We must, therefore, turn ourselves to some other quarter to seek the origin of that idea.

Though the several resembling instances, which give rise to the idea of power, have no influence on each other, and can never produce any new quality *in the object*, which can be the model of that idea, yet the *observation*

---

[7] Section 6.

of this resemblance produces a new impression *in the mind*, which is its real model. For after we have observed the resemblance in a sufficient number of instances, we immediately feel a determination of the mind to pass from one object to its usual attendant, and to conceive it in a stronger light upon account of that relation. This determination is the only effect of the resemblance; and, therefore, must be the same with power or efficacy, whose idea is derived from the resemblance. The several instances of resembling conjunctions lead us into the notion of power and necessity. These instances are in themselves totally distinct from each other, and have no union but in the mind, which observes them, and collects their ideas. Necessity, then, is the effect of this observation, and is nothing but an internal impression of the mind, or a determination to carry our thoughts from one object to another. Without considering it in this view, we can never arrive at the most distant notion of it, or be able to attribute it either to external or internal objects, to spirit or body, to causes or effects.

The necessary connection betwixt causes and effects is the foundation of our inference from one to the other. The foundation of our inference is the transition arising from the accustomed union. These are, therefore, the same.

The idea of necessity arises from some impression. There is no impression conveyed by our senses, which can give rise to that idea. It must, therefore, be derived from some internal impression, or impression of reflection. There is no internal impression which has any relation to the present business, but that propensity, which custom produces, to pass from an object to the idea of its usual attendant. This, therefore, is the essence of necessity. Upon the whole, necessity is something that exists in the mind, not in objects; nor is it possible for us ever to form the most distant idea of it, considered as a quality in bodies. Either we have no idea of necessity, or necessity is nothing but that determination of the thought to pass from causes to effects, and from effects to causes, according to their experienced union. . . .

As to what may be said, that the operations of nature are independent of our thought and reasoning, I allow it; and accordingly have observed, that objects bear to each other the relations of contiguity and succession; that like objects may be observed, in several instances, to have like relations; and that all this is independent of, and antecedent to, the operations of the understanding. But if we go any further, and ascribe a power or necessary connection to these objects, this is what we can never observe in them, but must draw the idea of it from what we feel internally in contemplating them. And this I carry so far, that I am ready to convert my present reasoning into an instance of it, by a subtilty which it will not be difficult to comprehend.

When any object is presented to us, it immediately conveys to the mind a lively idea of that object which is usually found to attend it; and determination of the mind forms the necessary connection of these objects. But when we change the point of view from the objects to the perceptions, in that case the impression is to be considered as the cause, and the lively idea as the effect; and their necessary connection is that new determination, which we feel to pass from the idea of the one to that of the other. The uniting principle among our internal perceptions is as unintelligible as that among external objects, and is not known to us any other way than by experience. Now, the nature and effects of experience have been already sufficiently examined and explained. It never gives us any insight into the internal structure or operating principle of objects, but only accustoms the mind to pass from one to another.

1. ANALYSIS OF CAUSATION

The relation of cause and effect is the only one which enables us to conclude to the existence of objects and the occurrence of events not immediately present to our senses. Precisely what the idea of causation involves can be discovered on Hume's principles only by seeking the original impression or impressions from which it is derived. In order to do this Hume analyzes the relation into three factors: (a) Contiguity in time and space of two events (the cause and the effect); (b) succession — cause preceeding effect. Having got so far Hume confesses that he can get no further. The idea of production is simply causation by another name and so contributes nothing to the analysis. Yet Hume concedes that contiguity and succession are not sufficient to yield the idea of causation, for one event may precede another immediately without being considered its cause. A third factor is wanting, and this he identifies as (c) *necessary connection.*

2. NECESSARY CONNECTION

But for necessary connection there is no discoverable precedent impression. There is nothing of which we are ever immediately aware that can be described as a necessary connection. No idea or impression, however closely scrutinized, affords in itself, and apart from associations we may have formed as the result of past experience, any information about any other impression or idea. No two impressions or ideas presented successively reveal any connection one with another.

The occurrence of any idea or impression could conceivably be followed by any other. No absurdity or contradiction is involved in imagining any event to be followed by any other. When I let go of my pen it might conceivably fly upward and adhere to the ceiling. I do not expect this to happen, but no contradiction is involved in the imagination of it. The same is true of any other imaginable sequence of events. And Hume has asserted as a general truth that whatever can be clearly imagined is a possible existent.[8] Similarly, of every sequence of events which does occur it is possible to imagine that it could have been other than it was. No connection, therefore, reveals itself between events, and if there is any, it is clearly not *necessary*, for if it were, we could not conceive the sequence to be other than it is or was.

Why then do we take cause and effect to be necessarily connected?

---

[8]*Treatise*, Book I, Part II, 2.

How do we establish the connection between causes and their effects? And from what impression does the idea of necessary connection between them originate?

(a) CONSTANT CONJUNCTION. No reasoning from any immediately presented fact to any other, past or future, is possible, Hume contends, except by means of the relation of cause and effect. But the inference from cause to effect or *vice versa* is not derived from the inspection of either, for no object or event logically implies the existence, or occurrence, of any other. It is only from experience that we could learn of any connection. Yet all we do learn from experience is that in the past events of one kind have repeatedly been followed by events of another kind (for example, lightning flashes by thunderclaps). We experience no necessary connections, but we do experience constant conjunctions, and when two events have occurred successively a sufficient number of times, the occurrence of an impression or idea of one of the objects or events produces by association the idea of the other. "Without any further ceremony," says Hume, "we call one the *cause* and the other the *effect*, and infer the existence of the one from that of the other." This, then, is the answer to our first question. We *assume* a necessary connection (that of cause to effect) whenever we experience a constant conjunction. We believe cause and effect to be necessarily connected because we find them constantly conjoined.

(b) INDUCTION. But can we establish the existence of any connection between objects and events the constant conjunction of which we experience? How could such a connection be established? It is usually held that we establish it by inductive reasoning.

What in fact we believe is that when we have frequently or invariably experienced events constantly conjoined in the past, they will always be so conjoined in the future. It is this that we have to establish—that what has been frequently conjoined is universally connected. But, Hume shows, no valid reasoning can ever produce this transition. The repetition of a conjunction is no more guarantee of its universality than a single occurrence, because it is always conceivable that on the next occurrence of the alleged cause the usual effect will not follow; and this possibility is not removed however many past repetitions have occurred. The argument is based upon a well-known rule of validity in traditional formal logic (to which, however, Hume never directly refers), that from particular premises no universal conclusion can validly be drawn. It is never valid to go from "This a is red," and "that a is red" to "All a's are red." It does not follow validly that because this bird is a swan and is white all swans are white, not even if we have found some other white swans. This sort of fallacy is familiar as unjustified generalization. But we commonly think that if we have found enough positive cases we can *justifiably* generalize. Hume, however, points out that no matter how many particular premises we accumlate, the transition to a universal conclusion is still fallacious.

If we can be sure that we have exhausted all possible examples of a particular class and have found all of them to have a particular property, we may truthfully judge that they all do have that property. If I know that all the people in this room are male, I can truthfully state that fact in what looks like a universal proposition. This is called perfect induction, or induction by complete enumeration. But there is a significant difference between such statements as "All the people in this room are male" and "All people are male," or "All the marbles in this bag are white" and "All marbles are solid." Even if the latter statement were true (which it need not be, for a marble might conceivably be made of a very viscous liquid), it would be a different kind of judgment, because it asserts something of all members of a potentially infinite class and makes no distinction between those we have counted and examined and those we have not. The first kind of "all" statement is usually called a factual universal. It just happens to be the case that all the marbles in the bag are white. The second kind is called a law-like statement, for it asserts, in effect, what all marbles at any time or anywhere *must* be like. Now it is clear that from the examination even of a large number of positive cases we can never *logically* conclude to the law-like statement (as in the case of the solidity of marbles). And this is Hume's point.

In inductive reasoning, what we are claiming is that cases of which we have had no experience will resemble those of which we have, that future instances must resemble past instances, that if A has been followed by B in the past, any future A will be followed by B. But this, as we have already seen, is not demonstrable, because the contrary is always conceivable (or in Hume's way of thinking, imaginable), and therefore possible, however many times the conjunction has occurred in the past. If the contrary is possible the connection cannot be necessary, so we cannot establish it by reason or demonstration.

Sometimes it is argued that the necessary connection of what have been found constantly conjoined follows from "the uniformity of nature." As nature follows settled laws (Berkeley might have said), when we have found A followed constantly by B in the past we may conclude that this will always happen. But the belief in the uniformity of nature is precisely what has to be established. How do we know that nature is uniform, that there is a settled order? Even Berkeley has assured us that we learn it only from experience; that is, because we find events frequently or constantly conjoined we *expect* that they will continue to be so "without further ceremony." We can give no proof that this expectation is right, and the past uniformity is no guarantee of the future.

Can we not argue, however, at least that the frequent past occurrence of conjoint events renders their future conjunction *probable*? Though the future will not necessarily resemble the past, yet it probably will. To say this, Hume shows, would be to beg the question. We consider events probable only because we expect past conjunctions to be repeated; the reason for expecting this, therefore, cannot be that we consider it probable. In other words, our belief in probability is precisely the same thing as our belief that future events will resemble past events—it is itself inductive reasoning, and it is not very helpful or convincing to argue that we believe that the future will (probably) resemble the past, because we commonly believe that it does. Equally we rate probability according to the frequency of past conjunctions, assuming that frequency to be a measure of probability—the more often AB has occurred in the past, the more probable we think its future repetition. But this is *because* we believe that the future will always resemble the past. So frequency of past conjunctions cannot be the reason for that belief.

Nor can we validly argue that because we have not been disappointed when we have in the past believed that frequently conjoined events will continue to be conjoined, therefore we can adopt the principle that the future always will resemble the past; because that again is to assume what we are seeking to prove—that because we have not been disappointed hitherto, we shall not be disappointed in the future, that what we have hitherto experienced will be repeated, that is, that the future will be like the past. However we argue we beg the question, or argue in a circle.

We must conclude, therefore, that the necessary connection of causes and effects cannot be validly demonstrated.

But obviously it cannot be learned from experience because we can only learn from experience what has happened in the past, not what has not yet happened. We cannot therefore learn from experience that what we have *not* experienced will resemble what we have.

There is therefore no way of establishing necessary connection.

This is what is known as the problem of inductive reasoning, the reasoning from past experience to general (or universal) laws. It is supposed to be the foundation of all empirical science, but Hume proves here irrefutably that any such reasoning, as reasoning, is invalid. Since Hume wrote, the problem has been repeatedly discussed, but nobody has succeeded either in revealing any flaw in Hume's argument or in providing a more reassuring account of inductive reasoning. Many writers have tried to justify it as "probable reasoning" and to bolster it up with a mathematical theory of probability, but all such theories overlook Hume's argument, that probability itself presupposes induction and that inductive reasoning cannot, in consequence, be established as probable.[9]

Some modern writers seek to escape from the difficulty by appeal to linguistic usage. They argue that when we speak of being reasonable in scientific or practical procedure we normally mean arguing from frequent recurrences in past experience to general conclusions; and if this is what it *means* to "be reasonable," it is futile either to seek a rational justification of this procedure (because it is its own justification), or to seek to prove that it is fallacious or irrational. But this way of meeting the difficulty is only an evasion, for two reasons. First, the fact that we normally consider it reasonable to argue from a number of similar instances to a universal conclusion is evidence only of the fact, admitted on all hands, that we do commonly accept such reasoning. It does nothing to show that the reasoning is valid and justifiable—that it really is in the proper sense rational. Or if we are to say that there is another proper sense of rational that applies to inductive argument, then we have on our hands two meanings of the same word which are mutually in conflict.

Others put forward a similar objection to Hume to the effect that he is seeking to assimilate inductive reasoning to deductive reasoning, but that this cannot be done and ought not to be attempted. The rules of validity to which he appeals are rules of deduction, but induction has its own rules and is valid so long as it adheres to them. But what are these rules of inductive validity? They seem to be no more than the general principle that what has happened regularly in the past will always happen; or, in other words, that a universal conclusion does follow validly from particular premises, as long as one has enough of them. There is, however, no rule stating how many is enough. In any case, this is the precise contradiction of the rule of deductive reasoning, that universal conclusions do not follow validly from any number of particular premises. What this defense of inductive reasoning amounts to, then, is simply that it is the opposite of deductive reasoning, or that it al-

---

[9]Bertrand Russell, one of the most illuminating modern writers on this subject, never makes this mistake.

lows what is deductively invalid, and that is an odd sort of justification.

At most, these modern attempts to solve the problem reduce to say-ing that there are two different ways of being reasonable, following rules which contradict each other, yet each in its own way is in some sense valid. One can hardly think of a less satisfactory account of reason-ableness.

(c) NECESSARY CONNECTION. If we never experience necessary con-nection and if we cannot validly establish it by reasoning, how is the prevalence of the belief in it to be explained? For as Hume admits, the relation of cause and effect is dependent upon it, and without that no reasoning about matters of fact is possible. Attempts to appeal to such notions as power or efficacy are of no avail, (a) because they are little if anything more than synonyms for causality, (b) because the same sort of inductive argument is required to establish the belief that what has a power to produce a certain effect in instances which we have experi-enced will continue to have that power in other instances not experienced —for, as Hume points out, we do not perceive the power but only take it to be associated with certain other qualities of the cause which we do perceive,—and (c) because the presumed relation between the as-sumed power and its effect is precisely that of necessary connection of which we can find no evidence.

Hume concludes, therefore, that cause and effect is nothing more nor less than the habitual association of ideas which have in the past been constantly conjoined. The idea of necessary connection we do indeed possess, and we can have no idea without some precedent impression; yet we have no impression of sensation corresponding to this idea, therefore its origin must be an impression of reflection. This is what Hume alleges. Whenever we are firmly accustomed to the conjunction of two impressions the occurrence of one of them leads us confidently to expect the other and our mind is, as it were, impelled toward it so that we have a (more or less) intense feeling of expectation. This feeling of expectation is the impression of reflection of which neces-sary connection is the idea. It is a determination of the imagination to recall a more lively idea of an object customarily associated with a pre-sented impression (be it the cause or the effect).

Thus causation is finally resolved into the threefold relation of conti-guity, succession, and a feeling of expectation.

(d) BELIEF AND ITS CAUSES. In the course of the foregoing argument the effect of custom which proves so important has been described as the increase in liveliness or force of the idea repeatedly associated with the precedent idea or impression. Thus, when we have often experienced heat following upon the bright light of a fire, a new experience of the brightness will more forcefully arouse the idea of the heat and we expect it to follow. This expectation is belief. We come to believe in a connection between the two perceptions and to regard one as the cause of the other.

According to Hume belief is not an additional idea, nor does it in any way alter ideas which we entertain, for their content is the same whether we believe them or not. It is nothing more nor less than a heightened degree of liveliness in perception. So we believe more strongly in the existence of present objects, of which we have immediate impressions, than of imaginary or even remembered objects, of which we have fainter ideas. We believe more readily what we directly remember than what we simply fancy, for the same reason—that the ideas of the former are stronger than those of the latter. Belief is thus a characteristic of the imagination. It is the vivacity or liveliness of the ideas we entertain.

Any relation or influence which strengthens our ideas or makes them more lively increases our belief in their reality. Frequent repetition of an impression or idea has this effect, or frequent repetition of a conjunction of impressions, because, Hume holds, when any impression is related to other ideas it conveys to those ideas "a share of its force and vivacity." Repetition is thus a great source of belief, and what we are told repeatedly we tend to believe in the absence of any other evidence. Similarly, in religion we reinforce our beliefs by associating them with sensible objects and actions which we repeat frequently in order to retain our faith. For when objects are commonly associated, the direct experience of some of them excites the lively imagination of the others and increases our belief in the existence of the latter, more so than does the mere imagination of the former objects when they are not present. So, we are told, superstitious people use relics and icons to "enliven their devotion" and confirm their beliefs.

Now belief is "nothing but a strong and lively idea derived from a present impression related to it"; this liveliness is produced equally by repetitions in which there is no causality, but only customary association (not what we should regard as a "scientific" connection), and by the constant conjunction of events between which we come to assume a causal nexus. It follows that the ultimate basis of scientific reasoning and of superstition is one and the same. For in scientific reasoning from cause to effect our belief in the necessary connection is due simply to custom and the strong expectancy of successive occurrence which results from frequent conjunction, and likewise in superstition our belief is due to custom and frequent association of ideas and impressions. Our confidence in inductive reasoning has the same source, namely, our belief that the future will resemble the past, which is due simply to custom and a determination of the imagination to expect such resemblance; and this again results in the strengthening of the expected idea.

Accordingly Hume tells us that probable reasoning is nothing but a species of sensation. " 'Tis not solely in poetry and music we must follow our taste and sentiment, but likewise in philosophy. When I am convinc'd of any principle, 'tis only an idea, which strikes more strongly upon me."[10]

Thus, in the *Treatise*, Book I, Part III, section 12, Hume writes:

> Let men be once fully persuaded of these two principles, *that there is nothing in any object, considered in itself, which can afford us a reason for drawing a conclusion beyond it*; and, *that even after the observation of frequent or constant conjunction of objects, we have no reason to draw any inference concerning any object beyond those of which we have had experience*; I say, let men be once fully convinced of these two principles, and this will throw them so loose from all common systems, that they will make no difficulty of receiving any which may appear most extraordinary.

These are the foundations of a thoroughgoing scepticism the nature and implications of which we are next to examine.

SUGGESTIONS FOR FURTHER READING

Bertrand Russell, *The Problems of Philosophy*, Chapter 6. New York: Oxford University Press, Galaxy Books, 1959.

Paul Edwards, "Bertrand Russell's Doubts about Induction" in *Logic and Language* (G. N. Flew, ed.). New York: Anchor Books, Doubleday, 1965.

L. Will, "Will the Future be Like the Past" in *Logic and Language* (G. N. Flew, ed.). New York: Anchor Books, Doubleday, 1965.

Max Black, *Problems of Analysis*, Chapters 10 and 11. Ithaca, N. Y.: Cornell University Press, 1954.

Nelson Goodman, *Fact, Fiction and Forecast*. Cambridge, Mass.: Harvard University Press, 1955.

A. C. Ewing, *The Fundamental Questions of Philosophy*, Chapter 8. New York: Macmillan 1958.

---

[10]*Treatise*, Book I, Part III, 8.

CHAPTER 26

Scepticism

Treatise Concerning Human Understanding

OF SCEPTICISM WITH REGARD TO REASON

(Book I, Part IV, Section 1)

In all demonstrative sciences the rules are certain and infallible; but when we apply them, our fallible and uncertain faculties are very apt to depart from them, and fall into error. We must, therefore, in every reasoning form a new judgment, as a check or control on our first judgment or belief; and must enlarge our view to comprehend a kind of history of all the instances, wherein our understanding has deceived us, compared with those wherein its testimony was just and true. Our reason must be considered as a kind of cause, of which truth is the natural effect; but such a one as, by the irruption of other causes, and by the inconstancy of our mental powers, may frequently be prevented. By this means all knowledge degenerates into probability; and this probability is greater or less, according to our experience of the veracity or deceitfulness of our understanding, and according to the simplicity or intricacy of the question.

There is no algebraist nor mathematician so expert in his science, as to place entire confidence in any truth immediately upon his discovery of it, or regard it as anything but a mere probability. Every time he runs over his proofs, his confidence increases; but still more by the approbation of his friends; and is raised to its utmost perfection by the universal assent and applauses of the learned word. Now, it is evident that this gradual increase of assurance is nothing but the addition of new probabilities, and is derived from the constant union of causes and effects, according to past experience and observation.

In accounts of any length or importance, merchants seldom trust to the infallible certainty of numbers for their security; but by the artificial structure of the accounts, produce a probability beyond what is derived from the skill and experience of the accountant. For that is plainly of itself some degree of probability; though uncertain and variable, according to the degrees of his experience and length of the account. Now as none will maintain that our assurance in a long numeration exceeds probability, I may safely affirm, that there scarce is any proposition concerning numbers of which we can have a fuller security. For it is easily possible, by gradually diminishing the numbers, to reduce the longest series of addition to the most simple question which can be formed, to an addition of two single numbers; and upon this supposition we shall find it impracticable to show the precise limits of knowledge and of probability, or discover that particular number at which the one ends and the other begins. But knowledge and probability are of such contrary and disagreeing natures, that they cannot well run insensibly into each other, and that because they will not divide, but must be either entirely present, or entirely absent. Besides, if any single addition were certain, every one would be so, and consequently the whole or total sum; unless the whole can be different from all its parts. I had almost said that this was certain; but I reflect that it must reduce *itself*, as well as every other reasoning, and from knowledge degenerate into probability.

Since, therefore, all knowledge resolves itself into probability, and becomes at last of the same nature with that evidence which we employ in common life, we must now examine this latter species of reasoning, and see on what foundation it stands.

In every judgment which we can form concerning probability, as well as concerning knowledge, we ought always to correct the first judgment, derived from the nature of the object, by another judgment, derived from the nature of the understanding. It is certain a man of solid sense and long experience ought to have, and usually has, a greater assurance in his opinions than one that is foolish and ignorant, and that our sentiments have different degrees of authority, even with ourselves, in proportion to the degrees of our reason and experience. In the man of the best sense and longest experience, this authority is never entire; since even such a one must be conscious of many errors in the past, and must still dread the like for the future. Here then arises a new species of probability to correct and regulate the first, and fix its just standard and proportion. As demonstration is subject to the control of probability, so is probability liable to a new correction by a reflex act of the mind, wherein the nature of our understanding, and our reasoning from the first probability, become our objects.

Having thus found in every probability, beside the original uncertainty inherent in the subject, a new uncertainty, derived from the weakness of that faculty which judges, and having adjusted these two together, we are obliged by our reason to add a new doubt, derived from the possibility of error in the estimation we make of the truth and fidelity of our faculties. This is a doubt which immediately occurs to us, and of which, if we would closely pursue our reason, we cannot avoid giving a decision. But this decision, though it should be favourable to our preceding judgment, being founded only on probability, must weaken still further our first evidence, and must itself be weakened by a fourth doubt of the same kind, and so on *in infinitum*; till at last there remain nothing of the original probability, however great we may suppose it to have been, and however small the diminution by every new uncertainty. No finite object can subsist under a decrease repeated *in infinitum*; and even the vastest quantity which can enter into human imagination, must in this manner be reduced to nothing. Let our first belief be never so strong, it must infallibly perish, by passing through so many new examinations, of which each diminishes somewhat of its force and vigour. When I reflect on the natural fallibility of my judgment, I have less confidence in my opinions than when I only consider the objects concerning which I reason; and when I proceed still further, to turn the scrutiny against every successive estimation I make of my faculties, all the rules of logic require a continual diminution, and at last a total extinction of belief and evidence.

Should it here be asked me, whether I sincerely assent to this argument, which I seem to take such pains to inculcate, and whether I be really one of those sceptics who hold that all is uncertain, and that our judgment is not in *any* thing possessed of *any* measures of truth and falsehood; I should reply, that this question is entirely superfluous, and that neither I, nor any other person, was ever sincerely and constantly of that opinion. Nature, by an absolute and uncontrollable necessity, has determined us to judge as well as to breathe and feel; nor can we any more forbear viewing certain objects in a stronger and fuller light, upon account of their customary connection with a present impression, than we can hinder ourselves from thinking, as long as we are awake, or seeing the surrounding bodies, when we turn our eyes towards them in broad sunshine. Whoever has taken the pains to refute the cavils of this *total* scepticism, has really disputed without an antagonist, and endeavoured by arguments to establish a faculty, which nature has antecedently implanted in the mind, and rendered unavoidable.

My intention then in displaying so carefully the arguments of that fantastic sect, is only to make the reader sensible of the truth of my hypothesis, *that all our reasonings concerning causes and effects, are derived from nothing but custom; and that belief is more properly an act of the sensitive, than of the cogitative part of our natures.* I have here proved, that the very same principles, which make us form a decision upon any subject, and correct that decision by the consideration of our genius and capacity, and of the situation of our mind, when we examined that subject; I say, I have proved that these same principles, when carried further, and applied to every new reflex judgment, must, by continually diminishing the original evidence, at last reduce it to nothing, and utterly subvert all belief and opinion. If belief, therefore, were a simple act of the thought, without any peculiar manner of conception, or the addition of a force and vivacity, it must infallibly destroy itself, and in every case terminate in a total suspense of judgment. But as experience will sufficiently convince any one, who thinks it worth while to try, that though he can find no error in the foregoing arguments, yet he still continues to believe, and think, and reason, as usual, he may safely conclude that his reasoning and belief is some sensation or peculiar manner of conception, which it is impossible for mere ideas and reflections to destroy.

But here, perhaps, it may be demanded, how it happens, even upon my hypothesis, that these arguments above explained produce not a total suspense of judgment, and after what manner the mind ever retains a degree of assurance in any subject. For as these new probabilities, which, by their repetition, perpetually diminish the original evidence, are founded on the very same principles, whether of thought or sensation, as the primary judgment, it may seem unavoidable, that in either case they must equally subvert it, and by the opposition, either of contrary thoughts or sensations, reduce the mind to a total uncertainty. I suppose there is some question proposed to me, and that, after revolving over the impressions of my memory and senses, and carrying my thoughts from them to such objects as are commonly conjoined with them, I feel a stronger and more forcible conception on the one side than on the other. This strong conception forms my first decision. I suppose, that afterwards I examine my judgment itself, and observing, from experience, that it is sometimes just and sometimes erroneous, I consider it as regulated by contrary principles or causes, of which some lead to truth, and some to error; and in balancing these contrary causes, I diminish, by a new probability, the assurance of my first decision. This new probability is liable to the same diminution as the foregoing, and so on, *in infinitum*. It is therefore demanded, *how it happens, that, even after all, we retain a degree of belief, which is sufficient for our purpose, either in philosophy or common life?*

I answer, that after the first and second decision, as the action of the mind becomes forced and unnatural, and the ideas faint and obscure, though the principles of judgment, and the balancing of opposite causes be the same as at the very beginning, yet their influence on the imagination, and the vigour they add to, or diminish from, the thought, is by no means equal. Where the mind reaches not its objects with easiness and facility, the same principles have not the same effect as in a more natural conception of the ideas; nor does the imagination feel a sensation, which holds any proportion with that which arises from its common judgments and opinions. The attention is on the stretch; the posture of the mind is uneasy; and the spirits being diverted from their natural course, are not governed in their movements by the same laws, at least not to the same degree, as when they flow in their usual channel.

If we desire similar instances, it will not be very difficult to find them. The present subject of metaphysics will supply us abundantly. The same argument, which would have been esteemed convincing in a reasoning concerning history or politics, has little or no influence in these abstruser subjects, even though it be perfectly comprehended; and that because there is required a study and an effort of thought, in order to its being comprehended: and this effort of thought disturbs the operation of our sentiments, on which the belief depends. The case is the same in other subjects. The straining of the imagination always hinders the regular flowing of the passions and sentiments. A tragic poet, that would represent his heroes as very ingenious and witty in their misfortunes, would never touch the passions. As the emotions of the soul prevent any subtile reasoning and reflection, so these latter actions of the mind are equally prejudicial to the former. The mind, as well as the body, seems to be endowed with a certain precise degree of force and activity, which it never employs in one action, but at the expense of all the rest. This is more evidently true, where the actions are of quite different natures; since in that case the force of the mind is not only diverted, but even the disposition changed, so as to render us incapable of a sudden transition from one action to the other, and still more of performing both at once. No wonder, then, the conviction, which arises from a subtile reasoning, diminishes in proportion to the efforts which the imagination makes to enter into the reasoning, and to conceive it in all its parts. Belief, being a lively conception, can never be entire, where it is not founded on something natural and easy.

This I take to be the true state of the question, and cannot approve of that expeditious way, which some take with the sceptics, to reject at once all their arguments without inquiry or examination. If the sceptical reasonings be strong, say they, it is a proof that reason may have some force and authority; if weak, they can never be sufficient to invalidate all the conclusions of our understanding. This argument is not just; because the sceptical reasonings, were it possible for them to exist, and were they not destroyed by their subtilty, would be successively both strong and weak, according to the successive dispositions of the mind. Reason first appears in possession of the throne, prescribing laws, and imposing maxims, with an absolute sway and authority. Her enemy, therefore, is obliged to take shelter under her protection, and by making use of rational arguments to prove the fallaciousness and imbecility of reason, produces, in a manner, a patent under her hand and seal. This patent has at first an authority, proportioned to the present and immediate authority of reason, from which it is derived. But as it is supposed to be contradictory to reason, it gradually diminishes the force of that governing power and its own at the same time: till at last they both vanish away into nothing, by a regular and just diminution. The sceptical and dogmatical reasons are of the same kind, though contrary in their operation and tendency; so that where the latter is strong, it has an enemy of equal force in the former to encounter; and as their forces were at first equal, they still continue so, as long as either of them subsists; nor does one of them lose any force in the contest, without taking as much from its antagonist. It is happy, therefore, that nature breaks the force of all sceptical arguments in time, and keeps them from having any considerable influence on the understanding. Were we to trust entirely to their self-destruction, that can never take place, until they have first subverted all conviction, and have totally destroyed human reason.

OF SCEPTICISM WITH REGARD TO THE SENSES

(Book I, Part IV, Section2)

Thus the sceptic still continues to reason and believe, even though he asserts that he cannot defend his reason by reason; and by the same rule he must assent to the principle concerning the existence of body, though he cannot pretend, by any arguments of philosophy, to maintain its veracity. Nature has not left this to his choice, and has doubtless esteemed it an affair of too great importance, to be trusted to our uncertain reasonings and speculations. We may well ask, *What causes induce us to believe in the existence of body?* but it is in vain to ask, *Whether there be body or not?* That is a point which we must take for granted in all our reasonings.

The subject, then, of our present inquiry, is concerning the *causes* which induce us to believe in the existence of body: and my reasonings on this head I shall begin with a distinction, which at first sight may seem superfluous, but which will contribute very much to the perfect understanding of what follows.

We ought to examine apart those two questions, which are commonly confounded together, viz., Why we attribute a *continued* existence to objects, even when they are not present to the senses; and why we suppose them to have an existence *distinct* from the mind and perception? Under this last head I comprehend their situation as well as relations, their *external* position as well as the *independence* of their existence and operation. These two questions concerning the continued and distinct existence of body are intimately connected together. For if the objects of our senses continue to exist, even when they are not perceived, their existence is of course independent of and distinct from the perception; and *vice versa*, if their existence be independent of the perception, and distinct from it, they must continue to exist, even though they be not perceived. But though the decision of the one question decides the other; yet that we may the more easily discover the principles of human nature, from whence the decision arises, we shall carry along with us this distinction, and shall consider, whether it be the *senses, reason*, or the *imagination*, that produces the opinion of a *continued* or of a *distinct* existence. These are the only questions that are intelligible on the present subject. For as to the notion of external existence, when taken for something specifically different from our perceptions, we have already shown its absurdity.[1]

To begin with the *senses*, it is evident these faculties are incapable of giving rise to the notion of the *continued* existence of their objects, after they no longer appear to the senses. For that is a contradiction in terms, and supposes that the senses continue to operate, even after they have ceased all manner of operation. These faculties, therefore, if they have any influence in the present case, must produce the opinion of a distinct, not of a continued existence; and in order to that, must present their impressions either as images and representations, or as these very distinct and external existences.

That our senses offer not their impressions as the images of something *distinct*, or *independent*, and *external*, is evident; because they convey to us nothing but a single perception, and never give us the least intimation of anything beyond. A single perception can never produce the idea of a double existence, but by some inference either of the reason or imagination. When the mind looks further than what immediately appears to it, its conclusions can never be put to the account of the senses; and it certainly looks further, when from a single perception it infers a double existence, and supposes the relations of resemblance and causation betwixt them.

If our senses, therefore, suggest any idea of distinct existences, they must convey the impressions as those very existences, by a kind of fallacy and illusion. Upon this head observe that all sensations are felt by the mind, such as they really are, and that, when we doubt whether they present themselves as distinct objects, or as mere impressions, the difficulty is not concerning their nature, but concerning their impressions as external to, and independent of ourselves, both the objects, and ourselves must be obvious to our senses, otherwise they could not be compared by these faculties. The difficulty then is, how far are we *ourselves* the objects of our senses.

It is certain there is no question in philosophy more abstruse than that concerning identity, and the nature of the uniting principle, which constitutes a person. So far from being able by our senses merely to determine this question,

---

[1] Part II, section 6.

we must have recourse to the most profound metaphysics to give a satisfactory answer to it; and in common life it is evident these ideas of self and person are never very fixed nor determinate. It is absurd therefore to imagine the senses can ever distinguish betwixt ourselves and external objects.

Add to this, that every impression, external and internal, passions, affections, sensations, pains, and pleasures, are originally on the same footing; and that whatever other differences we may observe among them, they appear, all of them, in their true colours, as impressions or perceptions. And indeed, if we consider the matter aright, it is scarce possible it should be otherwise; nor is it conceivable that our senses should be more capable of deceiving us in the situation and relations, than in the nature of our impressions. For since all actions and sensations of the mind are known to us by consciousness, they must necessarily appear in every particular what they are, and be what they appear. Everything that enters the mind, being in *reality* as the perception, it is impossible anything should to *feeling* appear different. This were to suppose, that even where we are most intimately conscious, we might be mistaken.

But not to lose time in examining, whether it is possible for our senses to deceive us, and represent our perceptions as distinct from ourselves, that is, as *external* to and *independent* of us; let us consider whether they really do so, and whether this error proceeds from an immediate sensation, or from some other causes.

To begin with the question concerning *external* existence, it may perhaps be said, that setting aside the metaphysical question of the identity of a thinking substance, our own body evidently belongs to us; and as several impressions appear exterior to the body, we suppose them also exterior to ourselves. The paper on which I write at present is beyond my hand. The table is beyond the paper. The walls of the chamber beyond the table. And in casting my eye towards the window, I perceive a great extent of fields and buildings beyond my chamber. From all this it may be inferred, that no other faculty is required, beside the senses, to convince us of the external existence of body. But to prevent this inference, we need only weigh the three following considerations. *First*, that, properly speaking, it is not our body we perceive when we regard our limbs and members, but certain impressions, which enter by the senses; so that the ascribing a real and corporeal existence to these impressions, or to their objects, is an act of the mind as difficult to explain as that which we examine at present. *Secondly*, sounds, and tastes, and smells, though commonly regarded by the mind as continued independent qualities, appear not to have any existence in extension, and consequently cannot appear to the senses as situated externally to the body. The reason why we ascribe a place to them shall be considered afterwards.[2] *Thirdly*, even our sight informs us not of distance or outness (so to speak), immediately and without a certain reasoning and experience, as is acknowledged by the most rational philosophers.

As to the *independency* of our perceptions on ourselves, this can never be an object of the senses; but any opinion we form concerning it must be derived from experience and observation: and we shall see afterwards, that our conclusions from experience are far from being favourable to the doctrine of the independency of our perceptions. Meanwhile we may observe, that when we talk of real distinct existences, we have commonly more in our eye their

---

[2]Section 5.

independency than external situation in place, and think an object has a sufficient reality, when its being is uninterrupted, and independent of the incessant revolutions, which we are conscious of in ourselves.

Thus to resume what I have said concerning the senses; they give us no
notion of continued existence, because they cannot operate beyond the extent,
in which they really operate. They as little produce the opinion of a distinct
existence, because they neither can offer it to the mind as represented, nor as
original. To offer it as represented, they must present both an object and an
image. To make it appear as original, they must convey a falsehood; and this
falsehood must lie in the relations and situation: in order to which, they must be
able to compare the object with ourselves; and even in that case they do not,
nor is it possible they should deceive us. We may therefore conclude with
certainty, that the opinion of a continued and of a distinct existence never
arises from the senses.

To confirm this, we may observe that there are three different kinds of
impressions conveyed by the senses. The first are those of the figure, bulk,
motion, and solidity of bodies. The second, those of colours, tastes, smells,
sounds, heat, and cold. The third are the pains and pleasures that arise from
the application of objects to our bodies, as by the cutting of our flesh with steel,
and such like. Both philosophers and the vulgar suppose the first of these to
have a distinct continued existence. The vulgar only regard the second as on
the same footing. Both philosophers and the vulgar, again, esteem the third to
be merely perceptions; and, consequently, interrupted and dependent beings.

Now, it is evident, that whatever may be our philosophical opinion, colour,
sounds, heat, and cold, as far as appears to the senses, exist after the same
manner with motion and solidity; and that the difference we make betwixt
them, in this respect, arises not from the mere perception. So strong is the
prejudice for the distinct continued existence of the former qualities, that when
the contrary opinion is advanced by modern philosophers, people imagine they
can almost refute it from their feeling and experience, and that their very
senses contradict this philosophy. It is also evident, that colours, sounds, etc.,
are originally on the same footing with the pain that arises from steel, and
pleasure that proceeds from a fire; and that the difference betwixt them is
founded neither on perception nor reason, but on the imagination. For as they
are confessed to be, both of them, nothing but perceptions arising from the
particular configurations and motions of the parts of body, wherein possibly
can their difference consist? Upon the whole, then, we may conclude that, as
far as the senses are judges, all perceptions are the same in the manner of their
existence.

We may also observe, in this instance of sounds and colours, that we can
attribute a distinct continued existence to objects without ever consulting
reason, or weighting our opinions by any philosophical principles. And, indeed,
whatever convincing arguments philosophers may fancy they can produce to
establish the belief of objects independent of the mind, it is obvious these
arguments are known but to very few; and that it is not by them that children,
peasants, and the greatest part of mankind, are induced to attribute objects to
some impressions, and deny them to others. Accordingly, we find that all the
conclusions which the vulgar form on this head, are directly contrary to those
which are confirmed by philosophy. For philosophy informs us that everything
which appears to the mind is nothing but a perception, and is interrupted and

dependent on the mind; whereas the vulgar confound perceptions and objects, and attribute a distinct continued existence to the very things they feel or see. This sentiment, then, as it is entirely unreasonable, must proceed from some other faculty than the understanding. To which we may add, that, as long as we take our perceptions and objects to be the same, we can never infer the existence of the one from that of the other, nor form any argument from the relation of cause and effect; which is the only one that can assure us of matter of fact. Even after we distinguish our perceptions from our objects, it will appear presently that we are still incapable of reasoning from the existence of one to that of the other: so that, upon the whole, our reason neither does, nor is it possible it ever should, upon any supposition give us an assurance of the continued and distinct existence of body. That opinion must be entirely owing to the *imagination*: which must now be the subject of our inquiry.

Since all impressions are internal and perishing existences, and appear as such, the notion of their distinct and continued existence must arise from a concurrence of some of their qualities with the qualities of the imagination; and since this notion does not extend to all of them, it must arise from certain qualities peculiar to some impressions. It will, therefore, be easy for us to discover these qualities by a comparison of the impressions, to which we attribute a distinct and continued existence, with those which we regard as internal and perishing.

We may observe, then, that it is neither upon account of the involuntariness of certain impressions, as is commonly supposed, nor of their superior force and violence, that we attribute to them a reality and continued existence, which we refuse to others that are voluntary or feeble. For it is evident our pains and pleasures, our passions and affections, which we never suppose to have any existence beyond our perception, operate with greater violence, and are equally involuntary, as the impressions of figure and extension, colour and sound, which we suppose to be permanent beings. The heat of a fire, when moderate, is supposed to exist in the fire; but the pain which it causes upon a near approach is not taken to have any being except in the perception.

These vulgar opinions, then, being rejected, we must search for some other hypothesis, by which we may discover those peculiar qualities in our impressions, which makes us attribute to them a distinct and continued existence.

After a little examination, we shall find that all those objects, to which we attribute a continued existence, have a peculiar *constancy*, which distinguishes them from the impressions whose existence depends upon our perception. Those mountains, and houses, and trees, which lie at present under my eye, have always appeared to me in the same order; and when I lose sight of them by shutting my eyes or turning my head, I soon after find them return upon me without the least alteration. My bed and table, my books and papers, present themselves in the same uniform manner, and change not upon account of any interruption in my seeing or perceiving them. This is the case with all the impressions whose objects are supposed to have an external existence; and is the case with no other impressions, whether gentle or violent, voluntary or involuntary.

This constancy, however, is not so perfect as not to admit of very considerable exceptions. Bodies often change their position and qualities, and, after a little absence or interruption, may become hardly knowable. But here it is observable, that even in these changes they preserve a *coherence*, and have a regular dependence on each other; which is the foundation of a kind of reasoning from causation, and produces the opinion of their continued existence. When I return to my chamber after an hour's absence, I find not my fire in the same situation in which I left it; but then I am accustomed, in other instances, to see a like alteration produced in a like time, whether I am present or absent, near or remote. This coherence, therefore, in their changes, is one of the characteristics of external objects, as well as their constancy.

Having found that the opinion of the continued existence of body depends on the *coherence* and *constancy* of certain impressions, I now proceed to examine after what manner these qualities give rise to so extraordinary an opinion. To begin with the coherence; we may observe, that though those internal impressions, which we regard as fleeting and perishing, have also a certain coherence or regularity in their appearances, yet it is of somewhat a different nature from that which we discover in bodies. Our passions are found by experience to have a mutual connection with and dependence on each other; but on no occasion is it necessary to suppose that they have existed and operated, when they were not perceived, in order to preserve the same dependence and connection, of which we have had experience. The case is not the same with relation to external objects. Those require a continued existence, or otherwise lose, in a great measure, the regularity of their operation. I am here seated in my chamber, with my face to the fire; and all the objects that strike my senses are contained in a few yards around me. My memory, indeed, informs me of the existence of many objects; but, then, this information extends not beyond their past existence, nor do either my senses or memory give any testimony to the continuance of their being. When, therefore, I am thus seated, and revolve over these thoughts, I hear on a sudden a noise as of a door turning upon its hinges; and a little after see a porter who advances towards me. This gives occasion to many new reflections and reasonings. First, I never have observed that this noise could proceed from anything but the motion of a door; and therefore conclude that the present phenomenon is a contradiction to all past experience, unless the door, which I remember on the other side the chamber, be still in being. Again, I have always found, that a human body was possessed of a quality which I call gravity, and which hinders it from mounting in the air, as this porter must have done to arrive at my chamber, unless the stairs I remember be not annihilated by my absence. But this is not all. I receive a letter, which, upon opening it, I perceive by the handwriting and subscription to have come from a friend, who says he is two hundred leagues distant. It is evident I can never account for this phenomenon, conformable to my experience in other instances, without spreading out in my mind the whole sea and continent between us, and supposing the effects and continued existence of posts and ferries, according to my memory and observation. To consider these phenomena of the porter and letter in a certain light, they are contradictions to common experience, and may be regarded as objections to those maxims which we form concerning the connection of causes and effects. I am accustomed to hear such a sound, and see such an object in motion at the same time. I have not received, in this particular instance, both these perceptions. These observations are contrary, unless I suppose that the door still remains, and that it was opened without my perceiving it: and this supposition, which was at first entirely arbitrary and hypothetical, acquires a force and evidence by its being the only one upon which I can reconcile these contradictions. There is scarce a moment of my life wherein there is not a similar instance presented to me, and I have not occasion to suppose the continued existence of objects, in order to connect their past and present appearances, and give them such a union with each other, as I have found, by experience, to be suitable to their particular natures and circumstances. Here, then, I am naturally led to regard the world as something real and durable, and as preserving its existence, even when it is no longer present to my perception.

But, though this conclusion, from the coherence of appearances, may seem to be of the same nature with our reasonings concerning causes and effects, as being derived from custom, and regulated by past experience, we shall find, upon examination, that they are at the bottom considerably different from each other, and that this inference arises from the understanding and from custom, in an indirect and oblique manner. For it will readily be allowed, that since nothing is ever really present to the mind, besides its own perceptions, it is not only impossible that any habit should ever be acquired otherwise than by the regular succession of these perceptions, but also that any habit should ever exceed that degree of regularity. Any degree, therefore, of regularity in our perceptions can never be a foundation for us to infer a greater degree of regularity in some objects which are not perceived, since this supposes a contradiction, viz., a habit acquired by what was never present to the mind. But it is evident that, whenever we infer the continued existence of the objects of sense from their coherence, and the frequency of their union, it is in order to bestow on the objects a greater regularity than what is observed in our mere perceptions. We remark a connection betwixt two kinds of objects in their past appearance to the senses, but are not able to observe this connection to be perfectly constant, since the turning about of our head, or the shutting of our eyes, is able to break it. What, then, do we suppose in this case, but that these objects still continue their usual connection, notwithstanding their apparent interruption, and that the irregular appearances are joined by something of which we are insensible? But as all reasoning concerning matters of fact arises only from custom, and custom can only be the effect of repeated perceptions, and extending of custom and reasoning beyond the perceptions can never be the direct and natural effect of the constant repetition and connection, but must arise from the co-operation of some other principles.

I have already observed,[3] in examining the foundation of mathematics, that the imagination, when set into any train of thinking, is apt to continue even when its object fails it, and like a galley put in motion by the oars, carries on its course without any new impulse. This I have assigned for the reason, why, after considering several loose standards of equality, and correcting them by each other, we proceed to imagine so correct and exact a standard of that relation as is not liable to the least error or variation. The same principle makes us easily entertain this opinion of the continued existence of body. Objects have a certain coherence even as they appear to our senses; but this coherence is much greater and more uniform if we suppose the objects to have a continued existence; and as the mind is once in the train of observing a uniformity among objects, it naturally continues till it renders the uniformity as complete as possible. The simple supposition of their continued existence suffices for this pur-

---

[3]Part II, section 4.

pose, and gives us a notion of a much greater regularity among objects, than what they have when we look no further than our senses.

But whatever force we may ascribe to this principle, I am afraid it is too weak to support alone so vast an edifice as is that of the continued existence of all external bodies; and that we must join the *constancy* of their appearance to the *coherence*, in order to give a satisfactory account of that opinion. As the explication of this will lead me into a considerable compass of very profound reasoning, I think it proper, in order to avoid confusion, to give a short sketch or abridgment of my system, and afterwards draw out all its parts in their full compass. This inference from the constancy of our perceptions, like the precedent from their coherence, gives rise to the opinion of the *continued* existence of body, which is prior to that of its *distinct* existence, and produces that latter principle.

When we have been accustomed to observe a constancy in certain impressions, and have found that the perception of the sun or ocean, for instance, returns upon us, after an absence or annihilation, with like parts and in a like order as at its first appearance, we are not apt to regard these interrupted perceptions as different (which they really are), but on the contrary consider them as individually the same, upon account of their resemblance. But as this interruption of their existence is contrary to their perfect identity, and makes us regard the first impression as annihilated, and the second as newly created, we find ourselves somewhat at a loss, and are involved in a kind of contradiction. In order to free ourselves from this difficulty, we disguise, as much as possible, the interruption, or rather remove it entirely, by supposing that these interrupted perceptions are connected by a real existence, of which we are insensible. This supposition, or idea of continued existence, acquires a force and vivacity from the memory of these broken impressions, and from that propensity which they give us to suppose them the same; and according to the precedent reasoning, the very essence of belief consists in the force and vivacity of the conception. . . .

I believe an intelligent reader will find less difficulty to assent to this system, than to comprehend it fully and distinctly, and will allow, after a little reflection, that every part carries its own proof along with it. It is indeed evident, that as the vulgar *suppose*, their perceptions to be their only objects, and at the same time *believe* the continued existence of matter, we must account for the origin of the belief upon that supposition. Now, upon that supposition, it is a false opinion that any of our objects, or perceptions, are identically the same after an interruption; and consequently the opinion of their identity can never arise from reason, but must arise from the imagination. The imagination is seduced into such an opinion only by means of the resemblance of certain perceptions; since we find they are only our resembling perceptions, which we have a propension to suppose the same. This propension to bestow an identity on our resembling perceptions, produces the fiction of a continued existence; since that fiction, as well as the identity, is really false, as is acknowledged by all philosophers, and has no other effect than to remedy the interruption of our perceptions, which is the only circumstance that is contrary to their identity. In the last place, this propension causes belief by means of the present impressions of the memory; since, without the remembrance of former sensations, it is plain we never should have any belief of the continued existence of body. Thus, in examining all these parts, we find that each of them is supported by the strongest proofs; and that all of them together form a consistent system, which is perfectly convincing. A strong propensity or inclination alone, without any present impression, will sometimes cause a belief or opinion. How much more when aided by that circumstance!

But though we are led after this manner, by the natural propensity of the imagination, to ascribe a continued existence to those sensible objects or perceptions, which we find to resemble each other in their interrupted appearance; yet a very little reflection and philosophy is sufficient to make us perceive the fallacy of that opinion. I have already observed that there is an intimate connection betwixt those two principles, of a *continued* and of a *distinct* or *independent* existence, and that we no sooner establish the one than the other follows as a necessary consequence. It is the opinion of a continued existence, which first takes place, and without much study or reflection draws the other along with it, wherever the mind follows its first and most natural tendency. But when we compare experiments, and reason a little upon them, we quickly perceive that the doctrine of the independent existence of our sensible perceptions is contrary to the plainest experience. This leads us backward upon our footsteps to perceive our error in attributing a continued existence to our perceptions, and is the origin of many very curious opinions, which we shall here endeavour to account for.

It will first be proper to observe a few of those experiments, which convince us that our perceptions are not possessed of any independent existence. When we press one eye with a finger, we immediately perceive all the objects to become double, and one half of them to be removed from their common and natural position. But as we do not attribute a continued existence to both these perceptions, and as they are both of the same nature, we clearly perceive that all our perceptions are dependent on our organs and the disposition of our nerves and animal spirits. This opinion is confirmed by the seeming increase and diminution of objects according to their distance; by the apparent alterations in their figure; by the changes in their colour and other qualities, from our sickness and distempers, and by an infinite number of other experiments of the same kind; from all which we learn that our sensible perceptions are not possessed of any distinct or independent existence.

The natural consequence of this reasoning should be, that our perceptions have no more a continued than an independent existence; and, indeed, philosophers have so far run into this opinion, that they change their system, and distinguish (as we shall do for the future) betwixt perceptions and objects, of which the former are supposed to be interrupted and perishing, and different at every different return; and latter to be uninterrupted, and to preserve a continued existence and identity. But however philosophical this new system may be esteemed, I assert that it is only a palliative remedy, and that it contains all the difficulties of the vulgar system, with some others that are peculiar to itself. There are no principles either of the understanding or fancy, which lead us directly to embrace this opinion of the double existence of perceptions and objects, nor can we arrive at it but by passing through the common hypothesis of the identity and continuance of our interrupted perceptions. Were we not first persuaded that our perceptions are our only objects, and continue to exist even when they no longer make their appearance to the senses, we should never be led to think that our perceptions and objects are different, and that our objects alone preserve a continued existence. "The latter hypothesis has no primary recommendation either to reason or the imagination, but acquires all its influence on the imagination from the former." This proposition contains two parts which we shall endeavour to prove as distinctly and clearly as such abstruse subjects will permit.

As to the first part of the proposition, *that this philosophical hypothesis has no primary recommendation, either to reason or the imagination,* we may soon satisfy ourselves with regard to *reason,* by the following reflections. The only existences, of which we are certain, are perceptions, which, being immediately present to us by consciousness, command our strongest assent, and are the first foundation of all our conclusions. The only conclusion we can draw from the existence of one thing to that of another, is by means of the relation of cause and effect, which shows that there is a connection betwixt them, and that the existence of one is dependent on that of the other. The idea of this relation is derived from past experience, by which we find that two beings are constantly conjoined together, and are always present at once to the mind. But as no beings are ever present to the mind but perceptions, it follows that we may observe a conjunction or a relation of cause and effect between different perceptions, but can never observe it between perceptions and objects. It is impossible, therefore, that from the existence or any of the qualities of the former, we can ever form any conclusion concerning the existence of the latter, or ever satisfy our reason in this particular.

It is no less certain that this philosophical system has no primary recommendation to the *imagination,* and that that faculty would never, of itself, and by its original tendency, have fallen upon such a principle. I confess it will be somewhat difficult to prove this to the full satisfaction of the reader; because it implies a negative, which in many cases will not admit of any postive proof. If any one would take the pains to examine this question, and would invent a system to account for the direct origin of this opinion from the imagination, we should be able, by the examination of that system, to pronounce a certain judgment in the present subject. Let it be taken for granted, that our perceptions are broken and interrupted, and, however like, are still different from each other; and let any one, upon this supposition, show why the fancy, directly and immediately, proceeds to the belief of another existence, resembling these perceptions in their nature, but yet continued, and uninterrupted, and identical; and after he has done this to my satisfaction, I promise to renounce my present opinion. Meanwhile I cannot forbear concluding, from the very abstractedness and difficulty of the first supposition, that it is an improper subject for the fancy to work upon. Whoever would explain the origin of the *common* opinion concerning the continued and distinct existence of body, must take the mind in its *common* situation, and must proceed upon the supposition, that our perceptions are our only objects, and continue to exist even when they are not perceived. Though this opinion be false, it is the most natural of any, and has alone any primary recommendation to the fancy.

As to the second part of the proposition, *that the philosophical system acquires all its influence on the imagination from the vulgar one;* we may observe that this is a natural and unavoidable consequence of the foregoing conclusion, *that it has no primary recommendation to reason or the imagination.* For as the philosophical system is found by experience to take hold of many minds, and, in particular, of all those who reflect ever so little on this subject, it must derive all its authority from the vulgar system, since it has no original authority of its own. The manner in which these two systems, though directly contrary, are connected together, may be explained as follows.

The imagination naturally runs on in this train of thinking. Our perceptions are our only objects: resembling perceptions are the same, however broken or uninterrupted in their appearance: this appearing interruption is contrary to the identity: the interruption consequently extends not beyond the appearance, and the perception or object really continues to exist, even when absent from us: our sensible perceptions have, therefore, a continued and uninterrupted existence. But as a little reflection destroys this conclusion, that our perceptions have a continued existence, by showing that they have a dependent one, it would naturally be expected that we must altogether reject the opinion, that there is such a thing in nature as a continued existence, which is preserved even when it no longer appears to the senses. The case, however, is otherwise. Philosophers are so far from rejecting the opinion of a continued existence upon rejecting that of the independence and continuance of our sensible perceptions, that though all sects agree in the latter sentiment, the former, which is in a manner its necessary consequence, has been peculiar to a few extravagant sceptics; who, after all, maintained that opinion in words only and were never able to bring themselves sincerely to believe it.

There is a great difference betwixt such opinions as we form after a calm and profound reflection, and such as we embrace by a kind of instinct or natural impulse, on account of their suitableness and conformity to the mind. If these opinions become contrary, it is not difficult to foresee which of them will have the advantage. As long as our attention is bent upon the subject, the philosophical and studied principle may prevail; but the moment we relax our thoughts, nature will display herself, and draw us back to our former opinion. Nay she has sometimes such an influence, that she can stop our progress, even in the midst of our most profound reflections, and keep us from running on with all the consequences of any philosophical opinion. Thus, though we clearly perceive the dependence and interruption of our perceptions, we stop short in our career, and never upon that account reject the notion of an independent and continued existence. That opinion has taken such deep root in the imagination, that it is impossible ever to eradicate it, nor will any strained metaphysical conviction of the dependence of our perceptions be sufficient for that purpose.

But though our natural and obvious principles here prevail above our studied reflections, it is certain there must be some struggle and opposition in this case; at least so long as these reflections retain any force or vivacity. In order to set ourselves at ease in this particular, we contrive a new hypothesis, which seems to comprehend both these principles of reason and imagination. This hypothesis is the philosophical one of the double existence of perceptions and objects; which pleases our reason, in allowing that our dependent perceptions are interrupted and different, and at the same time is agreeable to the imagination, in attributing a continued existence to something else, which we call *objects*. This philosophical system, therefore, is the monstrous offspring of two principles, which are contrary to each other, which are both at once embraced by the mind, and which are unable mutually to destroy each other. The imagination tells us that our resembling perceptions have a continued and uninterrupted existence, and are not annihilated by their absence. Reflection tells us, that even our resembling perceptions are interrupted in their existence, and different from each other. The contradiction betwixt these opinions we elude by a new fiction, which is conformable to the hypothesis both of reflection and fancy, by ascribing these contrary qualities to different existences; the *interruption* to perceptions, and the *continuance* to objects. Nature is obstinate, and will not quit the field, however strongly attacked by reason; and at the same time reason is so clear in the point that there is no possibility of disguising her. Not being able to reconcile these two enemies, we endeavour to set ourselves at ease as much as possible, by successively granting to each whatever it demands, and by feigning a double existence, where each may find something that has all the conditions it desires. Were we fully convinced that our resembling perceptions are continued, and identical, and independent, we should never run into this opinion of a double existence; since we should find satisfaction in our first supposition, and would not look beyond. Again, were we fully convinced that our perceptions are dependent, and interrupted, and different, we should be as little inclined to embrace the opinion of a double existence; since in that case we should clearly perceive the error of our first supposition of a continued existence, and would never regard it any further. It is therefore from the intermediate situation of the mind that this opinion rises, and from such an adherence to these two contrary principles, as makes us seek some pretext to justify our receiving both; which happily at last is found in the system of a double existence.

Another advantage of this philosophical system is its similarity to the vulgar one, by which means we can humour our reason for a moment, when it becomes troublesome and solicitous; and yet upon its least negligence or inattention, can easily return to our vulgar and natural notions. Accordingly we find that philosophers neglect not this advantage, but, immediately upon leaving their closets, mingle with the rest of mankind in those exploded opinions, that our perceptions are our only objects, and continue identically and uninterruptedly the same in all their interrupted appearances.

There are other particulars of this system, where we may remark its dependence on the fancy, in a very conspicuous manner. Of these, I shall observe the two following. *First*, we suppose external objects to resemble internal perceptions. I have already shown that the relation of cause and effect can never afford us any just conclusion from the existence or qualities of our perceptions to the existence of external continued objects; and I shall further add, that even though they could afford such a conclusion, we should never have any reason to infer that our objects resemble our perceptions. That opinion, therefore is derived from nothing but the quality of the fancy above explained, *that it borrows all its ideas from some precedent perception.* We never can conceive anything but perceptions, and therefore must make everything resemble them.

Secondly, as we suppose our objects in general to resemble our perceptions, so we take it for granted that every particular object resembles that perception which it causes. The relation of cause and effect determines us to join the other of resemblance; and the ideas of these existences being already united together in the fancy by the former relation, we naturally add the latter to complete the union. We have a strong propensity to complete every union by joining new relations to those which we have before observed betwixt any ideas, as we shall have occasion to observe presently.[4]

Having thus given an account of all the systems, both popular and philosophical, with regard to external existences, I cannot forbear giving vent to a certain sentiment which arises upon reviewing those systems. I begun this subject with

---

[4]Section 5.

premising that we ought to have an implicit faith in our senses, and that this would be the conclusion I should draw from the whole of my reasoning. But to be ingenuous, I feel myself *at present* of a quite contrary sentiment, and am more inclined to repose no faith at all in my senses, or rather imagination, than to place in it such an implicit confidence. I cannot conceive how such trivial qualities of the fancy, conducted by such false suppositions, can ever lead to any solid and rational system. They are the coherence and constancy of our perceptions, which produce the opinion of their continued existence; though these qualities of perceptions have no perceivable connection with such an existence. The constancy of our perceptions has the most considerable effect, and yet is attended with the greatest difficulties. It is a gross illusion to suppose that our resembling perceptions are numerically the same; and it is this illusion which leads us into the opinion that these perceptions are uninterrupted, and are still existent, even when they are not present to the senses. This is the case with our popular system. And as to our philosophical one, it is liable to the same difficulties; and is, over and above, loaded with this absurdity, that it at once denies and establishes the vulgar supposition. Philosophers deny our resembling perceptions to be identically the same, and uninterrupted; and yet have so great a propensity to believe them such, that they arbitrarily invent a new set of perceptions, to which they attribute these qualities. I say, a new set of perceptions: for we may well suppose in general, but it is impossible for us distinctly to conceive, objects to be in their nature anything but exactly the same with perceptions. What then can we look for from this confusion of groundless and extraordinary opinions but error and falsehood? And how can we justify to ourselves any belief we repose in them? This sceptical doubt, both with respect to reason and the senses, is a malady which can never be radically cured, but must return upon us every moment, however we may chase it away, and sometimes may seem entirely free from it. It is impossible, upon any system, to defend either our understanding or senses; and we but expose them further when we endeavour to justify them in that manner. As the sceptical doubt arises naturally from a profound and intense reflection on those subjects, it always increases the further we carry our reflections, whether in opposition or conformity to it. Carelessness and inattention alone can afford us any remedy. For this reason I rely entirely upon them; and take it for granted, whatever may be the reader's opinion at this present moment, that an hour hence he will be persuaded there is both an external and internal world; and, going upon that supposition, I intend to examine some general systems, both ancient and modern, which have been proposed of both, before I proceed to a more particular inquiry concerning our impressions. This will not, perhaps, in the end, be found foreign to our present purpose.

THE DEMOLITION OF KNOWLEDGE

Hume's scepticism affects three major factors in knowledge: deductive reasoning, our presumed knowledge of the external world (as acquired through the senses), and our knowledge of ourselves. All that escapes it is the stream of consciousness itself, the occurrence of which alone, of the atomic percepts that constitute it, remains indubitable. But in this stream, we must remember, "whatever objects are different are distinguishable, and whatever objects are distinguishable are separable"[9]; and "our distinct perceptions are distinct existences," and "the mind never perceives any real connection among distinct existences."[10]

1. Scepticism With Regard To Reason

Accordingly, even the reasonings based on direct intuition of relations between ideas becomes subject to dissolution and doubt, and is ultimately reduced to probable reasoning dependent upon cause and effect.

Hume admits the reasonings of algebra and arithmetic to be exact, because, he says, they depend ultimately on the conception of a unit as a precise standard of comparison. When we compare, add, subtract, divide, and multiply numbers, we are, in effect, counting units in different ways. But here Hume fails to adhere strictly to his own principles, for the idea of unity must be derived from some impression and none is to be found which is of any avail in mathematics. Most objects of which we have impressions are divisible into parts, so we may regard each of them as one or many. What then is the impression of a unit? If we are to be consistent we can only say (as Hume does)[11] that such subdivision can go on only until we reach the minimum sensible. But this cannot serve as the impression of the unit (or of unity), the idea of which is used in arithmetic as our standard, for we cannot and do not count *minima sensibilia* in making comparisons. Mathematics, as a whole therefore, and not only geometry, can ultimately be regarded only as an approximate science.[12]

But worse is to follow, for although Hume allows that the rules of demonstrative reasoning are certain and infallible, we can never be certain that we have followed them strictly and applied them accurately. Consequently, any conclusion we reach, even by mathematical calculation, might be wrong and we can check it only be repeating the reasoning or proving it by some other similar demonstrative method. Repeated checks, however, do not produce certainty, but can do no more than increase the *probability* that our reasoning has been accurate and so our conclusion true.

---

[9]*Treatise* Book I, Part I, section 7.

[10]*Treatise*, Appendix.

[11]Cf. *Treatise*, Book I, Part II, sections 1–3.

[12]Cf. the example sometimes given of the inexactitude of $2 + 2 = 4$, by supposing the units to be drops of oil.

In effect, checking a calculation is a resort to inductive argument for the experience of a constant (or frequent) conjunction of the same answer with the same series of steps in the calculation leads us to conclude that this is the only answer, and so the right one: in other words, we conclude that there is a necessary connection between calculation and result from the fact that we find them constantly conjoined. If I repeat a calculation three times and get a different result each time, I cannot say which, if any, is correct. If I repeat it twice more and get one of the first three answers again, twice over, the probability that this one is right is three-fifths. Yet even if all the repetitions give the same answer, its correctness is not certain, for further checking may reveal mistakes that were repeated in the earlier trials.

It is to be noticed that even modern calculating machines and computers are liable to error, if they are wrongly programmed, or if the input is wrongly encoded, or if they malfunction; and the mistake can be discovered only by external checks and by experience. Thus they are subject to the same limitations that Hume alleges. In certain circumstances we may say that the probability of their accuracy is very high, but we can never say that it is absolutely certain (although for practical purposes the difference between very high probability and certainty may be negligible).

Demonstration therefore is certain, at most, only in principle, never in fact, and whatever knowledge is derived from it is never more than probable in some degree, which by repetition may be increased but can never be made absolute. But Hume goes much further than this. He maintains that frequent reconsideration of any train of reasoning, so far from increasing its probability, reduces it. For our past experience of errors must make us aware of the fallibility of any opinions, however carefully derived, and so reduce, to some extent, our confidence in them. Yet again, our awareness of our own liability to error is only a probable conclusion derived from past experience and is itself liable to similar doubt. Thus each review of our reasonings and opinions reduces their probability, and, if we persisted, would diminish their credibility to nothing. We ought, therefore, to be brought to the point of utter scepticism and would deny the truth of all judgment—in short, refrain altogether from judging—but that "nature, by an absolute and uncontrollable necessity, has determined us to judge as well as to breathe and feel."

It is odd that Hume should speak of an absolute and uncontrollable necessity in nature so soon after he has demonstrated persuasively that there is no discoverable necessity in the conjunction of natural phenomena and that our belief in it is simply the result of habit. To press this point, however, to convict Hume of inconsistency and to seek to correct his doctrine by withdrawing the statement quoted above, would only make matters worse. For if we were not conditioned by nature to judge, we should, on Hume's showing, be overwhelmed by doubt; and whether we judge or not, Hume offers us no ground for confidence in the truth of our judgment, only the reverse.

As matters stand so far, judgment is a merely instinctive activity and is based on reasoning all of which finally reduces to probable reasoning from cause and effect. In a significant footnote to section 7 of Part III, Hume asserts, in opposition to the traditional logicians, that reasoning does not require more than two ideas (nor judgment more than one) and that reasoning from effect to cause is immediate and is "not only a true species of reasoning but the strongest of all others, and more convincing than when we interpose another idea to connect the two extremes."

But this form of reasoning — the strongest of all — has been shown to depend on no more than habitual expectation generated by the contingent occurrence of a constant conjunction. It is all inductive reasoning which Hume has shown to be unsupportable either by demonstration or by experience. Accordingly, our resultant beliefs are no different from and no better than superstitions and are produced psychologically in exactly the same way.

With our reasoning reduced to so parlous a condition what becomes of our knowledge of the persistence and reality of things in the world about us?

2. Scepticism With Regard to the Senses

The chapter with this heading is one of the longest, most interesting and most important in Book I of the *Treatise*. It contains Hume's theory of our knowledge of the external world and is full of important epistemological insights of positive value. Yet the general effect is sceptical, for Hume persistently castigates as fallacy and illusion every means, whether logical or psychological, by which we come to believe in the reality of external bodies.

In an earlier chapter[13] Hume has declared the impossibility of any idea of external existence. Every impression and every idea we experience is conceived of as existent and we have no separate impression or idea of existence as such. Similarly, as nothing is ever present to the mind but perceptions, we can have no idea except of a perception (that

---

[13]*Treatise*, Book I, Part II, section 6.

is, of an impression or another idea) and so no idea of any external existent separate from and independent of perceptions. This is just Berkeley's doctrine reemphasized and reinforced.

It is therefore "vain to ask, *Whether there be body or not?*" If we did ask this question, we should have no means of answering it and no source of evidence to support any answer. So, again, we simply take the answer for granted as an instinctive assumption. The only fruitful question that can be raised is, "What causes induce us to believe in the existence of body?"

The answer which Hume offers is that this belief is the work of the imagination. We experience similar impressions and because of their similarity the mind runs easily from one to the other; so, in imagination we identify them and assume that the intermittently occurring similars are mutually continuous during the intervals when they are not perceived. This gives us the belief in the continued existence of objects when we are not perceiving them. Along with this belief, as a sort of corollary to it, is the belief that the objects also exist independently of their being perceived, for how else could they exist in the intervals between perception?

Similarly, even when objects do not remain constant (when impressions of them are not similar at different times) but change in a regular fashion (as when a fire dies down in the course of time), we attribute constant regularity to them if the percepts occur in coherent groups. Then, if some members of the group occur without the rest, we imagine the rest as having occurred without being perceived. Thus, when we observe a blazing fire at 9 a.m. and again, after an absence of some time, a fitful glow among embers, we presume that the same series of changes has occurred in the interval as we have in the past observed when we have been continuously present throughout the process.

The account Hume gives of the way in which we conclude to the existence of a world of external objects from the constancy and coherence of certain of our perceptions is one of his most perspicacious contributions to the theory of knowledge. He recounts a train of reasoning by which he concludes to the external existence of a door behind him, a staircase outside his room, continents and oceans, and a friend living abroad, from the evidence before him, first of the sound of the door opening, then of the appearance of a porter with a letter, then of the contents of the letter which he reads. These, in conjunction with his rememberance of the past association of certain types of event (the sound of a door swinging on its hinges and the movement of the door itself; the normal inability of heavy bodies to rise of their own accord;

the experience of a staircase ascending to his room; and so forth), lead him to certain conclusions on pain of self-contradiction. The appearance of the porter is inexplicable unless he climbed the stair — or unless we are to believe contrary to experience that heavy bodies levitate. That a letter in a friend's well-known handwriting should have sprung into existence without the friend's having written it contradicts all experience, to avoid which we must take it as a product of the friend's activity. The letter reports that the friend is in a distant country, and that would be inconsistent with any belief in the nonexistence of far countries and the intervening space with the objects, for which we have other evidence, which it contains. Therefore we cannot reasonably believe otherwise than that these things exist.

Here Hume is describing an argument resting on coherence in a different sense from that in which he says our percepts are "coherent." By that he meant that the same train of percepts is frequently repeated in the same order. The coherence of percepts is a kind of extended constancy by which not just one percept or one group of simultaneous percepts constantly recur, but a series of different percepts constantly recurs in the same sequence. But in the case of the porter with the letter there is no constantly recurring sequence. Here the coherence is between beliefs. I believe, in consequence of past experience, that heavy bodies do not levitate, I now see a heavy body existing on a higher level than it was at a prior time. I therefore believe that it has not risen through the air but has climbed the stairs. This belief again coheres with my belief also derived from past experience that a stairway exists outside my room. I read a letter and so believe it to have been written by the friend who signed it, in conformity with what I already know of his handwriting and other habits. The letter informs me of his whereabouts and the date on which it was written. I interpret this evidence in the light of other beliefs about the geographical positions and extent of continents and oceans. I find them to cohere, for if the letter was written on the date stated and at the place alleged and had travelled (as it must have if all these beliefs are to be mutually consistent) by the means of transport which I know to exist, it would have reached me at about this time.

So I believe in the existence of an external world because all the detailed facts and events of which my immediate perceptions give evidence dovetail into and cohere with the facts and events of which my past experience has variously given evidence. The whole body of beliefs forms a coherent system and describes a structured world, so that the denial of any of them, in the face of the evidence, would undermine and destroy the basis of the whole structure.

This, as Hume was obviously aware, is the process of thought, seldom if ever made explicit, by which we actually do conclude to the
existence of a world of objects external to and independent of ourselves. But for some reason, Hume did not find this type of thinking
adequate for reliable knowledge. Perhaps it is because he confused the
coherence of beliefs with the "coherence" of perceptions, which he goes
on to argue is not a sufficient reason for the beliefs which he says we
base upon it. Or perhaps it is because the cohering and mutually
corroborating beliefs are almost all dependent upon past experience
and so on some form of inductive reasoning which Hume held to be
invalid. At all events, he lays little stress on the impressive and accurate
account he has given of coherent thinking as a support for perceptual
assurance and factual belief, and merely goes on to examine and
criticize the support which is or might be given to our common conviction of the existence of external objects based, as he holds, on the
constancy and coherence of perceptions.

These two characteristics of our perceptions, he maintains, cause us
to build up in our imagination a picture of a world of objects existing
continuously when not perceived, independently of the perceptions
and of the perceiving mind. As this imaginative construction has force
and vivacity we believe in the reality of this world, the belief and the
liveliness of the ideas being one and the same.

When we consider, however, what might be the rational basis of this
belief, Hume finds that no reasoning by which we try to support it is
sound. The reasoning is fallacious and the belief is illusory. If we then
try to base it on experience, he finds again that experience cannot
possibly support it because it goes beyond experience at all points, and
even beyond what customary arguments from cause and effect would
allow.

Clearly experience cannot tell us that resembling perceptions persist
unperceived between our experiences of them, for that would involve
the contradiction that we could experience what was the case when we
did not experience (or perceive) it. Further, when we perceive objects
the perceptions are single. We do not perceive something independently existing at the same time as some mind-dependent perception of
it. So from experience we can never get any idea of an independently
existing object.

Yet, again, we have no impression of ourselves as such but only
experience a stream of impressions and ideas of other things. So we
have no experience of separateness between our percepts and "ourselves." It is conceivable that any of these percepts might exist separate
and independent from the rest, but we cannot (and never do) experi-

ence them so. Or if we argue that the appearance of bodies at a distance from our own body is evidence of their existence independently of our perceptions, we have only to realize that our own bodies are themselves like the rest only groupings of impressions and ideas, to see that their spatial relation to other such groupings proves nothing relevant to the existence of anything independently of percepts.

The "coherence" of our impressions leads us by an argument similar to that from cause and effect to conclude that they occur and exist in our absence, when they are not perceived, but the argument goes beyond what causal arguments warrant. For we link events causally when we experience them as conjoined regularly. But here we attribute regularity to the events beyond what we experience and assume them to occur coherently even when they do not (as in the example of the fire). Now experience cannot support our beliefs, even about causal connection (because when we have frequently experienced a conjunction we believe it to obtain in cases not experienced), still less can it support the belief in the invariant coherence of what we do not experience with invariant regularity.

So much for experience. Now, what about reason? Clearly it is not on rational grounds that the ordinary unphilosophical person believes in the existence of external things. The philosophical reasons for doing so have never been heard or thought of by the majority. Moreover, what is commonly believed is not what philosophers maintain. The ordinary belief is that the perceived objects themselves persist unperceived, but philosophers, noting the inconstancy and intermittence of our percepts, recognize the belief as false. Yet they are so addicted to it that they allege a world of independently existing objects other than our percepts, which the percepts merely represent. The latter, they say, are dependent on and exist only in the mind, while the former are their causes.

Here we have a double conflict. On the one hand, the reasons given by philosophers are obviously untenable because we can infer from effects to causes only from experience – only in cases where we have experienced the constant conjunction in the past. But we experience only perceptions, never any conjunction between perceptions and other entities which are not perceptions. It is therefore impossible to infer from percepts to their causes. We have equally no grounds for alleging a relation of resemblance between perceptions and anything beyond. We cannot possibly compare the perceptions with bodies existing allegedly in independence of them and so unperceived, so that the assumed resemblance must be groundless. Moreover what the vulgar believe is the continued and independent existence unperceived of the perceptions themselves, whereas the philosophers admit the intermittent and irregular appearance of the perceptions but postulate a set of objects (or external bodies) to duplicate the percepts for which there is no possible evidence and which are suggested to them only by the vulgar belief which (in their philosophical moments) they reject, but which they can never wholly relinquish. On the other hand, the vulgar belief that perceptions persist when not perceived and are independent of the perceiving is palpably false, and there are cogent reasons which can be adduced against it (Hume here repeats and elaborates Berkeley's arguments). So that the reasoning which postulates unperceived objects causing and corresponding to percepts is groundless and is in conflict with the imagination, as well as with the common belief in the persistence of percepts unperceived, which is false.

Consequently, the whole structure of our belief in an external world, whichever way we look at it, is a texture of fallacy, error, and illusion. Hume concludes: "I cannot conceive how such trivial qualities of the fancy, conducted by such false suppositions, can ever lead to any solid and rational system . . . What then can we look for from this confusion of groundless and extraordinary opinions but error and falsehood? And how can we justify to ourselves the belief we repose in them?"[14]

What, then, are we to do? Must we reject our beliefs and our reasoning and deny the existence of the world? That we could not do if we would because we have a natural propensity to believe in its existence despite any criticism. Yet the critique set forth cannot be refuted and the consequent scepticism cannot be cured. Can we find any remedy for the confusion of our philosophical doctrines and the conflicts between sense, imagination, and reason? None—except "carelessness and inattention."[15]

Treatise of Human Nature

OF PERSONAL IDENTITY

(Book I, Part IV, Section 6)

There are some philosophers who imagine we are every moment intimately conscious of what we call our *self*; that we feel its existence and its continuance in existence; and are certain, beyond the evidence of a demonstration, both of its perfect identity and simplicity. The strongest sensation, the most violent

---

[14]*Treatise*, Book I, Part IV, section 2.
[15]*Treatise*, Book I, Part IV, section 2.

passion, say they, instead of distracting us from this view, only fix it the more intensely, and make us consider their influence on *self* either by their pain or pleasure. To attempt a further proof of this were to weaken its evidence; since no proof can be derived from any fact of which we are so intimately conscious; nor is there anything of which we can be certain if we doubt of this.

Unluckily all these positive assertions are contrary to that very experience which is pleaded for them; nor have we any idea of *self*, after the manner it is here explained. For, from what impression could this idea be derived? This question it is impossible to answer without a manifest contradiction and absurdity; and yet it is a question which must necessarily be answered, if we would have the idea of self pass for clear and intelligible. It must be some one impression that gives rise to every real idea. But self or person is not any one impression, but that to which our several impressions and ideas are supposed to have a reference. If any impression gives rise to the idea of self, that impression must continue invariably the same, through the whole course of our lives; since self is supposed to exist after that manner. But there is no impression constant and invariable. Pain and pleasure, grief and joy, passions and sensations succeed each other, and never all exist at the same time. It cannot therefore be from any of these impressions, or from any other, that the idea of self is derived; and consequently there is no such idea.

But further, what must become of all our particular perceptions upon this hypothesis? All these are different, and distinguishable, and separable from each other, and may be separately considered, and may exist separately, and have no need of anything to support their existence. After what manner therefore do they belong to self, and how are they connected with it? For my part, when I enter most intimately into what I call *myself*, I always stumble on some particular perception or other, of heat or cold, light or shade, love or hatred, pain or pleasure. I never can catch *myself* at any time without a perception, and never can observe anything but the perception. When my perceptions are removed for any time, as by sound sleep, so long am I insensible of *myself*, and may truly be said not to exist. And were all my perceptions removed by death, and could I neither think, nor feel, nor see, nor love, nor hate, after the dissolution of my body, I should be entirely annihilated, nor do I conceive what is further requisite to make me a perfect nonentity. If any one, upon serious and unprejudiced reflection, thinks he has a different notion of *himself*, I must confess I can reason no longer with him. All I can allow him is, that he may be in the right as well as I, and that we are essentially different in this particular. He may, perhaps, perceive something simple and continued, which he calls *himself*; though I am certain there is no such principle in me.

But setting aside some metaphysicians of this kind, I may venture to affirm of the rest of mankind, that they are nothing but a bundle or collection of different perceptions, which succeed each other with an inconceivable rapidity, and are in a perpetual flux and movement. Our eyes cannot turn in their sockets without varying our perceptions. Our thought is still more variable than our sight; and all our other senses and faculties contribute to this change; nor is there any single power of the soul, which remains unalterably the same, perhaps for one moment. The mind is a kind of theatre, where several perceptions successively make their appearance; pass, repass, glide away, and mingle in an infinite variety of postures and situations. There is properly no *simplicity* in it at one time, nor *identity* in different, whatever natural propension we may have to imagine that simplicity and identity. The comparison of the theatre must not mislead us. They are the successive perceptions only, that constitute the mind; nor have we the most distant notion of the place where these scenes are represented, or of the materials of which it is composed.

What then gives us so great a propension to ascribe an identity to these successive perceptions, and to suppose ourselves possessed of an invariable and uninterrupted existence through the whole course of our lives? In order to answer this question we must distinguish betwixt personal identity, as it regards our thought or imagination, and as it regards our passions or the concern we take in ourselves. The first is our present subject; and to explain it perfectly we must take the matter pretty deep, and account for that identity, which we attribute to plants and animals; there being a great analogy betwixt it and the identity of a self or person.

We have a distinct idea of an object that remains invariable and uninterrupted through a supposed variation of time; and this idea we call that of *identity* or *sameness*. We have also a distinct idea of several different objects existing in succession, and connected together by a close relation; and this to an accurate view affords as perfect a notion of *diversity* as if there was no manner of relation among the objects. But though these two ideas of identity, and a succession of related objects, be in themselves perfectly distinct, and even contrary, yet it is certain that, in our common way of thinking, they are generally confounded with each other. That action of the imagination, by which we consider the uninterrupted and invariable object, and that by which we reflect on the succession of related objects, are almost the same to the feeling; nor is there much more effort of thought required in the latter case than in the former. The relation facilitates the transition of the mind from one object to another, and renders its passage as smooth as if it contemplated one continued object. This resemblance is the cause of the confusion and mistake, and makes us substitute the notion identity, instead of that of related objects. However at one instant we may consider the related succession as variable or interrupted, we are sure the next to ascribe to it a perfect identity, and regard it as invariable and uninterrupted. Our propensity to this mistake is so great from the resemblance above mentioned, that we fall into it before we are aware; and though we incessantly correct ourselves by reflection, and return to a more accurate method of thinking, yet we cannot long sustain our philosophy, or take off this bias from the imagination. Our last resource is to yield to it, and boldly assert that these different related objects are in effect the same, however interrupted and variable. In order to justify to ourselves this absurdity, we often feign some new and unintelligible principle, that connects the objects together, and prevents their interruption or variation. Thus we feign the continued existence of the perceptions of our senses, to remove the interruption; and run into the notion of a *soul*, and *self*, and *substance*, to disguise the variation. But, we may further observe, that where we do not give rise to such a fiction, our propension to confound identity with relation is so great, that we are apt to imagine something unknown and mysterious,[5] connecting the parts,

---

[5]If the reader is desirous to see how a great genius may be influenced by these seemingly trivial principles of the imagination, as well as the mere vulgar, let him read my Lord Shaftesbury's reasoning concerning the uniting principle of the universe, and the identity of plants and animals. See his *Moralists*, or *Philosophical Rhapsody*.

beside their relation; and this I take to be the case with regard to the identity we ascribe to plants and vegetables. And even when this does not take place, we still feel a propensity to confound these ideas, though we are not able fully to satisfy ourselves in that particular, nor find anything invariable and uninterrupted to justify our notion of identity.

Thus the controversy concerning identity is not merely a dispute of words. For when we attribute identity, in an improper sense, to variable or interrupted objects, our mistake is not confined to the expression, but is commonly attended with a fiction, either of something invariable and uninterrupted, or of something mysterious and inexplicable, or at least with a propensity to such fictions. What will suffice to prove this hypothesis to the satisfaction of every fair inquirer, is to show, from daily experience and observation, that the objects which are variable or interrupted, and yet are supposed to continue the same, are such only as consist of a succession of parts, connected together by resemblance, contiguity, or causation. For as such a succession answers evidently to our notion of diversity, it can only be by mistake we ascribe to it an identity; and as the relation of parts, which leads us into this mistake, is really nothing but a quality, which produces an association of ideas, and an easy transition of the imagination from one to another, it can only be from the resemblance, which this act of the mind bears to that by which we contemplate one continued object, that the error arises. Our chief business, then, must be to prove, that all objects, to which we ascribe identity, without observing their invariableness and uninterruptedness, are such as consist of a succession of related objects.

In order to this, suppose any mass of matter, of which the parts are contiguous and connected, to be placed before us; it is plain we must attribute a perfect identity to this mass, provided all the parts continue uninterruptedly and invariably the same, whatever motion or change of place we may observe either in the whole or in any of the parts. But supposing some very *small* or *inconsiderable* part to be added to the mass, or subtracted from it; though this absolutely destroys the identity of the whole, strictly speaking, yet as we seldom think so accurately, we scruple not to pronounce a mass of matter the same, where we find so trivial an alteration. The passage of the thought from the object before the change to the object after it, is so smooth and easy, that we scarce perceive the transition, and are apt to imagine, that it is nothing but a continued survey of the same object.

There is a very remarkable circumstance that attends this experiment; which is, that though the change of any considerable part in a mass of matter destroys the identity of the whole, yet we must measure the greatness of the part, not absolutely, but by its *proportion* to the whole. The addition or diminution of a mountain would not be sufficient to produce a diversity in a planet; though the change of a very few inches would be able to destroy the identity of some bodies. It will be impossible to account for this, but by reflecting that objects operate upon the mind, and break or interrupt the continuity of its actions, not according to their real greatness, but according to their proportion to each other; and therefore, since this interruption makes an object cease to appear the same, it must be the uninterrupted progress of the thought which constitutes the imperfect identity.

This may be confirmed by another phenomenon. A change in any considerable part of a body destroys its identity; but it is remarkable, that where the change is produced *gradually* and *insensibly*, we are less apt to ascribe to it the same effect. The reason can plainly be no other, than that the mind, in following the successive changes of the body, feels an easy passage from the surveying its condition in one moment, to the viewing of it in another, and in no particular time perceives any interruption in its actions. From which continued perception, it ascribes a continued existence and identity to the object.

But whatever precaution we may use in introducing the changes gradually, and making them proportionable to the whole, it is certain, that where the changes are at last observed to become considerable, we make a scruple of ascribing identity to such different objects. There is, however, another artifice, by which we may induce the imagination to advance a step further; and that is, by producing a reference of the parts to each other, and a combination to some *common end* or purpose. A ship, of which a considerable part has been changed by frequent reparations, is still considered as the same; nor does the difference of the materials hinder us from ascribing an identity to it. The common end, in which the parts conspire, is the same under all their variations, and affords an easy transition of the imagination from one situation of the body to another.

But this is still more remarkable, when we add a *sympathy* of parts to their *common end* and suppose that they bear to each other the reciprocal relation of cause and effect in all their actions and operations. This is the case with all animals and vegetables; where not only the several parts have a reference to some general purpose, but also a mutual dependence on, and connection with, each other. The effect of so strong a relation is, that though every one must allow, that in a very few years both vegetables and animals endure a *total* change, yet we still attribute identity to them, while their form, size, and substance, are entirely altered. An oak that grows from a small plant to a large tree is still the same oak, though there be not one particle of matter or figure of its parts the same. An infant becomes a man, and is sometimes fat, sometimes lean, without any change in his identity.

We may also consider the two following phenomena, which are remarkable in their kind. The first is, that though we commonly be able to distinguish pretty exactly betwixt numerical and specific identity, yet it sometimes happens that we confound them, and in our thinking and reasoning employ the one for the other. Thus, a man who hears a noise that is frequently interrupted and renewed, says it is still the same noise, though it is evident the sounds have only a specific identity or resemblance, and there is nothing numerically the same but the cause which produced them. In like manner it may be said, without breach of the propriety of language, that such a church, which was formerly of brick, fell to ruin, and that the parish rebuilt the same church of freestone, and according to modern architecture. Here neither the form nor materials are the same, nor is there anything common to the two objects but their relation to the inhabitants of the parish; and yet this alone is sufficient to make us denominate them the same. But we must observe, that in these cases the first object is in a manner annihilated before the second comes into existence; by which means, we are never presented, in any one point of time, with the idea of difference and multiplicity; and for that reason are less scrupulous in calling them the same.

Secondly, we may remark, that though, in a succession of related objects, it be in a manner requisite that the change of parts be not sudden nor entire, in order to preserve the identity, yet where the objects are in their nature changeable and inconstant, we admit of a more sudden transition than would otherwise be consistent with that relation. Thus, as the nature of a river consists in the motion and change of parts, though in less than four-and-twenty hours these be totally altered, this hinders not the river from continuing the same during several ages. What is natural and essential to anything is, in a manner, expected; and what is expected makes less impression, and appears of less moment than what is unusual and extraordinary. A considerable change of the former kind seems really less to the imagination than the most trivial alteration of the latter; and by breaking less the continuity of the thought, has less influence in destroying the identity.

We now proceed to explain the nature of *personal identity*, which has become so great a question in philosophy, especially of late years, in England, where all the abstruser sciences are studied with a peculiar ardour and application. And here it is evident the same method of reasoning must be continued which has so successfully explained the identity of plants, and animals, and ships, and houses, and of all compounded and changeable productions either of art or nature. The identity which we ascribe to the mind of man is only a fictitious one, and of a like kind with that which we ascribe to vegetable and animal bodies. It cannot therefore have a different origin, but must proceed from a like operation of the imagination upon like objects.

But lest this argument should not convince the reader, though in my opinion perfectly decisive, let him weigh the following reasoning, which is still closer and more immediate. It is evident that the identity which we attribute to the human mind, however perfect we may imagine it to be, is not able to run the several different perceptions into one, and make them lose their characters of distinction and difference, which are essential to them. It is still true that every distinct perception which enters into the composition of the mind, is a distinct existence, and is different, and distinguishable, and separable from every other perception, either contemporary or successive. But as, notwithstanding this distinction and separability, we suppose the whole train of perceptions to be united by identity, a question naturally arises concerning this relation of identity, whether it be something that really binds our several perceptions together, or only associates their ideas in the imagination; that is, in other words, whether, in pronouncing concerning the identity of a person, we observe some real bond among his perceptions, or only feel one among the ideas we form of them. This question we might easily decide, if we would recollect what has already been proved at large, that the understanding never observes any real connection among objects, and that even the union of cause and effect, when strictly examined, resolves itself into a customary association of ideas. For from thence it evidently follows, that identity is nothing really belonging to these different perceptions, and uniting them together, but is merely a quality which we attribute to them, because of the union of their ideas in the imagination when we reflect upon them. Now, the only qualities which can give ideas a union in the imagination, are these three relations above mentioned. These are the uniting principles in the ideal world, and without them every distinct object is separable by the mind, and may be separately considered, and appears not to have any more connection with any other object than if disjoined by the greatest difference and remoteness. It is therefore on some of these three relations of resemblance, contiguity and causation, that identity depends; and as the very essence of these relations consists in their producing an easy transition of ideas, it follows that our notions of personal identity proceed entirely from the smooth and uninterrupted progress of the thought along a train of connected ideas, according to the principles above explained.

The only question, therefore, which remains is, by what relations this uninterrupted progress of our thought is produced, when we consider the successive existence of a mind or thinking person. And here it is evident we must confine ourselves to resemblance and causation, and must drop contiguity, which has little or no influence in the present case.

To begin with *resemblance*; suppose we could see clearly into the breast of another, and observe that succession of perceptions which constitutes his mind or thinking principle, and suppose that he always preserves the memory of a considerable part of past perceptions, it is evident that nothing could more contribute to the bestowing a relation on this succession amidst all its variations. For what is the memory but a faculty, by which we raise up the images of past perceptions? And as an image necessarily resembles its object, must not the frequent placing of these resembling perceptions in the chain of thought, convey the imagination more easily from one link to another, and make the whole seem like the continuance of one object? In this particular, then, the memory not only discovers the identity, but also contributes to its production, by producing the relation of resemblance among the perceptions. The case is the same, whether we consider ourselves or others.

As to *causation*; we may observe that the true idea of the human mind, is to consider it as a system of different perceptions or different existences, which are linked together by the relation of cause and effect, and mutually produce, destroy, influence, and modify each other. Our impressions give rise to their correspondent ideas; and these ideas, in their turn, produce other impressions. One thought chases another, and draws after it a third, by which it is expelled in its turn. In this respect, I cannot compare the soul more properly to anything than to a republic or commonwealth, in which the several members are united by the reciprocal ties of government and subordination, and give rise to other persons who propagate the same republic in the incessant changes of its parts. And as the same individual republic may not only change its members, but also its laws and constitutions; in like manner the same person may vary his character and disposition, as well as his impressions and ideas without losing his identity. Whatever changes he endures, his several parts are still connected by the relation of causation. And in this view our identity with regard to the passions serves to corroborate that with regard to the imagination, but the making our distant perceptions influence each other, and by giving us a present concern for our past or future pains or pleasures.

As memory alone acquaints us with the continuance and extent of this succession of perceptions, it is to be considered, upon that account chiefly, as the source of personal identity. Had we no memory, we never should have any notion of causation, nor consequently of that chain of causes and effects, which constitute our self or person. But having once acquired this notion of causation from the memory, we can extend the same chain of causes, and consequently the identity of our persons beyond our memory, and can comprehend times, and circumstances, and actions, which we have entirely forgot, but suppose in general to have existed. For how few of our past actions are there, of which we have any memory? Who can tell me, for instance, what were his thoughts and actions on the first of January, 1715, the eleventh of March, 1719, and the third of August, 1733? Or will he affirm, because he has entirely forgot the incidents of these days, that the present self is not the same person with the self of that time; and by that means overturn all the most established notions of personal identity? In this view, therefore, memory, does not so much *produce* as *discover* personal identity, by showing us the relation of cause and effect among our different perceptions. It will be incumbent on those who affirm that memory produces entirely our personal identity, to give a reason why we can thus extend our identity beyond our memory.

The whole of this doctrine leads us to a conclusion, which is of great importance in the present affair, viz., that all the nice and subtile questions concerning personal identity can never possibly be decided, and are to be regarded rather as grammatical than as philosophical difficulties. Identity depends on the relation of ideas; and these relations produce identity, by means of that easy transition they occasion. But as the relations, and the easiness of the transition may diminish by insensible degrees, we have no just standard by which we can decide any dispute concerning the time when they acquire or lose a title to the name of identity. All the disputes concerning the identity of connected objects are merely verbal, except so far as the relation of parts gives rise to some fiction or imaginary principle of union, as we have already observed.

What I have said concerning the first origin and uncertainty of our notion of identity, as applied to the human mind, may be extended with little or no variation to that of *simplicity*. An object, whose different coexistent parts are bound together by a close relation, operates upon the imagination after much the same manner as one perfectly simple and indivisible, and requires not a much greater stretch of thought in order to its conception. From this similarity of operation we attribute a simplicity to it, and feign a principle of union as the support of this simplicity, and the centre of all the different parts and qualities of the object.

Thus we have finished our examination of the several systems of philosophy, both of the intellectual and moral world; and, in our miscellaneous way of reasoning, have been led into several topics, which will either illustrate and confirm some preceding part of this discourse, or prepare the way for our following opinions. It is now time to return to a more close examination of our subject, and to proceed in the accurate anatomy of human nature, having fully explained the nature of our judgment and understanding.

CONCLUSION OF THIS BOOK

(Book I, Part IV, Section 7)

But before I launch out into those immense depths of philosophy which lie before me, I find myself inclined to stop a moment in my present station, and to ponder that voyage which I have undertaken, and which undoubtedly requires the utmost art and industry to be brought to a happy conclusion. Methinks I am like a man, who, having struck on many shoals, and having narrowly escaped shipwreck in passing a small frith, has yet the temerity to put out to sea in the same leaky weather-beaten vessel, and even carries his ambition so far as to think of compassing the globe under these disadvantageous circumstances. My memory of past errors and perplexities makes me diffident for the future. The wretched condition, weakness, and disorder of the faculties, I must employ in my inquiries, increase my apprehensions. And the impossibility of amending or correcting these faculties, reduces me almost to despair, and makes me resolve to perish on the barren rock, on which I am at present, rather than venture myself upon that boundless ocean which runs out into immensity. This sudden view of my danger strikes me with melancholy; and, as it is usual for that passion, above all others, to indulge itself, I cannot forbear feeding my despair with all those desponding reflections which the present subject furnishes me with in such abundance.

I am at first affrighted and confounded with that forlorn solitude in which I am placed in my philosophy, and fancy myself some strange uncouth monster, who, not being able to mingle and unite in society, has been expelled all human commerce, and left utterly abandoned and disconsolate. Fain would I run into the crowd for shelter and warmth, but cannot prevail with myself to mix with such deformity. I call upon others to join me, in order to make a company apart, but no one will hearken to me. Every one keeps at a distance, and dreads that storm which beats upon me from every side. I have exposed myself to the enmity of all metaphysicians, logicians, mathematicians, and even theologians; and can I wonder at the insults I must suffer? I have declared my disapprobation of their systems; and can I be surprised if they should express a hatred of mine and of my person? When I look abroad, I foresee on every side dispute, contradiction, anger, calumny, and detraction. When I turn my eye inward, I find nothing but doubt and ignorance. All the world conspires to oppose and contradict me; though such is my weakness, that I feel all my opinions loosen and fall of themselves, when unsupported by the approbation of others. Every step I take is with hesitation, and every new reflection makes me dread an error and absurdity in my reasoning.

For with what confidence can I venture upon such bold enterprises, when, beside those numberless infirmities peculiar to myself, I find so many which are common to human nature? Can I be sure that, in leaving all established opinions, I am following truth? and by what criterion shall I distinguish her, even if fortune should at last guide me on her footsteps? After the most accurate and exact of my reasonings, I can give no reason why I should assent to it, and feel nothing but a *strong* propensity to consider objects *strongly* in that view under which they appear to me. Experience is a principle which instructs me in the several conjunctions of objects for the past. Habit is another principle which determines me to expect the same for the future; and both of them conspiring to operate upon the imagination, make me form certain ideas in a more intense and lively manner than others which are not attended with the same advantages. Without this quality, by which the mind enlivens some ideas beyond others (which seemingly is so trivial, and so little founded on reason), we could never assent to any argument, nor carry our view beyond those few objects which are present to our senses. Nay, even to these objects we could never attribute any existence but what was dependent on the senses, and must comprehend them entirely in that succession of perceptions which constitutes our self or person. Nay, further, even with relation to that succession, we could only admit of those perceptions which are immediately present to our consciousness; nor could those lively images, with which the memory presents us, be ever received as true pictures of past perceptions. The memory, senses, and understanding are therefore all of them founded on the imagination, or the vivacity of our ideas.

No wonder a principle so inconstant and fallacious should lead us into errors when implicitly followed (as it must be) in all its variations. It is this principle which makes us reason from cause and effect; and it is the same principle which convinces us of the continued existence of external objects when absent from the senses. But though these two operations be equally natural and necessary in the human mind, yet in some circumstances they are directly contrary;[6] nor is it possible for us to reason justly and regularly from causes and effects, and at the same time believe the continued existence of matter? How shall we adjust those principles together? Which of them shall we prefer? Or in case we prefer neither of them, but successively assent to both, as is usual among philosophers, with what confidence can we afterwards usurp that glorious title, when we thus knowingly embrace a manifest contradiction?

This contradiction[7] would be more excusable were it compensated by any degree of solidity and satisfaction in the other parts of our reasoning. But the case is quite contrary. When we trace up the human understanding to its first principles, we find it to lead us into such sentiments as seem to turn into ridicule all our past pains and industry, and to discourage us from future inquiries. Nothing is more curiously inquired after by the mind of man than the causes of every phenomenon; nor are we content with knowing the immediate causes but push on our inquiries till we arrive at the original and ultimate principle. We would not willingly stop before we are acquainted with that energy in the cause by which it operates on its effect; that tie, which connects them together; and that efficacious quality on which the tie depends. This is our aim in all our studies and reflections: and how must we be disappointed when we learn that this connection, tie, or energy lies merely in ourselves, and is nothing but that determination of the mind which is acquired by custom, and causes us to make a transition from an object to its usual attendant, and from the impression of one to the lively idea of the other? Such a discovery not only cuts off all hope of ever attaining satisfaction, but even prevents our very wishes; since it appears, that when we say we desire to know the ultimate and operating principle as something which resides in the external object, we either contradict ourselves, or talk without a meaning.

This deficiency in our ideas is not indeed perceived in common life, nor are we sensible that, in the most usual conjunctions of cause and effect, we are as ignorant of the ultimate principle which binds them together, as in the most unusual and extraordinary. But this proceeds merely from an illusion of the imagination; and the question is, how far we ought to yield to these illusions. This question is very difficult, and reduces us to a very dangerous dilemma, whichever way we answer it. For if we assent to every trivial suggestion of the fancy, beside that these suggestions are often contrary to each other, they lead us into such errors, absurdities, and obscurities, that we must at last become ashamed of our credulity. Nothing is more dangerous to reason than the flights of the imagination, and nothing has been the occasion of more mistakes among philosophers. Men of bright fancies may in this respect be compared to those

---

[6]Section 4.
[7]Part III, section 14.

angels, whom the Scripture represents as covering their eyes with their wings. This has already appeared in so many instances, that we may spare ourselves the trouble of enlarging upon it any further.

But, on the other hand, if the consideration of these instances makes us take a resolution to reject all the trivial suggestions of the fancy, and adhere to the understanding, that is, to the general and more established properties of the imagination; even this resolution, if steadily executed, would be dangerous, and attended with the most fatal consequences. For I have already shown,[8] that the understanding, when it acts alone, and according to its most general principles, entirely subverts itself, and leaves not the lowest degree of evidence in any proposition, either in philosophy or common life. We save ourselves from this total scepticism only by means of that singular and seemingly trivial property of the fancy, by which we enter with difficulty into remote views of things, and are not able to accompany them with so sensible an impression, as we do those which are more easy and natural. Shall we, then, establish it for a general maxim, that no refined or elaborate reasoning is ever to be received? Consider well the consequences of such a principle. By this means you cut off entirely all science and philosophy: you proceed upon one singular quality of the imagination, and by a parity of reason must embrace all of them; and you expressly contradict yourself; since this maxim must be built on the preceding reasoning, which will be allowed to be sufficiently refined and metaphysical. What party, then, shall we choose among these difficulties? If we embrace this principle, and condemn all refined reasoning, we run into the most manifest absurdities. If we reject it in favour of these reasonings, we subvert entirely the human understanding. We have therefore no choice left, but betwixt a false reason and none at all. For my part, I know not what ought to be done in the present case. I can only observe what is commonly done; which is, that this difficulty is seldom or never thought of; and even where it has once been present to the mind, is quickly forgot, and leaves but a small impression behind it. Very refined reflections have little or no influence upon us; and yet we do not, and cannot establish it for a rule, that they ought not to have any influence; which implies a manifest contradiction.

But what have I here said, that reflections very refined and metaphysical have little or no influence upon us? This opinion I can scarce forbear retracting, and condemning from my present feeling and experience. The *intense* view of these manifold contradictions and imperfections in human reason has so wrought upon me, and heated my brain, that I am ready to reject all belief and reasoning, and can look upon no opinion even as more probable or likely than another. Where am I, or what? From what causes do I derive my existence, and to what condition shall I return? Whose favour shall I court, and whose anger must I dread? What beings surround me? and on whom have I any influence, or who have any influence on me? I am confounded with all these questions, and begin to fancy myself in the most deplorable condition imaginable, environed with the deepest darkness, and utterly deprived of the use of every member and faculty.

Most fortunately it happens, that since reason is incapable of dispelling these clouds, Nature herself suffices to that purpose, and cures me of this philosophical melancholy and delirium, either by relaxing this bent of mind, or by some

---

[8]Section 1.

avocation, and lively impression of my senses, which obliterate all these chimeras. I dine, I play a game of backgammon, I converse, and am merry with my friends; and when, after three or four hours' amusement, I would return to these speculations, they appear so cold, and strained, and ridiculous, that I cannot find in my heart to enter into them any further.

Here, then, I find myself absolutely and necessarily determined to live, and talk, and act like other people in the common affairs of life. But notwithstanding that my natural propensity, and the course of my animal spirits and passions reduce me to this indolent belief in the general maxims of the world, I still feel such remains of my former disposition, that I am ready to throw all my books and papers into the fire, and resolve never more to renounce the pleasures of life for the sake of reasoning and philosophy. For those are my sentiments in that splenetic humour which governs me at present. I may, nay I must yield to the current of nature, in submitting to my senses and understanding; and in this blind submission I show most perfectly my sceptical disposition and principles. But does it follow that I must strive against the current of nature, which leads me to indolence and pleasure; that I must seclude myself, in some measure, from the commerce and society of men, which is so agreeable; and that I must torture my brain with subtilties and sophistries, at the very time that I cannot satisfy myself concerning the reasonableness of so painful an application, nor have any tolerable prospect of arriving by its means at truth and certainty? Under what obligation do I lie of making such an abuse of time? And to what end can it serve, either for the service of mankind, or for my own private interest? No: if I must be a fool, as all those who reason or believe anything *certainly* are, my follies shall at least be natural and agreeable. Where I strive against my inclination, I shall have a good reason for my resistance; and will no more be led a wandering into such dreary solitudes, and rough passages, as I have hitherto met with.

These are the sentiments of my spleen and indolence; and indeed I must confess, that philosophy has nothing to oppose to them, and expects a victory more from the returns of a serious good-humored disposition, than from the force of reason and conviction. In all the incidents of life, we ought still to preserve our scepticism. If we believe that fire warms, or water refreshes, it is only because it costs us too much pains to think otherwise. Nay, if we are philosophers, it ought only to be upon sceptical principles, and from an inclination which we feel to the employing ourselves after that manner. Where reason is lively, and mixes itself with some propensity, it ought to be assented to. Where it does not, it never can have any title to operate upon us. . . . .

3. Scepticism with Regard to the Self

The history of modern philosophy begins with Descartes's proof of the indubitable existence of the conscious subject. *Cogito ergo sum* states in essence a proof of the existence of a self which was not questioned by any of Descartes's successors, until Hume laid down the principle that every idea is derivative from some precedent impression and asked from what impression the idea of the self (or the soul) could originate. He found none.

For my part, when I enter most intimately into what I call *myself*, I always stumble on some particular perception or other, of heat or cold, light or shade, love or hatred, pain or pleasure. I never catch *myself* at any time without a perception, and never can observe anything but the perception.

If there is no impression of the self, there can be no idea. What one calls *oneself* is "nothing but a bundle or collection of different perceptions, which succeed each other with an inconceivable rapidity, and are in a perpetual flux and movement."[16] In this flux of perceptions Hume finds no single thread of identity. He finds, equally, no sense in the hypothesis of an underlying substance in which the fleeting percepts inhere, any more than he finds any material substance in which the qualities inhere that we experience in bodies.

Locke found the idea of substance elusive — something, we know not what. Berkeley abandoned material substance but retained spiritual substances as active agencies; yet he declared that we had no ideas of them. Locke, however, had laid it down that all our experiences originate in simple ideas of sensation and reflection, so the spiritual substances and the mysterious Berkeleyan "notions" we are supposed to have of them are equally suspect. When Hume consolidates Locke's position by insisting that all ideas derive from impressions and can arise in no other way, Berkeley's "notions" and the spirits which are their supposed objects are swept away, and we are left only with the flux of perceptions.

We attribute identity to objects when changes in them either do not occur or occur gradually and continuously without abrupt transition. Our stream of consciousness is like this. The perceptions slide from one to another with easy continuous transition and so we attribute to them some sort of identity. Further, by memory we frequently repeat ideas resembling one another and the original impressions of which they are copies. Resemblance is a relation enabling us to make easy and smooth transition between the resembling ideas, and so we tend to attribute identity to them. Likewise, causation produces the same result: a series of states of affairs linked continuously as cause and effect are apt to be regarded as successive states of the same thing. So in the mind impressions cause ideas and ideas new impressions, and thoughts and percepts are mutually occasions for the recall one of another. Consequently, we attribute an identity to the mind as we do to material bodies.

But in both cases the identity is fictitious, and the contradiction

---

[16]*Treatise*, Book I, Part IV, section 6.

between the alleged identity and the constantly changing flux is so apparent to us that we separate them and imagine an unchanging, identical soul-substance underlying the fluid and changing perceptions. But it is a fiction generated by an illusion on a par with our fallacious beliefs in external existences.

What, we may ask, commits the fallacies, constructs the fictions, is deceived by the illusions, and is guilty of errors of judgment? It cannot be the self, of which no impression or idea properly exists and which at best is a fictitious entity with no real author to invent it.

4. The Problem of Self-Identity

Unsatisfactory as this conclusion obviously is, how can it be avoided? If Hume is wrong, where is his argument at fault? One fundamental error, inherited from Locke, is that he describes human experience as if it were a sort of magic lantern show of successive pictures on a screen played before a passive audience who contributes nothing to its production. Perception is treated as mere reception, as it was for Locke, who compared the mind to white paper, a mirror, or some merely passive receptacle with respect to its incoming ideas. Of course, these philosophers agree that the mind is active in some respects. It operates upon impressions and ideas once received; it revives, rearranges, separates, and recombines them. But, in merely perceiving, it is passive and inert.

Yet Hume alleges that we may be deceived, that we suffer from illusion, that we entertain fallacious beliefs, and in various ways fall into error, all of which is evidence that the mind is active; for to err is to judge (falsely) and to judge is to act. Belief itself is an activity of the mind, though Hume represents it merely as a lively perception. The fact is, that perception is never a mere passive acceptance but is always an activity of interpretation of received data (whatever these may turn out to be). This is apparent when different people perceive the same objects differently, according to their past experience. A farmer seeing something moving on a distant hillside will perceive it as a herd of cattle, a hunter will see it as a herd of deer, and a general may see it as a movement of troops. We need vague and ambiguous objects to reveal this activity in our perceiving, for when they are clear and close by it is performed so rapidly and automatically that we are not aware of its occurrence. But that such activity must occur even then is apparent from the fact that sense never gives us any material object complete or as a whole. We can see or feel only part of it at a time; we hear only sounds which are caused by it; and scent and taste give us still less. Yet when the object is familiar the very least of these clues leads to a perception of it, as a whole. What is missing from the datum is supplied by the mind. We must recognize, therefore, that even in perception the mind is active.

Hume is by no means altogether unaware of these facts, as his account of our belief in the existence of bodies gives witness. But what he does not seem sufficiently to have noticed is that where activity is performed there must be some agent, and that a mere bundle of impressions and ideas (like the play of pictures or patterns in a kaleidoscope) includes no agent. Such a bundle could hold no beliefs, make no judgments, commit no errors, entertain no deceptive illusions. Something essential has been overlooked, and Berkeley is surely on firmer ground when he insists on the existence of an active principle as the essence of the mind and the ultimate source of ideas. Whatever may be the solution of this problem of the nature of the self, this will surely be the pointer to it.

Nevertheless, the solution is not easy to come by. For what can it be that I refer to when I speak of myself? I take myself to be a single, unique personality, the same person now as I was a few moments ago, the same person as I was yesterday and have been as long as I can remember. Yet what is it in me that has remained the same? It is not my body, for that has changed and is constantly changing. Biologists assure us that within a relatively short time every cell in our bodies dies and is replaced, so that not a single one would remain the same after a few years. In fact, every living organism is materially in a state of constant flux, an open system constantly interchanging matter and energy with its surrounding environment. It is like a candle flame that retains in some measure a shape and a certain pattern of relationship between its parts, but the actual substance of which is constantly passing away and being renewed.

My body, therefore, does not answer to my idea of self-identity. Is it my memory that supplies the continuity of sameness? Certainly I must in some sense be the same now as I was before in order to remember anything at all — unless memory is sheer illusion. Bertrand Russell has suggested that it is logically possible for minds to spring into existence complete with memories of a nonexistent past. These, however, would be false memories and thus, strictly speaking, not memories at all; and certainly they could not be evidence of continued self-identity. This suggestion at once reveals the difficulty of our proposed answer to the question. If memory is deceived it cannot be reliable evidence of prior existence, and memory is certainly not always accurate and often we are uncertain whether some seemingly past experience is something we remember or merely imagine. In any case, memory is a present experience, although we refer it to the past; and how we bridge the gap between present and past remains a mystery, for the past cannot literally be revisited, nor can it literally be revived. So although memory seems to give some sort of evidence of continued identity through time, it is difficult to say what sort of evidence, and it is never conclusive.

What then is my abiding, identical self? I have certain habits and dispositions, foibles and idiosyncracies. These persist in some measure, but they are by no means unchanging. Moreover, they are even less what I habitually identify myself with. I am wholly unaware of some of them; others I may be inclined consciously to cultivate; yet others I may dislike and may try to rid myself of. In all cases I am apt to distinguish myself from them, as something over against them — their possessor — and I own them as mine, if at all, only so far as I can control or react in some way to my own awareness of them. They do not seem to supply any permanent core of my personality which I can call my actual self.

We may be inclined, in consequence of these failures to identify the self, to say that everything I am ever aware of — the sum total of my experience — is what constitutes me. But not only does this seem implausible (because much of my experience is purely accidental and seems to make little, if any, difference to what I regard as myself proper), but if we did adopt this view, we should simply be back in a position, much like Hume's, that the self is nothing but a bundle of experiences without any abiding, identical element.

No philosopher has yet provided any wholly satisfactory answer to this question, and we are indebted to Hume for making the problem apparent and for largely defining its character. Descartes and Berkeley, resting on the idea of a substance, do not help us, because they tell us nothing, or very little, of what such a substance could be. For Descartes it is merely *res cogitans* (something that thinks). For Berkeley it is an active spirit of which we have some vague kind of notion. But these accounts do not take us far. Hume strips them of their plausibility by asking precisely what the idea we have of them is — from what impression is it derived?

Nevertheless, the notions of thinking and activity may provide the right clues. What we are seeking must certainly be some kind of agent, and we saw that Hume's theory was incoherent for the lack of any subject to be the victim of the delusions he alleges. If the activity of the agent is thinking and if thinking is an activity of unifying differences — or of organizing a multiplicity of data (of whatever kind) into a single whole, there will have to be some principle of order which will give the whole its distinctive and unitary character. This principle would have to be the same throughout or it could not serve this unifying function. Possibly the self is some such principle of organizing or unifying activity pervading an individual experience, and so giving it a characteristic identity of its own.

While it is difficult to say just what this might be, there are analogies to which we could compare it. Physicists tell us that elementary particles may be wave packets of radiant energy. When a number of waves of different lengths overlap, they may reinforce one another in a certain region but cancel one another out elsewhere. So in that region there would be a wave pattern of a certain type that may maintain its identity for some time. This is a particle. But a wave is not a simple "substance" or a hard indestructible granule, and a wave packet is nothing but an enduring pattern or *gestalt* of flowing energy. What gives it identity is the structure or principle of order that determines that pattern, and nothing else.

The same is true of a living organism which is an open system. But here the organization of the system is so very complex, so partially known, and so highly integrated that the pattern and the principle of order involved are difficult in the extreme to specify and define. Yet we can see that in some manner there is one and that it makes the organism what it is and constitutes its life. A person is at least a living organism, and perhaps personality is just a higher and more intense manifestation of that same organizing activity which is at work in living process; or, if it is a different kind of activity it may well be, and pretty obviously is, analogous to it. In that case perhaps the self is just the active principle of organization working at such a pitch of intensity as to have become conscious and aware of itself.

This is no final answer and may even, by some, be thought to obscure the matter in hand rather than to illuminate it. But we are dealing here with a subject that is so difficult that we might well retort: "If you can suggest a better theory, and one that will not break down under scrutiny, please do!" With that we may return to Hume.

5. *Scepticism and its Collapse*

The depth and irremediable character of Hume's scepticism is revealed in the final section of Book I where he himself draws out its fatal consequences. All reliable criteria of truth have gone, all confidence in reasoning, all reliance upon experience or practice. Even this very conclusion is placed in doubt and jeopardy, but not to the advantage of any other or any contrary belief, only to plunge the philosopher

into an anarchy of disbelief and intolerable dilemma. Finally he gives
way to his own recommended specific, "careless and inattention."

Nature herself . . . cures me of this philosophical melancholy and delirium,
either by relaxing this bent of mind or by some avocation, and lively impression
of my senses, which obliterate all these chimeras. I dine, I play a game of
backgammon, I converse, am merry with friends; and when, after three or four
hours' amusement, I would return to these speculations, they appear so cold,
and strained, and ridiculous, that I cannot find in my heart to enter into them any
further.

Neither Hume's theoretical conclusions, nor his remedy for the
dilemmas and paradoxes with which they leave us, will ultimately stand
up. The remedy cannot be deliberately chosen, for if it is, it ceases to
be carelessness and inattention and becomes deliberate neglect of the
problems with which we are faced. Such deliberate choice implies a
reason for choosing and a reason requires theoretical support; but
scepticism, as we have seen, so far from providing support, destroys
the very means of producing it.

In general, the sceptical denial of truth undermines its own foundations. To impute error, fallacy, sophism, and illusion to opinion is at
once to presuppose (if not, by implication, to affirm) a positive criterion
by which to recognize sophistry, error, and illusion. The grounds for
rejection must themselves be credible before rejection can be made.
Scepticism, however, denies every positive criterion and destroys all
positive grounds. Moreover, deception implies a judging subject who is
deceived, yet the Humean sceptic denies the existence of any judging
agent and finds the subject of experience to be a mere fiction.

The source of Hume's scepticism is his psychological atomism which
reduces experience to a bundle, collection, or bare succession of particular percepts, each separate from every other and devoid of all
mutual connections. What, on this basis, becomes of the relations which
Hume listed at the outset and which he takes to provide the framework
of our knowledge? He devotes attention almost exclusively to causation
and that dissolves under his hand; but the same or worse would result
from analysis of identity, resemblance, spatial and temporal relations,
and the rest. Consider only the first two.

(a) IDENTITY. No two impressions or ideas are the same, therefore
none can be identical with any other. Identity must then be a relation of
a single percept with itself. But how is this possible unless we detect
some kind of duality in the percept to provide at least two terms which

may be related? If we do this, we must distinguish within one percept two aspects or elements, and what can be distinguished can be separated, and what can be separated must be separate existences, and what are two are not one—and so not identical. Yet if we have not two terms (at least) we have no relata, for a single term stands in relation to nothing. There can then be no relation of identity.

How then could we acquire the idea of identity? What is identical is just the single percept by itself; there is no attendant impression of identity any more than there is one of existence. Our idea of identity should thus be simply the copy of any impression we happen to experience, which is as much as to say that we have no distinct idea of identity at all.

(b) RESEMBLANCE. If ideas are copies of impressions they must (as indeed Hume says they do) resemble one another. Moreover, some impressions are mutually resembling and the repetition of similar percepts is the root of our imaginative construction of persistent objects, as well as of our notions of cause and effect. The greater part of Hume's analysis depends upon the explicit or implicit assumption of this relation of resemblance. But how is it possible among a congeries of separate, unconnected, particular percepts?

To say that one percept resembles another is to say that in both there is something which is the same. But as they are separate and distinct, what is it that they could have in common? Whatever it is it must either be identical in each of them, and that we have found impossible, or it must be something in one which is similar to something in the other. But then the same problem breaks out with respect to the two similar elements. Their similarity must consist of some identical aspect which they share, or it too must split up into separable elements—and so *ad infinitum*.

Further, either no two impressions or ideas have anything in common, in which case there can be no resemblance, or they do have common properties. Then what they have in common must either be the whole of each, or only part of it. If it is the whole, they will be identical and so not two impressions or ideas. If it is only part, we must distinguish that part in each which is common from that part which is not. But what we can distinguish must be separable and separate, and so we must have three or four percepts instead of two. If there are four, two of them must be alike and the problem repeats itself as to how we understand the relation of resemblance between them. If there are only three, one of them must be the common element. But then (a) it is not anything common to the other two (for it is separate from them), and *(b)* it is merely identical with itself and so not a resemblance of anything to anything else. Even apart from the difficulties already encountered with identity, this analysis leaves us with nothing corresponding to resemblance. We should then conclude that there is no such relationship.

Does my idea of a red patch resemble my impression of it? If so, how? It is, we say, a paler image. Does that mean that it is another paler red patch? If so, they differ in brightness (and so are not alike in that respect). But they are the same in hue. But this hue cannot be identical with the impression or any part of it, for if it were it could not also be identical with any part of the idea – because the impression is distinct from the idea and no part of either is identical with any part of the other. What then is this "redness" which they share? It cannot be another impression, nor yet another (abstract – Heaven forbid!) idea. If it were either, it would have to resemble both in some inexplicable way. This is the nemesis of nominalism and the denial of universal concepts.

There is no way of making these relations or our ideas of them intelligible on the basis of Hume's account of our experience as a stream of particulars. Yet, on these relations the whole of his account of our experience rests, and without them we could not have any experience of the sort that we do have. In short, there would be nothing to analyze. The analysis, therefore, destroys its own foundations and has nothing upon which to rest. The only reason why this does not become fully apparent in Hume's own writing, is that he does not carry out the analysis to the bitter end, but applies it only to causation, to our ideas of external reality, and to the self.

The greatness and permanent value of Hume's philosophy, however, lies precisely in the consistency and fearlessness with which he presses home his analysis as far as he does. No other writer, before or since, has developed so complete and self-consistent an empiricist theory. The sceptical conclusion which results is inherent in the premises from which the whole theory begins – Locke's insistence that the first beginnings of our knowledge are simple, particular ideas of sensation and reflection and that what can be built out of these constitutes all the material of knowledge. Hume takes these premises seriously, makes them more precise by distinguishing impressions from ideas, and develops their consequences relentlessly. If we begin with Locke we must end with Hume, and if we dislike his conclusion, the only proper method to find a way of escape is to return to the starting point and reassess the empiricist foundations.

SUGGESTIONS FOR FURTHER READING

D. Hume, *An Inquiry Concerning the Human Understanding*. New York: Oxford University Press; and Liberal Arts Press, 1955.

———, *A Treatise of Human Nature*, Book I. New York: Oxford University Press, 1955.

V. C. Chappell, *Hume (A Collection of Critical Essays)*. New York: Anchor Books, Doubleday 1966.

T. H. Green, Introduction to Hume, *Works of Thomas Hill Green*, 2d ed., Vol. I. New York: Kraus Reprint Corp., 1968.

E. E. Harris, *Nature, Mind and Modern Science*, Chapter 8. London: Allen and Unwin, 1954.

N. Kemp Smith, *The Philosophy of David Hume*. London: Macmillan 1964.

C. R. Morris, *Locke, Berkeley, Hume*. New York: Oxford University Press, 1931.

J. A. Passmore, *Hume's Intentions*. London: Cambridge University Press, 1952.

H. H. Price, *Hume's Theory of the External World*. New York: Oxford University Press, 1940.

PART IV

Kant

CHAPTER 27

Rationalism versus Empiricism

1. THOUGHT AND SENSE

Throughout the whole of the discussion so far undertaken, the question underlying almost every issue has been that of the relation between thought and sense. It is primarily an epistemological question, but its relevance is by no means confined to the theory of knowledge, for action is also dependent upon perception, upon thinking as well as feeling, so that the parts played by the rational and the sensuous elements in our activity will determine the nature of conduct and the principles which regulate it, as much as they do the nature of knowledge.

Plato addresses himself to the question of the relation of thought to sense in both of these major contexts. Sense perception he finds too changeable and inconstant to be relied on as a source of knowledge, and so, *a fortiori*, as a source of knowledge about how best to act. For him, therefore, the one satisfactory kind of knowing is pure intellection, the objects of which are Forms—purely intelligible entities. Sense perception gives us knowledge at all only because its objects in some way participate in or resemble the Forms and remind us of them. Our conduct must, in consequence, if it is to produce satisfactory results, be

445

guided by a knowledge of Forms and especially by knowledge of the Good; and so comes to be directed entirely toward the attainment of such prerequisite knowledge, for which end mastery and subordination of the sensual desires is an obvious condition.

The reason for this conclusion in Plato's theory is that sense perception, which affords us only particular percepts no two of which are exactly alike, none of which is repeated, and which are constantly passing and perishing, provides no principles of order and correlation such as are indispensable to the most elementary knowledge — no universal principles. Plato found the universal principles in the Forms, but had difficulty in explaining how they were related to the sense-given particulars. Thought and sense remained for him separate sources of knowledge and its materials, just as soul and body remained separate but somehow conjoined.

The deliverances of sense were no more satisfactory to Descartes than to Plato. He speaks of them as fluctuating evidences, and again what reduces them to order and intelligibility is only what the intellect can clearly and distinctly conceive. Descartes leaves the precise nature of such clear and distinct ideas otherwise undefined, though he too thinks they are, for the most part, innate, and he says that they are (in some sense) simple. Yet again, how these clearly conceived simple natures relate to the confused perceptions of sense remains obscure. At times Descartes speaks as if they were merely the simplest mechanical parts of what is sensibly perceived, but this is clearly not what he intends, for they are certainly not the *minima sensibilia* of which Hume speaks, nor the simple ideas of Locke. To judge from many of the examples given by Descartes, they are logical connections of some sort. Moreover, they are necessary, and what holds necessarily holds always and so universally. Once more we are concerned with universal principles.

Both Plato and Descartes are rationalists for whom knowledge proper is purely an activity of thought, and sense provides no more than the confused dross in which the grains of precious metal have to be discerned by intellectual insight. The empiricist approach, which takes sense perception to be the proximate means of information about the surrounding world, seems more natural and convincing at first sight. But, whereas the rationalist is hard put to discover the exact relation between the universal element in knowledge and the sensuous, the empiricist, admitting only the sensuous as the ultimate source of information, is hard put to discover any universal element at all. Consequently, as we saw in our examination of Hume's theory, the organizing principles on which coherent sense can be made of our experience are missing and knowledge disintegrates into a flurry of unconnected particulars.

The problem of the relation of thought to sense remains unsolved. The function in knowledge of the universal has been overstressed by one group of philosophers and underplayed by the other, leading in each case to results which are paradoxical. But what must be noticed is that they all begin from our common experience of the world and try to analyze it in order to discover the principles which make it intelligible as knowledge of a world. Plato and Descartes, each in his own way, are impressed by the unreliability and contradictory character of common beliefs. Yet the very fact that these beliefs pose as the truth indicates that there is in them some semblance of order and intelligibility — we do recognize sensible material objects as, for example, equal, as having mathematical properties and as structured entities — so that the task for the rationalist is to distinguish the element that makes this possible. The empiricist faces the same situation. Our senses furnish us with percepts of a world of objects. How, from a succession of particular sensations, can such an awareness of an orderly world be constructed? In short, what we seek to discover are the conditions on which it is possible to have the kind of experience which we undoubtedly have, the experience of an ordered world.

2. THOUGHT AND ACTION

Because we act in the world according as we experience it, our action is intimately dependent on the nature of our knowledge. And just as the sensuous appearances of things often conflict, hampering our effort to know the truth about them, so our feelings and appetites frequently collide, frustrating our efforts to attain satisfaction. The rationalist finds the remedy for knowledge in intellectual intuition of some sort, while for the empiricist the intellect simply inspects, compares, and rearranges sensuous material received from without. So, in action, the rationalist seeks to resolve conflicts of appetite and desire by subjecting them to rules laid down by reason. Plato thought this could be done by reference to Ideas (of Good, Justice, Courage, Temperance, and the like). On the other hand, the empiricist finds pleasure and appetite to be the determinants of action and sees reason merely as the instrument for discovering means to predetermined ends. By and large, reason for the rationalist is constitutive both of truth and of moral goodness and rightness; for the empiricist it is instrumental, goodness, the end of action, being determined ultimately by feeling.

In his famous simile of the cave[1] Plato depicts the ordinary, untu-

---

[1]*Republic*, Book VII, 514A – 518B.

tored man as chained with his back to the light watching the fluctuating shadows of objects behind him cast on the wall of the grotto by the light of a flickering fire. The objects are rough models of the real things which exist above in the open air and are visible in the sunlight to those, who, by arduous study and reflection, have released themselves from the chains of prejudice and opinion and climbed up the slope into the open. The conduct of men in the cave will be as confused, corrupt, and unsatisfying as their knowledge· is faulty, and the duty of the philosopher is to return from the sunlight into the darkness, not to improve his own way of life and knowledge but to correct and instruct those less enlightened.

The implication of this figure is that the good attainable by the philosopher is, in itself, a good which might be enjoyed by the individual in isolation from the society of other people: the life of contemplation and enjoyment of truth for its own sake. This is a natural and consistent conclusion to draw from the rationalist view of knowledge and is, in effect, the conclusion of the *Phaedo*, where we are told that the souls of the philosophers attain to the elysium in which, in company with the gods, they contemplate the intelligible forms. But the whole spirit of Plato's ethics, as set out in the *Republic*, runs counter to individualism. There we learn that the barest essentials of a good life are attainable only in society and by the cooperation of a group of persons, by means of the regulated and coordinated performance of interlocking functions. The philosopher, however, once he has attained the light, becomes independent of society, yet for the sake of others he must return to the cave and give them the benefit of his insight. What seems to have been overlooked here is that the philosopher's attainment is no less dependent upon his membership in society than is the happiness of the artisan and the farmer, and the importance of reason and knowledge for the good life, great though it is, is not separable from that of the physical and psychological satisfactions which human nature craves. Rationalism in ethics tends, therefore, to give us (as in epistemology) only half the picture.

Meanwhile, empiricism gives us only the other half; for it stresses the feelings as the determinants of good and evil. What attracts us is good, what repels us is evil. What we seek is pleasure and what we avoid is pain. The function of reason is to connect means with ends and to dictate the procedures by which the ends can be achieved. It follows from this that judgments of value are never in the last resort factual, but are only expressions of feeling and sentiment. In the last analysis there can be no rational justification of preferences, which depend upon feeling—for feeling is ultimately subjective and there can be no rational dispute about tastes. On this view, therefore, the ultimate choice of ends is arbitrary, and no final justification can ever be given of moral choice and moral approval. On this basis moral obligation becomes purely conditional and relative to feeling or taste and no objective morality can ever be rationally established. The position in ethics is similar to the position which Hume reaches in epistemology. Scientific conviction for him was on a par with any other form of belief or sentiment and no rational criterion of truth ultimately proved valid. So in ethics no rational criterion of goodness is forthcoming and moral judgment is simply an expression of emotion or some other form of noncognitive expression.

It should be obvious that both the rationalist and the empiricist forms of philosophical approach are unsatisfactory, as each emphasizes one side of the fact at the expense of the other, whereas the fact is complex and involves both. What is needed is a theory which combines both aspects coherently and without mutual conflict. In epistemology we find such a theory—or at least a close approach to it—in the philosophy of Kant, who saw that reason and sense were equally necessary and contributed concurrently to knowledge. "Thoughts without content are empty," he says, and "perceptions[2] without conceptions are blind."

Kant's theory provided a synthetic approach which made a significant advance in epistemology, although his ethics remained strongly rationalistic, for reasons inherent in his metaphysics. For, although he went far to overcome the antithesis of reason and experience, he did not go all the way, and came down, in the end, on the side of empiricism in his attitude toward metaphysics, denying it factual and scientific import. This denial, oddly enough, throws the judgments of morality on to the side of reason and divorces them from empirical conditions, so that Kant's ethics take the form of a somewhat rigid and uncompromising rationalism.

The complexities and intricacies of Kant's theory are too difficult for detailed study in an introductory text and we shall be able to do no more than sketch the main outlines of his doctrine. Greater elaboration and more intimate analysis must be reserved for more advanced courses in philosophy, in which the greatness of Kant's system may be explored and the penetration of his thought more fully appreciated.

---

[2]*Anschauungen* (intuitions).

CHAPTER 28

Reassessment of the Position

The Critique of Pure Reason[1]

This may well be called the age of criticism, a criticism from which nothing vi n
need hope to escape. When religion seeks to shelter itself behind its sanctity,
and law behind its majesty, they justly awaken suspicion against themselves,
and lose all claim to the sincere respect which reason yields only to that which
has been able to bear the test of its free and open scrutiny.

Metaphysic has been the battlefield of endless conflicts. Dogmatism at first ii
held despotic sway; but . . . from time to time scepticism destroyed all settled iii
order of society; . . . and now a widespread indifferentism prevails. Never has iv
xiv metaphysic been so fortunate as to strike into the sure path of science, but has
xv kept groping about, and groping, too, among mere ideas. What can be the
reason of this failure? Is a science of metaphysic impossible? Then, why
should nature disquiet us with a restless longing after it, as if it were one of our

------

[1]Numbers in the right hand margin refer to the page numbers in the first edition; those
in the left hand margin to those of the second edition of *Kritik der Reinen Vernunft*.

most important concerns? Nay more, how can we put any faith in human reason, if in one of the very things that we most desire to know, it not merely forsakes us, but lures us on by false hopes only to cheat us in the end? Or are there any indications that the true path has hitherto been missed, and that by starting afresh we may yet succeed where others have failed?

xvi   It seems to me that the intellectual revolution, by which at a bound mathematics and physics became what they now are, is so remarkable, that we are called upon to ask what was the essential feature of the change that proved so advantageous to them, and to try at least to apply to metaphysic as far as

xi   possible a method that has been successful in other sciences of reason. In mathematics I believe that, after a long period of groping, the true path was disclosed in the happy inspiration of a single man. If that man was Thales,

xii   things must suddenly have appeared to him in a new light, the moment he saw how the properties of the isosceles triangle could be demonstrated. The true method, as he found, was not to inspect the visible figure of the triangle, or to analyze the bare conception of it, and from this, as it were, to read off its properties, but to bring out what was necessarily implied in the conception that he had himself formed *a priori*, and put into the figure, in the construction by which he presented it to himself.

Physics took a much longer time than mathematics to enter on the highway of science, but here, too, a sudden revolution in the way of looking at things took place. When Galileo caused balls which he had carefully weighed to roll down an inclined plane, or Torricelli made the air bear up a weight which he

xiii   knew beforehand to be equal to a standard column of water, a new light broke on the mind of the scientific discoverer. It was seen that reason has insight only into that which it produces after a plan of its own, and that it must itself lead the way with principles of judgment based upon fixed laws, and force nature to answer its questions. Even experimental physics, therefore, owes the beneficial

xiv   revolution in its point of view entirely to the idea, that, while reason can know nothing purely of itself, yet that which it has itself put into nature must be its guide to the discovery of all that it can learn from nature.

xvi   In metaphysical speculations it has always been assumed that all our knowledge must conform to objects; but every attempt from this point of view to extend our knowledge of objects *a priori* by means of conceptions has ended in failure. The time has now come to ask, whether better progress may not be made by supposing that objects must conform to our knowledge. Plainly this would better agree with the avowed aim of metaphysic, to determine the nature of objects *a priori*, or before they are actually presented. Our suggestion is similar to that of Copernicus in astronomy, who, finding it impossible to explain the movements of the heavenly bodies on the supposition that they turned round the spectator, tried whether he might not succeed better by

xvii   supposing the spectator to revolve and the stars to remain at rest. Let us make a similar experiment in metaphysic with *perception*. If it were really necessary for our perception to conform to the nature of objects, I do not see how we could know anything of it *a priori;* but if the sensible object must conform to the constitution of our faculty of perception, I see no difficulty in the matter. Perception, however, can become knowledge only if it is related in some way to the object which it determines. Now here again I may suppose, either that the *conceptions* through which I effect that determination conform to the objects, or that the objects, in other words the experience in which alone the objects are known, conform to conceptions. In the former case, I fall into the same perplexity as before, and fail to explain how such conceptions can be known *a priori*. In the latter case, the outlook is more hopeful. For, experience is itself a mode of knowledge which implies intelligence, and intelligence has a rule of its own, which must be an *a priori* condition of all knowledge of objects presented to it.

xviii To this rule, as expressed in *a priori* conceptions, all objects of experience must necessarily conform, and with it they must agree.

Our experiment succeeds as well as we could wish, and gives promise that
xix metaphysic may enter upon the sure course of a science, at least in its first part, where it is occupied with those *a priori* conceptions to which the corresponding objects can be given. The new point of view enables us to explain how there can be *a priori* knowledge, and what is more, to furnish satisfactory proofs of the laws that lie at the basis of nature as a totality of objects of experience. But the consequences that flow from this deduction of our faculty of *a priori* knowledge, which constitutes the first part of our inquiry, are unexpected, and at first sight seem to be fatal to the aims of metaphysic, with which we have to deal in the second part of it. For we are brought to the conclusion that we never can transcend the limits of possible experience, and therefore never can realize the object with which metaphysic is primarily concerned. In truth,
xx however, no better indirect proof could be given that we were correct in holding, as the result of our first estimate of the *a priori* knowledge of reason, that such knowledge relates not at all to the thing as it exists in itself, but only to phenomena. For that which necessarily forces us to go beyond the limits of experience and of all phenomena is the *unconditioned*, which reason demands of things in themselves, and by right and necessity seeks in the complete series of conditions for everything conditioned. If, then, we find that we cannot think the unconditioned without contradiction, on the supposition of our experience conforming to objects as things in themselves; while, on the contrary, the contradiction disappears, on the supposition that our knowledge does not conform to things in themselves, but that objects as they are given to us as phenomena conform to our knowledge; we are entitled to conclude that what
xxi we at first assumed as an hypothesis is now established as a truth.

It may seem from this that the result of our critical investigation is purely *negative*, and merely warns us not to venture with speculative reason beyond the limits of experience. And no doubt this is its first use; but a *positive* result is obtained when it is seen that the principles with which speculative reason ventures beyond its proper limits, in reality do not *extend* the province of
xxv reason, but inevitably *narrow* it. For in seeking to go altogether beyond its true limits, the limits of sensibility, those principles threaten to supplant pure reason
xxvii in its practical aspect. Let us suppose that the necessary distinction which our criticism shows to exist between things as objects of experience and the same things as they are in themselves, had not been made. Then the principle of causality, and with it the mechanical conception of nature as determined by it, would apply to all things in general as efficient causes. Hence I could not, without palpable contradiction, say of the same being, for instance the human soul, that its will is free, and yet is subject to the necessity of nature, that is, is not free. But, if our criticism is sound and the object may be taken in two distinct senses, on the one hand as a phenomenon, and on the other hand as a
xxviii thing in itself; there is no contradiction in supposing that the very same will, in its visible acts as a phenomenon, is *not free*, but necessarily subject to the law

of nature, while yet, as belonging to a thing in itself, it is not subject to that law,
xxix but is *free*. Now, morality requires us only to be able to think freedom without
self-contradiction, not to understand it; it is enough that our conception of the
act as free puts no obstacle in the way of the conception of it as mechanically
necessary, for the act stands in quite a different relation to freedom from that in
which it stands to the mechanism of nature. From the critical point of view,
therefore, the doctrine of morality and the doctrine of nature may each be true
in its own sphere; which could never have been shown had not criticism
previously established our unavoidable ignorance of things in themselves, and
xxx limited all that we can *know* to mere phenomena. I have, therefore, found it
necessary to deny *knowledge* of *God*, *freedom*, and *immortality*, in order to find
a place for *faith*.

It is dogmatism, or the preconception that progress in metaphysic may be
made without a previous criticism of pure reason, that is responsible for that
xxxi dogmatic unbelief which is so hostile to morality. The first and most important
task of philosophy is to deprive metaphysic once for all of its pernicious in-
xxxv fluence by closing up the sources of its errors. Our critique is not opposed to
the dogmatic procedure of reason as a science of pure knowledge, which must
be strictly proved *a priori* from well-founded principles, but only to dogmatism,
that is, to the presumption that we may follow the time-honoured method of
constructing a system of pure metaphysic out of principles that rest upon mere
conceptions, without first asking in what way reason has come into possession
of them, and by what right it employs them. Dogmatism, in a word, is the
dogmatic procedure of reason *without any previous criticism of its own powers*.

The critique of pure reason is not a criticism of books and systems, but of the vi
faculty of reason in general, in so far as reason seeks for knowledge that is
independent of all experience. I have evaded none of its questions, on the plea
of the imbecility of human reason. In fact, reason is so perfect a unity that, if it vii
were in principle inadequate to the solution of even a single one of the questions which by its very nature it raises, we might at once with perfect certainty
xxxvii set it aside as incapable of answering any of the others. For as it is a true
organic unity, in which the whole exists for the sake of each of the parts, and
xxxviii each part for the sake of the whole, the slightest imperfection, whether it is due
to a flaw or to a defect, will inevitably betray itself in use.

INTRODUCTION

1. Distinction of Pure and Empirical Knowledge.

There can be no doubt whatever that all our knowledge begins with experience. By what means should the faculty of knowledge be aroused to activity
but by objects, which, acting upon our senses, partly of themselves produce
ideas in us, and partly set our understanding at work to compare these ideas
with one another, and, by combining or separating them, to convert the raw
material of our sensible impressions into that knowledge of objects which is
called experience? In the order of time, therefore, we have no knowledge prior
to experience, and with experience all our knowledge begins.

But, although all our knowledge begins *with* experience, it by no means follows that it all originates *from* experience. For it may well be that experience is itself made up of two elements, one received through impressions of sense, and the other supplied from itself by our faculty of knowledge on occasion of those impressions. If that be so, it may take long practice before our attention is drawn to the element added by the mind, and we learn to distinguish and separate it from the material to which it is applied.

It is, therefore, a question which cannot be lightly put aside, but can be answered only after careful investigation, whether there is any knowledge that is independent of experience, and even of all impressions of sense. Such knowledge is said to be *a priori*, to distinguish it from *empirical* knowledge, which has its sources *a posteriori*, or in experience.

The term *a priori* must, however, be defined more precisely, in order that the full meaning of our question may be understood. We say of a man who undermines the foundations of his house, that he might have known *a priori* that it would fall; by which we mean, that he might have known it would fall, without waiting for the event to take place in his experience. But he could not know it completely *a priori*; for it is only from experience that he could learn that bodies are heavy, and must fall by their own weight when there is nothing to support them.

By *a priori* knowledge we shall, therefore, in what follows understand, not such knowledge as is independent of this or that experience, but such as is *absolutely* independent of all experience. Opposed to it is empirical knowledge, or that which is possible only *a posteriori*, that is, by experience. *A priori* knowledge is *pure*, when it is unmixed with anything empirical. The proposition, for instance, that each change has its own cause is *a priori*, but it is not pure, because change is an idea that can be derived only from experience.

2. Science and Common Sense contain a priori Knowledge.

Evidently what we need is a criterion by which to distinguish with certainty between pure and empirical knowledge. Now, experience can tell us that a thing is so and so, but not that it cannot be otherwise. Firstly, then, if we find a proposition that, in being thought, is thought as necessary, it is an *a priori* judgment; and if, further, it is not derived from any proposition except which is itself necessary, it is absolutely *a priori*. Secondly, experience never bestows on its judgments true or strict universality, but only the assumed or comparative universality of induction; so that, properly speaking, it merely says, that so far as our observation has gone, there is no exception to this or that rule. If, therefore, a judgment is thought with strict universality, so that there can be no possible exception to it, it is not derived from experience, but is absolutely *a priori*. Necessity and strict universality are, therefore, sure criteria of *a priori* knowledge, and are also inseparably connected with each other.

Now, it is easy to show that in human knowledge there actually are judgments, that in the strictest sense are universal, and therefore pure *a priori*. If an example from the sciences is desired, we have but to think of any proposition in mathematics; if an instance from common sense is preferred, it is enough to cite the proposition, that there can be no change without a cause. To take the latter case, the very idea of cause so manifestly implies the idea of necessary connection with an effect, that it would be completely lost, were we to derive it, with Hume, from the repeated association of one event with another that precedes it, and were we to reduce it to the subjective necessity arising from the habit of passing from one idea to another. Even without appealing to such examples to show that as a matter of fact there are in our knowledge pure *a priori* principles, we might prove *a priori* that without such principles there could be no experience whatever. For, whence could experience derive the certainty it has, if all the rules that it follows were merely empirical and therefore contingent? Surely such rules could not be dignified with the name of first principles.

3. A Science is needed to determine the possibility, the principles, and the extent of all a priori Knowledge.

A far more important consideration remains than anything that has yet been stated. There is a sort of knowledge that even quits the field of all possible 3 experience, and claims to extend the range of our judgments beyond its limits, by means of conceptions to which no corresponding object can be presented in experience. Now, it is just in the province of this sort of knowledge, where experience can neither show us the true path nor put us right when we go 7 astray, that reason carries on those high investigations, the results of which we regard as more important than all that understanding can discover within the domain of phenomena. Nay, we are even willing to stake our all, and to run the risk of being completely deluded, rather than consent to forego inquiries of such moment, either from uncertainty or from carelessness and indifference. These unavoidable problems, set by pure reason itself, are *God, freedom,* and *immortality,* and the science which brings all its resources to bear on the one single task of solving them is *metaphysic.*

Now, one might think that men would hesitate to leave the solid ground of experience, and to build an edifice of truth upon knowledge that has come to them they know not how, and in blind dependence upon principles of which they cannot tell the origin, without taking the greatest pains to see that the foundation was secure. One might think it only natural, that they would long ago have raised the question, how we have come into possession of all this *a* 8 *priori* knowledge, and what may be its extent, its import and its value. But the 4 fact is, that a part of this knowledge — mathematical knowledge, for instance — has so long been established as certain, that we are less ready to suspect the evidence for other parts, although these may be of a totally different nature. Besides, when we are once outside the circle of experience, we are sure not to be contradicted by experience; and so strong is the impulse to enlarge our knowledge, that nothing short of a clear contradiction will avail to arrest our footsteps. Now, such contradiction may easily be avoided, even where we are dealing with objects that are merely imaginary, if we are only careful in putting our fictions together. Mathematics shows us by a splendid instance, how far a science may advance *a priori* without the aid of experience. It is true that by it objects and conceptions are considered only in so far as they can be presented in perception; but it is easy to overlook the limitation, because the perception in this case can itself be given *a priori*, and is therefore hard to distinguish from a mere idea. Deceived by this proof of the power of reason, we can see no limits 5 9 to the extension of knowledge. So Plato forsook the world of sense, chafing at the narrow limits it set to our knowledge, and, on the wings of pure ideas, launched out into the empty space of the pure understanding. He did not see that with all his efforts he was making no real progress. But it is no unusual thing for human reason to complete its speculative edifice in such haste, that it forgets to look to the stability of the foundation. The reason why we have no fear or anxiety while the work of construction is going on, but take it for granted that the foundation stands firm, is, that much of the work of reason, perhaps the greater part, consists in the *analysis* of conceptions which we

10 already possess. This analysis really gives us a kind of *a priori* knowledge that 6 is safe and useful. But, misled by this success, reason interpolates propositions of quite a different character, which but superficially resemble the others. I shall therefore at the very outset point out the distinction between these two kinds of knowledge.

4. The distinction between Analytic and Synthetic Judgments.

There are two ways in which the predicate of an affirmative judgment may be related to the subject. Either the predicate B is already tacitly contained in the subject A, or B lies entirely outside of A, although it is in some way con-

11 nected with it. In the one case I call the judgment *analytic*, in the other case *synthetic*. Analytic judgments are those in which the predicate is related to the 7 subject in the way of identity, while in synthetic judgments the predicate is not thought as identical with the subject. The former class might also be called *explicative*, because the predicate adds nothing to the subject, but merely breaks it up into its logical elements, and brings to clear consciousness what was already obscurely thought in it. The latter class we may call *ampliative*, as adding in the predicate something that was in no sense thought in the subject, and that no amount of analysis could possibly extract from it. "Body is extended," for instance, is an analytic judgment. For, to be conscious that extension is involved in the conception signified by the term body, it is not necessary to go outside that conception, but merely to analyze it into the various logical elements that are always thought in it. But in the proposition "Body has weight," the predicate is not implied in the very conception of body, but is a perfectly new view. The addition of such a predicate, therefore, yields a synthetic judgment.

Judgments of experience are all by their very nature synthetic. To say that I must have recourse to experience for an analytic judgment is absurd, because I can frame the judgment without going beyond the conception I already pos-

12 sess. I have, for instance, the conception of body, and by mere analysis I become aware of the attributes extension, impenetrability, figure, etc., which the thought of it involves. To enlarge my conception, I turn again to experience, from which the conception was originally derived, and, finding weight to be invariably connected with those attributes, I attach it to them by synthesis as a new attribute. The possibility of this synthesis of the attribute weight with the conception body therefore rests upon experience. The two ideas are quite distinct, but they yet are parts of the same experience, and experience is itself a whole in which a number of perceptions are synthetically though only contingently combined.

In *a priori* synthetic judgments, on the other hand, I can get no aid whatever 9

13 from experience. But, if it is here vain to look to experience for aid, on what other support am I to rely, when I seek to go beyond a certain conception A, and to connect B synthetically with it? Take the proposition, that every event

must have its cause. No doubt I cannot have the conception of an event without thinking of something as having a moment of time before it, and from this certain analytic judgments may be derived. But the conception of a cause lies entirely outside the conception of an event, and introduces an idea not contained in it. By what right, then, do I pass from the conception of an event to the totally different conception of a cause? How do I know that there is a necessary connection between the two conceptions, when I can perfectly well think the one without the other? What is here the unknown x, which gives support to the understanding, when it seems to have discovered an entirely new predicate B to belong necessarily to the subject A? Experience it cannot be, because the principle has a degree of universality that experience can never supply, as it is supposed to connect the new conception with the old in the way of necessity, and must do so entirely *a priori*, and on the basis of mere conceptions. And yet our speculative *a priori* knowledge must rest upon such 10 synthetic or ampliative propositions.

14 *5. The principles of all Theoretical Sciences of reason*
    are a priori Synthetic Judgments.

(1) All *mathematical* judgments, without exception, are synthetic. No doubt the mathematician, in his demonstrations, proceeds on the principle of contradiction, but it is a mistake to suppose that the propositions on which his demonstrations rest can be known to be true by that principle. The mistake arises from not observing that, while a synthetic proposition may certainly be seen to be true by the principle of contradiction, its truth is in that case evident, not from itself, but only because it is seen to follow from another proposition that has been previously obtained by synthesis.

The first thing to notice is, that no truly mathematical judgments are empirical, but always are *a priori*. They carry necessity on their very face, and therefore cannot be derived from experience. Should any one demur to this, I 15 am willing to limit my assertion to the propositions of *pure mathematics*, which, as everybody will admit, are not empirical judgments, but perfectly pure *a priori* knowledge.

At first sight it may seem that the proposition $7 + 5 = 12$ is purely analytic, and follows, by the principle of contradiction, from the conception of a sum of 7 and 5. But, when we look more closely we see that the conception of the sum of 7 and 5 is merely the idea of the union of the two numbers, and in no way enables us to tell what may be the single number that forms their sum. To think that 7 and 5 are to be united is not to have the conception 12, and I may analyze the idea of the possible sum as long as I please, without finding the 12 in it. To get beyond the separate ideas of 7 and 5, I must call in the aid of perception, referring to my five fingers, or to five points, and, starting with the conception 16 7, go on to add to it, unit by unit, the 5 so presented to me in perception. The propositions of arithemetic are therefore all synthetic. This is even more manifest if I take larger numbers, when it becomes at once obvious that without the aid of perception no mere analysis of my conceptions, turn and twist them as I may, could ever yield the sum.

Nor is any proposition of pure geometry analytic. That the straight line between any two points is the shortest, is a synthetic proposition. My idea of straight is purely an idea of quality, not of quantity. From no analysis of the conception of a straight line can the knowledge that it is the shortest be derived. Perception has to be called in to enable me to make the synthesis.

17   (2) The principles on which *physics* rests are *a priori* synthetic judgments. I shall content myself with citing two such judgments: first, that in all changes of the material world the quantity of matter remains the same; and, secondly, that
18 in the communication of motion, action and reaction are always equal. Both propositions, it is plain, are not only necessary, and therefore in their origin *a priori*, but they are also synthetic. The conception of matter does not include the idea of permanence, but merely signifies its presence in the space which it occupies. When, therefore, I say that matter is permanent in quantity, I add *to* the conception of matter an attribute which was not at first thought *in* it. Accordingly, the proposition is not analytic, but at once *a priori* and synthetic; and so with the other propositions of pure physics.

   (3) Unsuccessful as *metaphysic* may hitherto have been in solving the unavoidable problems set to it by human reason, its aim undoubtedly is to acquire *a priori* synthetic knowledge. That aim it certainly will never attain by merely dissecting the conceptions of things which we have in our mind *a priori*, and expressing them in analytic propositions. For it seeks to enlarge our *a priori* knowledge, and therefore it must try to show that there are judgments that add to a conception something not already contained in it, even if it should be led to venture into a region where experience cannot follow, as for instance in the proposition that the world must have had an absolute beginning. In its aim at least metaphysic therefore consists entirely of *a priori* synthetic propositions.

19 *6. The Problem of Pure Reason.*

   It is of very great advantage, to others as well as to one self, to be able to bring together various topics of investigation in a single problem. Now, the true problem of pure reason may be put in this way—*How are a priori synthetic judgments possible?*
20   Should this question be answered in a satisfactory way, we shall at the same time learn what part reason plays in the foundation and completion of those sciences which contain a theoretical *a priori* knowledge of objects. Thus we shall be able to answer the questions—*How is pure mathematics possible? How is pure physics possible?* As these sciences actually exist, we may fairly ask *how*
21 they are possible; for that they must be possible is proved by the fact that they exist. But as no real progress has as yet been made in the construction of a system that realizes the essential aim of *metaphysic*, it cannot be said that metaphysic exists, and there is, therefore, reason to doubt whether it is possible at all.

   Yet in one sense metaphysic may certainly be said to exist, namely, in the
22 sense that there is in man a natural disposition to seek for this kind of knowledge. But as all attempts to answer the questions which human reason is naturally impelled to ask, as, for instance, whether the world had a beginning, or has existed from all eternity, have always and unavoidably ended in self-contradiction; we cannot be satisfied with asserting the mere natural disposition to metaphysical speculation, or, in other words, with the bare ability of pure reason to construct some sort of metaphysic. It must be possible for reason to attain to certainty one way or the other: we must be able to ascertain whether reason can know the objects it seeks, or whether it cannot know them;

we must find a conclusive answer to the question whether pure reason is capable or incapable of determining the nature of those objects, and whether, therefore, its domain may with confidence be enlarged beyond the limits of experience, or must be restricted within them. Accordingly, the third and last question, which flows from the general problem of pure reason, may be correctly put in this way: *How is a science of metaphysic possible?* Thus a criticism of reason in the end necessarily leads to science, whereas the dogmatic employment of reason without previous criticism can lead only to groundless assertions, to which other assertions equally specious may always be opposed, the inevitable result being *scepticism*.

23

1. KANT'S PROBLEM

Empiricism as established by Locke led to a dead end, and the many attempts made since Hume to rehabilitate it by means of uneasy compromises and evasions have met with scant success. The first temptation was to appeal to "common sense" and to assert against Hume that without the notion of causation neither common experience of the world nor a scientific account of it would be possible. Hume would have agreed, as everyone must; but that is no solution of his problem, which was how, in an experience that comes to us only as a succession of contingent percepts, we can ever justifiably make judgments of necessary connection. If science depends on our doing so, then we must ask, How is science possible?

That necessary judgments, not only concerning causal connection, but also concerning other relations among sensory data, are indispensable to a coherent and scientific knowledge of a world was the firm conviction of Immanuel Kant, who began his career as a natural scientist. Kant had assumed unquestioningly the possibility of such judgments until (as he tells us) a reading of Hume "awoke him from dogmatic slumbers"; whereupon he set himself to reconsider Hume's problem and to seek a means of reconstructing what Hume's analysis seemed to have destroyed.

The important point to notice is that the kind of necessary judgments which science requires are not simply the sort resulting from the assertion of identity and difference, like "*A* is *A*" or "*A* is not not-*A*." These are said to be analytically true for they merely repeat, define, or analyze the subject term without giving any new information. What is needed is a synthetic judgment, which links the subject to a further and hitherto unsuspected term, such as "*A* causes *B*." The first, analytic type of proposition we know to be necessarily true independently of experience. It is, like Descartes's simple natures, self-evident, clear, and distinct in itself. So we say that we know it *a priori*, which means that it is necessarily and universally true. But the second, synthetic type of proposition is the sort the truth of which, Locke and Hume maintained, we could discover only from experience, or by induction, only *a posteriori*; and thus, as Hume tried to show, such propositions could never be necessary.

Kant's question, then, in the interests of the possibility of scientific knowledge, was "How are synthetic judgments possible *a priori*?"—a question which really involves another, which is even more fundamental.

Hume, in effect, had argued that synthetic judgments just cannot be *a priori* or necessary. But Hume gives a description of human experience and understanding which, as we have seen, if pressed, dissolves away all reliable knowledge of the world and of ourselves. If it were correct, we simply would not have the sort of experience of a world of objects in which we are ourselves members such as, in fact, we do have. Kant, therefore, in reopening the matter, is asking on what conditions it is possible to have the kind of experience which we do in fact enjoy, and we might reframe the question thus: How is an experience of a world of objects possible? or, What are the indispensable presuppositions of such an experience?

2. KANT'S "COPERNICAN REVOLUTION"

The presumption made unquestioningly by Locke was that the truth of our ideas depended upon their conformity to things in the world— our ideas of primary qualities resembled the primary qualities of external bodies, the complex ideas of substances, when true, combined the simple ideas as they were found to occur in nature; in short, our ideas conform to things. This presumption, as we have seen, proved self-defeating, for the nature and existence of things in themselves and apart from ideas is by hypothesis unknown to us, thus the conformity to them of our ideas (or their lack of conformity) remains equally unknown.

Kant accordingly asserts firmly that things in themselves are unknowable. It is therefore futile to maintain either that our ideas (or concepts) do or should conform to them. He proposes the hypothesis that our objects, on the contrary, must conform to our concepts and that only by discovering how this can be so can we learn the true nature of our knowledge. This, we shall find, is the condition on which an experience of a world of objects is possible. On any other assumption (as Hume's analysis proves) no coherent world of objects could be experienced at all. It is to this that Kant referred as his "Copernican revolution"—a transfer of point of view from the external world to the mind, similar to Copernicus's transfer of point of view from the earth to the sun.[2]

As soon as we consider the matter closely, we realize the importance and fruitfulness of Kant's suggestion. Our sensations, which were supposed by Locke to convey to us directly information about an external world, are in themselves merely subjective modifications of consciousness; as such they do not constitute objects in an external world at all. Further, as we have already noted, they come to us haphazard, without regular order and as a constant flux of fleeting changes in quality, which means nothing and represents nothing, unless and until it can be sorted out, until its elements can be related to one another in definite ways, and accurately referred to complex objects with specific and characteristic structure. Apart from such sorting, relating, and referring, the sensory flux is what Kant called "a mere manifold," which, as an experience of an objective world, was "as good as nothing." The manifold of sense is much the same as the "blooming and buzzing confusion" alleged by William James as the probable experience of a newborn baby. To become aware of a world of objects external to our bodies, distinctions have to be made within this confused mass of feeling, and elements within it have to be "objectified." Some are referred specifically to one's own body, others to bodies related to one's own in space; and the application of definite principles of order, or rules of relationship, is implied in this process of objectification. These rules and principles, Kant demonstrates, cannot be derived from experience. They are what Hume failed to find (though in some cases he tacitly assumes them). They are, according to Kant, concepts presupposed *a priori* and are supplied by the faculty of thinking. To such concepts, therefore, objects must conform in order to rank as external things. Thus, Kant says, it is not our knowledge that conforms to objects, but objects that conform to our knowledge.

3. *A PRIORI* AND *A POSTERIORI* KNOWLEDGE

In order to understand Kant's reasoning it is essential to grasp the distinction he makes between *a priori* and *a posteriori* knowledge, to which we have already referred. Strictly speaking, these phrases are

---

[2]Cf. *The Critique of Pure Reason.* Preface: "Our suggestion is similar to that of Copernicus in astronomy, who, finding it impossible to explain the movement of the heavenly bodies on the supposition that they turned round the spectator, tried whether he might not succeed better by supposing the spectator to revolve and the stars to remain at rest."

logical technical terms that were originally applied to forms of argument. A train of reasoning, which starts from first principles accepted as axiomatic and which proceeds deductively to necessary conclusions, was said to be *a priori*, because the conclusion was derived from truths taken to be logically prior. Such reasoning, once the axioms were accepted, was necessary and universal throughout, and each step followed logically from the preceding one without any appeal to experience. Accordingly, *a priori* knowledge is taken to be necessary and universal and prior to all experience, as that which can be posited with certainty by pure reason.

A posteriori reasoning, on the other hand, proceeds from particular cases to generalizations (or other particulars). It is essentially inductive and appeals to experience, and so the phrase is used to refer to knowledge which is possible only as the result of sense perception, and which is therefore always contingent and never properly universal. At best it can refer and apply only to what has already been observed, and so can never be asserted apodictically, or with necessity.

In his use of these phrases Kant tends to lay most stress on the dependence or independence of the kind of knowledge with which he is concerned upon sensory experience. What is known *a priori* is known (he tends to say) completely independently of experience, whereas what is the fruit of experience is known *a posteriori*. But he also insists that only what is known *a priori* is necessary and fully universal, following Hume in the admission and insistence that what we learn from experience can never be the foundation for necessary and universal judgments.

4. ANALYTIC AND SYNTHETIC JUDGMENTS

The next antithesis requisite to an understanding of Kant is his distinction between analytic and synthetic judgments, which is closely connected with that between *a priori* and *a posteriori*, but is not the same. An analytic judgment is one in which the predicate contains nothing which is not already implicit (as Kant puts it, already thought) in the subject. For instance, in the statement, "Bodies are extended," the very idea of a body implies that it is extended, and the judgment does no more than make this implication explicit.

A synthetic judgment, on the other hand, adds something new in its predicate which is not included in the idea of its subject. Kant's example is "Some bodies are heavy." Weight is not an essential attribute of bodies, though we may discover from experience that all the bodies with which we ever become acquainted are in fact heavy.

Obviously, analytic judgments are always necessary and are known to be universally applicable to their subjects independently of further experience once the concept of the subject is understood. They are therefore *a priori*. In some cases, however, the subject may be an empirical concept, derived only from experience. In others, it may be a conception which is altogether prior to experience, without which no experience would be possible. What such cases might be we shall see shortly.

A posteriori judgments are always, obviously, synthetic. What is discovered by experience is that some subject is qualified by some predicate which is not contained or implied in its concept. But the converse is not necessarily true, that all synthetic judgments are *a posteriori*. Kant maintains emphatically that synthetic judgments are made in the sciences which are both universal and necessary — which are, in short, *a priori*: for instance, that a straight line is the shortest distance between two points; or that two straight lines cannot enclose a space.

The task Kant sets himself is to show how it is possible for us to assert propositions which are both *a priori* (that is, necessary and universal) and synthetic, for if Hume's account of experience were correct this should never be possible. Wherever Hume found such propositions being commonly assumed, he attributed them to the imagination or to the effect of custom, a psychological propensity which could neither be explained nor logically justified. This, as we saw, led to scepticism, from which Kant, with his firm faith in the possibility of scientific knowledge, sought to save us.

He [Hume] . . . put his ship aground, to bring it into safety, on the shore of scepticism where it may lie and rot; instead of which what I want to do is to give it a pilot who will be able to sail the ship safely wherever he will, using sure principles of navigation drawn from knowledge of the globe, and equipped with a complete set of charts and a compass.[3]

5. PURE PERCEPTION

The German word *Anschauung* is usually translated "intuition," and it is used by Kant to refer to a form of cognition in which we are confronted with an object immediately and do not arrive at a conclusion discursively, by inference. Not all discursive thinking, however, is inferential, for Kant. The thinking required to synthesize an object out of data, according to certain rules of organization, he also describes as

---

[3]*Prolegomena to any Future Metaphysics*, Preface III (Lucas's translation).

discursive, and he says that we do this by means of conceptions. In contrast to such thinking there is the direct presentation of an object in intuition or perception, the form of apprehension which, he says, supplies us with the material or content of our knowledge.

Such matter or content is, however, sensuous and Kant thought it possible to think away all sensuous content and still to be left with an object of perception (or intuition). But this object would not be empirical, or derived from experience, but would be "pure". Moreover, as it is devoid of content, it would be purely formal. He calls it the pure form of perception (intuition - *Anschauung*) or the form of sensibility. There are two such objects of pure perception, namely, space and time. These, he proceeds to show, are independent of, and prior to, all sensuous experience, and it is to them that he first appeals in the search for the conditions of possibility of *synthetic a priori* judgments.

6. THINGS-IN-THEMSELVES

The Lockean philosophy fell foul of the epistemologist's fallacy, which Hume avoided by declaring firmly that the causes of our impressions were unknown. Kant argues more subtly for a position midway between Locke and Hume. That there are *a priori* synthetic elements in our knowledge he is sure, as they are to be found in mathematics and theoretical physics, but what is known *a priori* cannot, he maintains, be attributed to things-in-themselves because what pertains to them, if it could be discovered at all, would have to be conveyed to us *a posteriori*, through the senses. What is known *a priori*, therefore, must be imposed upon the object of knowledge by the character of our capacity (or faculty) of cognition. Consequently, the objects so determined cannot be things-in-themselves, but only things as they appear to us (phenomena). Moreover, we cannot know anything except what appears to us, so that all objects of knowledge are phenomenal, and things-in-themselves are altogether unknown and unknowable.

Nevertheless, Kant persistently asserts the existence of "bodies outside of us," which, he says, we know only through "representations that they effect in us when they affect our senses"; But "of what they may be in themselves we know nothing."[4] However, his position here is ambiguous because the "bodies outside of us" are said to be given to us as objects of the senses in space, and these are admittedly only phenomena. Yet that they are in some sense representations of things-in-

---

[4]See *Prolegomena*, Part I, Note I.

themselves is an opinion which Kant does not abandon. It has never entered his mind, he says in the *Prolegomena*, [5] to doubt the existence of things-in-themselves. Yet they are altogether unknown and unknowable.

Thus, by reference to things in themselves, Kant limits our knowledge (and especially the applicability of *a priori* knowledge) to phenomena. From the point of view of things in themselves phenomena and the *a priori* are subjective (or ideal). Criticism of our experience from this point of view is what Kant calls transcendental, a term which he explains as follows: " . . . the word transcendental . . . for me never means a reference of our knowledge to things, but only to our *faculty of knowing*."[6] The transcendental critique is one which prescribes limits to our knowledge from a point of view which lies beyond those limits (in things-in-themselves), although what lies beyond is said to be unknowable. To this extent, therefore, Kant also commits the epistemologist's fallacy. His insistence on the existence of things-in-themselves is a perpetual stumbling block. It provided him with a problem that exercised his mind throughout his philosophical career, and the conception of the thing-in-itself was continually modified as he proceeded, becoming something very different in the end from the bare external source (or "cause") of our sensations.

It is to be noticed that Kant's things-in-themselves correspond in part to Hume's unknown causes of our impressions, and in part to Locke's substance, the underlying something, we know not what, which supports qualities and which is also the basis of the internal constitution of things which we can never discover. If they are unknown, then allegations made about their relations to and effects upon our senses must be suspect; and we shall presently see that the conceptions of cause and effect cannot apply to them. To say, therefore, that they produce effects in us, or affect our senses, is illegitimate, as is any attempt to propound a theory (which is a claim to knowledge) about that which is at the same time held to be unknowable.

---

[5] *Prolegomena*, Part I, Note 3.
[6] *Prolegomena*, Part I, Note 3.

CHAPTER 29

Space and Time

Transcendental Aesthetic

1.

34   Sensation is the actual affection of our sensibility, or capacity of receiving   20
impressions, by an object. The perception which refers itself to an object
through sensation, is *empirical perception*. The undetermined object of such a
perception is a *phenomenon* (Erscheinung).

That element in the phenomenon which corresponds to sensation I call the
matter, while that element which makes it possible that the various determinations of the phenomenon should be arranged in certain ways relatively to one
another is its *form*. Now, that without which sensations can have no order or
form, cannot itself be sensation. The matter of a phenomenon is given to us
entirely *a posteriori*, but its form must lie *a priori* in the mind, and hence it must
be capable of being considered by itself apart from sensation.

35   This pure form of sensibility is also called *pure perception*. Thus, if from the
consciousness of a body, I separate all that the understanding has thought into
it, as substance, force, divisibility, etc., and all that is due to sensation, as impenetrability, hardness, colour, etc.; what is left over are extension and figure.   21
These, therefore, belong to pure perception, which exists in the mind *a priori*,
as a mere form of sensibility, even when no sensation or object of sense is
actually present.

36   The science of all the *a priori* principles of sensibility I call *Transcendental Æsthetic*, in contradistinction from the science of the principles of pure thought, which I call *Transcendental Logic*.

In Transcendental Æsthetic we shall first of all isolate sensibility, abstracting   22
from all that the understanding contributes through its conceptions, so that we may have nothing before us but empirical perception. In the next place, we shall separate from empirical perception all that belongs to sensation; when there will remain only pure perception, or the mere form of phenomena, the sole element that sensibility can yield *a priori*. If this is done, it will be found that there are two pure forms of sensible perception, which constitute principles of *a priori* knowledge, namely, Space and Time. With these it will now be our business to deal.

37 SECTION I. — SPACE

2. Metaphysical Exposition of Space.

In external sense we are conscious of objects as outside of ourselves, and as all without exception in space. In space their shape, size, and relative position are marked out, or are capable of being marked out. Inner sense, in which we are conscious of ourselves, or rather of our own state, gives us, it is true, no direct perception of the soul itself as an object; but it nevertheless is the one single form in which our own state comes before us as a definite object of   23
perception; and hence all inner determinations appear to us as related to one another in time. We cannot be conscious of time as external, any more than we can be conscious of space as something within us. What, then, are space and time? Are they in themselves real things? Are they only determinations, or perhaps merely relations of things, which yet would belong to things in them-
38 selves even if those things were not perceived by us? Or, finally, have space and time no meaning except as forms of perception, belonging to the subjective constitution of our own mind, apart from which they cannot be predicated of anything whatever? To answer these questions I shall begin with a metaphysi-cal exposition of space. An *exposition* I call it, because it gives a distinct al-though not a detailed, statement of what is implied in the idea of space; and the exposition is *metaphysical*, because it brings forward the reasons we have for regarding space as given *a priori*.

(1) Space is not an empirical conception, which has been derived from external experiences. For I could not be conscious that certain of my sensations are relative to something outside of me, that is, to something in a different part of space from that in which I myself am; nor could I be conscious of them as outside of and beside one another, were I not at the same time conscious that they not only are different in content, but are in different places. The con-sciousness of space is, therefore, necessarily presupposed in external percep-tion. No experience of the external relations of sensible things could yield the idea of space, because without the consciousness of space there would be no external experience whatever.

(2) Space is a necessary *a priori* idea, which is presupposed in all external perceptions. By no effort can we think space to be away, although we can quite   24

readily think of space as empty of objects. Space we therefore regard as a condition of the possibility of phenomena, and not as a determination dependent on phenomena. It is thus *a priori*, and is necessarily presupposed in external phenomena.

(3) Space is not a discursive or general conception of the relations of things, 25 but a pure perception. For we can be conscious only of a single space. It is true that we speak as if there were many spaces, but we really mean only parts of one and the same identical space. Nor can we say that these parts exist *before* the one all-embracing space, and are put together to form a whole; but we can think of them only as *in* it. Space is essentially single; by the plurality of spaces, we merely mean that because space can be limited in many ways, the general conception of spaces presupposes such limitations as its foundation. From this it follows, that an *a priori* perception, and not an empirical perception, underlies all conceptions of pure space. Accordingly, no geometrical proposition, as, for instance, that any two sides of a triangle are greater than the third side, can ever be derived from the general conceptions of line and triangle, but only from perception. From the perception, however, it can be derived *a priori*, and with demonstrative certainty.

40 (4) Space is *presented* before our consciousness as an infinite magnitude. Now, in every conception we certainly think of a certain attribute as common to an infinite number of possible objects, which are subsumed *under* the conception; but, from its very nature, no conception can possibly be supposed to contain an infinite number of determinations *within* it. But it is just in this way that space is thought of, all its parts being conceived to co-exist *ad infinitum*. Hence the original consciousness of space is an *a priori* perception, not a conception.

3. Transcendental Exposition of Space.

A transcendental exposition seeks to show how, from a certain principle, the possibility of other *a priori* synthetic knowledge may be explained. To be successful, it must prove (1) that there really are synthetic propositions which can be derived from the principle in question, (2) that they can be so derived only if a certain explanation of that principle is adopted.

Now, geometry is a science that determines the properties of space synthetically, and yet *a priori*. What, then, must be the nature of space, in order that 41 such knowledge of it may be possible? Our original consciousness of it must be perception, for no new truth, such as we have in the propositions of geometry, can be obtained from the mere analysis of a given conception (Introduction, 5). And this perception must be *a priori*, or, in other words, must be found in us before we actually observe an object, and hence it must be pure, not empirical perception. For all geometrical propositions, as, for instance, that space has but three dimensions, are of demonstrative certainty, or present themselves in consciousness as necessary; and such propositions cannot be empirical, nor can they be derived from judgments of experience (Introduction, 2).

How, then, can there be in the mind an external perception, which is antecedent to objects themselves, and in which the conception of those objects may be determined *a priori*? Manifestly, only if that perception has its seat in the subject, that is, if it belongs to the formal constitution of the subject, in virtue of which it is so affected by objects as to have a direct consciousness or perception of them; therefore, only if perception is the universal *form* of outer sense.

Our explanation is, therefore, the only one that makes the possibility of geometry intelligible, as a mode of *a priori* synthetic knowledge. All other explanations fail to do so, and, although they may have an external resemblance to ours, may readily be distinguished from it by this criterion.

42 *Inferences.*   26

(a) Space is in no sense a property of things in themselves, nor is it a relation of things in themselves to one another. It is not a determination that still belongs to objects even when abstraction has been made from all the subjective conditions of perception. For we never could perceive *a priori* any determination of things, whether belonging to them individually or in relation to one another, antecedently to our perception of those things themselves.

(b) Space is nothing but the form of all the phenomena of outer sense. It is the subjective condition without which no external perception is possible for us. The receptivity of the subject, or its capability of being affected by objects, necessarily exists before there is any perception of objects. Hence it is easy to understand, how the form of all phenomena may exist in the mind *a priori*, antecedently to actual observation, and how, as a pure perception in which all objects must be determined, it may contain the principles that determine beforehand the relations of objects when they are met with in experience.

It is, therefore, purely from our human point of view that we can speak of space, of extended things, etc. Suppose the subjective conditions to be taken
43 away, without which we cannot have any external perception, or be affected by objects, and the idea of space ceases to have any meaning. We cannot predicate spatial dimensions of things, except in so far as they appear in our 27 consciousness. The unalterable form of this receptivity, which we call sensibility, is a necessary condition of all the relations in which objects are perceived as outside of us, and this form, when it is viewed in abstraction from objects, is the pure perception that is known by the name of space. We are not entitled to regard the conditions that are proper to our sensibility as conditions of the possibility of things, but only of things as they appear to us. Hence, while it is correct to say, that space embraces all things that are capable of appearing to us as external, we cannot say, that it embraces all things as they are in themselves, no matter what subject may perceive them, and, indeed, whether they are perceived or not. For we have no means of judging whether other thinking beings are in their perceptions bound down by the same conditions as ourselves, and which for us hold universally. If we state the limitations under which a judgment holds of a given subject, the judgment is then unconditionally true. The proposition, that all things are side by side in space, is true only under the limitation that we are speaking of our own sensible perception. But, if we more exactly define the subject of the proposition by saying, that all things as external phenomena are side by side in space, it will be true universally and
44 without any exception. Our exposition, therefore, establishes the *reality*, or objective truth of space, as a determination of every object that can possibly 28 come before us as external; but, at the same time, it proves the *ideality* of space, when space is considered by reason relatively to things in themselves,

that is, without regard to the constitution of our sensibility. We, therefore, affirm the *empirical reality* of space, as regards all possible external experience; but we also maintain its *transcendental ideality*, or, in other words, we hold that space is nothing at all, if its limitation to possible experience is ignored, and it is treated as a necessary condition of things in themselves.

46 SECTION II. — TIME   30

4. Metaphysical Exposition of Time.

(1) Time is not an empirical conception, which has been derived from any experience. For we should not observe things to co-exist or to follow one another, did we not possess the idea of time *a priori*. It is, therefore, only under the presupposition of time, that we can be conscious of certain things as existing at the same time (simultaneously), or at different times (successively).   31

(2) Time is a necessary idea, which is presupposed in all perceptions. We cannot be conscious of phenomena if time is taken away, although we can quite readily suppose phenomena to be absent from time. Time is, therefore, given *a priori*. No phenomenon can exist at all that is not in time. While, therefore, phenomena may be supposed to vanish completely out of time, time itself, as the universal condition of their possibility, cannot be supposed away.

(3) Time is not a discursive, or general conception, but a pure form of sensible perception. Different times are but parts of the very same time. Now, the consciousness of that which is presented as one single object, is perception.   32 Moreover, the proposition, that no two moments of time can co-exist, cannot be derived from a general conception. The proposition is synthetic, and cannot originate in mere conceptions. It therefore rests upon the direct perception and idea of time.

48   (4) The infinity of time simply means, that every definite quantity of time is possible only as a limitation of one single time. There must, therefore, be originally a consciousness of time as unlimited. Now, if an object presents itself as a whole, so that its parts and every quantity of it can be represented only by limiting that whole, such an object cannot be given in conception, for conceptions contain only partial determinations of a thing. A direct perception must therefore be the foundation of the idea of time.

5. Transcendental Exposition of Time.

47   Apodictic principles which determine relations in time, or axioms of time in   31 general, are possible only because time is the necessary *a priori* condition of all phenomena. Time has but one dimension; different times do not co-exist but follow one another, just as different spaces do not follow one another but co-exist. Such propositions cannot be derived from experience, which never yields strict universality or demonstrative certainty. If they were based upon experience, we could say only, that it has ordinarily been observed to be so, not that it must be so. Principles like these have the force of rules, that lay down the conditions without which no experience whatever is possible: they are not learned from experience, but anticipate what experience must be.

Let me add here that change, including motion or change of place, is conceivable only in and through the idea of time. Were time not an inner *a priori* perception, we could not form the least idea how there should be any such thing as change. Take away time, and change combines in itself absolutely contradictory predicates. Motion, or change of place, for instance, must then be thought of as at once the existence and the non-existence of one and the same thing in the same place. The contradiction disappears, only when it is seen that the thing has those opposite determinations one after the other. Our conception of time as an *a priori* form of perception, therefore explains the possibility of the whole body of *a priori* synthetic propositions in regard to motion that are contained in the pure part of physics, and hence it is not a little fruitful in results.

6. *Inferences.*   32

(*a*) Time is not an independent substance nor an objective determination of things, and hence it does not survive when abstraction has been made from all the subjective conditions of perception. Were it an independent thing, it would be real without being a real object of consciousness. Were it a determination or 33 order of things as they are in themselves, it could not precede our perception of those things as its necessary condition, nor could it be known *a priori* by means of synthetic judgments. But the possibility of such judgments becomes at once intelligible if time is nothing but the subjective condition, without which we can have no perception whatever. For in that case we may be conscious of objects, and therefore *a priori*.

(*b*) Time is nothing but the form of inner sense, that is, of the perception of ourselves and our own inner state. As it has no influence on the shape or position of an object, time cannot be a determination of outer phenomena as such; what it does determine is the relation of ideas in our own inner state. And just because this inner perception has no shape of its own, we seek to make up for this want by analogies drawn from space. Thus, we figure the series of time as a line that proceeds to infinity, the parts of which form a series; and we reason from the properties of this line to all the properties of time, taking care to allow for the one point of difference, that the parts of the spatial line all exist at once, while the parts of the temporal line all follow one after the other. Even from this fact alone, that all the relations of time may thus be presented in an external perception, it would be evident that time is itself a perception.

(*c*) Time is the formal *a priori* condition of all phenomena without exception. Space, as the pure form of all external phenomena, is the *a priori* condition 34 only of external phenomena. But all objects of perception, external as well as internal, are determinations of the mind, and, from that point of view, belong to our inner state. And as this inner state comes under time, which is the formal condition of inner perception, time is an *a priori* condition of all phenomena: it is the immediate condition of inner phenomena, and so the mediate condition of outer phenomena. Just as I can say, *a priori*, that all external phenomena are in space, and are determined *a priori* in conformity with the relations of space, so, from the principle of the inner sense, I can say quite generally that all phenomena are in time, and stand necessarily in relations of time.

If we abstract from the manner in which we immediately perceive our own inner state, and mediately all external phenomena, and think of objects in themselves, we find that in relation to them time is nothing at all. It is objectively

true in relation to phenomena, because we are conscious of phenomena as *objects of our senses;* but it is no longer objective, if we abstract from our sensi- 35
bility, and therefore from the form proper to our perceptive consciousness, and
speak of *things as such.* Time is therefore a purely subjective condition of human
perception, and in itself, or apart from the subject, it is nothing at all. Nevertheless, it is necessarily objective in relation to all phenomena, and therefore also
52   to everything that can possibly enter into our experience. We cannot say that all
things are in time, because when we speak of things in this unqualified way,
we are thinking of things in abstraction from the manner in which we perceive
them, and therefore in abstraction from the condition under which alone we can
say that they are in time. But, if we qualify our assertion by adding that condition,
and say that all things as phenomena, or objects of sensible perception, are in
time, the proposition is, in the strictest sense of the word, objective, and is
universally true a *priori.*
    We see, then, that time is empirically real, or is objectively true in relation to
all objects that are capable of being presented to our senses. And as our
perception always is sensuous, no object can ever be presented to us in experience, which does not conform to time as its condition. On the other hand, we
deny to time all claim to absolute reality, because such a claim, in paying no 36
heed to the form of sensible perception, assumes time to be an absolute condition or property of things. Such properties, as supposed to belong to things in
themselves, can never be presented to us in sense. From this we infer the
transcendental ideality of time; by which we mean that, in abstraction from the
subjective conditions of sensible perception, time is simply nothing, and cannot
be said either to subsist by itself, or to inhere in things that do so subsist.

53   *7. Explanatory Remarks.*

    To this doctrine, which admits the empirical reality of time, but denies its
absolute or transcendental reality, there is one objection so commonly made,
that I must suppose it to occur spontaneously to everybody who is new to the
present line of thought. It runs thus: No one can doubt that there are real
changes, for, even if it is denied that we perceive the external world, together 37
with the changes in it, we are at least conscious of a change in our own ideas.
Now, changes can take place only in time. Therefore time is real.
    There is no difficulty in meeting this objection. I admit all that is said. Cer-
tainly time is real: it is the real form of inner perception. It has reality for me
relatively to my inner experience; in other words, I actually am conscious of
54   time, and of my own determinations as in it. Time is therefore real, not as an
object beyond consciousness, but as the manner in which I exist for myself as
an object of consciousness. But, if I could be perceived by myself or by any
other being without the condition of sensibility, the very same determinations,
which now appear as changes, would not be known as in time, and therefore
would not be known as changes. The empirical reality of time thus remains, on
our theory, the condition of all our experience. It is only its absolute reality that
we refuse to admit. Time is therefore nothing but the form of our inner perception. If we take away from it the peculiar condition of our sensibility, the idea of
time also vanishes; for time does not belong to objects as they are in themselves, but only to the subject that perceives them.   38
55   Time and space are two sources of knowledge from which a variety of *a*

priori synthetic judgments may be derived. Mathematics, especially, supplies a   39
56   splendid instance of such judgments, in the science of space and the relations of
space. Time and space are the two pure forms of all sensible perception, and as
such they make *a priori* synthetic propositions possible. And just because they
are mere conditions of sensibility, they mark out their own limits as sources of *a
priori* knowledge. Applying only to objects regarded as phenomena, they do
not present things as they are in themselves. Beyond the phenomenal world,
which is their legitimate domain, they cannot be employed in determination of
objects. But this limitation in no way lessens the stability of our empirical
knowledge; for, such knowledge, as depending upon necessary forms of the
perception of things, is just as certain as if it rested upon necessary forms of
things in themselves.
58   Transcendental Æsthetic cannot contain more than these two elements. This   41
is plain, if we reflect that all other conceptions belonging to sensibility presuppose something empirical. Even the idea of motion, in which both elements are
united, presupposes the observation of something that moves. Now, there is
nothing movable in space considered purely by itself; hence that which is
movable can be found in space only by experience, and is therefore an empirical datum. Similarly the idea of change cannot be put among the *a priori* data
of transcendental aesthetic. Time itself does not change, but only something that
is in time; hence the idea of change must be derived from the observation of
some actual object with its successive determinations—that is, from experience.

59   *8. General remarks on the Transcendental Aesthetic.*

62   (1) A distinction is commonly drawn between what belongs essentially to an   45
object, and is perceived by every one to belong to it, and what is accidental,
being perceived only from a certain position, or when a special organ is affected in a particular way. In the one case, we are said to know the object as it
is in itself; in the other case, to know it only as it appears to us. This, however,
is merely an empirical distinction. For, it must be remembered, that the empirical object which is here called the thing, is itself but an appearance. If this
were all, our transcendental distinction would be altogether lost sight of, and
we might imagine ourselves to know things in themselves when we knew only
phenomena. For the truth is, that, however far we may carry our investigations
63   into the world of sense, we never can come into contact with aught but appearances. For instance, we call the rainbow in a sun-shower a mere appearance, and the rain the thing itself. Nor is there any objection to this, if we mean
to state merely the physical truth, that from whatever position it is viewed the
rain will appear to our senses as a real object of experience. But, if we go
beyond the fact, that the sensible object is here the same for every one, and ask   46
whether the object is known as it is in itself, we pass to the transcendental point
of view, and the question now is in regard to the relation of our consciousness
of the object to the object as it exists apart from our consciousness. In this point
of view, not merely the rain-drops, but their round shape, and even the space
in which they fall, must be regarded as mere appearances, not as things in
themselves. Every aspect of the phenomenon, in short, is but a modification or
a permanent form of our sensible perception, while the transcendental object
remains to us unknown.
71   (2) It is recognized in natural theology, not only that God cannot be an object

of perception to us, but that He can never be an object of *sensuous* perception to Himself. At the same time, His knowledge must be *perception*, and not thought, for thought always involves limitations. Now, the natural theologian is very careful to say, that God, in His perception, is free from the limits of space and time. But, how can this possibly be maintained, if it has previously been assumed, that space and time are forms of things in themselves? It must then be held that, even if those things were annihilated, space and time would continue to be *a priori* conditions of their existence. And if they are conditions
72 of all existence, they must be conditions of the existence even of God. We can avoid this conclusion only by saying that space and time are not objective forms of all things, but subjective forms of our outer as well as of our inner perceptions. In fact our perception is sensuous, just because it is *not original*. Were it original, the very existence of the object would be given in the perception, and such a perception, so far as we can see, can belong only to the Original Being. Our perception is dependent upon the existence of the object, and therefore it is possible only if our perceptive consciousness is affected by the presence of the object.

Nor is it necessary to say, that man is the only being who perceives objects under the forms of space and time; it may be that all finite thinking beings agree with man in that respect, although of this we cannot be certain. But, however universal this mode of perception may be, it cannot be other than sensuous, simply because it is derivative (*intuitus derivativus*) and not original (*intuitus originarius*), and therefore is not an intellectual perception. An intellectual perception, as we have already seen reason to believe, is the prerogative of the Original Being, and never can belong to a being which is dependent in its existence as well as in its perception, and in fact is conscious of its own existence only in relation to given objects.

73 *Conclusion of the Transcendental Aesthetic.*

We have, then, in the Transcendental Aesthetic, one of the elements required in the solution of the general problem of transcendental philosophy: *How are a priori synthetic propositions possible?* Such propositions rest upon space and time, which are pure *a priori* perceptions. To enable us to go beyond a given conception, in an *a priori* judgment, we have found that something is needed, which is not contained in the conception, but in the perception corresponding to it, something therefore that may be connected with that conception synthetically. But such judgments, as based upon perception, can never extend beyond objects of sense, and therefore hold true only for objects of possible experience.

1. OUTER AND INNER SENSE

As Locke distinguished between sensation and reflection, so Kant distinguishes between outer and inner sense. Our sensory states occur in succession and we are aware of the continuous change from one to another. As they are purely sensory they are not spatial, but are incurably successive. So Kant says that the form of inner sense, of our awareness of sensory change, is time. But besides this awareness of change, some sensory objects are located outside of us and outside of one another in space. These are the objects of outer sense mutually related spatially.

2. SENSE AND UNDERSTANDING

Kant also distinguishes between sense and understanding as two sources of knowledge; the first provides (as Locke insisted) all the matter (or content) of experience; the second provides its form. By means of sense, objects are given to us; by means of understanding we think (or conceive) them. The parallel distinction is that between perception and conception. But although Kant asserts that objects are given to us by sense, the whole force of his argument is to the contrary. It establishes the impossibility of experiencing anything recognizable as an object apart from the formal characters supplied *a priori* by the mind. It is the ordering, relating, and organizing activity of consciousness that constitutes objects, though the material out of which it creates them is sensuous.

Kant, however, obfuscates this interdependence of sense and thought in knowledge, which his own insight and analysis are chiefly responsible for demonstrating, by asserting that space and time are themselves intuitions (or perceptions), albeit pure perceptions, devoid of sensuous content. These pure perceptions, he proceeds to show, are *a priori*, so that not even sensible objects are given to us wholly *a posteriori*.

3. THE TRANSCENDENTAL AESTHETIC

Kant proves that space and time cannot be ideas generalized from experience, but must be presupposed *a priori* in any experience of spatial and temporal objects, by means of four main arguments equally applicable to both space and time.

a. It is impossible to be aware of objects as outside of us and of one another, or of events as occurring before and after one another (or simultaneously) except on the presuppositions of space and time already envisaged as the framework within which these relations are apprehended. It cannot, therefore, be the case that we build up the ideas of space and time out of previously experienced spatial and temporal relations, for those relations already presuppose space and time as given wholes.

b. We can imagine empty space and empty time, but we can in no way conceive of a total absence of either space or time themselves. They are prior conditions of our experience of spatial and temporal objects.

c. Again, space and time cannot be general ideas under which particular objects are subsumed, because particular spaces (or times) are not just particular instances of a general concept, but are actual parts of one infinite space (or time).

d. Both space and time are thus infinite given wholes or magnitudes and no general idea can be that. General concepts do not *contain* their instances even if they do subsume an infinite number of instances under a single universal.

Space and time are not universal ideas but are objects of perception, though apart from their sensuous filling they are pure perceptions, the mere forms of sensibility supplied *a priori* by the mind prior to all experience. Accordingly, Kant argues, they are not characteristics of things in themselves but only of phenomena. They are empirically real but transcendentally ideal.

What Kant means by this he explains at some length. Sensations provide the given element in knowledge, but though they may be due to interaction between our minds and things-in-themselves, they do not present to us, or give us specific information about, things-in-themselves. They do not even give us a knowledge of objects, so far as they are no more than a sensory manifold. Nevertheless, they do supply the material of knowledge. The argument of the *Aesthetic* shows that, although it is passively received, this material can be received only in spatial and temporal forms. But these forms are only characteristics of our capacity to receive the sensible contents of our faculty of intuition. They are not the forms of things-in-themselves, but only of objects as they appear to us. As characteristics of such appearances (phenomena), space and time are real. We cannot perceive objects in any other way and, our capacity of receptivity (*Receptivitätsfähigkeit*) being what it is, space and time are empirically real (that is, for our experience and in reference simply to phenomena).

But relative to things-in-themselves these forms of perception are nothing. They belong to the mind and not to things. Viewed transcendentally, therefore, simply as the necessary conditions of any experience of objects, they are seen to be only ideal. They are real only as a mode or form of our perceiving.

4. HOW MATHEMATICS IS POSSIBLE

Having proved in this way that space and time are *a priori* forms of intuition, Kant proceeds to show that they are the foundation of synthetic judgments in mathematics which are, because of the *a priori* character of space and time, necessary and universally true. It is because space is a necessary form of perception and has a necessary structure which is the prior condition of any perception of external objects that we can affirm, necessarily and universally, without discovering it by measurement of particular instances, that two sides of a triangle are together greater than the third, and can prove deductively that the square on the hypotenuse of a right-angled triangle is equal to the sum of the square of the other two sides.

This is how it is possible to construct a science of mathematics capable of pronouncing *a priori* synthetic judgments, and this is the first stage of Kant's answer to the question he originally raised: "How are synthetic judgments possible *a priori*?"

5. THE CONDITIONS OF OBJECTIVE PERCEPTION

Space and time, however, have so far been treated as pure perceptions, and Kant always speaks of them as such. But the perception of spatiotemporal objects requires not merely the filling of space and time with sensuous qualities but the interrelation of such qualities in specific ways. They are quantitatively and qualitatively various so as to be susceptible of numerical comparison, and they have mutual dependence in various ways. These characteristics, moreover, are not just adjuncts of otherwise self-subsistent entities but enter into their very constitution. Kant goes on to consider the implications of these requirements for the experience of objects and discovers (to his readers, if not always to himself) that the very forms of space and time are dependent upon yet more fundamental conditions.

CHAPTER 30

A Priori Synthesis

The Critique of Pure Reason
(continued)

DEDUCTION OF THE CATEGORIES

Principles of a Transcendental Deduction.

There is a distinction in law between the question of right (*quid juris*) and the question of fact (*quid facti*). Both must be proved, but proof of a right or 117 claim is called its *deduction*. Now, among the variety of conceptions that make 85 up the very mixed web of human knowledge, there are certain conceptions that put in a claim for use entirely *a priori*, and this claim of course stands in need of deduction. It is useless to refer to the fact of experience in justification of such a claim, but at the same time we must know how conceptions can possibly refer to objects which yet they do not derive from experience. An explanation of the manner in which conceptions can relate *a priori* to objects, I 86 call a *transcendental deduction*; and from it I distinguish an *empirical deduction*, which simply tells us how a conception has been acquired by experience and reflection on experience. The former proves our right to the use of a certain conception, the latter merely points out that as a matter of fact it has come into our possession in a certain way.

We had no difficulty in explaining how space and time, although they are 89 themselves known *a priori*, are yet necessarily related to objects, and make possible a synthetic knowledge of objects which is independent of all experience. For, as it is only by means of these pure forms of sense that we can be 122 conscious of an object in empirical perception, space and time are pure perceptions, which contain *a priori* the condition of the possibility of objects as phenomena, and therefore synthesis in them has objective validity.

The categories of understanding, on the other hand, are not conditions under which objects are given in perception; hence objects might certainly be presented to us, even if they were not necessarily related to functions of understanding, as their *a priori* condition. Here, therefore, a difficulty arises that we did not meet with in the field of sensibility. The difficulty is, how *subjective conditions of thought* should have *objective validity*, or, in other words, how they should be conditions without which no knowledge of objects would be possible. Take, for instance, the conception of cause. Here we have a 90 peculiar sort of synthesis, in which something B is conceived as following upon something else quite different A, in conformity with a rule. It is hard to see why phenomena should be subject to such an *a priori* conception. Why should not the conception be perfectly empty, and without any phenomenal object corresponding to it?

123 We cannot avoid the toil of such investigations by saying that experience is 91 perpetually giving us examples of such conformity to law on the part of phenomena, and that we are thus enabled to form an abstract conception of cause, and to be certain of its objective validity. The conception of cause cannot possibly originate in that way; and hence we must either show that it rests 124 completely *a priori* upon understanding, or we must discard it altogether as a mere fiction of the brain. For the conception demands that something A should be of such a nature that something else B follows from it *necessarily*, and in conformity with an *absolutely universal rule*. No pure conception of understanding can be the product of empirical induction without a complete reversal of its nature and use.

126 The transcendental deduction of all *a priori* conceptions must therefore be 94 guided by the principle, that these conceptions must be the *a priori* conditions of all possible experience. Conceptions which make experience possible are for that very reason necessary. An analysis of the experience in which they occur 127 would not furnish a deduction of them, but merely an illustration of their use. Were they not the primary conditions of all the experience in which objects are known as phenomena, their relation to even a single object would be utterly incomprehensible.

Section II. — A Priori Conditions of Experience.[1]

It would be quite a sufficient deduction of the categories, and justification of 96 their objective application, to show that, apart from them, no object whatever is 97 capable of being thought. But there are two reasons why a fuller deduction is advisable: firstly, because, in thinking an object, other faculties besides understanding, or the faculty of thought proper, come into play; and, secondly,

---

[1]All that comes under this heading is taken from the *first* edition of the "Critique of Pure Reason," and forms what is called the "subjective deduction."

because it has to be explained how understanding can possibly be a condition of the knowledge of real objects. We must, therefore, begin with a consideration of the primary activities of the subject that are essential in the constitution of experience; and these we must view, not in their empirical, but in their transcendental character.

If consciousness were broken up into a number of mutually repellent states, each isolated and separated from the rest, knowledge would never arise in us at all, for knowledge is a whole of related and connected elements. When, therefore, I call sensible perception a synopsis, in order to mark the complexity of its content, it must be remembered that in this synopsis a certain synthesis is implied, and that knowledge is possible only if *spontaneity* is combined with *receptivity.* This is the reason why we must say that in all knowledge there is a three-fold synthesis: firstly, the *apprehension* in perception of various ideas, or modifications of the mind; secondly, their *reproduction* in imagination; and, thirdly, their *recognition* in conception. These three forms of synthesis point to three sources of knowledge, which make understanding itself possible, and through it all experience as an empirical product of understanding.   98

1. Synthesis of Apprehension in Perception.

Whatever may be the origin of our ideas, whether they are due to the influence of external things or are produced by internal causes, whether as objects they have their source *a priori* or in experience, as modifications of the   99 mind they must all belong to the inner sense. All knowledge is, therefore, at bottom subject to time as the formal condition of inner sense, and in time every part of it without exception must be ordered, connected, and brought into relation with every other part. This is a general remark, which must be kept in mind in the whole of our subsequent inquiry.

We should not be conscious of the various determinations that every perception contains within itself were we not, in the succession of our impressions, conscious of time. If each feeling were limited to a single moment, it would be an absolutely individual unit. In order that the various determinations of a perception, as, for instance, the parts of a line, should form a unity, it is necessary that they should be run over and held together by the mind. This act I call the *synthesis of apprehension.* It is *apprehension,* because it goes straight to perception; it is *synthesis,* because only by synthesis can the various elements of perception be united in one object of consciousness.

Now, this synthesis of apprehension must be employed *a priori* also, or in relation to determinations not given in sensible experience. Otherwise we should have no consciousness of space and time *a priori*, for these can be   100 produced only by a synthesis of the various determinations that are presented by sensibility in its original receptivity. There is therefore a pure synthesis of apprehension.

2. Synthesis of Reproduction in Imagination.

There is an empirical law of the association of ideas. When any two ideas have often followed, or accompanied each other, an association between them is at last formed, and they are so connected that, even when an object is not present, the mind passes from the one to the other in conformity with a fixed rule. But this law of repoduction presupposes that phenomena are themselves actually subject to such a rule, and that the various elements in these phenomena of which we are conscious should accompany or follow one another in accordance with certain rules. On any other supposition our empirical imagination would have nothing to reproduce in any way conforming to its own nature, and would therefore lie hidden in the depths of the mind as a dead, and to us unknown faculty. Were cinnabar, for instance, sometimes red and sometimes black, sometimes light and sometimes heavy; or were the same name given at   101 one time to this object, and at another time to that, without the least regard to any rule implied in the nature of the phenomena themselves, there could be no empirical synthesis of reproduction.

There must, therefore, be something which makes the reproduction of phenomena possible at all, something which is the *a priori* ground of a necessary synthetic unity. That this is so, we may at once see, if we reflect that phenomena are not things in themselves, but are merely the play of our own ideas, and therefore at bottom determinations of the inner sense. Now, if we can show that even our purest *a priori* perceptions can yield knowledge, only in so far as they involve such a combination as makes a thoroughgoing synthesis of reproduction possible, we may conclude that this synthesis of imagination, being prior to all experience, rests upon *a priori* principles. We must then assume a pure transcendental synthesis as the necessary condition of all   102 experience, for experience is impossible unless phenomena are capable of being reproduced. Now, if I draw a line in thought, or think of the time from one day to another, or even think of a certain number, it is plain that I must be conscious of the various determinations one after the other. But if the earlier determinations—the prior parts of the line, the antecedent moments of time, the units as they arise one after the other—were to drop out of my consciousness, and could not be reproduced when I passed on to the later determinations, I should never be conscious of a whole; and hence not even the simplest and most elementary idea of space or time could arise in my consciousness.

The synthesis of reproduction is therefore inseparably bound up with the synthesis of apprehension. And as the synthesis of apprehension is the transcendental ground of the possibility of all knowledge—of pure *a priori* as well as empirical knowledge—the reproductive synthesis of imagination belongs to the transcendental functions of the mind, and may therefore be called the transcendental faculty of imagination.

3. Synthesis of Recognition in Conceptions.   103

Were I not conscious that what I think now is identical with what I thought a moment ago, all reproduction in the series of ideas would be useless. The idea reproduced at a given moment would be for me a perfectly new idea. There would be no identical consciousness bound up with the act of producing one idea after another; and as without such consciousness there could be for me no unity, I should never be conscious of the various members of the series as forming one whole. If, in counting, I should forget that the units lying before my mind had been added by me one after the other, I should not be aware that a sum was being produced or generated in the successive addition of unit to unit; and as the conception of the sum is simply the consciousness of this unity of synthesis, I should have no knowledge of the number.

At this point it is necessary to have a clear idea of what we mean by an   104
object of consciousness. We have seen that a phenomenon is just a sensation of
which we are conscious, and that no sensation can be said to exist by itself as
an object outside of consciousness. What, then, do we mean when we speak of
an object as corresponding to our knowledge, and therefore as distinct from it?
It is easy to see that this object can be thought of only as something $= x$, for
there is nothing beyond knowledge that we can set up as contrasted with
knowledge, and yet as corresponding to it.

It is plain that in knowledge we have to do with nothing but the various   105
determinations of our own consciousness; hence the object $= x$, which corresponds to them is nothing to us — being, as it is, something that has to be distinct
from all our ideas — the unity which the object makes necessary can be nothing
else than the formal unity of consciousness in the synthesis of the manifold of
ideas. It is only when we have thus produced synthetic unity in the manifold of
perception that we are in a position to say that we know the object. But this
unity is impossible if the perception cannot be generated in accordance with a
rule by means of such a function of synthesis as makes the reproduction of the
manifold *a priori* necessary, and renders possible, a concept in which it is
united. Thus we think a triangle as an object, in that we are conscious of the
combination of three straight lines according to a rule by which such a perception can always be represented. This unity of rule determines all the manifold,
and limits it to conditions which make unity of apperception possible. The
concept of this unity is the representation of the object $= x$, which I think
through the predicates, above mentioned, of a triangle.

All knowledge demands a concept, though that concept may, indeed, be   106
quite imperfect or obscure. But a concept is always, as regards its form, something universal which serves as a rule. The concept of body, for instance, as the
unity of the manifold which is thought through it, serves as a rule in our
knowledge of outer appearances. But it can be a rule for perceptions only in so
far as it represents in any given appearances the necessary reproduction of
their manifold, and thereby the synthetic unity in our consciousness of them.
The concept of body, in the perception of something outside us, necessitates
the idea of extention, and therewith ideas of impenetrability, shape, etc.

All necessity, without exception, is grounded in a transcendental condition.
There must, therefore, be a transcendental ground of the unity of consciousness in the synthesis of the manifold of all our perceptions, and consequently
also of the concepts of objects in general, and so of all objects of experience, a
ground without which it would be impossible to think any object for our perceptions; for this object is no more than that something, the concept of which
expresses such a necessity of synthesis.

This original and transcendental condition is no other than *transcendental*   107
apperception. Consciousness of self according to the determinations of our state
in inner perception is merely empirical, and always changing. In this flux of
inner phenomena there can be no unchanging or permanent self. This form of
self-consciousness is usually called *inner sense* or *empirical apperception*. Now,
from empirical data it is impossible to derive the conception of that which must
necessarily be numerically identical. What we require, in explanation of such a
transcendental presupposition, is a condition that precedes all experience, and
makes it possible.

No knowledge whatever, no unity and connection of objects, is possible for us, apart from that unity of consciousness which is prior to all data of perception, and without relation to which no consciousness of objects is possible. This pure, original, unchangeable consciousness I call *transcendental apperception*. That this is the proper name for it is evident, were it only that even the purest objective unity, that of the *a priori* conceptions of space and time, is possible only in so far as perceptions are related to it. The numerical unity of this apperception is, therefore, just as much the *a priori* foundation of all conceptions as the various determinations of space and time are the *a priori* foundation of the perceptions of sense.

It is this transcendental unity of apperception which connects all the possible 108 phenomena that can be gathered together in one experience, and subjects them to laws. There could be no such unity of consciousness were the mind not able to be conscious of the identity of function, by which it unites various phenomena in one knowledge. The original and necessary consciousness of the identity of oneself is at the same time the consciousness of a necessary unity in the synthesis of all phenomena according to conceptions. These conceptions are necessary rules, which not only make phenomena capable of reproduction, but determine perception as perception of an object, that is, bring it under a conception of something in which various determinations are necessarily connected together. It would be impossible for the mind to think itself as identical in its various determinations, and indeed to think that identity *a priori*, if it did not hold the identity of its own act before its eyes, and if it did not, by subjecting to a transcendental unity all the synthesis of empirical apprehension, make the connection of the various determinations implied in that synthesis possible in accordance with *a priori* rules.

129 *15. Possibility of any Combination whatever.*[2]

Though a perception is merely sensuous or receptive, the various determinations of consciousness may be given, while the form, as simply the way in which the subject is affected, may lie *a priori* in the mind. But the combination (*conjunctio*) of those determinations can never come to us through the medium of sense, and therefore cannot be contained even in the pure form of sensible
130 perception. Combination is a spontaneous act of consciousness, and, as such, it is the especial characteristic of understanding, as distinguished from sense. All combination, therefore, whether we are aware of it or not, whether it is a combination of the various determinations of perception or of several conceptions, and whether the determinations of perception are empirical or pure, is an act of understanding. This act we call by the general name of *synthesis*, to draw attention to the fact that we can be conscious of nothing as combined in the object, which we have not ourselves previously combined. And as it proceeds entirely from the self-activity of the subject, combination is the element, and the only element, that cannot be given by the object. It is easy to see that this act must in its origin always be of one and the same nature, no matter what may be the form of combination; and that the resolution or *analysis*, which seems to be its opposite, in point of fact always presupposes it. If understanding has previously combined nothing, there is nothing for it to resolve; for without

---

[2]What follows (15–27) constitutes the "objective deduction" of the categories, as it appears in the *second* edition of the "Critique."

the combining activity of understanding there can be no consciousness of an object at all.

By combination, however, must be understood not merely the synthesis of the various determinations of sense, but also their unity. Combination is con-
131 sciousness of the *synthetic unity* of various determinations. The consciousness of this unity cannot be the result of the combination, for were we not, in being conscious of various determinations, also conscious of their unity, we should have no conception of combination at all. Nor must this unity, which precedes any conception of combination, be confused with the category of unity; for all categories rest upon logical functions of judgment, and, in these, combination, or the unity of given conceptions, is already implied. For an explanation of the unity in question, which is qualitative, we must go further back, and seek it in that which, as the ground of the unity of various conceptions in judgment, is implied in the possibility even of the logical use of understanding.

16. The original Synthetic unity of Apperception.

132   The "*I think*" must be capable of accompanying all my ideas; for, otherwise, I should be conscious of something that could not be thought; which is the same as saying, that I should not be conscious at all, or at least should be conscious only of that which for me was nothing. Now, that form of consciousness which is prior to all thought, is *perception*. Hence, all the manifold determinations of perception have a necessary relation to the "*I think*" in the subject that is conscious of them. The "*I think*," however, is an act of *spontaneity*, which cannot possibly be due to sense. I call it *pure apperception*, to distinguish it from *empirical apperception*. I call it also the *original apperception*, because it is the self-consciousness which produces the "*I think*." Now, the "*I think*" must be capable of accompanying all other ideas, and it is one and the same in all consciousness; but there is no other idea beyond the "*I think*," to which self-consciousness is bound in a similar way. The unity of apperception I call also the *transcendental unity* of self-consciousness, to indicate that upon it depends the possibility of *a priori* knowledge. For, the various determinations given in a certain perception would not all be in my consciousness, if they did not all belong to one self-consciousness. True, I may not be aware of this, but yet as they are determinations of my consciousness, they must necessarily conform to the condition, without which they are not *capable* of standing
133 together in one universal self-consciousness. In no other way would they all without exception be mine. From this original combination important consequences follow.

The absolute identity of apperception in relation to all the determinations given in perception, involves a synthesis of those determinations, and is possible only through consciousness of the synthesis. For, the empirical consciousness, which accompanies each determination as it arises, is in itself broken up into units, and is unrelated to the one identical subject. Relation to a single subject does not take place when I accompany each determination with consciousness, but only when I add one determination to the other, and am conscious of this act of synthesis. It is only because I am capable of combining *in one consciousness* the various determinations presented to me, that I can become aware that in every one of them the consciousness is the same. The
134 *analytic* unity of apperception is, therefore, possible only under presupposition

of a certain *synthetic* unity. The thought, that the determinations given in a perception all belong to me, is the same as the thought, that I unite them, or at least that I am capable of uniting them in one self-consciousness. This does not of itself involve a *consciousness of the synthesis* of determinations, but it presupposes the possibility of that consciousness. It is only because I am capable of grasping the various determinations in one consciousness, that I can call them all mine; were it not so, I should have a self as many-coloured and various as the separate determinations of which I am conscious. Synthetic unity of the various determinations of perception as given *a priori*, is therefore the ground of that identity of apperception itself, which precedes *a priori* every definite act of thought. Now, objects cannot combine themselves, nor can understanding
135 learn that they are combined by observing their combination. All combination is the work of understanding, and in fact understanding is itself nothing but the faculty of combining *a priori*, and bringing under the unity of apperception, the various determinations given in perception. The unity of apperception is, therefore, the supreme principle of all our knowledge.

This principle of the necessary unity of apperception, is no doubt in itself an identical and therefore an analytic proposition; but it also reveals the necessity for a synthesis of the various determinations given in perception, because without such synthesis the thoroughgoing identity of self-consciousness is inconceivable. In the simple consciousness of self, no variety of determination is given; such variety of determination can be given only in the perception which is distinguished from the consciousness of self, and can be thought only by being combined in one consciousness. An understanding in which the consciousness of self should at the same time be a consciousness of all the complex determinations of objects, would be *perceptive*; but our understanding can only think, and must go to sense for perception. I am conscious of my self as identical in the various determinations presented to me in a perception, because all determinations that constitute one perception I call mine. But this is the same as saying, that I am conscious of a necessary synthesis of them *a priori*, or that they rest upon the original synthetic unity of apperception, under which all the
136 determinations given to me must stand, but under which they can be brought only by means of a synthesis.

17. The synthetic unity of Apperception is the supreme principle of Understanding.

In the Transcendental Æsthetic, we have seen that the supreme principle, without which perception in its relation to sensibility is impossible, is, that all the determinations of perception should stand under the formal conditions of space and time. Now, the supreme principle, without which perception, in its relation to understanding is impossible, is, that all determinations of perception should stand under conditions of the original synthetic unity of apperception. Under the former stand all determinations of perception, in so far as they are *given* to us; under the latter, in so far as they must be capable of being *com-*
137 *bined* in one consciousness. Apart from the synthetic unity of apperception, nothing can be thought or known, because the determinations given in perception, not having the act of apperception, "*I think,*" in common, would not be comprehended in one self-consciousness.

Speaking quite generally, understanding is the faculty of *knowledge*. Knowledge consists in the consciousness of certain given determinations as related to an object. An *object*, again, is that, in the conception of which the various determinations of a given perception are *united*. Now, all unification of determinations requires unity of consciousness in the synthesis of the determinations. Hence, the unity of consciousness is absolutely necessary, to constitute the relation of determinations to an object, give them objective validity, and make them objects of knowledge; and on that unity therefore rests the very possibility of understanding.

The principle of the original *synthetic* unity of apperception, as being completely independent of all conditions of sensuous perception, is the first pure cognition of the understanding, upon which all its further use depends. Space, as the mere form of external sensuous perception, does not of itself yield any knowledge: it but supplies the various elements of *a priori* perception that are 138 capable of becoming knowledge. To know anything spatial, as, for instance a line, I must *draw* it, and so produce by synthesis a definite combination of the given elements. Thus, the unity of the act of combination is at the same time the unity of the consciousness in which the line is thought, and only in this unity of consciousness is a determinate space known as an object. The synthetic unity of consciousness is, therefore, an objective condition of all knowledge. It is not merely a condition which I must observe in knowing an object, but it is a condition under which every perception must stand, before *it can become an object for me at all*. Without this synthesis, the various determinations would *not* be united in one consciousness.

Although it is thus proved, that the synthetic unity of consciousness is the condition of all thought, the unity of consciousness, as has been already said, is in itself an analytic proposition. For, it says only, that all the determinations of which *I* am conscious in a given perception must stand under the condition, which enables me to regard them as *mine*, or as related to my identical self, and so to comprehend them as synthetically combined in one apperception, through the "*I think*" expressed in all alike.

But this is not the principle of every possible understanding, but only of an understanding, through the pure apperception of which, in the consciousness 139 "*I am*," no determinations are given. If we had an understanding, which, by its mere self-consciousness, presented to itself the manifold determinations of perception; an understanding, which, by its very consciousness of objects, should give rise to the existence of these objects; such an understanding would not require, for the unity of consciousness, a special act of synthesis of manifold determinations. But this act of synthesis is essential to human understanding, which thinks, but does not perceive. It is, indeed, the supreme principle of human understanding. Nor can we form the least conception of any other possible understanding, whether of one that itself perceives, or of one that is dependent upon sensibility for its perception, but not upon a sensibility that stands under the conditions of space and time.

18. Objective unity of Self-consciousness.

The transcendental unity of apperception is that unity through which all the determinations given in a perception are united in a conception of the object. It is, accordingly, called *objective*, and must be distinguished from the *subjective unity* of consciousness, which is a *determination of the inner sense*, through which the complex of perception is given empirically to be combined into an

object. Whether I shall be *empirically* conscious of certain determinations as
140 simultaneous, or as successive, depends upon circumstances, or empirical
conditions. Hence, the empirical unity of consciousness, through the association
of the elements of perception, is itself a phenomenon, and is perfectly contingent. But the pure form of perception in time, as merely perception in general,
stands under the original unity of consciousness just because the various determinations given it it are necessarily related to an "*I think.*" It therefore stands
under that original unity by means of the pure synthesis of understanding, which
is the *a priori* ground of the empirical synthesis. Only the original unity of apperception is objective; the empirical unity, with which we are not here concerned,
and which besides is only derived from the other, under given conditions *in
concreto*, is merely subjective. To one man, for instance, a certain word suggests
one thing, to another a different thing. In what is empirical, the unity of consciousness does not hold necessarily and universally of that which is given.

*19. The Logical Form of all Judgments consists in the objective unity
of the Apperception of the Conceptions they contain.*

141 A judgment is simply the way in which given ideas are brought to the *objec-*
142 *tive* unity of apperception. This is the force of the copula "*is*," which just marks
the distinction between the objective unity and the subjective unity of given
ideas. It indicates their relation to the original apperception, and their *necessary unity*. This holds good even if the judgment is itself empirical and therefore contingent. I do not mean, that, in the proposition, "Bodies are heavy," the
idea of *heavy* is *necessarily* connected with the idea of *body* in empirical
perception, but that they are connected with each other in the synthesis of
perceptions through the *necessary unity* of apperception. That is to say, the
two ideas are connected with each other in conformity with the principles by
which ideas are objectively determined and become knowledge. Now, those
principles are all derived from the supreme principle of the transcendental
unity of apperception. Through this principle alone, ideas are related in the
way of judgment, and become *objectively valid*. Thus we get a sufficient test of
the distinction between the relation of ideas in a judgment, and a relation of the
same ideas that is only of subjective validity, as, for instance, a relation depending upon the laws of association. In the latter case, all that I could say
would be, that if I lift a body, I have a sensation of weight, but not, that the
body is heavy. To say that the body is heavy, means, that the two ideas of
heavy and *body* are connected together in the object, whatever the state of the
subject may be, and not merely that they are contiguous in my observation,
repeat it as often as I please.

143 *20. All sensuous Perceptions stand under the Categories as conditions under which
alone their various determinations can come together in one Consciousness.*

The various determinations given in a sensuous perception stand under the
original synthetic unity of apperception, because in no other way could there
possibly be any *unity* of perception. But that act of understanding, by which
the determinations given in consciousness, whether these are perceptions
or conceptions, are brought under a single apperception, is the logical

function of the judgment. Hence, all the elements given in an empirical perception are *determined* by one of the logical functions of judgment, and thus
brought into one consciousness. But the categories are just the functions of
judgment, in so far as these are applied in determination of the various elements of a given perception. Therefore, the various determinations in a given
perception necessarily stand under the categories.

146   *22. The Category has no other application in Knowledge*
          than to Objects of Experience.

To *think* an object is not the same thing as to *know* it. Knowledge involves
two elements: firstly, the conception or category, by which an object in general
is thought; secondly, the perception by which it is given. If no perception could
be given, corresponding to the conception, I should no doubt be able to think
an object so far as its form was concerned, but as there would be no object in
which that form was realized, I could not possibly have knowledge of any
actual thing. So far as I could know, there would be nothing, and could be
nothing, to which my thought might be applied. Now, the Æsthetic has shown
to us that all the perception that we can have is sensuous; hence the thought of
an object in general, by means of a pure conception of understanding, can
147   become knowledge, only by being brought into relation with objects of sense.
Sensuous perception is either the pure perception of space and time, or the
empirical perception of that which is directly presented through sensation as
actually in space and time. By the determination of space and time themselves,
we can obtain that *a priori* knowledge of objects which mathematics supplies.
But this knowledge is only of the form of phenomena, and it is still doubtful if
actual things must be perceived in this form. Mathematical conceptions, therefore, can be called knowledge, only if it is presupposed that there are actual
things which cannot be presented to us except under the form of that pure
sensuous perception. Now, *things in space and time* are given to us only
through empirical observation, that is, in perceptions that are accompanied by
sensation. Hence, the pure conceptions of understanding, even if they are
applied to *a priori* perceptions, as in mathematics, do not yield a knowledge of
things. Before there can be any knowledge, the pure perceptions, and the
conceptions of understanding through the medium of pure perceptions, must
be applied to empirical perceptions. The categories, therefore, give us no
knowledge of actual things, even with the aid of perception, except in so far as
they are capable of being applied to *empirical perception*. In other words, they
are merely conditions of the possibility of *empirical knowledge*. Now, such
knowledge is called *experience*. Hence the categories have a share in the
148   knowledge of those things only that are objects of possible experience.

1. THE SYNTHETIC ACTIVITY OF THE UNDERSTANDING

Kant asserts that there are two sources of knowledge: perception, in
which an object is given to us, and conception, through which an object
is thought in relation to the impressions of sense. Yet at the same time
he insists that no perception yields knowledge without conception and

that both are involved in all knowledge. "Knowledge arises only from their united action."

If this is so, what has so far been established in the Aesthetic cannot be the whole truth of the matter. For there we were led to understand that objects could be perceived wholly by sense under the *a priori* forms of space and time. But now we are to be shown in detail that no sensuous objects can be apprehended without a synthesis of the given manifold according to rules and that the rules are supplied only by the intellect. Objects, in fact, are never merely given, even in sense. To apprehend them at all they must be *"thought* in relation to the impressions that arise in our consciousness."

The rules of synthesis are not and could not be derived from experience because all experience presupposes them and is possible only as a result of their application. They are essentially *a priori.* Kant calls such rules "principles of the understanding," which he claims to derive from a table of twelve categories allegedly deduced from the types of judgment distinguished in traditional logic. We need not enter into the niceties of Kant's derivation of this list of principles. What is more important is the argument by which he proves the inevitability of their use and their *a priori* character. Further, the significant point about this "deduction of the categories," as he calls it, is not that it establishes once and for all the necessity of just this list of concepts, but that it does demonstrate incontrovertibly the indispensability, for the apprehension of any object presented for perception, of the operation of a synthetic activity of thinking, proceeding according to universal and necessary principles.

The general force of this section of Kant's *Critique* is to revise and modify, if not actually to contradict, much that he laid down in his introduction. In particular, the rigid distinction between analytic and synthetic judgments is seen to be largely provisional, and every judgment of significance transpires as both analytic and synthetic, according to the way in which you look at it. Similarly, the distinction between *a priori* and *a posteriori* is largely rescinded, for what comes to us in experience is shown to be dependent for its intelligible character (that is to say, whatever recognizable character it has) upon *a priori* factors supplied by the understanding.

2. THE "SUBJECTIVE" DEDUCTION

Kant produced two versions of the argument by which he sought to prove the necessity of the synthetic activity of thinking in the apprehension of objects. The first, which appeared in the first edition of the

Critique of Pure Reason, is sometimes called the subjective deduction, because it concerns itself with certain subjective conditions of the experience of objects. The second, which appears in the second edition, is known as the objective deduction and deals with the formal conditions of all experience of objects.

Kant sets out to show, as he puts it, that "no object whatever is capable of being thought" without the categories. We may ask what is meant by thinking an object, for we usually speak only of thinking *about* objects, assuming that the object is first given to us in perception and that our thinking is then exercised upon its relations and properties. But what Kant is about to show is that no perception is even possible without an activity of synthesis that essentially involves thinking and therefore the categories.

He begins by laying down the conditions of any coherent knowledge whatsoever, in a general statement of a principle to which he constantly reverts. If each presentation to consciousness were completely isolated and separate from every other no knowledge would ever arise, because, Kant asserts, knowledge is a whole of interconnected and related presentations. This, in a sentence, is the answer to Hume, who regards experience as no more than a succession of distinct and separable percepts. But it is their coherence in a single interrelated system that constitutes knowledge, and Kant sets out forthwith to find the principles of synthesis which make a system of this sort possible. He then proceeds to distinguish the indispensable forms of synthesis that contribute to coherent knowledge.

(a) The synthesis of apprehension in perception.

Kant reminds us first that all representations are modifications of inner sense and are accordingly ordered in the sequence of time. He then points out that as every perception involves a multiplicity of presentations, and these occur in succession, they must, to be grasped as a multiplicity (or manifold), be held all at once before the mind as a unity. Hence the sequence of presentations has to be run over and held together, and this would be impossible if each presentation were confined to a single moment (as a unit in itself). The apprehension of even the simplest spatial object presupposes a synthesis of such presentations in a single percept.

The fact that space and time are, in themselves and without sensuous filling, *a priori* forms of pure perception implies that there is an *a priori* synthesis holding together, in this way, the multiple determinations involved in the idea of a spatiotemporal manifold. So it becomes plain that not even space and time are intuited purely and without the synthetic activity of thought.

(b) The synthesis of reproduction in imagination.

Here Kant draws attention to what all the empiricists in their account of the association of ideas overlook. A frequent conjunction of presentations by which one becomes habitually associated with the other presupposes an actual association, according to a fixed rule, between the phenomena themselves. The color we experience in cinnabar must always be red, midsummer must always be warm and green, for one percept, when presented, to call up in imagination its appropriate accompaniment. We must therefore, in the first instance, apprehend the ideas (or impressions) as connected, which we could not do if the first dropped out of our consciousness and disappeared before the second was experienced. There must, therefore, be *a priori* in the form of inner sense, a synthesis which makes possible the reproduction of the earlier presentation together with the apprehension of the later one. For example, in tracing a line in space, or counting a series of passing objects, or understanding a spoken sentence, or hearing a tune, the earlier parts of the sequence must somehow be retained and the whole sequence synthesized or no line, or sum, or sequence would be cognized at all.

The synthesis of apprehension is thus inseparably involved with that of reproduction in imagination.

(c) The synthesis of recognition in conception.

It follows from what has been said above that what is reproduced in imagination, to be of any use for association, must be recognized as the same as what was earlier experienced. If it were not, it would rank simply as a new experience and not as a reproduction of anything. In that case there could be no unity of consciousness in which a manifold of representations were successively produced. For if what was reproduced were not recognized there could be no synthesis in imagination, and if there were no synthesis in imagination there could be none in apprehension.

The whole succession of inner states can be known as such only for an identical consciousness, which is the fundamental condition of all coherent knowledge: that is, knowledge of related facts which can be subjected to universal rules. Kant here emphasizes the fact that the synthesis of the manifold, which is requisite to an experience of objects, is a synthesis according to rules. For instance, the general concept of

body is really a rule of synthesis of representations according to determinate spatial and temporal formulae which enables us to perceive (as
bodies), groups of sensa in what comes to us as a variegated mass of
sensation. Such a rule must be universal and necessary, for if the mode
of synthesis were variable or contingent our experience would not be
what it is. All universal and necessary rules are *a priori*, for what is
gathered *a posteriori* can be neither. Accordingly, any experience of
objects, involving as it must the three kinds of synthesis described,
implies *a priori* synthesis of representations (that is, synthesis accord-
ing.to universal and necessary rules).

Finally, Kant points out that all awareness of unity and all synthesis
presupposes a unitary consciousness which is not and cannot be experienced empirically, but which is the essential presupposition of all the
forms of synthesis we have been discussing. It is, therefore, logically
prior to all consciousness of objects, and he calls it the unity of transcendental apperception. This is the condition at once of the awareness
of self-identity and of the unity and interrelatedness of knowledge as a
whole.

3. THE "OBJECTIVE" DEDUCTION

In the second edition of the *Critique* Kant substitutes a new version
of the deduction, which begins by developing the last point made in the
"subjective" deduction. First, however, he points out that no combination can ever be given merely by sense, which may present a manifold
to be passively received, but not even in the pure forms of intuition
(space and time) is any conjunction or combination given. This is
tantamount to an admission that the forms of space and time themselves are dependent upon a prior conjunction or combination of the
determinations out of which they are constructed and which could only
be supplied by thought. By combination Kant means more than mere
collocation. He seems to include classification and correlation as well
under the term. It is closer to what we should call interpretation, for it
is what involves and makes possible a knowledge of laws — laws of
nature, which (as he says further on) make nature possible.[3] Such
combination, Kant says, is a spontaneous act of consciousness (*Vorstel-
lungskraft*). He calls it synthesis and maintains that it is presupposed
by any analysis. Where no synthesis has been made, no analysis is
possible.

---

[3]*Critique of Pure Reason*, second edition, pp. 159–160.

This is especially interesting, for it makes necessary a radical modification of the distinction between analytic and synthetic judgments. The implication is that what every analytic judgment analyzes must be the product of a prior synthesis which is the work of the understanding and not something simply given by sense. We may add by way of comment that awareness of any synthetic unity equally implies at least the possibility of analysis, for it is not possible to synthesize, or hold together, what has no distinguishable elements or parts within it. Analysis and synthesis thus turn out to be merely two aspects of the organizing activity of thinking, which are mutually dependent, and every judgment (as an act of thought) will be, in some sense, both analytic and synthetic.

The next point which Kant makes is subtle and important. We cannot be aware of a combination without being conscious of its unity, because a collection of totally discrete atomic representations cannot be cognized as one whole. Any combination has two necessary aspects: it is both one and many — one set of many members — and Kant is here insisting that unless it is cognized as one (as a unity) it cannot be known as a combination at all. The idea of unity cannot, therefore, be derived from the process of combining separate representations, as the latter is possible only on the presupposition of the idea of the former.

The source of this consciousness of unity lies deeper. Every conscious state — every idea or *Vorstellung* — is accompanied by "I think." It is mine. This is true of everything in consciousness, whether it comes *a posteriori* or is *a priori* in the understanding. Now the "I think" is a spontaneous act of thought which cannot possibly be due to sense. It accompanies all my states and is one and the same in all of them. If it were not, they would not all be states of my consciousness. This is what Hume never realized. When he said that, on looking into his mind he never came upon anything other than particular perceptions none of which was himself, he implied (but failed to notice) that whatever perception he might stumble upon was *his*. So, although he never experienced a perception of himself in introspection, whatever he did find was an element in a single continuous experience which he called his own — an experience in which he could have prefaced the description of each and every element with the judgment "I think . . . ." Consequently, we should be justified in saying that we never experience anything at all without at least the possibility of being conscious of ourselves (even though we may not be explicitly conscious of ourselves at all times). It was this self-consciousness that Descartes found it impossible to deny when he was forced to the conclusion: *Cogito ergo sum.*

This persistent identity of the knowing subject in relation to all representations implies a synthesis of those representations in a single experience, and the awareness of self-identity is possible only through consciousness of that synthesis. Empirical consciousness—that is, the stream of percepts as they come to us in fleeting succession—is discrete and does not in any of its states reveal the unity of the subject. Only when these experiences are combined by the subject's own act of thought into the experience of one consciousness is the identity of the thinker recognized as the necessary presupposition of all combination or synthesis and so as prior to all consciousness of objects.

The "original synthetic unity of apperception," therefore, is both the source of all unity in knowledge and the presupposition of all synthesis. Without synthesis there could not be an identical consciousness, and without the unity of the knowing subject there could be no synthesis of representations.

Now, says Kant, objects cannot combine themselves, nor can the understanding discover that they are combined by observing their combination *a posteriori*, because they are not so given. All combination is the work of the understanding, and the source of all combination is the original synthetic unity of apperception. It is therefore the supreme principle of all knowledge, and upon it rests the very possibility of the use of the understanding—the faculty of thinking—or of combining in thought.

What we have to remember in all this is that every object of experience, *qua* object, implies a synthesis, according to definite rules, of the passing flux of sensations; that objects are not just given, but imply a structure which has to be imposed upon the manifold of sense. Kant is arguing that the only possible source of this structure is thought—the activity of the understanding, synthesizing and combining according to rules (or categories), the detailed application of which he discusses at length in succeeding chapters of the *Critique of Pure Reason*.

Consequently, he defines the understanding as the faculty of knowing, and knowledge as the definite relation of given representations to an object. He then defines an object as that in the conception of which the various presentations (the manifold) of a given perception are united. All unity depends on the original synthetic unity of apperception; it is, therefore the fundamental condition of all knowledge of objects.

The unity of representations in an object must be distinguished from the subjective association of representations in the stream of consciousness. To be aware of an object we must be able to distinguish between the empirical succession of presentations as they come to us (as Kant would say, in the inner sense) and an objective succession. For example, if I look along a row of houses from left to right I experience a different succession of representations from that which I receive when I view them from right to left. But neither succession occurs in the objects. Whereas if a flock of sheep moves past me, the succession which I experience is objective. If all our experience were simply reducible to subjective association we should never be able to distinguish between the succession in the way we attend to phenomena and succession which occurs in the phenomena themselves. We could not then discover how representations were actually combined in objects as distinct from the contingent order in which they appear to us. This would mean that we could have no proper knowledge of objects at all.

The combination of representations in objects is combination according to fixed (universal) rules, to which subjective associations do not necessarily conform. These rules, Kant explains in detail, derive from the categories which the understanding imposes *a priori* upon experience. They cannot be discovered empirically, for what comes to us *a posteriori* involves only subjective associations. These *a priori* rules spring ultimately from the original unity of apperception, of which the categories are, as it were, specific applications. They are what make the experience of an objective world possible. Thus the original synthetic unity is the source of other *a priori* knowledge and the condition of the knowledge of objects, and so Kant calls it transcendental. It, and the categories or modes of synthesis derived from it, impose necessary and universal rules of combination upon the flux of sensuous presentations. In this way Kant reintroduced into knowledge that element of universality which Hume excluded.

4. KANT'S ANSWER TO HUME

In the Transcendental Deduction Kant has in principle refuted Hume's scepticism. The doctrine that whatever can be distinguished can be separated and whatever can be separated are separate existences has been replaced by the recognition that knowledge is a coherent whole involving a synthetic comprehension without which no objects can be cognized. Necessity and universality are reintroduced by making the rules of this synthesis *a priori*, or necessary presuppositions of knowledge. The identity of the self is posited as the ultimate condition and source of the awareness of a unitary experience and hence of unitary objects; and, on the basis of these principles, an objective knowledge of the external world of nature is firmly founded.

But the objective world which Kant reestablishes is not the real world of things in themselves, but only a world of things as they appear to us—a world of phenomena. Just as space and time are only the forms of sensuous appearance, so the laws of physics, and of nature generally, are only the forms in which the world appears to creatures with the sort of understanding we have.[4]

The implications of this feature of Kant's theory, though very important and far-reaching in its consequences, cannot be followed out in this introduction. We must content ourselves simply with a brief account of the way in which Kant shows in detail how the categories make a knowledge of objects possible, and glance at his explanation of the necessary connection between cause and effect, of which Hume gave so unsatisfactory an account.

---

[4]*Critique of Pure Reason*, p. 164: "Just as phenomena have no existence in themselves but only as relative to a being which has senses, so laws exist just as little in phenomena except as relative to a subject so far as it has understanding."

CHAPTER 31

Categories and Principles of The Understanding

The Critique of Pure Reason
(continued)

FIRST AND SECOND ANALOGIES OF EXPERIENCE

A. FIRST ANALOGY: PRINCIPLE OF THE PERMANENCE OF SUBSTANCE

In all changes of phenomena substance is permanent, and its quantum in nature neither increases nor diminishes.

Proof

Our apprehension of the various determinations of a phenomenon is always successive, and therefore is always changing. Hence there is nothing in apprehension, taken by itself, that enables us to say whether those determinations are, as an object of experience, co-existent or successive. An object of experience is possible only if there is something that *always is*, something *permanent* and *persistent*, all change and co-existence being nothing but so many modes of

497

time in which that permanent something exists. Only in the permanent can there possibly be the relations of simultaneity and succession, which are the sole relations in time. The permanent is therefore the *substratum* of the empir- 183 ical consciousness of time itself, and only in it is any determination of time possible at all. Permanence is time considered quite generally, as the constant correlate of all change and all concomitance of actual objects of experience. For, change does not affect time itself but only phenomena in time; just as co-existence is plainly not a mode of time itself, the parts of time not being together, but following one another. If it is said, that time itself comes into being part by part, we must suppose that there is another time in which it successively comes to be. Only through the permanent does *existence* in a number of successive moments acquire a *magnitude*, which we call *duration*. In mere succession, taken by itself, existence is always vanishing and appearing, and never has even the smallest magnitude. Apart from the permanent, there is therefore no relation of time. Now, time cannot be perceived by itself; hence 227 the permanent is the substratum of all the determinations of phenomena in time, and therefore the condition without which there could be no synthetic unity in our perceptions, that is, in experience. Thus we learn that all existence and all change in time must be regarded as simply a *modus* of the existence of that which does not change but persists. In all phenomena the permanent is therefore the object itself, that is, the substance (*phaenomenon*), while all that changes, or can change, pertains merely to the manner in which substance or 184 substances exist, and therefore to the determinations of substance.

229   The determinations of a substance are called *accidents*. They are always 186 real, because they are just the manner in which the substance exists, whereas negations are merely determinations which affirm that a substance does not 230 exist in a certain manner. If we wish to say, that what is real in a substance has a special sort of existence, as, for instance, that motion is the manner in which matter exists, we are wont to speak of this mode of existence as *inherence*, to distinguish it from the existence of the substance, which is called *subsistence*. But this is apt to lead to much misapprehension, and it is more precise and 187 more correct to say, that an accident is simply the manner in which the existence of a substance is positively determined. At the same time, the conditions under which understanding in its logical use operates, gives a kind of independence to that in the existence of a substance which can change while the substance remains unchanged, and this changing element we are led to view as standing in relation to the really permanent and radical element. It is for this reason that the category of substance is put among the categories of relation; for, although strictly speaking it does not itself contain a relation, it yet is the condition of relations.

The conception of *change* can be properly understood only by reference to the idea of permanence. Coming to be and ceasing to be are not changes of that which comes to be or ceases to be. Change is a mode of existence that follows upon another mode of existence of the very same object. All that changes is *permanent*, and only its *state alters*. As this alteration affects only the determinations, which can cease to be or begin to be, we may say, in words that sound somewhat paradoxical, that only the permanent changes, while the 231 changeable is subject to no change, but only to an *alternation*, in which certain determinations cease to be as others begin to be.

Change, then, can be observed only in substances. An absolute beginning or 188 cessation can by no possibility be observed, but only a determination of that which is permanent; because only by reference to that which is permanent can there be any consciousness of the transition from one state into another, and from not being to being. And these states can be known empirically only as alternating determinations of that which is permanent. If we suppose something absolutely to begin to be, we must also suppose that there was a point of time in which that something was not. But with what are we to connect this point of time, if not with something that already is? For, an empty time, if we suppose such to precede the point of time in question, is not a possible object of perception; and if we connect what is supposed absolutely to begin to be with things that existed before it, and continue to exist up to the moment of its origination, that which is supposed absolutely to begin to be must be really a determination of the permanent that existed before it. So, also, that which absolutely ceases to be requires us to presuppose the empirical consciousness of a time in which there was nothing to observe.

Substances, then, are the substrates of all determinations of phenomena in time. If some substances could come into being, and others cease to be, even the sole condition, under which the empirical unity of time is possible, would be
232 taken away. We should in that case be compelled to suppose, that phenomena were in two distinct times, and that existence flowed away in two parallel streams. But this is absurd, for there is *only one time*, and different times are   189 not side by side, but follow one another.

Permanence is therefore a necessary condition, without which phenomena
225 cannot be determined as things or objects in a possible experience. The permanent is the substance, or the real, in a phenomenon, which, as the substratum of all change, always remains the same. And as substance can be subject to no change in existence, its quantum in nature can neither increase nor diminish.

232 B. SECOND ANALOGY: PRINCIPLE OF CAUSAL SUCCESSION

All changes take place in conformity with the law of the connection of cause and effect.

Proof

234   The apprehension of the various determinations of a phenomenon is always successive. The ideas of the parts follow one another in consciousness. Whether the parts follow one another in the object also, is a different thing. Now, anything whatever of which we are conscious, anything of which we have an idea, we may certainly call an object; but it is not so easy to say what is
235 meant when the term object is applied to a phenomenon. In this case by an   190 object must be understood, not a mere idea, but only that in the idea which stands for an object. But in so far as by an object we mean merely our own ideas as objects of consciousness, there is no distinction between actual objects of sense and the apprehension or reception of them in the synthesis of imagination. So far we must therefore say that the various determinations of phenomena are always produced in the mind successively. Were phenomena things in themselves, no man could tell how the various determinations, as they arise

one after the other in consciousness, might be connected in the object. As we cannot go outside of our own consciousness, there is no possible way of knowing how things may be in themselves, apart from the ideas through which we are affected by them. But, although phenomena are not things in themselves, and yet are the only things that can be presented to us as knowledge, it is necessary to explain what there is in phenomena themselves that can connect their various determinations in time, while yet the consciousness of those determinations is in apprehension always successive. Thus, for instance, the apprehension of the various determinations contained in the perception of a house is successive. But no one would think of saying that the determinations 236 of the house itself are successive. Now, when I ask how an object is to be conceived from the transcendental point of view, I find that the house is not a thing in itself, but only a phenomenon, that is, it is the consciousness of some- 191 thing, the transcendental object of which is unknown. The question therefore is, what is meant by the connection of various determinations in the phenomenon itself, that phenomenon being yet no thing in itself. Here that which lies in the successive apprehension is considered as mere modes of my consciousness, while the phenomenon which is given to me, although it is nothing but a complex of these modes, is yet regarded as their object, and the conception which I derive from them is held to harmonize necessarily with that object. It soon becomes evident that, as truth consists in the agreement of knowledge with its object, the only question here must be in regard to the formal conditions of empirical truth. The phenomenon as an object can be opposed to apprehension as a series of states of consciousness, only on the ground that it is a unique mode of apprehension, which stands under a rule that necessitates the connection of its various determinations in a certain way. That in the phenomenon which contains the condition of this necessary rule of apprehension, is the object.

Let us now go on to our special problem. There can be no empirical observation that something has occurred, that is, that something, or some state, has 237 come to be which before was not, unless there has previously been observed something that does not contain this state in itself. For, an actual thing following upon an empty time, an absolute beginning preceded by nothing, can no more 192 be apprehended than empty time itself. Every apprehension of an event is therefore a perception that follows upon another perception. But, as this is true in all synthesis of apprehension, even in such a synthesis as that of the determinations of a house already instanced, there is nothing in the mere succession of perceptions to distinguish the apprehension of an event from any other apprehension. But I note further, that when I am conscious of a phenomenon as containing an event, the perception of the antecedent state A cannot follow the perception of the consequent state B, but, on the contrary, B, in my apprehension, always follows A, while A never follows B but can only precede it. I see, for instance, a ship moving down stream. I first observe it higher up the stream, and then lower down, and it is impossible that in the apprehension of the phenomenon I should first observe the ship lower down the stream and then higher up. The order in which the perceptions follow one another in my apprehension is here determined, and to that order my apprehension is tied 238 down. In the former example of the house, my apprehension might begin with a perception of the roof and end with the basement, but it might just as well begin from below and end above, or again the units of my empirical observa-

tion might be apprehended from right to left or from left to right. In that series   193
of observations there was therefore no fixed order that made it necessary for
my apprehension to begin at a certain moment in the empirical combination of
the various elements of perception. But, in the observation of any event, there
always is a rule that makes the order in which the elements of perception
follow one another in my apprehension a *necessary* order.

In this case, therefore, the *subjective succession* of apprehension must be
derived from the *objective succession* of the phenomena. Were it not so, there
would be nothing whatever to determine the order of succession in my apprehension, and to distinguish one sort of phenomenon from another. Viewed by
itself a mere succession of apprehension is quite arbitrary, and tells us nothing
about the connection of the elements of perception in the object. The objective
connection must therefore consist in the order in which the elements of perception follow each other, the order being this, that the apprehension of one
event follows the apprehension of another event *in conformity with a rule.*
Thus only am I justified in saying, that there is succession in the phenomenon,
and not merely in my apprehension, or, in other words, that I cannot possibly
have the apprehension in any other order.

239   In conformity with this rule, there must lie in that which precedes any event,
the condition for a rule by which the event always and necessarily follows; but
I cannot say, conversely, that I can go back from the event and apprehend   194
what precedes it. No phenomenon goes back from a given point of time to an
antecedent point of time, but it yet is related to *some antecedent point of time*;
on the other hand, the progression from a given time to the precise time that
follows is necessary. Now something certainly follows, and this I must necessarily refer to something else, which precedes it and upon which it follows
necessarily or in conformity with a rule. Accordingly, the event, as that which is
conditioned, points back with certainty to some condition, and this condition is
what determines the event.

240   When therefore we have experience of any event, we always presuppose
that something has gone before, on which the event follows according to a rule.
Otherwise I should not say that the object follows, for I am not justified in
saying that there is succession in an object merely because there is a succession   195
in my apprehension, but only because there is a rule that determines the
succession of my apprehension by relation to what precedes. It is therefore
always by reference to such a rule that I make my subjective synthesis or
synthesis of apprehension objective, and under this presupposition, and this
presupposition only, is even the experience of an event possible at all.

No doubt this seems to contradict the whole view of the course of thought
that the facts have always been held to warrant. The accepted doctrine is, that,
from the repeated observation and comparison of many cases in which certain
241   events follow certain antecedents, we are first led to the discovery of a rule
according to which the events invariably follow those antecedents, and then by
reflection on the rule, to the general conception of cause. But on that showing,
the conception of cause would be merely empirical, and the rule based upon it,   196
that every event has a cause, would be just as contingent as the experience
from which it was derived. Having no *a priori* foundation, but resting merely
on induction, it would have no genuine universality, but only a purely supposi-
tious universality and necessity. The truth is, that here the same principle
applies as in the case of other pure *a priori* elements, for instance, space and

time: the principle that we can derive a clear conception from experience, only because we have ourselves put it into experience, and, indeed, have thereby made experience possible at all. No doubt we cannot have a logically clear idea of cause, as a rule that determines the series of events, until we have made use of it in experience, but it is none the less true, that a tacit reference to that rule, as a condition of the synthetic unity of phenomena in time, was the foundation of experience itself, and therefore preceded it *a priori*.

244   No experience whatever is even possible without understanding, and the   199
first thing that understanding does, is not to make the conception of special
245   objects clear, but to make the very consciousness of an object possible. Now, this it effects by conferring upon phenomena and their existence order in time, assigning *a priori* to each of them as consequent a determinate position in time relatively to what precedes. Were such position in time not assigned to phenom-   200
ena, they would not harmonize with time itself, all the parts of which have their position determined *a priori*. Now, the determinate position of phenomena cannot be learned from the relation of phenomena to absolute time, for absolute time cannot be observed; on the contrary, it is the phenomena that must determine for one another their position in time, making the order in time in which each occurs necessary. That which follows or occurs, must follow in conformity with a universal rule, on that which was contained in a preceding state. Thus arises a series of phenomena, which, by the action of understanding, necessarily assumes in the series of possible perceptions the very same order and unbroken connection which are found *a priori* in time itself, as the form of inner perception in which all perceptions must have their position.

The perception of an event is therefore a possible experience, which becomes an actual experience, when I regard a phenomenon as determined to its position in time, and therefore as an object that can always be found in the
246   connection of perceptions in accordance with a rule. This rule, by which a thing is determined conformably with the succession of time, is, that in what precedes is to be found the condition under which an event always or necessarily follows.

The proof of this proposition rests entirely upon the following grounds. All   201
empirical knowledge implies the synthesis by imagination of various determinations. This synthesis is always successive, or, in other words, the various determinations always follow one another in consciousness. In this synthesis of imagination, however, there is no fixed order of succession, for the series of ideas may be taken just as well backwards as forwards. But, if this synthesis is a synthesis of apprehension, in which there is a consciousness of the various determinations contained in a given phenomenon, the order is determined in the object, or, more exactly, there is in our apprehension an order of successive synthesis that determines an object, and in conformity with that order something must necessarily precede, and if it exists, something else must necessarily follow. If, therefore, in my observation I am to obtain the knowledge of an event, that is, of something that actually takes place, my observation must carry with it an empirical judgment, in which the succession is thought as so determined that the event in question is preceded by something else, which it
247   follows necessarily or according to a rule. Were this not so, were I to determine the antecedent as existing, without being forced to recognize the event as following, I should be compelled to regard the succession as a mere subjective play of my imagination, or, if I still supposed it to be objective, I must call it a mere dream. Hence that relation of phenomena, that is of possible perceptions,   202

in which the consequent is necessarily determined in its existence in time by some antecedent in accordance with a rule—the relation, in a word, of cause and effect—is the condition of the objective validity of our empirical judgments with regard to the series of perceptions, and therefore the condition of experience. The principle of causality thus applies to all objects of experience that stand under the conditions of succession, just because it is itself the ground of the very possibility of such experience.

Hume drew attention to the relation of cause and effect and sought in experience for the necessary connection between them. But he assumed that the percepts which constituted the cause and the effect were received intact as objects, in themselves recognizable and knowable by the perceiver. Kant proceeds to show that, without the conception of principles of necessitation, not even the perception of objects is possible such as would constitute either cause or effect. Hume looked for the impression from which the idea of necessary connection was derived and found none among the impressions of sensation. Kant shows that not even an impression of reflection, an habitual tendency to associate ideas, will serve the required purpose. Implicit even in the perception of objects are concepts, not derived from sense experience, but presupposed *a priori*, necessarily determining the way in which we connect and order the manifold presentations of sense.

1. QUANTITY AND QUALITY

To begin with, all sensible objects are determined as to quantity and quality. All such objects are spatiotemporal, because space and time are the necessary forms of sensuous perception. But all spatial and temporal magnitudes are made up of distinguishable parts which must be summed or synthesized to constitute a quantity. A necessary characteristic of all objects, therefore, is that they have extensive magnitude. This notion of extension is thus *a priori*. Kant calls it an axiom of perception, and in consequence we can pronounce necessary synthetic truths, such as:

Anything that is colored is extended

and

Whatever endures has successive phases,

prior to any particular experience of sensible objects (apart, of course, from the need to learn from experience what color is). It is to be observed that ideas of extension as such, and duration as such, are what Berkeley and Hume rejected as abstract; but Kant argues that without them, as presupposed *a priori*, no particular perception would be possible. Thus they could not be derived by inductive generalization from particular instances.

Similarly, it is knowable *a priori* that every presentation in sense has intensive magnitude with respect to its quality. What quality it may have depends on experience and cannot be anticipated *a priori*. But that the sense quality must have some degree of intensity between 0 and infinity is a necessary condition of sensory presentation.

2. SUBSTANCE AND QUALITY

More important is the *a priori* requirement that all sensible qualities must be referred to some permanent substance to which they belong. The reason why this is important is that it provides the basis for the distinction, indispensable for knowledge, between the real and the merely apparent.[1]

We have already observed on several occasions that sense qualities are presented to us in no fixed or necessary order and arrangement. I am at present aware of a variegated expanse of colored shapes and at the same time I experience numerous tactual sensations and hear various sounds. How do I know which of all these sensory data go together in any one object? Locke's allegation that some of them go constantly together is false, for I do not always experience a cool, smooth sensation in my fingertips when I experience a rhomboid red patch, or a white serrated expanse when I hear a rustling sound. Nor is it true that the red rhomboid is always accompanied by a white margin along one side. On the other hand, once I make the assumption that what lies before me is a book I expect a certain colored shape to represent its cover, another the edges of its pages (when it is closed) and to hear a characteristic rustling sound when the pages are flicked, as well as to feel the appropriate tactual sensations. To say that I learn all this from experience begs the question because I could learn it from experience only if I already knew that certain sensory data belonged together in certain specific ways in the representation of a material object. If I did not, I should never be able to learn from the flux of sensory presentations what a material object was.

---

[1]In Kant's theory this distinction is complicated by the further distinction he insists on between phenomena and things-in-themselves. It is not necessary to discuss this complication here. We need only notice that within the realm of phenomena (as Kant is fully aware) a difference must be recognizable between what is objective and what is merely subjective.

Kant has already pointed out that subjective association of ideas implies a real (or necessary) connection of the corresponding qualities in the object. "Were cinnabar, for instance, sometimes red and sometimes black, sometimes light and sometimes heavy; or were the same name given at one time to this object and at another time to that, without the least regard to any rule implied in the phenomena themselves, there could be no empirical synthesis of reproduction." This necessary connection of qualities in objects cannot, therefore, be the consequence of subjective association. As we saw in considering Berkeley's theory, it is the condition and cannot be the result of the settled order of nature.

Kant calls our attention to this fact once more by pointing out that our consciousness presents us with a constantly changing series of determinations and never with anything permanent. But unless we presuppose a permanent object in which the changes occur, we could never distinguish between those determinations which coexist in actuality and those which succeed each other in time. To go back to the example of the book, I have to experience its various sides and the different surfaces of its pages one after another; I can never experience them all simultaneously. Yet I take them to be all coexistent determinations of one thing. In my experience they are successive and constantly changing, but I take them to belong to a permanent or persistent entity. This permanent substratum is never given in experience but it must be presupposed *a priori* if any experience of actual objects is ever to be possible. Without it, strictly speaking, there is not even an experience of objective change, because a succession of different qualities does not indicate a change in anything unless it is presumed that they are all qualities of the same thing. If I see a white expanse followed by a red expanse, I cannot judge that something has changed its color unless I assume that it is the same something which I was seeing on both occasions — otherwise, all that has changed is my sensation. Only what is permanent, says Kant, can change; hence the conception of permanence in substance is *a priori* presupposed in all experience of objects. For the same reason that which changes in its qualities, properly speaking, is the permanent substance, so that there is a sense in which it is also true that only what changes is permanent. (Permanence can be recognized only as identity, in some respect, persisting through changes.)

In the permanent substratum some determinations (or qualities) coexist and some vary with the passage of time. We can tell which do which only if we synthesize the deliverances of sense according to definite rules of order so that they are necessarily connected in specific ways. For, whether they are simultaneously coexistent or successive changes, they all appear to us successively through sense. Strictly speaking, these ways of organizing presentations define their relations in space and time, which provide a kind of schema into which we fit them. Space and time, we have been told, are *a priori* forms of sense perception; but we are now discovering that, even so, spatiotemporal relations can be specified only insofar as we synthesize the manifold of sense in conformity to rules supplied *a priori* by conceptions of the understanding (by thought).

To sum up, then, we can be aware of material objects such as books, or chairs, or ashtrays only on condition that we (tacitly or otherwise) presuppose the existence of a substance to which the various qualities presented successively in sensation belong; and these qualities must be collected together and attributed to things according to fixed rules which may not vary contingently, if our experience of the world is to be coherent and intelligible. One of the most important of such rules is that of causal connection, which we must consider next.

3. CAUSE AND EFFECT

Following upon the previous argument, Kant returns to the very fundamental distinction he made earlier between a subjective and an objective succession. We have just seen that subjectively presentations follow one another in constant flux, but we take the characters, which these successive experiences present, to be actually (or objectively) coexistent in some instances and successive in others. The various sides of a building, observed as one walks round it, are experienced successively but are apprehended as coexistent; but the sequence of appearances of a ship sailing downstream is actually (objectively) successive.

What marks the difference between the two cases is that in the first there is no necessity in the order of occurrence. I can go round a house from east to west or *vice versa*. I can view it from basement to roof or from roof to basement. But in the case of the ship I cannot experience it upstream after I have experienced it further down (if down is the direction in which it is moving). There is a necessity in the order of succession.

There can be necessity in the order of succession only if something in the nature of the preceding event determines the occurrence of the one that follows, if the latter follows the former according to a rule. This condition is satisfied if the first is the cause of the second (or if some other event can be identified as the cause of the sequence, for example, the force of the wind or the current in the stream determining the movement of the ship). And the rule by which the later follows the earlier must be a necessary rule. Thus it cannot be inferred inductively from subjective associations. If it were, it would be merely contingent. The necessary connection must therefore be presupposed (*a priori*) as the condition of the apprehension of an objective succession as opposed to the subjective succession in which all our percepts follow one another (whether of coexistent qualities or not).

Kant contends that, apart from such a rule of necessary connection between events, it would be impossible to date them precisely in the order of time. It would, in fact, be impossible to identify them as events; for the order of time is the order of objectively successive events. The merely subjective succession does not justify any judgment as to what follows what. Because I experience A before B it does not follow that A occurred first in time (the east side of the house does not occur before the south side, though I may experience them in that order). I am justified in saying that B is an event occurring after A only if I can point to a law of necessary succession connecting them in that order. Pure time by itself contains nothing to determine the position of events within it. That can be done only by the mutual relations between the events themselves. The position of an event in the series must therefore be determined by one or more antecedent events in accordance with a necessary rule. The prior event must *cause* that which succeeds as its effect. Some law of causal succession is therefore the necessary condition *a priori* of apprehending events as such; and, unless it is presupposed, the merely subjective succession of sensuous presentations cannot give us any pretext for alleging even a constant conjunction of events, for no objective events could be identified at all.

This, then, is Kant's ultimate reply to Hume and the conclusion to which we are brought is that sense impressions cannot be the sole source of knowledge, which is possible only if the sensory data are organized according to universal and necessary rules which sensory experience by itself does not (and cannot) supply. Knowledge, properly speaking, is at once both sensory and intellectual. Its most elementary objects are already the products both of sense and of thought. No consciousness of any object is possible without both.

CHAPTER 32

The Status of Metaphysics

The Critique of Pure Reason
(continued)

THE DISTINCTION OF PHENOMENA AND NOUMENA   235

295   We have seen that, whatever understanding produces from itself, it holds in   236
296   trust solely in the interest of experience. The principles of pure understanding,
whether as mathematical they are *a priori* constitutive principles, or as dynam-
ical merely regulative principles, contain nothing but what may be called the
pure schema for a possible experience. For experience derives its unity entirely   237
from the synthetic unity which understanding imparts, originally and spontaneously, to the synthesis of imagination in relation to apperception; and phenomena, as the data for a possible knowledge, must therefore stand *a priori* in
relation to that synthetic unity and in harmony with it.

297   Now the proposition that understanding can never make a transcendental   238
use, but only an empirical use, of any of its *a priori* principles, is seen to have
298   very important consequences, so soon as it is thorougly understood. A conception is employed transcendentally when it occurs in a proposition regarding
things *as such* or *in themselves*; it is employed empirically when the proposition
relates merely to *phenomena*, or objects of a possible experience. Only the
empirical use is admissible. Every conception requires, firstly, the logical form   239

of conception or thought, and, secondly, the possibility of an object being empirically given to which it may be applied. Where no such object can be given, the conception is empty and meaningless, containing nothing but the logical function which is necessary in order to form a conception out of any data that may be given. Now, the only way in which an object can be presented is in perception. And this perception must be empirical; for, although pure perception is possible *a priori* before the presentation of an object, yet, as it is a mere form, it can by itself have no object value ascribed to it. Hence all conceptions, and with them all principles, even when they are possible *a priori*, are none the less relative to empirical perceptions as the data for a possible experience. Apart from this relation they have no objective validity, but are a mere play of imagination or of understanding.

300   That this limitation applies to all the categories, and to all the principles   240
derived from them, is evident, if only from this, that we cannot give a *real* definition of even a single one of them, or in other words, make the possibility of their object intelligible, without directly referring to the conditions of sensibility, and therefore to the form of phenomena. The categories are thus neces-   241
sarily limited to phenomena as their sole object, and, if this limitation is taken away, all meaning or objective relation vanishes from them, and no possible instance of an object can be adduced to make the conception comprehensible.

303   There is therefore no way of avoiding the conclusion that the pure concep-   246
tions of understanding can never be employed transcendentally, but only empirically, and that the principles of pure understanding can apply only to objects of sense, as conforming to the universal conditions of a possible experience, and never to things as such, or apart from the manner in which we are capable of perceiving them.

The Transcendental Analytic has brought us to this important conclusion, that understanding can never do more than supply by anticipation the form for a possible experience; and, as nothing but a phenomenon can be an object of experience, it has taught us that understanding cannot possibly transcend the limits of sensibility, beyond which no objects are presented to us. The principles of pure understanding are merely exponents of phenomena, and for the   247
proud name of Ontology, as a science that claims to supply in a systematic doctrine *a priori* synthetic knowledge of things as such, must be substituted the more modest claims of an Analytic of Pure Understanding.

309   If from empirical knowledge is taken away all that thought contributes in its   253
categories, there is no longer any knowledge of an object. By mere perception nothing whatever is thought, and the mere fact that I am conscious of an affection of my sensibility does not entitle me to say that I am conscious of my affection as related to any object. On the other hand, even if all perception is taken away, there still remains the form of thought, or the manner in which the   254
various elements of a possible perception are capable of being combined in relation to an object. The categories have therefore in this sense a wider reach than perceptions of sense, that they think objects in general, without looking to the particular manner in which they may be presented. But although they are so far independent of sensibility, they do not determine a larger sphere of objects; for we are not entitled to say that non-sensuous objects can be presented, unless we can show that a sort of perception is possible that is not sensuous. Now this we cannot possibly do.

310   A conception which cannot be known in any way to have objective reality

may be called problematic, if it is not self-contradictory, and if it is bound up with the knowledge gained through certain conceptions the range of which it serves to limit. Now the conception of a *noumenon*, that is, of a thing that cannot be an object of sense, but is thought, by pure understanding alone, as a thing in itself, is certainly not self-contradictory; for we cannot know with certainty that sensibility is the only possible mode of perception. Moreover, the conception of a noumenon is necessary to prevent sensuous perception from claiming to extend to things in themselves, and to set a limit to the objective validity of sensuous knowledge. In the end, however, we are unable to under- 255 stand how such noumena are possible at all, and the realm beyond the sphere of phenomena is for us empty. We have indeed an understanding that *problem-atically* stretches beyond the sphere of phenomena, but we have no perception in which objects beyond the field of sensibility can be presented, nor can we conceive how such a perception is even possible. Hence understanding cannot be employed *assertorically* beyond the world of phenomena. The conception of

311 a noumenon is, therefore, merely the conception of a *limit*, a conception which is only of negative use, and but serves to check the presumption of sensibility. But although it is unable to establish anything positive beyond the sphere of phenomena, the idea of a noumenon is not a mere arbitrary fiction, but is connected in the closest way with the limitation of the sensibility to phenomena.

The *positive* division of objects into phenomena and noumena, and of the world into a sensible and intelligible world, is therefore quite inadmissible. Certainly, the distinction of conceptions as sensuous and intellectual is legiti-mate. But, as intellectual conceptions do not determine any object for them-selves, they can have no objective validity. If abstraction is made from sense, how shall it be made intelligible, that the categories, which are then the only 256 means of determining noumena, have any meaning whatever? The mere unity of thought is not the same thing as the determination of an object; for knowl-edge also requires that the object to which that unity can be applied, should be capable of being presented in a perception. At the same time, if the conception of a noumenon is interpreted in a problematic sense, it is not only admissible but indispensable, serving as it does to define the limits of sensibility. In that sense, however, a noumenon is not a special kind of object for our understand-ing, namely, an *intelligible object*; on the contrary it is problematic whether

312 there is any understanding that could have such an object actually before it. Such an understanding would not know its object discursively by means of categories, but intuitively in a non-sensuous perception; and how this is possi-ble we cannot form even the faintest conception. Still, in the conception of a noumenon our understanding gets a sort of negative extension; for in calling things in themselves *noumena*, and viewing them as not objects of sense it rather limits the sensibility than is limited by sensibility. At the same time, understanding cannot limit sensibility without also setting limits to itself, for it has instantly to add, that things in themselves cannot be known by means of categories, and all that remains is to think them under a name that indicates something unknown.

315   There are, therefore, no principles through which the conception of pure, 259 merely intelligible objects could ever be applied, for we cannot imagine any way in which such objects could be presented to us. The problematic thought, which leaves a place open for intelligible objects, serves only, as a sort of empty space, to limit the empirical principles, without containing within it or indicating 260 any object of knowledge that lies outside the sphere of those principles.

1. KANT'S "DIALECTIC" OF PURE REASON

Although Kant established the indispensability of thought to the apprehension, even in sensuous perception, of a world of objects, he insisted that those objects were no more than phenomena. They were, he maintained, the appearances of things to us, not the reality of things in themselves. The phenomenal objects result from the imposition of concepts on the flux of the sensuous manifold and these concepts are principles of order and structure, the logical implication of which is completeness and systematic unity. But the completion of the system is never attainable within the realm of phenomena — the scope of human experience. Reason demands such completion but cannot discover it among phenomena, so it goes beyond the range of experience and constructs ideas which are never and can never be presented to the senses. These ideas are of the soul and its immortality, the cosmos as an infinite whole, and God as the Ideal of rational completeness — objects which are not and could not be phenomena. They are the products of pure thought, and Kant calls them, therefore, noumena.[1] Noumena are not strictly objects at all, for they cannot be presented to us empirically, and we can have no idea how they might be presented to an intelligence different from our own but capable of intellectual intuition. We cannot, therefore, *assert* anything positively about the existence of noumena, but can speak of them only problematically as possible (if the conceptions of them are not self-contradictory). Our ideas of them are mere "ideas of reason" without objective validity. Such ideas of reason are only ideas; they are not objects, and we have no means of proving their existence. All our attempts to do so which form the subject matter of traditional metaphysics fall into paralogisms, antinomies, and fallacies, and metaphysics of this kind is not, and cannot be, scientific. The only sound metaphysics is the transcendental critique which demonstrates what can be known *a priori* about phenomena, and which sets the limits of that knowledge.

Nevertheless, although ideas of reason are not, and cannot be, *constitutive* of objects, they are not altogether futile and fallacious. They arise, Kant insists, inevitably and necessarily as a result of the application of the categories, first to experience, and then, as demanded by the understanding, beyond experience, to determine ideals toward which our knowledge asymptotically progresses. In this way the ideas of reason exercise a *regulative* function, directing our researches to extend the limits of our scientific knowledge within experience and to preserve its coherent and systematic character.

---

[1]From the Greek word *nous* = mind.

Further, in the second *Critique* (*of Practical Reason*) and in his ethical writings Kant went on to argue that man's mind is not merely cognitive, but is also conscious of itself as a moral agent. Such consciousness is not empirical. As agents, we are for ourselves "purely intelligible objects" and therefore noumena. We can of course observe our own actions as events in the world and the consequences which result from them, and as so observed they are phenomena. The self, as a series of psychological occurrences, is only phenomenal. But it has an altogether different character as directly apprehended by itself in the consciousness of its own activity. As such it does not fall, and cannot be brought, under the categories, but is purely intelligible—a noumenon—and the regulative influence of ideas of reason upon its action is the source of moral obligation. Similarly, the ideals of reason provide Kant with a criterion of teleological and esthetic judgment, a theory of which he develops in the third of the Critiques—the *Critique of Judgment*.

It is to be observed that all this theorizing is said to be critical. It does not claim to be metaphysical, for metaphysics, in Kant's view, is an illegitimate attempt to determine objects which cannot be presented in sensuous experience. It is a pseudo-science treating mere ideas of reason as if they were constitutive of objects and noumena as if they were assertorically[2] (not only problematically) real. Metaphysics is not a science, except so far as it confines itself to criticism—to defining the limits of experience and elucidating the legitimate regulative use of ideas of reason.

2. RETURN TO METAPHYSICS

Succeeding philosophers criticized Kant's distinction between phenomena and noumena (the second of which, as his philosophical position developed, he tended increasingly to identify with things in themselves). They argued that it is impossible to say anything at all about what is in the nature of the case unknowable—even that it exists. It is true that we cannot go beyond experience, and for that very reason we cannot make the distinction between phenomena and things in themselves, which are supposed to be beyond experience. Still less can we say what the relation is between the known and the unknowable. "Phenomena" therefore exhaust experience and there is no reason to

---

[2]In logic the assertoric form of proposition is the indicative, "*S* is *P*"; the problematic the subjunctive, "*S* may be *P*," and the apodictic is that which states necessity, "*S* must be *P*."

regard them as unreal. On the contrary, the categories which deter-mine them are the very principles of reality, which is what our thinking reveals to us.

Consequently, the demands of reason are not simply regulative, as Kant said, but constitutive. As the concepts of the understanding constitute the objects of the natural sciences, so the concepts of reason constitute the objects of metaphysics (and religion). This was the sort of critique offered by Hegel, and those who followed a similar line rein-stated metaphysics as a legitimate pursuit. Fichte rejected the thing-in-itself and made the transcendental ego the foundation of all knowl-edge and reality. Schopenhauer held our knowledge of the world to be a texture of ideas structured by innate principles, which serves as an instrument to the will in its insistent urge toward self-preservation and self-objectification. For him, the reality is will, manifesting itself in a gamut of natural forms which culminate in consciousness. For Hegel, the ultimate reality was subject and not substance. He called it Abso-lute Spirit and conceived it as generating out of itself the world of nature and finite spirit by a dialectical process, the principles of which (or categories) were at once the principles of thought (of logic) and of the real world, so that logic and metaphysics were, in Hegel's view, one and the same.

These philosophers had widespread influence in the latter half of the nineteenth century, and the most imposing representatives of idealistic philosophy in the English-speaking world at the turn of the century were F. H. Bradley in England and Josiah Royce in America. Bradley taught that reality was an all-inclusive experience which he identified with the Absolute. This somehow differentiated itself into innumerable finite centers in which the world appeared under various forms, differ-ing in degree of reality or adequacy to the complete nature of the Absolute. Only the Absolute as a whole was fully real, so all these different appearances were in varying degrees unreal; but the final truth and ultimate reality, except in broad and general outline, were unattainable by finite minds.

3. REALISM

There are many subtleties in Bradley's doctrine that we cannot now explore and also several serious difficulties. Some philosophers of his day reacted strongly against its seemingly paradoxical features and (in spite of Bradley's protestations to the contrary) its apparent implica-tions of subjectivism and even solipsism. The reaction took various forms but all, or most, of them went by the name of "realism" and were characterized by the insistence that consciousness and mind were only special characteristics of a small group of extraordinarily complex and versatile entities in a world of material things whose existence was in no way dependent upon that specially talented group, and was not at all affected by the knowledge acquired by conscious beings of their surroundings.

This position, stated as simply as that, is obviously far from unobjectionable, but it had a common sense appeal which was attractive, and one philosopher in particular, G. E. Moore, who was to exercise considerable influence upon contemporary trends, set himself to defend the main beliefs of common sense as quite certainly true. He argued that he himself knew quite certainly that an external world existed and contained other people who had bodies like his own and experiences similar to his; and, as he knew all this with certainty, it followed that it was equally certainly known to others. The only difficulty, he alleged, was the correct analysis of the statements in which such beliefs were expressed. In effect, this meant that while the beliefs were undoubtedly true, it was exceedingly difficult to state accurately and precisely what we mean when we express them in ordinary language.

Those who followed Moore and sympathized with his realistic position were thus led to pay a great deal of attention to what he and his followers called "analysis" of statements, and to the forms of linguistic idiom in which our common beliefs are expressed.

One of the philosophers who was, by his own admission, influenced early in his career by the arguments of G. E. Moore was Bertrand Russell, probably the most influential of all twentieth-century philosophers to date; and in the final section of this book we shall consider his main position and give some brief account of the developments to which it led. Realists generally, and Moore and Russell in particular, tend to revert to the empiricist position, to repudiate certain forms of metaphysics (in some more extreme cases to deny the possibility of metaphysics altogether) and to give precedence to sense perception. In some respects, therefore, their attitude is similar to Kant's, but on the whole it constitutes much more nearly a return to that of Hume.

4. POSITIVISM AND THE LATTER-DAY REPUDIATION OF METAPHYSICS

Like Hume, more recent philosophers have maintained that all direct knowledge of the world is confined to sense-given particulars, and that statements about the world (about matters of fact) have meaning only if they can be verified by sense observation—just as Hume had said that every idea must be traceable to some sense impression. Any statement the purport of which is factual but which claims to go beyond the range of sense perception, therefore, is nonsense. In consequence, metaphysics can tell us nothing about the world and its propositions have no literal significance. This is the doctrine of Positivism.

In one way there is a kind of agreement here with Hegel and his followers, for they too insist that "experience" and only experience gives us knowledge of the real, but they recognize and accept Kant's discovery that the experience of objects depends on *a priori* concepts. So they are prepared to respect the demands of reason to follow out the implication of those concepts. Positivists go back to Hume and deny the possibility of any *a priori* synthetic knowledge, presuming, in spite of Kant's detailed demonstration to the contrary, that coherent objects can be and are simply given in sense perception.

SUGGESTIONS FOR FURTHER READING

Selections from the Philosophy of Kant. New York: Modern Library edition or Scribner's, 1958.

I. Kant, *The Critique of Pure Reason*. N. Kemp-Smith translation. New York: St. Martin's Press, 1965.

———, *Prolegomena to any Future Metaphysics*. Indianapolis, Ind.: Liberal Arts Press, 1951.

Robert Adamson, *The Development of Modern Philosophy*. London: Blackwood, 1903.

R. G. Collingwood, *The Idea of Nature*. New York: Oxford University Press, 1965.

A. C. Ewing, *A Short Commentary on the Critique of Pure Reason*. Chicago: University of Chicago Press, 1950.

E. E. Harris, *Nature, Mind and Modern Science*, Chapter 9. London: Allen and Unwin, 1954.

A. D. Lindsay, *Kant*. New York: Oxford University Press, 1936.

H. J. Paton, *Kant's Metaphysic of Experience*. London: Allen and Unwin, 1936.

W. H. Walsh, *Reason and Experience*. New York: Oxford University Press, 1947.

S. Körner, *Kant*. Baltimore, Md.: Penguin Books, 1955.

PART V

Logic and Language

CHAPTER 33

Logical Atomism

The next text to be presented is an essay by Betrand Russell which in a remarkably comprehensive way anticipates almost all of the recent developments in what has come to be called analytic philosophy. Some of these developments, particularly those which confine philosophy to an analysis of language, Russell himself has rejected. Nevertheless, his own doctrines are their philosophical forbear and their exponents usually acknowledge the fact.

While we cannot enter into these theories in any detail, nor even discuss the many important facets of Russell's own views (he is one of the most prolific writers among contemporary philosophers), we shall indicate the main lines of development which issued from the position set out in this essay, to give some brief inkling of the general character of one contemporary stream of philosophical thinking. Its details and its more technical aspects must be left to the subsequent researches of the reader.

In selecting this contemporary movement for the concluding part of this book, we are far from wishing to suggest that there are no others. The major existentialist writers, however, are too difficult and obscure to introduce into a preliminary text, and the student must be left to explore their works at a later stage of his progress, when he has become more intimately acquainted with the nineteenth-century metaphysicians who influenced them (both positively and negatively). Equally we must leave to his further curiosity the works of such writers as Henri Bergson, Samuel Alexander, and Alfred North Whitehead (to mention no others) who have made significant and weighty contributions to the philosophy of the twentieth century.

Logical Atomism

The philosophy which I advocate is generally regarded as a species of realism, and accused of inconsistency because of the elements in it which seem contrary to that doctrine. For my part, I do not regard the issue between realists and their opponents as a fundamental one; I could alter my view on this issue without changing my mind as to any of the doctrines upon which I wish to lay stress. I hold that logic is what is fundamental in philosophy, and that schools should be characterized rather by their logic than by their metaphysic. My own logic is atomic, and it is this aspect upon which I should wish to lay stress. Therefore I prefer to describe my philosophy as "logical atomism," rather than as "realism," whether with or without some prefixed adjective.

A few words as to historical development may be useful by way of preface. I came to philosophy through mathematics, or rather through the wish to find some reason to believe in the truth of mathematics. From early youth, I had an ardent desire to believe that there can be such a thing as knowledge, combined with a great difficulty in accepting much that passes as knowledge. It seemed clear that the best chance of finding indubitable truth would be in pure mathematics, yet some of Euclid's axioms were obviously doubtful, and the infinitesimal calculus, as I was taught it, was a mass of sophisms, which I could not bring myself to regard as anything else. I saw no reason to doubt the truth of arithmetic, but I did not then know that arithmetic can be made to embrace all traditional pure mathematics. At the age of eighteen I read Mill's *Logic*, but was profoundly dissatisfied with his reasons for accepting arithmetic and geometry. I had not read Hume, but it seemed to me that pure empiricism (which I was disposed to accept) must lead to scepticism rather than to Mill's support of received scientific doctrines. At Cambridge I read Kant and Hegel, as well as Mr. Bradley's *Logic*, which influenced me profoundly. For some years I was a disciple of Mr. Bradley, but about 1898 I changed my views, largely as a result of arguments with G. E. Moore. I could no longer believe that knowing makes any difference to what is known. Also I found myself driven to pluralism. Analysis of mathematical propositions persuaded me that they could not be explained as even partial truths unless one admitted pluralism and the reality of relations. An accident led me at this time to study Leibniz, and I came to the conclusion (subsequently confirmed by Couturat's masterly researches) that many of his most characteristic opinions were due to the purely logical doctrine that every proposition has a subject and a predicate. This doctrine is one which Leibniz shares with Spinoza, Hegel, and Mr. Bradley; it seemed to me that, if it is rejected, the whole foundation for the metaphysics of all these philosophers is shattered. I therefore returned to the problem which had originally led me to philosophy, namely, the foundations of mathematics, applying to it a new logic derived largely from Peano and Frege, which proved (at least, so I believe) far more fruitful than that of traditional philosophy.

In the first place, I found that many of the stock philosophical arguments about mathematics (derived in the main from Kant) had been rendered invalid by the progress of mathematics in the meanwhile. Non-Euclidean geometry had undermined the argument of the transcendental aesthetic. Weierstrass had shown that the differential and integral calculus do not require the conception of the infinitesimal, and that, therefore, all that had been said by philosophers on such subjects as the continuity of space and time and motion must be regarded as sheer error. Cantor freed the conception of infinite number from contradiction, and thus disposed of Kant's antinomies as well as many of Hegel's. Finally Frege showed in detail how arithmetic can be deduced from pure logic, without the need of any fresh ideas or axioms, thus disproving Kant's assertion that "7 + 5 = 12" is synthetic—at least in the obvious interpretation of that dictum. As all these results were obtained, not by any heroic method, but by patient detailed reasoning, I began to think it probable that philosophy had erred in adopting heroic remedies for intellectual difficulties, and that solutions were to be found merely by greater care and accuracy. This view I have come to hold more and more strongly as time went on, and it has led me to doubt whether philosophy, as a study distinct from science and possessed of a method of its own, is anything more than an unfortunate legacy from theology.

Frege's work was not final, in the first place because it applied only to arithmetic, not to other branches of mathematics; in the second place because his premises did not exclude certain contradictions to which all past systems of formal logic turned out to be liable. Dr. Whitehead and I in collaboration tried to remedy these two defects, in *Principia Mathematica*, which, however, still falls short of finality in some fundamental points (notably the axiom of reducibility). But in spite of its shortcomings I think that no one who reads this book will dispute its main contention, namely, that from certain ideas and axioms of formal logic, by the help of the logic of relations, all pure mathematics can be deduced, without any new undefined idea or unproved propositions. The technical methods of mathematical logic, as developed in this book, seem to me very powerful, and capable of providing a new instrument for the discussion of many problems that have hitherto remained subject to philosophic vagueness. Dr. Whitehead's *Concept of Nature* and *Principles of Natural Knowledge* may serve as an illustration of what I mean.

When pure mathematics is organized as a deductive system—i.e. as the set of all those propositions that can be deduced from an assigned set of premises—it becomes obvious that, if we are to believe in the truth of pure mathematics, it cannot be solely because we believe in the truth of the set of premises. Some of the premises are much less obvious than some of their consequences, and are believed chiefly because of their consequences. This will be found to be always the case when a science is arranged as a deductive system. It is not the logically simplest propositions of the system that are the most obvious, or that provide the chief part of our reasons for believing in the system. With the empirical sciences this is evident. Electro-dynamics, for example, can be concentrated into Maxwell's equations, but these equations are believed because of the observed truth of certain of their logical consequences. Exactly the same thing happens in the pure realm of logic; the logically first principles of logic — at least some of them — are to be believed, not on their own account, but on account of their consequences. The epistemological question: "Why should I believe this set of propositions?" is quite different from the logical question: "What is the smallest and logically simplest group of propositions from which this set of propositions can be deduced?" Our reasons for believing logic and pure mathematics are, in part, only inductive and probable, in spite of the fact that, in their *logical* order, the propositions of logic and pure mathematics follow from the premises of logic by pure deduction. I think this point important, since errors are liable to arise from assimilating the logical to the epistemological order, and also, conversely, from assimilating the epistemological to the logical order. The only way in which work on mathematical logic throws light on the truth or falsehood of mathematics is by disproving the supposed antinomies. This shows that mathematics *may* be true. But to show that mathematics *is* true would require other methods and other considerations.

One very important heuristic maxim which Dr. Whitehead and I found, by experience, to be applicable in mathematical logic, and have since applied in various other fields, is a form of Ockham's razor. When some set of supposed entities has neat logical properties, it turns out, in a great many instances, that the supposed entities can be replaced by purely logical structures composed of entities which have not such neat properties. In that case, in interpreting a body of propositions hitherto believed to be about the supposed entities, we can substitute the logical structures without altering any of the detail of the body of propositions in question. This is an economy, because entities with neat logical properties are always inferred, and if the propositions in which they occur can be interpreted without making this inference, the ground for the inference fails, and our body of propositions is secured against the need of a doubtful step. The principle may be stated in the form: "Wherever possible, substitute constructions out of known entities for inferences to unknown entities."

The uses of this principle are very various, but are not intelligible in detail to those who do not know mathematical logic. The first instance I came across was what I have called "the principle of abstraction," or "the principle which dispenses with abstraction."[1] This principle is applicable in the case of any symmetrical and transitive relation, such as equality. We are apt to infer that such relations arise from possession of some common quality. This may or may not be true; probably it is true in some cases and not in others. But all the formal purposes of a common quality can be served by membership of the group of terms having the said relation to a given term. Take magnitude, for example. Let us suppose that we have a group of rods, all equally long. It is easy to suppose that there is a certain quality, called their length, which they all share. But all propositions in which this supposed quality occurs will retain their truth-value unchanged if, instead of "length of the rod x" we take "membership of the group of all those rods which are as long as x". In various special cases — e.g. the definition of real numbers — a simpler construction is possible.

---

[1] *Our Knowledge of the External World*, p. 42.

A very important example of the principle is Frege's definition of the cardinal number of a given set of terms as the class of all sets that are "similar" to the given set — where two sets are "similar" when there is a one-one relation whose domain is the one set and whose converse domain is the other. Thus a cardinal number is the class of all those classes which are similar to a given class. This definition leaves unchanged the truth-values of all propositions in which cardinal numbers occur, and avoids the inference to a set of entities called "cardinal numbers," which were never needed except for the purpose of making arithmetic intelligible, and are now no longer needed for that purpose.

Perhaps even more important is the fact that classes themselves can be dispensed with by similar methods. Mathematics is full of propositions which seem to require that a class or an aggregate should be in some sense a single entity — e.g. the proposition "the number of combinations of n things any number at a time is 2^n". Since 2^n is always greater than n, this proposition leads to difficulties if classes are admitted because the number of classes of entities in the universe is greater than the number of entities in the universe, which would be odd if classes were some among entities. Fortunately, all the propositions in which classes appear to be mentioned can be interpreted without supposing that there are classes. This is perhaps the most important of all the applications of our principle. (See *Principia Mathematica*, 20.)

Another important example concerns what I call "definite descriptions," i.e. such phrases as "the even prime," "the present King of England," "the present King of France." There has always been a difficulty in interpreting such propositions as "the present King of France does not exist." The difficulty arose through supposing that "the present King of France" is the subject of this proposition, which made it necessary to suppose that he subsists although he does not exist. But it is difficult to attribute even subsistence to "the round square" or "the even prime greater than 2". In fact, "the round square does not subsist" is just as true as "the present King of France does not exist." Thus the distinction between existence and subsistence does not help us. The fact is that, when the words "the so-and-so" occur in a proposition, there is no corresponding single constituent of the proposition, and when the proposition is fully analysed the words "the so-and-so" have disappeared. An important consequence of the theory of descriptions is that it is meaningless to say "A exists" unless "A" is (or stands for) a phrase of the form "the so-and-so." If the so-and-so exists, and x is the so-and-so, to say "x exists" is nonsense. Existence, in the sense in which it is ascribed to single entities, is thus removed altogether from the list of fundamentals. The ontological argument and most of its refutations are found to depend upon bad grammar. (See *Principia Mathematica*, 14.)

There are many other examples of the substitution of constructions for inferences in pure mathematics, for example, series, ordinal numbers, and real numbers. But I will pass on to the examples in physics.

Points and instants are obvious examples: Dr. Whitehead has shown how to construct them out of sets of events all of which have a finite extent and a finite duration. In relativity theory, it is not points or instants that we primarily need, but event-particles, which correspond to what, in older language, might be described as a point at an instant, or an instantaneous point. (In former days, a point of space endured throughout all time, and an instant of time pervaded all space. Now the unit that mathematical physics wants has neither spatial nor temporal extension.) Event-particles are constructed by just the same logical process by which points and instants were constructed. In such constructions, however, we are on a different plane from that of constructions in pure mathematics. The possibility of constructing an event-particle depends upon the existence of sets of events with certain properties; whether the required events exist can only be known empirically, if at all. There is therefore no *a priori* reason to expect continuity (in the mathematical sense), or to feel confident that event-particles can be constructed. If the quantum theory should seem to demand a discrete space-time, our logic is just as ready to meet its requirements as to meet those of traditional physics, which demands continuity. The question is purely empirical, and our logic is (as it ought to be) equally adapted to either alternative.

Similar considerations apply to a particle of matter, or to a piece of matter of finite size. Matter, traditionally, has two of those "neat" properties which are the mark of a logical construction; first, that two pieces of matter cannot be at the same place at the same time; secondly, that one piece of matter cannot be in two places at the same time. Experience in the substitution of constructions for inferences makes one suspicious of anything so tidy and exact. One cannot help feeling that impenetrability is not an empirical fact, derived from observation of billiard-balls, but is something logically necessary. This feeling is wholly justified, but it could not be so if matter were not a logical construction. An immense number of occurrences coexist in any little region of space-time; when we are speaking of what is not logical construction, we find no such property as impenetrability, but, on the contrary, endless overlapping of the events in a part of space-time, however small. The reason that matter is impenetrable is because our definitions make it so. Speaking roughly, and merely so as to give a notion of how this happens, we may say that a piece of matter is all that happens in a certain track in space-time, and that we construct the tracks called bits of matter in such a way that they do not intersect. Matter is impenetrable because it is easier to state the laws of physics if we make our constructions so as to secure impenetrability. Impenetrability is a logically necessary result of definition, though the fact that such a definition is convenient is empirical. Bits of matter are not among the bricks out of which the world is built. The bricks are events, and bits of matter are portions of the structure to which we find it convenient to give separate attention.

In the philosophy of mental occurrences there are also opportunities for the application of our principle of constructions *versus* inferences. The subject, and the relation of a cognition to what is known, both have that schematic quality that arouses our suspicions. It is clear that the subject, if it is to be preserved at all, must be preserved as a construction, not as an inferred entity; the only question is whether the subject is sufficiently useful to be worth constructing. The relation of a cognition to what is known, again, cannot be a straightforward single ultimate, as I at one time believed it to be. Although I do not agree with pragmatism, I think William James was right in drawing attention to the complexity of "knowing." It is impossible in a general summary, such as the present, to set out the reasons for this view. But whoever has acquiesced in our principle will agree that here is prima facie a case for applying it. Most of my *Analysis of Mind* consists of applications of this principle. But as psychology is scientifically much less perfected than physics, the opportunities for applying the principle are not so good. The principle depends, for its use, upon the existence of some fairly reliable body of propositions, which are to be interpreted by the logician in such a way as to preserve their truth while minimizing the element of inference to unobserved entities. The principle therefore presupposes a moderately advanced science, in the absence of which the logician does not know what he ought to construct. Until recently, it would have seemed necessary to construct geometrical points; now it is event-particles that are wanted. In view of such a change in an advanced subject like physics, it is clear that constructions in psychology must be purely provisional.

I have been speaking hitherto of what it is *not* necessary to assume as part of the ultimate constituents of the world. But logical constructions, like all other constructions, require materials, and it is time to turn to the positive question, as to what these materials are to be. This question, however, requires as a preliminary a discussion of logic and language and their relation to what they try to represent.

The influence of language on philosophy has, I believe, been profound and almost unrecognized. If we are not to be misled by this influence, it is necessary to become conscious of it, and to ask ourselves deliberately how far it is legitimate. The subject-predicate logic, with the substance-attribute metaphysic, are a case in point. It is doubtful whether either would have been invented by people speaking a non-Aryan language; certainly they do not seem to have arisen in China, except in connexion with Buddhism, which brought Indian philosophy with it. Again, it is natural, to take a different kind of instance, to suppose that a proper name which can be used significantly stands for a single entity; we suppose that there is a certain more or less persistent being called "Socrates," because the same name is applied to a series of occurrences which we are led to regard as appearances of this one being. As language grows more abstract, a new set of entities come into philosophy, namely, those represented by abstract words—the universals. I do not wish to maintain that there are no universals, but certainly there are many abstract words which do not stand for single universals—e.g. triangularity and rationality. In these respects language misleads us both by its vocabulary and by its syntax. We must be on our guard in both respects if our logic is not to lead to a false metaphysic.

Syntax and vocabulary have had different kinds of effects on philosophy. Vocabulary has most influence on common sense. It might be urged, conversely, that common sense produces our vocabulary. This is only partially true. A word is applied at first to things which are more or less similar, without any reflection as to whether they have any point of identity. But when once usage has fixed the objects to which the word is to be applied, common sense is influenced by the existence of the word, and tends to suppose that one word must stand for one object, which will be a universal in the case of an adjective or an abstract word. Thus the influence of vocabulary is towards a kind of platonic pluralism of things and ideas.

The influence of syntax, in the case of the Indo-European languages, is quite different. Almost any proposition can be put into a form in which it has a subject and a predicate, united by a copula. It is natural to infer that every fact has a corresponding form, and consists in the possession of a quality by a substance. This leads, of course, to monism, since the fact that there were several substances (if it were a fact) would not have the requisite form. Philosophers, as a rule, believe themselves free from this sort of influence of linguistic forms, but most of them seem to me to be mistaken in this belief. In thinking about abstract matters, the fact that the words for abstractions are no more abstract than ordinary words always makes it easier to think about the words than about what they stand for, and it is almost impossible to resist consistently the temptation to think about the words.

Those who do not succumb to the subject-predicate logic are apt to get only one step further, and admit relations of two terms, such as before-and-after, greater-and-less, right-and-left. Language lends itself to this extension of the subject-predicate logic, since we say "*A* precedes *B*", "*A* exceeds *B*", and so on. It is easy to prove that the fact expressed by a proposition of this sort cannot consist of the possession of a quality by a substance, or of the possession of two or more qualities by two or more substances. (See *Principles of Mathematics*, § 214.) The extension of the subject-predicate logic is therefore right so far as it goes, but obviously a further extension can be proved necessary by exactly similar arguments. How far it is necessary to go up the series of three-term, four-term, five-term . . . relations I do not know. But it is certainly necessary to go beyond two-term relations. In projective geometry, for example, the order of points on a line or of planes through a line requires a four-term relation.

A very unfortunate effect of the peculiarities of language is in connexion with adjectives and relations. All words are of the same logical type; a word is a class or series, of noises or shapes according as it is heard or read. But the meanings of words are of various different types: an attribute (expressed by an adjective) is of a different type from the objects to which it can be (whether truly or falsely) attributed; a relation (expressed perhaps by a preposition, perhaps by a transitive verb, perhaps in some other way) is of a different type from the terms between which it holds or does not hold. The definition of a logical type is as follows: *A* and *B* are of the same logical type if, and only if, given any fact of which *A* is a constituent, there is a corresponding fact which has *B* as a constituent, which either results by substituting *B* for *A*, or is the negation of what so results. To take an illustration, Socrates and Aristotle are of the same type, because "Socrates was a philosopher" and "Aristotle was a philosopher" are both facts; Socrates and Caligula are of the same type, because "Socrates was a philosopher" and "Caligula was not a philosopher" are both facts. To love and to kill are of the same type, because "Plato loved Socrates" and "Plato did not kill Socrates" are both facts. It follows formally from the definition that, when two words have meanings of different types, the relations of the words to what they mean are of different types; that is to say, there is not one relation of meaning between words and what they stand for, but as many relations of meaning, each of a different logical type, as there are logical types among the objects for which there are words. This fact is a very potent source of error and confusion in philosophy. In particular, it has made it extraordinarily difficult to express in words any theory of relations which is logically capable of being true, because language cannot preserve the difference of type between a relation and its terms. Most of the arguments for and against the reality of relations have been vitiated through this source of confusion.

At this point, I propose to digress for a moment, and to say, as shortly as I can, what I believe about relations. My own views on the subject of relations in the past were less clear than I thought them, but were by no means the views which my critics supposed them to be. Owing to lack of clearness in my own thoughts, I was unable to convey my meaning. The subject of relations is difficult, and I am far from claiming to be now clear about it. But I think certain points are clear to me. At the time when I wrote *The Principles of Mathematics*, I had not yet seen the necessity of logical types. The doctrine of types profoundly affects logic, and I think shows what, exactly, is the valid element in the arguments of those who oppose "external" relations. But so far from strengthening their main position, the doctrine of types leads, on the contrary, to a more complete and radical atomism than any that I conceived to be possible twenty years ago. The question of relations is one of the most important that arise in philosophy, as most other issues turn on it: monism and pluralism; the question whether anything is wholly true except the whole of truth, or wholly real except the whole of reality; idealism and realism, in some of their forms; perhaps the very existence of philosophy as a subject distinct from science and possessing a method of its own. It will serve to make my meaning clear if I take a passage in Mr. Bradley's *Essays on Truth and Reality*, not for controversial purposes, but because it raises exactly the issues that ought to be raised. But first of all I will try to state my own view, without argument.[2]

Certain contradictions — of which the simplest and oldest is the one about Epimenides the Cretan, who said that all Cretans were liars, which may be reduced to the man who says "I am lying" — convinced me, after five years devoted mainly to this one question, that no solution is technically possible without the doctrine of types. In its technical form, this doctrine states merely that a word or symbol may form part of a significant proposition, and in this sense have meaning, without being always able to be substituted for another word or symbol in the same or some other proposition without producing nonsense. Stated in this way, the doctrine may seem like a truism. "Brutus killed Caesar" is significant, but "Killed killed Caesar" is nonsense, so that we cannot replace "Brutus" by "killed," although both words have meaning. This is plain common sense, but unfortunately almost all philosophy consists in an attempt to forget it. The following words, for example, by their very nature, sin against it: attribute, relation, complex, fact, truth, falsehood, not, liar, omniscience. To give a meaning to these words, we have to make a detour by way of words or symbols and the different ways in which they may mean; and even then, we usually arrive, not at one meaning, but at an infinite series of different meanings. Words, as we saw, are all of the same logical type; therefore when the meanings of two words are of different types, the relations of the two words to what they stand for are also of different types. Attribute-words and relation-words are of the same type, therefore we can say significantly "attribute-words and relation-words have different uses." But we cannot say significantly "attributes are not relations." By our definition of types, since relations are relations, the form of words "attributes are relations" must be not false, but meaningless, and the form of words "attributes are not relations," similarly, must be not true, but meaningless. Nevertheless, the statement "attribute-words are not relation-words" is significant and true.

We can now tackle the question of internal and external relations, remembering that the usual formulations, on both sides, are inconsistent with the

---

[2]I am much indebted to my friend Wittgenstein in this matter. See his *Tractatus Logico-Philosophicus*, Kegan Paul, 1922. I do not accept all his doctrines, but my debt to him will be obvious to those who read his book.

doctrine of types. I will begin with attempts to state the doctrine of external relations. It is useless to say "terms are independent of their relations," because "independent" is a word which means nothing. Two events may be said to be causally independent when no causal chain leads from one to the other; this happens, in the special theory of relativity, when the separation between the events is space-like. Obviously this sense of "independent" is irrelevant. If, when we say "terms are independent of their relations," we mean "two terms which have a given relation would be the same if they did not have it," that is obviously false; for, being what they are, they have the relation, and therefore whatever does not have the relation is different. If we mean—as opponents of external relations suppose us to mean—that the relation is a third term which comes between the other two terms and is somehow hooked on to them, that is obviously absurd, for in that case the relation has ceased to be a relation, and all that is truly relational is the hooking of the relation to the terms. The conception of the relation as a third term between the other two sins against the doctrine of types, and must be avoided with the utmost care.

What, then, can we mean by the doctrine of external relations? Primarily this, that a relational proposition is not, in general, logically equivalent formally to one or more subject-predicate propositions. Stated more precisely: Given a relational propositional function "xRy", it is not in general the case that we can find predicates a, β, γ, such that, for all values of x and y, xRy is equivalent to xa, $y\beta$, $(x, y)\gamma$ (where (x, y) stands for the whole consisting of x and y), or to any one or two of these. This, and this only, is what I mean to affirm when I assert the doctrine of external relations; and this, clearly, is at least part of what Mr. Bradley denies when he asserts the doctrine of internal relations.

In place of "unities" or "complexes," I prefer to speak of "facts." It must be understood that the word "fact" cannot occur significantly in any position in a sentence where the word "simple" can occur significantly, nor can a fact occur where a simple can occur. We must not say "facts are not simples." We can say, "The symbol for a fact must not replace the symbol for a simple, or vice versa, if significance is to be preserved." But it should be observed that, in this sentence, the word "for" has different meanings on the two occasions of its use. If we are to have a language which is to safeguard us from errors as to types, the symbol for a fact must be a proposition, not a single word or letter. Facts can be asserted or denied, but cannot be named. (When I say "facts cannot be named," this is, strictly speaking, nonsense. What can be said without falling into nonsense is: "The symbol for a fact is not a name.") This illustrates how meaning is a different relation for different types. The way to mean a fact is to assert it; the way to mean a simple is to name it. Obviously naming is different from asserting, and similar differences exist where more advanced types are concerned, though language has no means of expressing the differences.

There are many other matters in Mr. Bradley's examination of my views which call for reply. But as my present purpose is explanatory rather than controversial, I will pass them by, having, I hope, already said enough on the question of relations and complexes to make it clear what is the theory that I advocate. I will only add, as regards the doctrine of types, that most philosophers assume it now and then, and few would deny it, but that all (so far as I know) avoid formulating it precisely or drawing from it those deductions that are inconvenient for their systems.

I come now to some of Mr. Bradley's criticisms (*loc. cit.*, p. 280 ff.). He says:

"Mr. Russell's main position has remained to myself incomprehensible. On the one side I am led to think that he defends a strict pluralism, for which nothing is admissible beyond simple terms and external relations. On the other side Mr. Russell seems to assert emphatically, and to use throughout, ideas which such a pluralism surely must repudiate. He throughout stands upon unities which are complex and which cannot be analysed into terms and relations. These two positions to my mind are irreconcilable, since the second, as I understand it, contradicts the first flatly."

With regard to external relations, my view is the one I have just stated, not the one commonly imputed by those who disagree. But with regard to unities, the question is more difficult. The topic is one with which language, by its very nature, is peculiarly unfitted to deal. I must beg the reader, therefore, to be indulgent if what I say is not exactly what I mean, and to try to see what I mean in spite of unavoidable linguistic obstacles to clear expression.

To begin with, I do not believe that there are complexes or unities in the same sense in which there are simples. I did believe this when I wrote *The Principles of Mathematics*, but, on account of the doctrine of types, I have since abandoned this view. To speak loosely, I regard simples and complexes as always of different types. That is to say, the statements "There are simples" and "There are complexes" use the words "there are" in different senses. But if I use the words "there are" in the sense which they have in the statement "there are simples," then the form of words "there are not complexes" is neither true nor false, but meaningless. This shows how difficult it is to say clearly, in ordinary language, what I want to say about complexes. In the language of mathematical logic it is much easier to say what I want to say, but much harder to induce people to understand what I mean when I say it.

When I speak of "simples" I ought to explain that I am speaking of something not experienced as such, but known only inferentially as the limit of analysis. It is quite possible that, by greater logical skill, the need for assuming them could be avoided. A logical language will not lead to error if its simple symbols (i.e. those not having any parts that are symbols, or any significant structure) all stand for objects of some one type, even if these objects are not simple. The only drawback to such a language is that it is incapable of dealing with anything simpler than the objects which it represents by simple symbols. But I confess it seems obvious to me (as it did to Leibniz) that what is complex must be composed of simples, though the number of constituents may be infinite. It is also obvious that the logical uses of the old notion of substance (i.e. those uses which do not imply temporal duration) can only be applied, if at all, to simples; objects of other types do not have that kind of being which one associates with substances. The essence of a substance, from the symbolic point of view, is that it can only be named—in old-fashioned language, it never occurs in a proposition except as the subject or as one of the terms of a relation. If what we take to be simple is really complex, we may get into trouble by naming it, when what we ought to do is to assert it. For example, if Plato loves Socrates, there is not an entity "Plato's love for Socrates," but only the fact that Plato loves Socrates. And in speaking of this as "a fact," we are already making it more substantial and more of a unity than we have any right to do.

Attributes and relations, though they may be not susceptible of analysis, differ from substances by the fact that they suggest a structure, and that there can be no significant symbol which symbolizes them in isolation. All proposi-

tions in which an attribute or a relation *seems* to be the subject are only significant if they can be brought into a form in which the attribute is attributed or
the relation relates. If this were not the case, there would be significant propositions in which an attribute or a relation would occupy a position appropriate
to a substance, which would be contrary to the doctrine of types, and would
produce contradictions. Thus the proper symbol for "yellow" (assuming for the
sake of illustration that this is an attribute) is not the single word "yellow," but
the propositional function "x is yellow", where the structure of the symbol
shows the position which the word "yellow" must have if it is to be significant.
Similarly the relation "precedes" must not be represented by this one word,
but by the symbol "x precedes y", showing the way in which the symbol can
occur significantly. (It is here assumed that values are not assigned to x and y
when we are speaking of the attribute or relation itself.)

The symbol for the simplest possible kind of fact will still be of the form "x is
yellow" or "x precedes y," only that "x" and "y" will be no longer undetermined variables, but names.

In addition to the fact that we do not experience simples as such, there is
another obstacle to the actual creation of a correct logical language such as I
have been trying to describe. This obstacle is vagueness. All our words are
more or less infected with vagueness, by which I mean that it is not always
clear whether they apply to a given object or not. It is of the nature of words to
be more or less general, and not to apply only to a single particular, but that
would not make them vague if the particulars to which they applied were a
definite set. But this is never the case in practice. The defect, however, is one
which it is easy to imagine removed, however difficult it may be to remove it in
fact.

The purpose of the foregoing discussion of an ideal logical language (which
would of course be wholly useless for daily life) is twofold: first, to prevent
inferences from the nature of language to the nature of the world, which are
fallacious because they depend upon the logical defects of language; secondly,
to suggest, by inquiring what logic requires of a language which is to avoid
contradiction, what sort of a structure we may reasonably suppose the world to
have. If I am right, there is nothing in logic that can help us to decide between
monism and pluralism, or between the view that there are ultimate relational
facts and the view that there are none. My own decision in favour of pluralism
and relations is taken on empirical grounds, after convincing myself that the *a
priori* arguments to the contrary are invalid. But I do not think these arguments can be adequately refuted without a thorough treatment of logical types,
of which the above is a mere sketch.

This brings me, however, to a question of method which I believe to be very
important. What are we to take as data in philosophy? What shall we regard as
having the greatest likelihood of being true, and what as proper to be rejected
if it conflicts with other evidence? It seems to me that science has a much
greater likelihood of being true in the main than any philosophy hitherto
advanced (I do not, of course, except my own). In science there are many
matters about which people are agreed; in philosophy there are none. Therefore, although each proposition in a science may be false, and it is practically
certain that there are some that are false, yet we shall be wise to build our
philosophy upon science, because the risk of error in philosophy is pretty sure
to be greater than in science. If we could hope for certainty in philosophy

the matter would be otherwise, but so far as I can see such a hope would be chimerical.

Of course those philosophers whose theories, *prima facie*, run counter to science always profess to be able to interpret science so that it shall remain true on its own level, with that minor degree of truth which ought to content the humble scientist. Those who maintain a position of this sort are bound — so it seems to me — to show in detail how the interpretation is to be effected. In many cases, I believe that this would be quite impossible. I do not believe, for instance, that those who disbelieve in the reality of relations (in some such sense as that explained above) can possibly interpret those numerous parts of science which employ asymmetrical relations. Even if I could see no way of answering the objections to relations raised (for example) by Mr. Bradley, I should still think it more likely than not that some answer was possible, because I should think an error in a very subtle and abstract argument more probable than so fundamental a falsehood in science. Admitting that everything we believe ourselves to know is doubtful, it seems, nevertheless, that what we believe ourselves to know in philosophy is more doubtful than the detail of science, though perhaps not more doubtful than its most sweeping generalizations.

The question of interpretation is of importance for almost every philosophy, and I am not at all inclined to deny that many scientific results require interpretation before they can be fitted into a coherent philosophy. The maxim of "constructions *versus* inferences" is itself a maxim of interpretation. But I think that any valid kind of interpretation ought to leave the detail unchanged, though it may give a new meaning to fundamental ideas. In practice, this means that *structure* must be preserved. And a test of this is that all the propositions of a science should remain, though new meanings may be found for their terms. A case in point, on a non-philosophical level, is the relation of the physical theory of light to our perceptions of colour. This provides different physical occurrences corresponding to different seen colours, and thus makes the structure of the physical spectrum the same as that of what we see when we look at a rainbow. Unless structure is preserved, we cannot validly speak of an interpretation. And structure is just what is destroyed by a monistic logic.

I do not mean, of course, to suggest that, in any region of science, the structure revealed at present by observation is exactly that which actually exists. On the contrary, it is in the highest degree probable that the actual structure is more fine-grained than the observed structure. This applies just as much to psychological as to physical material. It rests upon the fact that, where we perceive a difference (e.g. between two shades of colour), there is a difference, but where we do not perceive a difference it does not follow that there is not a difference. We have therefore a right, in all interpretation, to demand the preservation of observed differences, and the provision of room for hitherto unobserved differences, although we cannot say in advance what they will be, except when they can be inferentially connected with observed differences.

In science, structure is the main study. A large part of the importance of relativity comes from the fact that it has substituted a single four-dimensional manifold (space-time) for the two manifolds, three-dimensional space and one-dimensional time. This is a change of structure, and therefore has far-reaching consequences, but any change which does not involve a change of structure does not make much difference. The mathematical definition and study of structure (under the name of "relation-numbers") form Part IV of *Principia Mathematica.*

The business of philosophy, as I conceive it, is essentially that of logical analysis, followed by logical synthesis. Philosophy is more concerned than any special science with relations of different sciences and possible conflicts between them; in particular, it cannot acquiesce in a conflict between physics and psychology, or between psychology and logic. Philosophy should be comprehensive, and should be bold in suggesting hypotheses as to the universe which science is not yet in a position to confirm or confute. But these should always be presented *as* hypotheses, not (as is too often done) as immutable certainties like the dogmas of religion. Although, moreover, comprehensive construction is part of the business of philosophy, I do not believe it is the most important part. The most important part, to my mind, consists in criticizing and clarifying notions which are apt to be regarded as fundamental and accepted uncritically. As instances I might mention: mind, matter, consciousness, knowledge, experience, causality, will, time. I believe all these notions to be inexact and approximate, essentially infected with vagueness, incapable of forming part of any exact science. Out of the original manifold of events, logical structures can be built which will have properties sufficiently like those of the above common notions to account for their prevalence, but sufficiently unlike to allow a great deal of error to creep in through their acceptance as fundamental.

I suggest the following as an outline of a possible structure of the world; it is no more than an outline, and is not offered as more than possible.

The world consists of a number, perhaps finite, perhaps infinite, of entities which have various relations to each other, and perhaps also various qualities. Each of these entities may be called an "event"; from the point of view of old-fashioned physics, an event occupies a short finite time and a small finite amount of space, but as we are not going to have an old-fashioned space and an old-fashioned time, this statement cannot be taken at its face value. Every event has to a certain number of others a relation which may be called "compresence"; from the point of view of physics, a collection of compresent events all occupy one small region in space-time. One example of a set of compresent events is what would be called the contents of one man's mind at one time – i.e. all his sensations, images, memories, thoughts, etc., which can coexist temporally. His visual field has, in one sense, spatial extension, but this must not be confused with the extension of physical space-time; every part of his visual field is compresent with every other part, and with the rest of "the contents of his mind" at that time, and a collection of compresent events occupies a minimal region in space-time. There are such collections not only where there are brains, but everywhere. At any point in "empty space," a number of stars could be photographed if a camera were introduced; we believe that light travels over the regions intermediate between its source and our eyes, and therefore something is happening in these regions. If light from a number of different sources reaches a certain minimal region in space-time, then at least one event corresponding to each of these sources exists in this minimal region, and all these events are compresent.

We will define a set of compresent events as a "minimal region." We find that minimal regions form a four-dimensional manifold, and that, by a little logical manipulation, we can construct from them the manifold of space-time that physics requires. We find also that, from a number of different minimal regions, we can often pick out a set of events, one from each, which are closely similar when they come from neighbouring regions, and vary from one region to another according to discoverable laws. These are the laws of the propagation of light, sound, etc. We find also that certain regions in space-time have quite peculiar properties; these are the regions which are said to be occupied by "matter." Such regions can be collected, by means of the laws of physics, into tracks or tubes, very much more extended in one dimension of space-time than in the other three. Such a tube constitutes the "history" of a piece of matter; from the point of view of the piece of matter itself, the dimension in which it is most extended can be called "time," but it is only the private time of that piece of matter, because it does not correspond exactly with the dimension in which another piece of matter is most extended. Not only is space-time very peculiar within a piece of matter, but it is also rather peculiar in its neighbourhood, growing less so as the spatio-temporal distance grows greater; the law of this peculiarity is the law of gravitation.

All kinds of matter to some extent, but some kinds of matter (viz. nervous tissue) more particularly, are liable to form "habits," i.e. to alter their structure in a given environment in such a way that, when they are subsequently in a similar environment, they react in a new way, but if similar environments recur often, the reaction in the end becomes nearly uniform, while remaining different from the reaction on the first occasion. (When I speak of the reaction of a piece of matter to its environment, I am thinking both of the constitution of the set of compresent events of which it consists, and of the nature of the track in space-time which constitutes what we should ordinarily call its motion; these are called a "reaction to the environment" in so far as there are laws correlating them with characteristics of the environment.) Out of habit, the peculiarities of what we call "mind" can be constructed; a mind is a track of sets of compresent events in a region of space-time where there is matter which is peculiarly liable to form habits. The greater the liability, the more complex and organized the mind becomes. Thus a mind and a brain are not really distinct, but when we speak of a mind we are thinking chiefly of the set of compresent events in the region concerned, and of their several relations to other events forming parts of other periods in the history of the spatio-temporal tube which we are considering, whereas when we speak of a brain we are taking the set of compresent events as a whole, and considering its external relations to other sets of compresent events, also taken as wholes; in a word, we are considering the shape of the tube, not the events of which each cross-section of it is composed.

The above summary hypothesis would, of course, need to be amplified and refined in many ways in order to fit in completely with scientific facts. It is not put forward as a finished theory, but merely as a suggestion of the kind of thing that may be true. It is of course easy to imagine other hypotheses which may be true, for example, the hypothesis that there is nothing outside the series of sets of events constituting my history. I do not believe that there is any method of arriving at one sole possible hypothesis, and therefore certainty in metaphysics seems to me unattainable. In this respect I must admit that many other philosophies have the advantage, since in spite of their differences *inter se*, each arrives at certainty of its own exclusive truth.

1. THE RELATION OF KNOWLEDGE TO ITS OBJECTS

Quite apart from metaphysics, Kant's work suggested a new approach to logic. He believed the old traditional formal logic, developed by the medievals from Aristotle's foundations, to be a perfect and completed science, to which nothing could be added; but he claimed to have constructed a new "transcendental" logic which demonstrated the dependence of knowledge upon *a priori* categories. As we have seen, what he actually demonstrated was the impossibility of becoming aware of any objects, properly so called, without both a sensuous content (or matter) and the structural principles of thinking which ordered that matter into a coherent and intelligible system. This demonstration suggested a logic as much concerned with the nature and structure of the objects of knowledge as with the purely formal principles of reasoning.

The old logic disregarded the subject matter about which reasoning busied itself. It concentrated simply on the form of the proposition, or the syllogism. Thus the propositions

> All ravens are black,
> Some men are wise
> Plants are either monocotyledon or dicotyledon

differ in form. But we can see this without mentioning the subject matter, by writing them as follows:

> All A's are B's
> Some C's are D's
> X's are either Y or Z

(or, in the traditional symbolism, putting S for subject and P for predicate — "All S is P," and so on). Likewise with forms of inference, the subject matter can be simply replaced by symbols and the form remains apparent, thus for

> All ravens are black,
> Some *corvidae* are ravens,
> ∴ Some *corvidae* are black

we can write:

> All M is P
> Some S is M
> ∴ Some S is P

(M stands for what is called the middle term — the one that appears in both premises).

Thus, traditional logic is formal.

Kant's theory, however, implied that the subject matter of thinking was itself infected with the forms of thought. Although Kant had said that conception without perception was empty, he showed that unless sense data were linked and arranged by necessary rules, no objects could be apprehended, and so no subject matter would be forthcoming.

Later philosophers, following this lead, adopted the view that the validity of reasoning should depend as much on the categories operative in the construction of the subject matter (or content) of thought, as on its form. Consequently, they rejected formal logic as inadequate and attempted to construct a theory of assertion or judgment, and of inference in terms of the structure of the ideas which formed the subject matter of the thinking. That the objects of knowledge depended upon the forms of knowing, or categories supplied *a priori* by the mind, was a doctrine characteristic of theories called "idealist" and was held chiefly by philosophers who developed Kant's ideas by stressing the position he developed in his Transcendental Analytic, and by repudiating his teaching about things-in-themselves.

But other philosophers adhered more firmly to the idea that things-in-themselves are independent of our knowing them (as Kant would have agreed), but they diverged from Kant's view in declaring that as things are in themselves so they appear to us, at all events when our knowledge is true. They appear to us otherwise only when we make mistakes. This doctrine was expressed in the dictum that "knowledge makes no difference to the known." In short, to know an object is to know it as it is in itself, as it is apart from and independent of our knowing it.

If this were so, anything supplied by the mind which made a difference to what we should otherwise experience might well result in distortion and falsehood, and only what is immediately apprehended by direct acquaintance could be regarded as wholly reliable. This view is generally known as "realism," and is, in effect, a return to the position of Locke, but in the hands of contemporary philosophers, of whom Bertrand Russell is the most eminent, it becomes much more subtle and complicated and is brought into association with the elaborate techniques of mathematical logic.

2. RUSSELL'S THEORY OF ACQUAINTANCE

To give a detailed and adequate account of the historical context of Russell's theory is not part of our present purpose. It will be sufficient to sketch in outline the main ideas which have dominated his thought and which have been the source of certain important philosophical developments, even though Russell himself has vehemently opposed many of the more recent.

The basis of Russell's theory of knowledge is his doctrine of acquaintance, which may perhaps best be defined as the immediate awareness of a present object, so that the person apprehending it can give the object a proper name, or indicate it directly in some way which does not involve giving a description of it in terms of other known objects. Such direct experience would correspond to what Kant would have identified as a presentation either of inner or of outer sense, or to what Locke would have termed ideas of sensation or reflection.

For Russell, the objects of acquaintance constitute what he calls the "hard data" of knowledge, which in some of his writings he equates with sensations.[1] Upon them depends all other knowledge derived by inference or indicated by description. The objects of acquaintance to which we can assign proper names are, in the main, particulars, though in some places Russell asserts that we can be acquainted with universals and with relations; but it is doubtful whether these statements are consistent with his contention that any selected object of acquaintance can be given a proper name by the person experiencing it.[2] The objects which can thus be named are constituents of facts which are composed of things having properties or things in mutual relation, or both. If such a fact is not analyzable into component facts, but only into things, properties and relations, it is said to be atomic, and an assertion stating that an atomic fact is the case (that something x has a certain property, or properties; that something a stands in a relation R to b, or that several things are mutually related in a certain way), asserts an atomic proposition. This gives us the groundwork for both metaphysics and logic.

3. THE IDEAL LOGICAL LANGUAGE

Russell's criticism of the traditional logic is not (like that of the idealists) that it is too formal and neglects the character of the subject matter, but that it is not formal enough and restricts itself to propositional forms which mask and misrepresent the forms of the facts they assert. This fault he traces to the conventions and character of ordinary language which states almost everything in subject-predicate form. The traditional logic took this over and, in consequence, so Russell alleges,

---

[1] Cf. *Our Knowledge of the External World*, p. 90ff.
[2] Cf. "On The Nature of Aquaintance" in *Logic and Knowledge* (R. C. Marsh, ed.). London: Allen and Unwin, 1956.

traditional philosophy has been systematically misled by it. For the subject-predicate form is appropriate at most to propositions asserting the possession by a particular thing of an attribute. The fact that two things stand in a specific relation cannot suitably be stated in subject-predicate form and its use for that purpose misleads the philosopher into the belief that the relation is an attribute, or even worse, in some cases (for example, in Plato), that an attribute is some sort of thing—for instance, when one refers to a character by means of a noun and uses it as the subject of a sentence (as in, "Mortality is common to the human race").

The primary desideratum of logic is that the form of the proposition should mirror the form of the fact, and so one has to construct a special logical language to ensure that this will be so. In this language there will be different kinds of symbols for different types of terms (simples, attributes, relations, and so forth), others for quantifiers (indicating reference to "all" or "some," and so on), and others for the assertion of existence. If the language is suitably constructed it should be possible to state everything required with absolute clarity.

In this way all sorts of confusions would be avoided which have in the past misled philosophers into beliefs in bogus entities, such as universals, bogus problems, like that of the existence of the external world, and unwarrantable theories, like that of the unreality of time, space, relations, and what not. On the other hand, the clarification achieved by the new mathematical logic would enable the modern philosopher to dispose of many old problems and solve many new ones. It would give philosophy its long sought scientific status and method and replace interminable dispute with secure agreement as to facts and first principles.

Unfortunately, these confident expectations were not fulfilled, for reasons which will presently appear, but before we explore them we must draw further consequences from the position so far stated.

4. LOGICAL POSITIVISM

If the form of the fact is to be reflected in that of the proposition, how is it in the first place to be ascertained? Apparently by acquaintance, or direct inspection. Thus we revert to sensation as the primary source of indubitable information about the world; and Russell says in at least one place that hard data are what, while the experience of them lasts, cannot be doubted.[3] Consequently, it is to sense that all our knowledge

---

[3]*Our Knowledge of the External World*, p. 60ff.

must in the end be referred. The empiricist assumption is revived that objective information is given in sense perception without the assistance of thought, and that the verification of any factual statement is effected only by tracing it back to some set of sense data in which the state of affairs that it records must have been presented.

Subsequent philosophers argued from this that no proposition or statement the purport of which was factual could have any sensible meaning unless a possible observation could be deduced from it (along with other suitably chosen propositions) by which it could be verified. They concluded that no metaphysical statements could have any factual meaning, and that metaphysics was not a legitimate discipline. All factual propositions belong to one or other of the special sciences, natural and social, and none therefore could belong to philosophy. Russell had insisted that what was fundamental in philosophy was logic, and now it was maintained that philosophy could be nothing other than logic and that logic was concerned solely with language and the forms of its expression and usage. Accordingly, the only legitimate method of dealing with a philosophical problem came to be regarded as linguistic analysis, which would reveal how the usages of language obscured the facts so as to prompt bogus questions and suggest false answers, and how the clarification of the language would remove the puzzlement and refer any legitimate factual question to the appropriate special science.

This theory was known as logical positivism. The most important philosophers who contributed to its development were Ludwig Wittgenstein and Rudolph Carnap. Russell, in his turn, was influenced by them, but later developments went far beyond anything he could accept, and when, ultimately, logical atomism was rejected, as a metaphysical doctrine no more sensible than the rest, and ordinary language was taken, after all, to be the criterion of correct usage, Russell became one of the most vehement opponents of a philosophical vogue the original sources of which he had himself provided.

An outline of this later development will be given below. Let us now turn to Russell's essay of 1924 on Logical Atomism in which premonitions of many of the later doctrines appear.

5. PHILOSOPHY AND SCIENCE

At least since Descartes philosophers have tried to make philosophical arguments rigorous in a way that exempted them from criticism. Kant bewailed the failure of his predecessors and sought to put metaphysics on "the sure path of a science." In the essay on Logical Atomism (as elsewhere in his writings) we find Russell moved by the same aspiration. He seeks to realize it in two different ways: (a) by assimilating logic to mathematics and making that fundamental to all philosophy, and (b) by accepting natural science as more reliable than the "very subtle and abstract arguments" typical of the philosophy of the past, and by founding future philosophy upon the findings of science. These two moves are not so disconnected as they may appear at first sight, but their common foundation in empiricism is not immediately obvious.

The assimilation of logic to mathematics is represented by Russell as a reduction of mathematics to logic, but what precisely is meant by "logic" in this connection is not stated. It is clearly different from epistemology because Russell denies that his reason for believing in his ultimate metaphysical doctrine of pluralism is logical. He says it is empirical, and he says also that "our reasons for believing logic and pure mathematics are, in part, only inductive and probable," because of the observed truth of some of their consequences. We must not, he says, assimilate the logical to the epistemological order. Thus, what is logically necessary is not necessarily fact. What is true or false is what we discover empirically about matters of fact. Logic, it seems, can reveal only the formal relations between propositions and its own truths are not about the world (or facts) but are pure tautologies. Thus logical propositions are always and only analytic. Accordingly, Russell maintains that his (and Whitehead's) reduction of mathematics to pure logic shows that mathematics is throughout purely analytic and Kant must therefore have been wrong about the *a priori* synthetic character of arithmetic and geometry. We are thus back in a position very close to that of Hume: mathematics, so far as it is demonstrative, is purely intuitive and analytic, while all knowledge of matters of fact is derived from experience — acquaintance, or impressions — and so belongs to the natural sciences. But the problem of induction remains, and Russell (though he does not discuss it in this essay) does not shirk it. He sees it clearly for what it is, but can solve it only by forsaking strict empiricism. The principle of induction he concludes is *a priori*[4] — yet it is synthetic.

It follows that the main concerns of philosophy will be of two kinds, one quasi-mathematical in logic, which will be "scientific" in the same way and to the same extent as mathematics is scientific; and the other will be metaphysical, dealing with the general structure of the world[5]

---

[4]Cf. *The Problems of Philosophy* and *Human Knowledge*.
[5]Cf. *Logical Atomism*, p. 532 above.

and thus will be "scientific" just so far as it is based upon the findings of science. The task of philosophy is, however, essentially that of logical analysis, followed by logical synthesis; that is, uncovering possible logical conflicts between different sciences and proposing comprehensive hypotheses of how the sciences may be united.

That the main task of philosophy includes both analysis and synthesis has been commonly accepted at least since Plato and this modern statement of the position is in keeping with tradition. Analysis and clarification of concepts, discovery of hidden presuppositions, removal of implicit contradictions in tacitly assumed principles have always been regarded as the philosopher's primary tasks; and the attainment of a synoptic view of the scientific interpretations of factual experience has long been regarded as a major object of the metaphysician's endeavor. But later philosophers have understood the essential work of logical analysis as exclusive of metaphysics and the unification of science was seen as the reducibility of the languages of all the other sciences to the language of physics.[6]

6. THE NEW TECHNIQUES OF EMPIRICISM

The empiricist character of Russell's philosophy is more clearly revealed in the principle he advocates of substituting "construction" for inference. Inference to unobserved entities is to be reduced to a minimum; such as are needed must be "constructed" out of known entities — that is, entities with which we are acquainted, namable particulars. Thus, like Berkeley and Hume, he is able to dispense with abstraction. Abstract notions are to be replaced by a class, set, or group of particulars. Thus the "length" of a rod x is interpreted as "membership of the group of all those rods which are as long as x". And a number is defined as the class of all classes similar to a given class.

Even classes themselves are in the end abandoned by means of an analysis which can provide an interpretation of all propositions mentioning classes without assuming that there are any. For instance, all red things can be interpreted to mean all those things which are similar in color to a ripe tomato.

---

[6]This doctrine is known as Physicalism. By restricting its reference to language the philosophers who advocate it disguise the fact that it is no more than an alternative version of the older metaphysical doctrine known as Materialism.

The famous theory of definite descriptions is another example of this removal of all taint of universality in our discourse by reduction of universal notions to explicit references to particulars. When we use phrases such as "the author of Waverley" or "the King of France" we tend to think that they refer to some sort of entity with a being of its own and so to think that there is, for instance, an object called "the King of France," whether or not anybody actually holds that office in fact. This Russell contends is a delusion. Sentences such as "The King of France exists" must be translated into "There is one and only one object c, such that c is a king and c rules France." As this statement is false, there is no object c and no temptation to believe that any such object "subsists." The world is a world of particulars and any meaningful locution must ultimately refer to them alone. These particulars, moreover, are all the objects, or possible objects of acquaintance, and, if they are not actual sense data, are at least *sensibilia*.

· All the seeds of Logical Positivism are obviously here, and when Russell declares that a metaphysical doctrine like the ontological argument (along with most of its refutations) depends upon bad grammar, the door is thrown open to the whole range of linguistic philosophy that has since become influential in the English-speaking world. In fact, what Russell says in this essay of the influence of language upon logic and upon earlier philosophy and his whole doctrine of logical language marks the beginning of the development of the recent philosophy of linguistic analysis.

In this connection, a particularly interesting example of the use of construction is Russell's treatment of those "properties" of matter which seem to be logically necessary, such as the impossibility of two bodies occupying the same space. This, he says, is not discovered empirically but is the result of a logical construction determining what is meant by the term "matter" (or "body"). There is obviously something in common here with Kant's teaching that our apprehension of a body depends upon the application of certain logical categories. But Russell's followers interpreted the doctrine as meaning that the definition of matter arrived at in this way was simply the consequence of linguistic convention. The logical necessity arose from the way in which the word was used. If bodies interpenetrated (like gases) they simply would not be what we mean by the word "bodies." Hence, that two bodies cannot occupy the same space is really a tautological statement.[7]

But the instrument of Russell's analysis is mathematical logic and the

---

[7]Cf. A. J. Ayer, *Language, Truth and Logic* (New York, 1953), p. 58.

development of mathematical logic, as we shall see presently, produced a reversal of the original direction of the linguistic movement which has, in effect, undermined its philosophical foundation.

7. THE EFFECT OF THESE TECHNIQUES

The question naturally arises whether the devices introduced by Russell succeed. Does the construction he advocates really demonstrate the nonentity of the referents of the constructed terms or does it simply remove the mention of them from our discourse? If we substitute a group or "class" of particulars for the universal term which describes them, have we really dispensed with the universal conception? What class are we to substitute for it? How do we know which particulars belong to it? When we speak of "membership of the group of all those rods which are as long as x", what qualifies any rod for membership is a certain identifiable property common to it and to x—not just any common property (they may both be steel rods, or both silvery blue). How then do we identify the relevant property? All rods belonging to the group must be *as long as* x. In saying (and understanding) this have we really eliminated the concept of length, or that of equality, or have we just referred to it in a different way? Does not "as long as" mean precisely the same as "equal in length"? To identify all those rods equal in length to x we must use the notions of equality and of length, so substitution for these terms by membership of the group does not really dispense with them.

Frege's definition of number suffers from the same difficulty. If a number is the class of all those classes similar to a given class, in what respect is it similar? We can only say "in the number of its members" (for it is not to be similar in size or shape or even in symbolic representation—III, or 3, or γ, or x will all serve equally well). An attempt is made to get round this inconvenience by defining similar classes as those with a one-one relationship between their members. But this makes the definition of number circular, because we cannot know what constitutes one member of a class without using the conception of unity (or one-ness), and one is a number to which the general definition has to apply. A member of the class of all the things in this room is not my hand, or the desk top, or a chair leg, or a doorknob; it is whatever counts as a single thing for the purpose of enumeration, and what counts as one is a member of all those classes (or groups) which have only one member.

But to give, as the definition of "one," the class of these classes is obviously circular.[8] Yet to say simply "the classes similar to this class" (which has but one member) will serve only if we know what is to count as one. If "this class" is in fact a pen, do we identify its members as its nib and its holder, or the various materials of which it is made, or is the class the pen as a single whole? If the class is a stroke on paper (like this: /), is it as strokes that we count its members or as points in a line, or, like Hume, as *minima sensibilia*? If the membership of "this class" is to be recognized so that we can tell what classes are similar to it, we must be able to decide what counts as one, or in other words, we must be able to count the members. Thus the definition proffered already involves the implicit use of the notion of number, and in particular of the number defined—that of the given class.

The same obstacle presents itself in the attempt to dispense with classes. Though it may serve certain purposes to refer to red things as all those similar in color to a ripe tomato, and so to avoid mentioning the word red, one could only know what things were similar in the required respect if one knew what the color was; and without a conception of redness, as such, the reference would have no point.

Russell himself makes the point in *The Problems of Philosophy* that even if there were no other universals we should still be left inescapably with similarity, which is itself a universal that cannot be eliminated from our discourse. No good purpose would be served by speaking of the class of all similar things as all those things which resemble one another. Resemblance is as much a universal as any other.

The manifest aim of these techniques is to isolate as the legitimate subjects of clear discourse the simple particulars of which the world is supposed really to consist. Reference to classes or universals or definite descriptions (such as "the King of France") and numerous other alleged objects then becomes illegitimate, and they are castigated as bogus entities. From what has already been said it is clear that the existence of these pseudo-objects is suggested by linguistic forms; so the objective set before the philosopher is to construct a symbolism which will elimi-

---

[8]Mathematicians define one as the class of which zero is a member. Zero is the class of classes which have no members, and of these there is but one, the null class. Thus zero, the class of classes without members, has only one member (the null class). The class of classes similar to zero is, accordingly, one. But we can know this only if we can become aware of the uniqueness of the empty class, of the fact that it is the only one of its kind. Thus we must use the concept of one-ness in its own definition when we define it as the class of classes the members of which are unique. But this circularity in the definition is disguised by restricting its wording so as to mention only zero.

nate the bogus entities and clearly indicate the genuine ones — to construct an ideal logical language. What must not be overlooked is the
fact that the original ground for proceeding in this manner is the belief
that the world does in fact consist entirely of simple particulars in
relation; in short, of atomic facts. And that belief, again, is founded
upon the empiricist doctrine that sense data, the immediate objects of
sense, put us in direct contact with the outside world.

8. THE THEORY OF TYPES

In connection with the way in which symbols, verbal or otherwise,
represent objects and ideas, Russell lays great stress on the theory of
logical types. The referents of different words and phrases are of
different logical types, whereas, as he points out, the words which refer
to them are often all of the same type. This leads to confusion if language is not carefully scrutinized. Our symbolism, therefore, needs
reform so as to indicate differences of type and to obviate meaningless
forms of statement, which may be grammatically correct in common
speech, but which apply inappropriate predicates to types of objects
that are not susceptible to them. Thus relations are not of the same
logical type as the things which they relate. We may legitimately ask
how x is related to y, but to ask how the relation between these two
terms is related to either of them (as F. H. Bradley does in a famous
discussion of the topic[9]) is to ask a meaningless question, because
relations do not stand in relation to other things and are not things of
the same logical type as those that do.

Whether or not this theory can provide us with a satisfactory solution
of Bradley's problem is a discussion upon which we cannot here enter,
but the general notion of a hierarchy of types or categories within each
of which terms function differently from the way they do in others, is
one which in different forms has been put forward by other philosophers and is of considerable importance. Confusion between logical
types or categories can lead to serious philosophical errors. Gilbert Ryle
refers to it as the committal of category-mistakes and gives as an example the attempt to refer to the University of Oxford in the same way as
one refers to its constituent colleges, as if a tourist, on being shown the
buildings in which some institution functions, expected to be shown
another building which was the institution itself. He suggests further
that our traditional belief in body and mind as two entities of the same

---

[9]F. H. Bradley, *Appearance and Reality*, Chapter 3.

kind related to one another in some such way as two different mechanisms or as two different bodily organs are related, may be the result of a similar category-mistake. For mental events may well be of a different logical type from physical events. In our earlier discussions of the theories of Plato and Descartes we had reason to believe that this may well be the case.

Unfortunately, neither Russell nor any of his followers have made very fruitful use of this doctrine in metaphysics. Russell's own theory of body-mind relation follows quite a different course. He holds that each is simply a different kind of grouping, or logical construction, out of constituents which are neither physical nor mental.[10] It is a doctrine which has been severely criticized[11] and has not really served to remove the difficulties which cluster around this vexed question. On the whole, the theory has been passed over, largely because the main thrust of Russell's teaching has been in another direction. It has had the effect of discrediting altogether the discussion of metaphysical questions as arising invariably from the misuse of language, from category-mistakes and from infringement of logical rules imposed by the theory of types.

9. SUBSEQUENT DEVELOPMENTS

The work of mathematical logicians, on the one hand, and the later philosophical reflections of Ludwig Wittgenstein, on the other, produced drastic modifications of the views which developed out of the doctrines Russell put forward. Logical positivism, the first among these, soon began to crumble. The verification principle, that factually sensible statements must be verifiable by observation, gave continual difficulty. First, it became apparent that such verification even of bona fide empirical statements was not always practicable; then it was seen that even where practicable it could never be fully achieved, because an infinite number of observations would be needed. So modifications to the doctrine were made requiring only verification in principle, and later still less, merely confirmation by some sense observations. But then it came to be seen that the principle itself was neither an analytic proposition which was logically true, nor an empirical statement verifiable by observation and it became suspect.

Worse still, the doctrine of logical atomism, from which this entire

---

[10]Cf. *The Analysis of Mind* and *Our Knowledge of the External World*.
[11]Cf. Lovejoy, *The Revolt against Dualism*.

course of philosophical development had originated, was seen to be a
metaphysical doctrine. The first intimation of this was given by Wittgenstein in his *Tractatus Logico-Philosophicus*, where he stated the
metaphysical basis of the positivistic theory and then concluded by
asserting that his statements had no sense and should be disregarded
— the ladder on which he had climbed, he recommended, should be
thrown away. But if that were true, what should be the status of the
conclusions which he had reached? The doctrine, as G. J. Warnock has
said, lay like a timebomb in the foundations of logical positivism.[12]

Meanwhile, the mathematical logicians discovered that it was possible to construct a whole series of different logics, all logically unexcep-
tionable, by adopting different axiom sets. None, therefore, could make
good the claim to be the perfect logical language revealing the form of
the facts. The question then naturally became pressing whether the
facts had the form alleged — or, for that matter, any recognizable form
at all.

Wittgenstein, in his later reflections, rejected his own earlier views
about language. He saw that it was not possible to reduce much of what
is stated in ordinary language to atomic propositions on the truth or
falsehood of which compound propositions depended. One specially
troublesome case was that of subjunctive conditional statements, such
as "If it had rained yesterday I could not have come." According to the
accepted theory of mathematical logic, a conditional statement's truth
or falsity depended on that of its component propositions, and if the
antecedent was false, then the conditional was always supposed to be
true because from a false proposition any other (so the theory runs) can
be inferred. But in subjunctive conditionals the antecedent is always
false (in the example, it did not, in fact, rain yesterday), so all subjunctive conditionals should be true whatever the facts might be. In short,
they are in principle unverifiable observationally, yet always true and
obviously not all metaphysical. This is a conclusion that nobody could
accept.

Consequently, it seemed impossible to maintain either that the logical
language represented the ideal to which all other language should be
reduced, or that all sensible factual statements must in some way be
observationally verifiable. Wittgenstein accordingly put forward the
view that every language functioned according to its own rules, and
that persons using it were like the players of a game behaving according to the rules laid down. It was not always possible to translate one
language game into another. Philosophical problems would arise as a

---

[12]Cf. *English Philosophy since 1900* (Oxford University Press, 1966), pp. 41-42.

result of failure to keep or to understand the rules, and the task of the philosopher was now seen as examination of the functioning of the language so as to clarify the rules of its use and so dissolve away the problems. His own and Russell's earlier addiction to logical atomism was seen as the result of their having been misled by the language of mathematics into unwarranted beliefs about a special form inherent in the facts of the world.

What, in all this, seems to have been overlooked is that the reason why language was originally alleged to mislead us into metaphysical beliefs was that it obscured, instead of revealed, the form of the facts. But if this is not the case, how or why should language mislead? If it is that we do not understand the rules, what, we must ask, determines the rules? They surely cannot be quite arbitrary and they must surely bear some relation to the facts which we try to express by means of the language. The rules of ordinary language mainly reflect the ideas of common sense, but these are frequently belied by scientific discovery. Are we to say simply that scientists play a different language game? If so, which language game is to be preferred, and why? And might there, perhaps, be a metaphysical language game with merits of its own?

These questions can hardly be answered without some investigation into the nature of things and the way in which our languages (ordinary, scientific, and philosophical) enable us to express our beliefs about the facts. Still more important is the question, What determines the truth or falsehood of those beliefs? This being so, it would seem that philosophical investigation of the traditional questions is not wholly misplaced. On this note it may be as well to stop, leaving the student to pursue his researches further along such lines as the study of the foregoing texts and problems may suggest, and according to the demands which they may have made upon his own curiosity.

SUGGESTIONS FOR FURTHER READING

Bertrand Russell, *Analysis of Mind*. London: Allen and Unwin, 1949.

———, *Introduction to Mathematical Philosophy*. London: Allen and Unwin, 1950.

———, *Our Knowledge of the External World*, New York: Mentor Books, 1956.

A. J. Ayer, *Language, Truth and Logic*. New York: Dover, 1953.

———, *Foundations of Empirical Knowledge*. London: Macmillan, 1951, (1965, paper).

J. O. Urmson, *Philosophical Analysis*. New York: Oxford University Press, 1958, (1967, paper).

G. J. Warnock, *English Philosophy Since 1900*. New York: Oxford University Press, 1966.

A. Flew (ed.), *Logic and Language*. New York: Doubleday, Anchor Books, 1965.

H. D. Lewis (ed.), *Clarity is not Enough*. London: Allen and Unwin, 1963.

M. White (ed.), *The Age of Analysis*. New York: Mentor Books, 1964.

Feigl and Sellars (eds.), *Readings in Philosophical Analysis*. New York: Appleton, 1949.

G. R. Mure, *Retreat from Truth*. Oxford: Blackwell, 1958.

G. E. Moore, "A Defense of Common Sense" in *Contemporary British Philosophy*, second series. London: Allen and Unwin, 1953.

E. E. Harris, *Nature, Mind and Modern Science*, Chapters 14, 15, and 16. New York: Humanities Press, 1954.

———, "Scientific Philosophy," *Philosophical Quarterly*, vol. II, 1952.

———, "The End of a Phase." *Dialectica*, vol. 17, no. 1, 1963.

H. Reichenbach, *The Rise of Scientific Philosophy*. Berkeley, Calif.: University of California Press, 1951.

Index

DATE DUE

JUN 21			
JAN 15 '84			
GAYLORD			PRINTED IN U.S.A.